THE ILLUSTRATED HISTORY OF THE WORLD

THE ILLUSTRATED HISTORY OF THE WORLD

SIMON & SCHUSTER
YOUNG BOOKS

First published in Great Britain in 1994 by
Simon & Schuster Young Books
Campus 400
Maylands Avenue
Hemel Hempstead
Hertfordshire HP2 7EZ

First Published in eight volumes as
The Earliest Civilizations © 1991 Margaret Oliphant
Rome and the Ancient World © 1991 Mike Corbishley
The Dark Ages © 1991 Tony Gregory
The Middle Ages © 1991 Fiona Macdonald
The Age of Discovery © 1992 Hazel Mary Martell
Conflict and Change © 1992 Fiona Reynoldson
The Nineteenth Century © 1992 Michael Pollard
The Modern World © 1992 Stephen Hoare

A CIP catalogue record for this book is available from the British Library.

ISBN 07500 1524 1

Printed and bound in Portugal by Edições ASA

Typeset by Goodfellow & Egan Ltd, Cambridge

Editor Diana Russell
Designer Roger Hammond
Illustrators Deborah Kindred, Hussein Hussein, Abdul Aziz Khan, James Field, Larry Rostant, Sheilagh Noble, Paul Ellis, Simon Boulstone, James Orr
Picture research Dee Robinson

CONTENTS

363 Revolution and Empire

395 The Old World

427 Towards Today

459 The End of the Old Order

491 Creating a New World

HOW TO GET THE MOST FROM YOUR BOOK

This book contains a huge amount of information. It is presented in many different ways, to help you find your way around the sections easily. It has an extensive index, and there are cross-references within the text. Supplementing the main text are fact-boxes which give extra information on such things as inventions and clothes. Time charts tell what was happening in other parts of the world. These features will make this book easy to use and we hope it gives you enjoyment for years to come.

THE VIKINGS: CONQUERORS AND SETTLERS

In Western Europe, the Vikings were adaptable. In the Shetlands, Orkney and the Hebrides, where there was land to be had, they settled as farmers, with piracy as a side interest, in about AD 780. Further south, where the land was richer and already densely settled, they had to take another approach–full scale invasion.

THE SCALE OF THE VIKING INVASION About AD 840 Norwegian Vikings invaded Ireland. They set up trading towns at Dublin, Waterford, Wexford, Limerick and Cork. Here, in wooden houses by the riverside ports, they traded with the Irish and the rest of Europe and went raiding from time to time.

Meanwhile the Danish Vikings were loose in the North Sea and the English Channel. In AD 793 they had pillaged the monastery of Lindisfarne, an act which shocked Christian England. Holland, Belgium and France were their prey too, and great ports like London, Dorestadt and Quentovic were destroyed. Further south they were less lucky. The *Moors* of Spain were better prepared, and in AD 844 Viking corpses hung from the palm trees of Seville and Viking heads were sent as presents to Africa.

THE INVASION OF ENGLAND In AD 862 Danish raids on England turned to invasion. The east and north of England became *Danelaw*, the Danish kingdom, but in the south, Alfred, King of Wessex, held out and pushed them back. By AD 924 much of England was English again. It was around York that the Viking power lasted longest. Here the Norsemen had a settlement like the ones in Ireland, and archaeology has turned up the smallest details of their lives.

In AD 994 the Danes were back. From fortified camps, like Trelleborg in Denmark, the armies of Svein Forkbeard and his Norwegian ally Olaf Tryggvason attacked. Only blackmail payments of mountains of silver by King Ethelred held them off. Finally Cnut (Canute) became King of England and Denmark, and the two kingdoms were one for 26 years.

of the Franks set a thief to catch thieves, and gave part of his kingdom to Rollo and his Viking band. They wanted land and the Franks wanted protection from other Vikings; it was a fair bargain. In a few years this part of France took the Norsemen's name and became Normandy. Their war leader became the Duke of Normandy and they became Christians.

As fighting men they were in demand, and they were invited to Italy in 1016 to help settle local wars. They fought and they stayed, setting themselves up in a Norman kingdom that covered southern Italy.

Fifty years later, Duke William of Normandy launched the last great Viking raid. In 1066 his army crossed the Channel to England. At the Battle of Hastings they defeated the English and William became the king of England.

'Never before has such terror appeared in Britain as we have now suffered from a pagan race, nor was it thought that such an inroad from the sea could be made. Behold the church of St Cuthbert, spattered with the blood of the priests of God, despoiled of all its ornaments; a place more venerable than all in Britain is given as a prey to pagan peoples.' Alcuin AD 793.

Left. This Viking spear is made of bronze and has a highly decorated hilt. Though not known particularly for their arts and crafts, the Vikings have left behind some beautiful artefacts. Fine weapons were greatly prized amongst Vikings, and were handed down from father to son.

J Words picked out in text are explained more fully in the Glossary.

I Text clearly and accurately narrates the history of the world from the dawn of mankind to the space age.

H Maps give information on the way military campaigns were run, national borders changed and how peoples moved.

G Quotations from the works of some of the greatest contemporary writers graphically evoke everyday life and events in the past.

A Full-colour photographs of archaeological finds provide insights and access points into the development of art and technology through the ages.

B Information boxes illuminate items of special interest.

Right. Contrary to popular images of Vikings in horned helmets, this carved head shows the typical plain, conical helmets that were generally worn.

The Runic Alphabet

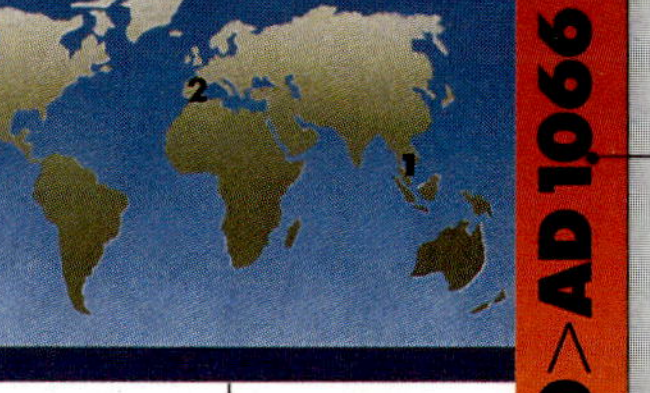

The Vikings used the Runic script. The origin of the Runic alphabet is uncertain, but probably dates from the first century BC or AD.

It is more than likely that runes had solely a monumental use. There is no certain evidence that they were ever used in a literary way–to record stories, legends or poems.

Three main varieties of the alphabet can be found on the 4000 inscriptions which have been found. The 'Old Teutonic' consisted of 24 letters. The Anglican *Futhark*, brought to Britain in the fifth and sixth centuries AD, increased the letters to 28. The alphabet was increased again to 33 letters in the ninth century AD, as the 'Old Teutonic' letters were not sufficient to represent all the old English sounds.

1 Between AD 860–890 the town of Angkor Thom was built by the Khmer ruler, Jayavarman III, in Cambodia. The town covered about 10 square kilometres and may have been home to as many as one million people. The town contained many temples; the central temple was called the Bayon. It was dedicated to the reigning king and the Buddha, and 200 great stone faces adorn its towers.

2 On 25 December AD 800, Charles, King of the Franks and Lombards, was pronounced Emperor of the Holy Roman Empire. This marked the first time since the fall of the Roman Empire that a ruler had emerged who was strong enough to unify Western Europe. His imperial coronation was an important sign that, after 400 years of invasions and chaos, Europe was on its way to recovery.

AD 780>AD 1066

Below. This is a reconstruction of what a typical Viking town probably looked like. Many of the streets would have been paved with logs. Houses varied in size and most would have had several storage huts or work places. These would all have been enclosed by a wooden fence.

C Date flashes provide quick and accurate reference to the time period covered on each double-page spread.

D Time charts (accompanied by a reference map) keep the reader in touch with events in the rest of the world at any one time.

AD	EUROPE	NORTH AND SOUTH AMERICA	REST OF WORLD
1834			The Great Trek from Cape Colony begins
1839>1842			Britain launches First Opium War against China
1850>1864			Taiping Rebellion in China
1851	The Great Exhibition is held in London		Gold found in New South Wales and Victoria in Australia
1852	Cavour becomes prime minister of Piedmont		
1853			US warships sail into Tokyo Bay
1856			South African Boers establish the independent republics of Orange Free State and Transvaal
1856>1860			Britain and France attack China: the Second Opium War
1859	War between Piedmont and Austria		
1860	Rebellion in southern Italy		
1861>1871			The Maori Wars against the British
1865>1868			Civil war in Japan
1866	Prussia defeats Austria in the Seven Weeks' War		
1867		USA establishes a naval base at Midway Island in the Pacific USA buys Alaska from Russia	Diamonds discovered on the border of Orange Free State
1869		North America's first transcontinental railway opens	The Suez Canal opens
1870	Unification of Italy complete except for Vatican City Outbreak of the Franco-Prussian War	Standard Oil Company founded in the USA	
1871	France surrenders to Prussia. Wilhelm I proclaimed Kaiser of the German Empire		Delegation leaves Japan for America and Europe to study Western technology
1873	James Clerk Maxwell publishes his paper on electricity and magnetism		
1874		Barbed wire invented in the USA	
1876		The Centennial Exhibition is held in Philadelphia	
1879			Britain fights the Zulu War
1880	In Germany, Siemens demonstrates the first electric train		
1882	First refrigerated cargo ship arrives in Britain from New Zealand		
1884			Gold discovered in the Transvaal
1884>1885			War between China and France, ending in Chinese defeat
1885	European powers agree on 'spheres of influence' in Africa		
1886		The Statue of Liberty completed in New York Harbor	
1888		Slavery abolished in Brazil	
1894>1895			War between China and Japan, ending in Chinese defeat
1896	Marconi begins experiments with radio		
1898			The Spanish-American War
1899			Britain declares war on the Boers
1899>1900			The Boxer Rising in China

E Time charts help the reader compare events around the globe, and find out what was happening in the world at any given time.

F Full-colour reconstructions of specific buildings, cities and events transport the reader back in time.

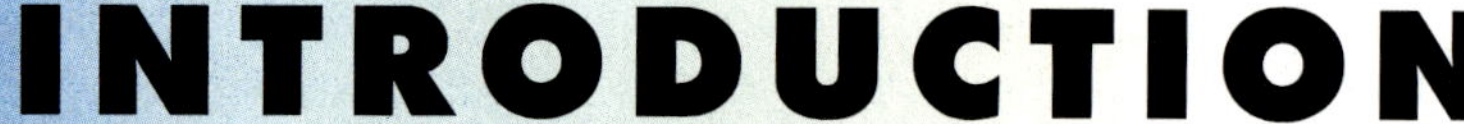

INTRODUCTION

Somebody once called the past 'a foreign country where people do things differently'. This is a helpful way of thinking about the past, for we can all imagine visiting another country and discovering how different it is. In this book we are going to find out about the past. Our journey begins millions of years ago when people first existed and ends with the end of the cold war in the 1980's.

But how do we actually know what happened so long ago? Well, knowledge of the past is based on *evidence*, much of which is found by *archaeologists* digging or excavating ancient sites. Non-written evidence such as skeletons of humans or animals, seeds and pollen, fragments of pottery or jewellery, stone or metal tools and weapons or the remains of buildings, are called *material remains*.

For the long period before the invention of writing, which is called *prehistory*, it is from the evidence of material remains that we can reconstruct what probably happened. For example, the fortifications built at Jericho in about 8000 BC show us that the city needed to defend itself, that it was wealthy enough to build such walls, and, because objects from distant places were found here, we can assume that there was extensive trade, which is probably why the city was wealthy.

But, without written evidence, we can know nothing of particular events. With the invention of writing and the keeping of records, the past becomes history filled with real people and the accounts of their actions. More recent events are reconstructed by historians using a variety of sources, such as paintings and photographs, letters, government records and relics. With these they can put together a good picture of what happened, and also what the people and places you will read about here looked like.

You can read this book from the beginning to try and understand the rise and fall of civilizations, or you can dip in and out of the book to learn about different events or cultures. The maps will help you to see where things happened and the timecharts will show you when they took place. We hope that using this book will give you pleasure for years to come.

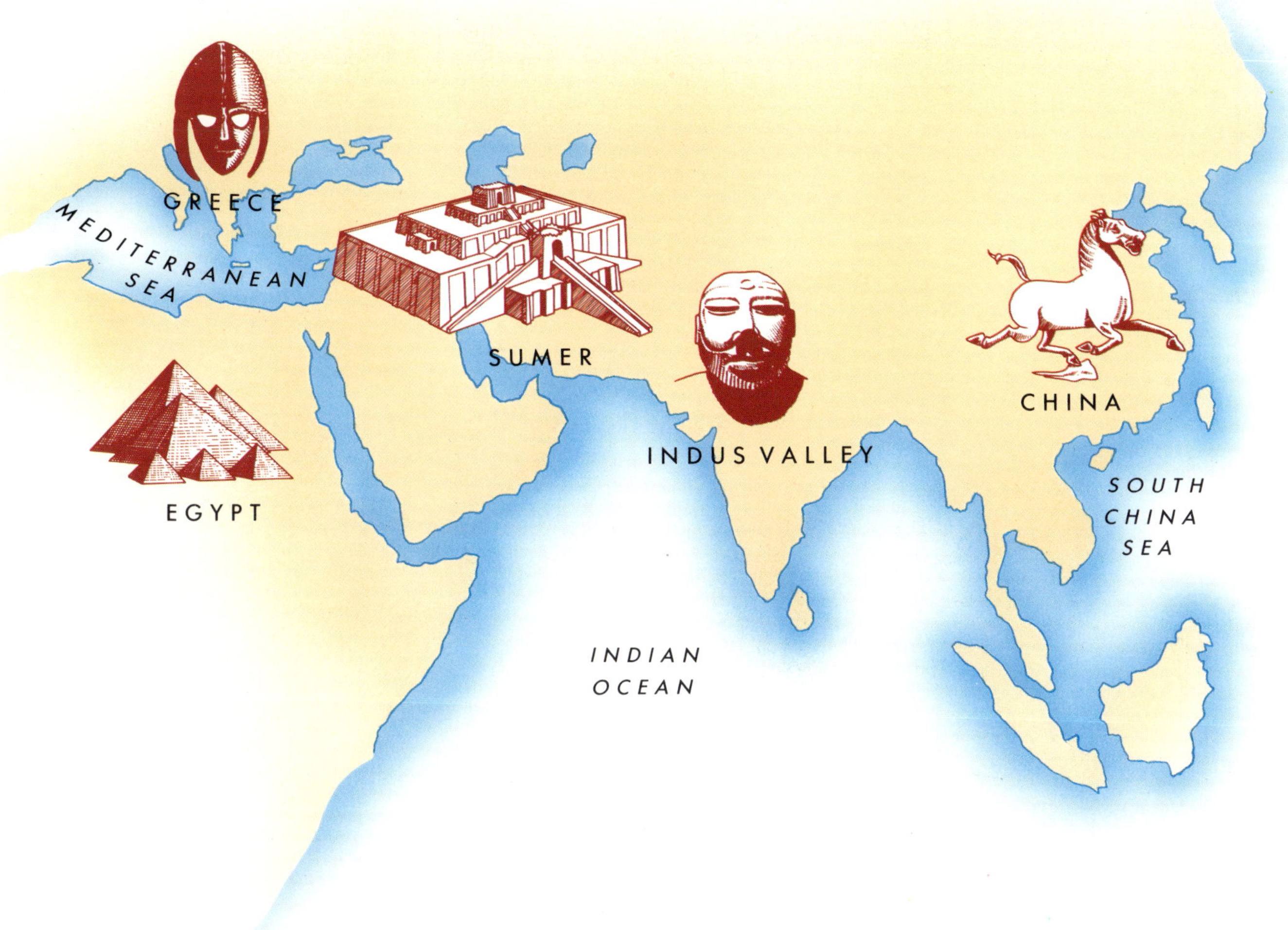

The First People

More than 5 million years ago, our ancestors first came down from the trees and became separated from the apes.

It took several more million years for our species, homo sapiens sapiens, to emerge. By then, our ancestors were making tools from pebbles and stones, and using fire.

Since that time, nearly 100,000 years ago, mankind's technological advances have been immense. However, it has only been in the last 10,000 years or so that so many skills that we take for granted have developed – such as the development of farming, metal-working and textile-making.

Whereas for thousands of years people have used ceramic plates and pots, and metal saucepans, nowadays our technology changes so rapidly that it is possible to imagine a very different world. A world in which plastic plates and dishes and microwave cookers replace the need for metal pans and ordinary cookers. Such changes have taken place in decades rather than, as formerly, in centuries.

Until recently – and even now in some countries – people used many tools and techniques little different to some of the inventions of the ancient world.

This section traces mankind's journey from our beginnings to the first cities and states. In between these two points, there was adaptation and invention as our ancestors evolved from nomadic hunter-gatherers to settler-farmers, and later to city-dwellers.

Stone and, later, metals were worked, and pottery and clothmaking developed. Prehistory ends with the invention of writing and the keeping of written records. From these we can learn something of the history of the earliest civilizations.

HOW MANKIND BEGAN

Man's history is very short compared with the history of Earth, which scientists think is about 4550 million years old. If you think of this book as containing the history of our planet, human history would fill the last 24 lines of the last page.

Although our existence is so relatively brief, nevertheless it took several million years for humans to develop. This process, called human evolution, was not only lengthy, but was also very complex and is still not fully understood.

THE PRIMATES The closest living relatives of humans are the great apes; both belong to the group of animals called primates, which includes monkeys. Humans however, differ from apes in three significant ways: their brains are larger, they walk upright on two feet, and use their hands with great dexterity.

THE SEPARATION OF APES AND HUMANS Once, man and ape had a common ancestor, but some time between eight and five million years ago, the separation of humans from apes took place. In a period of increasing dryness, the forests of Africa receded and the area of grasslands became greater. Apes lived in the trees of the forests and as the numbers of trees decreased, only the strongest apes remained in the forest, whilst those who were weaker were pushed out.

These weaker apes, who were the ancestors of man, had to adapt to a life in open grasslands. They had to learn to move quickly as they were more exposed and gradually their bodies became adapted to running and walking upright rather than swinging from trees.

Because they were less strong and less protected outside the forest, they learnt to use tools to protect themselves and to kill other animals. Their life was more difficult and complex than that of the ape in the forest and they were physically weaker, so their brains developed as they learnt more skills. So it was originally because they were physically weaker than the apes that our ancestors adapted and survived.

AUSTRALOPITHECENES From fossil remains we know that creatures called *australopithecenes* (southern apes), lived in Africa between four and 1.7 million years ago. They were 1.2 metres tall and had small brains, but they walked upright. A female skeleton found in Ethiopia – named Lucy after the Beatles' song 'Lucy in the Sky with Diamonds' – belongs to the earliest type or species of australopithecenes. Dated to 3.4 million years ago, her small body, whilst partly ape-like, had an upright posture and teeth with human characteristics. Some scholars think that Lucy's species was the ancestor to the earliest type of man. Others think that man, or homo, evolved separately. Man's origins are still uncertain and are the subject of much debate.

PREHISTORIC HANDYMEN By about two million years ago, australophithecenes and the earliest species of man, called homo habilis, 'handyman', were living at the Olduvai Gorge in Tanzania. 'Handyman' probably made the first stone tools, called Olduwan after the site. These simple tools made by chipping flakes from pebbles, are a landmark in human evolution. They show that homo habilis could plan, because he made special tools for particular tasks. This is something that other animals cannot do.

UPRIGHT MAN Homo erectus, 'upright man' was in Africa, China and Java by about 1.5 million years ago. By 700,000 BC Europe had been colonized. These people used fire, hunted large animals and made increasingly specialized tools.

WISE MAN By 120,000 BC early forms of homo sapiens, 'wise man', had emerged. These early stages of human development in the old *Stone Age* are called the Lower Palaeolithic period, from the Greek words for 'old' and 'stone'.

Skull Finds of Early Man

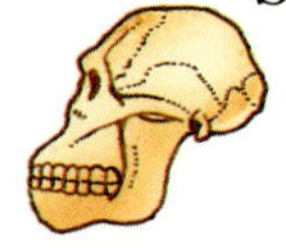

Australopithecene

Homo habilis

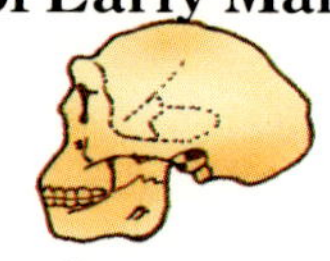

Homo erectus

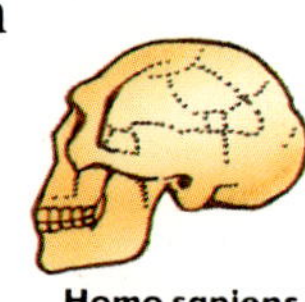

Homo sapiens

The remains of the oldest hominids have been discovered in Africa. Olduvai Gorge became especially famous following the first discovery of a skull of the homo habilis type made there by anthropologist, Louis Leakey, and his wife, Dorothy.

The fossil homo habilis could be distinguished by its larger brain, rounded skull and less ape-like face. Developments from the homo habilis skull show a progressive trend towards anatomical features that we can easily recognize as 'human'.

Ramapithecene	Australopithecene	Homo habilis	Homo erectus	Homo sapiens	Homo sapiens sapiens
11 million years ago	3.5 million years ago	1.5 million years ago	500,000 years ago	200,000 years ago	modern man

Remains of Hominids in Eurasia and Africa

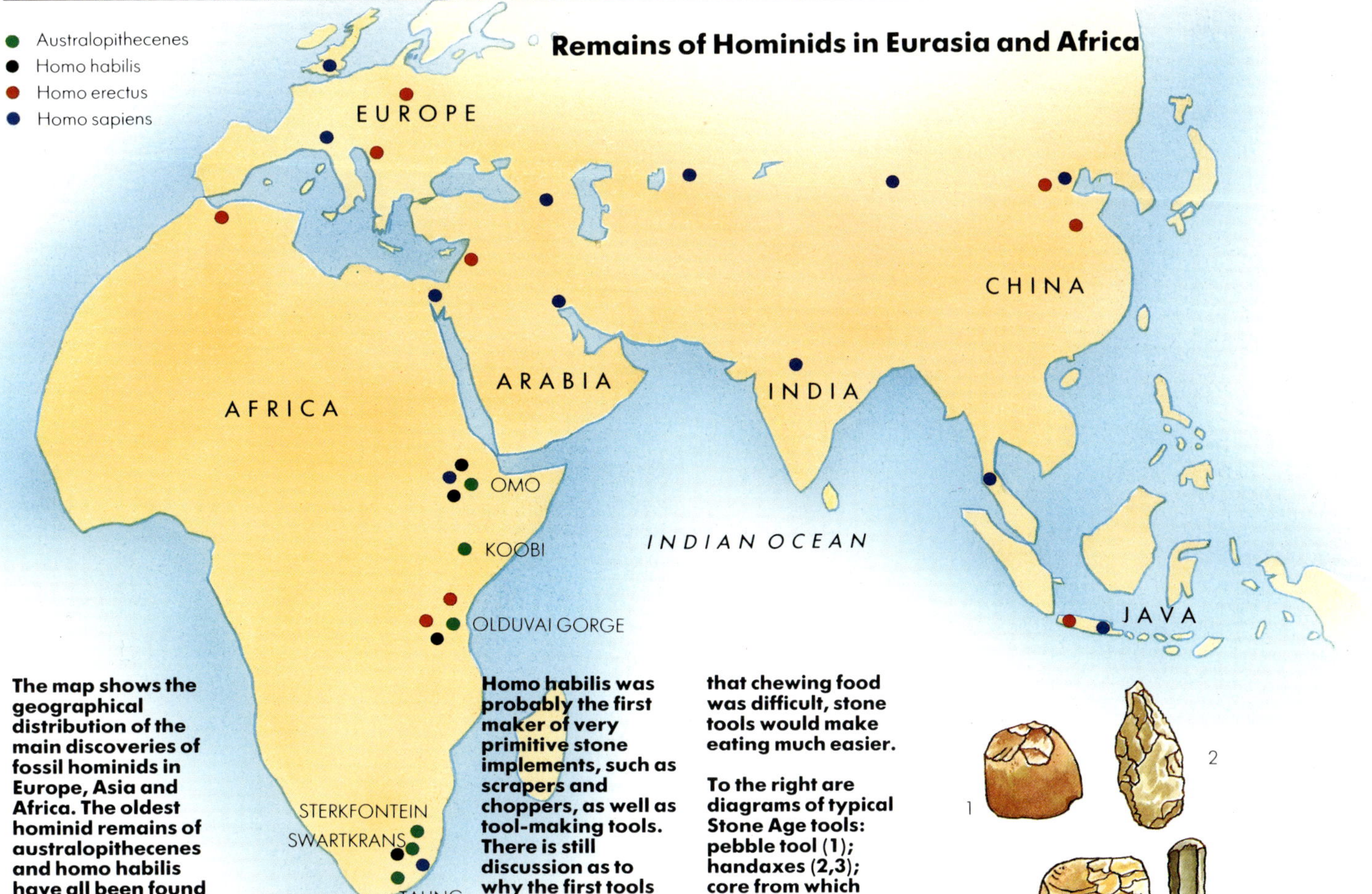

Australopithecenes
Homo habilis
Homo erectus
Homo sapiens

EUROPE
CHINA
ARABIA
INDIA
AFRICA
OMO
KOOBI
INDIAN OCEAN
OLDUVAI GORGE
JAVA
STERKFONTEIN
SWARTKRANS
TAUNG

The map shows the geographical distribution of the main discoveries of fossil hominids in Europe, Asia and Africa. The oldest hominid remains of australopithecenes and homo habilis have all been found in Africa. Within Africa, most of the oldest finds have occurred along the break in the earth's crust known as the Rift Valley.

Homo habilis was probably the first maker of very primitive stone implements, such as scrapers and choppers, as well as tool-making tools. There is still discussion as to why the first tools were made. The earliest tools were probably just sticks used to reach things that were otherwise out of reach. But stone tools may first have been used to help older members of the group. If teeth had been lost or worn down so much that chewing food was difficult, stone tools would make eating much easier.

To the right are diagrams of typical Stone Age tools: pebble tool (1); handaxes (2,3); core from which small pieces of flint have been chopped (4,6); knife (5).

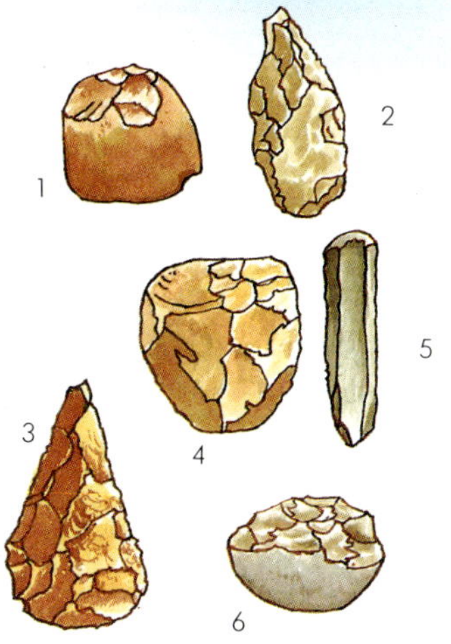

1
2
3
4
5
6

NOMADIC HUNTERS OF THE STONE AGE

During the Lower Palaeolithic period there were many changes in climate. The first of the four great *Ice Ages* began about 1.5 million years ago. During this time the weather was much colder, and snow and sheets of ice covered most of Northern Europe.

Because mankind's ancestors could think and plan ahead, they were able to survive the harsh conditions of the Ice Ages. Their tool-making skills developed, they used fire, made clothing and shelter and became more proficient at hunting animals and gathering plants. They lived in small groups as *nomads*, constantly on the move in search of food. Sometimes they would stop at certain places where there were many plants or animals to hunt.

NEANDERTHAL MAN The last Ice Age began about 70,000 BC, and during its early stages Europe and parts of Asia were inhabited by a species called Neanderthals. This period is called the Middle Palaeolithic and lasted until about 40,000 years ago.

Although they looked different to modern man, having a much heavier brow, their brains were the same size. Their way of life was more advanced than that of earlier humans. They hunted, lived in caves and used a variety of stone tools. Like us, they buried their dead. Perhaps they had some concept of an afterlife, for at the grave of an old Neanderthal man, flowers had been placed with the body.

THE EMERGENCE OF MODERN MAN By about 100,000 BC, the first modern humans, homo sapiens sapiens, had emerged in southern Africa. The descendants of these people, indistinguishable from ourselves, moved into Europe and replaced the Neanderthals some 35,000 years ago. The period to about 12,000 years ago is known as the Upper Palaeolithic, and much is known about it, especially in Europe.

Europe During the Ice Age

Much of Europe was covered with glaciers during the Ice Age. It was freezing cold and only stunted plants, lichens and mosses could grow. The climate became warmer some 10,000 years ago and as the ice sheets melted, the sea level rose, changing coastlines.

BRITISH ICE SHEET
SCANDINAVIAN ICE SHEET
ALPINE GLACIERS
MEDITERRANEAN SEA

These people lived together in cave entrances and rock shelters, or if there were no caves, they built large tents or huts, in which they had fires for heating and cooking. They hunted large animals such as mammoths, bison and reindeer, and gathered plants. They made tools from bone, antler and ivory, as well as stone. Apart from hunting, they used tools for a number of other tasks. They also invented the bow and arrow.

A reconstruction of what a community might have looked like in Upper Palaeolithic times. People either lived in caves or tents, such as these. Tents were made out of the skins of animals. The tents shown here are constructed on frames of mammoth bones. The woman on the left is pegging out a hide to let it dry before being used as a tent covering. The people are also wearing clothes made from animal hides. The temperature was much colder during this period so substantial clothing such as this would probably have been worn.

A wall painting from a cave at Lascaux in the Dordogne region of France, c. 15,000 BC. Bison, ibex, stags, horses and other animals were vividly depicted by the cave artists.

Hunting Weapons

Several new types of weapon came into use during the Stone Age, including the barbed harpoon and the spear. To throw spears a long distance, spear-throwers were used, which were attached to the hunters' wrists with leather thongs. The spearhead was placed on long wooden shafts whose bases fitted into the grooves of the throwers. Often these spear-throwers were beautifully carved with designs of animals.

Bone spearheads (1,2); barbed harpoons (3,4); harpoons attached to wooden shafts (5,6); double-headed harpoon (7); barbed spearhead (8).

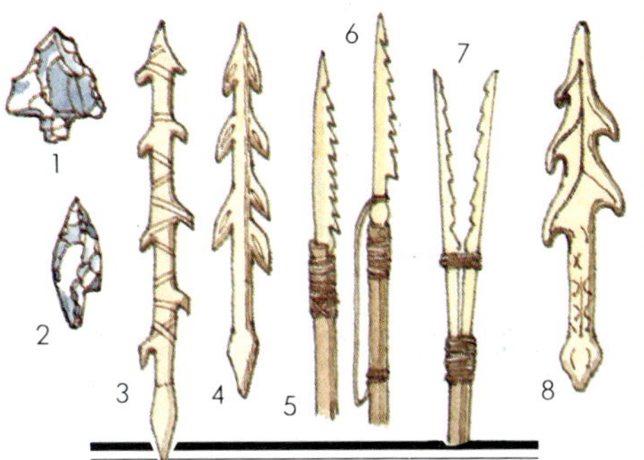

ART AND SCULPTURE The earliest known art was created by these Upper Palaeolithic hunters. The walls of caves and rock shelters were painted with pictures of animals such as deer, bison and horses. People are seldom shown, although they were sometimes painted wearing masks, antlers and animal skins; it is possible that these scenes are connected with hunting rituals. From what is known of communities that still live by hunting, which is done mainly by young men, these paintings might also be connected with ceremonies celebrating the entry of young hunters into the adult hunting group. The paintings were made with natural colour pigments crushed or ground from rocks or plants. Although cave paintings are known from elsewhere, many especially beautiful pictures are found in south west France and northern Spain.

These *hunter-gatherers* also engraved or carved animals and human figures in stone, ivory and bone antler. Whatever its original purpose, people still find the art of these ancient hunters very beautiful. Indeed, so many people have visited the caves at Lascaux in France that the paintings have started to decay, so a reconstruction has been created for people to visit.

FARMERS OF THE NEAR EAST

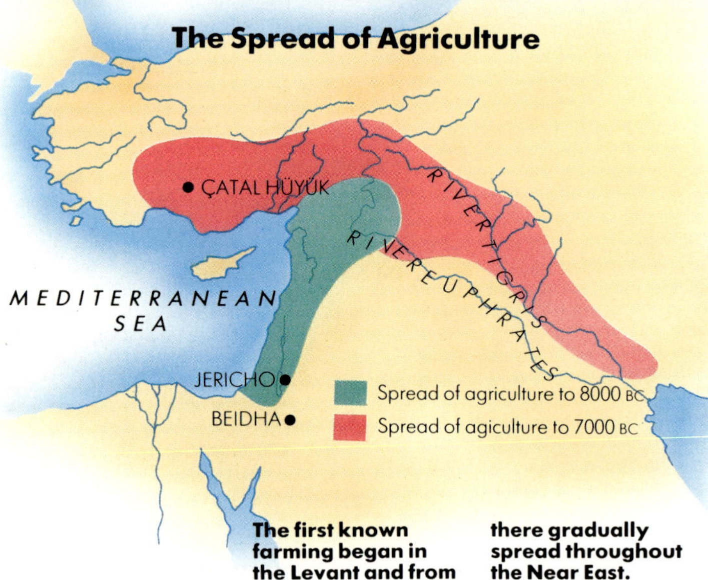

The first known farming began in the Levant and from there gradually spread throughout the Near East.

Around 10,000 BC the last Ice Age ended. As the ice sheets that had covered northern Europe receded, and temperatures rose, there were now more places where people could live and there were more food resources. This meant that the population grew. It also meant that, in spite of the improved conditions, in some places there were probably too many people living from hunting and gathering, and food was becoming harder to get.

One of the most important discoveries now took place. People learned that they could grow their own plants and rear animals themselves. In learning to farm, mankind took the first great step in controlling the world he lived in.

Up till now, people had followed the animals as they moved in search of new grazing. Similarly they had gathered wild plants, though from experience they would have known where and when there were plants ready to be harvested.

Now people became settled farmers, living in one place where they cultivated their crops and reared their animals. The terms agriculture and stock-breeding are used to describe these activities. This period of early farming is called *Neolithic* (New Stone Age).

Agriculture first developed in the Near East, in the uplands and grasslands of modern Iran, Iraq, Turkey and the Levant, which includes the Lebanon, Palestine and northern Syria.

We cannot be sure of exactly when people first began cultivating plants, but we do know that by 7000 BC, wheat, barley, peas and lentils were being grown in the Near East. Animals, such as goats, sheep and pigs, were also domesticated.

THE TOWN OF JERICHO In some places stock breeding and plant cultivation had started long before, as for example in the Jordan Valley at Jericho. This site was excavated in the 1950s by Dame Kathleen Kenyon and gradually she was able to piece together the town's history.

Here, in about 8000 BC, a fortified town covering some 4 hectares developed. Inside the town's wall was a large circular stone tower which still stands to a height of over 9 metres. The town was obviously wealthy enough to support a workforce to build the defensive wall and tower, and it is thought that this wealth probably came from trade.

The *archaeologists* there found turquoise from Sinai, cowrie shells from the Red Sea and obsidian from Turkey. Obsidian is a hard, black volcanic glass that was used for cutting. Because these precious objects came from elsewhere, we can be reasonably sure that the people of Jericho traded with other communities.

As time went by, a new group of people came to live here and they built rectangular shaped houses with plastered floors, which were often painted red.

One interesting discovery, which is thought to be connected to the worship of ancestors, was a group of human skulls. Faces of clay had been modelled on them and cowrie shells set into the eye sockets.

THE ECONOMY DEVELOPS Gradually in addition to farming, other specialized skills were developing. South of Jordan at Beidha workshops for various crafts and trades have been found. Tools, new materials and half-made objects of these ancient craftsmen and traders lay in their shops; one was a beadmaker, another a stonemason, and there was a butcher.

As we have seen, as people became settled farmers and food production increased, they were able to support some who did not work on the land. In this way specialization developed and work of such craftsmen in turn stimulated trade between communities.

A good example of this process is the obsidian trade which played a part in the economy of the large village of Çatal Hüyük in Turkey, which you can see in the picture.

Çatal Hüyük

Çatal Hüyük is the largest known Neolithic site in the Near East, and dates from about 6000 to 5000 BC. It covered some 13 hectares and about 5000 to 6000 people lived there.

It was the first community known to use *irrigation* to bring water to crops, and the people grew many different crops. They also made textiles and much attractive jewellery. The wealth came from obsidian, found nearby. It was prized for making axes, daggers and mirrors and was traded over long distances. The houses, made of mud, brick and wood, were built adjoining each other. People entered their houses from the flat roofs, along which they walked from one to another.

Some of the buildings seem to have been shrines or holy places for worshipping the gods. The walls were painted and there were bulls' heads modelled in plaster on the walls, perhaps representing a bull-god.

Left. This is a reconstruction of a funerary ritual in one of the many shrines that have been unearthed at Çatal Hüyük. The priestesses are disguised as vultures.

1 Around 8500 BC the first rock paintings in the Sahara appeared, showing wild, and later domestic animals. Around 7500 BC the first pottery appeared in the Sahara region.

2 The glaciers began to retreat c. 8300 BC, flooding lowland areas. Many new plants appeared that could be gathered by the hunter-gatherers. Around 6500 BC farming spread to the Balkans in southeast Europe, probably from Anatolia. Britain became separated from continental Europe by rising sea levels.

3 By 7500 BC farming had spread from western Asia to Pakistan. Also by this time, farming had developed independently in India. Farming villages had appeared in China by 6000 BC, and pigs and dogs had become domesticated. Rice cultivation began in China around 5000 BC.

4 The first evidence for plant cultivation in South America points to a date of 8500 BC. By 7500 BC crops were being cultivated in Mexico and the Upper Amazon region. Special grains for high altitudes began to be cultivated in Peru around 6300 BC, and potato cultivation began.

THE SPREAD OF FARMING TO EUROPE

Farming spread from Anatolia to the Balkans, that is south-east Europe, by about 6500 BC. Farming here was similar to that of the Near East as conditions were much the same. Wheat, barley, lentils and peas were grown and sheep, goats, pigs and cattle were bred by the people who lived here.

By 6200 BC there were farming villages in Sicily and southern Italy. These people lived in groups of huts which stood in large enclosures surrounded by ditches.

The new farming techniques spread only gradually further west along the Mediterranean coast. Here, communities of hunter-gatherers for whom fishing was also important, lived in caves and rock shelters. Even when they had started breeding sheep and goats people continued to hunt, fish and gather wild crops – probably because there were still plentiful supplies. But slowly cultivation increased and by about 5000 BC the first farming villages had developed in the south of France.

THE INFLUENCE OF CLIMATE Gradually farming techniques spread north west, and crops and stock had to be adapted to the cooler, more temperate weather. In central Europe the rich loamy soil was easily cultivated and was well suited to agriculture; the nearby forests were ideal for pigs. In this environment which was very different to the hotter and dryer Near East, pig and cattle herding replaced sheep and goats.

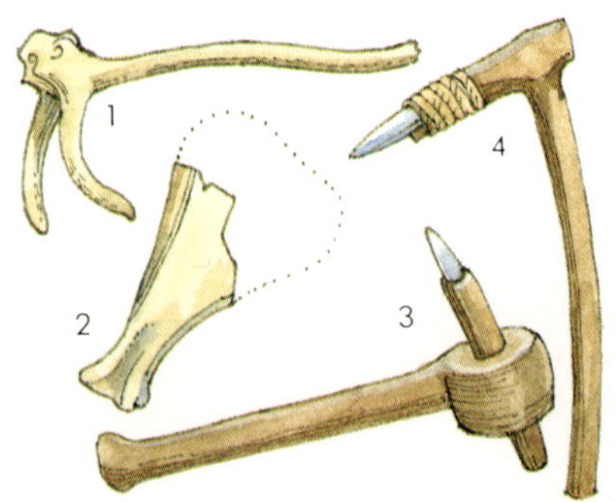

Although stone tools were still used, new woodworking tools for building and farming began to be made. Examples of these tools can be seen to the left as follows: a rake (1); a shovel made from a shoulder blade (2); small axes in wooden holders (3,4).

HOUSING Not only farming techniques, but also houses had to be adapted to a more rainy and cooler environment. The extensive forests provided plenty of timber for building. The villages of these farming people contained large longhouses which were sometimes as long as 45 metres. They were built of timber with thatched roofs and were usually divided into three parts. In the middle was the main living area; the cattle were kept in one end and the other was used for storage.

The houses were built in groups of two to five and each group had its own animal pens and rubbish pits.

Within two to three hundred years knowledge of farming had spread from central Europe to north-western Europe. We know this, because as well as the typical longhouses which in time were built from central Europe to the Netherlands, these people are also known from their distinctive lined pottery. Archaeologists call this early farming culture *Bandkeramik* after the pottery style first found in central Europe and later in the north and west.

As in the Near East, trade between different communities was carried out over long distances. Tombs in central Europe contained shells from the Aegean and the Adriatic as well as various stones not available locally.

NORTHERN EUROPE At the northern fringes of Europe, the hunter gatherer way of life continued for a long time because there was an abundance of food that could be gathered, hunted or fished. In general, farming was usually only adopted because there were no longer enough natural resources. In Denmark for instance, the disappearance of the oyster, which had been an important source of food in the spring and winter, led to the development of farming in order to provide food to replace it.

By about 4000 BC, farming was well established in Europe. Communities had increased in size, specialization of crafts developed and trading links expanded.

Styles of Pottery

Pottery is very important for helping archaeologists to understand the past. Different communities made distinctive styles of pottery, and as potsherds (broken pieces) are virtually indestructible, facts such as population movements, or length of habitation can be worked out by looking at pottery evidence. When people stay in one place there is more time to make pottery.

In antiquity, pottery was used for many purposes. Food storage and cooking were key among its uses.

Pottery was fired at very high temperatures in a kiln, after having been decorated with painted or engraved designs.

A painted vase from the Balkans (1); a Neolithic pot of a type known as 'clay flame' (2); pot with a face and a pedestal base from Hungary c. 4500 BC (3); a painted vase from Romania (4); Bandkeramik pot from Germany c. 4300 BC (5).

An early farming community in central Europe. The men on the left are making hurdles for fences and animal shelters. A longhouse is being re-thatched on the near left. Thatch was made from dried straw and laid on interwoven branches. The woman and child on the near left are making pottery with a banded decoration known as bandkeramik.

COPPER, GOLD AND THE DISCOVERY OF BRONZE

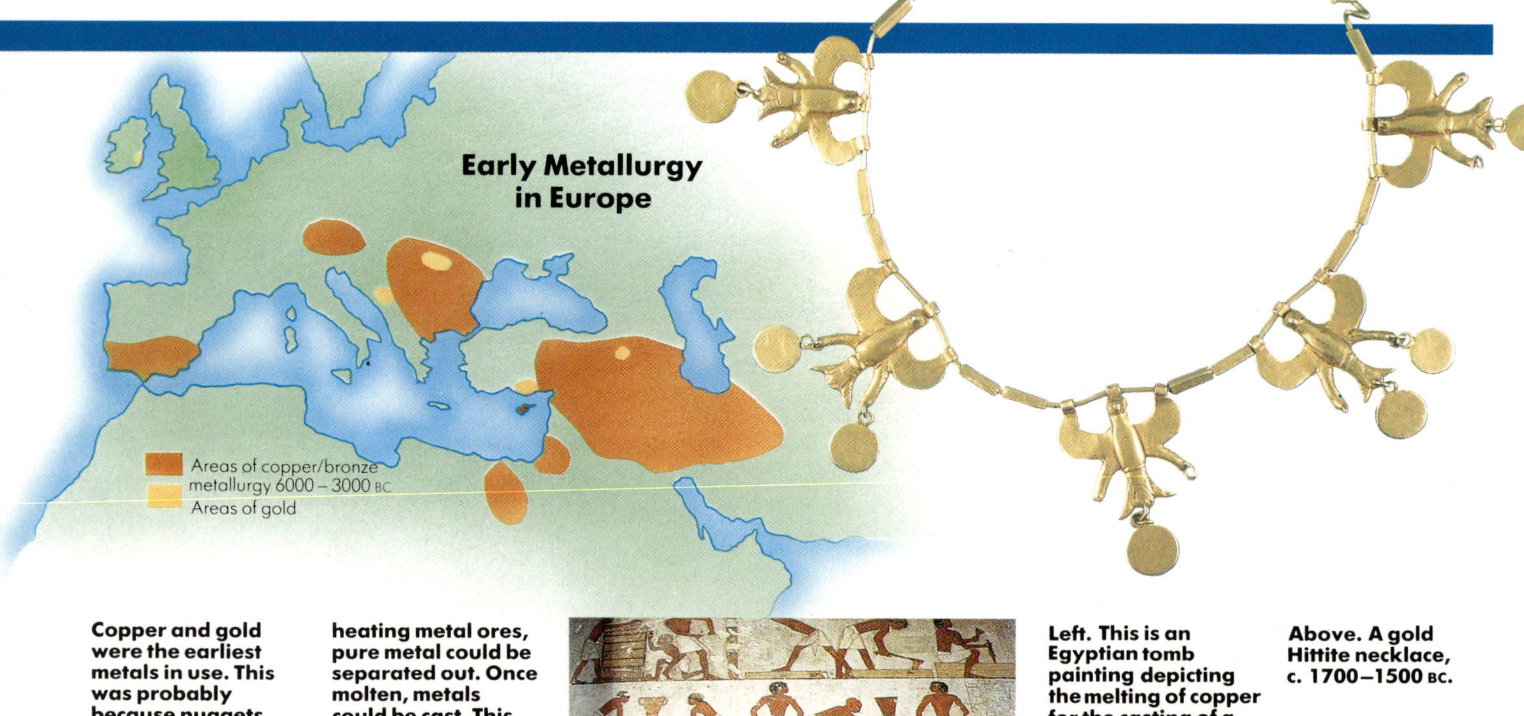

Copper and gold were the earliest metals in use. This was probably because nuggets of these occur naturally and could easily be formed into objects by hammering or cutting with stones. At some point, ancient man realised that by heating metal ores, pure metal could be separated out. Once molten, metals could be cast. This was the beginning of metallurgy and this stage was achieved at different periods in different parts of the world.

Left. This is an Egyptian tomb painting depicting the melting of copper for the casting of a pair of large temple doors. It dates from 2000 BC. The furnaces are being blown by pot bellows. It is one of the earliest records of metalworking.

Above. A gold Hittite necklace, c. 1700–1500 BC.

The discovery of metals and the development of metalworking further extended our ancestors' ability to control their environment. The earliest metals to be used were copper and gold. These metals were sometimes found in rivers and the sand as attractive nuggets soft enough to be hammered flat and cut with stone tools. Archaeologists have found beads and other ornaments made this way, together with stone and bone objects in Neolithic graves.

THE DISCOVERY OF METAL ORES But as *alluvial* (river) and surface gold deposits are fairly rare, it was the discovery that metal bearing rocks or ores could be heated to extract pure metal, that marks the beginning of true metallurgy (the term used to describe the science of metals).

This discovery seems to have been made separately in different places. In western Asia and the Balkans it was around 7000 to 6000 BC and in the Far East, some time before 2000 BC. From these regions the techniques spread to other parts of Europe, Africa and Asia.

Some of the first pieces of hammered and worked copper objects were made in Turkey in about 7000 to 6000 BC at Çayonu, an ancient site which lay only 21 kilometres from a copper mine. The earliest known metal object to be cast in a mould is a copper mace-head from Can Hasan in Anatolia (Turkey). To cast objects, the heated metal was poured into shaped stone moulds.

In Iran archaeologists have found traces of waste material from crucibles, and this evidence dates from about 4000 BC. Also found in Iran, and dating from about a thousand years later, were stone moulds used for casting copper tools. Evidence such as this tells us that both Turkey and Iran were early centres of copper mining and working, and would have been major suppliers of copper to other areas.

From archaeological remains and from written evidence, we know that copper was mined in ancient Dilmun, now Bahrain, and was exported to the cities of Southern Mesopotamia and the Indus Valley people. The Egyptians got their copper from Sinai and from Southern Palestine, where at Timna, near Eilat, copper mines and

Above. Necklaces and headbands from the early dynastic Royal Tombs of Ur in Sumer c. 2500 BC. The gold beads are made from a bitumen core and covered with gold foil.

furnaces have been found. Later, they imported copper from Cyprus; the name 'Cyprus' literally means the 'copper' island.

Although there was copper in the desert to the east of the Nile there were also the gold mines of the Wadi Hammamat. An ancient map on *papyrus* shows the mines to which the pharoahs sent large expeditions to bring back gold. Nubia, in the south, was another source of Egypt's gold.

THE BRONZE AGE Metals were at first used for ornament, but the discovery of bronze provided a much harder metal which could be used for weapons and tools. Bronze is an *alloy*, a mixture of copper and tin. Other alloys had been used, such as copper and arsenic, but true bronze was widely used in the Near East by about 2000 BC. It is possible that the tin came from as far as Cornwall, although some came from Afghanistan. The period when both stone and copper were used is called the *Chalcolithic* (meaning copper and stone) and was followed by the *Bronze Age*.

Early Mining and Smelting

Above are shown early miners extracting ores. The vertical shafts could extend to 12 m in depth. Light could always be provided either by lamps or by daylight. The miner on the right is shown digging with the aid of a deer's antler which is being used as a pick. His companion to the left collects together the ore and puts it in a crude net which is then hauled to the top of the shaft.

The diagram below shows an ancient copper mine that was worked using tunnels that were horizontal to the hillside.

In this Bronze Age copper mine, miners used bronze picks to excavate tunnels. They then used fire and water to break up the ore and bring it to the surface.

A shaft furnace used for smelting copper, seen from the side and above. Once smelted, the molten metal ran off through a hole in the side into an ingot.

THE PEOPLE OF THE NORTH

In 4000 BC most of Europe was still covered by forest, but within 1000 years much land had been cleared for farming. As in the Near East and elsewhere, the numbers of people grew with the spread of farming.

Farming techniques had gradually improved. The plough meant that more ground could be cultivated, which increased the supply of food. As metal became more widely used, farming implements became more efficient. For example, metal blades gave a sharper cutting edge to the sickle, which meant that more grain could be harvested.

THE MOUND PEOPLE Everything that is known about the prehistoric people of Europe, comes from their material remains. As there is no written evidence, we do not know what the various groups of people called themselves. Archaeologists however, have given names to some of them.

One group, who lived in Denmark over 3,000 years ago, is called the Mound People after their many round burial mounds. Much more is known about the customs of the Mound People than most other groups. This is because they were buried in boggy ground, which lacks oxygen and so their bodies and belongings have been preserved through time.

The women wore skirts and blouses, some of which were embroidered. The jewellery was of bronze, gold and silver, and included bracelets, arm rings, and finger rings. Most of the weapons were made of bronze and included swords and daggers. One of the coffins contained a vessel of birch bark which had held a mixture of beer and apple wine. Birch bark was also used for boxes, and ash wood was used to make folding seats.

Archaeologists have excavated the houses of people who lived next to lakes in Switzerland, northern Italy and eastern France. Some of these houses were very large, with up to 50 people living in them. They were rectangular in shape and were made from wood. They were thatched with reeds from the lakes.

THE MYSTERY OF THE MEGALITHS In Britain, Ireland and northwest France, there are the remains of monuments, whose functions are not always well understood. They are called *megaliths* because of the very large stones used to build them.

Some of these structures formed part of a burial complex, whilst others seem to have been used for ceremonial purposes, perhaps linked with the seasons and astronomy. But whatever their purpose, they could only have been built by well established and well organized communities: it has been estimated that it took about 15,700 manhours to build the longbarrows at West Kennet in Wiltshire.

One of the best preserved megalith constructions is Stonehenge. During the Bronze Age, about 1300 BC, an earlier ceremonial centre was made larger to create the site as we know it today. The huge stones that can still be seen, were set up, having been brought from the Marlborough Downs, about 29 kilometres away. The people who did this are called Beaker people.

The reconstruction to the right shows a typical burial mound, as used by the Mound People of Denmark. Many mound burials have survived because of the bog conditions.

When these people died they were wrapped in oxhide skins and then buried in oak coffins, such as the coffin shown at the far right of the diagram. They were buried with their clothes, jewellery, weapons and tools.

Above. A reconstruction of Stonehenge as it might have appeared during its construction. The labour and effort that must have been involved in the building of this ritual site was immense. Sarsen blocks each weighing an average of 26 tonnes, were brought from the Marlborough Downs some 29 km to the north. Their mode of transport was probably sledges using rollers and ropes, and it would have taken something like 1000 men to haul just one stone. Bluestones were the other type of stone used for construction, and these were quarried from the Prescelly Mountains in Wales, over 217 km away. The stones were raised into position by putting the lower edge over the posthole, and pulled upright using ropes.

Right. West Kennet (in Wiltshire, UK) is a Neolithic mound which has megalithic burial chambers at one end. It was used for 1000 years until c. 2500 BC, and was probably linked to death rituals. The remains of over 40 people have been found there.

Megalithic Tombs

NORTH SEA
STONEHENGE
WEST KENNET
ATLANTIC OCEAN
Early tombs c. 4500–4000 BC
Spread of tombs 4000 BC–2000 BC

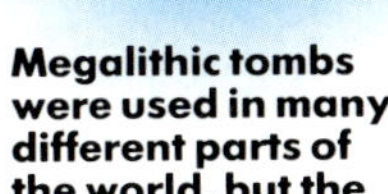

Megalithic tombs were used in many different parts of the world, but the main development occurred in Western Europe during the Neolithic period.

THE DEVELOPMENT OF WRITING

We all take writing for granted, but as with farming and metalworking, it is not something that people have always done, but it *is* another immensely important human invention.

The first known writing system was developed in Mesopotamia, the land between the Tigris and Euphrates rivers, in what is today Iraq. The earliest forms of this system date from around 3200 to 2800 BC. As the first examples of writing are of numbers of objects only, it seems that writing originated from the need to keep accounts and records.

PICTOGRAMS At first picture signs, called *pictograms* were used to indicate objects. A picture of a head or of grain, meant quite simply 'head' or 'grain'. Gradually this system expanded to suggest objects or ideas that could not be put into pictures. In this way, for instance, the Sumerian sign for 'mouth' came to also mean 'speak'. Another way of expressing actions or ideas was to combine two signs to mean a third; thus the sign for mouth and food was combined to mean 'eat'.

An important step was taken when a picture was used to represent the sound of the name and not the object it showed. These are called sound signs; for example, if we were using such a system, pictures of an eye and a saw would represent the sounds 'I saw' in English.

CUNEIFORM WRITING Because there was plenty of clay, people wrote on wet clay tablets with a sharpened reed or stylus. The tablet was left to dry in the sun. Gradually the picture forms became more abstract and a stylus with a triangular tip was used. This left wedge shaped impressions in the clay, hence the writing is called *cuneiform* from the Latin meaning 'wedge shaped'.

The cuneiform script was invented by the Sumerians. Later, other people in the Near East used this script to write their own very different languages. Akkadian, which was the earliest Semitic language, and the Indo-European Hittite were both written in cuneiform. Similarly, today all European languages are written in the same script that the Romans once used, although the languages are different.

OTHER WRITING SYSTEMS As you can see from the map, several different writing systems developed in various parts of the world. In Ancient Egypt they used a picture script which we call *hieroglyphic* in which the pictures represented both sounds and ideas. The Egyptians wrote with a brush and ink on *papyrus*, which was similar to paper and was made from the stem of the papyrus plant.

The first Chinese writing was also derived from pictures and was written on bones. Later, the Chinese invented paper. At about the same time that the Akkadians were writing in cuneiform, the people of the Indus Valley used a script that cannot yet be read.

All of these systems were complex and took many years to learn. Most people could not read or write, so that writing was done by a small group of *scribes* who were trained in the temple or palace schools. Around 1000 BC a much simpler form of writing emerged. This is called *alphabetic* and was first used by the Phoenicians. The Greeks adopted this system in which words are made from individual letters which stand for sounds. This is the system that the Romans borrowed and adapted and that we now use.

How Papyrus was Made

Papyrus was made from the stem of the papyrus plant which grew in the Nile delta. The diagrams below show how papyrus was actually made.

To form scrolls, several pieces of papyrus were stuck together. Papyrus continued in use until it was replaced by parchment, which was invented by the Hellenistic city of Pargamon.

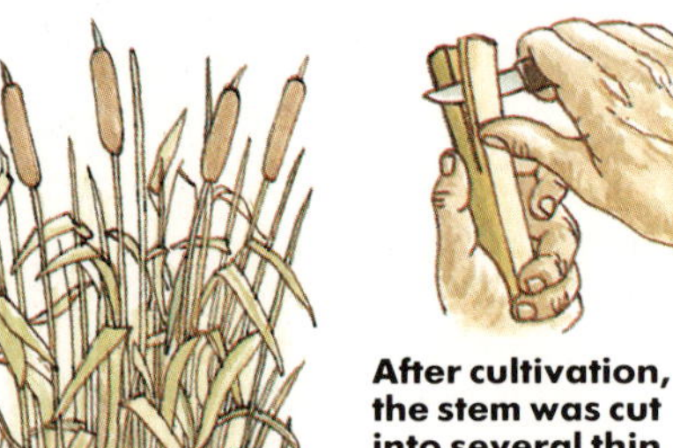

This shows the papyrus plant before cultivation.

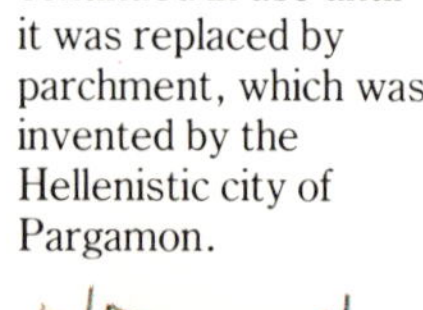

After cultivation, the stem was cut into several thin lengths, using a sharp tool.

These lengths were laid next to each other and layers were placed on top at right angles.

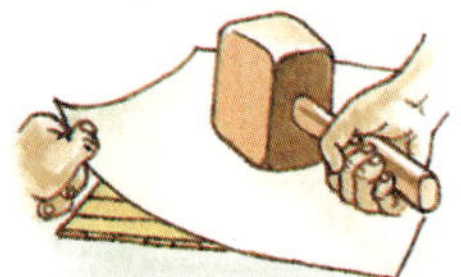

A piece of cloth was laid on top and was hammered gently to break down the fibres.

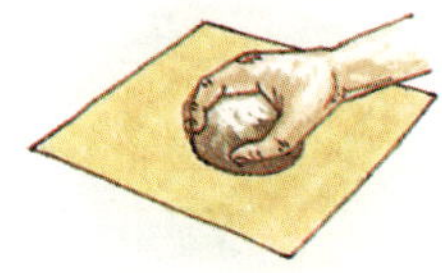

The papyrus was left to dry slightly, then rubbed smooth with a stone.

Below. This map shows the origin and development of early scripts. Most of the early scripts were pictographic, hieroglyphic or cuneiform.

An early Akkadian cylinder seal impression c. 2334–2000 BC. Seals such as this were worn for adornment and for sealing and signing documents, storage jars, etc. Often they were passed down in families. The inscription reads: 'Ubil-Eshtar, brother of the king; Kalki, the scribe, is your servant'.

The Spread of Writing

3500 BC Earliest writing in Mesopotamia
3000 BC Writing develops in Egypt
2500–1700 BC Scripts appear in the Indus Valley
1700–1200 BC Linear A and B develop in Greece
1500–600 BC Hieroglyphic and cuneiform scripts in Asia Minor and northern Syria
1400 BC Writing develops in China
1400 BC Early alphabets in Syria and Palestine

Cuneiform Writing

Cuneiform literally means 'wedge shaped writing'. It was written on damp clay tablets with a reed pen (as shown below). It was invented by the Sumerians and later adapted for Akkadian and other languages. It was used in the Near East until it was displaced by the Aramaic script. Cuneiform tablets have been found at many sites in western Asia and neighbouring lands.

The tablet above is an early administrative tablet from Jemdet Nasr c. 2900 BC. It is written in cuneiform and lists areas of fields and crops.

The chart below shows part of the developing stages of cuneiform from the original incised drawings of recognizable objects to more abstract strokes.

BIRD	WALK/ STAND	DONKEY	WATER	FISH

Below. This is the Rosetta Stone, inscribed by Egyptian priests in 196 BC. It provided the key to deciphering Egyptian hieroglyphics, since the inscription is written in two forms of Egyptian and in ancient Greek.

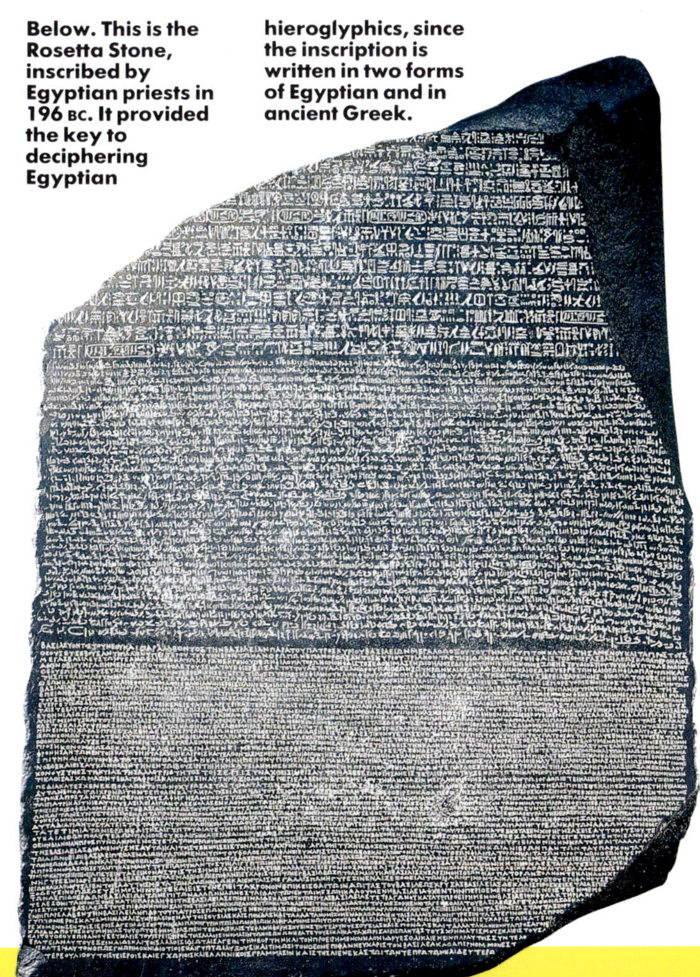

THE EMERGENCE OF CITIES

The first known cities were built by the Sumerians in about 3500 BC. The land of Sumer lay in what is today southern Iraq. This region, between the Tigris and Euphrates rivers, is also called Mesopotamia, from the Greek, meaning 'the land between the rivers'.

Elsewhere, urban civilization, that is, the civilization of cities, also developed next to great rivers. The Nile, the Indus and the Yellow river in China were all, independently, early centres of urban life.

Why did these early cities develop next to rivers? Why are the first cities not found in the regions where people had farmed since 7000 BC? To try and understand why urban life emerged in the river valleys, let us look at early Sumer.

Left. This white marble mask, almost life-sized, comes from the temple precinct of Eanna at Warka (Uruk).

Below. This shows the peace side from the Standard of Ur. Thought to be the sounding box of a musical instrument, this object has both peaceful and warlike scenes on either side of each other. The original wooden box was covered with bitumen and overlaid with a coloured mosaic of shell, lapis lazuli and red limestone. It dates from 2500 BC.

FARMING IN SUMER Before the Sumerians adopted agriculture they already had good supplies of food including fish from the rivers, wildfowl from the marshes and the fruit of the date-palm. We do not know precisely when these people began to farm, but by 4000 BC this region had become more productive than the earlier upland centres of farming.

One reason for this was the rich soil. Each year the rivers flooded the plain and left a layer of fertile soil brought down from the hills: this is called alluvium. There was, however, little rain and once the floodwaters receded, the earth dried out under the hot sun. No matter how rich the soil, nothing grows without water. If water could be led from the river to the soil, then crops would grow, and this is exactly what was done.

We call it irrigation farming and it is still used today. Water is fed to the fields from a dam or river, along artificial canals. Fertile soil and water provided plenty of food, which meant that more people survived and multiplied. The irrigation system itself required a degree

of organization and cooperation between communities. New canals had to be built and existing ones left clear. Also, as the network of waterways expanded, so communications increased. The rivers and canals acted like roads, with people travelling along them by boat.

BEGINNINGS OF SOCIETY Often there was more food grown than people could eat: this is called a surplus. It could either be stored to feed people after a poor harvest or it could be exchanged for goods not available locally. It could also feed specialists who no longer lived by farming but by their crafts or trading.

All these factors meant that society became more complex and small farming villages gradually became larger centres which had to be organized, protected and governed.

We do not know exactly how rulers, armies and government emerged. It is possible that as disputes over boundaries became more common between opposing tribes, a war-leader was appointed. In time, such leaders would have become kings in charge of large armies.

Because the earliest writings seem to record the delivery of food to temples, it is thought that the temples were rather like government departments, collecting taxes and organizing food supplies. Archaeologists have excavated some of these cities which had developed by about 3000 BC.

Some of the first cities appeared on the flat river plain of the Tigris and Euphrates rivers. Trade was extremely important to people living in this area, and all the major early towns are to be found on the rivers. The Sumerians traded over impressive distances — to Afghanistan, the Lebanon, Anatolia and Persia — and brought back goods such as timber, lapis lazuli, precious stones, and metal ores.

Above. A libation vase from Uruk c. 3000 BC. It is one of the earliest examples of Sumerian art where wild heroes of the countryside are shown protecting animals.

1 In 3118 BC Egypt was unified and the First Dynasty appeared. In 2800 BC construction work was begun on the pyramids of Giza, and the era of the Old Kingdom began. The Old Kingdom came to an end in 2100 BC, and the Middle Kingdom commenced in 2040 BC.

2 The first wheeled vehicles appeared in Europe in 3200 BC. Megalithic monuments become prominent in Britain and northwest France. The European Bronze Age began c. 2300 BC. By 2000 BC the main phase of building had begun at Stonehenge, and the palace centres of Minoan Crete had appeared.

3 By 3000 BC the plough was in use in China and farming had begun in Korea. Silk weaving in China began and the first bronze objects started to appear. The Indus Valley civilization, with great centres at Mohenjo-Dara and Harappa, had developed by 2500 BC.

4 By 3500 BC the llama was being used in Peru as a domestic pack animal; cotton was being grown in southern Peru and textiles were being made. From 2800–2300 BC, villages appeared in the Amazon region, temple mounds were built in Peru, and the earliest ceramics appeared in central America.

THE SUMERIANS

Most people in the first Sumerian towns were farmers. Each town or city lay at the centre of an area of cultivation. Barley, linseed and sesame were some of the main crops, as were date palms which grew in orchards along the river and canal banks. Oxen, pigs and sheep grazed on the land.

HOUSES AND TEMPLES At first houses were made of reeds, and indeed the Marsh Arabs of Iraq still live in houses of an almost identical style. In time however, they learned to build with mud bricks which they strengthened with straw and dried in the sun. In an area of little rainfall such houses can last for many years.

The most important buildings in the cities were the temples. The Sumerians believed that the gods who ruled the world, lived on mountains, and it is thought that their high terraced *ziggurats*, or temple towers, reflect this tradition. It was their belief that mankind existed to serve the gods and goddesses who had to be looked after like kings and queens. Priests served them in their temples and people brought food and clothes with which to feed and dress the gods. The priests were rich and powerful as they looked after all the wealth belonging to the gods.

The Sumerian cities were independent city states ruled by their kings who also headed the army. The temple priests administered the cities, collected taxes and were usually in charge of clearing the canals. Sometimes one city was stronger and controlled other cities, but until the time of Sargon of Agade there was no large unified state in the region.

SARGON OF AGADE In 2340 BC the first great age of the Sumerians ended when Sargon took control of the region. His capital was north of Sumer at Agade which has not yet been discovered. Sargon spoke Akkadian which is not related to the Sumerian language but is the ancestor of modern Arabic and is a Semitic language. Although Sargon led his armies to Anatolia, the Levant and Syria, his 'Empire' was shortlived

Near right. This bronze head is thought to be of Sargon of Agade. It was found at Nineveh in Assyria and dates from 2300–2000 BC. Far right. The Ziggurat at Ur was the core of the sacred precinct. It was dedicated to Nanna, the Moon God. Ziggurats were first built by Sumerians in the third millennium BC. They were monumental structures in the form of stepped towers, at the summit of which was a shrine. Ziggurats represented the sacred mountains where men communicated with the gods. The Ziggurat at Ur is the best preserved of all those that remain standing today.

Above. This plan of the world, with Babylon on the River Euphrates as the centre, was drawn to illustrate the campaigns of Sargon of Agade. According to later traditions, Sargon campaigned as far north as Anatolia and to the Levant in the west.

The Royal Tombs of Ur

A piece of jewellery and a dagger sheath from the Royal Tombs of Ur.

The city of Ur became one of the most important cities in Sumer during the third millennium BC. It was excavated between 1923–1934 by the British archaeologist, Leonard Woolley, and has since become famous for its royal tombs and ziggurat.

There are a total of 16 royal burials, and those of the greatest kings of Ur were located close to the ziggurat. The rulers were accompanied in their tombs by their retainers, and by some of the most beautiful jewellery and other objects which survive from ancient times.

and did not continue beyond his great grandson. Nevertheless, for the first time, the whole of Mesopotamia had been one political unity.

After the overthrow of Sargon's *dynasty* there was a revival of Sumerian civilization and for about a century from c.2100 BC, Ur became the most important Sumerian city. The Royal Tombs of Ur show how wealthy these people already were. After 2100 BC, the temples were rebuilt and were even larger and more impressive than earlier temples.

ANCIENT EGYPT

Egypt has been described as 'The gift of the Nile', for without the river, nothing would grow in the valley, which is bounded by desert on either side. But the annual flood made the land fertile, and by 5000 BC there were people living in farming villages along the river. Gradually two kingdoms developed, Lower Egypt in the north, and Upper Egypt in the south. They were unified by the first Pharaoh, Menes, around 3200 BC.

THE PHARAOHS The Egyptians believed that their king was a living god who had control over all aspects of life, including the Nile floods. The King lived in a palace called 'Per'ao' meaning 'the Great House'. The title Pharaoh comes from this word.

During his lifetime, the Pharaoh was believed to be the falcon headed sun-god, Horus. At death he became the mummified god of the underworld, Osiris. Because the Egyptians believed that death was the beginning of an afterlife, they regarded tombs as houses of eternity into which were placed everything needed for the next life.

The pyramids were the tombs of the Old Kingdom rulers, but because robbers stole from them, later pharaohs were buried in tombs hidden in the Valley of the Kings. But most of these were also robbed, except for the tomb of the boy-king Tutankhamun. This unplundered tomb was found by Howard Carter in 1922. There was so much treasure that it took several years for the tomb to be fully excavated. The many beautiful objects are now in the Cairo museum, but the King's *mummy* has been left in the tomb.

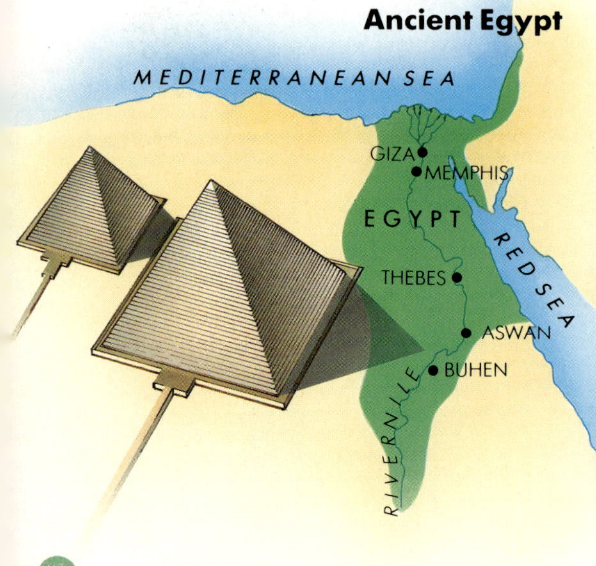

Ancient Egypt

MEDITERRANEAN SEA
GIZA
MEMPHIS
EGYPT
THEBES
ASWAN
BUHEN
RIVER NILE
RED SEA

The region controlled by Egypt shifted considerably throughout its history, but at its greatest extent Egypt extended as far as the Euphrates River. Despite shifts in its boundaries during some 3000 years, for the most part Egypt controlled the lands to the east of the Nile to the Red Sea, and on the west it bordered with Libya.

THE PRACTICE OF MUMMIFICATION People were mummified to preserve their bodies for the afterlife. After their intestines, lungs and liver and heart were removed and placed in *canopic jars*, the body was placed in *natron* for 40 days and then wrapped in resin-soaked bandages. Scientists and archaeologists sometimes study mummies to find out more about the health of the Egyptians.

The people and actions depicted in wall-paintings found in the tombs, which have been preserved in the dry desert conditions, give us a great deal of information about the Egyptians.

EGYPTIAN FARMING Most people lived in villages in flatroofed mud brick houses, farming the land close to the river. They grew wheat, barley and many types of vegetables, including peas, beans and lentils. Although cattle were raised and there were various domestic birds like ducks and geese, most people seldom ate meat but got their protein from lentils, eggs and fish.

When the land was flooded, they worked for the King, building pyramids, temples or palaces. As well as farmers, there were craftsmen such as jewellers, masons, carpenters, sculptors, painters, some of whom worked for the great nobles or the King. Some craftsmen worked only on the royal tombs, which began to be prepared at the beginning of each Pharaoh's reign.

DEVELOPMENT OF A WRITING SYSTEM The Egyptians were one of the first people to use a writing system: it is called *hieroglyphic*. Law cases, letters, medical and magical texts, stories, poems and hymns, all survive on *papyri*. These help to give us a picture of life and events. From the hymns and funerary texts we know that the Egyptians worshipped many gods.

The sun god Re' was also the falcon-headed Horus, the living Pharaoh, whose mother was Isis and whose father was Osiris. Isis and Osiris were also brother and sister. Seth, the god of storms, violence and lord of the desert was also their brother. Hathor the cow-goddess represented music, dancing and love.

Some gods were linked to places, such as Hapi the god of the Nile, or Ptah, the god of craftsmen and god of Memphis.

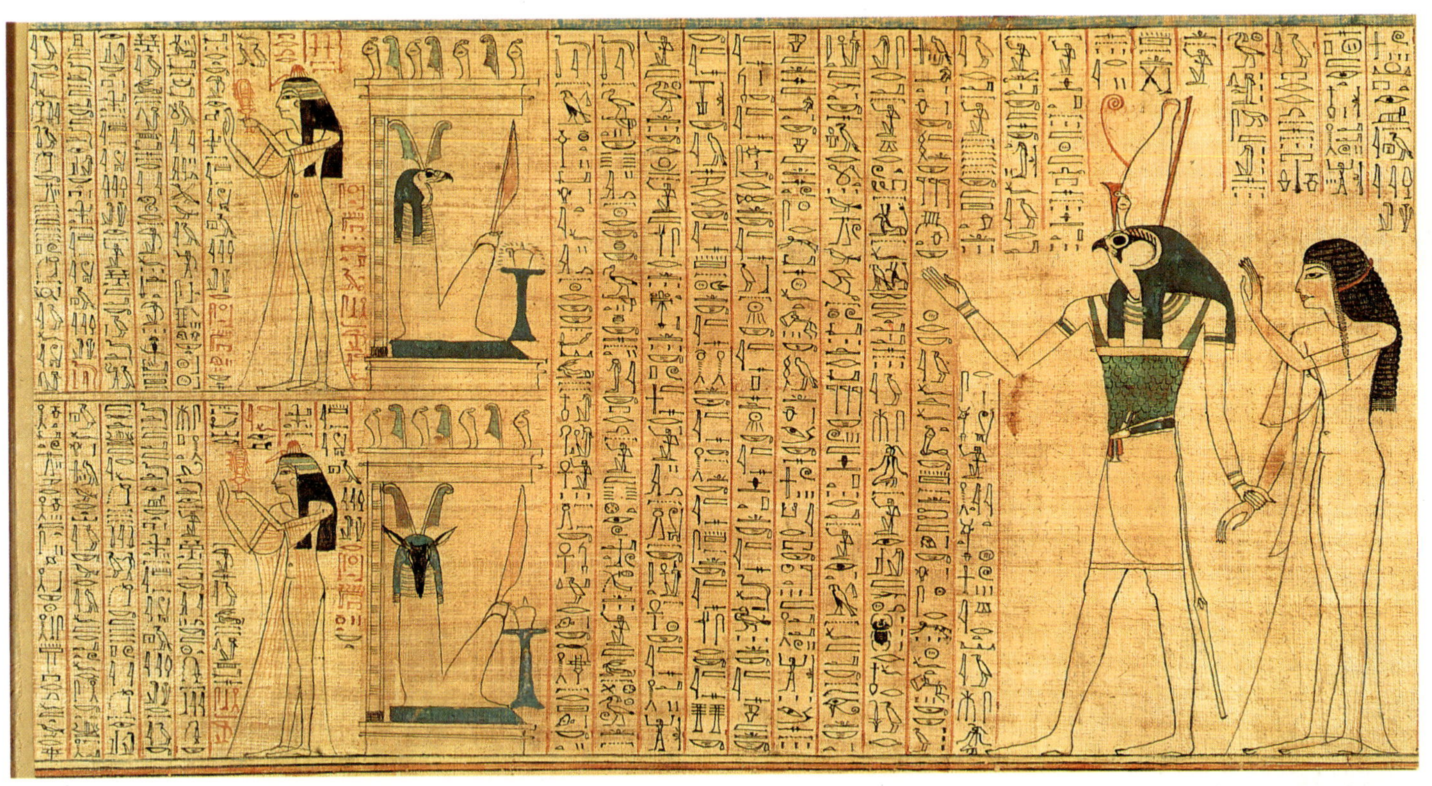

Above. This scene comes from the Book of the Dead, one of which was placed in each person's coffin.

Above. The tomb of Sennufer who was the royal gardener. The two people depicted are Sennufer and his wife. The tomb is most unusual in having the entire ceiling painted as a vine with hanging grapes. It dates from the 18th Dynasty.

Above and Left. This statue and frieze both depict Osiris, the Egyptian god of the dead. At death, Egyptian pharaohs were believed to become Osiris. He is shown here carrying the crook and flail which were symbols of kingship in Egypt.

Egyptian Arts and Crafts

Though most Egyptians were farmers, an important minority worked as craftsmen.

Painters and sculptors had to obey some very strict rules in their art. They had to draw everything to the right proportions, and only show people in certain poses. This was because a picture in a tomb was supposed to 'come alive' in the next world when the priests had said the right prayers and spells. The scenes shown were then believed to go on happening forever.

THE GOLDEN AGE OF EGYPT

Egypt's very long history is divided into three periods. These are called the Old, Middle and New Kingdoms. In the Old Kingdom (c. 2686 – 2181 BC) powerful pharaohs sent expeditions to Sinai for turquoise and copper from which they made marvellous jewellery and ornaments. They also traded with the Lebanon for cedarwood which they used to build boats. In time the local nobles became more and more powerful and rivalry between the regions resulted in chaos which brought the Old Kingdom to an end.

THE MIDDLE KINGDOM Egypt was reunited under a king from Thebes, Mentuhotpe, in 2040 BC, shortly after the beginning of the Middle Kingdom. This period also ended in confusion brought about by the arrival of the Hyksos. These people had entered Egypt from Syria from about 1674 BC, and had managed to assert their power over Egypt. The Egyptians fought with the Hyksos and eventually drove them out of the country. Egypt now entered her most powerful and wealthy era – the period of the New Kingdom.

THE NEW KINGDOM During this period Egypt controlled much of Syria and Palestine and also Nubia to the south. Tribute from the subject states and gold from Nubia made Egypt the richest nation in the ancient world.

Throughout the period of the New Kingdom, the

The Tomb of Tutankhamun

Tutankhamun's tomb was discovered in 1922. Although ancient robbers had left some disorder, the tomb was virtually unplundered and was full of beautiful objects.

In the burial chamber, within four golden shrines, lay the heavy stone sarcophagus. Inside were three coffins, the innermost of solid gold, 2.5 cm thick and exquisitely decorated.

The dried, embalmed body of Tutankhamun was wrapped in bandages. Over his face was a superb gold funerary mask, decorated with precious stones and glass.

Right. The goddess Isis on the inside of the door of a golden shrine. Isis has winged arms to receive the dead. Far right. The golden coffin belonging to Tutankhamun. Below. A funerary bedhead in the form of a cheetah, from one of the beds in the antechamber of Tutankhamun's tomb.

pharaohs ruled from Thebes. Instead of pyramids which were visible and could be plundered, the pharaohs were buried in tombs cut out of the rock.

The area used for burial was called the Valley of the Kings, and it lies on the west bank of the Nile. It was here that Howard Carter discovered the unplundered tomb of Tutankhamun in 1922. Although he was not an important pharaoh, it took three years for archaeologists to excavate and record the immense riches of his tomb.

EGYPT UNDER THREAT Although still prosperous, towards the end of the New Kingdom Egypt's borders became threatened. Early in the thirteenth century BC, the Egyptians, under Ramesses II, fought the Hittites at the battle of Qaddesh. The result was indecisive, but Ramesses had his victory recorded on temple reliefs which still exist today.

In about 1200 BC there was turmoil in the countries bordering the Mediterranean. Troy and the Mycenaean cities of Greece were destroyed. The Hittite Empire collapsed suddenly and the cities of the Levant were laid waste. Finally, Egypt was attacked by groups of raiders called the Sea People. Twice the Egyptians defeated them and saved their country from invasion. But already Egypt's period of greatness was over. After the New Kingdom rival kings ruled from different cities and civil war broke out.

The Egyptian Army

During the Old Kingdom, the army was more like a *militia*, composed of contingents from the different 'nomes' or regions. It consisted entirely of light and heavy infantry. Later, *mercenaries* were recruited from Nubia and Libya, and they formed the greater part of the army.

In the Middle Kingdom, the army began to be recruited. Although each nome provided a quarter of the recruits, they were now permanent soldiers. There were still mercenaries, but far fewer than there had been formerly. This too was an infantry army of spearmen and archers.

Following the expulsion of the Hyksos, the army of the New Kingdom was quite different, both in composition and in equipment. The nomes still provided their contingents for the regular army, but after a period of service, others took the place of these men so that there was now a trained reserve. The Hyksos had introduced the chariot and new weapons and equipment. There were now mounted forces as well as infantry. Armour was worn and the composite bow and a new form of axe were used. A few mercenaries were used at the beginning of the New Kingdom, but by the 20th Dynasty the Egyptian element in the army had again decreased.

An Egyptian soldier of the New Kingdom.

The Tombs of the Valley of the Kings

On the west bank of the Nile, some miles from Thebes, in the 'Land of the Dead', have been found the tombs of 62 rulers. The desolate valley was chosen so that the tombs would remain hidden. In fact, only the tomb of Tutankhamun remained virtually intact.

In order to keep the position of the tomb secret, the funerary temples for the worship of the dead rulers were built elsewhere. The most impressive of the tombs is that of Seti I, and it is illustrated below.

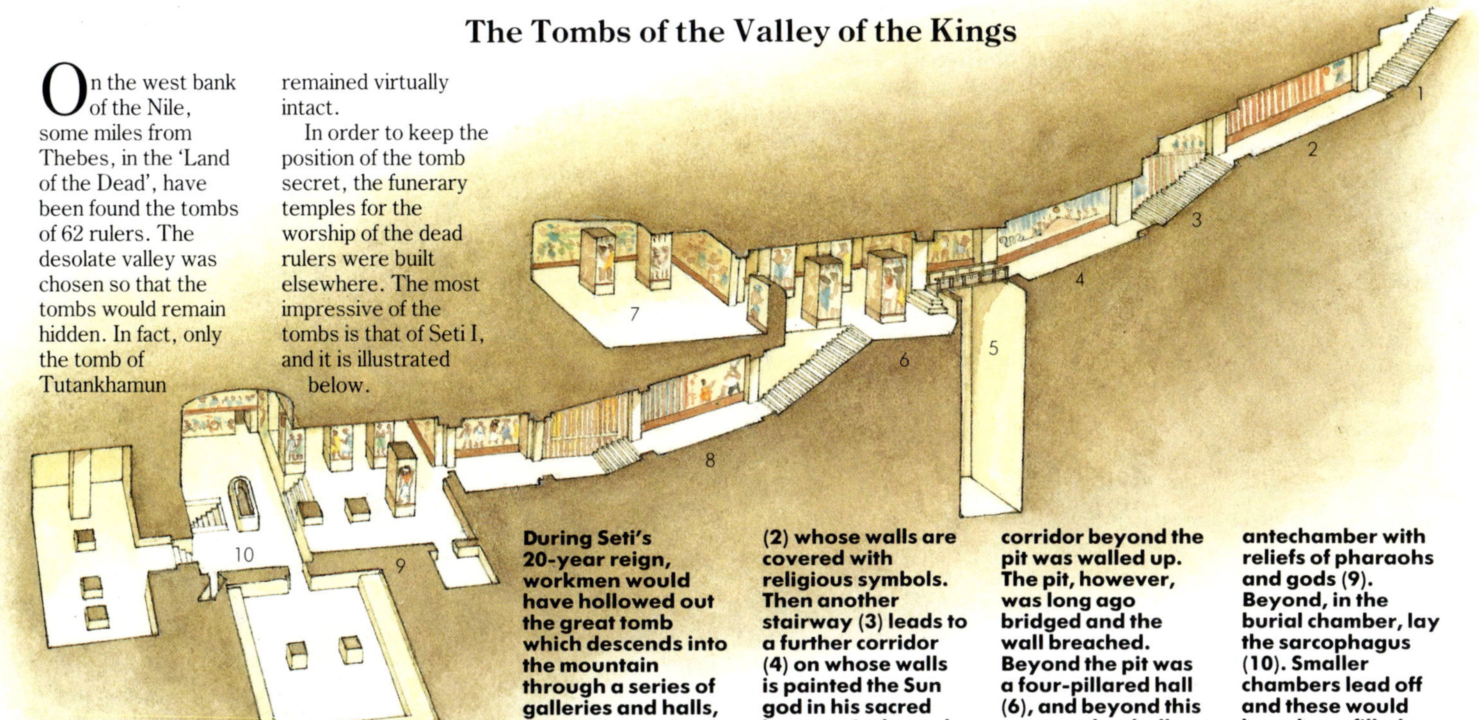

During Seti's 20-year reign, workmen would have hollowed out the great tomb which descends into the mountain through a series of galleries and halls, over 120 m in depth. From the entrance, a broad flight of steps (1) leads down to a sloping corridor (2) whose walls are covered with religious symbols. Then another stairway (3) leads to a further corridor (4) on whose walls is painted the Sun god in his sacred barque. At the end is a pit (5) which is 12 m deep. This was intended to keep out burglars, for the corridor beyond the pit was walled up. The pit, however, was long ago bridged and the wall breached. Beyond the pit was a four-pillared hall (6), and beyond this was another hall (7). A further staircase and corridors (8) lead down to an antechamber with reliefs of pharaohs and gods (9). Beyond, in the burial chamber, lay the sarcophagus (10). Smaller chambers lead off and these would have been filled with funerary furnishings.

KNOSSOS AND THE MINOAN CIVILIZATION

According to Greek legend, King Minos of Crete took an annual *tribute* from Athens of seven young men and seven girls. They were sacrificed to the Minotaur, a creature half-bull and half-man. The Minotaur lived in a maze under the palace of Knossos called the labyrinth.

The hero Theseus, whose father was the King of Athens, was selected as one of the seven youths. In Crete, Ariadne, the daughter of Minos, fell in love with Theseus. She gave him a ball of thread with which he was able to find his way out of the labyrinth after he had killed the Minotaur.

We do not know whether Minos was a real king or a mythical ruler, but such legendary stories do not seem as strange as they once did, before the long lost ancient civilization of Crete was discovered at the beginning of this century.

THE EXCAVATION OF KNOSSOS In March 1900 Arthur Evans, a wealthy scholar, began excavations at Knossos. Gradually an extraordinarily rich and lively world was revealed. Evans called this civilization *Minoan*, after King Minos.

The palace at Knossos was built in about 2000 BC on the site of an earlier village. Other palaces have been found to the east of Knossos on the coast, at Mallia, and in the south of the island at Phaestos. There was also a palace in the east, at Zakro.

The palaces were several storeys high with large rooms, and they were built around central courtyards. The royal apartments were painted with scenes of courtly life and naturalistic plants and animals. As well as being royal residences, the palaces were centres for the administration of the area.

Basement store-rooms or *magazines* housed the surplus produce of grain, oil, wine and honey in stone boxes and large jars called *pithoi*. Craftsmen also worked at the palaces making beautiful jewellery and pottery.

Many paintings and engravings have been found of bull-leaping ceremonies, which probably took place in the palace courtyards. Young men and women would grasp the bull's horns and somersault over the animal.

The Minoans did not build temples, but worshipped the great mother goddess. They also had shrines to the snake goddess in their houses.

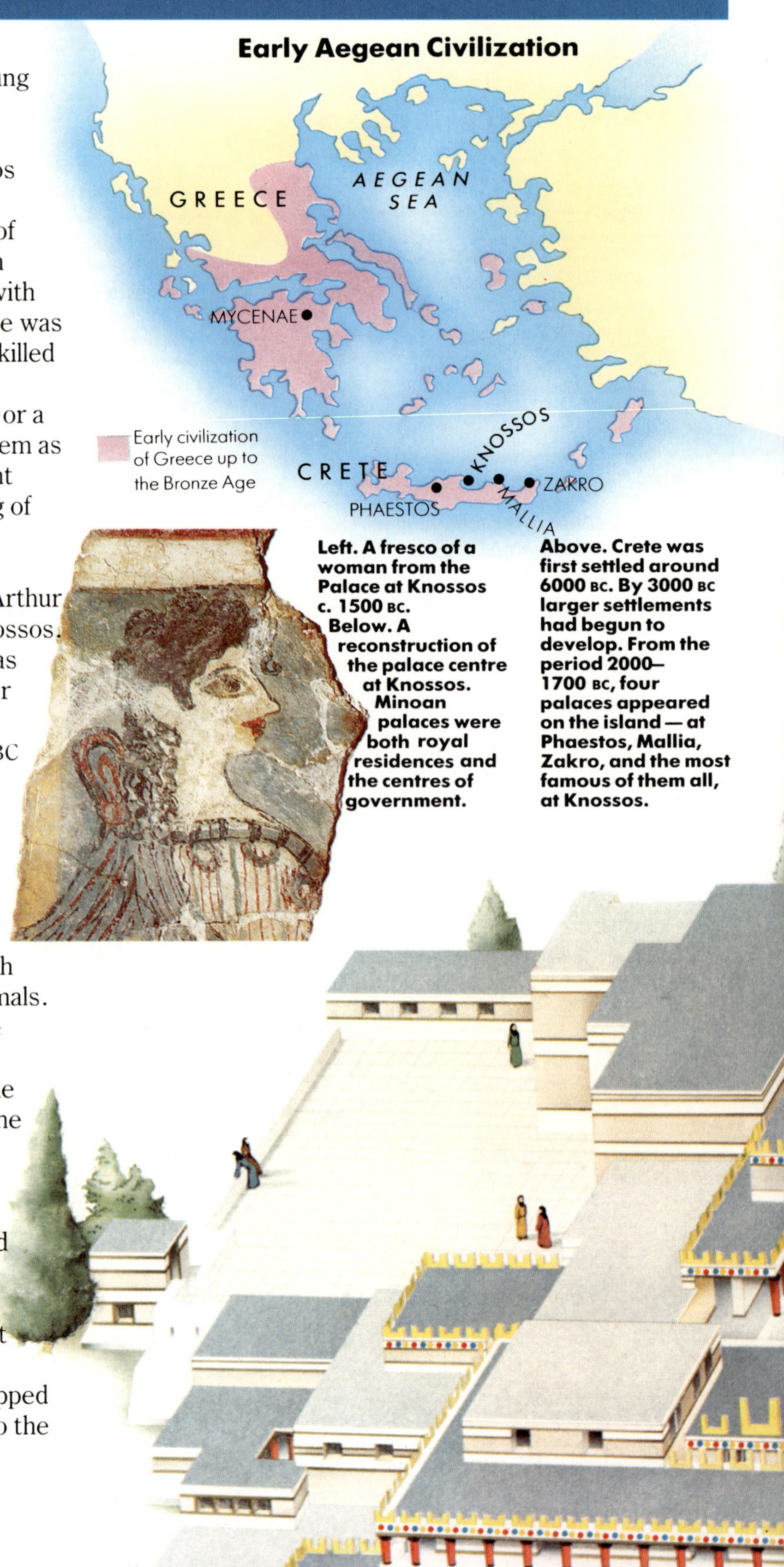

Left. A fresco of a woman from the Palace at Knossos c. 1500 BC.
Below. A reconstruction of the palace centre at Knossos. Minoan palaces were both royal residences and the centres of government.

Above. Crete was first settled around 6000 BC. By 3000 BC larger settlements had begun to develop. From the period 2000–1700 BC, four palaces appeared on the island — at Phaestos, Mallia, Zakro, and the most famous of them all, at Knossos.

Left. This shows the fresco of the dolphins in the so-called Queen's apartments at Knossos. The fresco dates from c. 1500 BC. Minoan artists painted in a flowing and naturalistic style, frequently depicting plants and animals.

Above. This fresco depicts a bull-leaper in the act of somersaulting over the bull's back. There appears to have been a cult in Minoan Crete linked to the bull. It is thought that the bull-leaping took place in the large courtyard at the palace. In Minoan art, women are shown in white and men in red. So, you can see here that the bull-leaper is in fact a man. The fresco dates from 1500 BC and is 70 cm in height.

The Minoans also had settlements on the islands of Thera and Kythera. From Cretan objects found in Egypt and elsewhere in the Near East, we know that Crete traded with these lands. Large houses with colourful paintings and household objects have been found on Thera. One very interesting painting shows a naval expedition setting out to sea.

The Minoan writing system, called Linear A, has not yet been deciphered; it was used from about 1900 BC to 1450 BC.

Another script, Linear B, was found at Knossos and was used from about 1450 to 1400 BC. The palaces and towns of Crete had been destroyed, probably by an earthquake, and abandoned in about 1450 BC.

Knossos however, was reoccupied for some fifty years by a new group of people from the Greek mainland. They adapted the Cretan Linear A script to write their own language.

TROY AND THE MYCENAEAN WORLD

The people from the Greek mainland who occupied Knossos in about 1450 BC are called Mycenaeans, after the town of Mycenae in southern Greece.

THE TROJAN WAR Homer's great poem, the *Iliad*, tells the story of the Greek expedition against Troy, led by King Agamemnon of Mycenae and other kings to recapture Helen. She was the beautiful wife of King Menelaus of Sparta, and had been abducted by the Trojan prince, Paris, whose father, Priam, was the king of Troy. The Trojan war lasted for 10 years and only ended when the Greeks used a trick to get into the city. They pretended to give the Trojans a gift of a wooden horse. Once the horse was in the city, the Greek soldiers hidden inside it broke out of the horse's body and attacked the Trojans.

This story was thought to be only legend, but in 1868 Heinrich Schliemann, who had made his fortune from trade, set out to find Troy. The site was identified as Hissarlik in Turkey, where a town was discovered which had existed from the early Bronze Age to the Roman era.

LEARNING ABOUT MYCENAE Homer's poems also include traditions about Mycenae, describing the city as 'rich in gold'. Although the poems were written at a much later date, about 800 BC, the information would have been passed down orally, by word of mouth. Schliemann's discoveries at Troy led him to excavate Mycenae, and he found remains of a splendid war-like people which bore out Homer's descriptions.

The late Bronze Age Mycenaean civilization existed from about 1600 BC to 1150 BC. There were a number of

The wooden horse of Troy shown in relief on a Greek terracotta amphora c. 670 BC. The story of how the Greeks tricked the Trojans after the 10-year long siege of the city is famous. It was Odysseus, the hero of Homer's great epic poem, the *Odyssey*, who devised the plan to get inside the city walls. The Greek fleet sailed away, leaving a huge wooden horse standing on the shore. The unsuspecting Trojans thought that this marked an end to the war and hauled the horse inside the city walls. But at midnight, the Greeks who were hiding inside the belly of the horse crept out. They opened the gates of Troy to let in the men from the Greek fleet, which had returned to Troy under the cover of darkness. The Greeks then destroyed Troy and Helen was reunited with her husband, Menelaus, king of Sparta.

small kingdoms, each with its central palace or *citadel*. These had often started as hillside villages which only later developed great fortifications.

At Mycenae, the huge walls were built around 1300 and extended in 1250 BC, when conditions were becoming increasingly troubled. Other towns such as Tiryns and Gla were also surrounded by immense walls. This type of wall in which huge stones were used, is called *Cyclopaean*, after the Cyclops, the giants of legend, thought by the Greeks to have built the walls.

MYCENAEAN PALACES The rooms of the palaces were arranged around courtyards. The floors and walls were plastered and painted, often with scenes of daily life. The most important room in each palace was the *megaron*, a large hall with a central hearth and a roof supported on four wooden columns.

These palaces had many store rooms for produce and equipment. As elsewhere, the palace also had craft workshops producing beautiful ivory, gold and other objects. The influence of Cretan craftsmanship is clear, especially in the wall painting and pottery. However, warfare was an important part of Mycenaean society and unlike Cretan art, much of the Mycenaean pottery, painting, ivories and inlaid designs on swords, depict soldiers armed with spears and large shields. There are also remains of weapons and armour, including a helmet with boars' tusks, of a type that is mentioned in the Iliad.

From the palace of Pylos and from the latest period at Knossos, are the remains of archives of clay tablets. These are written in the Linear B script, an early form of Greek. Linear B was a development of Linear A, the script used in Minoan Crete. The Mycenaens had adopted Linear A and had developed it to represent Greek.

These texts give a picture of centralized government. Various types of workers are mentioned, including metal-workers, cattle-herders and shepherds, sailors and weavers. Priests, soldiers and rulers also appear. From the archaeological remains and the texts we get a picture of a world of warlike and wealthy kings of independent cities to whom people paid taxes in kind.

All the Mycenaean palaces and towns were destroyed or abandoned by the end of the twelfth century BC. Although there appear to have been invasions, some scholars think that there might have been internal rebellions. However, we do not know what caused the end of this civilization, though we do know it suffered a violent end.

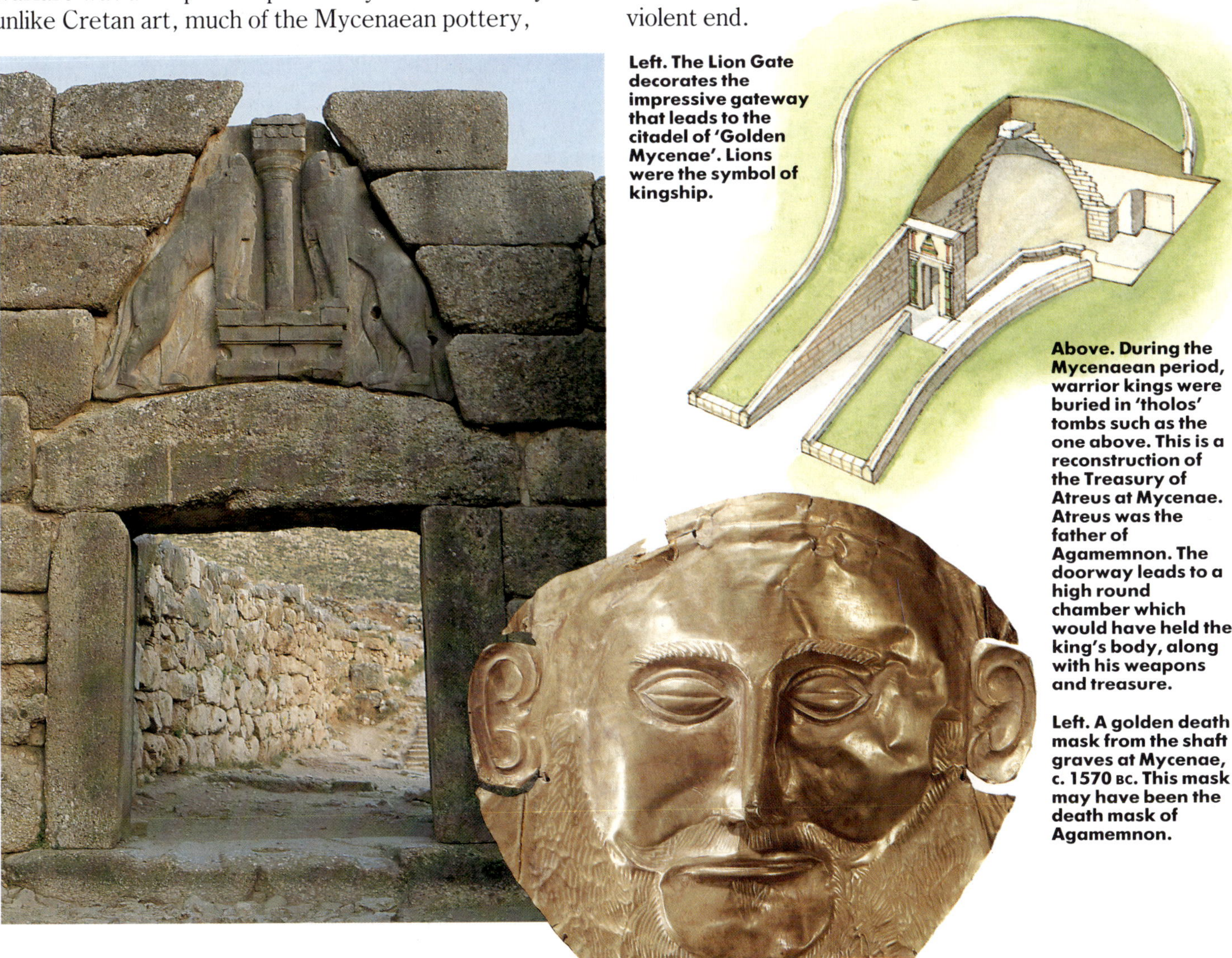

Left. The Lion Gate decorates the impressive gateway that leads to the citadel of 'Golden Mycenae'. Lions were the symbol of kingship.

Above. During the Mycenaean period, warrior kings were buried in 'tholos' tombs such as the one above. This is a reconstruction of the Treasury of Atreus at Mycenae. Atreus was the father of Agamemnon. The doorway leads to a high round chamber which would have held the king's body, along with his weapons and treasure.

Left. A golden death mask from the shaft graves at Mycenae, c. 1570 BC. This mask may have been the death mask of Agamemnon.

THE INDUS VALLEY CIVILIZATION

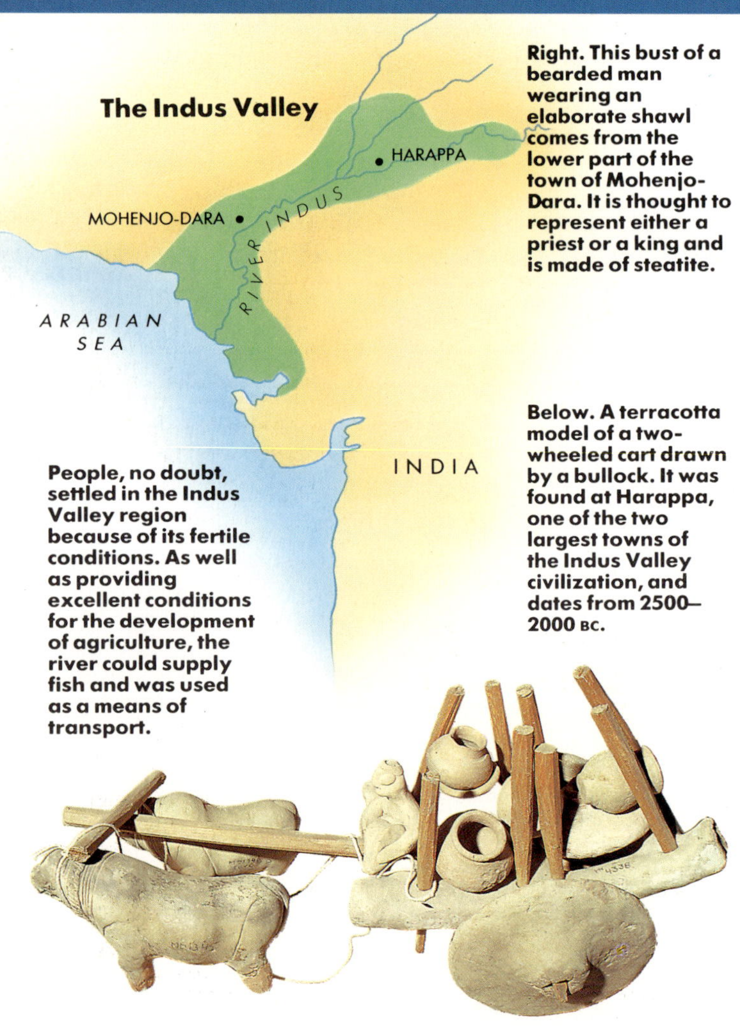

People, no doubt, settled in the Indus Valley region because of its fertile conditions. As well as providing excellent conditions for the development of agriculture, the river could supply fish and was used as a means of transport.

Below. A terracotta model of a two-wheeled cart drawn by a bullock. It was found at Harappa, one of the two largest towns of the Indus Valley civilization, and dates from 2500–2000 BC.

Right. This bust of a bearded man wearing an elaborate shawl comes from the lower part of the town of Mohenjo-Dara. It is thought to represent either a priest or a king and is made of steatite.

Far to the east of the Aegean, Egyptian and Near Eastern worlds lay another great centre of civilization. It is known as the Indus Valley civilization after the Indus River near to which many of its towns were built.

Covering 1.3 million square kilometres, it was the largest known Bronze Age civilization in the world. More than 150 sites are known and many have been excavated. The two largest are Mohenjo-Dara and Harappa, which were probably the main centres, each with populations of about 30,000 to 40,000 people. As elsewhere, this urban civilization developed from the Neolithic settlements of farming communities, which began around 3500 BC. Gradually, walled towns, trade and specialized crafts emerged, and by 2500 BC the villages and towns of this vast region were all part of the same civilization.

ORGANIZATION OF THE CITIES Mohenjo-Dara, Harappa and several of the smaller towns had similar plans. The town walls were made of baked brick, and in the centre of the town there was a raised area or citadel where the most important buildings were constructed. At Mohenjo-Dara there was a great bath, which may have been used for ritual bathing, rather like the tanks of holy water for bathing in many Indian temples today. Nearby was a building thought to be a granary.

There were no palaces in these cities. The citadel looked over the rest of the town, where there were streets and blocks of houses. The larger houses were arranged around courtyards and had stairs up to a flat roof. Poorer people lived in one-roomed houses.

Most buildings were of baked brick, which were the same size in all the towns. The streets had drains

Right. The probable granary, shown here in reconstruction, was situated on the citadel at Mohenjo-Dara on a steep verge. The granary was built of huge timber pieces which were set upon a high brick base, 27 blocks deep. The criss-cross arrangement of the passages between the blocks ensured that the air could circulate beneath it. This was vital to keep the grain fresh. The granary was originally 45 m long and 23 m wide but was later extended. A loading platform outside the main building facilitated moving the grain in and out of the stores.

Above. This is a reconstruction of the Great Bath at Mohenjo-Dara. The building was 12 m long, 7 m wide and 3 m deep. At the north and south ends, brick steps led down to the floor, with wooden treads which were set in bitumen or asphalt. The bath itself was lined with asphalt in order to make it waterproof. The bath was enclosed contained a well, perhaps the source for the water used in the bath. There was also a group of cells with private baths. These are thought to have been used by priests.

Above. The main blocks of buildings were subdivided by small streets or lanes running parallel to, or at right angles to, the main streets. Some houses were large, such as this one, and consisted of several rooms around a courtyard. There were stairs to an upper storey. Such houses also had a lavatory on the ground or upper floor, a bathroom and a private well. Brick drains were another feature of the Indus Valley towns and they even had their own inspection holes. The house above would have belonged to one of the more wealthy townspeople. Poorer people lived in single-room tenements.

covered in brick, with holes for inspection. Some houses also had bathrooms and lavatories leading to the street drains. Large houses had their own wells. There were also hearths for household fires.

In the lower part of town there were also the workshops of many craftsmen – metalworkers, bead-makers, potters, masons and textile-makers. A standard system of weights and measures was used and many stone weights have been found.

Beautiful sealstones, carved with animals, were used to seal bales of goods. Some have been found in Iraq, showing that the people of the Indus Valley and Sumer traded with each other. From cuneiform texts, we know that the island of Bahrain, which was called Dilmun, was a centre through which this trade passed.

The seals also have hieroglyphic inscriptions on them. These may be the names or titles of merchants but as yet this writing system has not been deciphered. Without written evidence, our knowledge of these people is limited. We still have no idea why the towns were suddenly abandoned and the civilization came to an end about 1700 BC.

LIFE AND DEATH IN ANCIENT CHINA

The civilization of ancient China emerged in the valleys of the Yellow River and Wei River in northern China. Of all the civilizations of the old world, Europe, Asia and Africa, it was the most isolated and owed little to contacts with other regions.

By 6000 BC farmers were working the fertile river valleys. The main crop here was millet and the people reared pigs. These early people made pottery which was beautifully painted.

THE LONGSHAN PERIOD The period from 2500 to 1800 BC is called the Longshan period. During this era people lived in towns which were walled for defence. They made metal tools and turned pottery on a wheel. Even then, there were always some people who were far wealthier than others. Archaeological evidence for these developments has been provided by burial practices of the period.

China in the Shang Era

The Shang culture embraced a large area, and rich burials and oracle bones have been unearthed at many of the Shang sites marked on this map. Near Anyang, which was the capital from the 14th to the 11th centuries, are the graves of the last Shang kings, who were buried with their attendants, horses and other animals.

Left. Examples of the many fine bronze vessels found by archaeologists, dating from the Shang period.

THE SHANG CIVILIZATION The uplands near the fertile valley contained metals which were mined by the people of the early Bronze Age civilization which had developed by about 1800 BC. It is called the Shang civilization, from the name of the dynasty of kings who ruled the region.

The Shang capital was moved several times. Zhengzhou was one of the earliest and was founded around 1700 BC. There was a large rammed-earth platform, creating a raised area, on which the palace buildings stood. A wall of 7 kilometres long surrounded this area, and parts of it, about 9 metres high, still survive.

Outside the palace and ceremonial area, were private houses in suburbs, and many workshops. During the Shang period, the skill of the craftsmen advanced dramatically, and beautiful bronze vessels were cast from pottery moulds. Amongst the workshops at Zhengzhou were pottery kilns and foundries for bronze casting. Several hoards of bronze objects were also found.

Anyang, which became the royal capital in 1400 BC, is the most important Shang site. Here too, was a ceremonial centre with palaces, as well as workshops and houses. When the palaces were built, both people and animals were sacrificed and buried in the building foundations and special pits, presumably to make the gods look favourably on the new city. No fewer than 852 people, 35 dogs, 18 sheep, 15 horses, 10 oxen and five chariots have been found in these pits.

BURIALS AND RELIGION Near to the town were cemeteries, which include the tombs of the last Shang kings. Although many of the tombs were robbed thousands of years ago, the surviving objects give us some idea of the wealth of these rulers.

The king's servants were sacrificed and buried with the body, as were his horses and dogs. They also buried the king's chariots, and many bronze and jade objects.

Ancestor worship was an important part of the Chinese people's religion. The ancestors were consulted through the oracle bones. These were animal bones or tortoise shells on which questions to the ancestor spirits and the gods were carved. Thousands of oracle bones have been found at Anyang and elsewhere.

The Shang dynasty collapsed in the eleventh century when the Zhou conquered the state. However, many traditions continued, passing into later Chinese civilization.

People of the Shang culture were skilled craftsmen, and used a variety of materials—gold, jade and lacquer, amongst them. This axe head is made of bronze and dates from c. 1200–1100 BC. It was of ceremonial use, and is highly decorated.

1 In Egypt, the Middle Kingdom comes to an end in 1783 BC, and the Hyksos take control. The New Kingdom begins in 1570 BC; it is during this period that the rock-cut tombs are built in the Valley of the Kings. Thebes becomes the new capital. Tutankhamun is buried in 1337 BC.

2 Palaces are built in Minoan Crete at Knossos, Phaestos and Mallia c. 2000 BC. Cretan hieroglyphic writing begins. The period in Greek history known as 'Mycenaean' begins c. 1550 BC. Mycenaeans take control of Crete c. 1450 BC. The Mycenaean period comes to an end c. 1150 BC.

3 The Indus Valley civilization collapses c. 2000 BC. On the steppes in central Asia, horses are used to pull carts c. 1850 BC, and pastoral nomads herding cattle on horseback appear c. 1400 BC. The bronze industry begins in central Asia c. 1200 BC.

4 The first metalworking begins in Peru c. 1500 BC. The first cities appear in central America c. 1200 BC, inhabited by people of the Olmec culture.

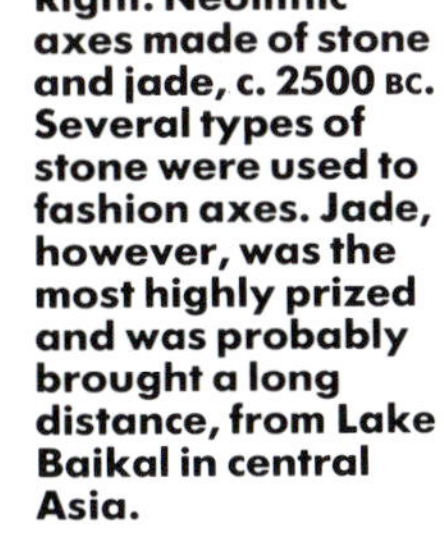

Right. Neolithic axes made of stone and jade, c. 2500 BC. Several types of stone were used to fashion axes. Jade, however, was the most highly prized and was probably brought a long distance, from Lake Baikal in central Asia.

Above and right. Two bronze ritual vessels of the Shang period. The one above was a libation vessel used for pouring offerings of wine, c. 1200–1100 BC. The one to the right was a food vessel. There were many different styles of Shang bronze ritual vessels used to hold either food, wine or water. Their decoration was often very ornate and symbolic.

The First People
TIME CHART

4.5 million BC – 100,000 BC Evolution of Man in Africa, Spread of Man from Africa and Palaeolithic Era
10,000 BC – 4000 BC Neolithic: Spread of Farming/Early Metalworking

BC	NEAR EAST	AFRICA/EGYPT	EUROPE/GREECE	CHINA/INDIA
6500			Neolithic farming	
6000	Copper-working in Anatolia	Cattle domesticated		Farming
5000	Irrigation farming		Metalwork in Balkans	
4500				Agriculture
4000		Sail first used in Egypt		
3500	First towns			
3118		Unification of Egypt		
3100	First writing			
2686>2181		Old Kingdom		
2600>2400	Royal Graves of Ur			
2500>1800				Longshan Neolithic culture in Taiwan
2372>2255	Akkadian Empire			
2133>1633		Middle Kingdom		
2113>2006	Third Dynasty of Ur			
2000>1900			Greek speaking tribes	
1792>1750	Hammurapi of Babylonia			
1674>1567		Hyksos invaders		
1650>1450			Minoans and Mycenaeans on mainland	
1587>1085		New Kingdom		
1500>1027				Shang dynasty centred on Anyang
1460>1180	Hittite Empire			
1450			Cretan civilization ends	
1300	Iranians move into Iran			
1200	Raids of Sea Peoples			
1197>1165		Ramesses III defeats Sea Peoples		

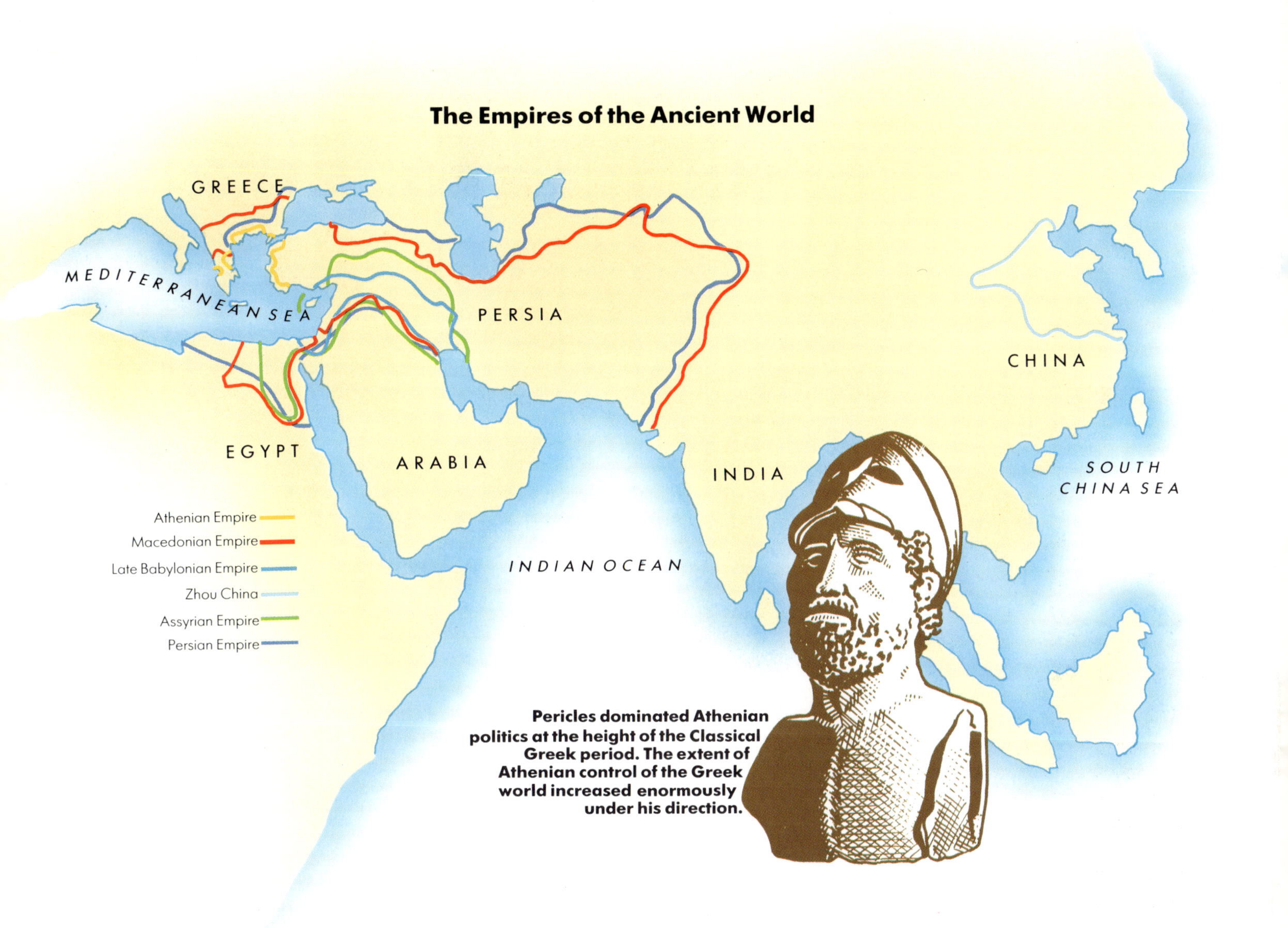

The Empires of the Ancient World

GREECE
MEDITERRANEAN SEA
PERSIA
CHINA
EGYPT
ARABIA
INDIA
SOUTH CHINA SEA
INDIAN OCEAN

Athenian Empire
Macedonian Empire
Late Babylonian Empire
Zhou China
Assyrian Empire
Persian Empire

Pericles dominated Athenian politics at the height of the Classical Greek period. The extent of Athenian control of the Greek world increased enormously under his direction.

The Great Empires

The thousand years, or millennium, before the beginning of our era was the period when iron began to be used in the Near East and when the manufacture of iron goods spread through Europe and Asia. This was a major development; iron is found in many places and it is stronger than copper or bronze for tools and weapons.

Better tools meant improved farming and more food, which resulted in more people. In some places, as the population grew, there was not enough land, so people moved on, seeking new places to live. This is one of the reasons why the Greeks, for instance, started colonies in the Black Sea area and around the southern coast of Italy and elsewhere. It is also the reason for the various movements of people on the fringes of the civilized world.

Iron also meant that armies were better equipped. The need for more land was sometimes backed by armed force, and in time some countries took control of others and formed empires. The Assyrians did this, so did the Babylonians and later, the Persians.

There were other inventions that changed life. The development of a keel on ships meant that sailors could take their vessels into the open sea and travel further. The alphabet made writing simpler and much easier to learn, so writing became increasingly widespread and more information was written down. This means among other things, that there is far more written evidence from which historians can gather facts, including accounts of events by Greek historians. From these, and from poetry, plays and other works, we have far more detail about what life was like for these people than for those who lived earlier.

THE PHILISTINES AND ISRAELITES

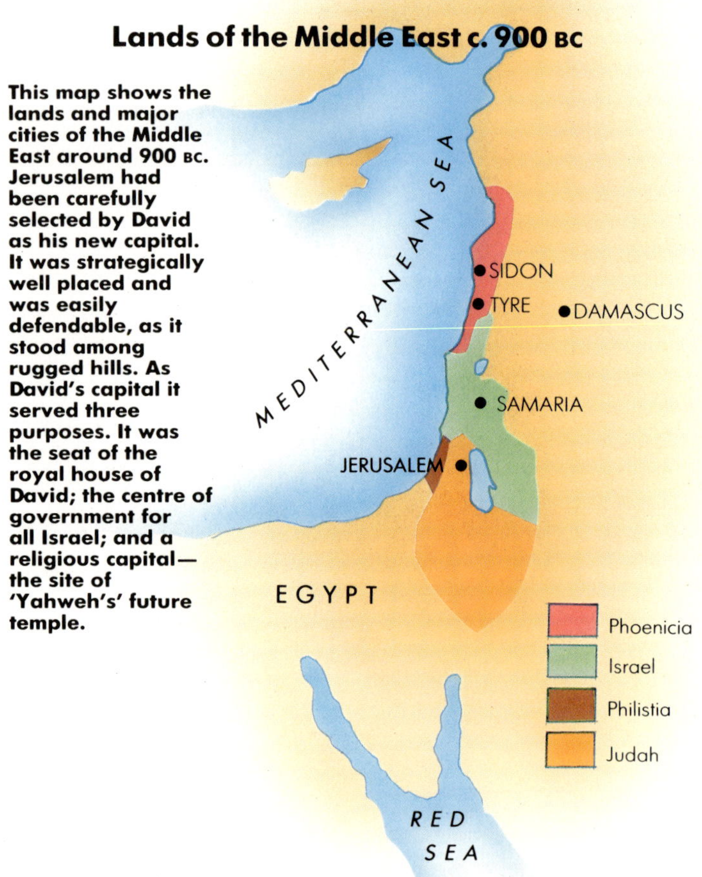

This map shows the lands and major cities of the Middle East around 900 BC. Jerusalem had been carefully selected by David as his new capital. It was strategically well placed and was easily defendable, as it stood among rugged hills. As David's capital it served three purposes. It was the seat of the royal house of David; the centre of government for all Israel; and a religious capital—the site of 'Yahweh's' future temple.

In about 1200 BC there were great upheavals in the lands of the Eastern Mediterranean Sea. The Hittite empire vanished suddenly and cities of the Levant were laid waste.

THE SEA PEOPLE It is generally thought that these disturbances were caused by groups of roving marauders called 'the Sea People'. It is possible that the Sea People were linked to the destruction and abandonment of the Mycenaean centres of the Aegean and Troy, but nothing is known for certain.

From Egyptian accounts we know that the Sea People attacked Egypt but were defeated. Pharaoh Ramesses III had his victory recorded: '*The foreign countries made a plot in their islands . . . no land could stand before their arms, beginning with Khatti (the Hittites) . . . They came, onwards to Egypt . . . as for those who reached my boundary . . . their hearts and their souls are finished unto eternity– those who entered unto the river mouths were confined . . . butchered and their corpses hacked up*.'

Some settled on Egypt's borders and later became mercenaries for the Pharaoh. Others, the Peleset, settled in southern Canaan around Gaza. Known as the Philistines, they gave their name to Palestine.

Events in the century before the first millennium BC (one thousand years), are not very clear and there is a break in the archaeological record. What is known, is that by 1000 BC there were several new groups of people living in the Near East. Also, the Great Powers such as Egypt and Babylonia had grown weaker.

THE CULTURE OF THE ISRAELITES Because there was no powerful state in control, groups of migrating nomads were able to settle in Syria and Palestine. Amongst them were the Israelites, the group whom we know most about.

The Israelites believed in the power of their god 'Yahweh' above all others. They despised other gods and in time they believed that no other god existed. From the eighth century BC, they wrote down their history and laws. These books were preserved, some as part of the Christian Old Testament. *Monotheism*, the belief in one god, was of great importance, because it was from this tradition that both Christianity and Islam were to come.

Apart from religion, their lives were no different to other people in this region. They were farmers living in villages and small, walled towns. They were also sturdy fighters and after arriving in Canaan, had fought the Philistines and the Canaanites.

The Israelites' greatest period was during the reigns of David and Solomon, from 1000 – 926 BC when there was one kingdom with its capital Jerusalem in Judah. David had captured and refortified the city and Solomon had a splendid temple and palace built here by Phoenician craftsmen.

In 926 BC the Kingdom was divided into Israel (north) and Judah (south). King Omri of Israel built himself a new capital at Samaria which had a beautiful palace. Later, Israel became an Assyrian province, and in 597 BC the Babylonians took Jerusalem, and in the process the king and his nobles were exiled to Babylon.

Left. Human-shaped or anthropomorphic coffins were used by the Philistines. This sarcophagus lid dates from the 12th century BC. It is made of clay and is typical of the styles made during this period.

Above. A household shrine of the Israelite period, but probably Philistine. Such shrines were widely used amongst the people of this region. The voluted columns resemble the proto-Ionic columns used on some buildings of this period.

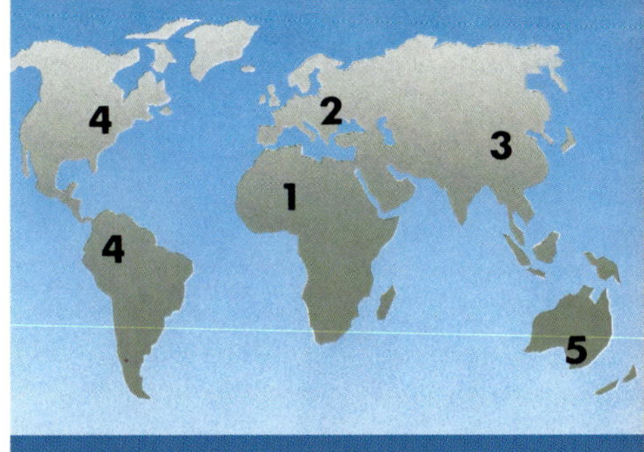

1 1085 BC marked the end of the New Kingdom in Egypt. The country was effectively divided with Upper Egypt controlled from Thebes, and Lower Egypt under the control of competing dynasts, including descendants of Libyan chiefs. The Kingdom of Kush (Nubia) was founded in 900 BC. This date also marked the beginning of the Nok culture of Nigeria.

2 By 1000 BC, hillforts were in use in western Europe, and iron was widely in use in the Aegean and central Europe. The period known as the 'Dark Ages' in Greece ended in 900 BC. In Italy, the settlement of Rome began c. 850 BC.

3 In China, the Zhou Dynasty replaced the Shang Dynasty in 1027 BC. Bronze-working spread from China to Korea.

4 Larger communities appeared in the central and south Andes of South America c. 1000 BC. At the same period in North America, the Indians of the Adena culture in the east began the practice of richly furnishing their burials. Grave goods such as bracelets, rings, beads, tobacco pipes and polished stone tools were commonly placed with the corpse under the burial mound.

5 Around 1000 BC long distance trade networks for raw materials developed. In the southeast of Australia, villages with round stone houses appeared.

Solomon's Temple

The temple built by Solomon was finished in the eleventh year of his reign. It is not possible to know how it looked exactly, though some idea can be gained from the description in the Bible, and from what is known about Canaan art in this period.

The walls were of stone blocks and were plain on the outside, but covered on the inside with cedar wood and carved figures of winged creatures, palm trees and rosettes.

Two large bronze pillars stood either side of the gold-inlaid, olivewood doors. There were also bronze basins on ornamental wheeled pedestals for washing burnt offerings. At the back of the interior were steps leading to the 'Holy of Holies' where stood the ark of the covenant containing the 10 commandments written on stone tablets.

THE PHOENICIANS

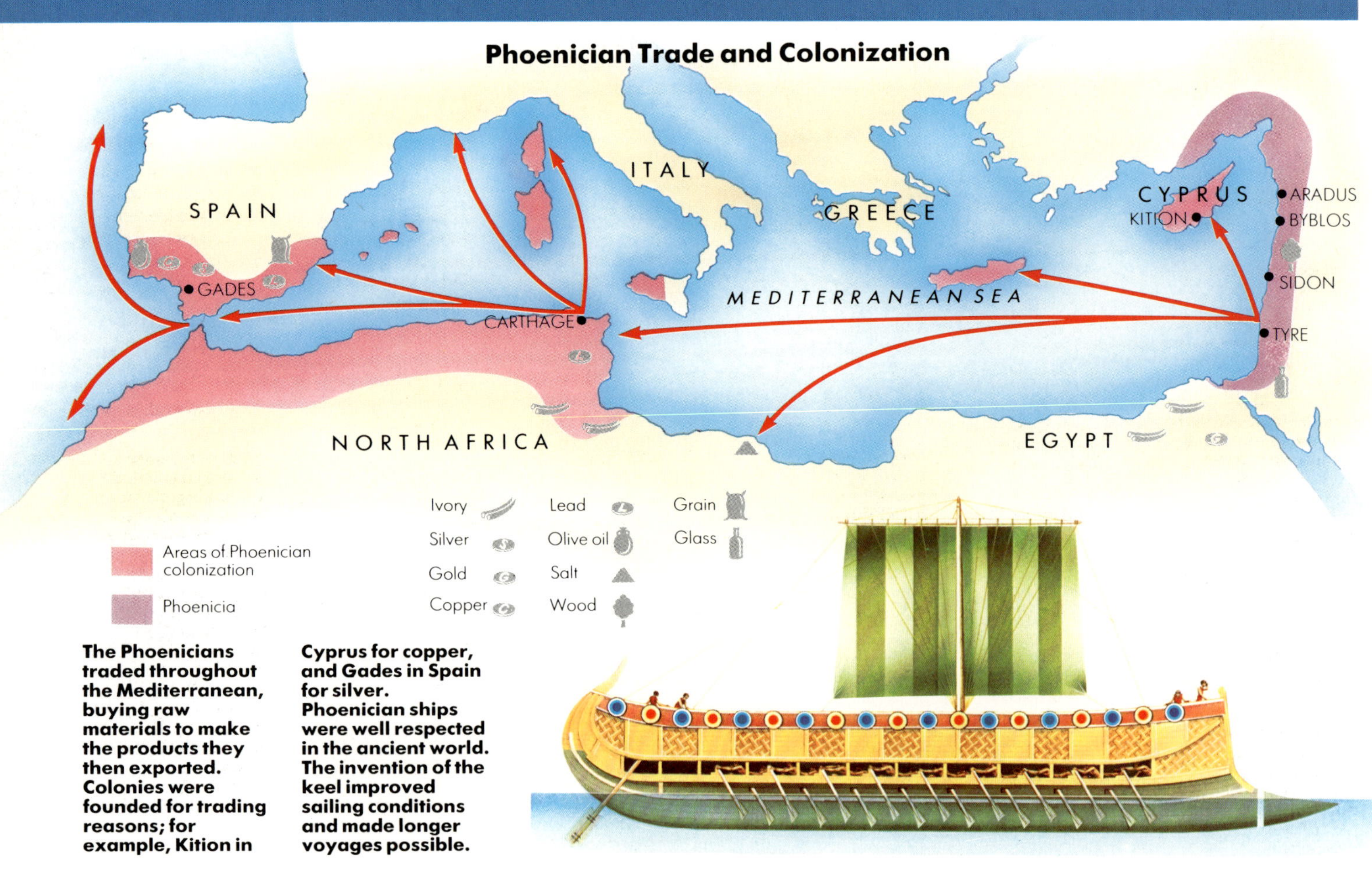

The Phoenicians traded throughout the Mediterranean, buying raw materials to make the products they then exported. Colonies were founded for trading reasons; for example, Kition in Cyprus for copper, and Gades in Spain for silver. Phoenician ships were well respected in the ancient world. The invention of the keel improved sailing conditions and made longer voyages possible.

In the Eastern Mediterranean, ancient peoples had long been linked by sea-borne trade. In 2000 BC Egyptian and Minoan ships sailed between Egypt, the Levant and Greece. Later, the Mycenaeans took to the sea, trading wine, honey, fine oils, pottery and metals.

This trade was brought to an end when the Sea People laid waste the lands of the Eastern Mediterranean. As on land, so on the sea, there was no longer one great power. Thus the cities of the Levant and Syrian coast were able to take control of the seaborne trade.

The people of these cities were the Phoenicians, known to the Greeks as 'Phoinikes', the purple men. They were perhaps called this because of the famous Tyrian purple dye with which they dyed the cloth that they exported.

The Phoenicians called themselves 'Kinahu' or 'Canaanites', after the name of the whole region, although they lived on the narrow coastal strip which today forms Israel and Lebanon. Here, cedar and fir trees grew on the mountains that divided the coast from the inland regions. From this timber the Phoenicians built themselves sturdy ships.

PHOENICIAN SOCIETY AND TRADE The Phoenician cities were each independent states, although sometimes they would form alliances with each other. The most important cities were Tyre, Sidon, Byblos and Aradus.

High stone walls and towers protected the towns. These were sometimes built on islands for further protection, or on land jutting out to the sea. The invention of lime mortar for water cisterns meant that cities like Tyre could be situated on islands where there was no water. The houses were double storied with balconies.

As early as 3000 BC cedars of Lebanon were exported to Egypt, where there was little good timber. Apart from wood and dyed fabrics, the Phoenicians

Above. The Phoenicians were famous for their skill with ivory. Elephants were extinct in Syria by 1000 BC, so stocks had to be imported from India or Africa. This piece depicts a sphinx and dates from the ninth century BC.

Right. Glassmaking developed in the second millennium BC. From about 600 BC the Phoenicians produced glass vessels that were almost colourless. They also produced coloured glass such as this bottle shown here. Coloured glass was made by adding pigments during the glassmaking process.

Above. 'The woman at the window' was a popular subject for ivory carvers. She is thought to represent the sacred prostitute of the cult of Ashtart. The woman is dressed in an Egyptian wig and clothing. This ivory dates from the ninth/eighth century BC.

Tyrian Purple

Tyrian purple was a highly prized dye. It was made from a gland found in the 'murex' — an offshore mollusc, or shellfish. The gland secretion was boiled up with various fixatives, and the intensity of the colour depended on the length of time the fabric was treated.

Colours could range from pink to deep purple — the famed 'Royal Purple of Tyre'. In antiquity, purple was the colour of royalty.

Left. This ivory depicts a lioness attacking a slave in a thicket of lotus and papyrus. It is one of a pair which were probably originally used as furniture panels on a throne or elaborate chair. The subject matter was originally Egyptian, symbolizing Egypt defeating the foreigner, but became a Phoenician decorative theme.

The Phoenician Alphabet

𐤇 𐤊 𐤋 𐤌 𐤍 𐤒

H K L M N Q

The alphabet was first developed in the Middle East about 1600 BC. The earliest known alphabet is called the North Semitic. Two other alphabets stemmed from it: the Aramaic and the Canaanite.

It was from the Canaanite that the Phoenicians developed their alphabet. Almost all present-day alphabets are derived from the Phoenician. Their alphabet consisted entirely of consonants, and it was the Greeks who added vowels at a later date. The Romans gave it the form that we use today.

traded glass and ivory carvings. When Omri of Israel built his palace at Samaria it was decorated with Phoenician ivory carving. They were also famous for their stone carving and Phoenician craftsmen built Solomon's temple at Jerusalem. The Phoenicians also acted as middlemen in trade – that is buying and selling goods from elsewhere, that they had not produced.

Metal ores were very important as they were used for weapons, tools and jewellery. Copper came from Cyprus, where the Phoenicians founded a colony. They also discovered rich deposits of silver in Spain where they founded a colony at Gades, modern Cadiz.

In 814 BC Carthage in North African was founded by the city of Tyre. At first it was only a staging post on the long journey to Spain, but it grew to be a great city.

The greatest legacy of the Phoenicians was their alphabetic writing system. This was adopted by the Greeks with whom they competed as traders. From the Greeks it has gradually passed down in time to us.

THE SCYTHIANS – NOMADS OF THE STEPPES

The Scythians were nomadic people of the *steppes*, the enormous belt of grassland stretching across Asia from Manchuria to Russia. Broken in parts by the desert, the steppes border forest to the north and desert and dry regions to the south.

Unlike the farmers and town-dwellers of the settled lands, the Scythians lived by stock-breeding and some hunting. They raised herds of sheep, cattle and horses. They practised *transhumance*, which means moving their herds from summer pasture on higher ground, to winter pasture on lower ground each year.

As they were on the move twice a year, the horse and wagon were very important for carrying the people and their belongings, all of which were portable.

MOVING ON In the eighth century BC, they were driven westward, probably by the activities of a stronger group than themselves. As they moved across this vast area, they came into contact, and often conflict, with the civilized lands to the south.

Some moved into south Russia, where they came into contact with the Greeks of the Black Sea towns. The Greek writer Herodotus wrote an account of them in his history.

Those who settled in northern Iran fought the Medes, whilst their presence in Armenia brought about the downfall of Urartu. Many settled for a long period in Anatolia.

Other groups settled east of the Caspian Sea, creating problems for the Persians. A related group, called the Cimmerians, fought with the Medes and Babylonians against Assyria.

SWIFT WARRIORS The picture given by the Chinese and Greek accounts, is of fierce and highly mobile warriors, almost one with their small swift horses. They fought on horseback, using the bow and arrow. According to one account, they scalped their enemies and kept the hair as a trophy.

LEARNING ABOUT THE PEOPLE Once again, we can learn much about these people from their graves. These have been found in southern Russia, as well as northern Mongolia, south of Lake Baikal and in the Altai Mountains. Because they were nomadic, there are no remains of towns to investigate. The other source of evidence comes from the written records of the people who came into contact with them, particularly the Chinese in the east and the Greeks in the west.

Some of their tombs have been very well preserved by ice which effectively sealed the tombs. Rich hangings, carpets, cushions and saddlecloths with lovely designs have been found in the tombs, as well as beautiful silks. The bodies of the dead were covered with elaborate tatoos.

When a chief died, his wife and servants were killed and buried with him, as were his horses. Many very beautiful golden objects have been found in Scythian burials, which give an idea of their wealth.

Above. This magnificent gold comb from a grave of the burial mound, or 'kurgan', at Solocha, was made in the late fifth/early fourth century BC. The handle shows details of Scythians in battle.

Right. Details from the frieze of figures on the amphora from the Čertomlyk 'kurgan' in the USSR. The horses are being trained and one is having its legs hobbled before being put to pasture.

Tattooing

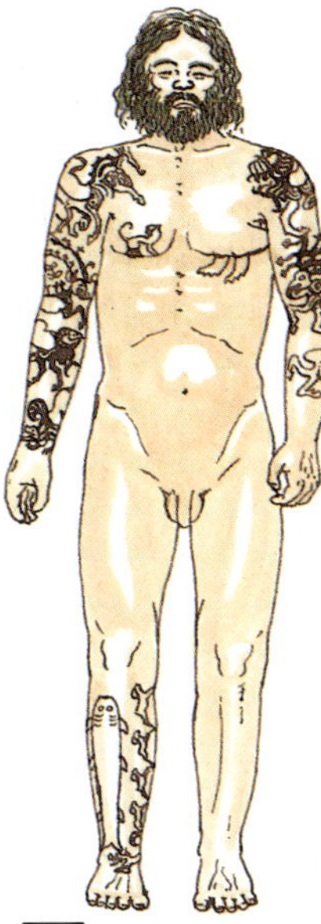

The picture above shows the tattooing on a body found at the second 'kurgan' at Pazyryk in the USSR. Bronze mirrors were also found in the tomb, which indicates that the Scythians cared about their appearance.

According to the Greek historian, Herodotus, tattooing was the mark of high birth, and the lack of it a mark of low birth. Often the designs were carefully arranged so that the person was a 'living' work of art.

Scythian Burials

When dead, the Scythians were placed in graves within 'kurgans', or burial mounds. Some were 'catacomb'-type tombs hollowed out of the ground as in the diagram above. Scythian chiefs and warriors were buried with their horses and carts. Their retainers and wives were also buried with them. Many very wealthy Scythians were buried with huge quantities of grave goods of gold and silver.

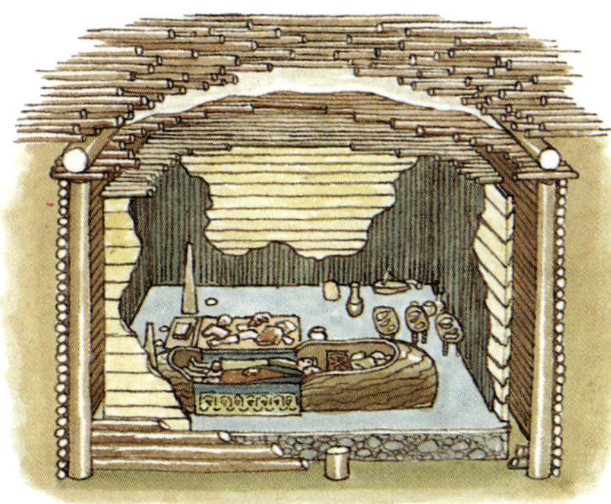

Above. The burial chamber of a rich Scythian with all his riches alongside.

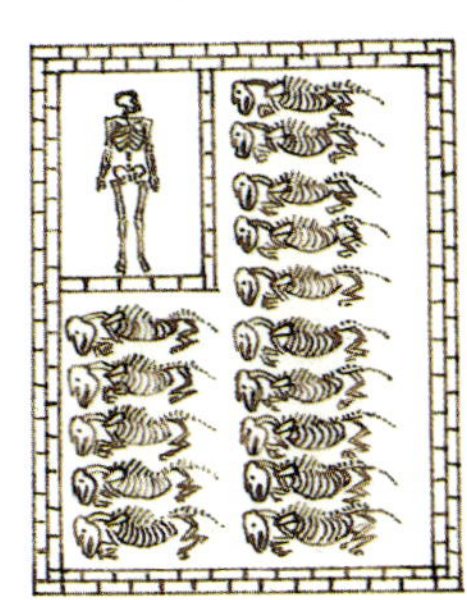

Right. Two burial chambers showing horses buried with their owners.

THE ASSYRIAN EMPIRE

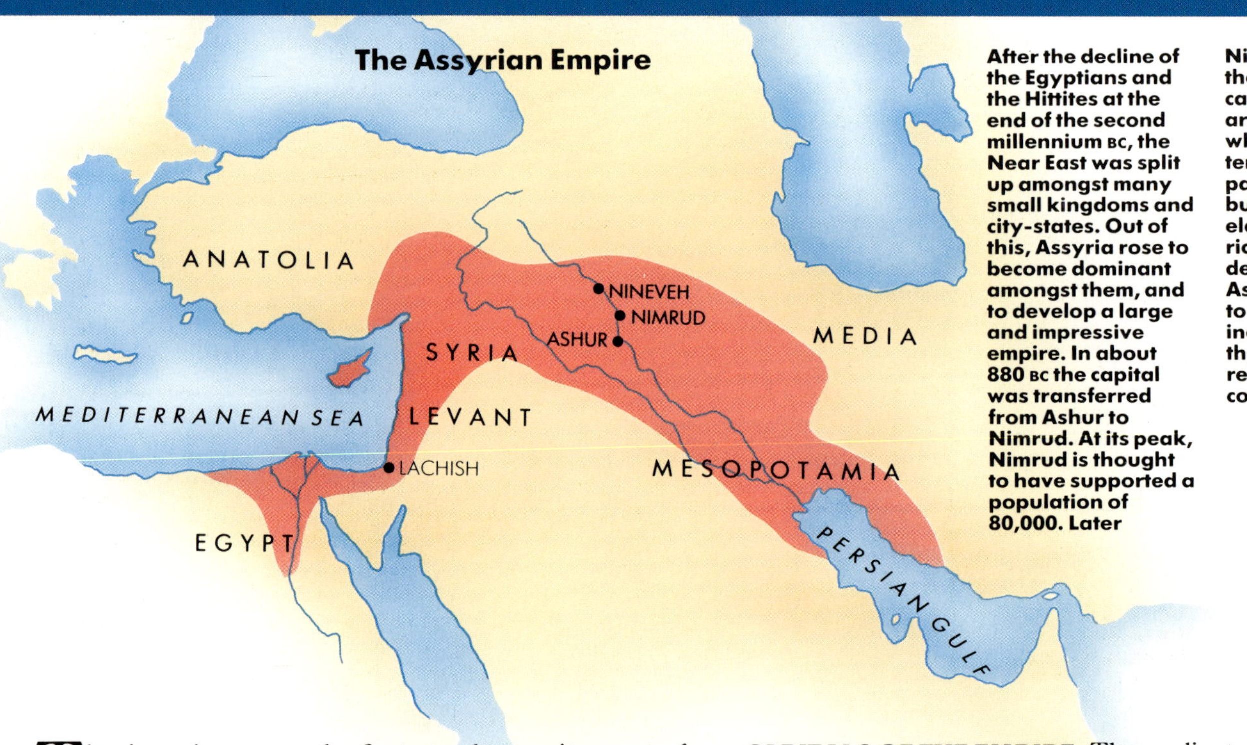

After the decline of the Egyptians and the Hittites at the end of the second millennium BC, the Near East was split up amongst many small kingdoms and city-states. Out of this, Assyria rose to become dominant amongst them, and to develop a large and impressive empire. In about 880 BC the capital was transferred from Ashur to Nimrud. At its peak, Nimrud is thought to have supported a population of 80,000. Later Nineveh became the capital. All the capitals were based around a citadel which housed temples and palaces. These buildings were elaborately and richly furnished and decorated. The Assyrians managed to maintain and increase the limit of the empire through relentless military conquest.

The Assyrians were the first people to unite most of the Near East under imperial control. Both the Hittites and Egyptians had expanded their territories and controlled foreign subjects by telling their rulers what to do.

Where the Assyrian Empire differs from these earlier empires is that its conquests and the extent of its power were on a much wider scale. The heartland of Assyria was situated in northern Mesopotamia. The climate of this region was different to that of the south, with enough rain to grow plenty of crops for an expanding city.

In the ninth century BC, the Assyrians began to expand their territory under a series of strong kings. At first they took control of northern Syria from the Armaeans. Then they battled with Urartu to the north, and later with the Egyptians and Babylonians. The Empire expanded until Assyria controlled much of the area from the Persian Gulf to Egypt.

To control this Empire, a system of provincial administration was set up. All provinces were obliged to offer tribute. A governor who was responsible for tax collection ruled each province from his palace in the provincial capital. These establishments were much smaller but similar to the royal palaces in Nimrud and Nineveh.

CAPITALS OF THE EMPIRE The earliest capital had been Ashur, where the kings were always buried. Ashurnasirpal II moved his capital to Nimrud. He enlisted workmen from all over his Empire to build a great palace there. When the building was finished, he gave a banquet. An inscription has survived which describes the banquet: there were 70,000 guests and they drank 10,000 skins of wine and ate 14,000 sheep and many other things. Later Nineveh became the royal centre, where Sennacherib (704–681 BC) built his 'palace without rival'. This had beautiful gardens, watered by streams led from the river.

THE ARMY The Assyrian army was well organized. At first, the soldiers were peasants and were positioned mainly in the capital alone. But as the Empire grew, there were detachments of soldiers enlisted from the provinces as well.

Garrisons were stationed in the provinces to maintain Assyrian control. Good roads and grain storage facilities were built so that messengers could move quickly and get fresh horses and food supplies.

Internal strife and external pressure, brought about by rebellions of the member states of the Empire, gradually weakened Assyria. In 612 Nineveh fell to the Medes and Babylonians and by 609 the Empire had fallen.

The Siege of Lachish

The siege of Lachish was the final act in Sennacherib's campaign to take control of Judah. Although documentary evidence about the siege is not complete, reliefs from Sennacherib's palace at Nineveh (see right) provide a rich record of events and military technology used.

The Assyrian army included archers, slingmen and spearmen. Archers were the main arm of the military unit, and soldiers with large shields were used to protect the archers when under fire. The Assyrians also used siege engines and battering rams.

Left. This relief from the palace at Nineveh depicts part of Sennacherib's siege of the Israelite city of Lachish. A siege engine can be seen battering the walls of the city, and prisoners are coming from the gate.

Below. An aerial view of the ancient city of Lachish. Excavations at the site have yielded some of the actual stones thrown by the stoneslingers during the siege of the city in 701 BC.

Right. A scene from the siege of Lachish. Israelite captives are being flayed alive on stakes outside the city. This relief is from the Nineveh palace at Nineveh and is dated c. 700 BC.

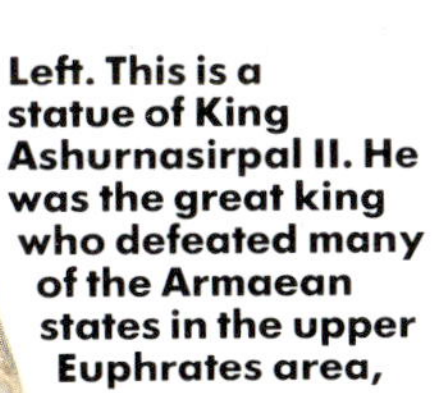

Left. This is a statue of King Ashurnasirpal II. He was the great king who defeated many of the Armaean states in the upper Euphrates area, and extended the boundaries to the great bend of that river. He moved the capital from Ashur to Nimrud, where he built a great palace. This statue comes from Nimrud and shows him holding the mace of kingship.

1 The earliest archaeological evidence points to the Phoenician founding of Carthage in 814 BC. In 600 BC the Nubian capital moves to Meroë. Northern Africa becomes a major ironworking centre.

2 From 900–750 BC the city-states begin to emerge in Greece, and from 800 BC in central Italy the Etruscan city-states begin to develop. The first Olympic Games are held in Greece in 776 BC. The first Greek alphabet inscription, adapted from the Phoenician alphabet, is dated to 750 BC. The Etruscan script is developed from Greek c. 690 BC. Around 600 BC the first Greek coins are used. During this period Rome develops into a town and the Latin script is first used.

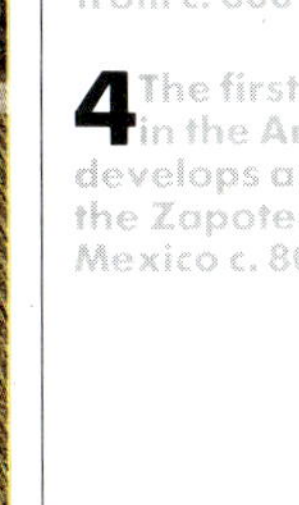

3 Cities in the Ganges valley in India emerge c. 800 BC and rice cultivation begins. Elephants are used for warfare in India from c. 600 BC.

4 The first writing in the Americas develops among the Zapotecs of Mexico c. 800 BC.

THE LATE BABYLONIAN EMPIRE

After the fall of the Assyrian Empire, the ancient city of Babylon became the centre of an empire which reached to the borders of Egypt.

THE CREATION OF AN EMPIRE Nabopolassar, the first of the Neo-Babylonian rulers, had defeated Assyria with the help of the Medes at Nineveh in 612. Then he and his son, Nebuchadrezzar II, took control of the Assyrian provinces in the west.

Above. Detail of the mythical 'Marduk' that once adorned the Ishtar Gate of Babylon.

Below. Under Nebuchadrezzar, Babylon was splendidly rebuilt and extended. In the centre stood the great ziggurat and the Temple of Marduk.

Within a few years Nebuchadrezzar had created a great empire, which included Judah. To maintain control of Judah, the Jewish king and nobles of Jerusalem were taken into captivity and were exiled to Babylon.

The provinces were ruled by Babylonian governors, although some were left in the care of local rulers who were loyal to Babylon. The temples had to give one tenth of their income (from temple lands) to the king. They resented this and it is possible that the dissatisfaction of the priests later resulted in their support of King Cyrus of Persia, who took the city without a battle in 539 BC.

The fall of Babylon is dramatically told in the Biblical story of 'Balshazzar's feast' where Daniel is called to interpret the writing on the wall. Although it is a story and not an historical incident, we know from cuneiform texts that Balshazzar was in fact the Crown Prince, and he died fighting the Persians outside Babylon.

THE GREAT CITY OF BABYLON Babylon was so famous that the Greek historian Herodotus wrote a detailed description of the city. Most of the building was done by Nabopolassar who had defeated the Assyrians, and his son Nebuchadrezzar. They made Babylon far more splendid than it had formerly been.

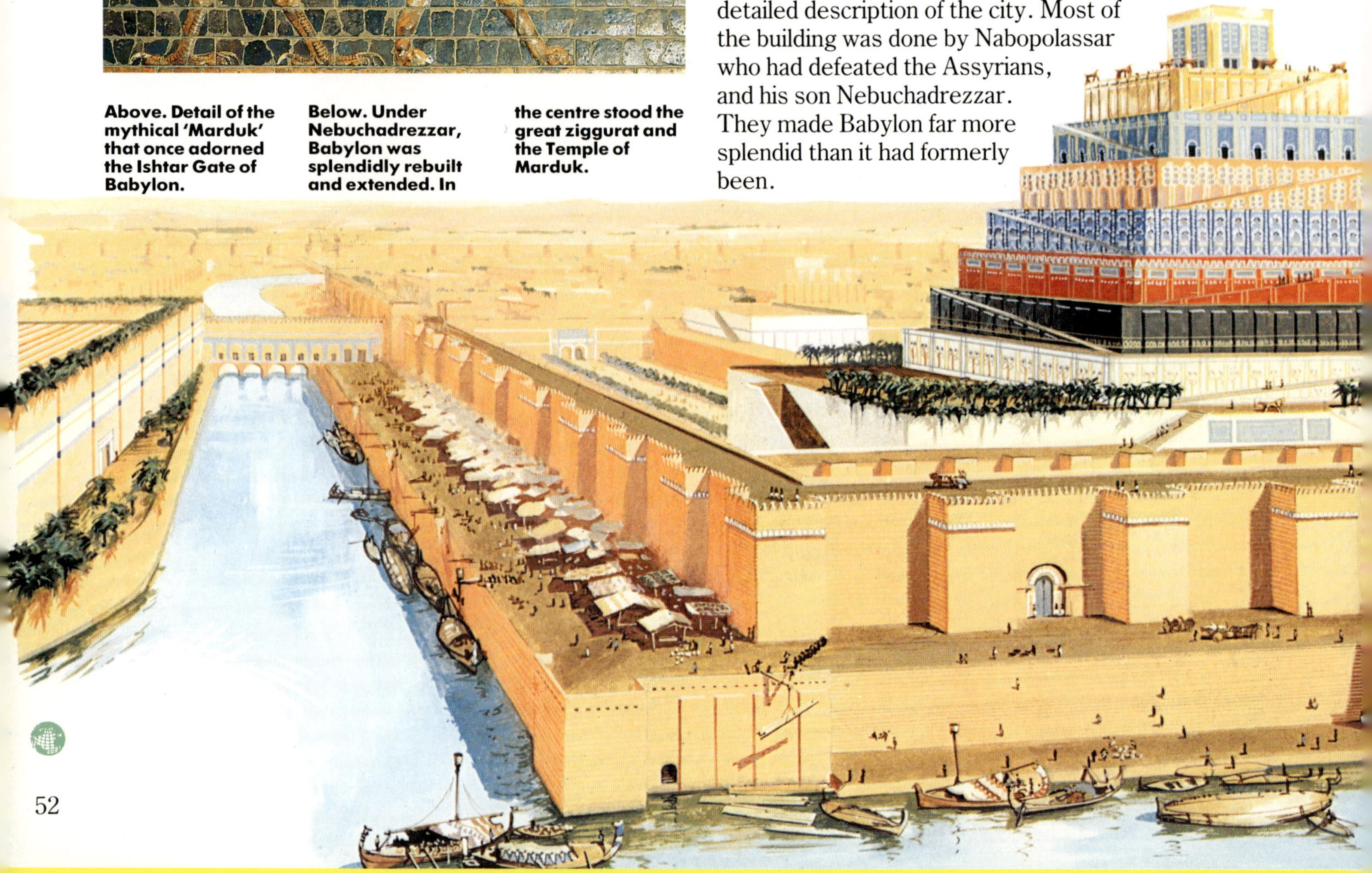

Above. This is a reconstruction of the gateway of Marduk. Marduk was the city god who became prominent in the 17th century BC. He is represented in the form of a dragon.

Key Dates

729 BC	Tiglathpileser became king of Babylon
689 BC	Sennacherib of Assyria destroyed Babylon
625–605 BC	Nabopolassar led fight against Assyrians with Persian support
605–562 BC	Nebuchadrezzar ruled Babylon
539 BC	Babylon captured by the Persians

Huge walls surrounded the city and the inner ones were so wide that a chariot with four horses could travel along them. There were several city gates, each named after one of the gods. The goddess of love and war was Ishtar, and from the great Ishtar Gate a long processional way led to the temples and palaces.

Both the gate and the sacred way were covered with brilliant blue glazed tiles on which were raised reliefs of lions, bulls and dragons. Each animal was linked to a god: the lion to Ishtar; the bull to Adad, god of the sky and weather; and the dragon to Marduk, the god of the city.

Within the city were numerous temples and palaces. The great temple of Marduk stood next to the *ziggurat* or temple tower. Near the river was the palace, which was also beautifully decorated with glazed tiles. Here were the famous Hanging Gardens that stood on man-made terraces. The garden was originally created for a Median princess who missed the trees and cooler weather of her homeland. The gardens were one of the Seven Wonders of the Ancient World.

As the city grew it extended to the other side of the river. There were numerous houses and shops for the large population.

Nowadays, all that remains are the mud brick foundations, for later the river shifted its course, causing Babylon to be abandoned.

IRAN AND THE RISE OF PERSIA

From their homeland the Persians spread throughout the Near East to eventually form the largest empire the world had ever seen up till then. (For the full extent of the Empire, see map on page 57.) Their earliest conquests included Lydia, Assyria and Babylon.

Above. A view of the acropolis at Sardis. The acropolis was fortified during the Lydian period, but during construction, one small area where there was a narrow steep drop was left unfortified. This proved to be the Lydians' undoing during the Persian attack. It was through this gap that a Persian soldier climbed to open the city gates for the army.

Iran, which lies to the east of the Mesopotamian valley was the homeland of the Medes and Persians. It is very different from the lands between the Tigris and the Euphrates rivers. Parts are desert, although the valleys between the mountains are fertile.

The southwest of the country is part of the Mesopotamian plain and here, as in Sumer, were some of the earliest cities in the world. This was the kingdom of Elam, and these people had a pictographic script, which cannot yet be read, so little is known of their history.

MEDES AND PERSIANS Because it can be easily reached from Central Asia, many nomads came to Iran, including the Iranians, an *Indo-European* people. They came from the steppes in about 1300 BC, and spread throughout the land. Amongst those who settled in the west were the Medes and Persians. Because much time was spent on horseback, the Medes wore trousers and felt hats similar to those of other nomads in Asia.

Gradually these people became powerful and in

Left. Strip of gold of unknown purpose. The style is of Scythian or Russian influence c. 800–700 BC. Above. Part of a necklace of gold and pearl beads from Pasargadae in Iran. Very few pearls have survived from an early date. These pearls probably came from the Persian Gulf.

Croesus, the Last King of Lydia

According to legend, Croesus, the defeated Lydian king, was saved by Apollo from execution at the last minute.

Herodotus, the Greek historian, tells us that Cyrus had already changed his mind about the execution, and demanded that the fire that had been lit under Croesus be put out.

The flames, however, had already taken hold. Croesus then called upon Apollo to save him. At this point, clouds gathered and a storm broke out with such violent rain that the fire was extinguished. The illustration on this amphora shows the pyre being lit.

The tholos at Delphi was built c. 400 BC in the sanctuary of Athena below the oracular shrine. By the beginning of the seventh century BC, the practice had begun of oriental kings making dedications at Delphi to win the favour of Apollo. Even before the time of Croesus the Phrygian king, Midas, and an earlier Lydian king, Gyges, are reported to have made offerings to the Delphic oracle. The offerings of Croesus however totally eclipsed all former dedications. Croesus had sent a lion made of pure gold weighing a quarter of a tonne, and vessels of gold and silver. This generosity of Croesus' was made with a view to gaining favourable oracular responses. The responses of the oracle were a serious matter in ancient Greece, and the oracle would be consulted on such important issues as whether to go to war with another state.

612 BC the Medes helped the Babylonians to defeat Assyria. The Persian king, Cyrus the Great, whose mother was a Mede, united the Medes and Persians. He then began the conquests that made the Persian Empire the largest of the ancient empires. First he defeated Lydia which was in Anatolia. Lydia was ruled by the immensely wealthy king, Croesus from his capital at Sardis. The Lydians were the first people to use coins – that is, a standard weight of metal guaranteed by the state. Lydia's wealth came from the gold of the Pactolus river which flowed through Sardis.

THE ORACLES Before the conflict with Cyrus, Croesus asked for advice from the Delphic oracle. An oracle was a kind of prophecy that told what would happen. These prophecies were made by priests or priestesses attached to sacred places like Delphi, situated in Greece, which was home to the oracle of the Greek god Apollo. Because the Lydians were neighbours of the Greeks, and in general on good terms, they also consulted Greek oracles.

Sometimes the priests were bribed to give helpful oracles. Often the oracles were not clear and could be interpreted in various ways – as happened to Croesus. He was told somewhat confusingly, that if he crossed the Halys river a great empire would fall. Taking this to mean Cyrus' Empire, Croesus crossed the Halys and was himself defeated. Cyrus is said to have spared Croesus' life.

The conquest of Lydia meant that Cyrus now controlled the Greek cities of the coast of Asia Minor. He returned to Persia and then captured Babylon in 539 BC. He took the Babylonian throne, not as a conqueror, but ruling according to local customs. This was very important as it meant that he gained the support of many Babylonians and their former subjects. He allowed the Jews to return to Jerusalem in 537 BC and to rebuild their temple there.

By the time of his death in 530 BC, Cyrus had laid the foundations of the Persian Empire.

DARIUS I AND THE EMPIRE

The remains of the Palace of Darius at Persepolis. The Palace overlooked the plain and rose very high. The door and window frames of polished dark stone now stand alone, as the mud brick walls have perished.

Cambyses, the son of Cyrus, conquered Egypt in 526 BC, as his father had planned to do. The Persian Empire now reached from the Indus River to the Nile.

THE ORGANIZATION OF THE EMPIRE The next ruler was Darius I who reorganized the empire, after he had put down the rebellions against his taking of the throne. He created *Satrapies*, or provinces, which were ruled by loyal Persians. There were 20 Satrapies in total, each ruled by a Persian noble or member of the royal family. A separate official, in charge of the army, collected the tribute from each province. This could be paid in many ways: in gold, silver, animals, slaves, incense from Arabia, ivory from Ethiopia or even camels from Bactria.

A system of roads was built, to make travel throughout the Empire easier. On the Royal Road from Susa in Persia to Ephesus in Anatolia, a royal courier could travel the 2700 kilometres in a week. Fresh horses were kept at stables along the way.

Darius also had a canal cut from the Red Sea to the Nile, so that ships could travel from the Indian Ocean to the Mediterranean in a much quicker time. He also built an entire fleet.

The Behistun Relief

In 522 BC Darius I had a large inscription placed 120 metres high on the great rock of Behistun. The king stands with his foot on the would-be usurper Gaumata. Two attendants are behind him and facing him are the nine rebel kings. The cuneiform inscription is in three languages, old Persian, Akkadian and Elamite.

It was the copying and deciphering of the old Persian version, that led to the decipherment of cuneiform.

WAR WITH THE SCYTHIANS In 512 BC Darius set out to the Black Sea area to fight against the Scythians. His aim was to stop them sending timber to the Greeks for their ships. He crossed the River Danube, but the Scythians had burnt the crops, so he could get no supplies for his

Right. Many of the decorations on the buildings at Persepolis were very elaborate. Though this carving now lies in the sand, it was once the top of a column. The carving shows a double-headed eagle.

Left. This is a relief from the Treasury at Persepolis showing King Darius receiving homage from Median and Persian nobles.

Above. A reconstruction of the Apadana, or audience hall, at the Palace. The Apadana had 36 interior columns, and leading off it were three porticoes, each with 12 columns. It was probably hung with tapestries inside, as shown here. The purpose of the buildings at Persepolis is not known, for there seem to be no places where people could actually have lived. It would appear that it served only as a ceremonial centre. When in attendance, the court and visitors would have stayed in specially erected tents.

The Persian Empire depended on good communications. Greek writers refer to the presence of the Royal Road from Susa to Ephesus and we can map its probable route. But little trace is left of the Road today.

army. However, he had managed to add Thrace to his empire, which meant that he now controlled the narrow straits, the Dardanelles, between Asia and Europe.

PERSIAN PALACES Darius treated his subject people fairly. Many foreign craftsmen worked at the palaces he built at Susa and Persepolis. He moved his capital to Susa, which was warmer in winter than the old capital Pasargadae. In gratitude to the army for its support, he had his bodyguard, the 'Ten Thousand Immortals', portrayed on the palace walls at Susa.

At Persepolis the king celebrated the Persian New Year festival. The palace was built on a raised terrace of 13.5 hectares. On the terrace were two reception halls. Darius began the great 'Apadana' of 60 metres square, but it was finished by his son, Xerxes. Its 36 columns were made of cedarwood. The second hall, 70 metres square, was built by Xerxes.

It was here that Alexander the Great held a feast before burning down the palace.

THE FALL OF THE PERSIAN EMPIRE

The death of Darius I in 486 BC marked the end of the greatest days of the Empire. Unfortunately, much of what is known of events after Darius I comes from the Greeks, and may not be fair to the Persians, as there was always strong rivalry and hostilities between the Greeks and Persians.

In 480 BC Xerxes led an army of 70,000 against the Greeks across the Dardanelles on a bridge of boats. Although he was successful at first, the war ended in failure.

THE START OF THE DECLINE From the late fifth century BC, there was strife and rebellion within the Persian Empire. Civil war broke out in the fourth century, and from late in this century, several rulers were murdered. Court intrigues had long been a problem for the Achaemenid kings. Darius III, the last ruler of the Empire, was placed on the throne in 336 BC by the manipulations of the eunuch Bagoas.

Five years later the Empire was lost to Alexander the Great, and the once mighty Persian Empire was now to become part of the new Hellenistic world.

The Greeks regarded the Persians as a people who had become decadent and luxury-loving since the great days of Cyrus. The many beautiful objects of gold and silver made by their craftsmen are indeed luxurious and reflect the great wealth of the Persian king and his satraps and nobles.

Key Dates of the Persian Empire

550 BC	Cyrus becomes king of the Medes and Persians.
530 BC	Death of Cyrus and accession of Cambyses II.
522–520 BC	Accession of Darius and internal rebellion.
490 BC	Invasion of Greece. Persians defeated at Marathon.
480–479 BC	Persians defeat Greeks at Thermopylae, but are defeated at Salamis and Plataea.
336–330 BC	Rise of Alexander and defeat of Persia. Persepolis burned.

A detail from the 'Alexander Sarcophagus' from the Royal Cemetery at Sidon, c. fourth century BC. A Greek cavalryman is shown attacking a Persian. The Persians are depicted wearing trousers and Persian headdress.

The Oxus Treasure

Right. A hollow fish beaten from flat gold sheet. It might have been used as a flask or bottle. It dates from the sixth century BC.

Above. Gold jug with a lion-headed handle. The lion is represented as biting the rim of the fluted body. It dates from the fifth century BC.
Below. A shallow gold bowl, c. sixth century BC. It depicts pairs of lions on their hind legs with their forearms outstretched.

Right. Gold armlet with winged-horned griffin finials, originally inlaid with glass and coloured stones. It dates from the fifth/fourth centuries BC.

The Oxus Treasure contains some 170 items of gold and silver dating from the sixth-fourth centuries BC. It is said to have been found on the banks of the Oxus River (near the borders of modern Afghanistan and the CIS) in 1877.

The origins of the treasure are not known, nor is it known who concealed it or why. Although most pieces date from the Hellenistic period, some are of Achaemenid date or even earlier, and the objects show a wide range of styles.

We are fortunate to have the treasure, since three years after it was found it was nearly lost when bandits attacked merchant ships. The robbers were caught and the treasure reclaimed, although some pieces had already been cut up in preparation for melting down.

EARLY GREECE

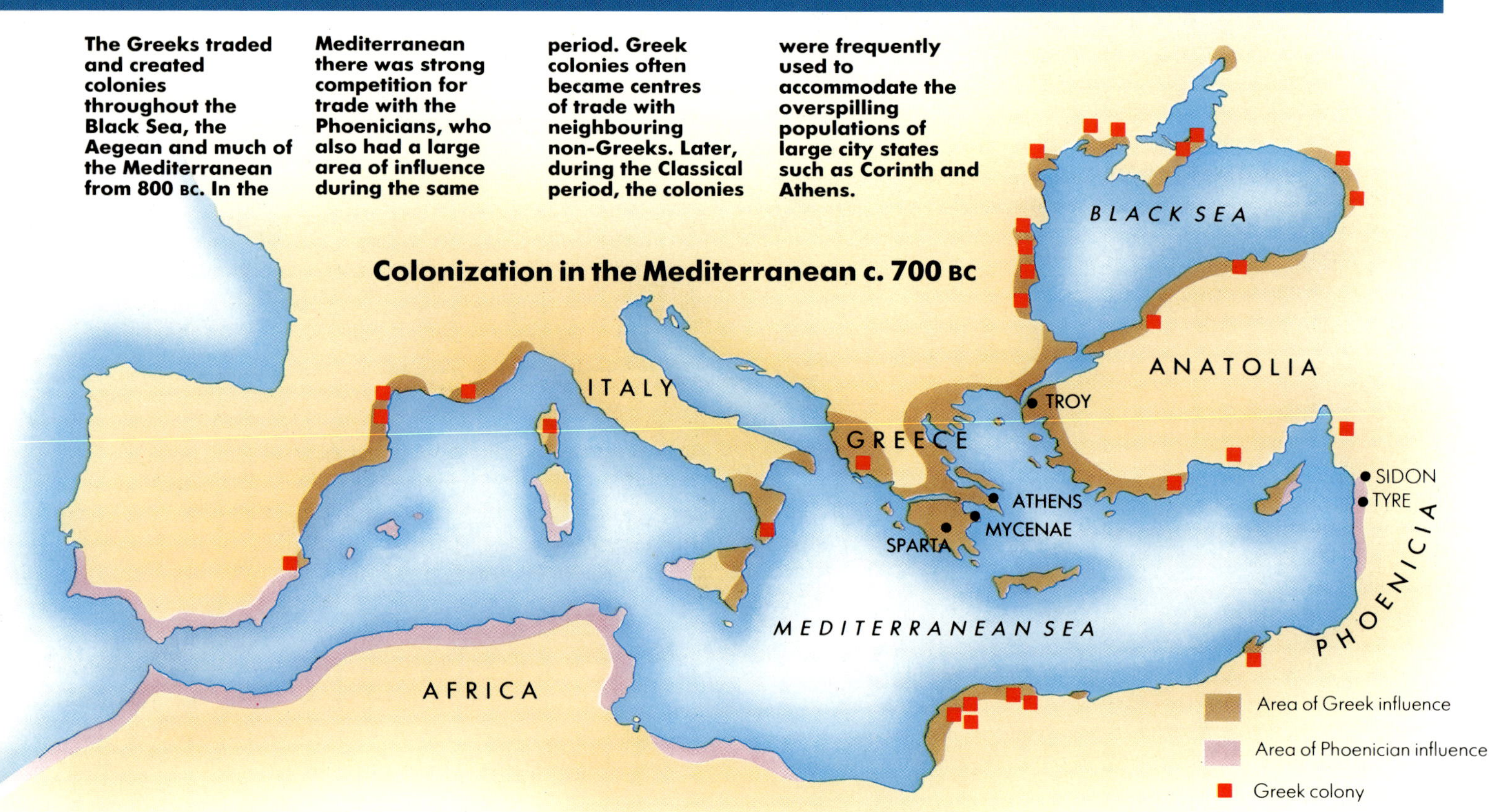

The Greeks traded and created colonies throughout the Black Sea, the Aegean and much of the Mediterranean from 800 BC. In the Mediterranean there was strong competition for trade with the Phoenicians, who also had a large area of influence during the same period. Greek colonies often became centres of trade with neighbouring non-Greeks. Later, during the Classical period, the colonies were frequently used to accommodate the overspilling populations of large city states such as Corinth and Athens.

After the collapse of the Mycenaean world, around 1200 BC, a new group of people came into Greece. They are known as the Dorians and they spoke a dialect of Greek.

Little is known about the period up to the ninth century, and for this reason it is called the 'Dark Age of Greece'. The country was very poor and the population had declined, perhaps to as little as a tenth of what it had been in Mycenaean times. From about 1000 BC, poverty led people to migrate from the mainland to the coast of Asia Minor and the Aegean islands, looking for a better life.

EPIC POETRY Many skills had been lost, in particular people no longer wrote things down until the society eventually became illiterate. Nevertheless, the origins of two of the world's greatest poems date back to this period. Although the *Iliad* and the *Odyssey* were written by Homer some time in the mid-eighth century, they are *epic poems* that had been passed down orally through the centuries.

The poems contain references to many artefacts of the Mycenaean world, now known to us from archaeological finds – boars' tusk helmets, gold drinking cups and enormous shields. 'Golden Mycenae' is a world of riches long gone, but still celebrated in the epic poems of Homer.

The *Iliad* tells of the warriors who attacked Troy (see page 36). The *Odyssey* recounts the warrior Odysseus' journey home to the island of Ithaca after the ten-year seige of Troy. His journey is long and fraught with dangerous adventures until he is finally reunited with his faithful wife, Penelope. Although there are elements of the Mycenaean age, the world of Odysseus also reflects a picture of the late Dark Ages.

PROSPERITY RETURNS In about 900 BC the Greeks began to trade with the Near Eastern countries of the Mediterranean and with Italy. Life gradually became more prosperous and the population began to increase. The Near Eastern contact influenced artistic design in both pottery and metalwork. The Greeks also acquired an alphabet, adapted from that of the Phoenicians, which brought literacy back to Greece.

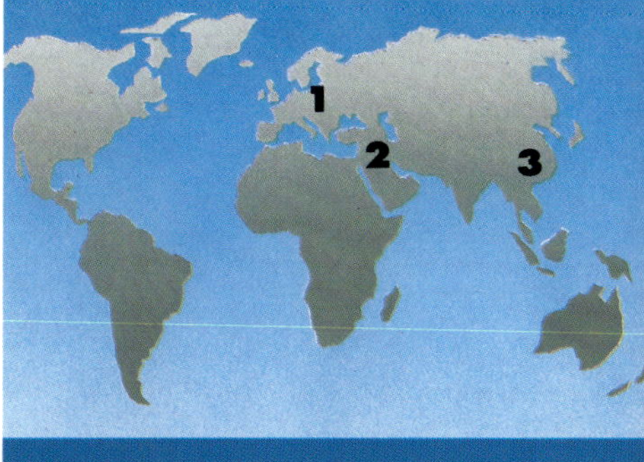

1 The iron industry becomes established in the Aegean and central Europe c. 1000 BC, and spreads to Britain c. 750 BC. The Celtic culture emerges north and east of the Alps c. 800 BC, and this marks the first phase of the Celtic Iron Age.

2 The Hittite Empire collapses c. 1200 BC. The Assyrian Empire is formed c. 950 BC and it goes on to unite almost all of the Near East.

3 The Zhou Dynasty begins in China in 1027 BC, replacing the Shang. This marks the beginning of the Western Zhou period. The beginning of the Eastern Zhou period in China starts in 770 BC, and the capital is moved to Loyang.

Above. This vase painting depicts Odysseus bound to the ship's mast so that he would not succumb to the seductive voices of the sirens.

Below. Odysseus and his men blinding Polyphemus, the one-eyed monster known as the Cyclops.

Right. A bronze bust of a siren from Olympia c. 700–600 BC. The figure once formed the handle of a bowl or cup.

The Greek Alphabet

Α Β Γ Δ Ε Ζ Η Θ Ι Κ Λ Μ
A B G D E Z E Th I K L M
Ν Ξ Ο Π Ρ Σ Τ Υ Φ Χ Ψ Ω
N X O P R S T U Ph Kh Ps O

The Greeks derived their alphabet from the Phoenician. We do not know, however, where and when the Greek alphabet came into existence. The earliest Greek inscriptions date from c. 750 BC, but the Greeks may have been writing earlier than that.

When the Greeks took over the Phoenician script, they adapted it and made changes in the pronunciation and form of the letters. For instance, they had to adapt some consonant signs and use them as vowel signs, as the Phoenician script did not employ signs for vowels.

Those who traded imported grain, timber, salted fish and luxury goods such as purple dye and papyrus. The Greeks exported wine, olive oil and pottery.

THE GREEKS SPREAD ABROAD The poet Hesiod, who lived in the late eighth century, described the hard work and difficult life of the farmers. One way to escape this life and get rich was to go to sea, and many Greeks did.

Much of Greece is mountainous and the soil is poor. In times of hardship, some left their homes and emigrated to places where larger areas of more fertile land were available. They went in groups and formed colonies in the new regions. You can see the large number of colonies that the Greeks established by looking at the map. In this way Greek influence spread throughout the Mediterranean.

By about 700 BC the towns were expanding. Because the many hills and mountains made transport and communication difficult, each town with its surrounding territory needed to be a self-sufficient, independent unit. As wealth increased and the towns grew they developed into *city states*.

CLASSICAL GREECE

The acropolis of Athens as it would have appeared during the Classical era. The building at the top was the Parthenon.

There were many city states with different traditions and forms of government. The Greek city state was called a 'polis', from which comes our word 'political'.

The two most powerful states were Athens and Sparta. Sparta in particular was quite unlike other great states. Its customs were very severe and designed to produce soldiers; all male citizens had to be full-time soldiers.

Boys were taken from their mothers when they were seven and brought up together under very harsh conditions. They had no extra clothes in winter and were only fed porridge. The young men lived together and trained to be soldiers, hunted, and supervised the serfs (called *helots*) who did all the work for them.

ATHENIAN DEMOCRACY Athens had a *democracy* which meant government by the people. All citizens had the right to attend a monthly 'Assembly' and to vote on matters of the city. Only adult men who had been born in Athens were 'citizens', and so women and slaves were not allowed to vote. So great was the power of the citizens or 'demos', the people, that they could send a politician into exile, or ostracize him. This could happen if a minimum of 4000 citizens wrote the politician's name on an ostrakon which was a piece of broken pottery. There were no lawyers and people represented themselves in court. To show the verdict, the jury used small discs for indicating 'guilty' or 'not guilty'.

THE PERSIAN WARS Athens' wealth came from the silver mine at Laureion and her natural harbour, the Piraeus. The Athenians used some of the silver to build a fleet to protect themselves against Persian attack.

In 490 BC the Persian king Darius invaded Greece. The Persians, however, were quickly defeated at the battle of Marathon in 490 BC. The news was carried to Athens over 40 kilometres away by one runner. The race we know as the 'Marathon' gets its name from this historical event. Ten years later, the Persians attacked again. At the battle of Thermopylae, 300 Spartans and their allies died fighting. The Persians advanced to Athens. At the naval battle of Salamis the Greek ships finally defeated the Persians.

After the Persian defeat, Athens became leader of an alliance set up against the prospect of another Persian attack. States contributed funds to be used to drive the Persians from the Greek cities of Asia Minor. The Athenians used this money to beautify their city. They built the Parthenon—the temple of Athena, the city goddess. This was on the top of the *acropolis*, meaning the 'high city', where many other city buildings were situated.

The Athenian Democratic System

These pieces of broken pottery, or potsherds, were called 'ostraka'. When a total of 4000 Athenian citizens scratched the name of the same politician on these ostraka, that politician would be exiled from Athens—or 'ostracized'.

These metal discs were used as jurors' ballots in the law courts. If a juror was voting for the acquittal of a defendant, he would place a disc that had a solid hub into the ballot box. If voting for condemnation , a disc with a hollow hub was used.

The device above was a water clock which was used to mark the length of time a speaker might be allowed in the Assembly of the people. When the water had flowed from the higher pot into the lower pot, his time was up.

The Greek Achievement

The Greeks were great experimenters and innovators in many areas such as *philosophy*, architecture, literature, sculpture and politics. Their theories about science and medicine, though often wrong, were accepted by western Europe up until a few hundred years ago. Below are listed some of the key areas of Greek achievement.

Philosophy Socrates was an Athenian philosopher who devoted his life to enquiring into what the best way is for a person to conduct his/her life. Socrates himself did not write books, but his followers included Plato, another great philosopher in his own right, who recorded various of Socrates' philosophical dialogues.

Socrates was but one of a number of thinkers who have greatly influenced western thought. Other great philosophers of this period included Plato, Aristotle and Pythagoras.

Historians It was the Greeks who began the practice of recording history. Herodotus wrote his great work, the *Historia*, which was an account of the conflict between the Greeks and Persians and how it had come to happen. Thucydides was an Athenian general who wrote an account of the Peloponnesian War between Athens and Sparta.

A mural from a Roman villa at Ephesus in Turkey depicting Socrates.

Dramatists Greek drama was rooted in the ritual festivities of various gods. By the fifth century BC various forms of drama had evolved, including tragedies, comedies and satires. Competitions were held to assess the best work of drama, and writers such as Sophocles, Aeschylus and Euripides wrote tragedies that are still played and adapted today. The great comedic writer of this period was Aristophanes.

Sculpture The art of sculpture became increasingly naturalistic in this period. Just as the Greeks delighted in intellectual pursuit, so the human body was to be admired. The greatest sculptor of this period was Praxiteles.

A modern bronze statue of Leonidas, the Spartan king who died in 480 BC whilst defending the pass of Thermopylae against the Persians.

Key City States in Classical Greece

MACEDONIA
DELPHI
THEBES
CORINTH
OLYMPIA
ATHENS
ARGOS
SPARTA
AEGEAN SEA

Area of Classical Greek civilization

The Greek civilization was small when compared with the empires of the Persians, Chinese and Indians. The area occupied by the city states of Classical Greece was not much larger than a Persian satrapy. Only a quarter of the land could be cultivated, and so ancient Greece never exceeded a population of 2,000,000.

THE RISE OF MACEDON

The Macedonian Army

Far left. In the Macedonian phalanx, soldiers kept the enemy at bay by using their very long thrusting spears called 'sarissas'. This allowed the cavalry to charge at a weak spot in the enemy line, so breaking up the ranks.

Left. Macedonian soldier wearing helmet, cuirass and greaves, and carrying a spear and shield.

The Macedonian army was largely the product of the efforts of Philip II. As a young man in Thebes he had studied Greek military methods.

He decided that the best opposition to the Greek hoplites would be the *phalanx*. This was armed with a new weapon called the 'sarissa'. It was a pike twice as long as an ordinary spear.

These were carried by ranks of soldiers standing further apart than the hoplite soldiers. In this way, the sarissas of the men behind stuck forward between the soldiers in the front ranks. The effect was that of a cluster of sharp objects, like a hedgehog.

In addition there was an armoured cavalry and a siege-train of heavy weapons, including catapults, to back up the phalanx. The Macedonian army was very formidable.

Left. Greek bronze helmet c. fifth century BC from Salonika.

As Athens became more powerful and exerted control over other Greek states, these states looked to Sparta for help. This led to the Peloponnesian War which lasted for 27 years until Sparta defeated Athens in 404 BC. During its course, the struggle raged over the whole of the Greek world. Thucydides, an Athenian historian, wrote an historical account to explain why it happened. As he pointed out, the war was prolonged and on an immense scale. All the states involved were exhausted at the end.

Sparta was now the ruling power amongst the Greeks. Sparta's political system was called *oligarchy* – the rule of the few over the many – and the Spartans despised democracy. Democrats were killed and in many other ways the Spartans abused their power. The other cities turned against them and in 371 BC Thebes rose up and defeated the Spartans. Soon afterwards the *helots* revolted successfully and Sparta's power was broken.

MACEDON BECOMES POWERFUL For a short while Thebes dominated Greece, but conflict soon broke out again which exhausted the Greek states. Their weakness now enabled King Philip of Macedon to take advantage of this situation and gain control of Greece.

Macedonia lay to the northeast of Greece and was very wealthy because it controlled a gold mine. The Greeks had always regarded Macedonia as a barbaric backwater, and were scornful of its claim to be Greek. It was on the fringes of Greece, and most people were hillsmen and shepherds until Philip's victories.

Macedonia was still a kingdom, a form of government long abandoned by Greeks. Many Greeks, particularly

Macedonian Wealth

Recent excavations at Vergina, where the Macedonian royal family were buried, have shown how wealthy they were. Splendid gold funeral wreaths, jewellery, diadems, a gold bow case or *gorytas* of Scythian style are among the objects found. There is a beautiful gold box or *larnax* containing human bones, thought to be those of Philip. A pair of *greaves* (worn to protect the front of the legs from knee to ankle – rather like hockey pads – only made of metal) is also thought to have belonged to him, because one is longer than the other and Philip is known to have had a bad leg. There are also bronze and silver drinking vessels, and even fragments of silk cloth.

Above. Gold wreath from the Royal Tombs at Vergina. Such wreaths, of thin gold foil, were made as funerary wreaths.

Above. Iron cuirass (breastplate) from the Royal Tombs at Vergina c. 350–325 BC. It is decorated with gold and features lion's heads which were a symbol of royalty. Right. Gold larnax, or chest, containing human bones. These are thought to be the bones of Philip of Macedon. It is from the Royal Tombs at Vergina.

Key Dates

359 BC	Accession of Philip II of Macedon.
356–5 BC	Philip defeats a coalition of northern barbarians; birth of Alexander.
352 BC	Philip victorious in Thessaly.
346 BC	Peace and alliance sworn to Philip and his descendants by Athens and her allies.
343–2 BC	Aristotle becomes Alexander's teacher.
338–7 BC	Philip enters Peloponnese; founds the peace alliance of the League of Corinth.
336 BC	Murder of Philip. Alexander succeeds him.
334 BC	Alexander crosses to Asia. Battle of Granicus.
332–331 BC	Alexander in Egypt. Foundation of Alexandria.
327 BC	Invasion of India by Alexander.
323 BC	Alexander dies in Babylon.

Right. Ivory head of Philip II from the Royal Tombs at Vergina.

the Athenians, disliked kingship and were proud of their democracy.

KING PHILIP SPREADS MACEDONIAN INFLUENCE

Under Philip, Macedon had grown strong and expanded. A new weapon, a long spear called the sarissa, had revolutionized the army's fighting tactics. Philip also had trained his army well and led them courageously in battle, even losing an eye in one battle.

Philip now began to buy support in the Greek states. In 338 BC he advanced to Chaeronaea in central Greece and defeated the Thebans and Athenians. He returned, victorious to Macedon only to be murdered in 336 BC. He had planned to fight against the Persians in Asia Minor to spread Macedonian influence even further, but this task was left to his son, Alexander, to carry out.

THE CONQUESTS OF ALEXANDER THE GREAT

On the death of Philip II of Macedon in 336 BC, his 20-year old son Alexander succeeded him. After making sure his kingship would not be taken away, he invaded Asia Minor in 334 BC. It is not certain whether Alexander planned to conquer the Persian Empire at the outset. But as time went by this certainly did become his aim.

The main part of his army consisted of 12,000 Macedonians and 12,000 Greeks. The troops were well trained and followed Alexander loyally. He was a brave and courageous commander and always led his men into battle. He narrowly escaped death on several occasions.

THE PERSIAN AND MACEDONIAN ARMIES The Persian King Darius III was an inexperienced military leader compared with Alexander who had fought under his father and had commanded troops even in his youth. The Persians took enormous baggage trains and even the royal ladies on their military campaigns. All the tents, furnishings and luxuries were a hindrance to swift movement.

By contrast, the Macedonian army was highly trained and efficient. The Macedonian *phalanx* was a formidable unit designed to break through the enemies ranks. It could also take up defensive positions when it was under attack. Pikes (the Macedonian sarissa, introduced by Philip) held by the front ranks formed the attack, whilst behind the soldiers held their shields up to deflect missiles.

THE CONQUEST OF PERSIA AND EGYPT Following Alexander's victory at Granicus, he moved along the west of Asia Minor taking cities such as Miletus which had withstood him. He wintered in Anatolia before reaching Issus (see map). Here he defeated a huge Persian army. After beseiging Tyre for several months, he took control of the city and then moved south to Egypt.

Alexander was welcomed in Egypt because the former Persian rulers had been harsh. He then turned north and east, winning his major victory at Gaugamela in northern Mesopotamia. Darius fled north to Bactria and was murdered by Bactrian nobles.

Persia and Egypt were now Alexander's, but still the conquests continued. The troops, however, were weary after fighting in the most distant region of northern Iran. Finally, in northern India, Alexander's army refused to go any further.

Now master of the Persian Empire, Alexander attempted to unite the Greeks, Persians and Macedonians. He married Roxanne, the daughter of a Bactrian nobleman, and encouraged his soldiers to marry Persian women. Gradually he adopted Persian dress and behaved like an Eastern ruler, which his Macedonian and Greek troops did not like.

He was planning a campaign to Arabia, when he died in Babylon in 323. His son, born after his death, was killed by ambitious generals. Alexander's Empire was divided into kingdoms ruled by his former generals, to avoid any one getting too much power. These were called the 'Successors', and for many years war raged across Greece and the Near East as they each established their control.

The Education of Alexander

From the age of seven, Alexander had been in the care of a strict tutor who had trained him in very Spartan ways. Very quickly he could ride well and had proved his prowess with Bucephalus, his beloved horse. He could also play the lyre and sing, and could recite Homer's *Iliad*.

A 12th century AD carving depicting Aristotle.

An engraving depicting Plato who had been Aristotle's teacher.

When he was 13 years old, Aristotle, the great Athenian philosopher, became his teacher. Aristotle had studied under Plato, who in turn had studied under Socrates (see page 63). Aristotle's approach to philosophy was scientific, and he taught Alexander botany and zoology.

All his life, Alexander was to maintain an interest in science, and also in medicine. Alexander benefited from learning under Aristotle for four years, and the knowledge he gained helped him to become a great leader and military strategist.

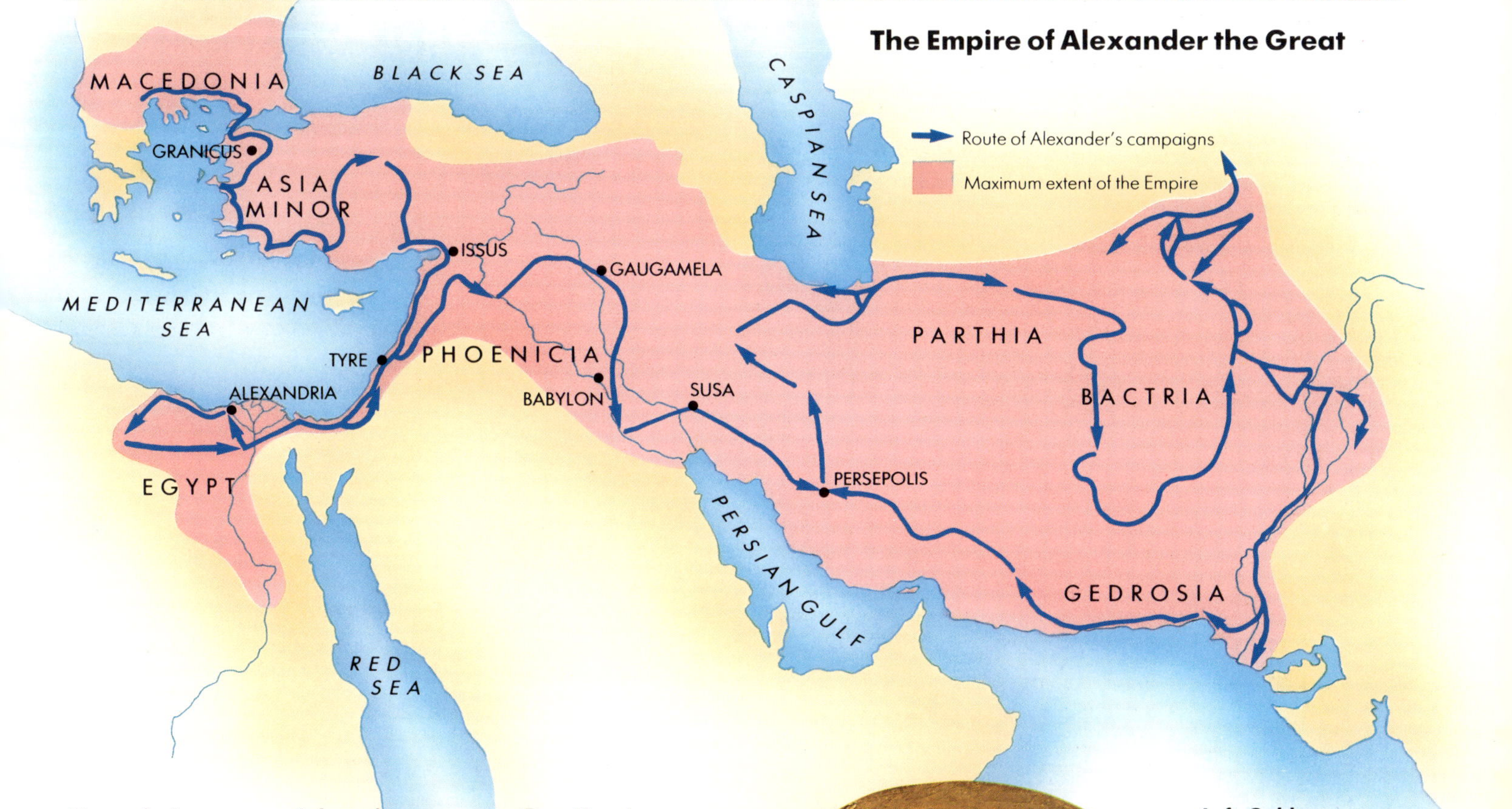

The Empire of Alexander the Great

MACEDONIA
BLACK SEA
CASPIAN SEA
Route of Alexander's campaigns
Maximum extent of the Empire
GRANICUS
ASIA MINOR
ISSUS
GAUGAMELA
MEDITERRANEAN SEA
PARTHIA
TYRE
PHOENICIA
BABYLON
SUSA
BACTRIA
ALEXANDRIA
EGYPT
PERSEPOLIS
PERSIAN GULF
GEDROSIA
RED SEA

Alexander's campaign to extend the Macedonian Empire reached from the Macedonian homeland to India. The campaign lasted for 11 years and in that time he defeated every great nation against whom he led his army. He is believed by many to have been the greatest warrior the world has ever seen.

Top. Mosaic showing the Battle of Issus from Pompeii in Italy. Alexander is shown on the left and Darius is in the chariot on the right.

Left. Gold medallion from the Aboukir Treasure depicting Alexander the Great.

THE SPREAD OF GREEK INFLUENCE

The 300 years from Alexander's death to the start of Roman Empire are called the *Hellenistic Age*. This means 'Greek', from Hellas, the name the Greeks gave to their country.

Because the eastern Mediterranean and parts of the Near East were ruled by Greek kings, there was naturally a strong Greek influence in that region.

Alexander's conquest took Greek soldiers as far as India. Along the way he founded towns in which some soldiers stayed behind, making new lives, and usually marrying local women. This was one way in which the east became Hellenized.

THE DISCOVERY OF AI KHANUM Some years ago, the King of Afghanistan was out hunting near the border with Russia. He noticed some Greek column fragments. French archaeologists excavated and found a completely Greek town. This town is called Ai Khanum, and you can see on the map how far it is from Greece. Here, in distant Bactria, Greeks visited the gymnasium to box and wrestle; they saw Greek plays and spoke the *koine*, the 'common language', the most widely used language of the time and the one in which part of the Christian New Testament was written.

Ai Khanum was only a village compared with the new Greek cities nearer to the Mediterranean. The Greek rulers of Babylonia built a new capital, Seleucia, to replace the ancient city of Babylon.

ALEXANDRIA In Egypt, the ruling family – the Ptolemies – ruled from the new Greek city of Alexandria (named for Alexander the Great) on the Mediterranean. Here there were splendid harbours with ships bringing luxury goods from all over the known world. In the huge royal granary the grain of Egypt was stored.

The city had the most famous library of the ancient world, with 700,000 roles of papyrus. Scientists and mathematicians all worked here, including Euclid whose geometry was still taught in schools until recently. At the first museum in the world, the Mouseion, scholars were paid generously to carry out their research.

Life was less pleasant for manual workers in the gold mines. Working conditions were terrible and children worked alongside slaves.

For the wealthier members of the community, there were many ways of relaxing. On holidays they could visit the theatre as well as attend processions with dancing

The Lighthouse at Alexandria

The great lighthouse was designed in the early Ptolemaic period and was dedicated by Sostratus of Cnidus in 279 BC. It was known as the 'Pharos' and was one of the Seven Wonders of the Ancient World.

No remains are left today of the lighthouse, though an approximate appearance can be reconstructed from various ancient accounts. It stood on a rock at the end of a causeway which divided the two large harbours of Alexandria. It was built with three storeys and was 120 m high. A fire burned permanently at the top, and was magnified and projected by a reflector so that it could be seen from a long distance. Horses were probably used to cart the fuelwood to the top, up a series of ramps.

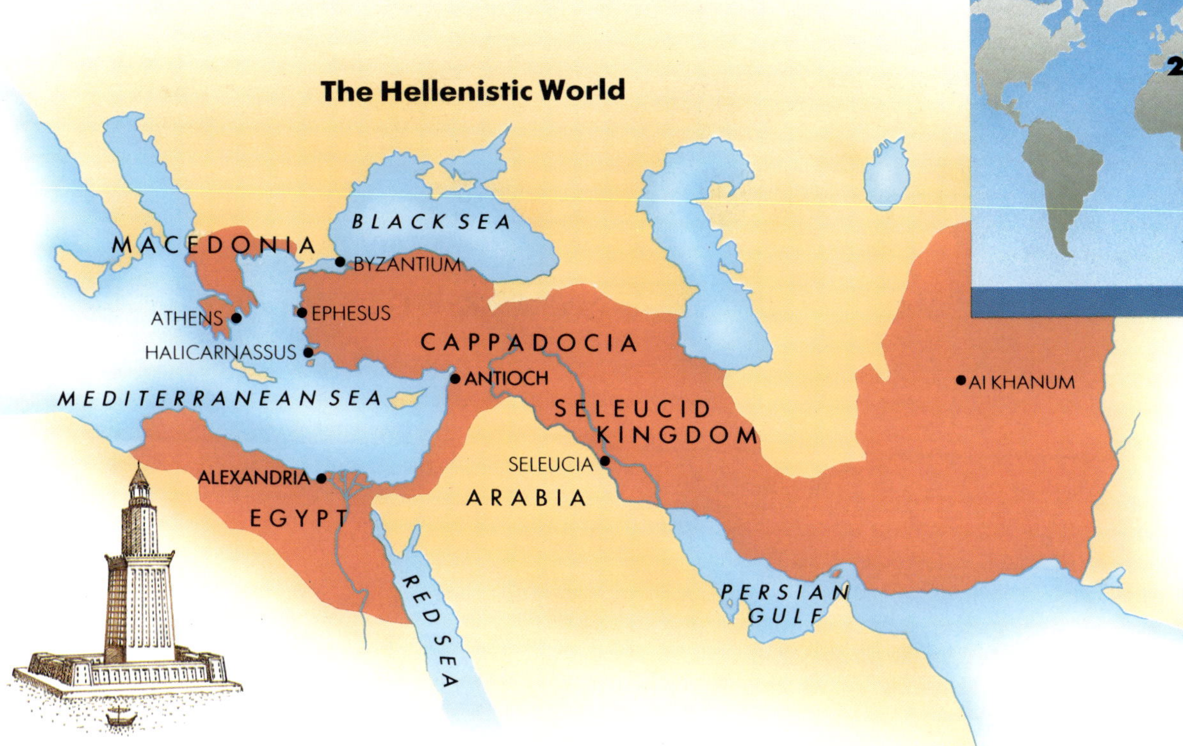

The Hellenistic world covered a vast area. Archaeological remains showing Greek influence have been found as far away from Greece as Ai Khanum in present-day Afghanistan. The Pharos (lighthouse) at Alexandria was one of the great architectural achievements of this period.

Left. Part of the frieze from the Great Altar of Zeus at Pergamon in Asia Minor. It depicts the fight between the gods and giants. It dates from c. 180–150 BC.

Below. A fine example of a Hellenistic statue of a boy athlete from Tralles. It dates from the third century BC.

and music. Games and chariot racing were held in the stadium, and men and boys exercised and met their friends at the gymnasium. Around the bustling market square were wine and food shops and stalls, selling everything from oil lamps to leather sandals and sweetmeats.

NEW LANDS At Pergamon in Asia Minor, beautiful gardens were created and sick people came to be healed at the sancturary of Aesclepius.

The wealth of these new lands attracted Greeks from the homeland. In time the eastern Greeks learned non-Greek ways, and many changed their religion. They even worshipped the ruler as a god king, something which would have been unthinkable in the Classical Greek world.

AN INTERNATIONAL AGE In some ways this age was like ours: restless, urban, open to change and above all, cosmopolitan.

1 Alexander conquers Egypt in 331 BC, and the town of Alexandria is founded. After Alexander's death, Egypt is ruled by Ptolemy Lagus and his descendants. Carthage in northern Africa is destroyed by the Romans in 146 BC.

2 Rome gains control of Italy c. 250 BC. Greek states are destroyed by the Romans in 146 BC and many Greek statues, paintings and books are plundered and taken back to Rome. Augustus becomes sole ruler of the Roman Empire in 27 BC.

3 In India, the Mauryan Empire is founded by Chandragupta in 322 BC. The first alphabetic Brahman script is used in India c. 250 BC.

4 China is unified under the Ch'in Dynasty in 221 BC. The building of the Great Wall of China commences. Around 100 BC, Indian religions begin to spread to China along trade routes.

ARYAN INDIA

Some time after 2000 BC people known as *Aryans* settled in northwest India. Gradually they moved east, until by 1000 BC they had also settled in the upper valley of the Ganges river. Their language was an Indo-European one, an old form of *Sanskrit* which forms the basis of the north Indian languages spoken today.

Apart from language, some aspects of today's Indian culture, for instance the *caste system*, can be traced back to the Aryans. There are also Aryan elements in the *Hindu* religion, such as certain gods. We know about Aryan gods and about the social structure of these people from literature that was passed on orally until it was written down in about AD 1300.

The *Rig Veda* is a collection of hymns. It portrays a picture of Aryans living in farming communities together with the original non-Aryan people, whom they dominated.

THE CASTE SYSTEM Early Aryan society was divided into four social groups. The first were the priests, called Brahmans. Next were the warriors or Kshatriyas. Third, the merchants, farmers and craftsmen, known as the Vish, and lastly the Shudras who were labourers and servants. Even lower were the non-Aryans in India.

This social group system eventually developed into the caste system. Eventually there were hundreds of castes and sub-castes. The non-Aryans were regarded as 'unclean' and became the outcasts or untouchables, as they were known. They did all the unpleasant work.

Images of the Buddha in human form, as shown here, began to appear from the first century AD. The Buddha is generally shown meditating or preaching. Here the Buddha sits in the traditional cross-legged pose. The very act of making images of the Buddha was highly respected and valued. Wherever Buddhism spread, a great many images were sure to proliferate, and many of these images have survived to the present day. This image can be seen today at the Lahore Museum in Pakistan.

HOMES AND CITIES There are no remains of the homes of these Aryans, but we know from their poems that they lived in houses of wood and bamboo. These decay quickly, leaving no archaeological evidence.

Large cities, the capitals of some 16 separate states, had been established in northern India by about 600 BC. Their names are known from two Sanskrit epics, the *Mahabharata* and the *Ramayana*. A number of such sites, one with a beautiful palace, have been excavated. As elsewhere, ironworking became widespread and the new tools increased food production. Other developments such as rice growing date from about 500 BC when people began to write and to use coinage.

THE SPREAD OF BUDDHISM In 563 BC the *Buddha*, meaning 'the Enlightened one', whose name was Siddhartha Gautama, was born in India. He lived the life of a rich nobleman until he was 29. Then he set out to try and understand what lay behind human existence. Gautama meditated and fasted and spent the rest of his life as a wandering preacher. He rejected the Brahmans' emphasis on rituals. The priestly class of Brahmans – who studied the sacred literature – performed all the sacrifices and rituals of the Vedic religion.

Gautama preached a very simple philosophy. Nirvana, or Enlightenment, could be achieved by following a life of good conduct. The Buddha died in 483 BC and this religion spread through much of India and the eastern world.

INVADERS OF INDIA In 533 BC northwest India was invaded by the Persians. The site of the city of Taxila, now in Pakistan, dates from this time. Persian influence can be seen in some early Indian sculpture.

In 326 BC Alexander the Great reached the Punjab in northwest India. Here he fought against Poros. Although he did not stay long, Greek influence remained in the Indo-Greek cities of northwest India and Afghanistan. Shortly after Alexander's death, Chandragupta Maurya drove the Greeks out of the Punjab and founded the Mauryan *dynasty*, whose capital was at Pataliputra on the Ganges. These rulers united India.

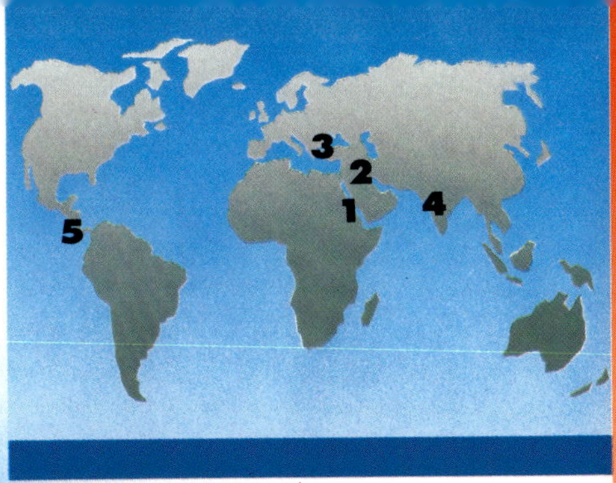

The Spread of Buddhism

By the time the Buddha died, thousands of people in India had become his followers. This process was helped by the conversion of the Mauryan Emperor Asoka to Buddhism in the third century BC. Until Asoka died in 232 BC, India enjoyed a golden period of Buddhist rule. Hinduism was restored in India in about 183 BC, when an army general, named Pusyamitra Sunga, seized power from the last of the Mauryan emperors. The Kushan Empire, which extended from central Asia to northern India, reinstated Buddhism in India at the end of the first century AD. During the next centuries Buddhist teaching spread throughout most of Asia. It mingled with the traditional beliefs of many countries. Today there are well over 500 million Buddhists, mainly in such countries as India, Nepal, China, Japan, Korea, Tibet, Cambodia, Laos, Vietnam, Malaysia, Burma, Thailand and Sri Lanka.

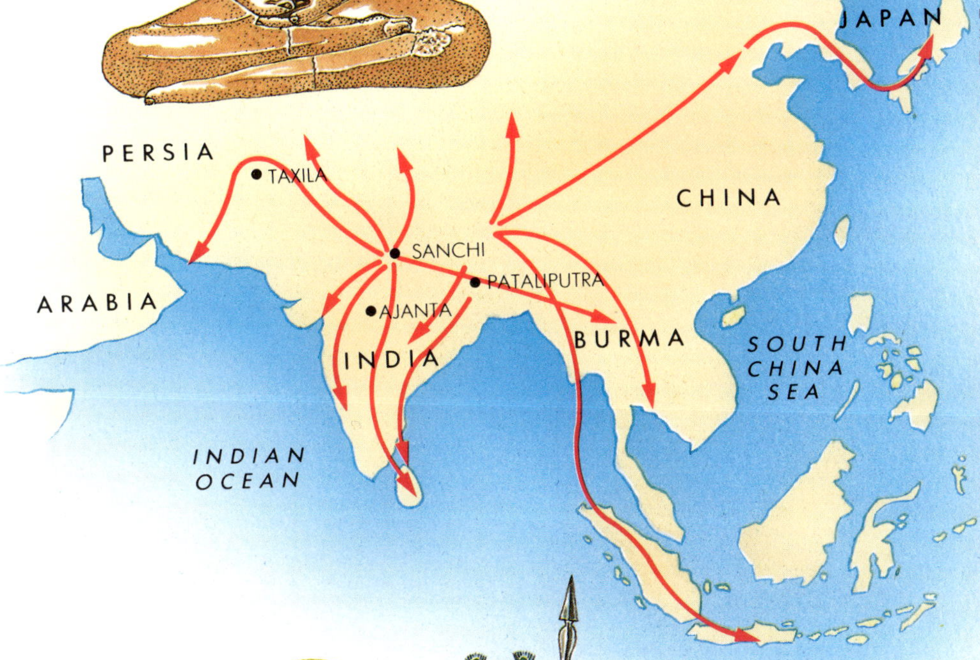

1 States begin to arise in the Red Sea area, exporting frankincense and myrrh c. 550 BC. The first copper smelting begins in Niger and Mali c. 500 BC.

2 The Assyrian Empire comes to an end in 609 BC. The New Babylonian Empire emerges in 600 BC, and the rise of the Persian empire commences c. 550 BC. In 334 BC Alexander the Great begins his conquests and the Persian Empire soon falls.

3 480 BC marks the beginning of the Classical period in Greece. The Parthenon comes to completion on the Athenian acropolis.

4 Siddhartha Gautama, the Buddha, is born in northern India in 563 BC. Iron production begins in China c. 550 BC, and the first coinage appears in 500 BC. Round the same period, Taxila in northern India becomes an important city, and it develops its own style of art, called Gandhara.

5 Early hieroglyphic writing appears at Monte Alban and Oaxaca in Mexico c. 500 BC. The Chavin temple complexes are completed in Peru c. 400 BC.

The Caste System

Aryan society was rigidly divided into different groups. This is called the caste system. The original four groups were the priests, or Brahmans, the soldiers, or Kshatriyas, the merchants, or Vish, and the labourers and servants, or Shudras.

Brahmans did not trade or work as other groups did, but went through various stages of development to become completely pure and holy.

The Kshatriya is shown here in battle dress with a spear, sword and helmet. His weapons are made of iron.

The Vish worked in trade and were often, but not always, prosperous. Many of this caste in fact converted to other religions which did not divide society so rigidly.

The Shudras were the poorest and least educated group. If a Shudra cast his shadow on a member of another caste, that person would undergo various ritual purification and cleansing acts to rid themselves of 'pollution'.

These four figures each represent one of the groups of the caste system.

THE FIRST EMPIRES OF CHINA

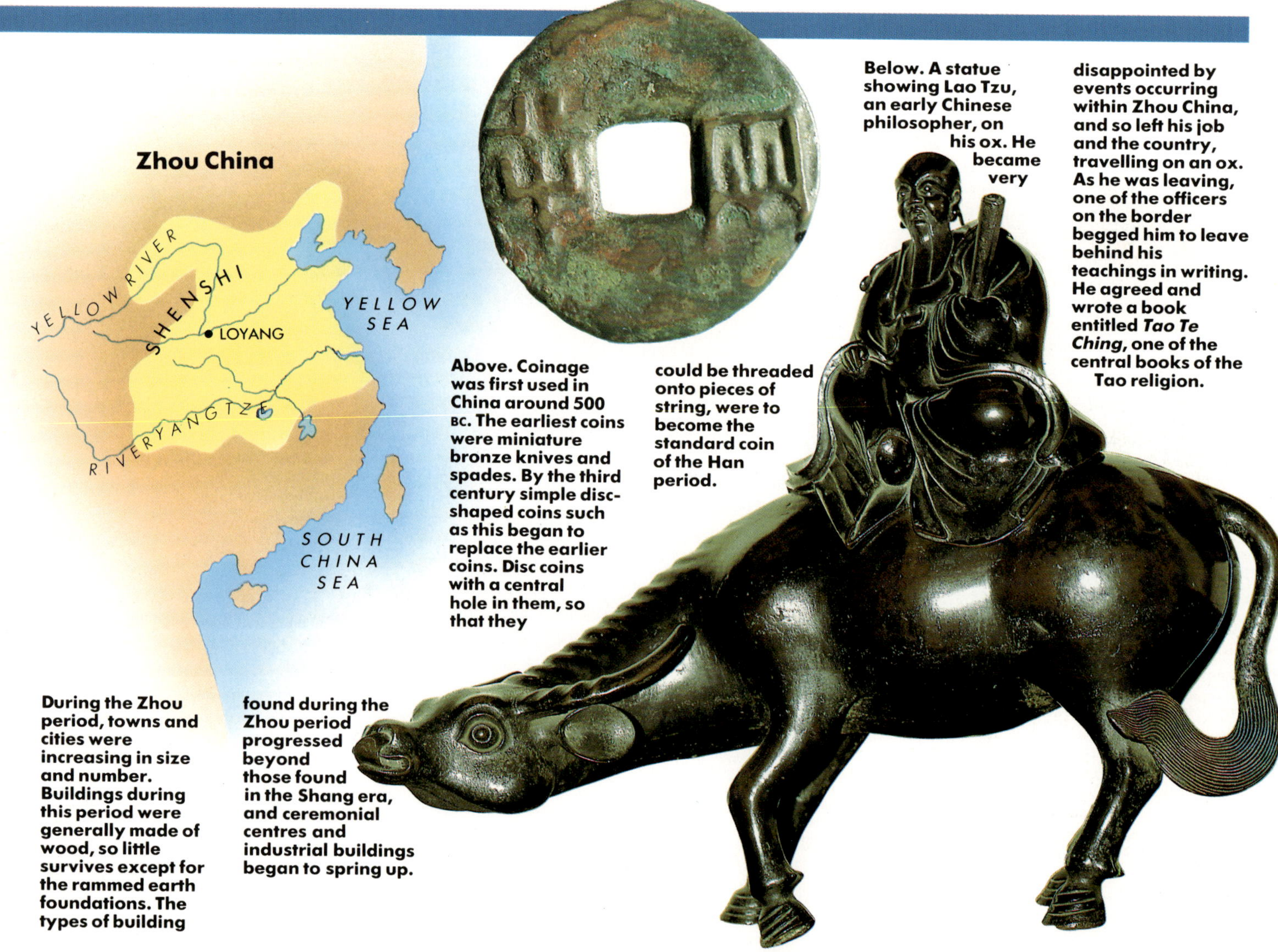

Below. A statue showing Lao Tzu, an early Chinese philosopher, on his ox. He became very disappointed by events occurring within Zhou China, and so left his job and the country, travelling on an ox. As he was leaving, one of the officers on the border begged him to leave behind his teachings in writing. He agreed and wrote a book entitled *Tao Te Ching*, one of the central books of the Tao religion.

Above. Coinage was first used in China around 500 BC. The earliest coins were miniature bronze knives and spades. By the third century simple disc-shaped coins such as this began to replace the earlier coins. Disc coins with a central hole in them, so that they could be threaded onto pieces of string, were to become the standard coin of the Han period.

During the Zhou period, towns and cities were increasing in size and number. Buildings during this period were generally made of wood, so little survives except for the rammed earth foundations. The types of building found during the Zhou period progressed beyond those found in the Shang era, and ceremonial centres and industrial buildings began to spring up.

The dynasty of the Zhou, which overthrew the Shang rulers in about 1100 BC, lasted for nearly 1000 years. The first part of this period is called the Western Zhou as the capitals were in Shenshi (see map). From 771 BC to 481 BC was the Eastern Zhou period, and the capital was near Loyang in Honan. The final phase is called the Warring States period, which ended in 221 BC.

THE POWER OF FEUDAL ESTATES Although these 1000 years are named after the Zhou dynasty, their control of the whole country ended in the eighth century BC. The Western Zhou state was really a continuation of the Shang *feudal*-style government. The Zhou kings kept power by granting feudal estates to relatives and trustworthy nobles, who in turn gave them political and military allegiance. Gradually, the king lost his power as the feudal lords became stronger and combined against each other or against the king.

These lords had complete control over their territories. They grew wealthy from the profits of the salt and iron trades.

In the Eastern Zhou period there was a struggle for supremacy, which shifted from state to state. By the fifth century, the beginning of the Warring States period, no fewer than seven kingdoms had emerged.

NEW DEVELOPMENTS In spite of the unsettled political situation, the period from the eighth century was one of new developments and change. Iron technology was just one development, and from about 500 BC the Chinese

Left. Confucius was China's most honoured philosopher. His Chinese name was K'ung Ch'ui. During his lifetime he travelled from one noble's court to another telling them how people ought to behave. Most of the nobles would not listen to him. Later on, however, some of his disciples gained important positions and were able to put his teachings into practice.

Right. Ritual vessel of the Zhou Dynasty. It is made from bronze with a gold sheet overlay.

Chinese Writing

The chart below shows how Chinese characters developed from early picture signs to less recognizable symbols. Several thousand different pictures were used as words during the Zhou Dynasty.

	SUN	MOON	TREE	BIRD	HORSE
ABOUT 1500 BC					
BEFORE 213 BC					
AFTER AD 200	日	月	木	鳥	馬

were making enormous quantities of iron tools and weapons.

The new and better tools increased food production, as did improved forms of irrigation. In turn, the population grew, and so did the size and number of towns and cities. China became wealthier and coinage was introduced in this period.

The use of writing spread beyond oracle bones, which fell from use. In the large cities, official records and archives were kept. Writing was done either on strips of bamboo or on lengths of silk.

CONFUCIUS This was also a time when literature began to develop. In 551 BC *Confucius* was born. As a young man he began to teach his philosophy. His work of Chinese history, *Spring and Autumn Annals*, was written shortly before he died in 479 BC. He claimed no original ideas, but believed that people could become good by the virtuous example of others – particularly those in positions of authority. Eventually his teachings became widely accepted.

LAO TZU Lao Tzu was another influential thinker. He believed that people should go back to leading a simple life, without any government interference, and in harmony with nature. He and his followers taught Tao, 'the way of nature', as a way of life. Both Lao Tzu and Confucius were reacting to the confusion of their time, which culminated in the conquest of all the other states by the *Ch'in* ruler in 221 BC.

The Great Empires
TIME CHART

BC	NEAR EAST	AFRICA/EGYPT	EUROPE/GREECE	CHINA/INDIA
1150			Dorians invade Greece	
1140		First Phoenician colony in North Africa		
1027				Defeat of Shang and start of Zhou Dynasty
1000>926	Israel's Monarchy			
900>750			Rise of city-states	
814		Phoenician city of Carthage founded		
745>609	Assyrian Empire			
700>600			Athenians expel kings	
700>500				Weakening of Zhou
625>539	Neo Babylonian Empire			
612	Nineveh sacked			
600				Early cities in Ganges valley
563				Birth of Buddha
551				Birth of Confucius
539	Cyrus conquers Babylon			
533				Achaemenid invasion of India
525>404		Egypt ruled by Persians		
507			Athenian democracy	
490>479			Persian Wars	
481>221				Warring States period – China
431>404			Peloponnesian War	
364>324				Nanda Dynasty – India
360	Weakening of Persia			
356			Philip in Greece	
343>332		Egypt's second period of Persian rule		
336>323			Alexander the Great	
334>323	Alexander the Great's campaigns			
334	Alexander invades Persian Empire			
332	Alexander conquers Mesopotamia	Alexander the Great invades Egypt		
326				Alexander in India
324>187				Mauryans drive out Greeks
323	Alexander dies in Babylon			
304>64	Seleucids into Mesopotamia			
304>30		Ptolemaic period		
256>221				Ch'in unify empire – China
247>227	Parthian kingdom established			
232				Asoka's death – India
206				Collapse of Ch'in Dynasty

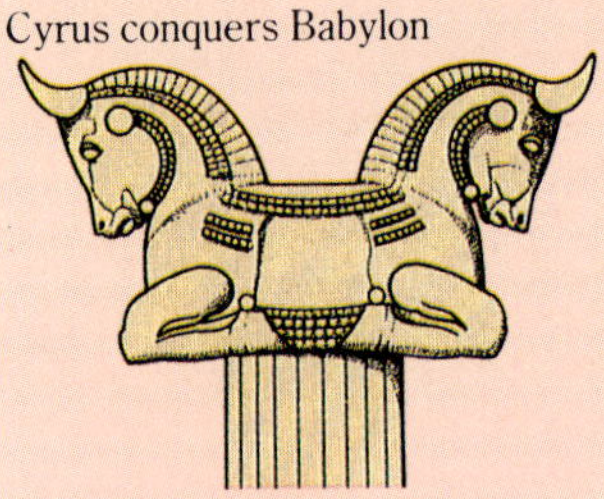

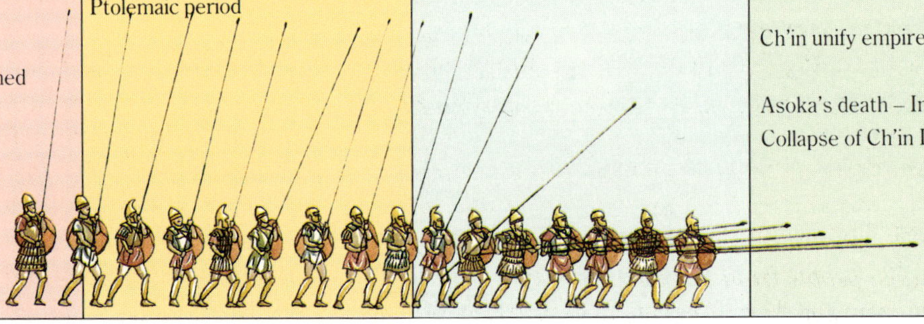

The eagle was the symbol of the Roman Empire.

The Roman Empire in AD 200

The Roman World

The map on this page shows the world known to the Romans in the second century AD. They created a huge empire. A small group of people in Italy were able to become a world power. You can see the area they conquered with their armies, but beyond that, in all directions, were lands and peoples the Romans traded with. For example, they imported silks from as far away as China.

The world of the Romans was not only big, it also lasted a very long time. Although it is difficult to say exactly when Rome began to develop, the Romans themselves used to teach their children that the city was founded in 753 BC. It was over a thousand years later that the Roman Empire came to an end.

FROM ALL OVER THE EMPIRE In AD 80 the Roman poet Martial wrote about people from all over the Empire coming to the opening of Rome's greatest amphitheatre, the Colosseum.

'There are farmers from the Balkans here, natives from southern Russia bred on horses' blood, people who drink the Nile's waters and even those from far away Britain. Arabs, people from the shores of the Red Sea, as well as those from southern Turkey, have hurried here and German tribesmen and Ethiopians each with their own peculiar hairstyles.'

THE IDEA OF BEING ROMAN Martial himself lived for over 30 years in Rome, the capital city of the Empire. But he grew up in Bilbilis in Spain, a new town created by the Romans in one of their *provinces*.

One of the important things which helps make people feel they belong to an empire is a single language. The language of the Roman Empire was Latin. The 60 million people living in the Roman Empire did not all speak Latin as their first language. But Latin was the official language and if you wanted to do well you had to master it.

EVIDENCE FOR THE ROMAN PAST How do we know about the Romans and their world? Writing and literature give us part of the evidence. The other important sources of evidence are the things that remain. Many Roman buildings can still be seen above ground, and archaeologists have excavated many others, as well as the thousands of Roman objects you can see today in museums. If you live in or visit countries that were once part of the Roman world, you are never far away from the Romans themselves! Read on.

THE FOUNDING OF ROME

This is an antefix which decorated the ridge line of a building in the Etruscan town of Veii and dates from the sixth century BC. It was made of clay and fired in a kiln and was once even more highly painted.

To understand the early history of the Romans we must first look back to a people known as the Etruscans. They lived in an area north of Rome, called Etruria, which was hilly but fertile. By the seventh century BC, these Etruscans had formed themselves into 12 independent states. Each state had its own capital city, but the people all thought of themselves as Etruscans. Together they began to conquer lands beyond Etruria and by the sixth century BC there were Etruscan cities from Salerno in the south to Mantua in the north.

THE SKILFUL ETRUSCANS The Etruscans were farmers who grew grain, olives and grapes. They also made money by trade (selling their extra corn, for example) with peoples such as the Greeks. They were skilled metalworkers and potters. Their cities were properly planned out with streets, *aqueducts* (for bringing water) and sewage systems.

We know quite a lot about the Etruscans from the beautifully decorated tombs which have been discovered. The Etruscans believed in a life after death and the rich built underground tombs for their dead. They buried them with objects such as vases, statues and jewellery. The walls of the tombs were painted with scenes of Etruscan life.

OTHER TRIBES The Etruscans were not the only people in this part of Italy at this time, although they were the most powerful. Other tribes were called the Samnites, the Umbrians, the Sabines and the Latins. The Latins were the biggest of the tribes and had arrived in this area, probably from across the Alps, before the eighth century BC. Their name, of course, shows that they spoke the Latin language.

THE CITY OF ROME The Latins lived around and in the city of Rome – 'Roma' was originally an Etruscan word. The early history of the city of Rome shows the complicated history of Italy at this time. Rome was governed first by a Sabine, then a Latin, another Sabine and then three Etruscan kings. The Romans themselves believed that their first ruler or king (*rex*) was Romulus who had founded the city of Rome on 21 April 753 BC. Perhaps you have read the story of the twins, Romulus and Remus, who were left to die as babies in a basket floating on the River Tiber. The story tells how they were brought up by a she-wolf. Romulus later killed his brother Remus in an argument.

The city of Rome was originally separate villages built on seven hills overlooking the River Tiber. They were the Quirinal, Viminal, Esquiline, Caelian, Aventine, Palatine and Capitoline hills. The Etruscans combined the villages into the first proper town of Roma. The valleys in between the hills began to be occupied with houses, shops and businesses. The River Tiber connected the growing town with the sea which meant easy trade with the rest of Italy and abroad. Later a port called Ostia was established at the mouth of the River Tiber.

This bronze statue of the wolf which suckled Romulus and Remus was made by an Etruscan craftsman in the sixth century BC. The twins were added in the sixteenth century AD.

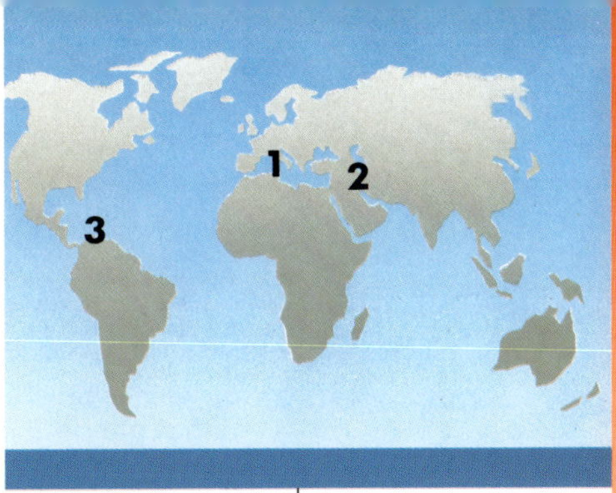

Italy in 241 BC

The Romans gradually increased their control over Italy with the help of their allies. Colonies were set up by Roman citizens. The dates of these colonies are given on the map. Other peoples were made Roman either by giving them full or half citizenship.

ARIMINUM 268
SPOLETIUM 241
COSA 273
ROME
AESERNIA 263
BENEVENTUM 268
BRUNDISIUM 244
PAESTUM 273
ADRIATIC SEA
TYRRHENIAN SEA

Roman territory (full citizenship)
Roman territory (half citizenship)
Roman colony
Romanized peoples
Allies of Rome
Date of colony 268

1 2 3

1 From about 1500 BC to 100 BC (when the Etruscans first appeared in Italy) there were a number of small kingdoms on mainland Greece and on other islands. There were royal palaces at Mycenae, in the Peloponnese south of Athens, and at Knossos on Crete. By about 1450 BC the Mycenaeans had taken over the civilization on Crete. The cities in mainland Greece became important. In the fifth century BC they were threatened by the Persian Empire. At a famous battle in the Bay of Marathon the Persians were defeated in 490 BC, and again at Salamis in 480 BC.

2 The Phoenicians were descendants of the Canaanites (from Israel) and were known throughout the ancient world as sea traders. From the ninth century BC onwards they established colonies in the southern Mediterranean. The most famous is at Carthage in north Africa.

3 Between 1200 BC and 300 BC the villages in parts of central America became the centres of complex civilizations. One of the most famous were the Olmec people, known for their art carved in stone. They occupied a relatively small area on the southern shores of the Gulf of Mexico between 1200 BC and 300 BC.

The Etruscans liked highly decorated objects. On the left is a vase of fired clay of a type known as bucchero which was grey all the way through. On the right is a little gold pot from the tomb of a wealthy Etruscan buried in Praeneste. It dates from the seventh century BC.

THE ROMAN REPUBLIC

The forum in Rome, seen from the Capitoline Hill, was the centre of political life. In the background is the Colosseum.

The Latin-speaking people of the city of Rome had been governed by rulers from other tribes in the earliest part of its history. The first kings had divided the population of Rome into different tribes. A king had a group of men to advise him. Later, people were allowed to vote on important matters in an assembly. They had rights according to how rich they were.

ETRUSCAN KINGS The third of the Etruscan kings of Rome, called Lucius Tarquinius, was nicknamed 'the Proud'. He was hated for his harsh rule and was thrown out by the Roman people. A much later ruler of Rome, the Emperor Claudius, wrote,

'Then, after what King Tarquinius the Proud did, he came to be hated by the people of Rome. We were all thoroughly fed up with being ruled by kings and the government was put in the hands of officials who were elected each year'.

THE REPUBLIC OF ROME Roman historians tell us that the date a completely new form of government was created was 509 BC. It was called res publica, which literally meant 'a matter for the people'. From it comes our word republic. A republic is a form of government where all the officials who govern are voted into office by the citizens. This is what happened in Rome.

ELECTED OFFICIALS The Romans hated the word 'king' and so their first act was to make it impossible for one person to have complete power – even if that person was voted into office. So they created two officials called *consuls*. They had much the same power as kings and were in charge of the government and the army. But they were only in office for one year and had to agree their decisions with each other.

To cope with a serious emergency, the consuls could appoint a *dictator* who held absolute power for a period of six months. It was specially useful in war to have just one supreme commander. The dictator had a second-in-command called a *magister equitum* (it means 'master of the horse') who was in charge of the *cavalry*.

THE ROMAN SENATE In normal circumstances a parliament, called the *senate*, made up of ex-officials, helped the consuls to reach decisions, and discussed all the important issues of the day.

There were four other chief officials of the government. *Praetors* were the chief judges of the Roman Republic elected each year. They were the most important officials of government after the consuls. Every five years *censors* were elected, originally to take a census, or count, of the citizens. The two censors held office for eighteen months. They registered all citizens and their properties and put them into tribes and classes for voting and military service. *Quaestors* were first appointed by the consuls as assistants to help as magistrates in the courts of law. Later four quaestors were elected and two of them looked after the state's finances. *Aediles* were four officials who were in charge of all public works and public records. For example, they were responsible for ensuring a proper water supply to the city through aqueducts.

PATRICIANS, PLEBEIANS AND EQUITES The people of Rome were divided into classes – at first there were two and then a third was added. The wealthy people who owned land were called *patricians*. They could trace their origins back to the noble families of early Rome. The patricians could vote and could become government officers, such as consuls. All the ordinary people were known as *plebeians*. They could vote but could only hold minor posts in the government. The plebeians were able to elect ten officials, called *tribunes*, each year who looked after their interests in the government.

The third class of people in Rome was created later from the growing number of business men who owned property. They were called the *equites* ('knights').

Not every adult person in the Roman Republic could vote. Women and slaves were excluded.

Plebeians formed the largest class in Roman society – workers who usually owned no property. They organized themselves, made protests and won the right to hold some political offices by 287 BC.

Patricians were the aristocracy of Rome – the privileged class. They held all the most important political and religious offices.

Equites was the name for the second rank of Roman nobles who were rich enough to provide a horse and equipment for the cavalry. The Emperor Augustus allowed any free man of blameless character to become a 'knight' on payment of 400,000 sesterces.

The Government of Rome

Praetors were the highest level of magistrates in Roman courts of law.

Normally in wars the two consuls would take charge of the army.

The Senate was the place where the affairs of state were discussed – similar to a modern parliament.

Consuls held the supreme power of both the civilian government and the army. During the Republican period the consuls were voted in by the assembly of the people. But they had to be proposed by senators from their own ranks. They retained power for a year (beginning on 1 January) until the period of the emperors when they remained in office for two to four months only.

An aedile's job involved the care for the city's water supply.

Censors were first appointed in about 443 BC to compile the census of the male property-owning population.

Aediles had the job of looking after public buildings and the state archives.

Tarquin the Proud

According to tradition and Roman sources the last three kings of Rome were all Etruscan. Many stories were told about the early years of Rome – not all can possibly be true. One, which was a favourite for Roman children, was about the last king of all – Lucius Tarquinius – who murdered the former king, Tullius. He acted as cruel dictator from the start of his reign. He took rights away from the people and put to death the patricians whose land or wealth he wanted for himself. He was nicknamed 'Superbus' (the Proud) by the Roman people, who hated him. He increased the power of Rome by defeating neighbouring tribes, including the Volscians. After 24 years of this tyrant's rule the people banished him in 510 BC. He fled to the Etruscan town of Caere. He led various uprisings against Rome but eventually died at Cumae.

THE ARMY IN THE REPUBLIC

Rome had always needed an army to protect its own citizens from other tribes. The Romans also wanted to conquer lands around the city, and later further afield. When the Romans were ruled by kings, each of the three Roman tribes provided 1000 men for an infantry regiment and 100 men with horses for a cavalry squadron. The size of the army increased as the state became bigger. But during the Republic it was not a permanent army; it was called together in times of trouble.

THE CALL-UP The heads of state, the consuls, appointed officers, called *tribuni militum* ('military tribunes'). It was the tribunes' job to recruit the right number of men for the regiment, or *legio* ('legion') as it was called. Any free citizen who owned property had to assemble in Rome and could be chosen by the tribunes to join the army for a particular campaign.

WEAPONS AND WARFARE The infantry soldiers of the legions – legionaries – were put into different fighting units according to their age and physical strength. The front line troops were fully armed and carried two javelins to hurl against the enemy. Behind them came the older men, used in emergencies in the battle. They each carried a long spear. The last group were the skirmishers. These were the poorest citizens who could only afford to equip themselves with light armour and carry short javelins.

OFFICERS AND CAVALRY Each part of each legion had a number of officers to command the men and control the battle. A cavalry squadron was formed from the wealthiest citizens – those who could afford both the horse, weapons and armour. Because the Roman citizens could never afford enough cavalry, the allies of Rome provided the largest number of mounted soldiers in the army as well as an equal number of infantrymen.

ON CAMPAIGN On the march, the soldiers of the allies marched first, followed by the rest of the army. They went in battle order if they were in hostile territory. At the end of each day, one of the tribunes chose a suitable site for the camp. To make the camp, the legionaries dug

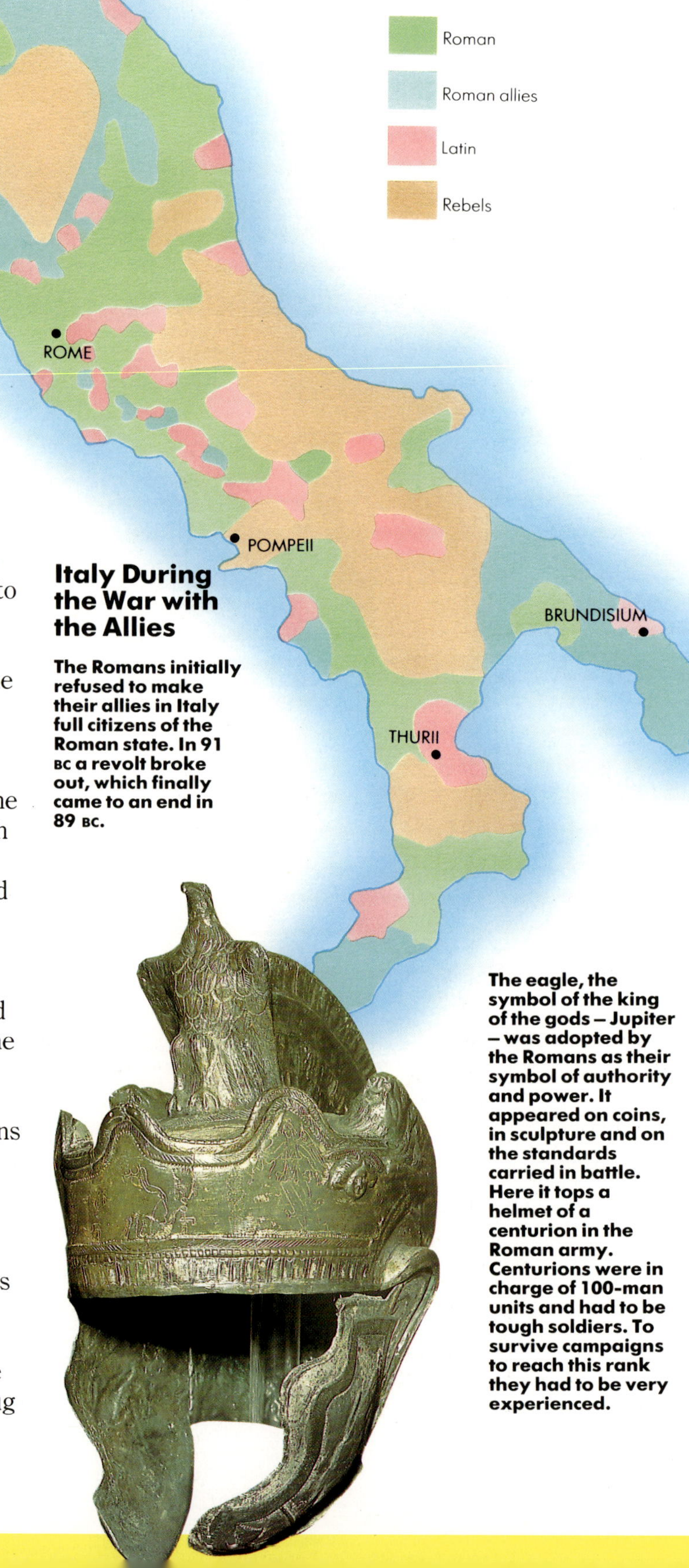

Italy During the War with the Allies

The Romans initially refused to make their allies in Italy full citizens of the Roman state. In 91 BC a revolt broke out, which finally came to an end in 89 BC.

The eagle, the symbol of the king of the gods – Jupiter – was adopted by the Romans as their symbol of authority and power. It appeared on coins, in sculpture and on the standards carried in battle. Here it tops a helmet of a centurion in the Roman army. Centurions were in charge of 100-man units and had to be tough soldiers. To survive campaigns to reach this rank they had to be very experienced.

Lined up for battle the Roman army was a formidable sight for their enemies. On the left you can see the three types of foot soldiers. The triarius (standing left) were so called because, as experienced soldiers, they formed the rear rank in battle. The two front lines were formed by the hastatus or princeps (kneeling), less experienced but still young enough to fight. The velites (standing right) were lightly armed with helmets (this one has a wolf skin over it) and spears. They were used as skirmishers. In front of the troops (below) you can see a horn blower who gave out orders from the commanders. On the right is a standard bearer. There was one standard bearer for each legion, and one for each centuria (a century = 100 men). This is one of the century standard bearers.

The Organization of the Army

Two centuries made up one manipulus. Within each century were the following officers and soldiers:
Centurion: unit commander
Optio: second-in-command
Cornicen: trumpeteer
Signifer: standard bearer

The organization of the soldiers in a legion, headed by six tribunes.

Tesserarius: guard commander
Hastati: foot soldiers
Principes: foot soldiers
Velites: foot soldiers/ skirmishers

A legion was made up of 10 manipuli of the following types of soldiers:
Hastati: front line foot soldiers
Principes: second line foot soldiers
Triarii: rear line foot soldiers
10 squadrons of cavalry.

The legion was commanded by six tribunes.

a deep ditch and formed a bank, called the *rampart*, to protect the army. On top of the rampart a strong wooden fence was made of stakes. Each soldier carried two stakes. Everyone knew exactly where to pitch their tents inside the camp because it was always laid out in the same way.

INTO BATTLE The Romans were careful to adopt tried-and-tested battle procedures that they could use again and again. Normally the consuls would set out their army in this way: in the centre of the battle line were the legions. On each side were the legions of the allies and on the wings were the cavalry squadrons. At the start of the battle the light-armed troops and cavalry would try to unnerve the enemy by fast attacks in small groups. Then in the centre the main army would advance, first hurling their spears and then fighting at close quarters. Each legionary carried a short sword and a dagger as well as a long shield. The army commanders made sure that their men were trained in formation fighting, and that they were disciplined and obeyed orders in battle.

ENEMIES OF ROME: GAULS, SAMNITES AND GREEKS

The Gauls and the Geese

When the Gauls, who were fierce warriors, reached Rome and besieged the city the people fled and took refuge on one of the high points of the city called the Capitoline Hill. The Gauls crept up on the sleeping Romans at night but, as the Roman historian, Livy, tells us:

'One by one the Gauls pulled themselves up the side of the hill and reached the top. They were so silent that not even the guard dogs were woken up . . . but the Gauls could not escape the notice of the geese, which were sacred to the goddess Juno. These geese saved the Romans by their cackling and the flapping of their wings'.

The Latin people of Rome needed a large army in order to remain the most powerful tribe in their area. In the area closest to the city of Rome there were three tribes they had to conquer. The Sabines lived to the north-east. The Aequi lived in the mountainous areas in central Italy. The Volsci lived close to Rome itself. The Romans had conquered all these peoples by 304 BC.

The Etruscans were still powerful in Italy and the Romans had to deal with them, too. They proved difficult to conquer but were eventually defeated.

THE GAULS Celtic tribes called the Gauls came across the Alps in about 400 BC to look for new land in Italy. One Roman historian, Polybius, said that they:

'*spent their time in war or farming and that their only possessions were cattle and gold because this is what they could carry about with them*'.

In 390 BC these Gauls became a real threat to the city of Rome itself. They besieged the city and would have broken in by night if they had not been spotted in time. Eventually the Romans were forced to pay them a very large sum of gold to leave the country.

THE SAMNITES A greater threat to the Romans than the Gauls were the Samnites who lived in villages in central Italy south of Rome. Originally the Romans had signed a treaty with the Samnites to help them both conquer the Volsci. But they were both powerful peoples and only one could take overall control. War broke out in 343 BC and lasted for 50 years. Samnite warriors were difficult to

This sculpture comes from the tomb of Mausolus, the Greek ruler of Caria in Asia. It shows the story of the Greeks fighting the Amazons. You can see that the Greeks wore little armour except for helmets and round shields.

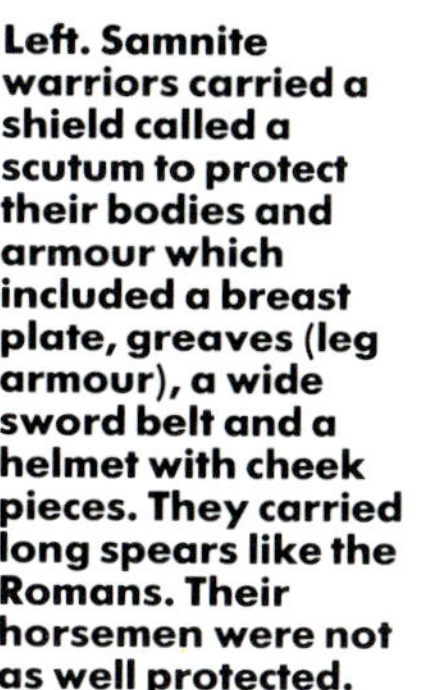

Left. Samnite warriors carried a shield called a scutum to protect their bodies and armour which included a breast plate, greaves (leg armour), a wide sword belt and a helmet with cheek pieces. They carried long spears like the Romans. Their horsemen were not as well protected.

Above. A captured Gaul is shown chained to a tree which is hung with weapons collected from battle. It is part of an arch built at Carpentras, in the south of France, to celebrate the defeat of the Celtic peoples in Gaul by the Romans.

Right. Typical Greek soldiers. 'The greatest defeat of the day was caused by the unstoppable force of the elephants of King Pyrrhus', wrote the historian Plutarch. Elephants were trained to charge the enemy and sometimes carried an armoured box for soldiers as here.

fight against because they were very heavily armed. The Romans copied the Samnite idea of a long rectangular shield. The Romans suffered several defeats in their wars against the Samnites but eventually conquered them in 290 BC when the Samnites agreed to become allies of Rome.

THE GREEKS Throughout the fourth and third centuries BC the Romans established their superior position in Italy by a combination of conquest, *alliances* with other tribes and by establishing *colonies*, or new towns. The people of these new colonies had a territory to control around it and this was a good way of introducing the Roman way of life to that area.

Other peoples had also set up colonies. In the south of Italy the Greeks had established a new Greek land called *Magna Graecia* ('Great Greece') which contained many Greek colonies. The Romans wanted to force these Greek colonies to join them. The colonies objected and asked the Greek king of Epirus, Pyrrhus, for help. In 280 BC he came with a huge force – 25,000 soldiers and 20 war elephants. Pyrrhus also enlisted the help of enemies of Rome in southern Italy. The Romans raised about the same number of troops and although they lost 7,000 men in the first battle with Pyrrhus they eventually won. In 275 BC Pyrrhus returned to Greece with only about two-thirds of his army.

The Romans were now in control of all of Italy. But they were about to face their biggest threat – the Carthaginians.

ENEMIES OF ROME: HANNIBAL AND THE CARTHAGINIANS

A sea-trading people called the Phoenicians established the city of Carthage in north Africa. Its people, the Carthaginians, established their control over the large area of the Mediterranean, including the island of Sicily.

THE FIRST WAR The first war with Carthage lasted 23 years and began in 264 BC. It started when the Carthaginians moved out of the territory they held in the south-west of Sicily and occupied the town of Messana (now modern Messina). This was the closest town to the mainland of Italy. The Romans sent two legions and beat their enemy.

But the Romans did not defeat the Carthaginians easily or quickly. The Romans were not good at fighting at sea and had to build two huge fleets to overcome the Carthaginian navy. When the war was over the Romans forced them to pay a huge fine in silver.

HANNIBAL – CARTHAGINIAN COMMANDER-IN-CHIEF After this first war with Rome, the Carthaginian commander, Hamilcar Barca, led his forces into Spain in 237 BC to defend the settlements established there and win some more territory. It was here that his son, Hannibal, became commander-in-chief of the Carthaginian forces at the age of 25.

The Romans considered these new campaigns in Spain and southern Gaul (now southern France) a threat to them, especially when Hannibal besieged the town of Saguntum on the north-east coast. The Romans had made a treaty with Saguntum and sent two armies against Hannibal. One went to Africa from southern Italy, the other to Massilia (now Marseilles) to confront Hannibal's army.

HANNIBAL CROSSES THE ALPS Unfortunately for the Romans, Hannibal left southern Gaul before they arrived and began an incredible journey across the Alps to reach Italy and the heart of the Romans' territory. Hannibal's army had about 40,000 men in it as well as 37 war elephants. The journey was so difficult that by the time it finally reached Italy the army had been reduced to about 26,000 men and 12 elephants.

At first Hannibal was successful against the Romans

Hannibal lost an enormous number of men and animals, crossing the Alps into the heart of Roman territory.

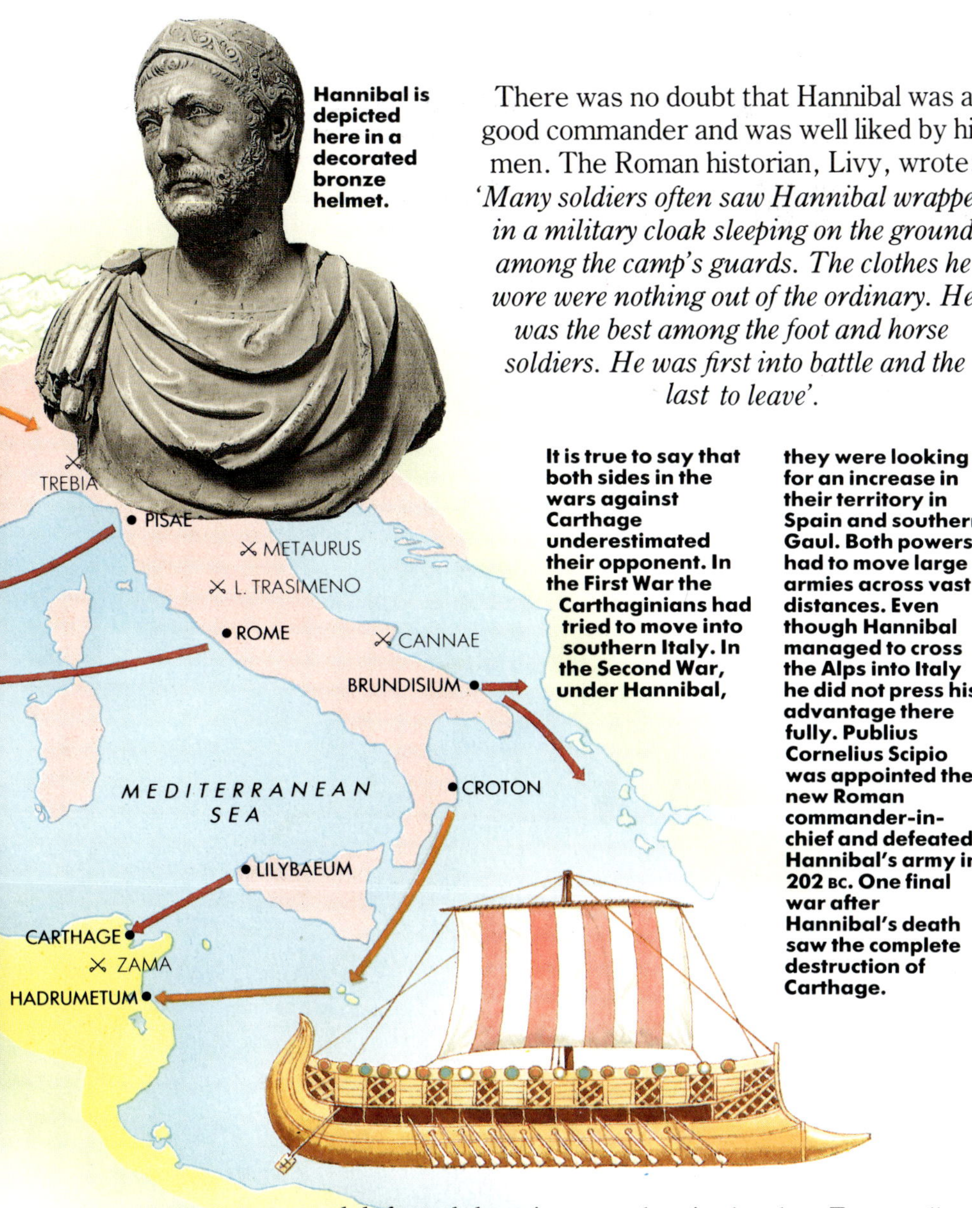

Hannibal is depicted here in a decorated bronze helmet.

There was no doubt that Hannibal was a good commander and was well liked by his men. The Roman historian, Livy, wrote: *'Many soldiers often saw Hannibal wrapped in a military cloak sleeping on the ground among the camp's guards. The clothes he wore were nothing out of the ordinary. He was the best among the foot and horse soldiers. He was first into battle and the last to leave'.*

It is true to say that both sides in the wars against Carthage underestimated their opponent. In the First War the Carthaginians had tried to move into southern Italy. In the Second War, under Hannibal, they were looking for an increase in their territory in Spain and southern Gaul. Both powers had to move large armies across vast distances. Even though Hannibal managed to cross the Alps into Italy he did not press his advantage there fully. Publius Cornelius Scipio was appointed the new Roman commander-in-chief and defeated Hannibal's army in 202 BC. One final war after Hannibal's death saw the complete destruction of Carthage.

and defeated them in several major battles. Eventually the Romans won a battle in Italy and then attacked Carthage itself. Carthage was taken in 146 BC and its inhabitants, 50,000 in all, were made slaves. Carthage and the territory it had once held became the new Roman province of Africa.

The Carthaginian Wars

Under Carthaginian control, 218 BC

Under Roman control, 218 BC

Carthaginian army

Roman army

× Major battle

Key Dates in the Carthaginian Wars

First War

264 BC	Carthaginians occupy Messana in Sicily
260	Full-scale war
241	Carthage surrenders

Second War

221	Hannibal made Carthaginian commander
219	Saguntum captured. Romans declare war
218	The march across the Alps. Roman defeats
204	Romans invade north Africa
202	Carthaginian army defeated at Zama
183	Hannibal commits suicide

Third War

149	War breaks out
146	City of Carthage completely destroyed

1 The earliest towns and cities in southeast Asia are in Vietnam where the fortified town of Co Loa is dated to the third century BC. The civilization developed here from complex societies living in village settlements but producing fine quality metal and fired clay goods. Towns like Co Loa were not densely occupied with houses but served as religious and trading centres for large areas around. The fortifications are in the form of stone walls and sometimes moats.

2 The Maya were a people who occupied the Yucatan peninsula in Central America, creating their wealth from maize which they regarded as the greatest gift of the gods. By 300 BC they were building great ceremonial centres for their religion and their administration. These centres developed into full-scale cities by AD 300. The city of Tikal, for example, had a population of 50,000 at this time. The Maya built stepped pyramids with temples on the top where they carried out elaborate ceremonies. They believed that certain days were controlled by particular gods and chose the time carefully to carry out their activities. They developed writing, astronomy, and mathematics. Their numbering system had units of our calendar system) in August 3114 BC.

3 At this time in Britain, society was well developed with the country divided between a number of tribes whose names we know from Roman literature. Some people lived in centres which were well fortified with walls, banks of earth and ditches. Some of these were hilltop settlements, now called hillforts. One of the largest and most famous is Maiden Castle in Dorset, where the local people resisted the Romans after their invasion in AD 43. Art was well developed and skilled craftspeople made pottery, jewellery and weapons.

THE END OF THE ROMAN REPUBLIC

The final defeat of the Carthaginians did not bring peace for the Romans. They had chosen to control peoples in Italy as well as to conquer new territories in many other parts of the Mediterranean.

After the wars with Carthage, there were other threats to Rome's new territories. The Cimbri, Teutones and Ambrones, tribes from north-western Europe, invaded northern Italy and Gaul. King Mithradates VI, who ruled the lands south of the Black Sea, was defeated by the Romans in 63 BC. Pirates threatened Roman trade in the eastern Mediterranean. Nearer to home the Romans had to cope with uprisings of slaves and revolts of allies in Italy.

By 100 BC they controlled many of the lands surrounding the Mediterranean, including Spain, southern Gaul, Corsica, Sardinia, Carthage, Sicily, Greece and Asia (what is now Turkey). The Romans called these new territories *provinces* and each was governed by either an ex-consul (if the territory was important from a military point of view) or an ex-praetor.

It was during this time that the greatest strain was put on the republican form of government. In the senate house and in other public buildings (this is a basilica or public hall) politicians argued with each other or formed factions. Power had been held by such a few powerful families for so long. Tribunes of the people, like Tiberius and Gaius Gracchus, fought to give poorer people both land and some political rights.

THE NEED FOR LAND During these campaigns to acquire new territories the Roman state took control of a huge amount of farming land. This was normally given or let to farmers who were already rich. Poor smallholders often had land taken away from them and free farm workers were replaced by slave labour. There was a need for changes in the law to protect the poorer people. A tribune, Tiberius Gracchus, proposed a law which allowed this newly-acquired land to be given to poor farmers. Wealthy Romans in positions of power in the government opposed this law and had Tiberius murdered. His brother Gaius took up the reform but he too was murdered.

POLITICS IN ROME Apart from his strong views about land reform, Gaius was murdered because he wanted to reform the government and take some power away from one of the powerful groups in Rome – the senate. At this time in Rome there were two political parties. The Roman lawyer and politician Cicero explains the situation:

'In the Roman state there have always been two groups of people eager to take part in, and be leaders of, public life. One group wished to be known as the populares, the other as the optimates.'

You can almost work out what these two groups stood for from their names. The optimates (the word 'optimum' means best) were a group of very wealthy men who wanted to keep their wealth and their power. They tried to make sure that their chosen candidates were voted in to important positions. They particularly opposed the senate. The populares (think about the words 'popular' and 'population') were those who wanted reforms for ordinary working people and who wanted to take power away from the patricians and the senate.

CIVIL WARS This rivalry lead to clashes, street gangs, murders and eventually civil wars in the first century BC. Gaius Marius, for example, tried to win support for himself from the senate and ordinary people and marched on Rome with his army. He appointed himself consul seven times – completely illegal acts. He was opposed by Lucius Sulla who landed in Italy with a loyal army of 40,000 soldiers in 83 BC and began a civil war against Marius.

The whole idea of the Roman Republic with its officials voted in each year was beginning to fall apart as powerful politicians, backed by huge armies, took power for themselves as dictators. The second civil war was fought between Gnaeus Pompeius, better known by the name he gave himself – Magnus 'Pompey the Great' – and Julius Caesar. Pompey fought for the senate but his army, finally led by his son, was defeated in 45 BC.

The system of rule by kings, which the early Romans had been so against, had almost returned in the rule of dictators. Julius Caesar finally declared himself 'dictator for life' in 44 BC. He was murdered the same year. This did not stop the breakdown of the republican system. After more civil war the system finally changed and the Romans got a king again – although this time he was careful to call himself by a different name, Emperor of Rome.

Key People and Dates in the Civil Wars

Cicero 106–43 BC (left). Marcus Tullius Cicero was the most well known of Roman public speakers. Originally a lawyer, he moved into politics. He sided with Pompey in the Civil War against Julius Caesar and was eventually put to death by Octavian who later became the Emperor Augustus.

Pompey 106–48 BC (below). Gnaeus Pompeius, now known as Pompey, fought with Sulla in the Civil War against Marius.

Marius 157–86 BC (above). Gaius Marius was elected consul many times. He defeated the Cimbri, the Teutones and the Ambrones.

Sulla 138–78 BC (above). Lucius Cornelius Sulla brought about the Civil War in 83 BC by marching on Rome. He declared himself dictator and threw out the elected government, which had declared him a 'public enemy'.

123–122	Gaius Gracchus voted tribune
105	Romans defeated by Cimbri and Teutones
104–100	Consulships of Marius
102	Teutones defeated
101	Cimbri defeated
87	Revolt of Marius in Rome
82–81	Sulla created dictator
70	Consulship of Pompey and Crassus
63	Consulship of Cicero
60	Coalition of Pompey, Caesar and Crassus
59	Caesar voted consul
49–46	War between Caesar and his opponents
48	Death of Pompey
44	Assassination of Julius Caesar

INCREASING THE LIMITS OF THE EMPIRE

Julius Caesar became a consul in 59 BC. After he had held the highest position in the government of Rome he went to be governor of the provinces in northern Italy and Gaul. Caesar was a professional soldier and decided to invade the territories of the Celtic peoples in Gaul, Germany and Britain. By 54 BC he had established the northern boundary of the Roman world at what is now called the English Channel.

The politician Cicero spoke about Caesar in the senate:

'Before, members of the senate, we had only a route through Gaul. All the

The Celtic peoples in Britain, tattooed and with wild war cries, fiercely resisted Caesar's invasions. 'Their usual method of fighting,' wrote Caesar, 'was from chariots dashing about all over the battlefield hurling their javelins.'

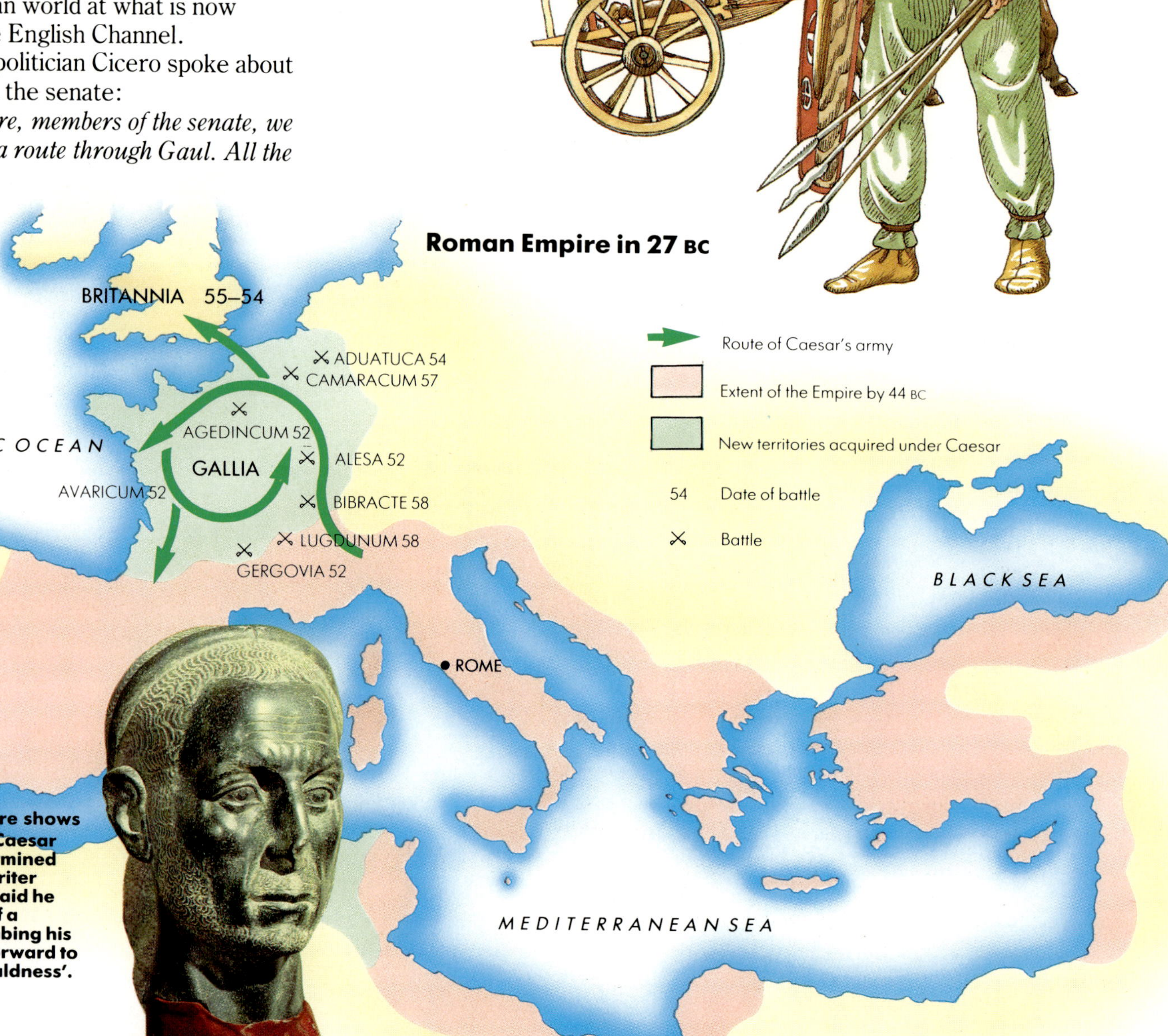

The sculpture shows that Julius Caesar was a determined man. The writer Suetonius said he was 'a bit of a dandy, combing his few hairs forward to cover his baldness'.

This marble statue of the Emperor Augustus shows him at the age of 45 in the full uniform of a Roman general. On his breast plate is pictured the sun god Apollo whom Augustus regarded as his special protector.

other territories were occupied by peoples who were hostile to us or could not be trusted. Caesar has fought very successfully against the fiercest of peoples in great battles and made them part of the Roman state.'

INVADING BRITAIN During his campaigns, Caesar invaded the island of Britain twice, in 55 and 54 BC. He felt that the tribes there were helping the peoples in northern Gaul, allowing safe refuge for campaigns across the Channel. In his first invasion in 55 BC he landed somewhere near Deal in Kent with about 12,000 troops and forced the chieftains there to accept the authority of Rome and promise not to give help to his enemies in Gaul.

This silver coin shows Julius Caesar in 44 BC.

The next year he invaded again with about 37,000 men and got as far as Hertfordshire, defeating a powerful tribe there. He did not leave any troops in Britain but he had made the new province of northern Gaul a safer part of the Roman state.

The information Caesar collected was useful to the Emperor Claudius when he decided to invade and conquer Britain in AD 43.

AFTER JULIUS CAESAR After the murder of Julius Caesar, his adopted son, Octavian, eventually beat all his enemies and became the most powerful man in Rome. In 27 BC he was given the special title of Augustus by the Roman senate. He governed on his own as emperor and his new name, Augustus, became the official name for emperor after that.

GOVERNING THE PROVINCES Augustus was careful to choose people he could trust to govern the provinces and be in command of the armies there. He allowed the senate to choose the governors of a few provinces, but all the rest had his own friends as governors. One very rich country, Egypt, he kept just for himself.

By Augustus' death in AD 14 the Roman state, or Empire as it can now be called, included all the lands and seas from Spain to Syria, from the Rivers Rhine and Danube to the Sahara Desert.

TRADE IN THE ROMAN EMPIRE

Small ferry boats like this unloaded cargo from ships moored in the harbour. This boat, called the Isis Giminiana, is being loaded with grain under the watchful eye of the 'magister' (the captain) named Farnaces.

The map opposite shows how vast the Roman Empire had become by the second century AD. Somewhere between 50 and 60 million people lived inside Rome's frontiers. People needed to travel within the Empire for different reasons – legions to guard the frontiers and keep down revolts, governors and their staff to administer the provinces and traders to sell their goods. The people and goods moving from place to place needed good roads and routes of communication. The Romans created both.

ROADS AND COURIERS The first roads in a new province were constructed by the army. The routes were direct and the roads as straight as possible, at least in stretches. The Emperor Augustus established an official courier service, called the *cursus publicus*, to carry official documents. There were also official 'hotels' for travellers on public business on all major routes throughout the Empire.

TRAVELLING BY SHIP Although a great deal of produce was carried on land by carts and camels, much heavier loads could more easily be transported by ship. The trade in corn for bread was probably the most important of all. Vast quantities of corn were shipped from Egypt and north Africa. Huge amounts were needed to keep the poor in the city of Rome from rioting – there were 200,000 poor people registered for free food handouts by 2 BC.

Large merchant ships traded all over the Mediterranean Sea. Heavy pottery storage jars called *amphorae* were used for olive oil, wine and fish sauce. A ship might carry as many as 6000 amphorae. But it was not just food which was transported. There were materials like stone and wood for building, metal for tools, horses for the army and haulage, and wild animals for the cruel 'sport' in the *amphitheatre*. These, as well as luxury items such as silks, came from all over the Roman Empire and beyond – from as far away as India and China.

One interesting cargo was discovered by archaeologists working at Kenchreae near Corinth in the Roman province of Greece. They found wooden crates containing a special type of marble flooring, called *opus sectile*, inside. It was in sections, laid on a backing of plaster, resin and pieces of broken amphorae – ready made to lay down. Because of an earthquake recorded at Kenchreae in AD 375 we know when the work was supposed to have been carried out.

SAFE HARBOURS AND PORTS Throughout the Roman world engineers and builders constructed harbours for all this trade. The most important was at Ostia about 25 kilometres from Rome. It was here that Rome's River Tiber flowed out to sea. It had been a base for the Roman navy until the reign of the Emperor Augustus.

The Emperor Claudius began the work to create a new harbour near the little port of Ostia. He even established a detachment of firemen to protect the port. This *corpus vigilum* was part of the military organization of the Roman state, and as well as fighting fires it provided police protection at night.

In AD 103 Emperor Trajan made Claudius' harbour even bigger and connected it to Ostia by a deep channel.

By the second century AD, about 50,000 people lived in Ostia. Shipping firms established themselves there and built great warehouses for the goods which passed through the port.

Sixty-one of the wealthy shipping merchants and other trades connected with shipping built a chamber of commerce for themselves.

A ROMAN WRITER CALLED AELIUS ARISTIDES DESCRIBED TRADE IN THE SECOND CENTURY AD: *'So many merchant ships arrive in Rome with cargoes from everywhere, at all times of the year, and after each harvest, that the city seems like the world's warehouse. The arrival and departure of ships never stops – it's amazing that the sea, not to mention the harbour, is big enough for these merchant ships.'*

PEOPLE OF THE ROMAN WORLD

Longinus's tombstone is typical of those made for cavalry officers in the Roman Empire. The top of the stone shows a sphinx – a mythical creature part winged lion, part woman. On each side is a lion entwined with a snake.

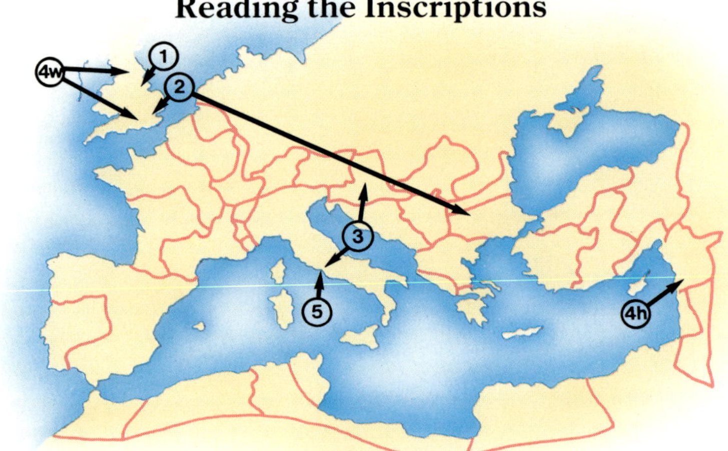

Here are some examples of Latin abbreviations to help you with the tombstones on these pages:
D M – short for DIS MANIBUS means 'To the Gods of the Dead'.
H S E – short for HIC SITUS EST means 'He lies buried here'.
FECIT – means 'made', that is put up the tombstone.
VIX – short for VIXIT means 'lived'.

1 Julia Velva from Rome buried in York.
2 Longinus from Bulgaria buried in Colchester.
3 Titus from Hungary buried in Rome.
4 Regina from Hertfordshire buried at South Shields. Husband Barathes from Palmyra buried at South Shields.
5 Vergilius from Rome buried in Rome.

A passer-by in one of the graveyards in Rome might have noticed these words on a tombstone:

'Stranger, my message is short. Stand here and read it. Here is the unlovely tomb of a lovely woman. Her parents gave her the name of Claudia. She loved her husband with all her heart. She bore two sons, one of whom she leaves on earth, the other she has placed under the earth. She was charming to talk to and gentle to be with. She looked after the house and spun wool. That's my last word. Go on your way.'

As we do today, the Romans often put information about the dead person on their tombstone. This one does not say how old Claudia was when she died, but others can tell us a lot about Roman people – if you can understand the code behind the words and the sculpture. Look at the pictures of tombstones and read on.

JULIA VELVA The scene shown on this tombstone found in York in northern Britain is quite common. It pictures the ceremonial feast at the burial of the dead woman who is reclining on a couch holding a glass. Food for this feast is laid out on the three-legged table in front of her. Above the scene are two pine cones which were usually burnt at funerals to give off a rich sweet-smelling odour.

The inscription under the sculpture tells us more. We see her name is Julia Velva and that she 'lived most dutifully for 50 years'. The person who inherited her property is called Aurelius Mercurialis, perhaps her son-in-law. He is standing on the right. His wife is seated on the left and the little boy is probably Julia's grandson.

LONGINUS Also buried in Britain is this junior officer (DVPLICARIUS on the tombstone) from a cavalry regiment, who died in the town of Colchester. He belonged to a squadron from the district of Sardica which is now in Bulgaria. He was the son of Sdapezematygus and died at the age of 40 after serving 15 years in the army.

Right. Julia Velva's tombstone shows a typical scene: the funeral feast. Even today many peoples have the same tradition after the burial. Scenes like this provide lots of evidence about the Romans. Look at the details of clothes, hairstyles and furniture.

Above. The inscription on the tombstone of Titus tells us that two friends, who were his heirs, put up the stone for him. They were Titus Flavius Marcellinus, a standard bearer, and Titus Aurelius Secundinus.

Right. On the far left of Vergilius' tomb you can see the bread being baked in an oven. Originally on this monument, but not shown here, were relief sculptures of Vergilius and his wife.

Above. The tombstone of Regina is unusual in Britain because it was carved in the style of her husband's place of origin – Palmyra in Syria. It is possible that it was carved by a stonemason who came from Palmyra. From the carving on the tombstone we can also see that Regina wove cloth. The inscription about her is carved in Latin but the last line is Palmyrene script.

The carving is interesting for two reasons. It was very common for a cavalry officer to have this picture showing him riding over the cowering body of a naked Celtic warrior. The other interesting thing is that the tombstone has been damaged – in Roman times. Longinus has had his face broken off. We know that this happened during the revolt of Queen Boudica against Roman rule in AD 60.

TITUS The dead person shown on this tombstone is reclining on a couch while a man leads his horse away below. His full name was Titus Aurelius Saturninus. He is an EQ SING – an *eques singularis*, a member of the mounted bodyguard for the emperor. He was born in the province of Pannonia (now Hungary) and died at the age of 30 in Rome after serving 11 years in the army.

REGINA Regina died at the age of 30 (AN XXX) at the Roman town of Corstopitum, now South Shields, just south of Hadrian's Wall in northern Britain. She had been bought as a slave and came from the southern tribe of the Catuvellauni whose chief town was Verulamium, now St Albans in Hertfordshire.

Her husband, who freed his wife, had this tombstone carved for her. His name was Barathes and he came from Palmyra, a very wealthy city in the Syrian desert. Barathes was also buried in Corstopitum.

VERGILIUS EURYACES Standing now just outside one of the gates of Rome put up by the Emperor Claudius is this impressive monument. It is the tomb of Vergilius Euryaces, a wealthy baker who died in 30 BC. He also provided supplies for the state, including bread for the poor of Rome.

The large holes you can see represent the standard-size containers which bakers used for measuring out flour. The frieze along the top shows Vergilius overseeing the workers in his factory making dough out of flour.

LIVING IN A ROMAN TOWN

Above top. A Roman housewife is ordering meat at the butcher's using the shopping list on her wax tablet. Notice the scales to weigh the meat.

Above. Two trades are pictured here. On the left is a ropemaker. On the right a shoemaker works in front of his cupboard with a range of shoes and sandals on top.

Roman towns were busy, noisy, bustling places. One Roman writer, Juvenal, said the streets were *'jammed with carts, crowded with people pushing and shoving, pavements and roads filthy to walk on'.*

HOUSES AND FLATS Most people lived in small apartments in blocks of flats or above their shops or workshops. In Rome these blocks might be six storeys high. In other places the buildings were only two storeys high. Apartment blocks were usually built of wood, at least above the ground floor, and there were often serious fires in towns. Some towns had their own fire service, complete with fire crews and pumps.

Those in towns who could afford it lived in houses. They were kept private from the noisy streets by few windows and inner courtyards to keep the rooms cool and airy during the summer. Unlike the cramped flats, these houses gave the families and their slaves who lived in them complete privacy.

IN THE STREET Where it was possible, streets in Roman towns had stone or gravel surfaces and had pavements. Although there were no supermarkets, shopping was easy because you went to a particular district or street to buy goods. The leather workers, for example, would be all in one street, shops selling jugs and plates in another.

Of course there were no large panes of glass for shop windows then, so Roman shops opened on to the street. A shopkeeper might advertise with a shop sign or a notice painted on the outside wall. All towns had restaurants and take-away food bars. The most common was called a popina.

Some goods, such as wine in its great storage jars called *amphorae* were brought into towns from outside. Most things were made on the premises. At the baker's you could watch the flour being ground, made into dough and baked in the ovens. An ironmonger would make you a kitchen knife, or repair one on the spot.

GOING TO SCHOOL If you were up and about at dawn you would see boys and girls going off to school. There were usually more boys than girls because some parents did not believe that it was important to educate their daughters. A teacher, called a *magister ludi*, set up a school in a room somewhere, perhaps near a public square. Children from the age of seven attended schools

'How can anyone sleep in lodgings here? It's only the rich who get any sleep. The noise of the carts thundering along the narrow streets and the language of the drivers when they get stuck in a traffic jam would wake even the heaviest sleeper.' The writer Juvenal expresses the thoughts of many people who had to live in the middle of town.

like this and there was strict discipline, with a beating if they did not pay enough attention.

After five years children went on to a secondary school run by a teacher called a *grammaticus*. Here the children learnt about the literature of the Romans and the Greeks, history, arithmetic, geometry and astronomy.

A few pupils, usually boys, went on to complete their education with professors who offered lessons and discussions. The boy's family could choose from several towns to send their son to receive this higher education. One of the favourite places was Athens in Greece. The Greeks already had a number of centres of education long before the Roman period and the Romans admired Greek literature and art. The Roman lawyer and politician Cicero spent two years at various 'universities'.

Roman Writing

Fragments of Roman writing can be seen in many museums today. But these are usually in the form of inscriptions carved on stone. Handwriting is less common because it is harder to preserve. You can sometimes find names, words or phrases scratched on to roof tiles, and graffiti on walls. For example, a worker in a tile factory in Roman London wrote this about his workmate, 'Austalis has been skiving off by himself every day for the last thirteen days'!

In a Roman school or office you would find writing on three types of material. Papyrus was made into scrolls from the leaves of a plant that grows near rivers, especially in Egypt. Pens and ink were used on papyrus. Wax tablets were shallow wooden boxes filled with wax. Romans used a sharp metal point called a stylus to scratch out their words.

Little 'notebooks' were made from very thin pieces of wood, joined together with leather thongs, which were written on with pens and ink.

Writing instruments and 'paper' in the form of a wax tablet and rolls of papyrus. The inkwell can be hung up to be used more easily.

ROME: CAPITAL OF THE EMPIRE

Part of the main forum in Rome, called the Forum Romanum. On the left are the remaining columns of the Temple of the god Saturn.

Anyone living inside the Roman Empire would have expected to see towns in all the provinces with much the same facilities. It was all part of being civilized. When new towns were built in the provinces, the townspeople would want the sorts of buildings and amenities they had seen, or heard about, in the capital of the Empire – Rome.

THE BEGINNINGS OF A CITY It was under the Etruscan kings that the various villages became the single town of Rome on the west bank of the River Tiber. By the time of Julius Caesar there were nearly one million people living on the seven hills of Rome and in the valleys leading down to the river.

In the city centre there were buildings for government, religion, trade and entertainment.

PUBLIC SERVICES The Romans were good at engineering and from the earliest periods laid out good routes of communication. Major roads led out from the city centre to other parts of Italy. A good water supply was essential, especially for such a huge population. Great stone *aqueducts* carried water in channels over arches across the city. The first aqueduct was built by the politician Appius Claudius in 312 BC and named after him, the Aqua Appia. Each town needed an official, called a *curator aquarum*, to look after the water supply.

Water was brought to public fountains and tanks alongside main streets to supply people and industries. It was also needed in huge quantities for the public baths. Each town had at least one major bath where large numbers of people could enjoy the various forms of bathing – hot, steamy rooms, cold dips and saunas, as well as exercise halls.

THE FORUM At the centre of the town was the *forum*.

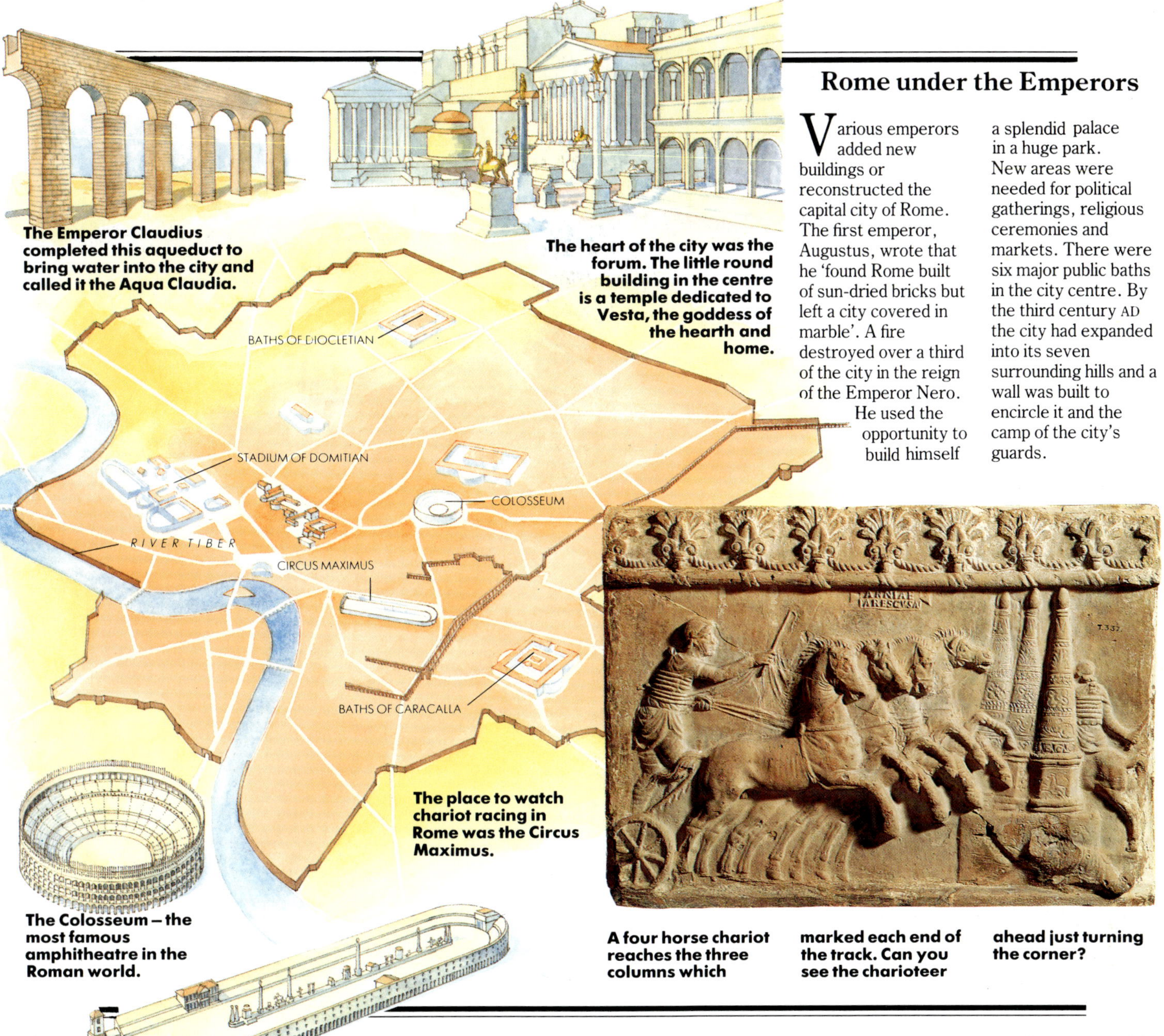

The Emperor Claudius completed this aqueduct to bring water into the city and called it the Aqua Claudia.

The heart of the city was the forum. The little round building in the centre is a temple dedicated to Vesta, the goddess of the hearth and home.

The place to watch chariot racing in Rome was the Circus Maximus.

The Colosseum – the most famous amphitheatre in the Roman world.

A four horse chariot reaches the three columns which marked each end of the track. Can you see the charioteer ahead just turning the corner?

Rome under the Emperors

Various emperors added new buildings or reconstructed the capital city of Rome. The first emperor, Augustus, wrote that he 'found Rome built of sun-dried bricks but left a city covered in marble'. A fire destroyed over a third of the city in the reign of the Emperor Nero. He used the opportunity to build himself a splendid palace in a huge park. New areas were needed for political gatherings, religious ceremonies and markets. There were six major public baths in the city centre. By the third century AD the city had expanded into its seven surrounding hills and a wall was built to encircle it and the camp of the city's guards.

This was a large open area where markets could take place and the people could carry on the business of the town. Around the forum were the buildings for the government of the town, and in Rome itself, for the government of the state. Public halls, called *basilicas*, with aisles on each side of the long building, were used for law courts and public meetings. The forum was also the place where you would find temples to the gods of the city and the most important of the Roman gods and goddesses.

PLACES FOR ENTERTAINMENT A Roman might tell you that any decent town would be able to provide the people who lived there some public entertainment. There were three very popular forms of entertainment in the Roman world. The most popular took place in the *amphitheatre*. In these huge oval-shaped stadiums as many as 50,000 spectators watched trained fighters called *gladiators* battle to the death. It was here too that gladiators would hunt and hope to kill wild beasts, such as lions, bears, deer, elephants and snakes.

The bloodthirsty spectators also enjoyed watching convicted criminals fight to the death or be torn apart by wild animals. Sometimes amphitheatres were flooded to recreate sea battles.

Theatres were for smaller audiences. As many as 5000 people might watch a series of Greek or Roman plays lasting all day. There were other types of performances though, including the *mimus* which was a short sketch, and the *pantomimus* which was a sort of ballet with music.

Finally there was the thrill of watching chariot racing in the *circus*. The biggest of all was the Circus Maximus in Rome. In the first century BC it could hold 100,000 people, but by the fourth century AD it had been enlarged to a capacity of 350,000!

LIVING ON A COUNTRY ESTATE

You may have come across the Latin word *villa* before. Today it is often used to mean a countryside or seaside house where you spend your holidays. The Romans used the word villa for the same thing, but it also meant a farm.

RICH LANDOWNERS If you were wealthy enough to afford more than one house, you would be able to choose which of your houses to spend your time in. You might say, like the Roman poet Martial, '*Whenever I'm worn out with worry and want to get some rest, I go to my villa*.' Country houses with farming land brought in a great deal of wealth for some people. The houses the wealthy built for themselves on their farming estates were often grand and certainly had the facilities required for gracious living – courtyards with covered walks, formal gardens, bath houses and several dining rooms. The Romans had a special name for the owner's house on a farming estate – the villa urbana.

THE WORKING FARM BUILDINGS Many people who owned large farms chose not to live on them all through the year. When this happened they employed a farm manager, called a vilicus, to look after the work. The house of the farm manager was called a villa rustica. If the farm manager was married, his wife was probably also employed on the farm as the vilica – that is the manager, or housekeeper in charge of the household slaves. The vilicus and the vilica would probably be slaves, too.

Gaius Plinius to his dear friend Gallus: '*Greetings! You are amazed that I am so fond of my Villa at Laurentum. You won't be when you see how charming it is – on a fine stretch of seashore and only 17 miles (27.3 km) from Rome. I can spend the night here after a full day's work in the city*'.

Villas often grew a variety of produce as well as breeding animals. On the right oxen are pulling a cart full of baskets of fruit. On the left is an area in the farmyard set aside for large storage jars. These jars, called amphorae, stored the harvest of wine or olive oil. Later the produce or animals were taken to local markets or shipped direct to Rome itself.

All the other farm buildings were given the name villa fructuaria, which literally means the places where produce was kept.

One Roman writer, Columella, tells us that there should be *'rooms for oil, for the oil presses, for wine, for hay-lofts, granaries and storage places for wine and oil ready to go to the market'*. In some parts of the Empire the farming estates produced one main crop, such as wheat.

A *mosaic* from Tunisia in north Africa shows the house of the owner – the villa urbana – with its towers and colonnades. In the foreground are ducks on the edge of a pond, geese and pheasants. Surrounding the villa are fruit trees, bushes and roses.

FARM WORKERS Those who worked on large farms were usually slaves. The work was very hard and the hours long. The farm manager had to be tough to control a workforce like this.

Besides the work needed to plant and harvest the produce on the farm or look after the animals, a villa needed to be as self-sufficient as possible. Managers obviously tried to grow all the food they needed for the workforce but other jobs, such as maintaining buildings and machinery, were also carried out by the slaves. Often travelling craftspeople would come to the farm to offer special skills such as pottery, tile making or ironworking.

The house of the villa owner – the villa urbana – often contained parts which were similar to town houses, like this one from Pompeii. This is the garden of the House of the Vetii brothers which had all the latest styles of decoration. In a typical villa urbana the garden would have been in front of the house.

RELIGION AND THE GODS OF THE ROMAN WORLD

Religion was a very important part of people's lives in Roman times. They believed that their gods and goddesses and spirits surrounded them and controlled everything they did. They even treated the emperors as gods. People believed that they had to make sacrifices and offerings to keep the gods and spirits friendly. There were altars and statues everywhere – not only inside temples but in the streets and in houses too.

This list of sacrifices from a document found at Dura-Europus in the Roman province of Syria shows how important sacrifices and ceremonies were to the military garrison stationed there in AD 224:

January 3. Our vows fulfilled and offered for the preservation of our lord Emperor Marcus Aurelius Severus Alexander Augustus and for the eternity of the Empire of the Roman people. Sacrificed to Jupiter Best and Greatest, an ox; to Juno, a cow; to Minerva, a cow; to Jupiter Victor, an ox; to Father Mars, a bull; to Victory, a cow . . .

January 24. Birthday of the deified Emperor Hadrian. Sacrificed to the deified Hadrian, an ox.

TEMPLES AND PROCESSIONS The Romans believed

Above. Sculpture found on Hadrian's Wall showing the birth of the god Mithras from an egg. Around him are the signs of the zodiac.
Right. The Roman town of Sufetula (now Sbeitla) in Tunisia. Through the arch you can see the impressive front of the Temple of Jupiter.
Below right. Statue of Diana, the woodland goddess of hunting, now in Istanbul (Constantinople).

that their gods and goddesses took human forms and had special responsibilities. For example, Juno was the patron goddess of women. They built temples for their gods and a priest, called a *pontifex*, carried out ceremonies and sacrifices on behalf of the worshippers. The ceremony might involve a procession through the town ending in the sacrifice of animals at the altar of the temple.

LIFE AFTER DEATH The Romans believed in a life after death. The dead went to the underworld to live with the *manes*, the gods of the dead.

Offerings were made to the gods by pouring out wine or leaving food such as honey cakes at the grave side. These ceremonies were held nine days after burial and then at special times throughout the year.

GODS FROM OTHER COUNTRIES As the Romans conquered more and more territories they came into contact with other gods and goddesses. Most of these new gods they adopted into their own 'family' of gods. Some of them became very important gods to the Romans. For example, the Egyptian goddess Isis and the god Serapis were both worshipped all over the Empire. The Persian god Mithras had temples built for him by soldiers and merchants in most provinces.

CHRISTIANITY Not all foreign religions were liked or accepted by the Romans. They outlawed the worship of the Druids, which took place in Britain and in Gaul and involved human sacrifice. There were several wars with the Jews. Christianity was practised secretly in many parts of the Empire. Christians were persecuted and often massacred in amphitheatres.

In the end, the religion survived and was made the official religion of Rome by the Emperor Constantine I in AD 312. However, many Romans still went on worshipping the other gods.

Temples of the Romans

Various types of temple were built by the Romans. The first (top) copied the idea from Greek temples. Built on a platform, it had an imposing front entrance. Columns lined the front and sides of the building inside, called the cella. Sometimes temples were enclosed in a sacred courtyard area (middle) called a temenos. Statues and altars would be put up here and ceremonies and processions held inside its walls.

In Gaul and in Britain a different type of temple (bottom) was often built. This is known as a Romano-Celtic temple because it was built for the Celtic gods and goddesses adopted by the Romans. The cella of this type of temple is surrounded by a colonnaded terrace. They were sometimes built inside a temenos.

Roman Gods and Goddesses

Venus was the goddess of beauty and love. Julius Caesar built her a temple in Rome because he claimed to be a descendant of the hero Aeneas, who was the son of the divine Mars (god of war) and Venus.

Bacchus (also called Dionysus) was a god who was worshipped by the Greeks. He was a god of fertility, especially of the fruit of trees. This included grapes which made wine. He is often shown drinking, as here.

Diana, the goddess of hunting, is usually pictured hunting with bow and arrows. She was worshipped as a goddess of fertility in wooded places. She was also one of the goddesses associated with women.

Juno was the most important goddess of women and the wife of Jupiter. In early Roman times she was only associated with childbirth. Later she became one of the main goddesses of the Roman state.

Mercury was the Roman god of traders and merchants. His Greek counterpart is the god Hermes. Hermes was the messenger god and, like Mercury, is usually shown with a winged helmet and sandals.

Jupiter, the king of all the gods, is shown here on his throne with his emblem – the eagle. The eagle was adopted by the Roman state as their symbol of power. Zeus is his Greek counterpart.

GUARDING THE FRONTIERS OF THE EMPIRE

You have read how the Romans needed a large army to conquer their Empire. It was just as important to have a large force to control it and keep their enemies outside its limits. In the second century AD, when there were between 50 and 60 million people living in the Roman Empire, there were only about 450,000 soldiers in the army.

FRONTIERS OF THE EMPIRE About 28,000 of these soldiers were on patrol in the province of Africa which supplied Rome with an enormous amount of grain. Here, as in other provinces, there was a network of good roads and strong permanent forts. The Roman emperors tried to establish frontiers wherever they could. In the deserts of Arabia and Syria, the Emperor Trajan built a large number of roads and forts to form the easternmost boundary of the Empire.

In the north there was a need for more permanent frontiers to keep out the *barbarians*, as uncivilized neighbours were called. A permanent barrier, called the *limes*, of a bank, a ditch, and a wooden fence with watch towers and forts, was constructed between the River Rhine and the Danube. On the northern edge of Roman territory in Britain, the Emperor Hadrian had a stone wall constructed – known now as Hadrian's Wall.

Roman soldiers had more to do than just fight the enemy. A legionary soldier would often find himself on regular patrol but would also have to guard important places such as quarries and mines or act as customs officer at frontier crossing points. There were other jobs too as these records from a legion posted to Egypt in about AD 80 show:

'Titus Flavius Valens . . . assigned to papyrus manufacture January 15, returned. Assigned to coin mint January 17, returned. Assigned to the granary at Mercurium . . .'

This fine stretch of Hadrian's Wall shows one of the guard posts built at every mile (1.6 km). Gates allowed civilians and soldiers to pass through this frontier line.

THE PERMANENT FORT The size of a fort depended on the size of the army unit based there. Some forts were enormous and could house an entire legion of about 6,000 men. As you would expect, the forts were laid out in a very regular way with streets between buildings to give easy and quick access to the surrounding ramparts and walls. Strongly built and defended gateways and guard towers were placed on the walls. The barrack buildings were long and put together in groups. In the centre was the headquarters building for the commander-in-chief and his officers. It was here that the administration of the unit was carried out, and here the pay and the standards of the unit were kept safely.

Other buildings inside the fort would include granaries and storehouses, cookhouses and lavatories, workshops and a hospital and sometimes the commander's own house. Outside there might be a bath house for the troops.

Beyond the walls of the permanent forts a civilian settlement usually grew up. The Romans called this the *canabae*. Roman soldiers were not allowed to marry and have families while on active duty, although many did. Shops and other services for soldiers, such as taverns, were a regular feature of canabae.

DOCUMENTS AND LETTERS Out of the pay a soldier received from the army he had to pay for his food and clothes. We know that army units had to keep a careful account of supplies sent in to the fort. Two records recently discovered at the fort of Vindolanda on Hadrian's Wall give a list of items delivered: *'barley, Celtic beer, wine, fish-sauce, pork-fat, spices, salt, young pig, ham, wheat, venison, roe-deer . . .'*

Perhaps even more interesting was this letter which has partly survived on the wooden backing of a wax tablet, also from Vindolanda:

'I have sent you . . . pairs of woollen socks, two pairs of sandals and two pairs of underpants . . .'

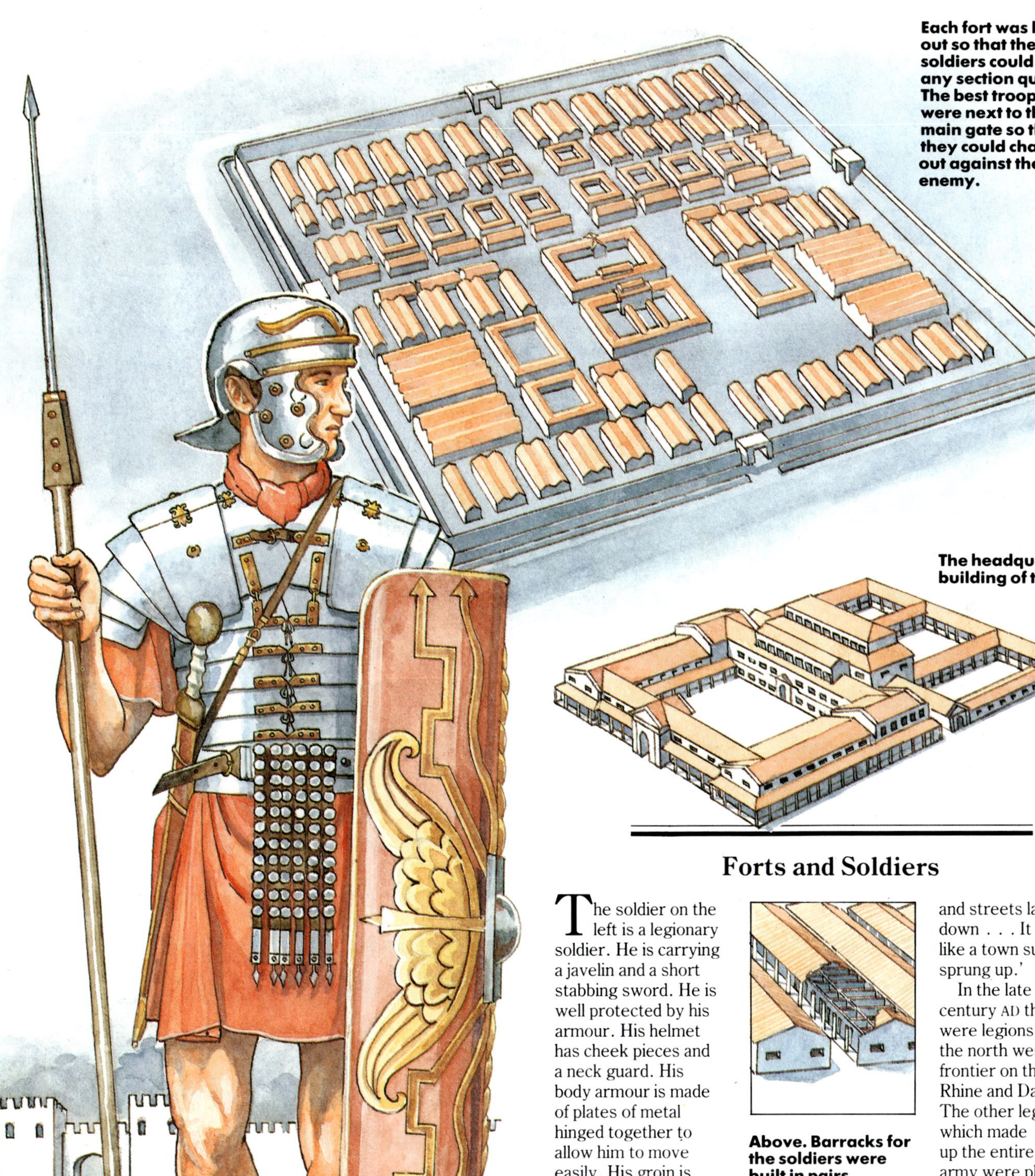

Each fort was laid out so that the soldiers could reach any section quickly. The best troops were next to the main gate so that they could charge out against the enemy.

The headquarters building of the fort.

Forts and Soldiers

The soldier on the left is a legionary soldier. He is carrying a javelin and a short stabbing sword. He is well protected by his armour. His helmet has cheek pieces and a neck guard. His body armour is made of plates of metal hinged together to allow him to move easily. His groin is protected by an apron of metal discs riveted on to leather straps. His shield is wooden with a layer of linen or leather on the outside and a bronze or iron centre boss.

On a march in hostile territory the army would build a camp each night. It was the same layout as the drawing of the permanent one above. The Roman writer Josephus said, 'The inside is measured out and streets laid down . . . It seems like a town suddenly sprung up.'

Above. Barracks for the soldiers were built in pairs opening out onto a corridor. Each barrack had 11 rooms – one for the centurion and 10 for the 80 men under his command.

In the late first century AD there were legions guarding the north west frontier on the rivers Rhine and Danube. The other legions which made up the entire Roman army were placed in trouble spots mainly in the eastern Mediterranean. Each legion had its own number and name – taken from the place where it was raised, or named after an emperor or a victory, for example LEGIO I ITALICA or LEGIO II AUGUSTA or VI VICTRIX.

THE EMPIRE COMES TO AN END

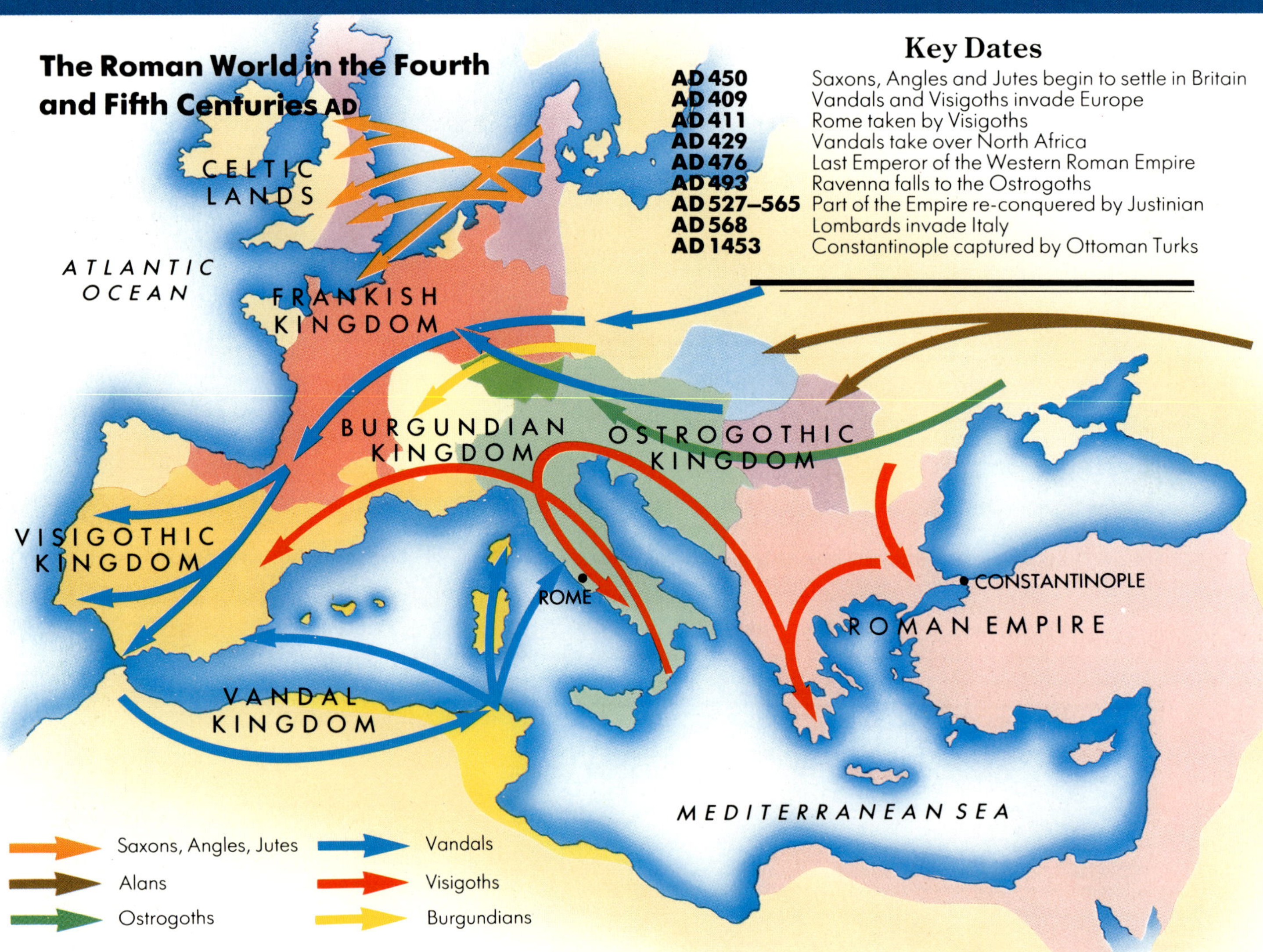

The Roman Empire grew gradually from a town in central Italy to a world power. It was difficult to control such a huge area and even more difficult to keep out those many enemies who were waiting beyond the boundaries. Even so, the Empire maintained control for several centuries.

COASTAL ATTACKS During the third century AD there were attacks along the coasts of Britain and Gaul. A series of new forts had to be built and a strong naval force patrolled the coastline.

THE EMPIRE REORGANIZED In AD 286 the Emperor Diocletian made an important change to the way his Empire was ruled. He divided the huge Roman territory in two. He ruled the eastern part from the city of Nicomedia in Bithynia, while his friend, Maximian, ruled the western part from Rome. To help govern the Empire, Diocletian established twelve districts called *dioceses*. Each district had a governor called a *vicarius*. At the same time the army was enlarged but divided into two new groups. From now on there were permanent troops stationed on the frontiers and small mobile units which could be moved to trouble spots very quickly.

RETURN TO ONE EMPEROR The Roman Empire returned to the rule of one emperor in AD 324 when Emperor Constantine finally defeated his enemies. However he moved his capital to Constantinople (now Istanbul in Turkey) in AD 330.

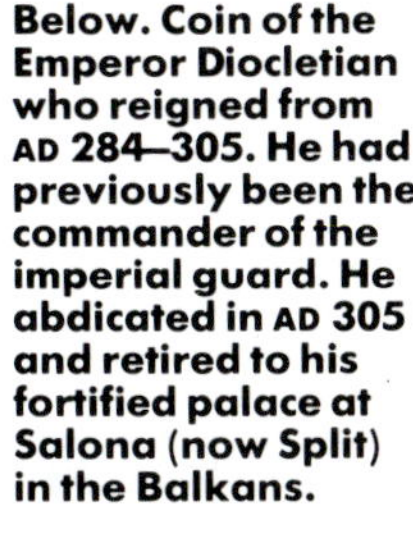

Below. Coin of the Emperor Diocletian who reigned from AD 284–305. He had previously been the commander of the imperial guard. He abdicated in AD 305 and retired to his fortified palace at Salona (now Split) in the Balkans.

Left. Most Roman traditions continued in the Eastern Empire. This is part of a fine floor mosaic laid in the imperial palace at Constantinople during the reign of Justinian. It shows two gladiators fighting wild animals in an amphitheatre.

Below. The head from a colossal statue of the Emperor Constantine I, called 'The Great', who reigned from AD 306–337. The statue was carved in about AD 315 in Rome.

Emperors of the Later Roman Empire

West	
287–305	Maximian Augustus
293–306	Constantius I
306–307	Severus
306–337	Constantine I
East	
284–305	Diocletian Augustus
293–305	Galerius
305–311	Galerius Augustus
305–313	Maximinus Augustus
308–324	Licinius
324–327	Constantine I, sole ruler of whole Empire

Above. Coin showing the Emperor Justinian who reigned from AD 527–565. The coin celebrates the victory of his general, Belisarius, over the Vandals in AD 535.

A RE-DIVIDED EMPIRE After the Emperor Theodosius died in AD 395, the Empire was again divided into two, with capitals at Constantinople and Rome. The Western Empire suffered most at the hands of its enemies. Waves of barbarian tribes began to swarm over Europe, causing disruption and destruction. By the mid-fifth century the Saxons, Jutes and Angles from Belgium, Holland, Germany and southern Scandinavia had settled in eastern Britain. From the north and east, enemies such as the Visigoths and Huns began to occupy large areas of the Roman Empire. For example, the Visigoth chief Alaric took Rome itself in AD 410. The last Emperor in the west, Romulus Augustulus, only reigned from AD 475 to 476. In this year Odovacar led German armies into Italy and declared himself king.

THE EASTERN EMPIRE The rulers in Constantinople were not as hard pressed by enemies beyond their borders. In fact the Emperor Justinian in AD 527 began to re-conquer some of the old Roman Empire which had been lost to the barbarians. Justinian's armies re-occupied parts of Africa, Spain and Italy.

After Justinian's death the attacks began again and the Lombards invaded Italy in AD 568. In the late seventh century the Muslims took over Africa and then Spain. The Eastern Roman Empire, which was also known as the Byzantine Empire, continued to be ruled by emperors until AD 1453. This was the year the capital of the Eastern Empire, Constantinople, was captured by the Ottoman Turks. This signalled the fall of one of the greatest empires ever seen.

The Roman World
TIME CHART

	THE CITY OF ROME	THE ROMAN DOMAIN
BC		
753	Legendary foundation of Rome	
509	Etruscan kings thrown out Roman Republic established	
390	Gauls besiege Rome	
343>290		Wars with the Samnites
280>275		Greeks invade Italy
264>241		First war with Carthage
237>202		Second war with Carthage
149>146		Third war with Carthage
146		Carthage destroyed
133>122	Land reforms of Tiberius and Gaius Gracchus	
83>82		Civil war
49>45		Civil war
44	Julius Caesar 'Dictator for Life'. Murdered same year	
31>29		Civil war
27	Augustus begins reign as Emperor.	
AD		
14	Augustus dies	
43		Emperor Claudius invades Britain
80		Vesuvius erupts. Pompeii and Herculaneum destroyed
79	Colosseum opens	
114	Emperor Trajan builds his column in Rome	
122		Hadrian's Wall begun
212		All men in provinces made citizens of Rome
286	Empire divided into two. Ruled from two capitals.	
312	Christianity made official religion of Rome	
330		Emperor Constantine moves capital of Empire to Constantinople
402		Western capital moved to Ravenna
410	Rome sacked by Visigoths	
455	Rome attacked by Vandals	
476	Last Emperor in Rome thrown out by German armies	
540	Eastern Empire forces recapture Italy	
1453		Turks capture Constantinople. Fall of the Holy Roman Empire

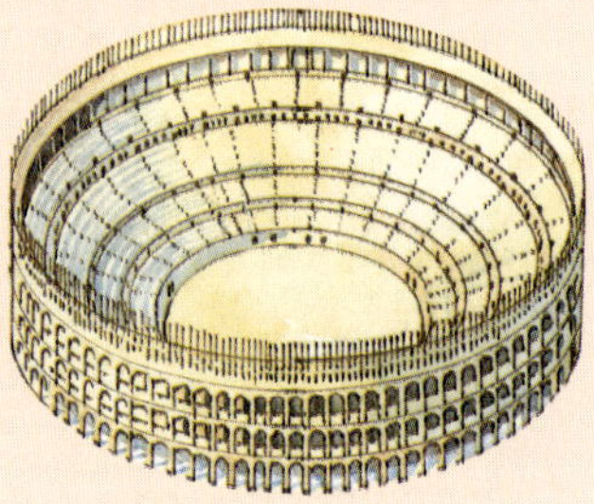

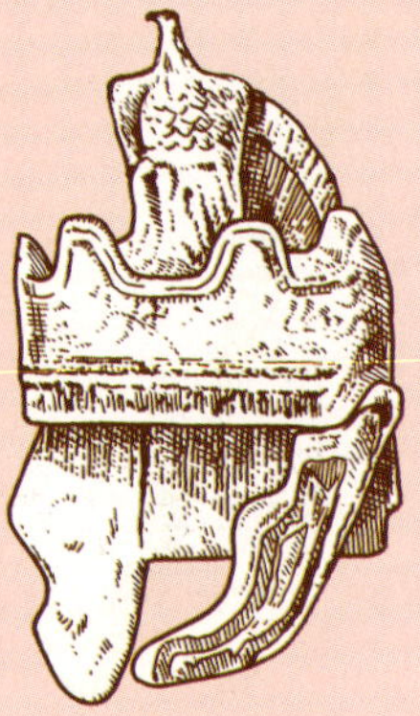

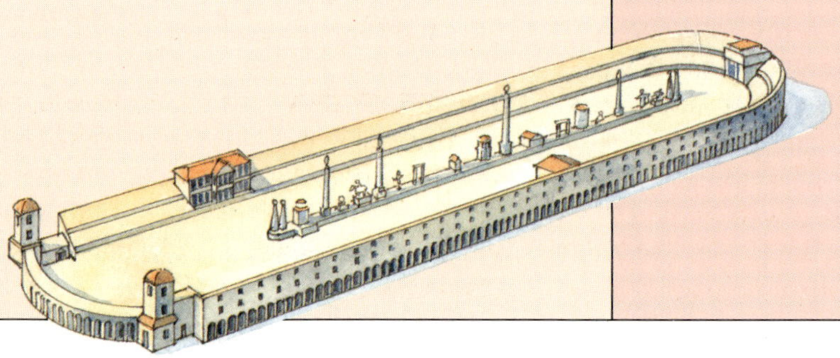

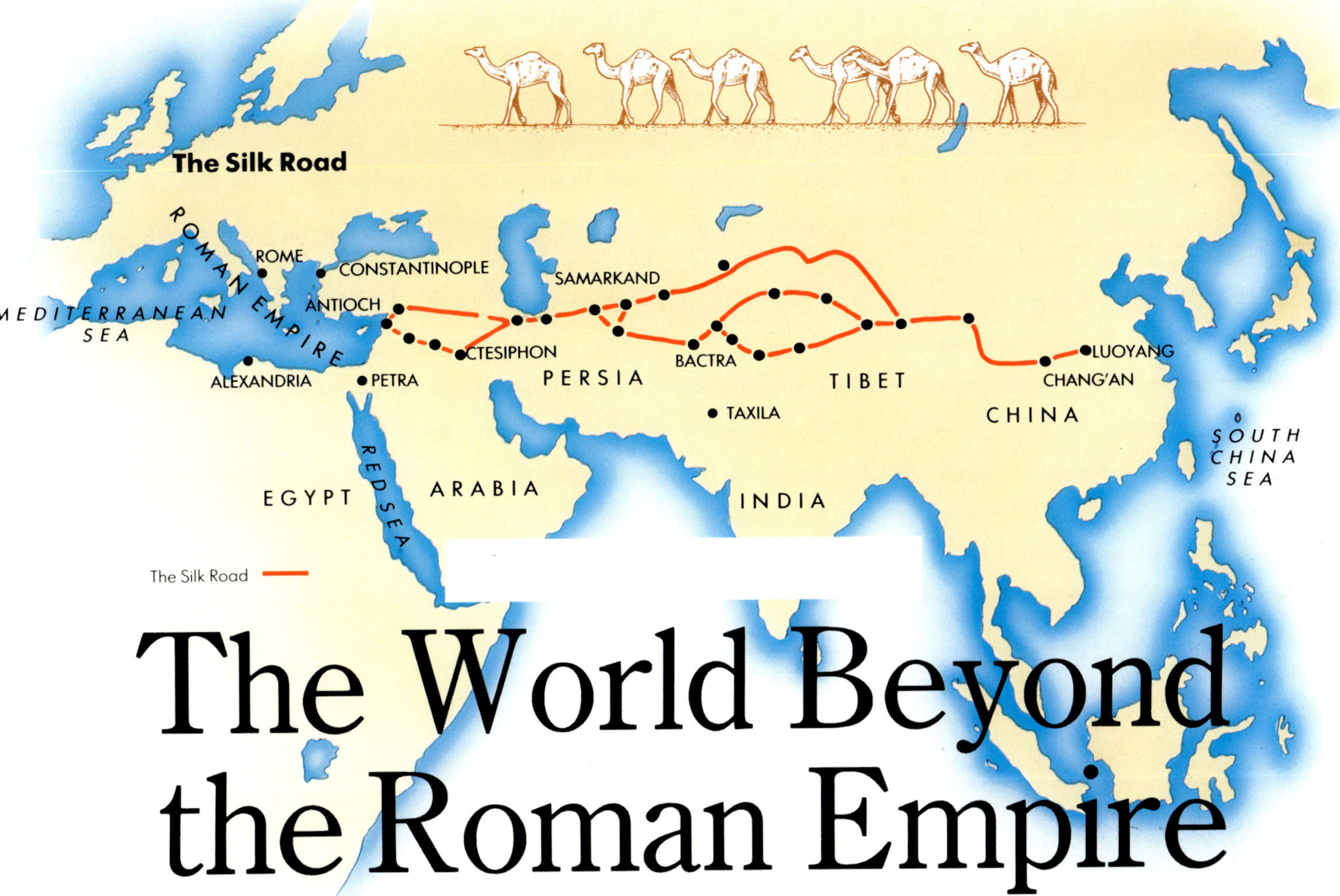

The World Beyond the Roman Empire

Now we are going to look at the world beyond the boundaries of the Roman Empire. All the civilizations you will read about in this section have some connection with Rome – usually through trade, but sometimes because they were conquered by the Romans.

Just before he died in AD 14, the Roman Emperor Augustus deposited in the state archives a manuscript called *Res Gestae Divi Augusti*, 'The Achievements of the Divine Augustus'. In it he says:

'Royal embassies from India, never seen before by any Roman general, were often sent to me.'

But India was not the furthest place with which Rome was connected. Exotic goods came from as far away as China.

THE SILK ROAD The map shows the way the Far East was connected with Europe over a route known as the Silk Road. The term is odd because it was not really a road but a series of *caravan* routes between towns and oases. Nor did the merchants carry only silk, but a great variety of expensive goods.

Chinese silk was especially popular – if you could afford it. Fragments have been found in sixth century graves in Athens and in Iron Age burials in Germany. The Romans bought these luxury goods in large quantites. One Roman writer, called Pliny the Elder, said in the first century AD:

'India, China and the Arabian states drain our Empire of a huge amount of money every year – this is what our luxuries and our women are costing us.'

The trade traffic was two-way, of course. In exchange for all these luxury items from the east, the Romans must have sent gold and silver coins, fine pottery, glass vessels and precious stones.

TRAVEL OVER LAND Travel over land was dangerous and slow, at least by modern standards. Roman writers reckoned that a camel train could cover about 34 kilometres in one day.

Very few traders covered the whole route. Most worked shorter distances passing goods on to other traders. Many places, such as Taxila (see page 126) and Petra (see page 136), became wealthy simply because of their positions as trade centres.

TRAVEL BY SEA The sea routes for trade were also extremely important. A great deal of silk came to India and from there by sea to Europe. Roman coins and objects such as pottery have been found in southern India. There was even a Roman trading station at Arikamedu on the south-eastern coast of India.

THE HAN DYNASTY

The civilization of China began very early in history. By 6000 BC there were villages in China where farmers bred pigs, kept dogs and grew millet. Later soya beans and rice were introduced. We know that from 2700 BC the Chinese had discovered how to produce silk from silkworms. From about 1800 BC there were cities in China which were defended against their enemies. In these cities Chinese craftworkers were producing fine quality pottery and metal objects. After 1500 BC the Chinese had invented a system for writing.

THE EMPEROR CH'IN The Chinese cities fought each other as well as outside enemies. After centuries of civil war one man became the most powerful. He was the Emperor Ch'in Shi-huang-ti. In 221 BC he united the vast country into one Empire and gave China its name. His own family, or *dynasty*, did not rule China for very long – only 11 years – but the system of government he set up lasted until 1912.

This bronze figure of a horse is typical of the fine art of the Eastern Han Dynasty of the second century AD. It is only 34.5 cm high but shows the horse at a 'flying' gallop. The horse is neighing and is carefully balanced on a swallow in flight.

THE GREAT WALL The Emperor Ch'in is probably best known for the massive stone wall, the Great Wall, which he built on the northern borders of China. Some of the northern states had built walls to protect themselves but Emperor Ch'in joined several together to form a unified frontier.

The Chinese Empire was divided into a number of provinces, each with its own governor and military commander.

THE HAN DYNASTY The military campaigns and costly building projects like the Great Wall made people hostile to the rule of Ch'in and a new civil war began in 210 BC. After the war a new dynasty emerged called the Han Dynasty.

The most important of China's enemies were the Xiongnu tribes to the north of the Great Wall. Under the Han Dynasty there were campaigns against these tribes. The Great Wall was extended to the north-west to protect the important trade route into central Asia. Trade with the West began at this time.

The Han Empire was also extended to the east into Korea to include those states on the edge of the South China Sea. The princes who had ruled their own small territories were gradually taken into the Empire and ruled from the capital.

CHANG'AN – CAPITAL OF CHINA The earliest surviving count of the people (called a census), taken in the Han Dynasty in AD 1, gives 57 million as China's population. This vast population was controlled from the capital city, which was Chang'an. The city was more like an enormous imperial court than a city. More than two-thirds of the area was taken up by royal palaces. Little now remains of the buildings of Chang'an. However, it is known that high pavilions were popular in the Han period, and a pavilion 115 metres high is said to have been built in Chang'an.

Han China

As early as the third century BC fortifications, mainly of earth, were built in the north to keep the 'barbarians' out of China. The Emperor Ch'in joined them together, reinforced them and made the Great Wall of China. It stretches for about 2300 km and stands about 7.5 m high with towers and defended gateways.

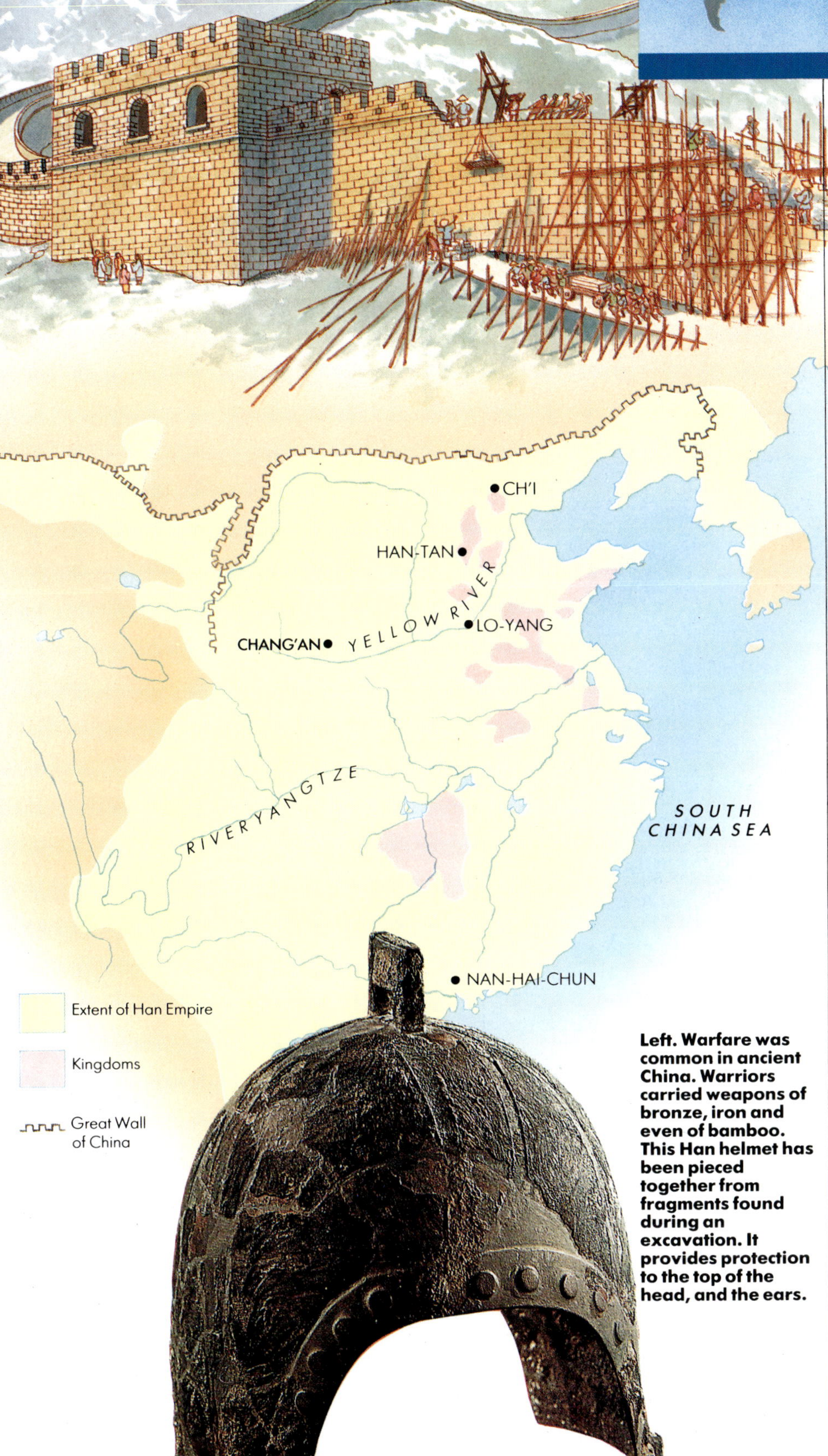

Left. Warfare was common in ancient China. Warriors carried weapons of bronze, iron and even of bamboo. This Han helmet has been pieced together from fragments found during an excavation. It provides protection to the top of the head, and the ears.

Key Dates

Shang Dynasty 1600–1027 BC
There were constant wars and their enemies, if captured, could be slaughtered in the royal tombs.

Zhou Dynasty 1027–771 BC
King Wu of Zhou overthrew the Shang Dynasty and established his capital at Hao-ching.

Warring States 481–221 BC
There was constant warfare in this period.

Ch'in and Western Han Dynasties 221 BC–AD 8
Emperor Ch'in united the country.

Hsin Dynasty AD 9–23
Wang Mang took control and became emperor.

Eastern Han Dynasty AD 24–220

1 The early peoples in the Andes Mountains were called Chavin and were building huge ceremonial temples from about 1200 BC. The Nazca people established themselves from about 200 BC. There is still a great mystery about the Nazca people because of the 'lines' they created. They cleared soil from the ground to reveal the underlying rock, making parallel lines or geometric shapes. Sometimes monkeys, birds or spiders were drawn out. Their real purpose is unknown and most can only be appreciated from the air. They may have been 'offerings' to their gods.

2 In the southwest of north America from about 1000 BC people hunted and gathered food but also practised some small-scale farming. The climate was dry and the people are known, from what has been preserved, as the 'Basketmakers'. By AD 1 they were building very small villages with houses which had floors sunk below ground. Most of the food they ate was gathered or hunted, but some plants, like maize, were cultivated.

BURIAL IN THE HAN DYNASTY

Above. The bodies of Prince Liu Sheng and his wife Tou Wan were encased in suits made from pieces of jade, which the Chinese believed prevented decay. Archaeologists found the suits collapsed but were able to reconstruct them. Right. From the first century AD pottery models of buildings were placed in tombs.

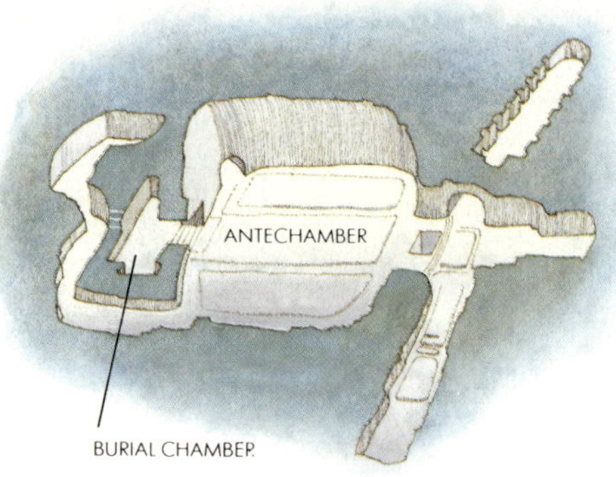

Left. Prince Liu Sheng and Princess Tou Wan were buried in different tombs. This is Tou Wan's tomb carved out of the solid rock. An entrance gallery on the right led to two chambers which contained beautiful objects. A main chamber led to the place of burial at the far end.

The ancient Chinese believed in a life after death. They also believed that life would be just the same after death so they took their possessions with them. In earlier dynasties the Chinese killed their servants and buried them with their dead masters and mistresses to continue to serve them in the next world. Later on, models of servants and soldiers were placed in graves.

Archaeologists have been able to discover an enormous amount about the Chinese way of life in the early periods from the burial tombs. Objects were carefully placed with the person who was buried – even food for the next world.

THE BURIAL OF THE FIRST EMPEROR Perhaps the most spectacular of the Chinese burials was that of Ch'in Shi-huang-ti. His royal tomb was discovered quite by accident in 1974 by farmers digging wells for water. At Mount Li in the Shansi province they found huge pits containing life-size models of 7000 warriors – each with a different face. They must have been modelled on the real warriors.

BURIAL IN THE HAN DYNASTY The tombs of the Han Dynasty were very elaborate. Tomb walls were often decorated with scenes of everyday life – in the kitchen, on the farm or working at industries such as salt mining.

THE PRINCE AND THE PRINCESS Two of the finest tombs ever discovered from the Han Dynasty are those of Prince Liu Sheng and his wife the Princess Tou Wan. The tombs were discovered at Mancheng which is 150 kilometres south-west of Beijing (Peking).

Part of the tomb of China's first emperor, Ch'in Shi-huang-ti showing some of the 7000 pottery models of warriors. Also buried are pottery horses and chariots.

Tomb Facts

The tomb of Emperor Ch'in Shi-huang-ti:

- was discovered in March 1974 at Mount Li by farmers digging a well for water
- was under a huge mound of earth 1400m square
- contained 7000 warriors, 3000 footsoldiers, six chariots with horses as well as bowmen, spearmen and officers
- took about 700,000 forced labourers 36 years to build.

The tombs of Liu Sheng and Tou Wan:

- were discovered in June 1968 at Mancheng when soldiers fell into a hole that led underground
- were sealed under a layer of molten iron
- contained over 2800 objects which included the burial suits. Tou Wan's suit had 2156 jade pieces sewn together with over 700 grams of gold wire.

Archaeologists, local people and soldiers took months to clear the passageways and chambers of the two tombs. All the hard work was worth it – the tombs had lain untouched since they were built in 113 BC.

CONSTRUCTING THE TOMB Prince Liu Sheng, who was the brother of the Emperor Wu-ti, had ordered the tombs to be built before his death. They were cut into the hillside out of solid rock. Not only was there a special chamber for each of the bodies of the Prince and Princess but there were three other chambers and long entrance passageways.

There was always the danger of tomb-robbing in ancient China so the Prince had taken special precautions. On his own tomb he had the walls sealed with rocks and molten iron.

BURIED WITH THE DEAD Inside the two tombs the archaeologists found more than 2800 objects. There were jars to hold food and wine; gold and bronze vessels, weapons, lamps, incense burners and little figures of animals. One particularly interesting find was a collection of figures of acrobats, musicians and spectators.

BURIAL SUITS OF JADE The bodies of the Prince and Princess were placed in carefully made suits of jade. Jade is a very hard semi-precious stone. Each suit was made from over 2000 small tablets of jade held together with gold wire.

As the bodies inside rotted away, the suits collapsed. Archaeologists constructed dummies of the right size and reconstructed the suits around them so that we can see what they would have looked like.

ART AND CRAFTS OF THE HAN DYNASTY

Industry and trade were important in the Han Dynasty. Two of the most important industries – ironworking and salt production – were controlled by the state.

MAKING IRON The production of iron was made a state industry in 119 BC. The ancient Chinese were well ahead of the rest of the world in their knowledge of iron. Cast iron (that is poured into a mould) had been made since about 500 BC. Cast iron was not used in the western world until the Industrial Revolution in the nineteenth century.

Iron ore had to be dug from the ground, then melted at very high temperatures. The Chinese ironworkers used charcoal and, later, coal to heat the ore. We know that in the Han Dynasty there were 49 blast furnaces to produce cast iron. The furnaces were built of heat resistant bricks.

The Chinese of the Han period could make an even harder type of iron – steel. They did this by introducing carbon into the cast iron. Chinese archaeologists have excavated a number of iron furnaces and experimented on the site of one at Wenxian.

OBJECTS MADE OF IRON Iron could be used for all sorts of objects. At Wenxian the furnaces produced vast quantities of belt buckles and horse harness fittings. Weapons, tools and parts of ploughs and other objects for farming were also made of iron.

ART AND CRAFTS You have read about Han burials. The tombs contained the best evidence we have for the quality of craftwork in ancient China. Artists worked in bronze and gold with inlays of other metals and stone.

Made during the Han period, these lacquerwork boxes show obedient sons and daughters along their sides.

LACQUERWORK *Lacquerwork* objects have been found from before the Han period. Lacquer is a substance which comes from the tree called Rhus verniciflua which only grows in the Far East. A coating of lacquer will seal an object and preserve it. Lacquer also gives a brilliant shine to an object and brings out the colours. Wooden objects such as bowls, trays, boxes and even room screens were lacquered.

PICTURES FROM THE PAST Much of our detailed evidence for daily life comes from wall paintings and engravings in tombs. Favourite scenes are kitchens, with details of food preparation, and banquets. We can learn more about what the ancient Chinese ate from the detailed lists recorded in tombs and the labels put onto the food containers.

In the Han period the commonest foods were: rice and flour noodles; soup with meat and vegetables; vegetables – lotus roots, soya beans, leeks, yams, bamboo shoots, radishes; fruits – melons, plums, oranges, mandarins, peaches, pears, apricots, water chestnuts; meat – horse, dog, wild boar, beef, lamb, hare, chicken and game; spices and flavourings – sugar, honey, garlic, onion, cinnamon, ginger, salt, vinegar, soya sauce; drinks – milk, beer, also drinks made from fruits like plums.

The Chinese had to become skilled in cavalry fighting to defeat the nomads in the north. This influenced the artists who produced heads like this one of jade, as well as decorated horse trappings.

Below. The decoration on this horse harness made of bronze is of an elk. The idea of this sort of decoration came from the nomadic tribes in the Ordos region north of the Great Wall of China.

Above. A pottery model of a ferocious-looking guard or hunting dog. You can see the strong breast strap and the eye for attaching the lead. Other animals were often subjects for these little models, which were placed in tombs. One strange creature looked like a cross between a rhinoceros and a hippopotamus.

One of the many objects found buried with the Princess Tou Wan (see page 110). This shows the head of a servant girl, made of bronze. It is part of a little statue of the girl who is holding a lamp.

Silk Weaving

Silk is a fibre which comes from the cocoon of the silkworm. The silkworm feeds on the leaves of the mulberry tree and is 'farmed'. The drawing on the right shows the silkworms feeding on leaves placed on racks.

The larvae of the silkworms grow to about 8 cm in length after five weeks of eating mulberry leaves. Then they begin to spin their cocoons. Each cocoon is made up of two continuous fibre threads, about 900 m in length, stuck together with a gum called seracin. To remove the silk fibre the cocoons are softened in hot water in a vat and the cocoons are unwound. They can then be twisted together ready to be woven.

The very fine silk was then woven into cloth on a loom. Garments made of silk were very fashionable and expensive in the Han period, as they are today.

LANGUAGE AND WRITING IN ANCIENT CHINA

Writing was invented in the Near East so that people could keep records and accounts of their goods and transactions. Various forms of scripts were used. The earliest writing found so far is from Mesopotamia. Clay tablets with a picture script have been dated to 3200 BC. These *pictograms*, as they are called, are of fish, grain, cows, water and other things. They form lists of goods in store or for trade.

CUNEIFORM AND HIEROGLYPHIC WRITING The next form of writing is called *cuneiform* and is also found in Mesopotamia for the first time in about 2800 BC. The writing is also found on clay tablets but it is a series of wedges to form symbols which represent words.

Later on a different form of writing was developed by the Egyptians called *hieroglyphic* script. It was a sort of picture writing, too. The Egyptians eventually made up about 700 hieroglyphs.

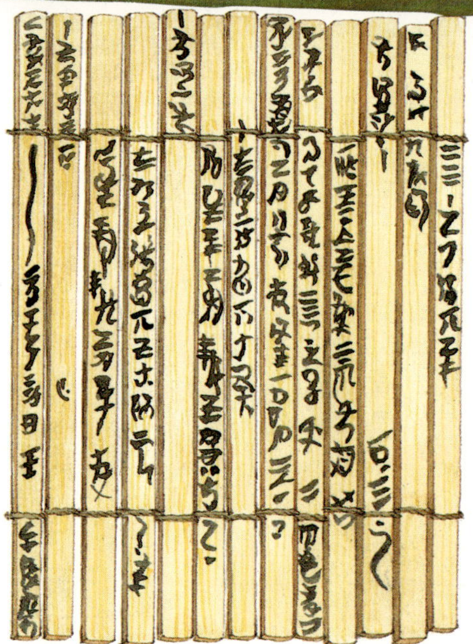

The T'ang Dynasty of China lasted from AD 618 to 906 and was a very prosperous and peaceful period in Chinese history. This period was the first to produce printed books. This one (above), which shows the Buddha addressing his disciples, was printed from a wood block on a scroll in AD 868. Before paper was invented characters were painted on to wood strips like this bamboo book (left). Strips of bamboo were tied with string and rolled into a 'book'.

Left. The names of the Buddha printed on paper found at Dunhuang dated to the 10th century AD. Right. Oracle bones have been found with inscriptions carved on them. The cracks are formed when the bone is touched by heated bronze points. The shape of the cracks gave the 'answers' of the oracle. The inscription on the right records the correct animals to be sacrificed to dead ancestors and reads 'Get ready the officers, Father second a pig, son a pig; Mother ninth a pig. . .'

CHINESE WRITING The Chinese probably developed their own form of writing without any knowledge of writing from other civilizations. Inscriptions are known from 1500 BC onwards. There are four different sorts of script.

Pictographs are simplified pictures of objects. In simplified pictographs, the pictographs were slightly changed and the original pictures indicated by one or more lines. This made writing simpler and quicker.

The third and fourth types of script indicated the sound of the word as well as its idea. The last group is the most commonly found with about 9000 characters in use in AD 100. This script is still used today but now has about 60,000 characters.

The Art of Calligraphy

Calligraphy is the art of writing. Chinese artists and scholars used brushes and ink to draw both words and pictures. A hard block of ink is rubbed on a stone palette with water to liquefy it.

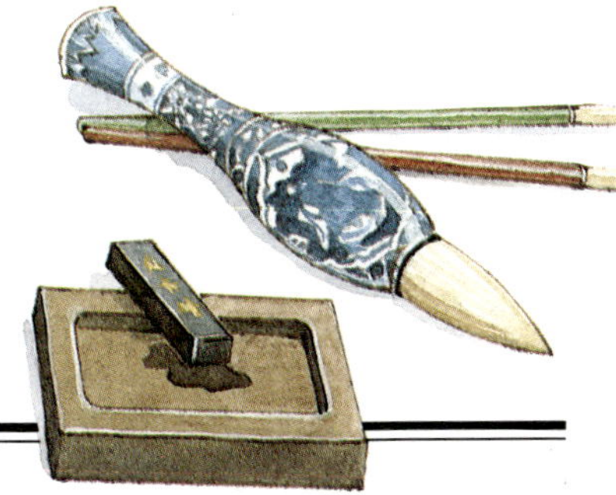

ORACLE BONES A great deal of ancient Chinese writing has been found on oracle bones. These are usually the flat shoulder blades of cattle. They were used to foretell the future by observing the cracks in the bone caused by touching the bone with a metal point heated by fire.

Writing is also found on paper made from rags and cellulose and on bamboo, wood and silk. Large numbers of manuscripts have now been found during excavations of tombs.

THE MAURYAN EMPIRE

Pakistan, in the north-western part of the subcontinent of India, was home to one of the world's earliest civilizations. The land around the River Indus was fertile enough to support a very large population of farmers. The river gives its name to the civilization – the Indus civilization – which developed around 2300 BC and had two main cities, Harappa and Mohenjo-Daro.

INDIAN STATES AT WAR After the cities of the Indus civilization had developed and declined, other parts of India flourished. The areas around other major rivers, like the Ganges, produced wealth from rice growing. By 600 BC there were at least 16 small states in the Ganges plain. During the fifth century BC they were at constant war with each other. The strongest took over the smaller, weaker ones and eventually they were all taken into the kingdom of Magadha.

THE MAURYAN EMPIRE ESTABLISHED The throne of the kingdom of Magadha was seized by Chandragupta Maurya at the end of the fourth century BC. He could be called the first real Emperor of India, as the Mauryan Empire which he established covered most of the subcontinent. Under his rule the Empire spread north-west into the area around the River Indus, south into central India and even into what is now Afghanistan.

His son, Bindusara, extended the Empire again but it was Bindusara's son, Asoka, who extended the Mauryan Empire furthest.

THE EMPEROR ASOKA Asoka took over from his father in about 270 BC and reigned until his death in 232 BC. Apart from the far south, he controlled most of the subcontinent of India. It was a rich Empire; most of the population were farmers. Asoka's grandfather had established a system of governing the Empire which was actually published in a book. Asoka developed this system, including a complicated way of collecting taxes.

TRAVEL AND TRADE Roads were an important way to control and administer the huge Empire. There was a special group of officials in the Mauryan government just for that. Major roads included the Royal Highway which ran from the capital city of Pataliputra to the north-west. The Roman Empire imported a number of goods from India. The Romans liked the cotton cloth made in India as well as the spices of southern India and its precious stones.

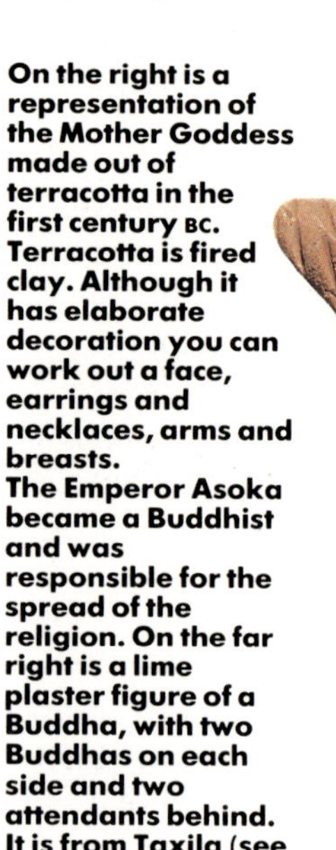

On the right is a representation of the Mother Goddess made out of terracotta in the first century BC. Terracotta is fired clay. Although it has elaborate decoration you can work out a face, earrings and necklaces, arms and breasts. The Emperor Asoka became a Buddhist and was responsible for the spread of the religion. On the far right is a lime plaster figure of a Buddha, with two Buddhas on each side and two attendants behind. It is from Taxila (see page 126).

Mauryan India

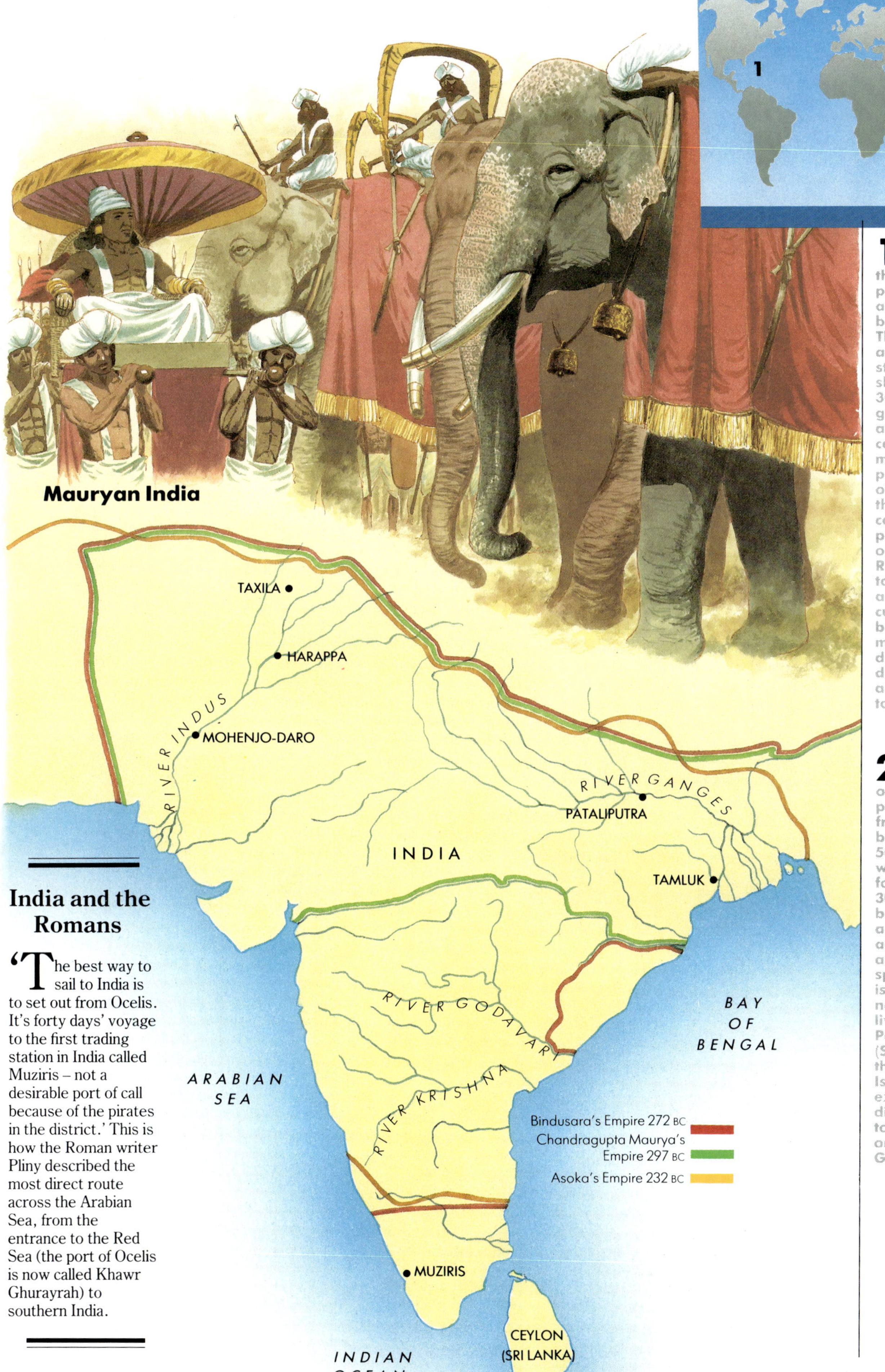

India and the Romans

'The best way to sail to India is to set out from Ocelis. It's forty days' voyage to the first trading station in India called Muziris – not a desirable port of call because of the pirates in the district.' This is how the Roman writer Pliny described the most direct route across the Arabian Sea, from the entrance to the Red Sea (the port of Ocelis is now called Khawr Ghurayrah) to southern India.

1 The earliest people to live in the Caribbean were probably hunting and food gathering by around 5000 BC. They made tools and weapons of stone, bone and shell. From about 3000 BC various groups who knew about agriculture can be identified – mainly from their pottery and art objects. One of these groups we call the Saladoid peoples. They occupied Puerto Rico and the islands towards Trinidad and Guyana. They cultivated crops, baked bread and made pottery decorated with designs based on animals, such as tortoises and frogs.

2 Australia was probably first occupied by peoples coming from southeast Asia by sea as early as 50,000 BC. These were hunters and food gatherers. By 3000 BC people were beginning to settle and use the land for agriculture. People and ideas soon spread to the islands to the northeast. Those living in the Polynesian islands (Samoa, Tonga and the Solomon Islands, for example) spoke different languages to those in Australia or Papua New Guinea.

GOVERNING THE MAURYAN EMPIRE

Left. An irrigation canal at Taxila (see page 126). Irrigation was essential for the early farmers trying to establish their farming communities. They undertook enormous projects to divert water supplies from rivers to their fields which were often built as terraces on hillsides (below). Traditional methods of construction and engineering were improved by those introduced by new peoples, such as the Greeks under Alexander. Canals and irrigation schemes can still be seen today in Pakistan and further north in Afghanistan dating from Mauryan, Kushan and Greek periods.

One of the signs that a civilization exists is the building of cities. The Mauryan Empire had many cities and was divided into four provinces so that the huge territory could be governed more easily. Each province had its own ruler, called a *viceroy*, appointed by the emperor. Asoka had been the viceroy of one province when his father was emperor. He ruled his province from the city of Taxila (see page 126). Asoka sent inspectors to tour the provinces every five years to check on the finances and administration.

THE ARTHASHASTRA Kautalya, who was the chief advisor to Chandragupta Maurya (see page 116), probably invented the basis of the Empire's tax system. He wrote a reference work on government called the Arthashastra. This work has survived and tells us a great deal about the way the government worked.

PAYING STATE TAXES The people in the cities and the farming population paid very high taxes to keep a vast standing army and a huge civil service to administer the Empire.

The two important posts in the administration were the Treasurer, who kept an account of the income from taxes, and the Chief Collector, who kept the tax records. The Chief Collector had a large number of clerks to assist him. Superintendents were in charge of each department:

'The Superintendent of Commerce should work out the demand or the lack of demand for various kinds of merchandise, and the rise or fall in their prices, whether the merchandise is brought by land or by water. The Superintendent will also work out the most suitable time for the merchandise to be distributed, held centrally, purchased and sold.' Arthashastra

A ruined *stupa*, dating to about 200 BC, at Dhamekh in India. This one has ornamental stonework around it (where it has not been removed), but stupas originally developed from simple mounds.

Left. The Emperor Asoka set up very tall pillars throughout his empire. They probably marked places which were already considered sacred. Asoka used the inscriptions on these pillars and on rocks to make proclamations. Part of one inscription reads '. . . Herbs for medicine, for people and animals, where they were lacking, have been imported and planted everywhere. Along the roads wells have been dug and trees planted for the enjoyment of people and animals.'

Above. Some of the decorative stonework and sculpture on stupas was very fine. These examples are from the stupa of the Jaulian monastery at Taxila (see page 126). It has now been brought inside a protective building to keep it secure. You can see that some of the stonework has already been damaged.

IN THE COUNTRYSIDE Most of the people in Mauryan India lived as farmers in small villages, growing crops and keeping animals. The land was owned by the Emperor and people paid taxes on the land, its produce and the animals. Large areas of land were cleared for agriculture, on the command of the Emperor. Frequently, people were moved by force from areas where the population was too large.

One of the most important developments during the period of the Mauryan Empire was irrigation. Reservoirs, tanks, wells and canals were all constructed. In western India one provincial governor built a dam across a river near Girnar and constructed a large lake for his region. Records show that this reservoir of water was maintained for 800 years. The Arthashastra mentions a water tax which was collected whenever the state provided help with irrigation.

TOWNS AND INDUSTRY Towns in Mauryan India were often defended. The capital of Pataliputra, near Patna, had a rampart with a huge timber frame which writers of the day said stretched for 14 kilometres along the Ganges.

The Arthashastra gives a record of what such a town was supposed to be like:

'Royal teachers, priests, the sacrificial place, the water reservoir, and ministers shall occupy sites east by north to the palace . . . the Royal kitchen, elephant stables and the store-house shall be situated on the sides east by south . . . on the eastern side will be the merchants trading in scents, garlands, grains and liquids . . . to the west the manufacturers of worsted cloth, cotton threads, bamboo mats, skins, armour, weapons and gloves . . . either to the north or the east burial or cremation cemeteries shall be situated.'

RELIGION IN THE MAURYAN EMPIRE

A wall painting from one of the caves at Ajanta. Most of the paintings illustrate events from the life of Gautama Buddha. This section shows the Buddha as a child being taught by other children.

Buddhism

The father of Siddhartha Gautama (Buddha) was the ruler of the Sakya tribe in northern India (modern Nepal). There are many legends about his birth, but he seems to have been a very gifted child. At the age of 29 he received four signs which proved a turning point in his life. He saw a sick man, an old man, a corpse, and a man with a shaven head wearing a yellow robe. These signs he interpreted and called **Dukkha** (sick man) or 'suffering', **Anicca** (old man) or 'change', **Anatta** (corpse) or 'becoming impersonal', and finally 'passing into a state of serenity' (shaven-headed man). This represents the whole of a person's existence.

Gautama decided to leave home and search for what he called the True Wisdom. He searched for six years and finally spent the night in meditation, passing through various stages of awareness until he reached Enlightenment and became the Buddha, which can be translated as 'The Enlightened One'.

For 45 years after this he wandered around India preaching that the middle way, or **Dhamma**, between extremes was the right way for people.

Siddhartha Gautama (Buddha) was born around 563 BC in one of the small states which became part of the Mauryan Empire. He founded one of the world's greatest religions, called Buddhism. He believed that each person should do good works, be disciplined in their life and meditate. After his death a group of his followers established an order of monks and began to spread this religious belief.

THE CONVERSION OF ASOKA During his reign, the Emperor Asoka became a convert to the Buddhist religion. He gave up conquering by war and lived by the new ideas of Buddhism. It became the main religion of the Empire and spread out beyond the borders, first to Sri Lanka. Buddhist monks travelled widely taking their religion to south-east Asia, China and Japan.

The first monuments and monasteries of Buddhism were put up during the reign of Asoka. Asoka spread the word of the Buddha by inscriptions carved on pillars and flat rock surfaces all over the Empire. Asoka also built monasteries with a special central building, called a *stupa*, for the rituals. The stupa changed its shape over time. It was originally a simple mound of earth. It soon became a round stone building.

THE MONASTERY OF AJANTA In central India on the edge of the River Waghora are some of the most impressive monuments of the Buddhist religion. Cut into the rock of the cliff are a number of temples and monasteries. Two temples and three monasteries were created there in the second or first centuries BC and all the rest constructed in the fifth century AD.

Below. In plan form you can see the temples and monasteries at Ajanta set in a horseshoe-shape around the River Waghora. Ajanta was an important place in the first and second centuries BC but became very important in the fifth century AD. The various religious buildings here contain some of the best Buddhist carvings and wall paintings in existence.

Above. Caves had been used for religious purposes before the Mauryan period. The caves at Ajanta were adapted by the Buddhist monks and decorated (see right) with elaborately carved columns, windows and Buddhas.

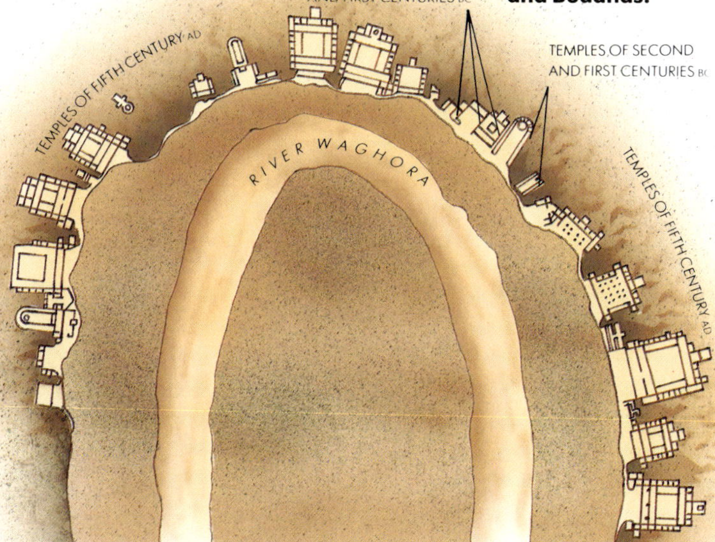

Temples were built to cover small stupas which often contained holy relics. The temples at Ajanta, in the early period, were long hall-like buildings with the stupa at one end which was half-round in shape.

Images of the Buddha and scenes from his life were usually found in temples and the wall paintings from Ajanta are some of the finest known. The first people from Europe saw them in 1819.

The buildings for the monks in the second century BC are simple in their plan. There was a central courtyard hall where the monks could gather together. Off this courtyard were the monks' individual rooms, or *cells*, with bed platforms cut out of the rock. The later monasteries were slightly more elaborate, some having two storeys.

INVADERS FROM CHINA

The continent of India was invaded many times by foreigners who established kingdoms or even empires. The campaigns of Alexander the Great reached India; in 327 BC he conquered Gandhara, the valley of the River Kabul in present-day Afghanistan. By 325 BC he was marching home having conquered most of what is now Pakistan. The Greeks were not able to hold the region for long. The area was soon taken over by the Mauryan Emperor Chandragupta Maurya (see page 116).

NEW INVADERS IN NORTHERN INDIA The strongest, and most successful, invaders of India were a nomadic tribe from China. In the west they were known as the Tochari but their proper name seems to have been the Yueh-chih. We know of them first of all in 165 BC living near the Great Wall of China. The Yueh-chih tribe was defeated by its neighbours and was forced to move west and settle in the region where the present-day countries of India, Pakistan, China, Afghanistan, Turkmenistan, Tajikistan, Uzbekistan and Kirgizia meet.

THE KUSHANS One part of the tribe of the Yueh-chih took over control and eventually established a very large empire. Their Chinese name was Kuei-shang which became known as Kushan. The Kushan Empire was established around AD 60. The greatest of the rulers was Kanishka I who began ruling in about AD 78, although we are not certain about dates at this time.

THE EMPIRE OF THE KUSHANS The Kushans eventually established an empire which stretched from the River Ganges in the east to the Caspian Sea in the west, from the River Jaxartes which flows into the Aral Sea in the north to the mouth of the Indus Valley in the south. To their west was the Empire of the Parthians (see page 128). Further west were the Romans. The Kushans were in a good position to trade with the Romans and their territory lay on the 'Silk Road' between Rome and China.

CITIES OF THE KUSHANS Kanishka I made the capital of his Empire the city of Purushapura close to the Hindu Kush mountain range north of the River Indus. The second most important city of the Empire was at Mathura, further east on the River Jumna.

Kushan rulers took grand titles for themselves which they borrowed from the Persians and the Chinese. The most usual were Maharajatiraja meaning King of Kings and Daivaputra meaning Son of Heaven. One ruler called himself Kaisura – Caesar – obviously wishing to be as powerful as a Roman emperor.

Kushan Empire in AD 150

The Kushan Empire of the ruler Kanishka I was situated in a key position between the states of India and the Parthian Empire. This position gave them access for trade with the Roman world.

Left. The reverse, or back, of a silver coin of Ardashir I who took over the Parthian Empire in about AD 224 (see page 128). He attacked neighbouring peoples, including the Kushans. The coin shows a fire altar.

THE END OF THE KUSHAN EMPIRE The great Kushan Empire lasted from the middle of the first century to the third century AD. The Empire was invaded by the Persians and almost destroyed. In the fourth century a new ruler revived it but by the following century the region had been taken over completely by new foreign invaders – the Huns – coming from the north.

Left. A group of gods of the sea from northern India in Gandharan style. These carvings of the Kushan period show the influence of Greek and Roman art.

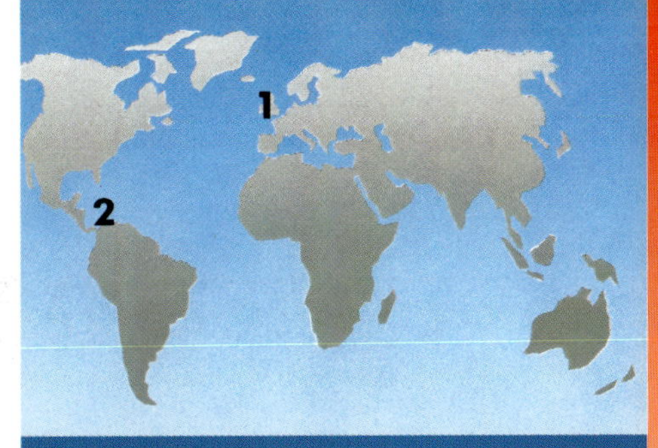

1 The year AD 60 was a significant date in the history of the Romans in Britain. The tribes in the east of Britain considered themselves hard pressed during the winter when the Roman tax collectors demanded payment. The fierce queen of the Iceni tribe, called Boudica, rose up against the Romans. She led an army of 100,000 through East Anglia and destroyed the towns of Colchester, Verulamium (now St Albans) and London. She went on to annihilate a Roman legion which was sent against her. She was stopped eventually and Roman order imposed again.

2 The city of Teotihuacan developed over a period of 600 years. By AD 500 it was the sixth largest city in the world with a population of about 200,000. The city was laid out on a grid system and covered over 20 square km. The people believed this was the birthplace of the Sun and the Moon gods. There is a square dedicated to the Moon and the famous Pyramid of the Sun.

Alexander's Empire

Greek influences appeared in India because of the invasion of the Greek ruler Alexander the Great (see also page 66). The map shows his invasion route and the empire he established to the borders of the Mauryan kingdom. Notice how many of the names of towns begin with or are called Alexandria – Alexander's town.

Left. This sculpture in relief in the Gandharan style of the third century AD shows a group of ascetics. These were followers of religion who denied themselves any luxuries and lived an extremely simple and austere life.

ART IN THE KUSHAN EMPIRE

During the period of the Kushan Empire artists and architects working in different materials produced some fine work. Art was influenced by contacts with Greece because of the invasions of Alexander the Great. Bronze sculptures and plaster-work were imported into the Kushan Empire from Alexandria. The Buddhist religion provided plenty of scenes and saints as subjects for art. Art in northern India became a combination of Indian and Greek ideas and styles and is known as Graeco-Indian or Graeco-Buddhist art.

GANDHARA ART The art of this period is usually known as Gandharan art, named after the area in the northern part of the Kushan Empire. The Buddha himself (see page 120) was represented in sculpture rather like a Greek mother-figure. Indian artists also modelled the Buddha on the Greek god Apollo.

There were sculptures in stone but also in fired clay, or *terracotta*, for those who could not afford expensive stone. Little terracotta figures were used as toys and as decoration in the home. A form of decorative moulded plasterwork, called *stucco*, was introduced from Alexander's Empire and used to decorate Kushan monasteries throughout the East.

This is part of a free-standing gate to the Great Stupa at Sanchi in central India. It was built in about the first century BC. It is covered with elaborate sculpture and carving in a realistic style showing Buddhist legends. At the bottom right is a female native spirit, called a yaksi, which guarded treasures. The spirals suggest the rolled ends of scrolls on which stories were written.

Left. A sculpture of the Buddha, as the 'Enlightened One', in the Gandharan style from the second or third centuries AD.

Below. A carved relief showed the Buddha (see page 120) as he grew up. In it, he is travelling in a chariot pulled by two rams.

Gautama is going to his lessons with his schoolfellows who are carrying writing boards and ink pots.

Above and right. The female was a favourite subject in Indian art. Both these objects are from Mathura near Delhi. Artists from Mathura developed a lively form of art and introduced the first images of the Buddha. These objects are both from around 150 BC. You can see (above) a terracotta which decorated a building and (right) the figure of a woman, also in terracotta.

THE CITY OF TAXILA

The excavated ruins of the cities at Taxila are now open to visitors.

The ancient city of Taxila is in modern Pakistan north-west of Rawalpindi. The location of Taxila meant that it was an important trading city for nearly 1000 years. Major trading routes passed through Taxila and its merchants traded not only between the Romans and India but also provided goods from China.

Taxila began to be prosperous in the sixth century BC when it was part of the Persian Empire. The Persians built the first roads there to govern their empire and for trade. By Alexander the Great's time Taxila was an independent kingdom. We know that Alexander the Great visited the city in 326 BC.

THE THREE CITIES At three different times cities were built at Taxila. The first is called the Bhir Mound and must have been the one which Alexander the Great visited. This was the site of the original Persian city. It was part of the territory conquered by the first Mauryan Emperor, Chandragupta Maurya. The city of the Mauryan period lies over the Persian one. The city has not been fully excavated but some of the narrow main streets lined with houses and shops have been uncovered.

SIRKAP After the Mauryan Empire Taxila was conquered, around 189 BC, by Greeks who had settled in Bactria (now northeast Afghanistan). A Greek city was laid out across the river from the original settlement at a place known as Sirkap.

Sirkap was laid out like new Greek cities in other countries with straight streets cutting across each other at right angles. Houses and shops were built inside the rectangular blocks which the streets created. Also typical of a Greek city was a high point called an *acropolis* enclosed by a wall. The most famous acropolis is the one in Athens, capital of ancient and modern Greece. The

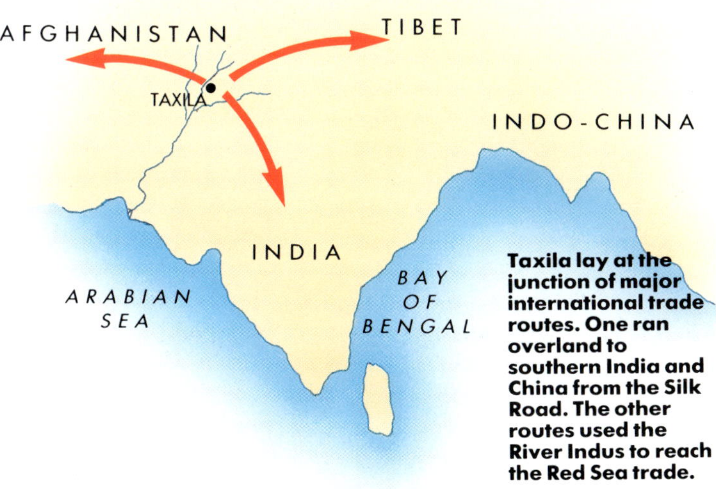

Taxila lay at the junction of major international trade routes. One ran overland to southern India and China from the Silk Road. The other routes used the River Indus to reach the Red Sea trade.

SIRSUKH
JANDIAL TEMPLE
SIRKAP
BHIR MOUND

There were a number of stupas and monasteries at Taxila both inside the city and around it. The sculpture above comes from a monastery there. The plan on the left shows the location of the three cities at Taxila. Excavations to uncover the city began in the 1920s but later archaeological work has shown how extensive the settlement was and how complex was its history.

whole city was surrounded and defended by a wall. Outside the city walls, at Jandial, the Greeks built a great temple.

The defences of Sirkap were not enough to stop it being attacked, and taken, by a nomadic tribe called the Shaka in the early first century BC and then again by the Parthians around AD 19. Both peoples occupied Sirkap.

SIRSUKH The final settlers at Taxila were the Kushans in the mid first century AD. They occupied Sirkap at first but then built a new city at Sirsukh. It was built like the cities in the country they had originally come from. Its shape, marked out by a wall for defence, was a parallelogram – that is, a rectangle where the opposite sides are parallel but the corners do not form right angles.

Around the three cities were a number of stupas and temples built by the Mauryan and Kushan peoples.

SHAPUR I AND THE DEFEAT OF ROME

Two peoples, the Medes and the Persians, came from central Asia into what is now Iran. The Persians became the controllers of the land after their King Cyrus defeated the king of the Medes in 550 BC. The Persian Empire grew to cover a vast area stretching from northern Greece to north Africa and east to India. Under two of their emperors, Darius and Xerxes, they tried to conquer Greece. Darius was defeated at the famous Battle of Marathon in 490 BC and Xerxes at the Battle of Salamis in 480 BC.

Part of the column put up in Rome by the Emperor Trajan to celebrate his victory over the Dacians in AD 114.

ALEXANDER THE GREAT The great Persian Empire came to an end much later in 331 BC. Alexander, a ruler from Macedon in northern Greece who became known as Alexander the Great, marched right through Persian territory to its easternmost limits – the River Indus in Pakistan.

THE PARTHIANS After Alexander's Empire had broken up at his death, various peoples and rulers took parts for themselves. Among these were the Parthians. They were originally a nomadic people from the eastern side of the Caspian Sea. They gradually took over more and more territory and established their own empire which was partly eastern and partly Greek. The Parthians were noted for their skill with horses and as cavalry fighters.

The limits of their Empire in the west touched the Roman Empire. At first they were unconquered by the Romans who were forced to negotiate with them. Under the Roman Emperor Trajan in AD 114 some of their territory was taken over.

THE SASSANIANS The Parthian Empire was finally taken over in the third century AD by the people who came to be known as the Sassanians. From one part of the Parthian Empire on the Persian Gulf, Persis, Sassanian princes built a new empire.

The first, called Prince Ardashir, led a revolt against Parthian rule and killed the last Parthian king, Artabanus V, in about AD 224. From then on Ardashir attacked the other peoples around, including the Romans and the Kushans.

His son, Shapur I, conquered most of the territory of the Kushan Empire and defeated three Roman emperors. Gordian III was killed in battle, Philip was forced to make peace and the Emperor Valerian was captured and executed in about AD 260. Shapur shamed the Romans by forcing Roman prisoners of war to resettle in a new city which he called Veh-Antiok-Shapur, which means 'The city of Shapur, better than Antioch'. Antioch was the Roman capital city of the province of Syria.

Left. A rock carving at Naqsh-i Rustam near Persepolis. It shows the king, Shapur I, on horseback towering over two Romans. They are the Roman emperors Philip (shown kneeling) and Valerian (standing). They are both paying homage to Shapur.

Above. This silver-gilt dish, now in the Hermitage Museum in St Petersburg in Russia, shows the Sassanian king, Ardashir III who reigned from AD 628 to AD 630. You can see the king is hunting on horseback.

1 After the collapse of the Han Dynasty in China in AD 220, the country broke into small states which were often at war with each other. For 45 years there were three states. Then the power shifted to two states – the Northern Wei and the Ch'i state in the south. China was not re-united as a country again until the first Sui Emperor came to power in AD 581.

2 Some 4,000 km from the coast of Chile lies Rapanui, or Easter Island – famous for its gigantic statues 3m to 10m high. The name of the island comes from a Dutch navigator, Jacob Roggeveen, who was the first European to visit it on Easter Day in 1722. The island remained uninhabited until about AD 500 when Polynesians settled there. They took plants with them and cultivated the banana, palm, taro and yam. The statues found there, called moai, are images of the head and the top half of the body cut into volcanic rock.

THE ART OF THE SASSANIAN EMPIRE

Far left. A fine example of gold craft showing a Sassanian king in relief.
Top. An eagle made from glass crystal.
Below. Bronze figure of a monster dated to the seventh/eighth century AD. Creatures like this dragon are often found in the art of the Sassanian period.

Ardashir was known as Shahanshah, which means 'king of kings'. The government of the Sassanian Empire was established in a very formal way; serving below the King of Kings were various 'grades' of officials and peoples. There were nobles, priests, warriors, civil servants and farming peoples. The religion, called Zoroastrianism, founded by the Persian prophet Zoroaster, became the official state religion.

CHINA AND THE SASSANIANS The links between the Sassanian Empire and China were very close. There was a great deal of trade between the two peoples along the Silk Road. China imported works of art in gold, glass, crystals and textiles. Chinese art was influenced by what was imported from the west. Chinese work in gold was begun during this period and goldsmiths from the Sassanian Empire must have travelled to China to work. Archaeologists have found more than 1200 Sassanid coins in China, most of them from Xinjiang.

SASSANIAN ART The Sassanian period is particularly noted for its fine works of art, often in precious metals and stones. Moulding in glass became an art form and gem-stones were cut into shapes. Cups, bowls and dishes of silver were made with people – especially kings – animals and plants shown in *relief*, where the figures stand out from the background. Examples of the different art forms are shown here.

Left. This relief sculpture is carved out of brick on the wall of a temple. Some features have also been enamelled. It pictures Ahuramazda, the god of gods, at the top. Ahuramazda was often shown giving the right of ruling to the Sassanian kings. Ahuramazda is shown as having a dish-shaped body with large symmetrical wings and the vertical tail of a bird. He hovers in the heavens above the earth. Below the god are two winged sphinxes.

Below. A very fine example of Sassanian artistry in silver. This horse's head shows every detail of the harness with its decorated trappings.

Left. This cameo shows the Sassanian King Shapur I (see page 128) capturing the Roman Emperor Valerian. This victory over the Romans, and Shapur's defeat of Gordian and Philip, were often the subject for sculpture and decoration on a variety of objects.

THE PEOPLE OF THE NOK CULTURE

In Europe people had discovered how to use stone, then copper and bronze and finally iron to make tools and weapons. In Africa, south of the Sahara, the period when stone was used was followed by an iron age. Iron was used for most tools and was introduced by two very different routes. The River Nile was the first route by which the idea of using iron travelled from Egypt, in about 500 BC, to the Kingdom of Meroë. In about 450 BC iron-working came from the Carthaginian cities of north Africa to where the rivers Niger and Benue meet in the land now called Nigeria. The earliest furnaces for smelting iron ore in Nigeria are at Taruga.

In this area one particular way of life has been identified and called the Nok Culture. It lasted from the eighth century BC until the second century AD.

The people living in the region around the rivers Niger and Benue were farmers. By about 1000 BC they had been gathering food, hunting and fishing and had begun to produce food by farming as well. Cattle, sheep and goats were all introduced to the area from elsewhere. We know about these animals not only from bones found on archaeological excavations but from rock paintings and figurines. Crops like sorghum and millet, which were found wild, were also grown.

The people of the Nok Culture were discovered in the middle of this century when a large number of their works of art turned up in tin mining operations. Little is known about their villages or towns. Only one has been properly excavated at Samun Dukiya in the Nok Valley. This site was occupied in the third century BC. No houses had survived but plenty of objects – arrow and spear heads, bracelets, pounding and grinding stones for food, fired-clay pots as well as animal bones – were found.

Religious shrines were set up on the edges of land which was cultivated. The shrines were usually washed away each year as the rivers flooded. In fact, as these iron-working people cut more and more trees down for the furnaces, so land was eroded and washed away.

THE ART OF THE NOK These people of Nok are now best known for their art which tells us so much about the way people looked then. Their art came in the form of terracotta figurines – some lifesize. Usually only the heads have survived. Some figurines are of monkeys, elephants and snakes.

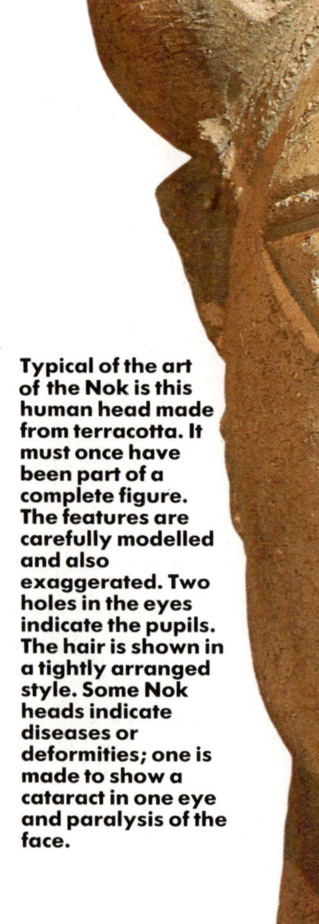

Typical of the art of the Nok is this human head made from terracotta. It must once have been part of a complete figure. The features are carefully modelled and also exaggerated. Two holes in the eyes indicate the pupils. The hair is shown in a tightly arranged style. Some Nok heads indicate diseases or deformities; one is made to show a cataract in one eye and paralysis of the face.

It is thought that the Nok heads and figurines were used in some ritual or religious way. This one (above) is of a kneeling man. Figurines are often shown with the head out of proportion to the body. Animals were also a favourite subject for terracottas as this elephant (left) shows. The artist has taken care to mould the detail of its features.

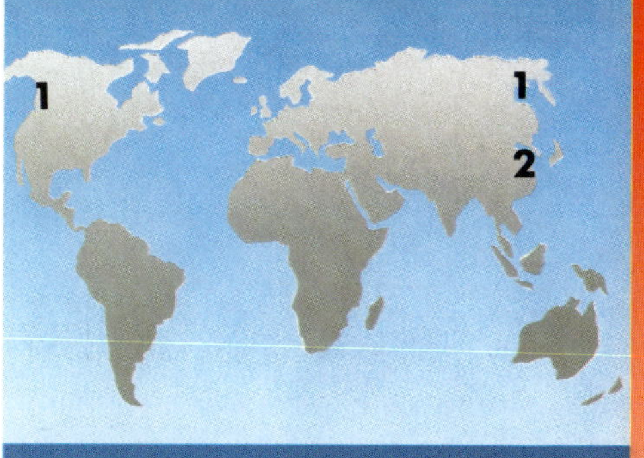

1 Hunters were living in the Arctic since the end of the last Ice Age. Groups moved across the land bridge in the Bering Sea in about 10,000 BC. These Inuit (or Eskimo) were found all around the Arctic Ocean from Greenland to Siberia. The Inuit made stone tools and used them to make both weapons and tools out of bone and also to carve objects. At the same time in Lappland a people called the Saami were living as hunters and fishers.

2 From about 300 BC to AD 300 the Yayoi spread from the Kyushu area of southern Japan to Honshu in the north. The Yayoi people were rice farmers. They also grew crops such as wheat, barley and melons and hunted and fished. They built a variety of houses – some partly below ground, others on stilts – in small settlements. The coastal fishing people, called the Jomon, resisted this settled agricultural way of life at first but had adopted it by about AD 300.

CARTHAGE
RED SEA
RIVER NILE
ADULIS
MEROË
AXUM
NOK
RIVER NIGER
Iron routes
Area of the Nok culture

The idea of using iron for tools and weapons spread down from the northern coasts of Africa to the area where the people of the Nok culture lived. The knowledge was probably brought south by the nomadic Berbers who learnt about ironworking from the Carthaginians.

Ironworking in Ancient Africa

To make objects out of iron it is necessary to melt down iron ore at a high temperature. Iron ore is not pure iron but a mixture of iron and another material such as silicates. 'Smelting' the ore removes everything except the iron. A temperature of 1150°C is needed to make the waste, called 'slag', run off.

Various types of furnaces survive which were used to smelt iron ore. The simplest is just a hollowed out space in the ground lined with clay. The iron ore is placed in layers interleaved with charcoal. Bellows help firing.

It is more efficient to smelt the iron ore in a 'reducing' atmosphere and so more complex furnaces were invented. This type of furnace has a clay cover with an in-built draught which makes the process more efficient. Two types of furnaces are shown here. On the left a clay dome is built over the hollow. The one on the right has a funnel-shaped cover. Both produce a draught aided by bellows inserted into the dome or funnel by means of a fired clay pipe called a tuyère

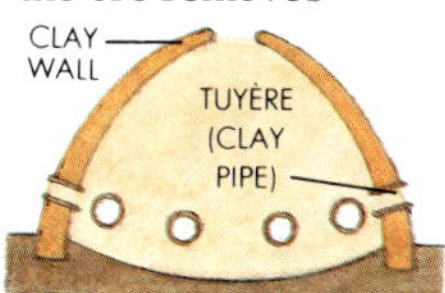

Charcoal is needed to produce iron. The nomadic Berbers in northern Africa may have traded their goods with the Nok people for charcoal, and introduced ironworking that way.

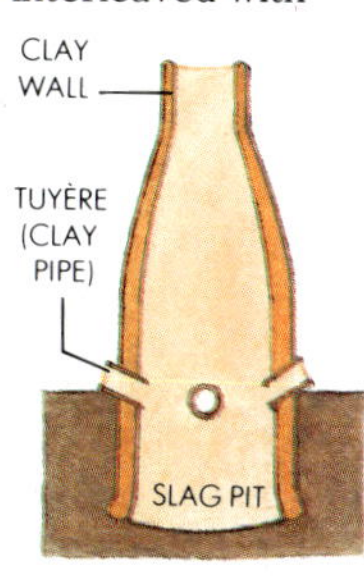

AXUM: ANCIENT KINGDOM OF ETHIOPIA

The Kingdom of Axum played an important part in the trade with Rome and with the Kushan Empire of India (see page 122) and lasted from around AD 100 to AD 1000. It was the centre of a network of trade routes.

The name Axum is first recorded in a guide for seafarers and traders written at the end of the first century AD. The author of the *Periplus Maris Erythraei*, which means 'Circumnavigation of the Erythrean Sea', was an Egyptian merchant.

THE PORT OF ADULIS The *Periplus* mentions the port of the Kingdom of Axum:

'Adulis is a large village three days' journey from Koloe, a town in the interior of the country and the chief market for ivory. From Koloe to the city of the Axumites, Axum, is another five days' journey. Here is brought all the ivory from the land beyond the Nile and from here it is taken to Adulis.'

THE IMPORT AND EXPORT TRADE IN AXUM The Kingdom of Axum, in Ethiopia on the coast of the Red Sea, was not only in an excellent position to trade with the Roman world, Arabia and India but it also had a variety of goods and produce which people wanted. The most important export was ivory from elephants' tusks, used to carve luxury items. The other exports included slaves, gold, rhinoceros horn, hippopotamus teeth and hides, monkeys and other live animals, obsidian, emeralds, tortoise shell and spices.

The Axumites imported iron, objects of precious metals, glass ointment jars from Egypt, Roman amphorae (wine and oil containers), clothes and textiles, sugar-cane, vegetable oil and spices.

THE PEOPLE OF AXUM Most of the population of Axum were farmers. They grew wheat and other cereal crops and kept herds of cattle, sheep and goats. They also had mules and asses. They hunted elephants for their tusks but also captured and trained them for their kings to use. Many were skilled in crafts such as metal-working and pottery or trades such as building.

The people were ruled by a King of Kings in Axum itself. Minor kings in charge of the smaller kingdoms around were subject to him and had to pay a yearly tax or tribute – collected from the people. The King of Axum would often collect this tribute in person.

Tall, thin standing stones, called *Stelae*, are a feature of Axum. This one is carved from a single block of granite and is over 21 m high. Stelae were carved to represent multi-storey buildings and stand over underground tombs.

Christian Axum

The Kingdom of Axum was one of the earliest states in Africa to be converted to Christianity. Two Christians called Aedesius and Frumentius were received by King Ella Amida in AD 257. Frumentius became the tutor of the crown prince, Ezana. After journeying to Alexandria, Frumentius returned to Axum as its bishop in AD 315 when Ezana was king.

Right. This elaborate gold crown, decorated with delicate metalwork and jewels, formed an important part of religious processions.

The Gods of the Axumites

The building shown below was probably a royal palace. Around it would have been public buildings including temples. The people of Axum worshipped a number of gods:

Hawbas was the moon god. Symbols of the moon and the sun can be seen on the *stelae* at Axum.

Mahrem was the supreme god. He represented war and the kings.

Astar was a representation of the planet Venus.

Ancestors were also worshipped, especially the dead kings of Axum. Stelae were often put up in their honour. Sacrifices were made to the gods, typically animals such as bulls and rams.

Remains of monumental stone buildings have been found at Axum. Archaeologists have drawn this reconstruction of one of them. The evidence they started from included: the excavated palace buildings with walls standing up to 5 m high; building construction observed in surviving churches; and descriptions from the past. One sixth century AD visitor described what he saw as 'a royal dwelling with four towers'.

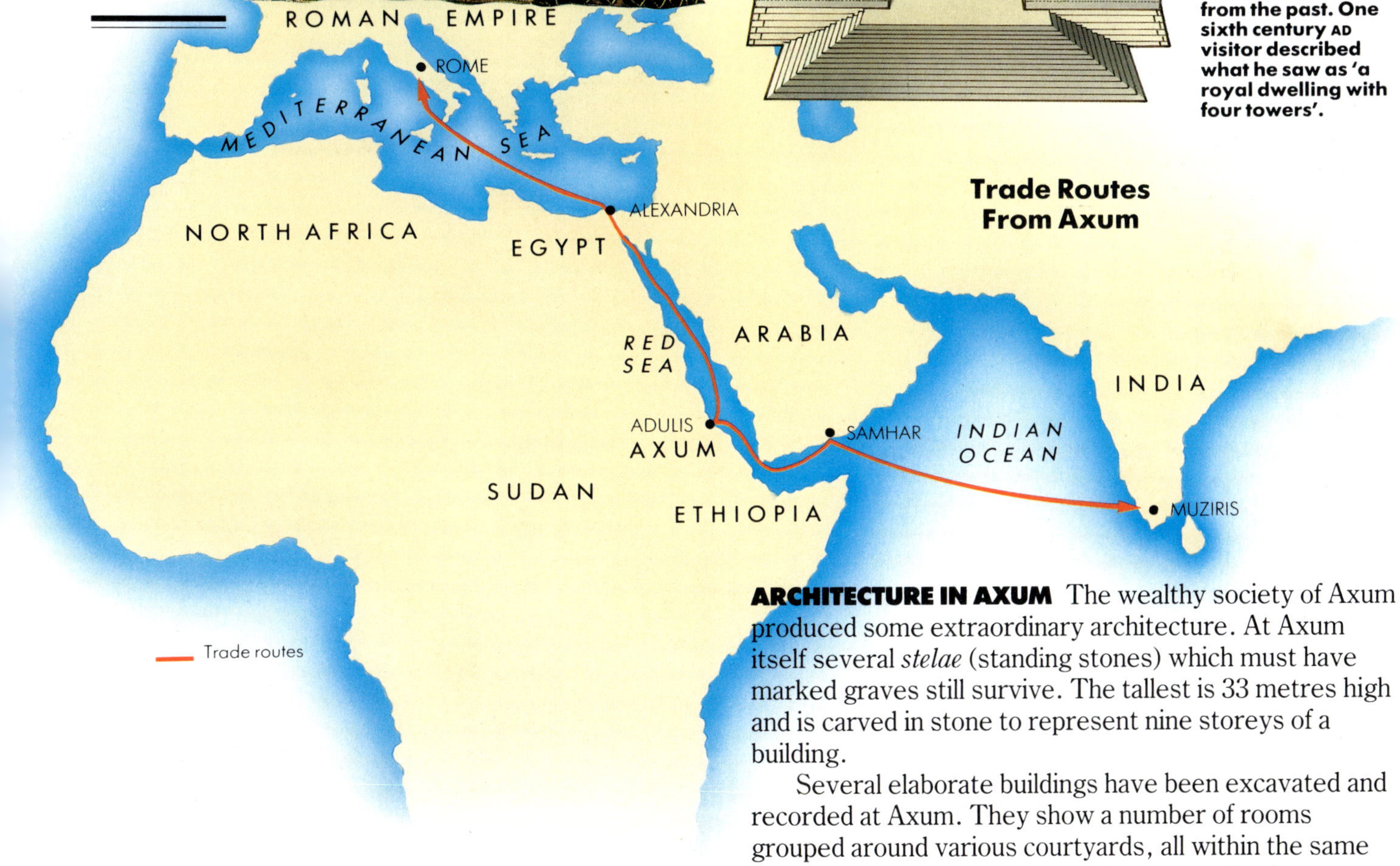

Trade Routes From Axum

ROMAN EMPIRE
ROME
MEDITERRANEAN SEA
ALEXANDRIA
NORTH AFRICA
EGYPT
ARABIA
RED SEA
ADULIS
AXUM
SAMHAR
INDIAN OCEAN
INDIA
SUDAN
ETHIOPIA
MUZIRIS

Trade routes

ARCHITECTURE IN AXUM The wealthy society of Axum produced some extraordinary architecture. At Axum itself several *stelae* (standing stones) which must have marked graves still survive. The tallest is 33 metres high and is carved in stone to represent nine storeys of a building.

Several elaborate buildings have been excavated and recorded at Axum. They show a number of rooms grouped around various courtyards, all within the same building. The skilful builders of Axum used both stone and timber in construction.

PETRA: CAPITAL OF THE NABATEANS

The peoples who lived on the eastern edges of the Roman Empire were in a good position to trade their own goods and produce. They also acted as merchants providing goods from further away for the Romans. This was especially so of the people called the Nabateans in southern Arabia.

THE NABATEANS The Nabateans were nomadic people who drove herds of animals and traded goods. They took the land south of Jerusalem from the Edomite tribe in the fourth century BC and began to settle in the valleys.

The Nabateans grew rich and powerful from their trade. They lived on the most important routes from India, the Red Sea, Egypt and Europe. They were in a position to control this trade and to impose taxes on traders who passed through their lands. They invented a special saddle for camels and became skilled in camel-back fighting.

FRANKINCENSE AND MYRRH The incense states or kingdoms along the Red Sea grew produce which could not be obtained anywhere else. Frankincense and myrrh were among the gifts offered to the child Christ and were in demand in the ancient world long before Christ's time.

Frankincense is the gum resin from a tree grown around the Red Sea and was used to burn as incense in religious ceremonies. It produces a pleasant smell when burnt. It was also used for *embalming* or preserving bodies. The Egyptians, living on the western side of the Red Sea, bought large quantities of frankincense.

Myrrh is similar to frankincense. It is also a gum resin from a tree and was also used for incense and embalming. Myrrh was also used in making perfumes and cosmetics.

Frankincense and myrrh trees were grown in large numbers in these incense states. Fields were created and irrigation systems constructed.

Nabatea and the Areas of Incense Cultivation

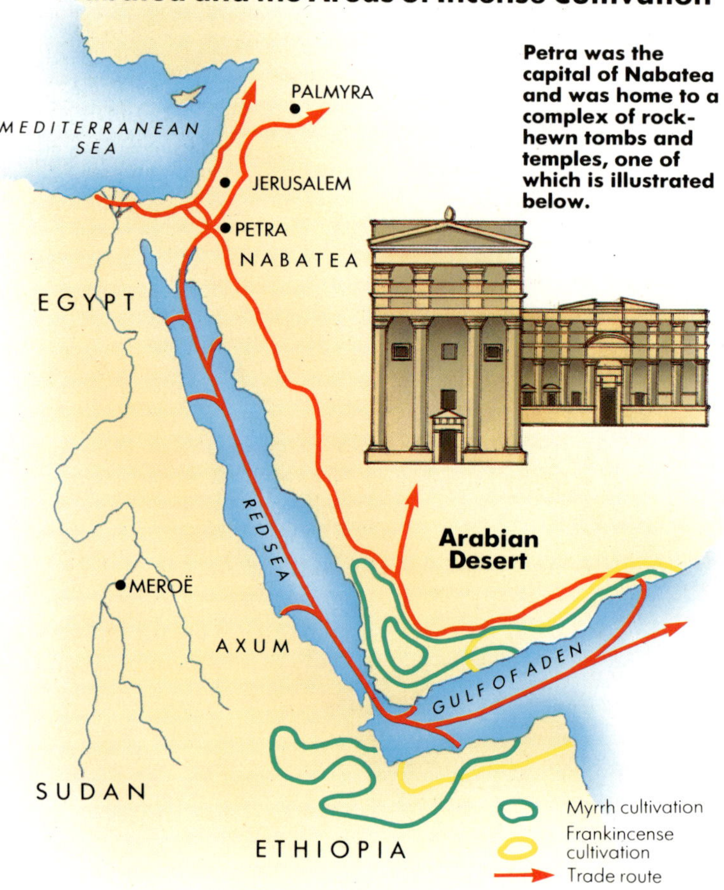

Petra was the capital of Nabatea and was home to a complex of rock-hewn tombs and temples, one of which is illustrated below.

Opposite left. **This is the Khasneh, or Treasury, built in the first century BC. Local people believed the treasure was in the urn 40 metres above ground and peppered the monument with gunshots.**

Above. The rock cut royal tombs at Petra on the cliff face of the Esh Shara mountains. Many tombs were elaborately carved.

Right. The largest rock-cut monument at Petra is called El Deir – 'The Monastery' – but is in fact an elaborate tomb built in the first century AD. The doorway measures 8 metres high, and leads to a large inner chamber.

PETRA The city of Petra was the capital of the kingdoms of the Edomites and the Nabateans. Its wealth came from its unique position on major trade routes. In the desert, but with a good water supply, the city lies in a valley between mountain ranges. It must have been a trading centre as early as the fifth century BC, but was most prosperous between 100 BC and AD 150.

The Nabateans traded with the Romans but eventually were taken over by them. The Roman General Pompey campaigned against them in 63 BC but they did not finally lose their independence until AD 106 when the Emperor Trajan made their territory the province of Arabia.

The city is famous today for its fine buildings in the middle of the desert. It was called the 'rose red city' because of the colour of the stone. It has about 4000 tombs carved into the rock cliffs which surround the city.

The World Beyond the Roman Empire

TIME CHART

	CHINA	MAURYAN KINGDOM/ KUSHAN EMPIRE	PARTHIAN AND SASSANIAN EMPIRES	AFRICA
BC				
800		Rise of cities and states in Ganges Valley		Beginnings of Nok Culture
600		16 states established. Elephants used in war		Nubian capital moves to Meroë
563		Birth of Siddartha Gautama, founder of Buddhism		
500	Cast iron first used. First coinage			
450				Iron-working from Carthage to Nigeria
403	Inter-state wars			
350	Crossbow invented			
331			Persian Empire comes to an end	
326		Alexander the Great in India		
321		Chandragupta founds Mauryan Empire		
270		Asoka takes over Mauryan throne		
240			Parthian Empire begins in northern Persia	
232		Asoka dies		
221	China unified under Ch'in Shi-huang-ti			
210	Emperor Ch'in buried			
206	Han Dynasty begins			
146				Rome destroys Carthage. West coast explored
115			Parthia controls Persia	
53			Parthia stems Roman expansion east	
AD				
50				Kingdom of Axum develops
60		Kushan Empire established		
105	First paper used			
106				Nabatean lands made a Roman province
114>6			Trajan's war with Parthians	
150	Buddhism reaches China			
200	Rise of small states. Han Dynasty threatened			
220	Han Dynasty comes to an end			
240		Empire taken over by Shapur I		
260			Roman Emperor Valerian captured by Shapur I, Sassanian king	
320		Founding of Gupta Dynasty. Kushan Empire re-established		
325				Axum destroys kingdom of Meroë
429				Vandals invade N. Africa
500		Decline of Gupta Dynasty. Huns take over Kushan Empire.		
641				Arabs conquer Egypt and invade north Africa
642			Sassanian Empire taken over by Arabs	

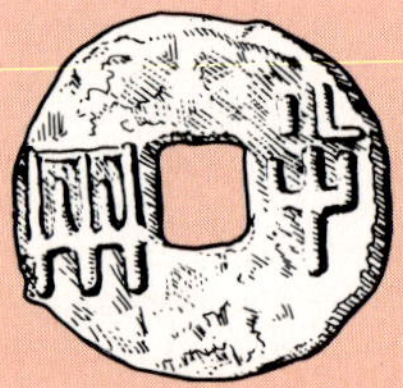

PART ONE

Europe in Confusion

The map on this page shows the way that Europe looked during the Dark Ages–and it is in Europe that the term, 'Dark Ages', is most appropriate. For many centuries the Roman Empire had ruled half of Europe as well as parts of Asia and Africa.

THE END OF THE ROMAN EMPIRE But for the tribes of the Asian steppes, and the people that they pushed in front of them, the Roman Empire was the end of a long road, and here they had to stop. This brought the Empire to an end. How did it happen? Was it just because Roman armies collapsed and tribes broke in? No, of course it was more complicated than this. The Roman Empire was held together by its administration, its roads, seaways and trade as much as by its armies. The Emperor in Rome could send instructions to his generals in Britain or Iraq by way of his official couriers on the Roman roads. Civil servants all over the empire saw that these roads were maintained, bridges built, and taxes collected to pay for it all. Food for Rome was brought in ships from as far as Egypt, and the Mediterranean was busy with traders carrying essentials and luxuries from one end of the empire to the other.

NEW PEOPLES The new peoples who took over the old Roman Empire were very different. They were small tribes, who were often at war with each other. Their aim was to carve new land for themselves out of the Empire. During the Dark Ages these tribes gradually turned into settled kingdoms.

Some swallowed up their neighbours to found larger kingdoms, like England. Others, like the Franks, who turned Roman Gaul into medieval France, became *superpowers*.

Charlemagne, the greatest of the Frankish kings, founded his *Holy Roman Empire* as a successor to the old one.

THE SPREAD OF CHRISTIANITY Religion was one of the driving forces of the age: the invading tribes were pagans, but the Christian Church survived the collapse of the Roman Empire and quickly converted them. *Missionaries* went out in all directions to preach to others, and travelled further afield until even the Vikings in Scandinavia became Christian. Between them, the Christian Church and the new kingdoms laid the foundations of modern Europe.

STIRRINGS ON THE STEPPES

Right. A circular plaque showing a yak among trees, c. 100 BC. Craftsmanship among the steppe nomads was highly developed, and a distinctive art style evolved in which wild animals, such as the yak shown here, and hunting scenes featured strongly. This plaque is made from silver and measures 13.5 cm across.

Warfare seems to have been a constant feature of steppe life. Warriors typically fought on horseback using a bow, though and lances also used. Some of the steppe nomads are known to have scalped their enemies, keeping their hair as a trophy. The steppe warriors must have appeared as a terrifying threat to the relatively settled communities of Europe, India and China which they began to invade c. 300 BC.

Imagine a flat plain as far as your eye can see, covered in grass like a great green ocean. The nearest hills are hundreds of kilometres away, and trees are very scarce. This is the steppe country, from Hungary to the north of China, 6500 kilometres of grass.

THE TRIBES OF THE STEPPES Fifteen hundred years ago, the empires of Rome and Persia were getting old; but on the steppes the tribes were young and full of life. The world was about to undergo an enormous change.

Hundreds of thousands of people, perhaps millions, lived on these plains. Some, like the *Alans*, were closely related to the Persians. Others, like the *Huns*, were much more like the Chinese, and looked very Asiatic. They spent their lives on the move: their homes were wagons pulled by oxen, sometimes with huge woollen tents on board. They depended for their livelihood on their flocks and herds, cattle, sheep and, most especially, horses. Everyone rode, men, women and children, and horses provided milk, meat and skins too.

This section of Trajan's column depicts the cavalry of the Samartians, one of the steppe tribes that attacked the Roman Empire.

THE DOMINO EFFECT This nomadic way of life was well organized; each tribe had its own land, and it moved with its animals to different areas at different times of the year. In the winter, southward to escape the cold, and in the summer, northward to follow the sprouting grass. But it would only take one tribe to break the pattern, to try to move into its neighbour's land, and the system would break down, each tribe pushing its neighbour out of the way.

Somehow, perhaps around AD 200, this had started to happen. A hundred years later it was in full swing. Perhaps there were some particularly cold winters or hot dry summers north of China, and the tribes started to push out looking for better land. In Asia, they started to move south towards Persia and India, and east into China, and the ancient civilizations started to weaken.

Others headed west, through Russia into Europe. Here, from Germany to Hungary, there was already restlessness. Tribes of Germanic people, called *Franks*, *Lombards*, *Vandals*, *Visigoths* (West Goths) and *Ostrogoths* (East Goths) were on the move themselves. For 100 years or more they had looked jealously at the rich lands of the Roman empire, separated from them by the River Rhine and the River Danube and protected by the Roman armies. They had already been raiding the Roman empire, but now as the eastern tribes pressed on them, their raids became more determined.

Owing to constant movement in search of new pasture, the steppe nomads have left very few settlement remains. As they moved from one area of good pasture to the next, some tribes mounted their woollen tents, called 'yurts', onto wagons. Teams of oxen were used to move these early 'mobile homes'.

THE OLD EMPIRES

This rock relief shows the Persian King Shapur I in triumph over the defeated Roman Emperor Valerian.

By now the Romans had ruled most of the Mediterranean area for more than 700 years. France (Gaul to the Romans) had been Roman for more than 400 years and Britain (or Britannia) for 350 years. It was an old empire and cracks were starting to show.

THE PERSIANS Further to the east in Mesopotamia (modern Iraq) and Persia (Iran) there had been civilization for over 3000 years and many empires had risen and fallen–Sumerian, Assyrian, Babylonian, Parthian. Now the Persians ruled from Iraq to Afghanistan and defended their borders with an army of heavily armed cavalry. These soldiers, archers and lancers in chain-mail shirts and steel helmets, were a match for the Romans.

The religion of the Persians was *Zoroastrianism,* named after their *prophet* Zoroaster. They worshipped the good god Ormuzd, who was constantly struggling with Ahriman, the evil one. In this way their religion and Christianity had a lot in common. But to the Zoroastrians earth, air, fire and water were sacred, and must not be polluted. To avoid polluting the earth, dead bodies were not buried, but laid out on the top of high wooden towers, to be eaten by vultures and eagles.

To the east, the Persian frontiers were menaced by the tribes of the steppes. In the west there was almost continuous war with Rome; their battlegrounds were Syria, Turkey and Iraq, where Roman and Persian armies fought and died in the deserts.

THE ROMANS Persia was not Rome's only enemy. There had been wars along the northern frontiers of the Roman Empire for many years too. Germanic tribes had

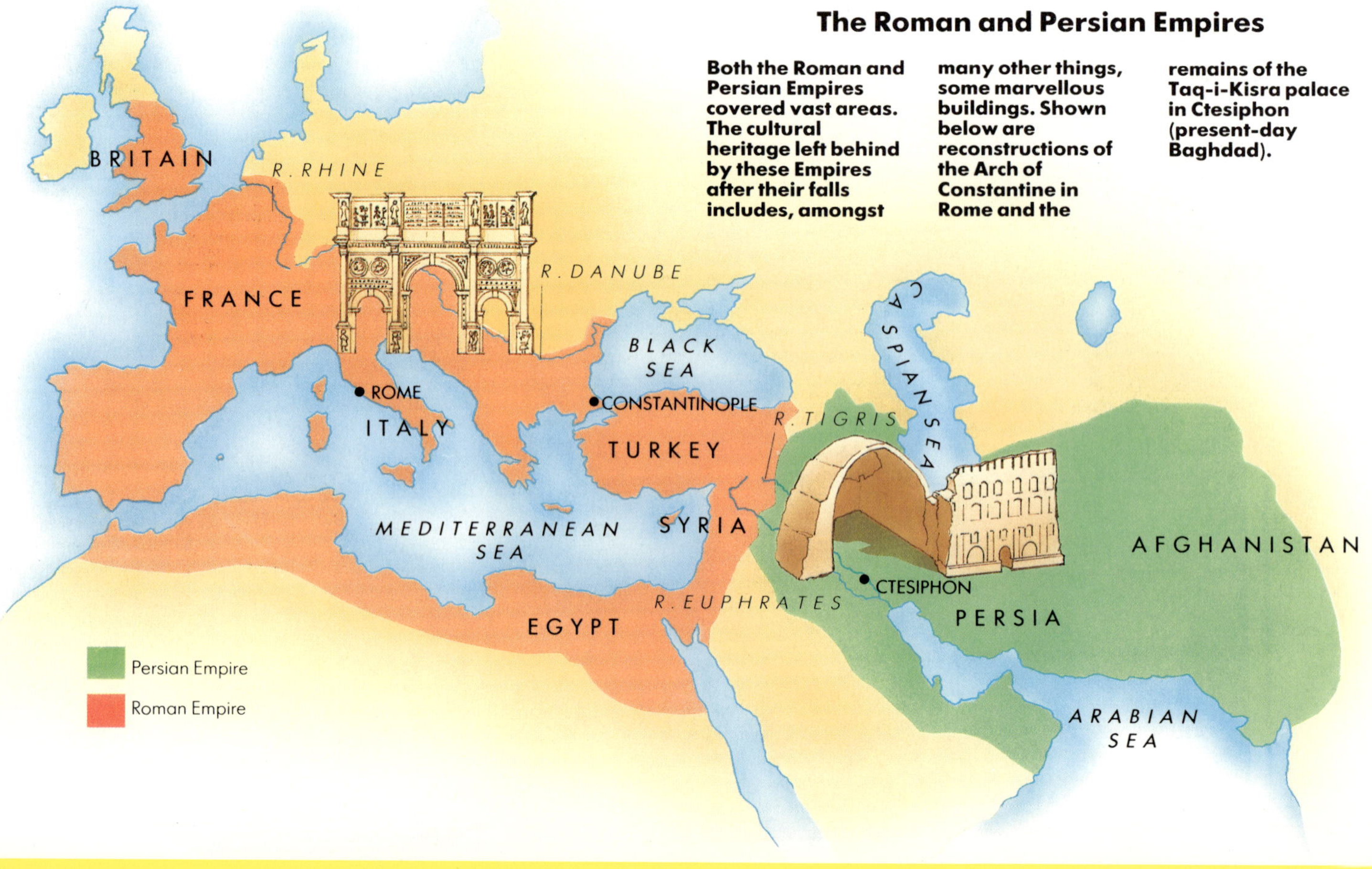

The Roman and Persian Empires

Both the Roman and Persian Empires covered vast areas. The cultural heritage left behind by these Empires after their falls includes, amongst many other things, some marvellous buildings. Shown below are reconstructions of the Arch of Constantine in Rome and the remains of the Taq-i-Kisra palace in Ctesiphon (present-day Baghdad).

BRITAIN
R. RHINE
FRANCE
R. DANUBE
BLACK SEA
ROME
CONSTANTINOPLE
ITALY
TURKEY
R. TIGRIS
CASPIAN SEA
MEDITERRANEAN SEA
SYRIA
AFGHANISTAN
CTESIPHON
R. EUPHRATES
EGYPT
PERSIA
ARABIAN SEA
Persian Empire
Roman Empire

been crossing the Rivers Rhine and Danube, that formed the empire's frontier, to burn and destroy the land. Often the results were disastrous for Rome. Refugees fled from the frontier provinces, from Austria, the Balkans, Hungary and Bulgaria (called Noricum, Illyricum, Pannonia and Moesia by the Romans). These were the areas where Rome recruited its best soldiers. In the great battles of this period, tens of thousands of soldiers died, and understandably young men were reluctant to join the army. So how could Rome recruit more troops?

The answer was found in the German tribes themselves. Many of them crossed into the empire and were settled as allies in the frontier areas. Here they provided recruits for the army, a solution which worked for some time. Gradually the tribesmen became more and more important to Rome, but they could also cause trouble.

Trouble could come from the army itself, too. Generals, in command of thousands of victorious soldiers, easily became over ambitious, and had their men declare them emperor in competition to the official ruler. So civil wars were not uncommon, and they did as much to destroy the empire as wars against invaders.

RELIGION IN THE ROMAN EMPIRE Religion was another source of trouble. In the fourth century AD Christianity became the Empire's main religion, but it was one of many varieties. Different groups had different beliefs, often about very minor details; the differences came out in riot, bloodshed and civil war.

Zoroastrianism

The central prophet of this ancient Persian religion was called Zoroaster. He probably lived around 600 BC. Zoroastrians believe that the prophet was chosen by God to receive his unique revelation. This is contained in 17 hymns, called the Gathas.

Fire is the focus of Zoroastrian rites, and many fire temples have been built, such as the one shown below. In such temples, a sacred fire is kept burning in a large vessel, sometimes as high as 2 metres. The temples are totally bare except for the fire which represents the living image of God.

1 Around AD 50, the Tiahuanaco and Huari Empires began to dominate much of the central and southern Andes in South America. Although the two civilizations were about 750 kilometres apart, they were most certainly in contact. They shared an art style and perhaps their religion. Both expanded their empires at the same time, becoming more powerful. Both civilizations had died out by AD 1000.

2 Around AD 400, the city of Jenne-jeno, situated on an island in the River Niger, began to be settled. It is the oldest known city of the Sahara Desert. The city wall, built between AD 400–800, was up to 11 metres wide and had a circumference of 2 kilometres. The city was a centre for local trade. Iron ore and grinding stones were imported, and food, especially fish and cereals, was exported to the new towns emerging on the fringes of the desert.

Key Dates

AD 260 Roman Emperor Valerian defeated by Persian King Shapur I
AD 298 30 years' peace treaty between King Narses and Emperor Galerius
AD 363 Emperor Julian invades Persia. Romans win battle of Ctesiphon
AD 364 30 years' peace treaty signed between Shapur II and Emperor Jovian
AD 527–32 War between Emperor Justinian of Byzantium and King Kavadh of Persia
AD 571–591 War between Persia and Byzantium
AD 573 Persians invade Syria
AD 603 Persians invade Byzantine Empire
AD 622 Heraclius, Emperor of Byzantium, attacks Persia
AD 626 Persians besiege Byzantium
AD 627 Byzantines invade Persia
AD 628 Peace signed between Persians and Byzantines
AD 636–642 Persian Empire falls to the Arabs

This coin of the Roman Emperor Magnus Maximus (left) and silver dish showing a typical Persian king contrast the different artistic styles of the two empires.

THE INVADERS

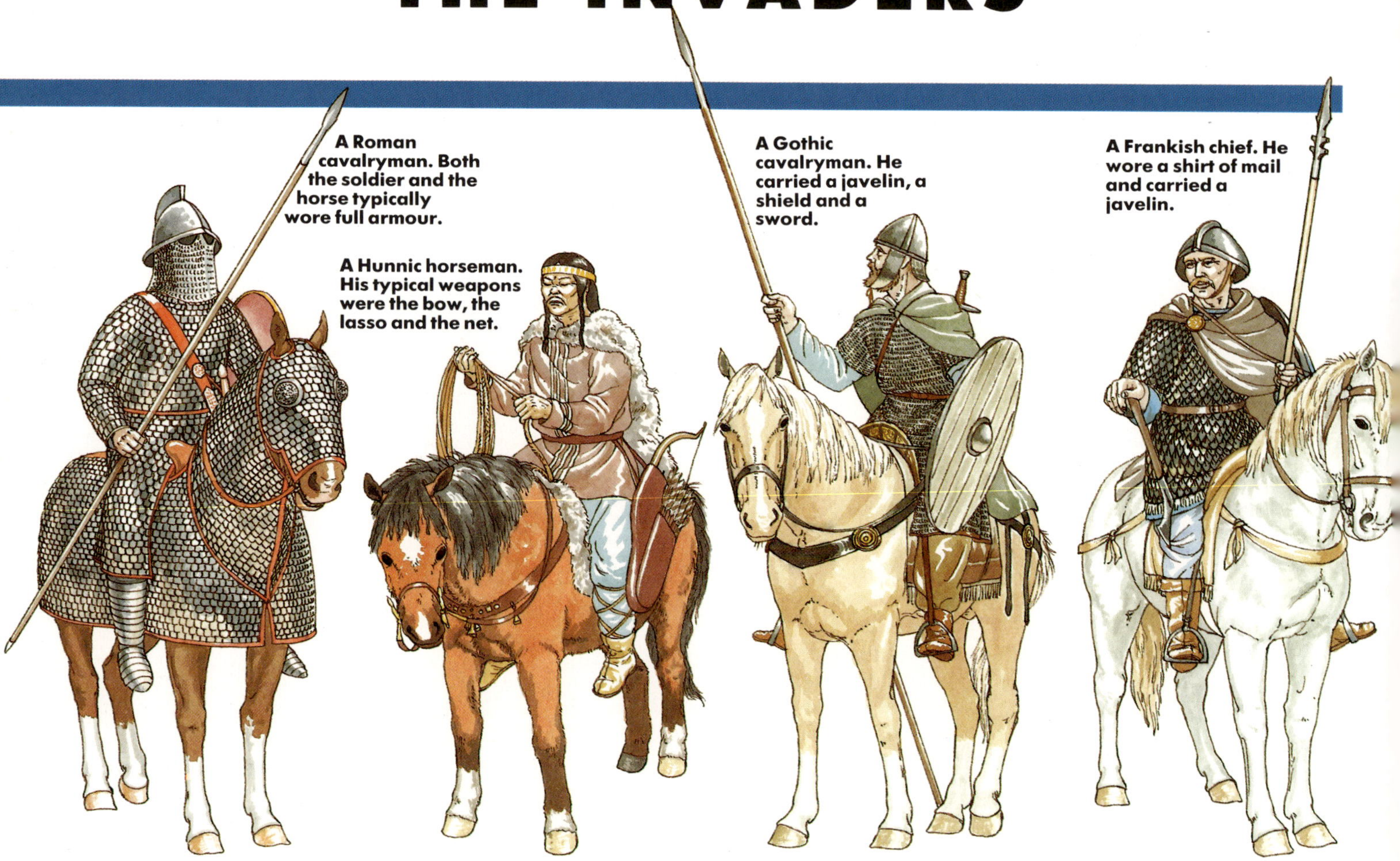

A Roman cavalryman. Both the soldier and the horse typically wore full armour.

A Hunnic horseman. His typical weapons were the bow, the lasso and the net.

A Gothic cavalryman. He carried a javelin, a shield and a sword.

A Frankish chief. He wore a shirt of mail and carried a javelin.

Armour and Weapons of the Invaders

Despite being less well-equipped, the invading armies proved to be very effective in defeating the Roman army.

The Huns, in particular, were superb horsemen and had mastered the use of the bow and arrow. To the Romans, they appeared to live on horseback: '*They are unable to put their feet on the ground: they live and sleep on their horses*', said one Roman historian.

The main weapons of the Franks and Goths were the sword and the javelin. Body armour was rarely worn, and probably only chiefs rose to it. Ordinary soldiers entered battle naked or clad only in a cloak, or in trousers. Their main means of defence was the shield. This was usually made of wood with an iron boss in the centre.

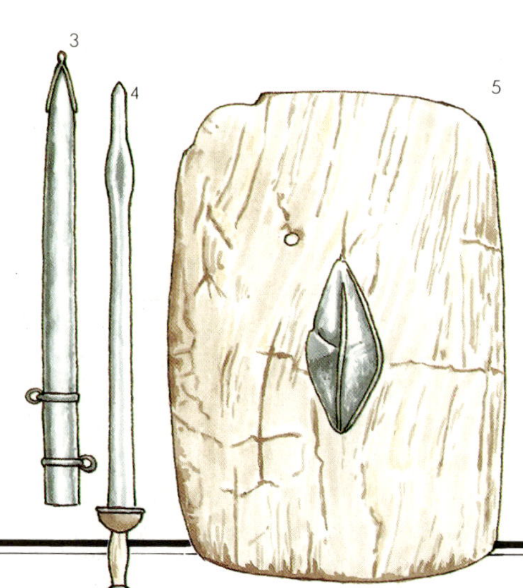

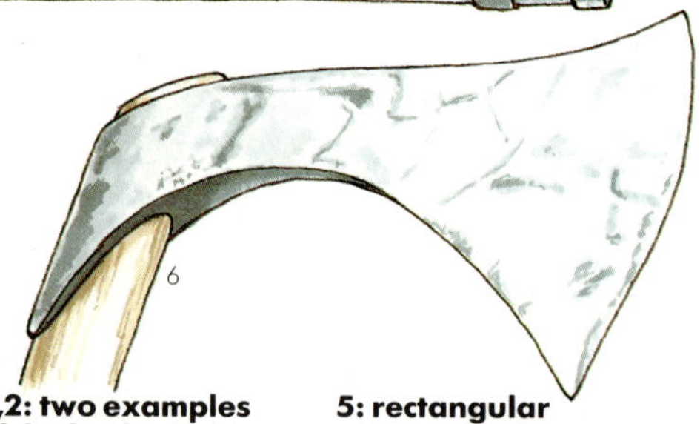

1,2: two examples of the barbed javelins used particularly by the Franks.
3,4: typical Frankish double-edged sword and sheath, fashioned after the Roman design.

5: rectangular wooden shield with a central iron boss.
6: a 'franciska', or throwing axe. Such axes would be hurled at the enemy immediately before contact, and proved extremely effective.

Some of the tribes which threatened the Roman frontiers were Christians; they had been converted by Roman missionaries. Others continued their traditional *pagan* worship. But they were all regarded by the Romans as *barbarians*. This is an interesting word, that was originally used by the Greeks to mean everyone who did not speak Greek; their language, the Greeks thought, sounded like 'ba-ba-ba'. The Romans adopted this, and to them, any people outside the empire, whether they were nomadic Huns or imperial Persians, became 'barbarians'.

INVADING THE EMPIRE Barbarians came at Rome all along the northern frontier, Franks over the Rhine and Goths, Alans and Huns across the Danube. They were very different tribes, but they shared one thing–the use of the horse for war. This had originally started with the tribes of the steppes; Huns and their relatives spent a great deal of time on the backs of their small shaggy ponies, and children learned to ride at the same time as they learned to walk.

Arts and Crafts of the Barbarians

Little survives of the craftwork of the early invading tribes. From what has been unearthed, it seems that the tribes frequently made use of artefacts looted from the Romans. There have been found, however, some beautiful pieces of metalwork and woodwork which attest to their artistic skills.

Above left. A Frankish bed, made for a boy. It is made of wood and is decorated with balusters.
Above right. A bird brooch of Frankish type.
Left. A Hunnic bronze stewpot from the fifth century AD.

DIFFERENCES IN MILITARY TACTICS For centuries the Roman army had relied on its footsoldiers, the heavily armed legionaries, but they now suffered heavy losses at the hands of Gothic and Hunnish *cavalry*. They soon learned the lesson, and by the fourth century the Roman armies had cavalry too.

In AD 378 a great battle was fought at Adrianople in Bulgaria, when the Goths wiped out most of the Roman army. It was the Gothic cavalry that made the difference. They sat in saddles, with their feet firmly anchored in stirrups, and charged with lances. It was the saddle and the stirrup, which were far superior to the equipment of the Roman cavalry, that made so much difference.

THE WARRIOR TRIBES The Roman world was divided into soldiers who fought and civilians who did not. In the barbarian tribes it was different: all free men were warriors. Chiefs and nobles had bands of young fighting men around them. These fighting men owed everything to their chief who fed and housed them and led them into battle. The richer and more warlike the chief, the more warriors he supported and the more powerful he became.

So war was a way of life in the tribes. They were restless, always seeking more plunder, more power and more land for their families and their herds.

In some ways, the barbarians seemed to have all the advantages; their cavalry was a formidable weapon, and their way of life encouraged the raiding and warfare which wore down the Roman Empire. But they learned quickly too; tribes who fought in the Roman army were quick to learn Roman tactics and methods; when the time was convenient, they turned on their old masters, and the Empire seemed powerless before them.

Left. This silver plaque from the fourth century AD depicts the Roman Emperor, Theodosius I, surrounded by German mercenary bodyguards. As the barbarians invaded the Empire, many of them joined the Roman army, as the Romans admired their fighting prowess.

AN EMPIRE DIVIDED

The Roman empire was huge: it stretched more than 6500 kilometres from Britain to Egypt and from Spain to Iraq. Even with the Roman system of roads and safe seaways it took many days to get a message from the emperor in Rome to a general on the frontier. How could an empire like that be controlled? Generals were all too easily tempted to set themselves up as emperors in revolt.

In AD 286 the Emperor Diocletian tried to solve the problem: he split his empire in two. The eastern half was to be ruled by him, from a capital at Nicomedia in Turkey. The western half was given to his co-emperor, Maximian, who ruled not from Rome but from Milan. This sort of arrangement lasted until AD 324 when Constantine I, Constantine the Great, found himself sole emperor after many years of civil war.

A NEW CAPITAL Constantine set his sons up as Caesars, or princes, to help him with the job of running the immense empire But where would the capital be? The enemies of Rome were closing in, in Persia and on the River Danube. The emperor had to be in his capital, but near enough to the theatres of war to direct operations. So, where should the capital be?

The map shows the areas of the frontiers of the Eastern and Western Roman Empires that were threatened most. The Vandals, Franks and Alans opposed the Romans in northern Europe; the Huns in central Europe; and the Persians in the east. With the fall of Rome in AD 410, the long era of Roman domination of the Mediterranean world finally came to an end.

On the Bosporus, a narrow channel that separates Europe from Asia, was the old town of Byzantium. Here were the crossroads of the Empire. Constantine dreamed up a scheme to turn this small town into the greatest city in the world. He built palaces, churches, official buildings and houses, and an immense racetrack– the *Hippodrome*. The greatest works of art of the empire were brought to adorn the new city. At its heart he set up the True Cross, the wooden cross on which Christ was said to have been crucified, brought back from Jerusalem by Constantine's mother Helena.

CONSTANTINOPLE On 11 May AD 330, after 40 days of celebrations, the new city was dedicated, with the name of Constantinople (Greek for 'the city of Constantine'– over the years this name has gradually changed to Istanbul). Carved on stone pillar was the slogan 'the new Rome'. But it was a city with a Greek name, and its people spoke Greek, so how could it be a new Rome?

The Empire had always had two official languages, Latin in Italy and the west, and Greek in the east. There was rivalry between the speakers of the two languages, and the division of the Empire recognized this. It was a division that proved good for the east, and bad for the city of Rome and the west. The Romans of the eastern empire, from the capital at Constantinople, beat back the Goths from the Danube and the Persians from the eastern frontier: the western empire fared much worse.

The Goths turned away from the east: Alaric and his tribes of Visigoths invaded Italy, while another *barbarian* army of Vandals and Alans crossed the frozen River Rhine into France. In AD 410 Alaric captured Rome, the first time that the city had fallen to barbarians for 800 years. The Goths burned and destroyed the city and then marched south. The city of Rome came back to life, but it would never again be the capital of a great empire. From now on, western Europe belonged to the Germanic tribes, and it began to take the form that lives on in modern-day Europe.

Left. A detail of the obelisk of Theodosius from Constantinople (Istanbul), showing Theodosius holding a wreath for a victorious charioteer. Theodosius was Emperor of the Eastern Empire from AD 379–395.

Above. Constantine I is portrayed here on a gold coin minted at Nicomedia in AD 335. The artist who created the image for the coin intended that Constantine should be seen looking upwards. This was so that he should appear 'as though speaking with God' as Eusebius, Constantine's biographer, records.

Right. Bust of the Emperor Diocletian found at Nicomedia. Diocletian's main reform was to divide the Empire into two. He ruled the east from Nicomedia, and Maximian ruled the west from Rome.

THE END OF THE WORLD?

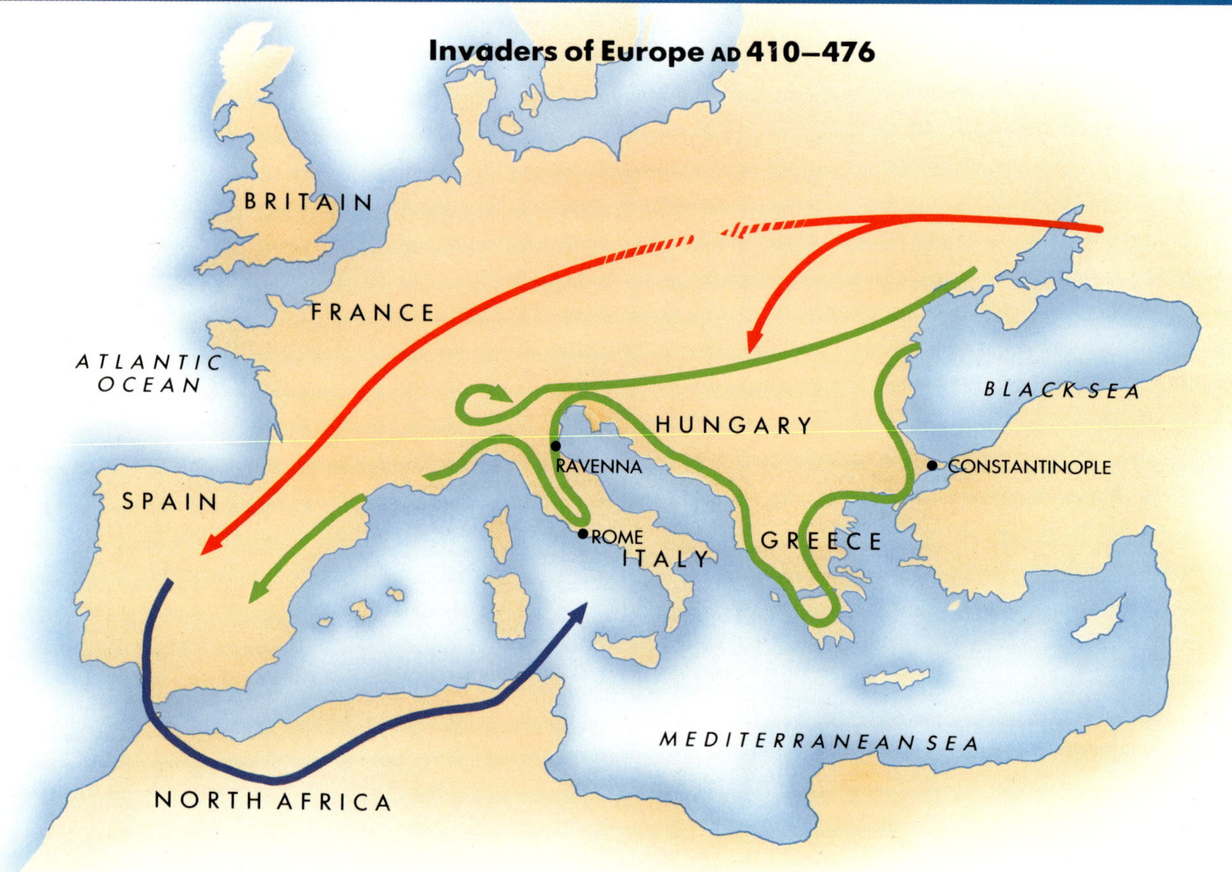

Invaders of Europe AD 410–476

BRITAIN
FRANCE
ATLANTIC OCEAN
SPAIN
HUNGARY
RAVENNA
ROME
ITALY
GREECE
CONSTANTINOPLE
BLACK SEA
MEDITERRANEAN SEA
NORTH AFRICA

Huns
Vandals
Goths

All the great civilizations of the Classical world came under pressure from the barbarian tribes of northern and central Europe, and from pastoral nomads who formed huge and mobile cavalry armies. Most affected of all, though, was the Roman Empire in the west which suffered under wave after wave of invaders. Though not shown on this map, China, Persia and India also suffered under the same onslaught, as the Huns, in particular, radiated out in all directions.

By AD 410 the frontiers of the western empire had crumbled; the Visigoths were in Italy and the Alans and Vandals had taken over France. Also in France were the Franks, tribes from Holland and North Germany who had been given land there by the Roman authorities more than 100 years before. In Britain the Roman army declared its own commander as emperor, Constantine III. He crossed the Channel, joined up with the Franks and crushed the Alans and Vandals.

But then, to make things even more confusing, the Visigoths, who had just sacked Rome, marched into the south of France and established their own kingdom there. Meanwhile the Alans and Vandals slipped into Spain. There were barbarians all over Europe.

The western Roman Empire was now comprised of Italy and parts of North Africa–a poor shadow of what it had once been. From its capital at Ravenna, supplied with corn from North Africa, it was small yet still an empire; but not for long.

In AD 429 the Vandals, 80,000 of them under their king, Gaeseric, crossed the straits of Gibraltar by ship

The Fortress of Divitia

The Fortress of Divitia, near modern-day Cologne in Germany, was built on the east bank of the River Rhine to defend the Empire against barbarian attacks. It was large enough to hold a garrison of 900 soldiers.

The Romans built 45 such fortresses on their frontiers. Despite their efforts, the barbarians still managed to go around Roman defences to attack the Empire.

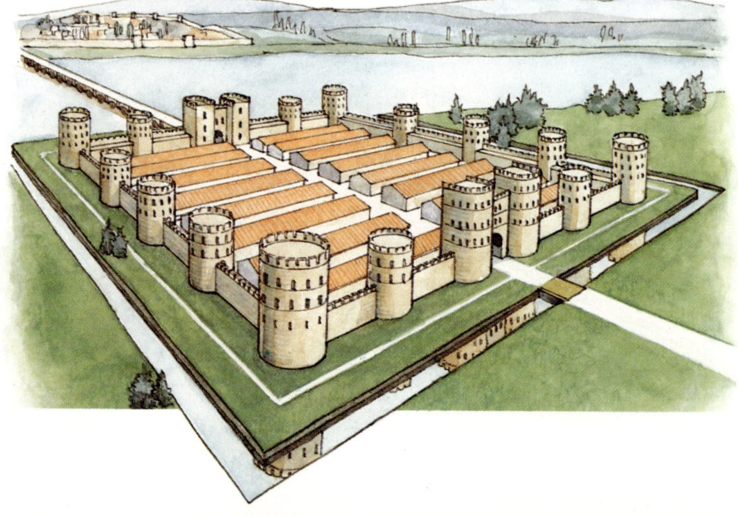

Left. A Visigothic votive crown made in the second half of the seventh century AD. It is made of gold and is inlaid with precious stones. Most of the invading tribes were converted to Christianity. This crown was made by Visigoths who had been converted to Christianity in northern Spain.

Above. A Hunnic brooch depicting a cicada from the fourth/fifth centuries AD. Such brooches were used as a sign of rank among the Huns. It is made from gold and is inlaid with precious stones.

and arrived in Africa. By AD 435 they had captured all the Roman possessions from Morocco to Tunisia. First they tightened the noose on Italy by cutting off the corn supplies, then they raided Italy itself.

ATTILA AND THE HUNS Meanwhile there was another invader at hand, the fiercest and most terrifying of all, the Huns. They had worked their way into Europe and had set themselves up in Hungary under their king Attila, whose name even today is associated with terror and savagery. In AD 451 Attila swept through France until, at the battle of Moirey, he was stopped by an extraordinary allied army–the Roman army from Ravenna, the Franks from northern France and Visigoths and Alans from the south. They had all united against the ultimate threat.

Attila was beaten off and had to retreat into Hungary. But the next year he was back, this time in Italy and threatening to destroy Rome. Only the threat of an army from Constantinople and a personal visit from Pope Leo stopped him. A few months later he was dead, and Europe could breathe easily again.

THE SACK OF ROME But Rome was far from safe. In AD 455, only three years after the Huns had been diverted, the Vandals sailed across from Africa, where they had taken control of all Roman African territories, and invaded Italy and sacked Rome. They spared the lives of the inhabitants but looted and destroyed the buildings. Even now their name is used to mean acts of wanton destruction. They soon withdrew, leaving Italy to a Roman emperor, supported by an army of German *mercenaries*. Finally in AD 476 the Roman Emperor, Romulus Augustulus, was deposed and a German king Odovocar, took over the shadow of the empire.

For centuries Rome had ruled Italy, and Italy had ruled much of the known world; now it was over. The Old World was coming to an end, but a new one was starting: there was a new 'Roman' Empire, ruled by 'Roman' emperors, in the east based at Constantinople (modern-day Istanbul). And, more important still, the German tribes that had brought Rome to its knees were creating their own states, laying the foundations of modern Europe.

WRITING, READING AND DIGGING

Much of the history we have knowledge of is due to the painstaking efforts of clergymen such as these. This ivory depicts Pope Gregory who held office from AD 590–604.

We talk confidently about wars and invasions, about the savagery of the Huns, and the destruction caused by the Vandals. But how do we know? Our memories do not reach back that far. But in a way they do.

Historians, passing down knowledge about the past from one generation to the next, give us a sort of memory. For 2500 years history has been written–by Greeks, Romans, Franks, Arabs, and all sorts of people–recording the worlds that they knew and the history behind them. These histories give us unique insights into the past.

WRITTEN HISTORY Some of their books, written out by hand and painstakingly copied by *scribes*, have survived through the centuries, many of them in the libraries of monasteries. The invention of printing made it possible to spread them all over the world. But some have been lost, burnt in fires, or just thrown away, and a part of our memory has gone.

History can also be confusing. Authors disagree with each other and leave us different versions of the same event. Also, depending on their nationality and other factors, authors can use bias in their books to give a more or less favourable version of events. So historians have to untangle a very twisted web to get to the truth. Copying has not helped; imagine that you are a scribe, copying by hand a long and badly written manuscript: you miss bits out; you make mistakes; you even change bits, or add your own comments. So there can be many versions of the same history book, each slightly different.

On top of this there were places and times when there were very few historians; this happened in the west of Europe in the fifth, sixth and seventh centuries. So this period of time has come to be called the 'Dark Ages', not because it was uncultured or backward, but because written information is scarce.

Some buildings have survived almost intact from many hundreds, even thousands, of years ago. The aqueduct of Valens, built in Istanbul (Constantinople) in the fourth century AD has survived particularly well. Large-standing structures such as this can tell us much about earlier times.

Unearthing an Anglo-Saxon Village

The pictures here show the kind of artefacts archaeologists discover, and how they can put their knowledge to use.

West Stow in Suffolk, England, was home to an Anglo-Saxon village. All the original buildings were made of wood and had thatched roofs, so little trace of them has been left behind.

Skilled archaeological excavation, however, managed to detect the trenches and holes that were dug to take the wooden posts that formed the walls of the buildings.

By digging these out again, archaeologists could tell how the buildings were constructed and were able to build accurate reconstructions.

Left. It took painstaking excavation to unearth these Anglo-Saxon foundations at West Stow. Though this may not seem to reveal much about the Anglo-Saxons to the untrained eye, archaeologists were able to piece together the whole structure and shape of the community. Such excavations tell us a great deal about the history of the 'Dark Ages'.

Far left. This bone comb was found in an Anglo-Saxon burial at West Stow. A mole had burrowed through the middle. The Anglo-Saxons must have been quite proud of their hair and their appearance.

Left. An Anglo-Saxon house at West Stow constructed on its original site. A house such as this would have accommodated one family.

Above. Near the village at West Stow was a cemetery where the villagers were buried. Several burials like this have been unearthed.

ARCHAEOLOGICAL INVESTIGATIONS So we have to look for another source, and luckily there is a very rich one–archaeology.

This is the investigation of material remains–objects that people used, the buildings that they lived in, and the remains of the sites where they lived. They might be huge, like the *aqueduct* at Constantinople, or tiny, like coins; but each one has a story to tell.

The stories about ordinary people, Roman citizens or German tribesmen, how and where they lived, what they ate, and so on, can only really come from archaeology. So digging the sites of towns, villages and farms is vital. They are lying buried, often only a few centimetres deep. They are there not because they were buried in some catastrophe, but simply because people moved away somewhere else, and the houses fell down; or they built new ones on top and buried the old.

The rubbish that they left behind, broken pieces of pottery, fragments of jewellery, even charred wood and bone, help archaeologists to put together a picture of how they lived.

Faint traces of the foundations of wooden houses, drainage ditches and pits full of rubbish have as much to tell us as the writings of ancient historians.

ANGLES, SAXONS AND JUTES

This seventh century AD Germanic carving shows Wotan, lord of the Teutonic gods. He was the god of war, and is shown here wearing a helmet and armed with shield, sword and spear.

Right. Anglo-Saxon spearheads found in England. The Saxons were known to be the cruellest of the invaders. Each band followed its war-lord and were eager to fight and die, if they must, when he died in battle.

While the Goths and the other tribes were surging over the old Roman frontiers, the people of the north were restless too.

THE PEOPLES OF NORTHERN EUROPE On the north coast of Holland and Germany lived the Frisians and Saxons, and Denmark was home to the Angles and Jutes. They were all Germanic peoples, farmers and seafarers who were intent on adventure and plunder. Summer raiding was probably part of the way of life of their men, who were farmers, sailors and soldiers at the same time.

Their raids probably started in the third century AD, when the Roman authorities built forts along the coasts of England and France–the forts of the Saxon Shore. By AD 300 the Saxons were the menace of the North Sea, and in AD 367 they crossed it in force. At the same time, tribes from Scotland and Ireland invaded Roman Britain. Much of the country was devastated. But the invaders, having plundered and destroyed, returned home.

THE URGE TO ROAM Why were the people of Denmark and Germany on the move? It was partly because they were affected by the mood of unrest all around them. But also, as we know from archaeology, living conditions at home were getting worse. Until about AD 200 the weather had been comparatively warm and dry, and farms prospered. Then a colder, wetter period set in and life became much more difficult. There seems to be evidence that the sea began to encroach more and more on the low-lying lands of northern Europe. Food would have been harder to come by; the young men looked overseas, and Britain looked a likely target.

Every year the raids became more destructive. While the Roman Empire was strong they were a nuisance, but little more. Some tribesmen were allowed

A prow from a Saxon ship.

The Saxon Invasions of Britain

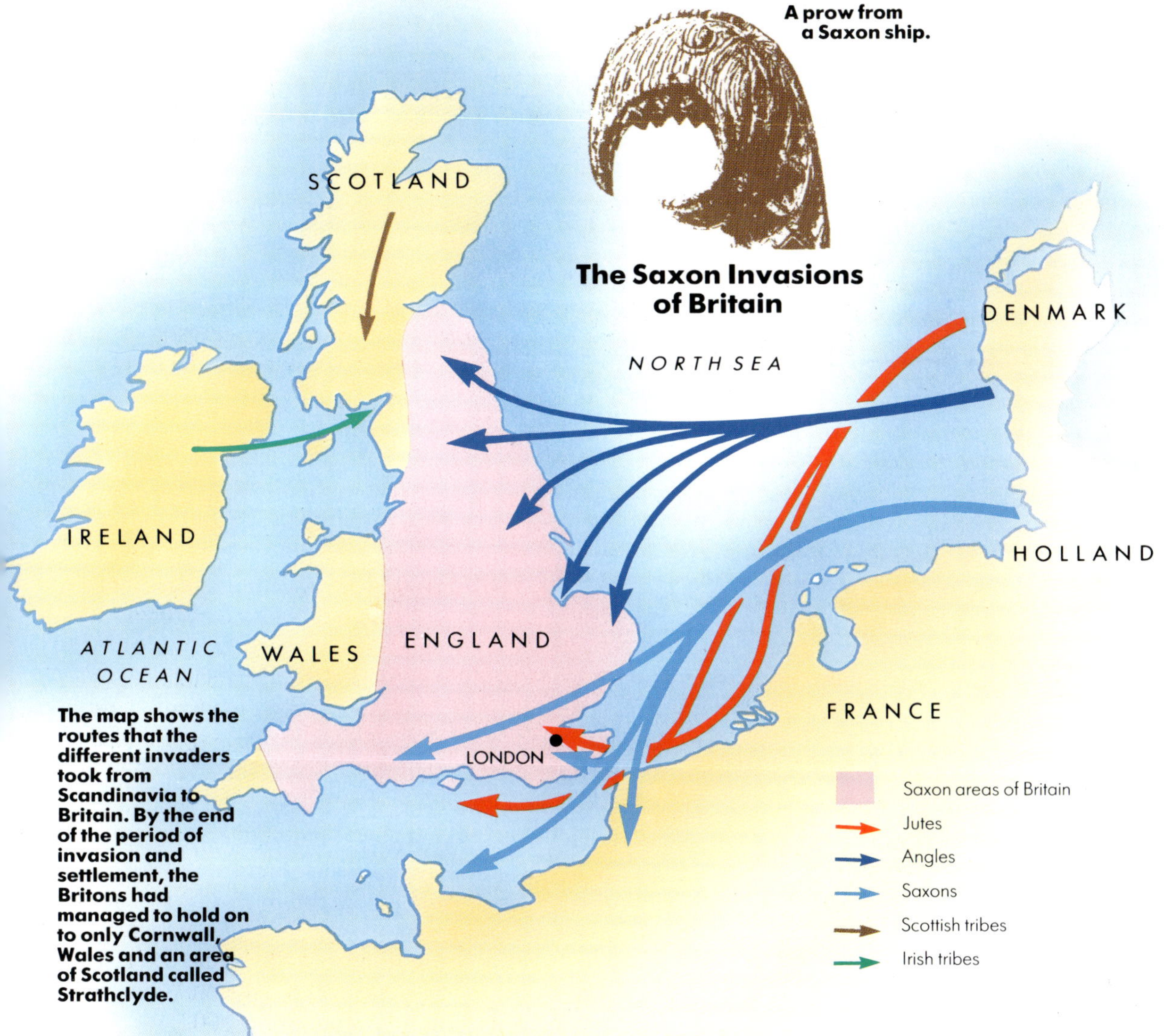

SCOTLAND
IRELAND
ATLANTIC OCEAN
WALES
ENGLAND
LONDON
NORTH SEA
DENMARK
HOLLAND
FRANCE

Saxon areas of Britain
Jutes
Angles
Saxons
Scottish tribes
Irish tribes

The map shows the routes that the different invaders took from Scandinavia to Britain. By the end of the period of invasion and settlement, the Britons had managed to hold on to only Cornwall, Wales and an area of Scotland called Strathclyde.

The New Language

With the invaders themselves came a new language. The native language of the Anglo-Saxons pushed back the language of the Britons to the Celtic fringes. In the process, it almost totally obliterated the influence of Celtic from what came to be known as 'Old English'.

Today, when using modern English, it is almost impossible to write a sentence without using Anglo-Saxon words. Basic words, such as 'the', 'is', and 'you' are Anglo-Saxon in origin. The word 'man' is a descendant of Anglo-Saxon 'mann' and 'house' is derived from 'hus'. Computer analysis of modern English has shown that the 100 most commonly used words are of Anglo-Saxon origin.

to settle in Britain as allied troops. But by AD 410 Britain was the least of the empire's worries. Goths were loose in Italy, and the Romano-Britons had to fend for themselves.

We know little of the details, but we can imagine the raiders getting bolder, and Romano-British troops retreating into the walled towns, leaving the *barbarians* to roam the countryside at will. Soon the towns, too, were captured, or were deserted as civic order collapsed. To add to all this, *plague* and famine came too.

FROM ROMANS TO ANGLO-SAXONS It took 40 or 50 years for the raiders to become settlers, so the change was gradual. By about AD 450 the Angles, Saxons and Jutes (who probably had Frisians with them) were building their farms and villages in Britain; they were the new ruling classes. But ordinary Romano-Britons survived. They simply swapped wealthy Roman bosses for new Germanic ones. They adopted the invaders' languages and customs. Roman Britain became Saxon England.

Left. This longboat, reconstructed from the remains of a boat found at Nydam in Denmark, is the kind of vessel in which the Anglo-Saxon invaders crossed to Britain. It was rowed by 14 pairs of oarsmen, and could carry a total of 30–40 warriors.

ANGLO-SAXON ENGLAND

By AD 500 the Anglo-Saxons were masters of most of eastern England, but then they met a setback. Around that year they were defeated in battle at Mons Badonicus, somewhere in the southwest of England, by a British war leader, Ambrosius Aurelianus. He was probably just one of a number of British rulers opposing them–another might well have been the legendary King Arthur. It was only a temporary setback, however, and eventually the whole country became Anglo-Saxon.

LIFE IN ENGLAND The old Roman towns, like London and St Albans, were almost deserted. A few of the old buildings were still used, but most were allowed to fall down, and the land was used for fields and gardens. It was out in the countryside that most of the new settlements appeared. These were typically farms and villages like the ones that the tribes had left behind in their homelands.

Here they grew corn and tended herds of cattle, sheep and pigs. The main houses were large timber halls, as big as barns; here the family lived in one end, and used the other end for storage and to keep animals over the winter. Nearby were smaller buildings and sheds, often with wooden floors over pit-like cellars; these were used for storage and as workshops. A pen for animals completed the farm, and nearby there might be a wooden shrine where *pagan* gods were worshipped.

All the men of the community were warriors who could be called to war by their chief. Armed with shields, spears and swords they would march to join the local king.

THE NEW KINGDOMS The settlers had broken up into a host of small states, many of them no bigger than modern English counties. The Jutes took Kent and the Isle of Wight. The Saxons established a number of kingdoms in the rest of southern England, where their names still survive–Essex (East Saxons), Middlesex (Middle Saxons), and Sussex (South Saxons).

To the north were the Angles–the Northfolk (Norfolk) and Southfolk (Suffolk) in East Anglia. There were many small Anglian kingdoms further west and north which, in the sixth century, came together as Mercia and Northumbria. It was a time of warring kings and kingdoms, each one getting the upper hand for a while, and then another taking over. It was not until the ninth century that the kings of Wessex could claim to be the kings of all England.

By now it had become 'England' (Angleland). Germanic languages were spoken almost everywhere, and Germanic laws had replaced Roman ones. The foundations of modern England were being laid.

A typical Saxon village in England had groups of single-roomed buildings for sleeping, workshops and storehouses. Each group was centred around a 'hall' or house/cow shed, such as the one shown here on the far right. There was probably one hall for each family. The whole family met and lived in their hall: uncles and aunts, brothers, sisters and slaves.

King Arthur

Few facts are known about King Arthur and today there is still great debate about whether he actually ever lived.

Even though King Arthur's existence cannot be proved, what does seem clear is that around AD 500, a leader of the Britons defeated the Anglo-Saxons.

According to legend, Arthur, the son of the British King, Uther Pendragon, was brought up in secret by the wizard Merlin. Years later he proved himself the rightful King when he alone was able to pull a sword out of a block of stone. The sword was called 'Excalibur'. Arthur's royal court was at Camelot where he was served by a company of knights. They dined at a round table and often rode away to carry out noble deeds.

Left. The Round Table in the Great Hall at Winchester was once thought to have been Arthur's table. We now know, however, that it was made in the thirteenth century.

Below. The Iron-Age hillfort at South Cadbury in Somerset is now commonly believed to have been Arthur's Camelot.

THE CELTS

Above. This ring fort at Staigue, County Kerry, Ireland, is one of the best examples of the characteristic Celtic dwellings of the Iron Age. Right. A tenth century AD Celtic stone cross.

THE CELTS IN PREHISTORY Long before the Germanic tribes swept across Europe, others had done the same. The Celts, also known as Gauls and Galatians, spread over the European continent perhaps as much as 3000 years ago. By the height of the Iron Age, between about 600 BC and the time of the Roman Empire, they covered Britain, Spain, France, south Germany, the Czech Republic and Slovakia. Also, from time to time they descended on Italy, Greece and Turkey.

They were warlike, colourful and extravagant. At the same time they were great craftsmen in iron and bronze. Their kings held splendid *barbaric* courts where *bards* regaled feasting warriors with songs and poems of magic and heroes, and with the *epic* tales of their past.

One by one the Celtic tribes fell to the Roman Empire until, by AD 100, only Ireland (where the Scots, or Scotti, lived) and the north of Scotland, home of the Picts, remained independent.

CELTIC IRELAND While their cousins in Britain took on Roman ways, the Irish carried on to develop a very special Celtic culture. Their lives, like those of the Germans, revolved around the duties that they owed to their kings. Celtic kings ruled from strongholds defended by stone walls or earth ramparts.

They carried on the old traditions, raiding the Roman Empire by descending on the west coast of Wales and England. As Roman power declined, Irish successes increased, and they founded settlements in Wales, and in Scotland where their name (Scots) was soon given to the whole country.

CONVERSION TO CHRISTIANITY It was on one of these raids, perhaps around AD 410, that a young Christian Briton called Patrick (Patricius) was captured and taken as a slave to Ireland. He escaped, but went back about AD 432 as one of the earliest Christian *missionaries*. He and his colleagues were spectacularly successful, and soon Christianity was a powerful force in Ireland.

Meanwhile, Anglo- Saxons were taking over England and Christianity was disappearing there. So it was the Irish who, in AD 563, first brought the faith back to Britain. An Irish missionary, Columba, founded a monastery on the isle of Iona, off the west coast of Scotland. Celtic Christianity spread quickly. Eventually Irish monks and their new English converts were travelling throughout western Europe, founding more monasteries abroad.

Celtic Lands AD 450–600

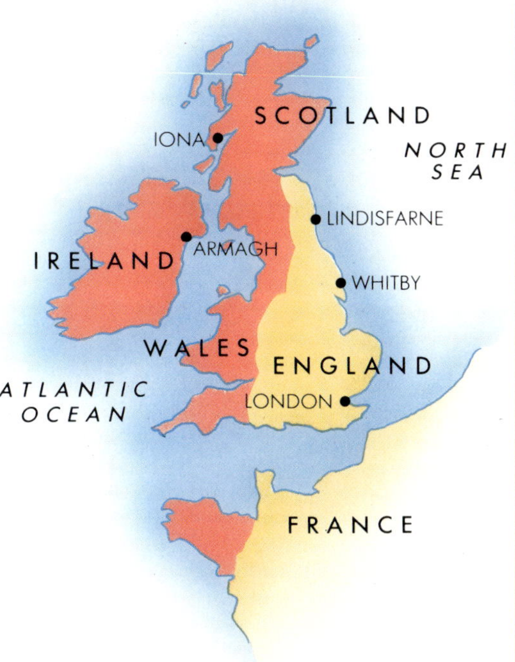

Above. By the mid-fifth century AD, the lands held by the Celts had dwindled to a very small area. Celtic communities had occupied most of western Europe during the first millennium BC. The rise of Rome and frequent invasions by European tribes had beaten the Celts back to the western extremities of the British Isles and France. Today, Celtic heritage is still very much alive in the languages and the folklore of Wales, Scotland, Ireland, and Brittany in western France.

Illuminated Manuscripts

One of the most beautiful artforms to emerge from the Dark Ages is the art of illuminated manuscripts. At a time when life was crude and harsh, when barely one man in a thousand could read or write, monks of the Celtic Church were producing beautifully written and illustrated books.

They worked in tiny unheated cells. They accepted this total lack of comfort because their books were for the glory of God and the Christian religion.

You can see from looking at this page from the Book of Kells, produced in the eighth century AD, just how intricate and fine the monks' work was.

It seems incredible that this could have been produced by hand.

A reconstruction of a typical secluded site of an Irish monastery on a distant, tiny island. Irish monks lived lives of absolute poverty and simplicity. They owned nothing and they ate, drank and spoke as little as possible.

A NEW EUROPE

This front plaque of a gilt bronze helmet, c. AD 600, shows the Lombard King, Agilulf, enthroned and surrounded by courtiers.

By AD 476, the west had settled into a number of more or less stable kingdoms. The Vandals had been established in North Africa since AD 435. The properties of the old Roman landowners there were shared out between the Vandals, but the 'Romans'–mostly Romanized Africans–ran the civil service and worked the land. They lived under Roman law, and the Vandals under Vandal law, side by side.

In Spain and the south of France, the Visigoths used a similar system. Goths were forbidden to marry into the native population and the two peoples were kept separate. Some signs of what the Romans would have called 'civilization' began to appear–the Visigothic laws were translated into Latin, for example.

The New Languages of Europe

Latin had been the official language of the Roman Empire. People throughout the Empire spoke one of two forms: educated people spoke classical Latin, and ordinary people spoke vernacular Latin.

As invaders settled into the old lands of the Empire, the vernacular Latin spoken in different areas began to be influenced by the languages of the new settlers.

The Franks and Burgundians, for example, who had settled in France, eventually influenced the language so much that by AD 800 an early form of French was being spoken. The Goths and the Lombards in Italy contributed to the emergence of the Italian language.

Other *Romance languages*–those derived from vernacular Latin–include: Spanish, Portuguese and Romanian.

CATHOLICS AND ARIANS Like the people of Roman France and Spain, the Franks were Catholics by religion. The Goths and Vandals, on the other hand, had been converted long before to a different brand of Christianity, Arianism. To the Catholics, this made them *heretics*, but at least the Franks were of the right religion. Between the Franks and the Visigoths were the Burgundians. They were Arians who quickly converted to Catholicism. This did not save them from the Franks, however, who took them over in AD 534 leaving only their name behind, in Burgundy.

THEODERIC AND ZENO In Italy, Theoderic, king of the Ostrogoths, had murdered Odovacar by treachery, and Italy joined Switzerland and the Balkans in his kingdom. This had the support of the Emperor at Constantinople, Zeno. Theoderic repaid the Emperor's support by continuing the traditions of Rome; under the Visigoths public building in the Roman style, as well as Roman arts and crafts, were encouraged.

But Zeno's support did not last long. In AD 530 an army from Constantinople landed in North Africa, defeated the Vandals and then turned on Italy. Belisarius, the Roman general, seemed about to bring Italy into the Eastern Empire, and for a while Italy was ruled from Constantinople. But this did not last long.

DEAD BUT NOT FORGOTTEN When Lombards invaded Italy from the north in AD 568, the Roman world seemed to be dead–but much of it was still remembered. The

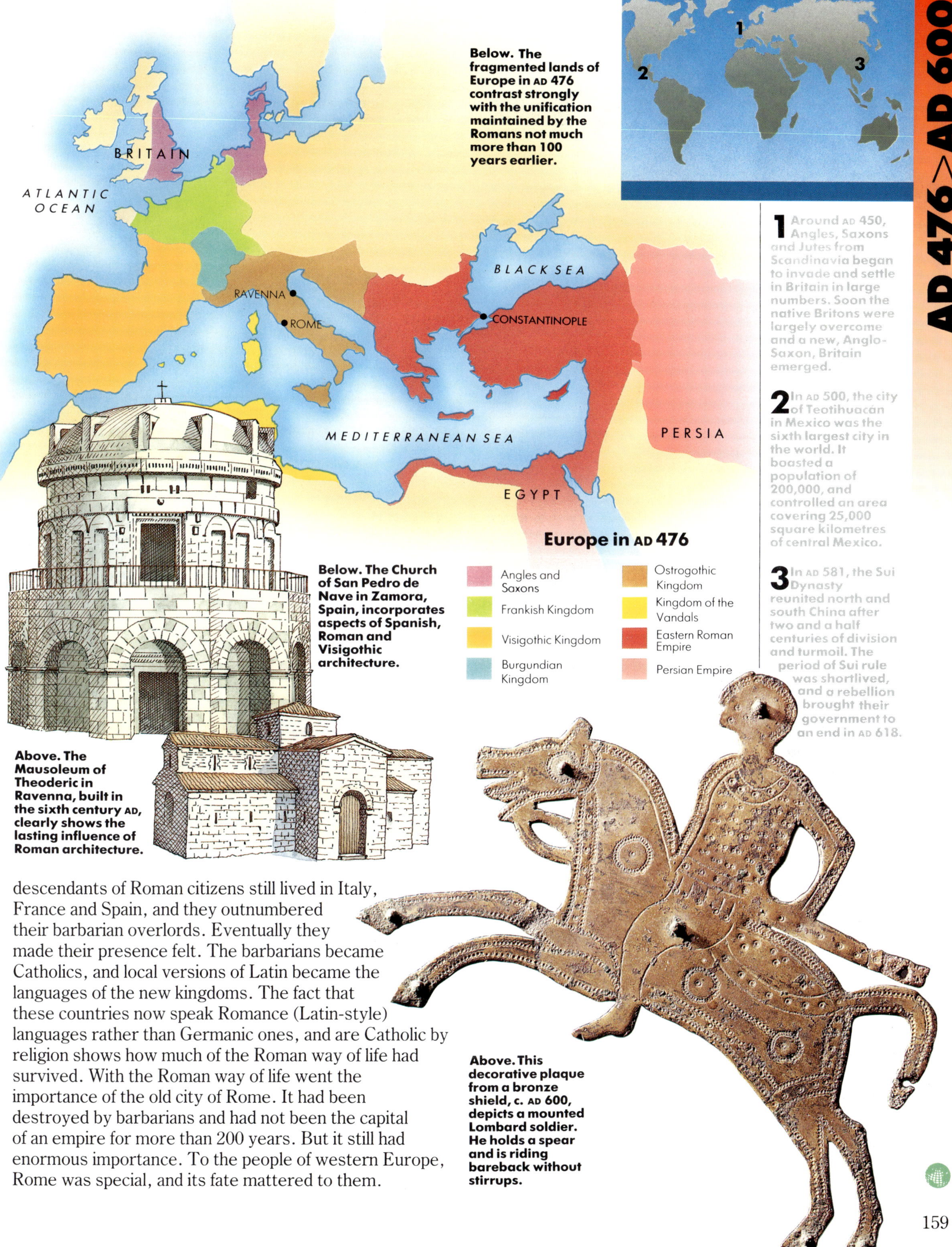

Below. The fragmented lands of Europe in AD 476 contrast strongly with the unification maintained by the Romans not much more than 100 years earlier.

AD 476>AD 600

1 Around AD 450, Angles, Saxons and Jutes from Scandinavia began to invade and settle in Britain in large numbers. Soon the native Britons were largely overcome and a new, Anglo-Saxon, Britain emerged.

2 In AD 500, the city of Teotihuacán in Mexico was the sixth largest city in the world. It boasted a population of 200,000, and controlled an area covering 25,000 square kilometres of central Mexico.

3 In AD 581, the Sui Dynasty reunited north and south China after two and a half centuries of division and turmoil. The period of Sui rule was shortlived, and a rebellion brought their government to an end in AD 618.

Below. The Church of San Pedro de Nave in Zamora, Spain, incorporates aspects of Spanish, Roman and Visigothic architecture.

Above. The Mausoleum of Theoderic in Ravenna, built in the sixth century AD, clearly shows the lasting influence of Roman architecture.

descendants of Roman citizens still lived in Italy, France and Spain, and they outnumbered their barbarian overlords. Eventually they made their presence felt. The barbarians became Catholics, and local versions of Latin became the languages of the new kingdoms. The fact that these countries now speak Romance (Latin-style) languages rather than Germanic ones, and are Catholic by religion shows how much of the Roman way of life had survived. With the Roman way of life went the importance of the old city of Rome. It had been destroyed by barbarians and had not been the capital of an empire for more than 200 years. But it still had enormous importance. To the people of western Europe, Rome was special, and its fate mattered to them.

Above. This decorative plaque from a bronze shield, c. AD 600, depicts a mounted Lombard soldier. He holds a spear and is riding bareback without stirrups.

THE CHURCH

As Irish Christianity spread southwards in Britain, Catholicism came north to meet it. In AD 597, Augustine landed in Kent, and the conversion of southern England began. It was only in England that Christianity had been submerged by *pagan* invaders.

In Italy, France and Spain all the invaders had been Christians of a sort. The Christianity of the Roman Empire survived and made sure that Roman law and Latin languages continued.

POPE GREGORY One man played an enormous part in this: Pope Gregory, who sent Augustine to England in AD 597. His efforts had also led to the conversion of the Visigoths in Spain from Arian to Catholic ways. He was a great supporter of the monks and monasteries. Their importance for the next 1000 years as centres of learning and culture is due largely to him.

Key Dates in the Spread of Christianity

AD 590–604	Gregory the Great, Pope
AD 590–615	St Columban teaching in Lombardy and Burgundy
AD 597	Benedictine monks from Rome begin mission in Kent under St Augustine of Canterbury
AD 632	Conversion of East Anglia in England begun
AD 663/664	Synod of Whitby resolves differences between English and Celtic Christianity. Roman obedience confirmed
AD 680s	St Willibrod converts the Frisians of Holland
AD 719–741	St Boniface sent from Winchester to convert Germans
AD 754	Martyrdom of St Boniface
AD 860–5	Methodius converts the Bulgarians
AD 967	Christianity introduced in Poland
AD 988/989	Beginning of conversion of Russia to Christianity
AD 995–1000	Olaf Trygvasson introduces Christianity into Norway
AD 1076	Synod of Worms: bishops depose Pope Gregory. Beginning of a power struggle between the Popes and the Holy Roman Emperor

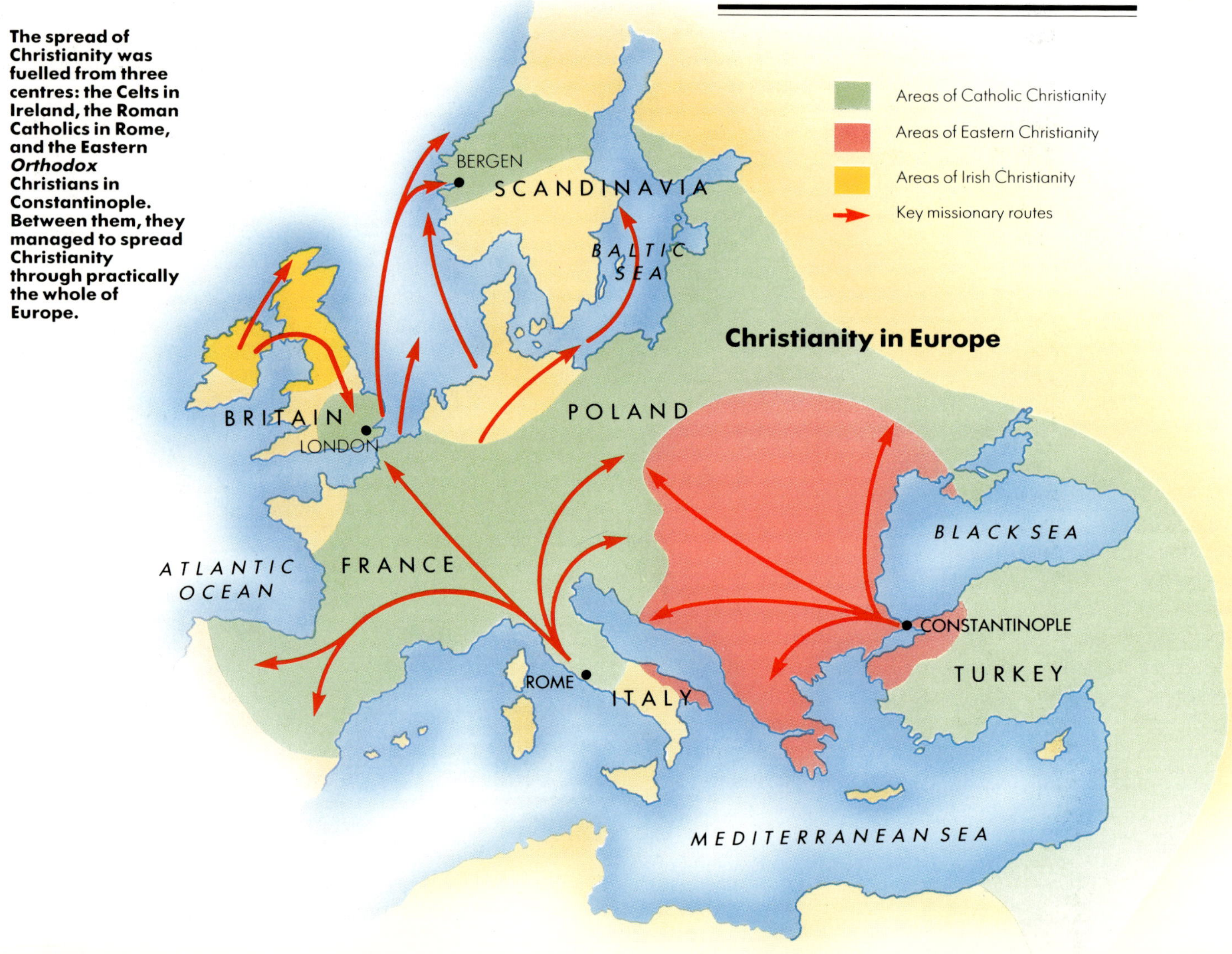

The spread of Christianity was fuelled from three centres: the Celts in Ireland, the Roman Catholics in Rome, and the Eastern *Orthodox* Christians in Constantinople. Between them, they managed to spread Christianity through practically the whole of Europe.

THE MISSIONARIES To the Catholic Church, the conversion of the *heathen* was a high priority. After the Arian *heretics* had been won over, the next targets were the tribes outside the old Roman frontiers. The monks went out on dangerous missions. St Gall, an Irishman, was one of the first, and with Frankish monks he founded monasteries in Bavaria, in South Germany.

In the AD 680s an English monk, Willibrod, converted the Frisians of Holland. It was one of his followers, Boniface, who was the most famous monk of all. From AD 719 to 741 he travelled through Germany, baptizing pagans by the thousand, closing their shrines and felling their sacred trees. He brought his new converts into the Catholic Church, recognizing the Pope as its head. It was because of men like Boniface and Gregory that the power of the Popes took hold. From now on the Pope was to be the spiritual leader of the western world.

Above. To the early Christians, conversion of the 'heathens' was a high priority. First they would send missionaries out to convert the people, then they would construct lasting structures to make sure that Christianity endured. This monastery of St Bishoi in Al Wadi El Natrun in Egypt was built for this purpose.

THE EASTERN CHURCH Constantinople sent out its missionaries too, into Asia and eastern Europe. Most famous were Cyril and his brother Methodius, who converted the Bulgarians in AD 860-5. The Bulgarians were an illiterate tribe as savage as Attila's Huns. As well as religion, Cyril gave them letters, the *Cyrillic alphabet*, which is still used in Bulgaria and Russia today.

BEYOND CONSTANTINOPLE In the world even further east, in the centuries after Christ's crucifixion, Christianity had spread south and east. In Egypt the *Coptic* church ruled, and further south the kingdom of Ethiopia was Christian too. From Syria to Persia, and even further afield, almost as far as Mongolia, there were *Nestorian* Christians. These were followers of Nestorius who had been expelled from Constantinople as a heretic. They survived in the depths of Asia for many centuries, living in peace with Muslims and *Buddhists*.

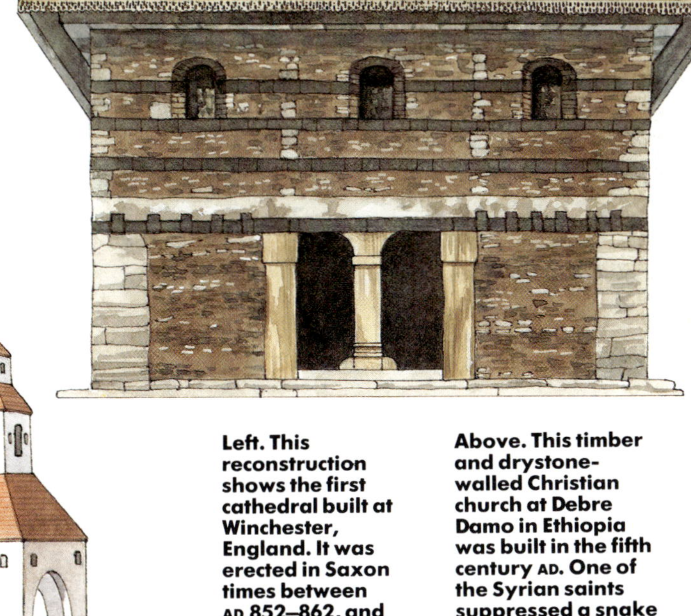

Left. This reconstruction shows the first cathedral built at Winchester, England. It was erected in Saxon times between AD 852–862, and was known as the Saxon Cathedral Church of St Swithin. It was replaced by a Norman cathedral in 1070–98.

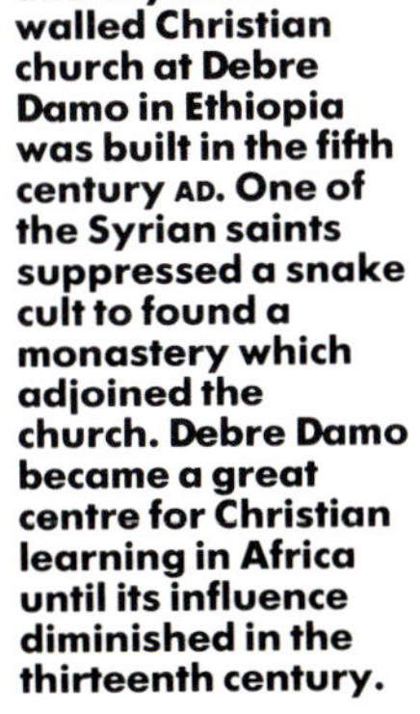

Above. This timber and drystone-walled Christian church at Debre Damo in Ethiopia was built in the fifth century AD. One of the Syrian saints suppressed a snake cult to found a monastery which adjoined the church. Debre Damo became a great centre for Christian learning in Africa until its influence diminished in the thirteenth century.

CHARLEMAGNE AND THE FRANKS

This statue of Charlemagne (centre) forms part of his tomb. It was built at Aachen in present-day Germany in AD 1215.

At the beginning of the eighth century AD, the European kingdoms looked secure: 100 years later, everything had changed. In AD 711 an Islamic army of *Moors* (the tribes of North Africa) and Arabs arose. By AD 720 they had completely overrun the Visigothic kingdom and looked set to sweep north.

At the same time, Charles, ruler of the Franks, was expanding his power to the south. In AD 732 Abd-ar-Rahman, the governor of Spain, and Charles clashed at Tours in the south of France. The Moors were defeated and the governor killed. Their advance had been stopped and Charles was given the nickname 'Martel'–Charles the Hammer.

FRANKS AND ROME Charles' son, Pepin the Short (AD 751-768), pushed on again. The Pope, ruler of the city of Rome as well as the head of the church, was under attack from the Lombards, a Germanic people who held the north of Italy. In 755 Pepin moved in, rescued the Pope and Rome, and established a special relationship between Rome and the Franks. Next he turned on the south of France and soon his realm, Francia, covered all of what is now France.

In AD 768 the crown passed to his son, Charles. Again there was trouble with the Lombards, and Charles marched across the Alps into Italy in AD 774. His victory made him King of the Franks and Lombards and, effectively, ruler of Rome.

A NEW EMPIRE Charles continued his conquests, but combined them with a sort of rough missionary work. In north Germany were the old Saxons, part of the tribe that had not gone to Britain. They were conquered and converted. In the south he took the northern part of Spain from the Moors, but not before Roland, one of his commanders, was killed at Roncevalles in the Pyrenees. This event soon become the favourite subject for songs and poems.

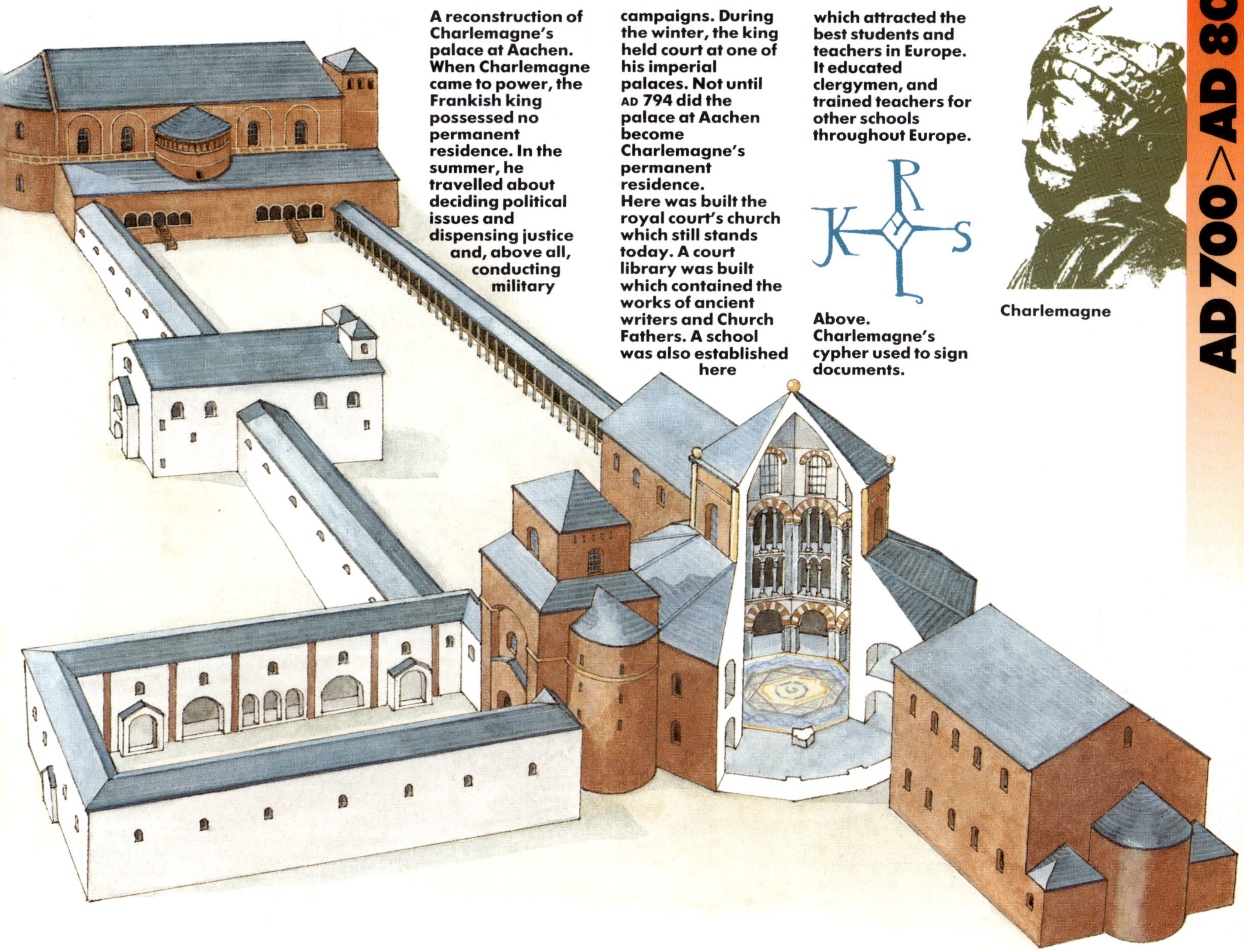

A reconstruction of Charlemagne's palace at Aachen. When Charlemagne came to power, the Frankish king possessed no permanent residence. In the summer, he travelled about deciding political issues and dispensing justice and, above all, conducting military campaigns. During the winter, the king held court at one of his imperial palaces. Not until AD 794 did the palace at Aachen become Charlemagne's permanent residence. Here was built the royal court's church which still stands today. A court library was built which contained the works of ancient writers and Church Fathers. A school was also established here which attracted the best students and teachers in Europe. It educated clergymen, and trained teachers for other schools throughout Europe.

Above. Charlemagne's cypher used to sign documents.

Charlemagne

Feudalism

In Charlemagne's time, almost all people made their living by farming. Few people had much money and the government and laws of the old Roman Empire had disappeared.

Charlemagne improved conditions by granting large estates to loyal nobles, such as dukes and counts who, in return, provided military and political services to the king.

These nobles employed ordinary people to work on their land.

Members of the church also became important members of the community.

This arrangement, called *Feudalism*, became the basic political and military system of Europe for the next 400 years.

By AD 800 Charles ruled France, the west of Germany, and the north of Italy. On Christmas day, in St Peter's Church in Rome, Pope Leo III placed a crown on his head and declared him 'the great and peace-bringing Emperor of the Romans'. Charles of Francia had become 'Charlemagne', Charles the Great, Holy Roman Emperor.

THE REIGN OF CHARLEMAGNE Under Charlemagne the Franks dominated the west of Europe. He was a great supporter of the church and he used it to encourage learning and culture. His court, travelling through the kingdom from one palace to the next, contained learned monks, like the English monk, Alcuin, and the Visigothic poet, Theodulf. Charlemagne himself could not write, yet he could understand Greek and Latin. He had the unwritten laws of his subjects collected and written. What the Roman emperors had done almost 1000 years before, he did again for his new empire.

THE VIKINGS: AT HOME AND ABROAD

Some 500 years after the Anglo-Saxons had descended on the old Roman Empire, more men of the north attacked the new Holy Roman Empire. They were *pagans*, looting and destroying Christian lands. History was repeating itself.

RAIDERS BY SEA This time they came from Norway and Denmark–the Norsemen, or Vikings. The popular picture of a Viking, a savage in a horned helmet, bent on total destruction, is picturesque, but wrong. Horned helmets had gone out of fashion 2000 years before. And although they were pirates and raiders, they were no different in this from most of the other peoples of their day. They were just better at it.

At home they were farmers and herdsmen, scratching a living from the poor land of Scandinavia. In the summers they became warriors and seamen, the most adventurous of the day.

Their longships are legendary, but we know more about them than legend: some have been preserved for more than 1000 years. One of the best known is a great ship buried in a grave at Gokstad in Norway. It was 24 metres long with a mast for the great red and white sail, and 34 oars.

THE GREAT JOURNEYS In 1893 a replica of this great ship was built, and in 28 days it safely sailed from Bergen in Norway to Newfoundland in Canada. This voyage was undertaken to prove that the legends of Viking voyages to America are more than myth.

About AD 870 they settled in Iceland, then an island almost deserted apart from a few Irish monks. In AD 982 Eirik the Red, an outlaw, settled in Greenland, cold and forbidding, but not so different from his homeland. Nineteen years later his son, Leif Eiriksson, took the next step and landed in Newfoundland. Eiriksson called this land Vinland. A present-day site at L'Anse aux Meadows is probably one of his winter camps. But there was no permanent settlement in America at this time.

VIKINGS IN THE EAST Swedish Vikings tended to travel east of their homeland. They traded first in the Baltic Sea for fur, slaves, timber and honey, and finally travelled up the great rivers of Poland and Russia. Many of them settled in towns like Novgorod and Kiev, where they were known as *Rus*. It was these Vikings who gave their name to the whole country, Russia. From here, they dragged their ships overland and sailed down the southward-flowing rivers into the Black Sea and Caspian Sea, trading and raiding as they went.

But they found other work too. Their fighting skills were well known to the eastern empire and to the Islamic world, and they were taken on as *mercenaries* there. The emperor in Constantinople was protected by the *Varangian* Guard, made up entirely of Vikings. Whether it was raiding, trading or soldiering, the Vikings were never slow to take their opportunities.

The Gods of the Vikings

The Vikings believed that the world was ruled by gods who lived in a heavenly place called Asgard. The greatest of their gods was Odin. He was the god most respected by Viking warriors, as they believed that he could give them courage, victory and wisdom.

The red-bearded Thor was the god of wind, rain and farming. Vikings believed that when he rode across the sky in his chariot drawn by goats, there was thunder and lightning. He carried a huge stone hammer, called 'Mjollnir', which legend tells us he hurled at giants and trolls.

Frey was the god of marriage and growing things. When Vikings sowed their crops, they scattered bread and poured wine or beer on the ground. This please Frey who would then make the crops grow tall and strong.

A ninth century AD stone head of Thor.

A ninth century AD stone head of Frey.

Odin is shown above on an 8-legged horse. The soapstone below features the face of Loki, a god associated with destruction.

Far right. The Vikings built fine defensive fortifications. Four fortifications such as this have been excavated in Denmark. They may have been used as either training bases or as places of refuge for soldiers.

Right. A typical Viking warrior. Their main weapons were the long-sword and the axe. Though the Vikings wore mail-shirts, some warriors, known as 'bareserks' would fight bare-chested. 'Bareserk' is the origin of the word 'berserk'.

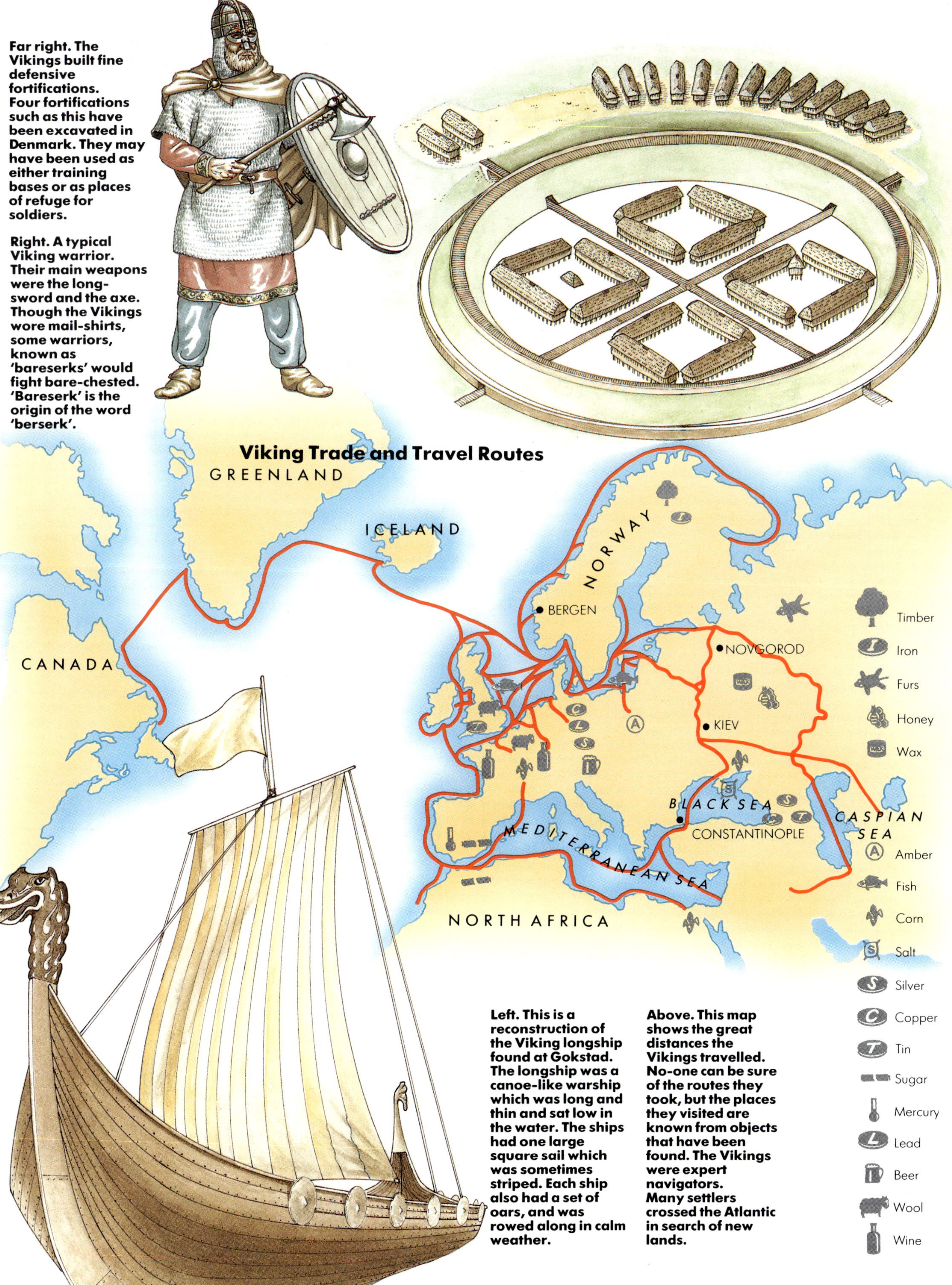

Left. This is a reconstruction of the Viking longship found at Gokstad. The longship was a canoe-like warship which was long and thin and sat low in the water. The ships had one large square sail which was sometimes striped. Each ship also had a set of oars, and was rowed along in calm weather.

Above. This map shows the great distances the Vikings travelled. No-one can be sure of the routes they took, but the places they visited are known from objects that have been found. The Vikings were expert navigators. Many settlers crossed the Atlantic in search of new lands.

THE VIKINGS: CONQUERORS AND SETTLERS

In Western Europe, the Vikings were adaptable. In the Shetlands, Orkney and the Hebrides, where there was land to be had, they settled as farmers, with piracy as a side interest, in about AD 780. Further south, where the land was richer and already densely settled, they had to take another approach–full scale invasion.

THE SCALE OF THE VIKING INVASION About AD 840 Norwegian Vikings invaded Ireland. They set up trading towns at Dublin, Waterford, Wexford, Limerick and Cork. Here, in wooden houses by the riverside ports, they traded with the Irish and the rest of Europe and went raiding from time to time.

Meanwhile the Danish Vikings were loose in the North Sea and the English Channel. In AD 793 they had pillaged the monastery of Lindisfarne, an act which shocked Christian England. Holland, Belgium and France were their prey too, and great ports like London, Dorestadt and Quentovic were destroyed. Further south they were less lucky. The *Moors* of Spain were better prepared, and in AD 844 Viking corpses hung from the palm trees of Seville and Viking heads were sent as presents to Africa.

THE INVASION OF ENGLAND In AD 862 Danish raids on England turned to invasion. The east and north of England became *Danelaw*, the Danish kingdom, but in the south, Alfred, King of Wessex, held out and pushed them back. By AD 924 much of England was English again. It was around York that the Viking power lasted longest. Here the Norsemen had a settlement like the ones in Ireland, and archaeology has turned up the smallest details of their lives.

In AD 994 the Danes were back. From fortified camps, like Trelleborg in Denmark, the armies of Svein Forkbeard and his Norwegian ally Olaf Tryggvason attacked. Only blackmail payments of mountains of silver by King Ethelred held them off. Finally Cnut (Canute) became King of England and Denmark, and the two kingdoms were one for 26 years.

NORMAN NORSEMEN The coast of France was suffering too. But in AD 911 the King of the Franks set a thief to catch thieves, and gave part of his kingdom to Rollo and his Viking band. They wanted land and the Franks wanted protection from other Vikings; it was a fair bargain. In a few years this part of France took the Norsemen's name and became Normandy. Their war leader became the Duke of Normandy and they became Christians.

As fighting men they were in demand, and they were invited to Italy in 1016 to help settle local wars. They fought and they stayed, setting themselves up in a Norman kingdom that covered southern Italy.

Fifty years later, Duke William of Normandy launched the last great Viking raid. In 1066 his army crossed the Channel to England. At the Battle of Hastings they defeated the English and William became the king of England.

'Never before has such terror appeared in Britain as we have now suffered from a pagan race, nor was it thought that such an inroad from the sea could be made. Behold the church of St Cuthbert, spattered with the blood of the priests of God, despoiled of all its ornaments; a place more venerable than all in Britain is given as a prey to pagan peoples.' Alcuin AD 793.

Left. This Viking spear is made of bronze and has a highly decorated hilt. Though not known particularly for their arts and crafts, the Vikings have left behind some beautiful artefacts. Fine weapons were greatly prized amongst Vikings, and were handed down from father to son.

Right. Contrary to popular images of Vikings in horned helmets, this carved head shows the typical plain, conical helmets that were generally worn.

Below. This is a reconstruction of what a typical Viking town probably looked like. Many of the streets would have been paved with logs. Houses varied in size and most would have had several storage huts or work places. These would all have been enclosed by a wooden fence.

The Runic Alphabet

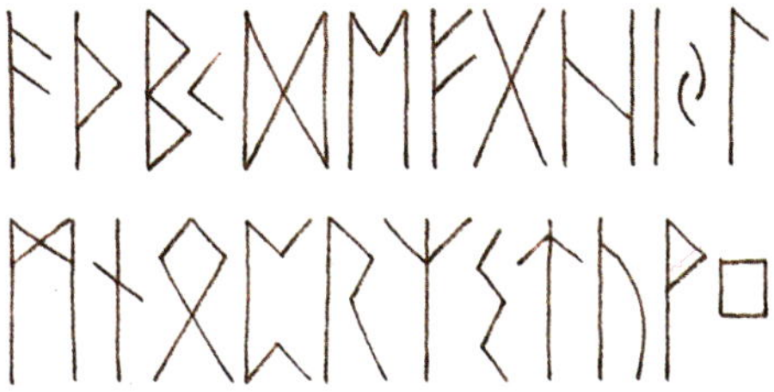

The Vikings used the Runic script. The origin of the Runic alphabet is uncertain, but probably dates from the first century BC or AD.

It is more than likely that runes had solely a monumental use. There is no certain evidence that they were ever used in a literary way–to record stories, legends or poems.

Three main varieties of the alphabet can be found on the 4000 inscriptions which have been found. The 'Old Teutonic' consisted of 24 letters. The Anglican *Futhark*, brought to Britain in the fifth and sixth centuries AD, increased the letters to 28. The alphabet was increased again to 33 letters in the ninth century AD, as the 'Old Teutonic' letters were not sufficient to represent all the old English sounds.

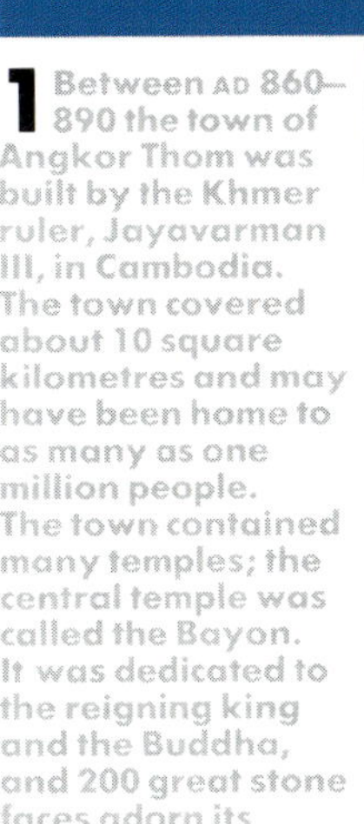

1 Between AD 860–890 the town of Angkor Thom was built by the Khmer ruler, Jayavarman III, in Cambodia. The town covered about 10 square kilometres and may have been home to as many as one million people. The town contained many temples; the central temple was called the Bayon. It was dedicated to the reigning king and the Buddha, and 200 great stone faces adorn its towers.

2 On 25 December AD 800, Charles, King of the Franks and Lombards, was pronounced Emperor of the Holy Roman Empire. This marked the first time since the fall of the Roman Empire that a ruler had emerged who was strong enough to unify Western Europe. His imperial coronation was an important sign that, after 400 years of invasions and chaos, Europe was on its way to recovery.

ARTS AND CRAFTS OF THE DARK AGES

Above. This purse lid was found in the Anglo-Saxon Sutton Hoo treasure. It is gold and is decorated with garnets and millefiori enamels.
Below. This silver brooch is typical of the intricate and fine work that Viking craftsmen produced.

From Scandinavia to Spain and from Britain to Bulgaria, the people of the Dark Ages all had their own art styles, ways of building and handicrafts. But they were all very different from the Roman ways that had gone before and which survived in the East.

MATERIALS IN USE Gold, enamel (a sort of coloured glass), and jewels were used lavishly on the most important objects. The art of the Anglo-Saxons, the Lombards and the Vikings is alive with squirming interlacing animals, in gilded bronze, gold, ivory or wood. On the other hand, the Franks, Visigoths and Vandals favoured gaudier colours and their art glows with red and green jewels and enamel on gold backgrounds.

Whatever was important at the time was lavishly decorated. Anglo-Saxon pottery urns to contain the ashes of the dead have extravagant curving or stamped decoration. The hilts of the swords were alive with gilded twisting animals twined around each other.

When Christianity took hold, time and attention were lavished on bibles and on reliquaries–boxes to hold the sacred *relics* of the saints.

Above. This beautiful gold and enamel jewel is generally thought to have been owned by Alfred the Great, a British Saxon King. A Saxon inscription around the jewel reads 'Aelfred mec heht gewyrcan' which means 'Alfred had me made'.

Above. This page from the *Lindisfarne Gospels* shows how fine the work was of the monks who toiled over these beautiful hand-made books during the Dark Ages. Many manuscripts were beautifully decorated in bright colours—often gold or silver leaf was used on the initial letters and the decoration. Such manuscripts were called 'illuminated' because they looked as if they were lit from inside.

Below. This Merovingian brooch dates from the seventh/eighth centuries AD. It is typical of the art of the European settlers who used bright jewels and enamels to decorate their jewellery.

Europe in Confusion

TIME CHART

AD	THE MEDITERRANEAN	NORTHERN EUROPE
200		Barbarian invasions begin
286	Administrative separation of the eastern and western halves of the Roman Empire	
330	Foundation of Constantinople	
378	Battle of Adrianople	Angles and Saxons raid Britain
408		The Romans leave Britain
410	Visigoths capture Rome. Western Roman Empire collapses	
432		St Patrick converts Ireland to Christianity
452	Attila and the Huns in Italy	Angles and Saxons settle in Britain
476	Last Roman Emperor deposed	
500		Villages of northern Europe abandoned due to flooding. Germanic peoples migrate eastwards and southwards
530	Byzantines invade Italy	
532	Haghia Sophia, the great domed cathedral of Constantinople, built by Justinian	
542		Bubonic plague in Europe
590	Gregory I, 'The Great', becomes Pope	
597		St Augustine in England
610	The Eastern Roman Emperor, Heraclius, Hellenizes the Empire. From now on it is known as the Byzantine Empire	
625		Sutton Hoo burial in Suffolk, England, contains grave goods from Sweden, France and Constantinople
700		Willibrod and Boniface preaching in Germany
711	Arabs invade Spain	
732		Charles Martel halts the Arab advance into Europe
751	Ravenna captured by the Lombards	
762	Abbasid capital of Baghdad founded	
800	Charlemagne becomes Holy Roman Emperor	Viking raids begin
843	Treaty of Verdun divides Holy Roman Empire into three parts	
870		Vikings in Iceland
882		Vikings set up a state in Russia, centred on Kiev
969	Fatimids conquer Egypt and found Cairo	
982		Eirik the Red settles in Greenland
1001		Leif Eiriksson travels to America

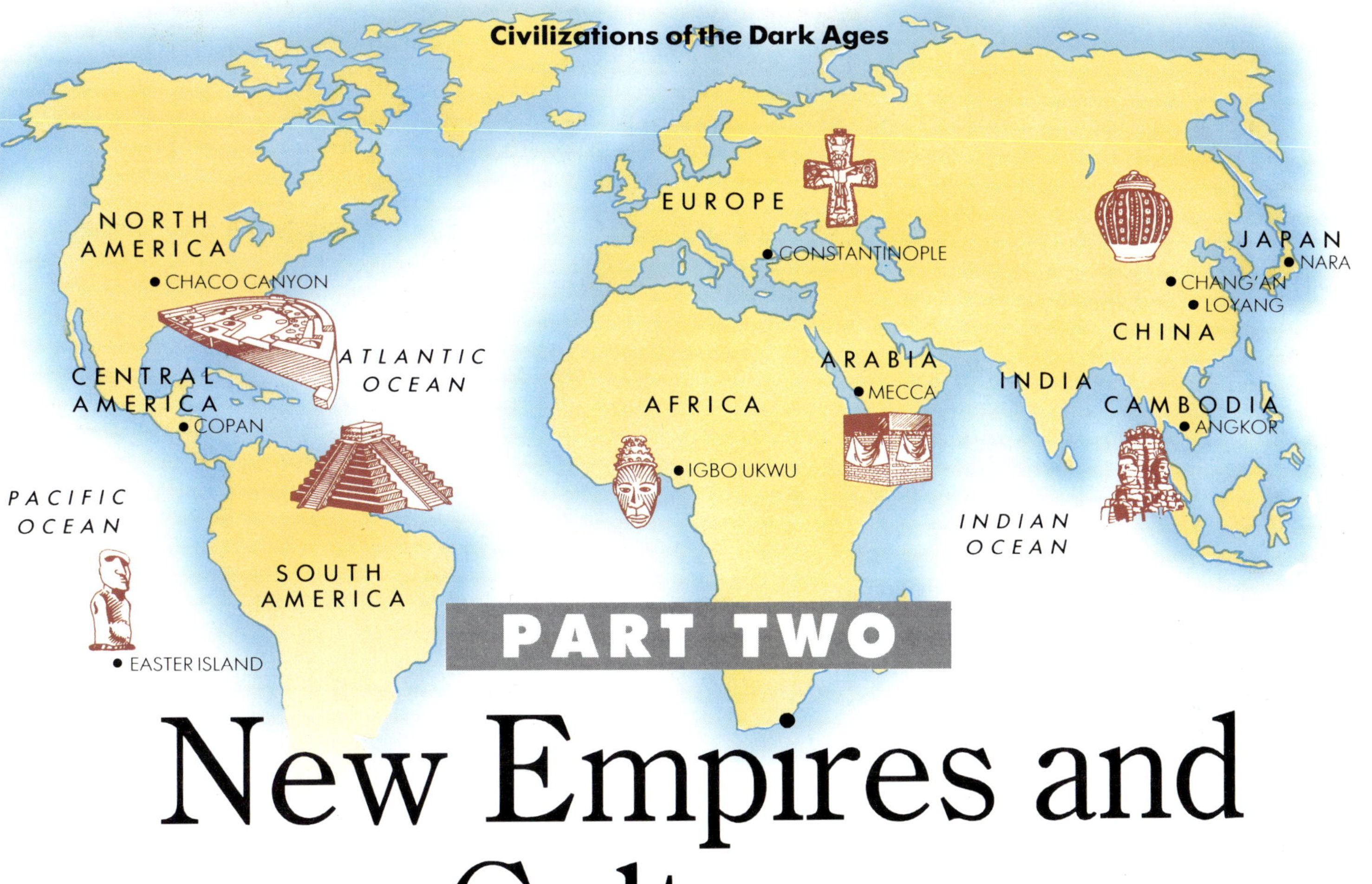

PART TWO

New Empires and Cultures

While Europe was in its 'Dark Ages', what was happening in the rest of the world? It was faring much better. In what had been the eastern part of the Roman Empire, the Byzantines ruled an empire, part-Roman and part-Greek, from Turkey to Egypt, where much of the learning of the Greeks and Romans was kept alive. But enemies were pressing in on the Byzantines all the time–first the Persians and then the Islamic Empire.

THE BIRTH OF ISLAM The founding of the religion of *Islam* was perhaps the most important event that happened in this period. Three of the world's great faiths had already been founded–Hinduism, Buddhism and Christianity. The fourth, Islam, now appeared.

In the twentieth century we all know how much power Islam wields, and how dedicated its followers are. At the beginning it was the same, or even more so. In less than 150 years Islam had spread all over the Middle East, through Persia to India in the east, and in the west along the north coast of Africa into Spain. Here Islamic Arabs, or *Moors*, were to rule until the Middle Ages. What sort of religion was it that inspired such conquests? Was it just a military machine? What was the cultural and intellectual life of Islam like? All these questions will be answered in the following pages.

EASTERN EMPIRES India and China suffered barbarian invasions like Europe, but managed to absorb them. They continued to develop glorious cultures and civilizations, spreading their own influence into Korea, Japan and Southeast Asia.

Trade flourished in this period, both by sea, from China to India and Arabia and so into Europe, and overland too. The great Silk Road, from China to the shores of the Mediterranean Sea, connected the west with the farthest countries of Asia, bringing silk, perfume and other luxury goods into Dark Age Europe.

NEW CULTURES Even further afield progress continued. Intrepid explorers from Southeast Asia made daring journeys into the unknown to settle the Polynesian islands of the Pacific Ocean. Rich civilizations and empires sprang up in Africa, and in America the huge temple-cities of the Olmecs and Maya, as ambitious and splendid as anything that Europe had ever produced, were being built in the jungle.

MEDITERRANEAN TRADE

The Roman Empire had lived on its trade. Great cities like Rome, Carthage in North Africa, Alexandria in Egypt, Antioch in Syria and Constantinople at the crossroads of Europe and Asia, had been the centres of great networks. Goods flooded in to them from inside and outside the Empire. They were bought, sold and shipped on. The end of the Roman Empire did not mean the end of the trade, but with so many kingdoms on the north side of the Mediterranean it became more complicated. Each one had its own rules and levied its own taxes, thus trade became more expensive.

ISLAMIC EMPIRE But after the seventh century AD the south side of the Mediterranean was held together by the Islamic Empire, which protected and promoted trade just as the Romans had done. Much of the trade here was in the hands of Jewish merchants, who could pass freely from one end of the empire to the other, always able to speak their own language to brother merchants, always sure of a friendly reception wherever they went.

These ancient *amphorae* were found in Turkey. Goods such as oil and wine would have been transported in amphorae like these throughout the Mediterranean.

THE NORTH AFRICAN ROUTE A new trade route grew up from Spain to Asia, along the north coast of Africa, and new cities like Tunis and Kairouan grew up to serve it. The sea was still the cheapest means of transport. A shipload of goods took 30 days to travel from Alexandria to Marseilles in France, but ships could only sail between April and October for fear of storms.

In North Africa, trade goods were mostly carried by camels. *Caravans* of camels had been crossing North Africa ever since the Roman period, and under the Arabs they carried wine, salt, oil and European goods eastwards, and eastern luxuries westwards.

THE NORTH European trade came into the system by several routes. Some from the North Sea area went to ports like London, Dorestad and Quentovic and then by sea to Spain. Another route led up the French rivers and overland to the Alps.

From the Alps, trade routes from all over Europe converged on Italy. At the head of the Adriatic Sea, a small city was beginning to build up a trading empire. This was Venice, and soon it had a firm grip on trade links with the Islamic world. Frankish swords, furs, tin, lead, wax, honey and timber were all shipped south out of Venice. But one other trade was even more important–the slave trade to Byzantium and the cities of the East. Many of these slaves were Slavs from eastern Europe who were often prisoners of war. The word 'slave' is the same as the word 'Slav'—which shows how many Slavs must have been bought and sold.

The trade from Venice connected into the main east-west trade route. The details had changed since the Roman period, but the Mediterranean market still thrived and lived on.

Though this is a modern-day caravan, carrying salt from Niger in Africa, the caravans transporting goods in the Dark Ages period probably looked little different.

This map gives a strong sense of the distances covered for trading purposes, and the variety of goods that were in demand.

Left. A typical Byzantine cargo ship. Such ships had to be wide and deep, in comparison to the narrow boats used for warfare, so that more trade goods could be stored in the hold.

FROM CONSTANTINOPLE TO BYZANTIUM

This thirteenth century Greek manuscript shows the Byzantines using the chemical weapon known as Greek Fire against the Arabs.

While the Western Roman Empire was changing into the new kingdoms of Europe, life in the east was very different.

ROMAN OR GREEK In the fifth century AD, Constantinople ruled an empire of Greece, the Balkans, Romania, Bulgaria, Turkey, Syria, Israel, Egypt and Lybia. Even in the heyday of Rome these countries had been as much Greek as Roman, and in a century or so after the decline of the Roman Empire, there was little Roman about them at all. To outsiders the empire of Constantinople was peopled by 'Greeks'. We refer to the empire as 'Byzantine', after the name of the original Greek city, Byzantium, which the Roman Emperor Constantine had rebuilt and renamed after himself–Constantinople.

THE EMPIRE LIVES ON The Byzantine Empire lasted a thousand years longer than the Roman one, until AD 1453. How was this achieved? It was attacked from the outside many times. In AD 441 and AD 447 Huns plundered the whole of Greece; in the AD 460s and AD 470s the Ostrogoths were as much of a threat. Even when Zeno, the Byzantine Emperor, distracted the Huns by sending them to attack Italy in his name, and so took the pressure off Byzantium, the Avars and the Bulgars replaced them and menaced the Byzantine Empire for centuries after.

PERSIANS AND ARABS In the east the great threat was Persia. Warfare between the Persians and Byzantines across the deserts of Syria and Iraq lasted, on and off, until Persia was conquered by the Arabs in AD 648. At the same time, the Arabs took Lybia, Syria and Israel from the Byzantines. Even worse than this, the Arabs took control of Egypt, where most of the food supplies of Constantinople came from.

So great were the Empire's losses that by AD 700 it was only a shadow of what it had formerly been, covering little more territory than Turkey and Greece. But still it survived.

THE BYZANTINE NAVY Part of the reason for its survival was its sea power. The Byzantine navy was the most powerful of its day, and was equipped with a horrific chemical weapon known as Greek Fire. This was a mixture of pitch, naphtha and sulphur which could be shot, like a flame thrower, at enemy fleets. It could just as easily be packed into pottery bombs–the earliest form of hand grenades.

THE WALLS OF CONSTANTINOPLE The city of Constantinople was magnificently defended: even when enemies conquered Greece or Turkey, the city remained intact behind its immense walls, resisting attack like a rock in the ocean. In AD 626 it held out against a combined attack by Avars from Greece, and Arabs who had invaded Turkey.

Every year from AD 674 to AD 677 it was attacked and besieged by Arabs, and one year the siege lasted more than a year. But still the city survived, defended by its fleet and by its army, many of whom were *Varangians*–Vikings from Scandinavia and Russia. For the last few centuries the Byzantine Empire steadily shrank, but from time to time a warrior-emperor like Basil II would arise and reconquer some of its old land.

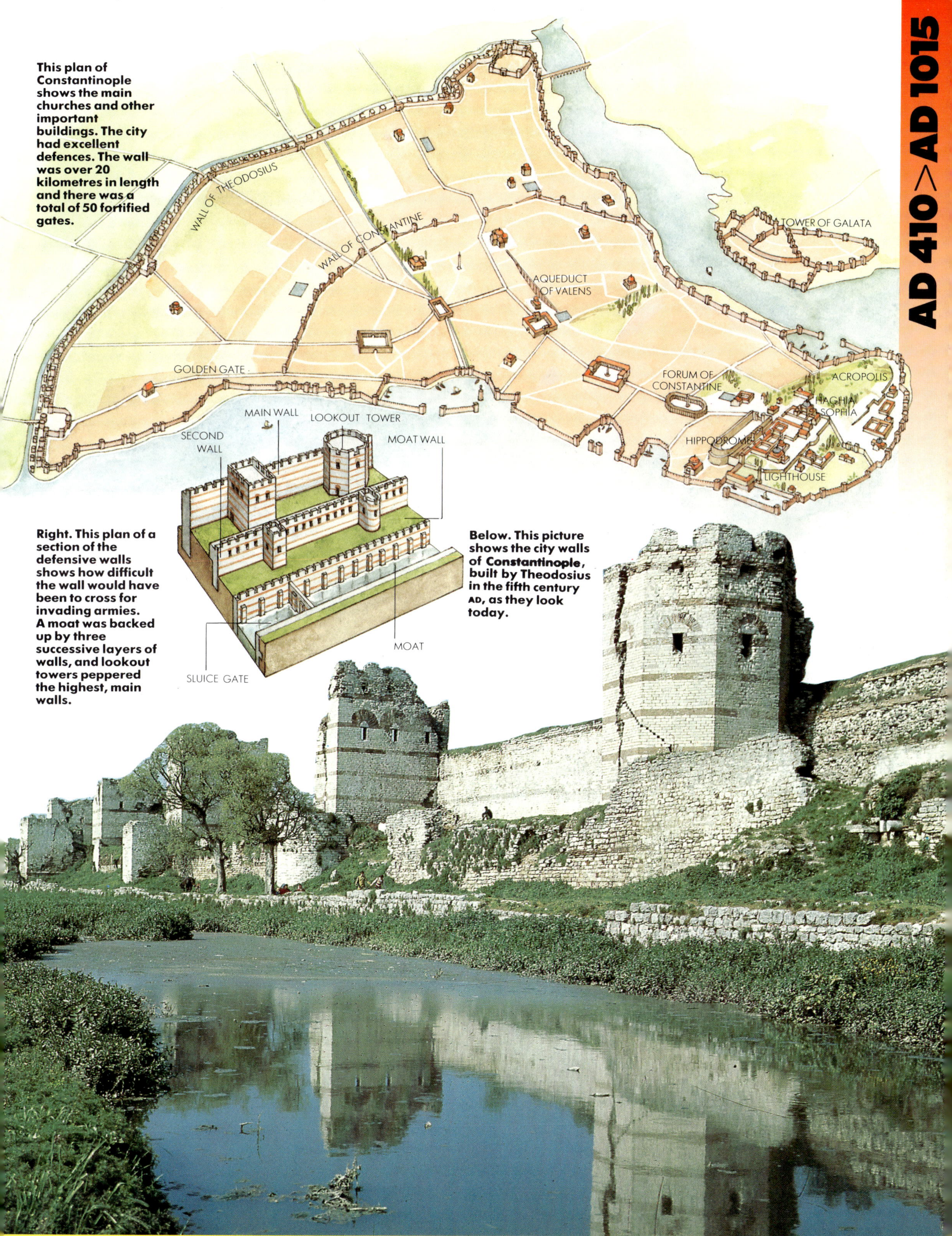

This plan of Constantinople shows the main churches and other important buildings. The city had excellent defences. The wall was over 20 kilometres in length and there was a total of 50 fortified gates.

Right. This plan of a section of the defensive walls shows how difficult the wall would have been to cross for invading armies. A moat was backed up by three successive layers of walls, and lookout towers peppered the highest, main walls.

Below. This picture shows the city walls of Constantinople, built by Theodosius in the fifth century AD, as they look today.

BYZANTINE ART AND CULTURE

Above. The Church of Haghia Sophia at Istanbul (Constantinople) as it appears today. The Emperor Justinian began its construction in AD 532. The church towered over all other buildings in the city. Its interior measures 30 metres wide and 60 metres high, and, when built, was the largest of any church in Europe.

When we look at what the Byzantines left behind them, it is easy to see what they thought was important. Their art and their buildings tell us a great deal.

LIVING ON THE LAND Outside the great cities, the Byzantines were farmers, like the Romans before them. Peasants grew corn, grapes and olives, and looked after flocks of sheep and goats. Rich landowners adorned with gold jewellery toured their estates supervising the work, and lived in luxury.

IMPERIAL MAJESTY At the centre of the Byzantine world was the Emperor: his face and figure were shown in art and on coins in the way that he wanted it to be seen. So the Emperor Anastasius, shown on an ivory panel as a young soldier receiving ambassadors from India, was actually about 70 at the time that the panel was created. It was important in the Byzantine world to create an image of power and youthfulness.

Left. This Byzantine ivory diptych depicts men fighting bears at the games, watched by the court. It dates from the fifth century AD.

The Art of Mosaic

Above. This is a detail of the mosaic shown opposite, enlarged. You can see the great skill that is involved in creating mosaics.

Mosaics were first used for decoration by the Ancient Greeks, but it was the Romans who developed the art of mosaic extensively.

Influenced by Roman artforms, the Byzantines went on to create some of the finest mosaics ever produced.

Mosaics of religious scenes were used to decorate the walls and ceilings of many Byzantine churches. Craftsmen used *tesserae* (the pieces from which the mosaic was formed) of gold, silver, glass, stone and terracotta to produce some breathtaking effects.

Above. A detail of a floor mosaic in the Great Palace at Istanbul, c. AD 565. Byzantine mosaics featured a wide variety of subject matter, from simple scenes such as this man feeding his donkey, to depictions of Jesus Christ.

Right. This ninth century AD cross is a very fine example of Byzantine craftsmanship in enamel.

CHRISTIAN GLORY The splendour of the emperors was matched by the glory of the Church. Monasteries and churches of the Byzantine Empire, which we would now call Greek Orthodox, were beautiful places. Where the treasures and furnishings have survived years of looting by Turks, Vikings and other Christians, they are astonishingly rich. The Church of Haghia Sophia marked a pinnacle of Byzantine architecture. This beautiful building towered over the city at the height of the Empire and was the largest of any church in Europe.

Byzantine ideas rubbed off onto neighbouring lands, too. Barbarian tribes like Slavs, Bulgars and Avars who attacked or traded with the Byzantines borrowed much from them, including their language, writing and art. The new barbarian art was often as beautiful as anything that the Empire itself could produce.

JUSTINIAN AND THEODORA

Above. This mosaic from the Basilica of San Vitale in Ravenna depicts the Emperor Justinian (crowned) and his court.
Left. The Empress Theodora from a mosaic accompanying the one above in the Basilica of San Vitale. Both mosaics date from the sixth century AD.

Of all the characters of the Byzantine Empire, the most colourful are the Emperor Justinian and his Empress Theodora. In their reign the empire reached its greatest extent and saw its most stirring times.

PEASANT EMPERORS Justinian's uncle, Justin, a peasant from Bulgaria who had made his name as a soldier, was made Emperor by the army in AD 518. Because he was uneducated and illiterate, his nephew acted as the power behind the throne. When Justin died, Justinian replaced him as Emperor with his wife becoming Empress.

Theodora was ambitious and determined to wield power in the Empire. The portraits of these two characters, in the mosaics of Ravenna, show them as imperial rulers, bedecked with finery.

RIOTS IN THE HIPPODROME The first crisis during their period of rule occurred in AD 532. Chariot racing in the *hippodrome* (the racecourse) was a national craze.

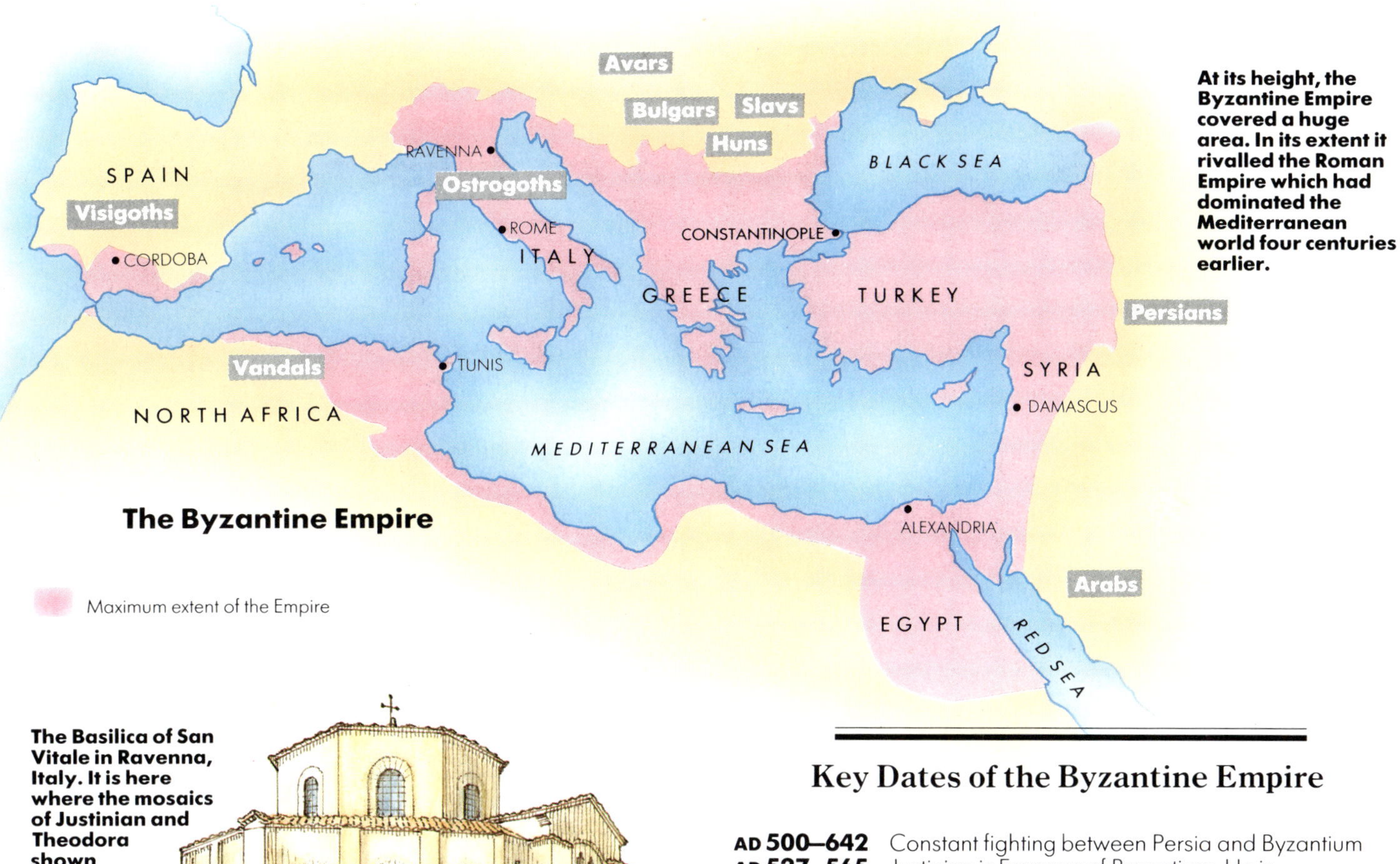

At its height, the Byzantine Empire covered a huge area. In its extent it rivalled the Roman Empire which had dominated the Mediterranean world four centuries earlier.

The Basilica of San Vitale in Ravenna, Italy. It is here where the mosaics of Justinian and Theodora shown opposite can be seen today. This Basilica houses some of the finest mosaics of the Byzantine period.

Key Dates of the Byzantine Empire

AD 500–642	Constant fighting between Persia and Byzantium
AD 527–565	Justinian is Emperor of Byzantium. He is responsible for modifying Byzantine laws
AD 534	Belisarius conquers the Vandals of North Africa
AD 535–554	Byzantium reconquers Italy
AD 542–546	Plague spreads in Byzantine Empire
AD 565–578	Justin II, Emperor of Byzantium
AD 572–628	Persians control Arabia
AD 626	Emperor Heraclius of Byzantium expels Persians from Egypt
AD 642	Final defeat of Persians by Arabs at Nehawand

The whole city was divided between the supporters of one team, the Blues, and the other, the Greens. Regularly the two groups of rival supporters came to blows, and the trouble had to be put down by force.

Unfortunately, Justinian went too far on this occasion, and found the two sides united against him. Blues and Greens together rampaged through the city and much of it was burnt to the ground.

In the emergency, Justinian called on his best and most trusted general, Belisarius, who had just returned from fighting against Persia. He marched into the hippodrome and slaughtered 30,000 rioters, putting an end to the crisis.

VANDALS, GOTHS AND PERSIANS Justinian had one great amibition: to restore the old Roman Empire and to rule it. He sent an army, with the great general Belisarius to lead it, to start the reconquest in AD 533. First to fall were the Vandals of Tunisia in AD 534.

For the next 19 years Byzantium was at war. First, Belisarius fought his way up through Italy, taking control of Rome from the Ostrogoths in AD 536, and taking Ravenna, in northern Italy, in AD 540.

At this point Justinian recalled Belisarius for service on the eastern frontier, where a new Persian king, Chosroes, was destroying Byzantine cities and armies. Not even Belisarius could stop the Persian King; only bubonic plague in Persia, and huge payments of Roman gold brought his attacks to an end.

At the same time, Huns and Slavs were invading the Empire from the north; four times between AD 540 and AD 558 they were beaten back.

In AD 551, the Ostrogoths fought back in Italy to try to reestablish their control. This time Justinian sent his court chamberlain, an 80 year-old with little military experience, called Narses. Despite his age and lack of qualifications, the old man succeeded and secured Italy. He then went on, after taking Italy, to add part of Spain to the Byzantine Empire.

By the time Justinian died, in AD 565, he had rebuilt a huge empire, extending from Syria to Spain. This was the golden age of the Byzantine Empire.

THE BIRTH OF ISLAM

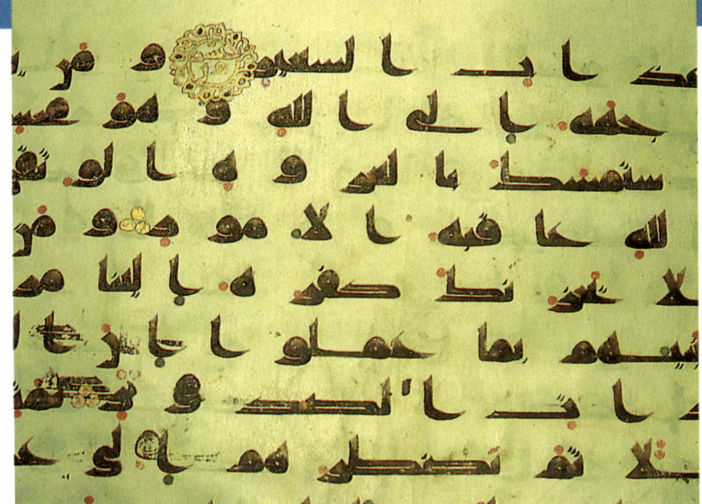

Muslims believe that the words of Allah were dictated to Muhammad by the angel Gabriel a little at a time. He learned them by heart, and repeated them to his followers. Some of them, who could write, took the words down 'on date leaves and pieces of white stone'. Others

The Qur'an

learned them by heart. Eventually they were collected into a single book, the *Qur'an*, which contains the central teachings of Islam.

The *Qur'an* is divided into chapters, called suras. The longest suras come first and contain

Above. This is a page from a ninth century AD *Qur'an*. It is written in an early Kufic script and is ornamented with gold.

instructions about how Muslims should carry out their daily life. The shortest suras at the end give warnings about the Day of Judgement.

The Arabian Desert was the home of nomadic tribes with cities in the fertile oases. These cities had grown rich on the trade in spices and frankincense, and in AD 525 the kingdom of Axum sent its army across the Red Sea to conquer southern Arabia. Thirty-six years later, in the Year of the Elephant (AD 571), a great battle was fought near Mecca, and the combined Arab tribes defeated the Axumites.

THE HOLY CITY AND THE PROPHET Mecca was already sacred to the Arabs, who came as pilgrims to the Ka'ba, a shrine containing a sacred black stone. It was a centre for the worship of the desert gods, a religion which had a lot in common with that of another desert people, the Jews.

In AD 610, there was a rich merchant of Mecca, named Muhammad. He was a deeply religious, mystical man, who believed that God had spoken to him with a new message: 'There is One God (Allah) and Muhammad is his *Prophet*'. He preached a new religion of obedience and equality, in which earlier prophets–Isaiah, Elijah, and Christ–all had a place. But his teachings, like those of other prophets before him, were revolutionary, and on 24 September, AD 622 he was forced to flee his home town to the nearby city of Medina.

THE BEGINNING OF ISLAM This flight, the *Hegira*, marks the beginning of Islam. At Medina, Muhammad

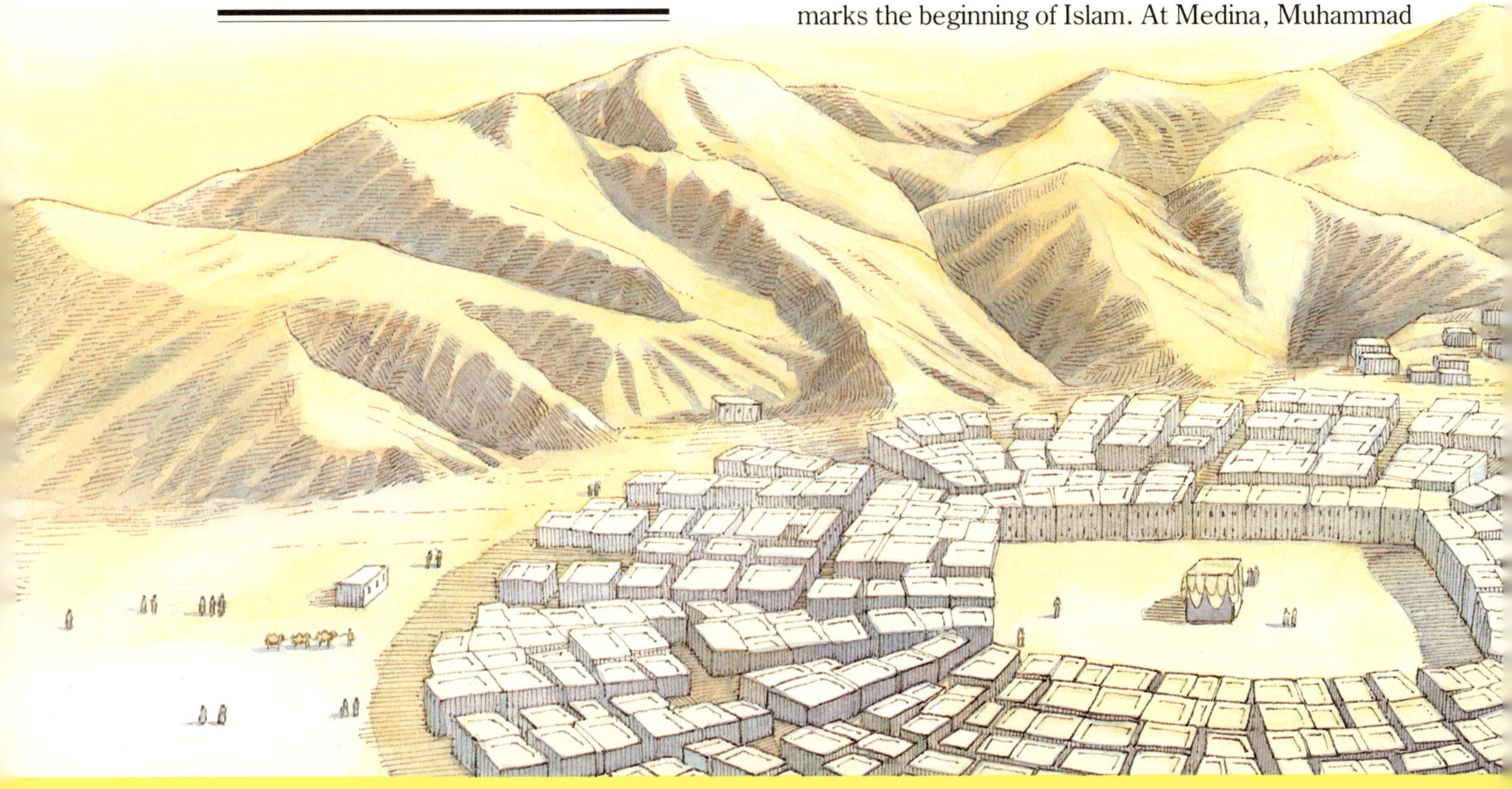

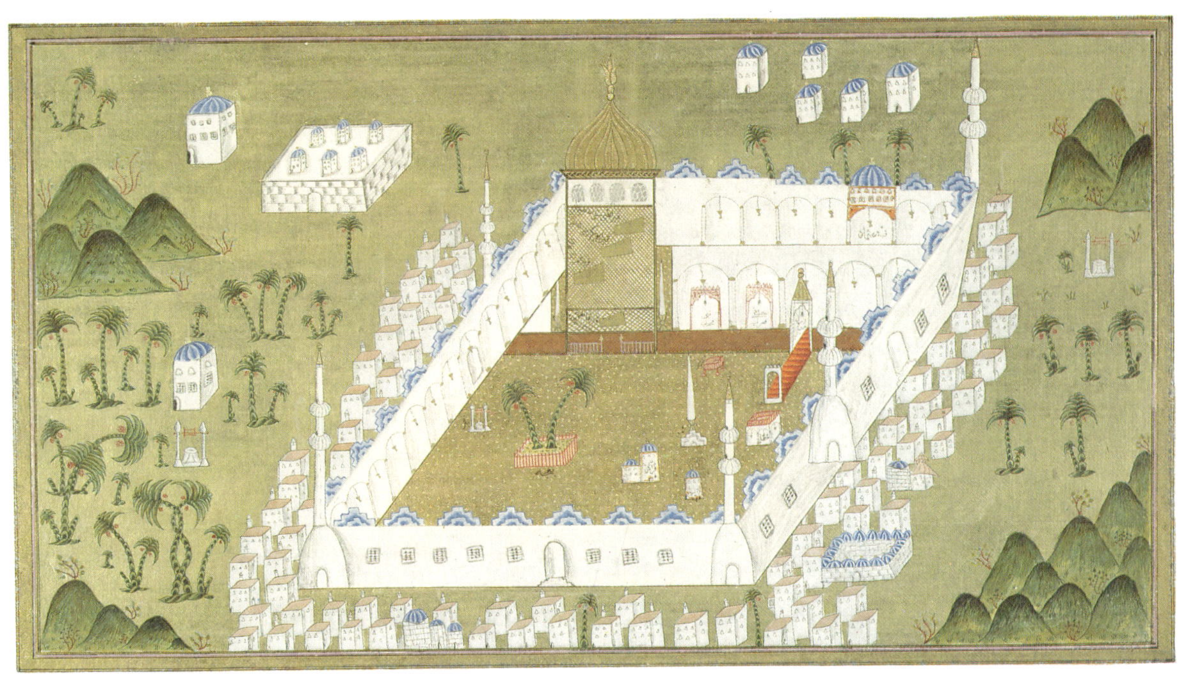

Left. This beautiful Islamic tile shows the original Holy Mosque of the Prophet Muhammad at Medina. When Muhammad fled Mecca in AD 622 he went to Medina, where he set up the first Islamic government. This was the first Islamic mosque ever built, and a mosque of the same name still stands on the site today. The Mosque houses Muhammad's tomb, making Medina one of the most important centres of the Islamic faith. Because of this, pilgrims will generally also visit Medina when they make their pilgrimage to Mecca.

and his followers devised the laws of their new way of life. Soon, he was the ruler of Medina, and had created an Islamic society which combined strict religious rules with commandments to protect the weak–particularly women, slaves and orphans.

The Arabs were a warlike people, and it was natural that their new religion should be spread by war and conquest rather than by peaceful conversion. In AD 630 Muhammad captured Mecca and led 10,000 warriors into the city on *pilgrimage*. It now became the holy city of Islam, and the Ka'ba, the old pagan shrine, was its most sacred spot.

Muhammad, who had been a refugee, died in AD 632 as the ruler of most of Arabia. He left behind the beginnings of a mighty empire, and something else even more important.

A NEW WAY OF LIFE The tribes of Arabia had been warlike and quarrelsome, with fierce loyalty to their families. Muhammad took this loyalty and turned it to himself and to the new religion, which has now spread all over the world. The western idea of Islam is often one of a conquering, warlike religion. But it was also a religion that allowed Jews, Christians and Buddhists to live in peace as respected citizens. Islam took the best of what it found and turned that into something very special. Muhammad is probably one of the most important men who ever lived.

Left. A reconstruction of how Mecca may have looked in the early years of Islam. The Ka'ba is the small square building in the centre of the picture. Until AD 630 it housed the stones and other objects held sacred by the tribes of Arabia, in an inner chamber. All except the sacred 'Black Stone' were removed by Muhammad in AD 630 when he retook the city of Mecca. At this point, the Ka'ba became the centre of the Muslim world. Even today, Muslims must make a pilgrimage to Mecca at least once in their lifetimes.

THE HOLY WAR

The conquests of Islam led to mosques being constructed in territory controlled by the Arabs. This mosque—the Ibn Tulun Mosque—was built in Cairo, Egypt, in the ninth century AD.

When Muhammad died in AD 632, one of his most loyal followers, Abu Bakr, was elected to follow him as *Caliph*, or representative. From now on Islamic rulers were given the title, *Caliph*, meaning the representative of Muhammad on earth.

Until AD 655, former disciples of Muhammad ruled the Islamic lands from Medina, but then, after six years of civil war, the tribe of the Umayyads took control, and ruled the empire of Islam from their capital at Damascus in Syria.

THE CONQUESTS The Umayyads kept control until AD 749 when the Abbasids took over the empire. They ruled from a splendid new capital at Baghdad, in Iraq. In the 117 years since the death of Muhammad, an extraordinary thing had happened: Islam had grown from covering a small part of Arabia to ruling an immense empire which spread from the Atlantic Ocean to India.

The advance of the Arabs was even more devastating than the eruption of the Huns into the west. First they moved on the Byzantine Empire: by AD 642 they had conquered Syria and Egypt. Here, in trading cities like Alexandria, the Arabs acquired navies, and willing native peoples who were often pleased to be rid of the Byzantines.

AFRICA AND THE EAST The Byzantine Empire in Asia was now based mainly on Turkey, but even here the Arabs sometimes reached as far as Constantinople.

In the east, they swept through Persia and Asia. In AD 750 they defeated a Chinese army. In the other

Left. This fine example of Islamic craftsmanship in ivory depicts two men on horseback picking dates from a palm tree.

Right. Many of the first Muslim soldiers rode camels or horses. Their favoured weapons were lances, swords, and bows and arrows. Shirts made of mail or of leather gave protection against enemy attack.

Arabs often defeated their enemies in battle by pretending to be beaten, and riding away. When the enemy chased after them, the Arabs would turn on them and make an unexpected and deadly attack.

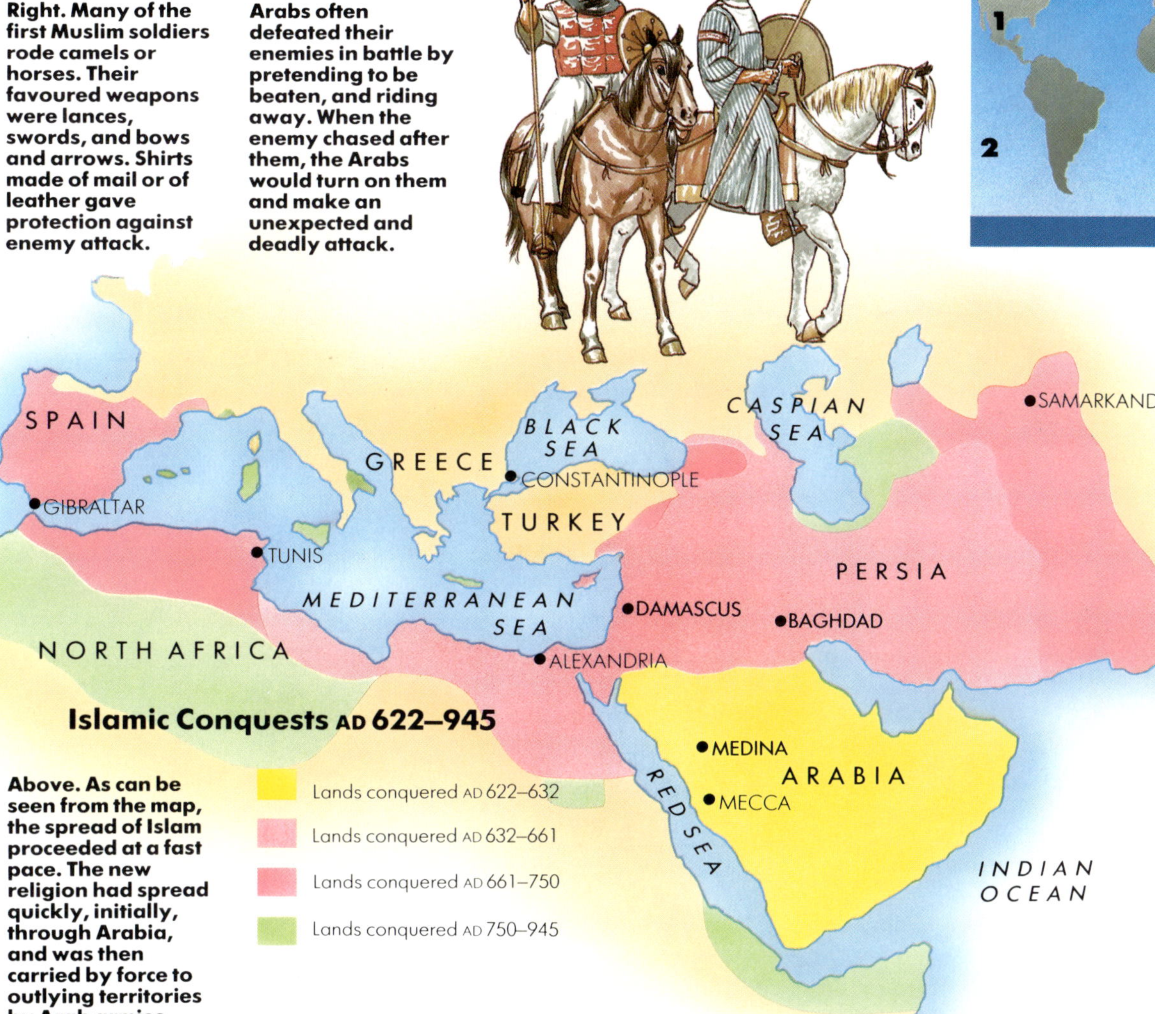

Above. As can be seen from the map, the spread of Islam proceeded at a fast pace. The new religion had spread quickly, initially, through Arabia, and was then carried by force to outlying territories by Arab armies.

direction they added Africa to their empire, defeating the Byzantines and the warlike nomads, the Berbers. By AD 700 all of Africa north of the Sahara Desert was theirs.

ISLAM IN EUROPE The sea was no obstacle: in AD 711, an army of Arabs and Berbers under the general Tariq Ibn Ziyad landed in Spain near a great rock which came to be named after him—Jebel-al-Tariq–the rock of Gibraltar. A few years later Spain was a province of Islam, called al-Andalus, the land of the Vandals, which gives us the modern name, Andalusia.

Now it was only the Franks in France and the Byzantines in Greece and Turkey who kept Islam at bay. But the empire was stretched to its limit now; it was far greater than the Arabs could control. It needed all the skills of their subject peoples–Egyptians, Syrians and Persians–and the fighting power of armies of slave soldiers to hold it together.

Because of this, when the Islamic people had conquered new territory, they administered it in a way which took account of the local culture, to keep unrest at bay.

The Arab conquest of Spain led to the birth of the Moorish culture. Buildings constructed by the Moors represent some of the finest examples of Islamic architecture. This is part of the highly decorated interior of the Grand Mosque at Cordoba.

1 By AD 700 three principal cultures had emerged in the southwestern region of North America: the Mogollon, the Anasazi and the Hohokam. Their territories covered much of present-day Utah, Colorado, Arizona and New Mexico. Early settlements of these cultures consisted of shallow pit-houses that were half below ground. By AD 900 canals up to 16 kilometres long were being built. These provided irrigation, ensuring the harvest of two crops per year.

2 By AD 650 the Polynesians had reached all the major Pacific island groups, with the possible exception of New Zealand. The settlement of the Pacific islands had begun around 1000 BC and ended around AD 1000. The Polynesians were, without doubt, the world's greatest explorers and covered vast distances to reach and settle tiny islands.

ISLAMIC SCHOLARS AND ARTISTS

A detail of the wooden panelling from the walls of a Fatimid palace from the tenth century AD. The scene depicts two musicians. It was unusual to show the figures of human beings or animals in Islamic designs, as it was thought that only Allah, the god of Islam, had the right to design such figures.

For the thousand years before the birth of Islam, Greece and the lands influenced by the Greeks, had been the centre of science and learning, and had been the intellectual centre of the Roman Empire. Philosophers and mathematicians such as Aristotle, Ptolemy and Archimedes had written about the way that the world worked. Scientists such as Hippocrates and Galen had written medical textbooks.

Their works had been collected and copied by Greeks, Romans and Byzantines. But many of these scholars became branded as *heretics* at home, and fled to Persia. Here, Greek learning mixed with the science and philosophy of India and China, to reach an even more advanced state.

THE NEW SCHOLARS It was through Persia, once the bitter enemy of Greece and Rome, that a lot of the ancient wisdom was preserved. The *Caliphs* brought scholars from Persia, Syria, Egypt, and all over their new empire, to the courts at Damascus and Baghdad. It mattered little to them whether the scholars were Jews, Christians or Muslims. What counted most was their learning, particularly in philosophy, science and literature.

Mathematicians and astronomers were also highly prized and were put to good use in surveying and agriculture.

THE TRANSLATORS The old knowledge was translated from its original Greek into Arabic, often by way of Persian or Syrian, and so it spread easily through the Empire.

In Spain, although the rulers were Muslims, Christian monasteries flourished. Islam was far more tolerant of Christianity than vice versa. Pope Sylvester III had studied in a Spanish monastery, and it was here that Greek books, now in Arabic, were translated into Latin. This is the tortuous way that learning gradually spread to France, Britain and Germany.

SIMPLE NUMBERS We take our numbers for granted. But Roman numerals, the counting system of the old Roman Empire, were very different, and difficult to use. Adding CIX to LIV to get CLXIII seems a lot more difficult than adding 109 to 54 to make 163. The latter counting system is, of course, the one we use today and is the product of Islam.

The system actually originated in India, but it was Islamic science that spread it through Europe. In fact, in the early days, these numbers were called 'algorisms', after the ninth-century mathematician, Al-Khwarizmi. The numbering system allowed Arab scientists to do complicated calculations.

The Muslims advanced the science of astronomy, particularly by developing instruments like the *astrolabe*, which was to become an essential aid to navigation at sea.

ARCHITECTS AND ARTISTS Arab engineers and builders have left us buildings of breath-taking beauty, including mosques with tall minarets and majestic domes and cool palaces with arcaded courts. The details of the buildings are exquisite.

The Arabs used abstract patterns, especially curving 'arabesques' which might be carved, painted or inlaid. Passages from the *Qur'an* were often worked into the patterns, so that Islamic *calligraphy* became an art in itself.

Left. The Dome of the Rock in Jerusalem, also called the Mosque of Omar, was built between AD 669–692. It covers the spot from which Muhammad is believed to have risen to heaven. It is without doubt one of the most exquisite examples of Islamic architecture. You can see how fine the abstract designs are all around the mosque. It is regarded as the most beautiful building in Jerusalem.

Above. Muslim artists were discouraged from painting people or animals. Thus, they created abstract designs and geometric patterns, such as these.

Above. A reconstruction of the *minaret* of the Great Mosque at Samarra, begun by al-Mutawakkil in AD 847. This circular minaret with a spiral ramp follows the scheme of the temple towers, or *ziggurats*, of ancient Assyria. The mosque is the largest in the Islamic world.

Famous Muslim Scholars

The early Islamic world produced a remarkable number of learned and influential scholars. There follow descriptions of some of the most famous.

Ibn Sina (known in Europe as Aricenna) was born in AD 980 near Bukhara in central Asia. He studied medicine, mathematics, astronomy, climatology and philosophy. His writings helped to spread Muslim scientific and medical knowledge to Europe. His book on medicine, entitled al-Qanun, was one of the most widely used medical textbooks during the Middle Ages. In it, he accurately describes the symptoms and spread of many serious diseases, and lists 760 different drugs used by Muslim physicians.

Al-Razi (known in Europe as Rhazes) was a physician in charge of the Baghdad hospital during the AD 900s. He was famous as the most skilful doctor of his generation. He developed several new and effective treatments for illnesses, and wrote a comprehensive medical encyclopedia.

Above. A detail from a page of a book on medicine written by a doctor in Baghdad in the eleventh century. Marrows were used to quench the thirst and cleanse the bowels.

Al-Khwarizmi lived in ninth century Khurason in central Asia. He wrote many books on mathematical topics. The word 'algebra' as used today, comes from the title of one of his books.

Al-Masudi, who lived in tenth century Egypt, studied the natural world, and wrote on geography, geology and biology. He suggested a theory of evolution, almost 900 years before Charles Darwin developed the theory in the western world. He was a great traveller and wrote a 30-volume encyclopaedia describing all the countries he had visited.

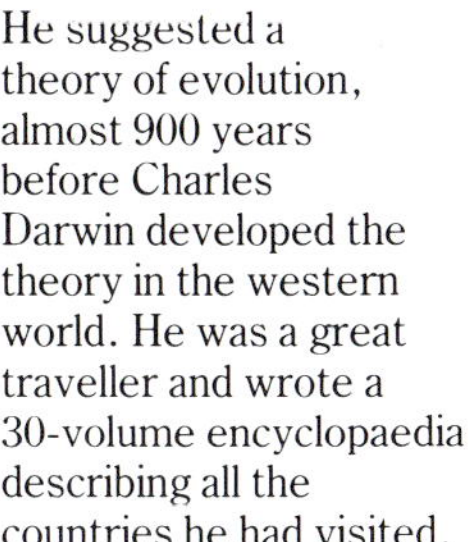

Left. The astrolabe is believed to have been invented by a Greek scientist named Hipparchus in 150 BC. Islamic scholars developed the instrument, and it became the chief instrument for navigational purposes, until superseded in the fourteenth century. This astrolabe dates from about the ninth century AD.

INDIA AND SOUTHEAST ASIA

While Rome ruled the west, the Kushan Empire, which lasted from AD 78–500 ruled northern India, Pakistan and Afghanistan. This was a period of great achievement and prosperity, but the explosion of barbarians which put an end to the Roman Empire also brought chaos to India.

HUNS AND ARABS The Huns poured into India around AD 500 and the Kushan civilization was wrecked. India became a land of many kingdoms, often at war with each other. Then around AD 700 Arabs fought their way into India and the first Muslim states were founded.

Throughout this period of chaos, Indian culture carried on. Beautiful Hindu temples and statues were erected. Poets, philosophers and historians carried on writing, and Buddhism spread far afield from India to Nepal, Tibet, China, Japan and Southeast Asia.

THE GREAT PILGRIMAGE Pilgrims travelled enormous distances to India, the home of Buddhism. In the seventh century Hsuan-tsang, a Chinese Buddhist, left his home and trekked around the north of the Himalayas across deserts and mountains to reach Kanauj, the capital of the Buddhist King, Harsha, on the River Ganges in northeast India. After several years of study he returned home with a precious baggage of holy books and flower seeds; his pilgrimage had lasted for 16 years.

INTO SOUTHEAST ASIA The Romans had traded with India, during the period of the Empire, and to supply this trade Indians had explored Southeast Asia, Burma, Thailand, Malaya, Sumatra, Java and Borneo in search of gems and spices. After the traders went priests, and the great religions of India–Hinduism and Buddhism–were taken up by native peoples. Chinese traders came to the area too, and the mixture of foreign civilizations and native traditions produced a spectacular culture.

Left. This Khmer sandstone statue from the tenth century AD depicts the Hindu god, Brahma. He was considered to be the father of mankind in general, and to be the god of wisdom. This view of the statue shows three of his four heads.

Below. This is a reconstruction of the Khmer capital of Angkor Wat. This great temple is perhaps the largest religious structure ever built.

THE KINGDOM OF THE KHMER In Cambodia the results were particularly spectacular, and the Kingdom of the Khmer (Cambodians) soon ruled huge areas of Southeast Asia. Their kings conquered new lands and seized slaves and tribute. The wealth from these conquests can still be seen in the great cities and temples of the Cambodian jungle.

The Khmer Kingdom began in the eighth century AD. The Khmers built cities like Banteay Srei, large and beautifully decorated buildings for the worship of Hindu gods as well as for the running of the kingdom. Eventually the Empire came to be centred at Angkor where King Suryavarman (AD 1113–1150) built Angkor Wat, the most splendid of all the temples, richly decorated with carvings and towers.

RICE AND WATER Around the Khmer temples were lakes–not just for decoration, but because the cities depended on them. The basic food, rice, was grown in wet paddy fields, and artificial irrigation was the only way to bring enough water to the fields. Whole rivers were diverted, and huge reservoirs, one 7 km long and 2 km wide, were created to support the great cities of the Khmer.

Right. A detail of the fine and intricate carvings at Angkor Thom today.

Southeast Asia and the Kingdom of the Khmer

The map shows the location of the ancient kingdom of the Khmer, in Southeast Asia.

CHINA: ANARCHY TO EMPIRE

This beautiful Tang painting of camels running through the trees is typical of the high standard of the art produced during the era of Tang dominance.

The history of China is the story of different *dynasties* coming to power and creating great empires which eventually collapsed. The Han Dynasty came to an end in AD 220, when the Roman Empire was at its peak, and after its demise, the vast land of China broke up into many small kingdoms. This lasted until AD 529 when a general, We Ti, conquered the whole country to initiate his own, Sui, Dynasty.

THE BEGINNING OF THE TANG DYNASTY By AD 618, China was again slipping into anarchy. In that year the Sui Emperor was assassinated, and Liu Yiian, the first Emperor of the Tang Dynasty, took over.

He founded a dynasty which would last until AD 907. This time was one of the peaks of Chinese civilization, marked by its art, culture and organization. After AD 907 the Empire split into warring states again until it was reunited by Chao Kwang Yin, first Emperor of the Sung Dynasty, in AD 960.

THE ALL-POWERFUL EMPEROR The Chinese world during this period was organized to give complete power to the Emperor and his civil service. All adult men paid tax to the Emperor for their land, and some of this tax was extracted in the form of forced labour. In AD 607 more than a million men were called up to 'pay' their taxes by repairing part of the Great Wall of China; in the 20 days that they worked, many died.

The same forced labour was used to build the Grand Canal, which was used to bring food from the rice fields on the Yangtze River more than 1000 kilometres to the capitals at Loyang and Chang'an. Roads and bridges, beautifully engineered, were also built, using forced labour, and were overseen and managed by the skilled administrators of the civil service.

Later, the Sung Emperors were to devise entrance examinations to set a high academic standard for their administrators, so important did the role of the civil service become.

The Tang Empire

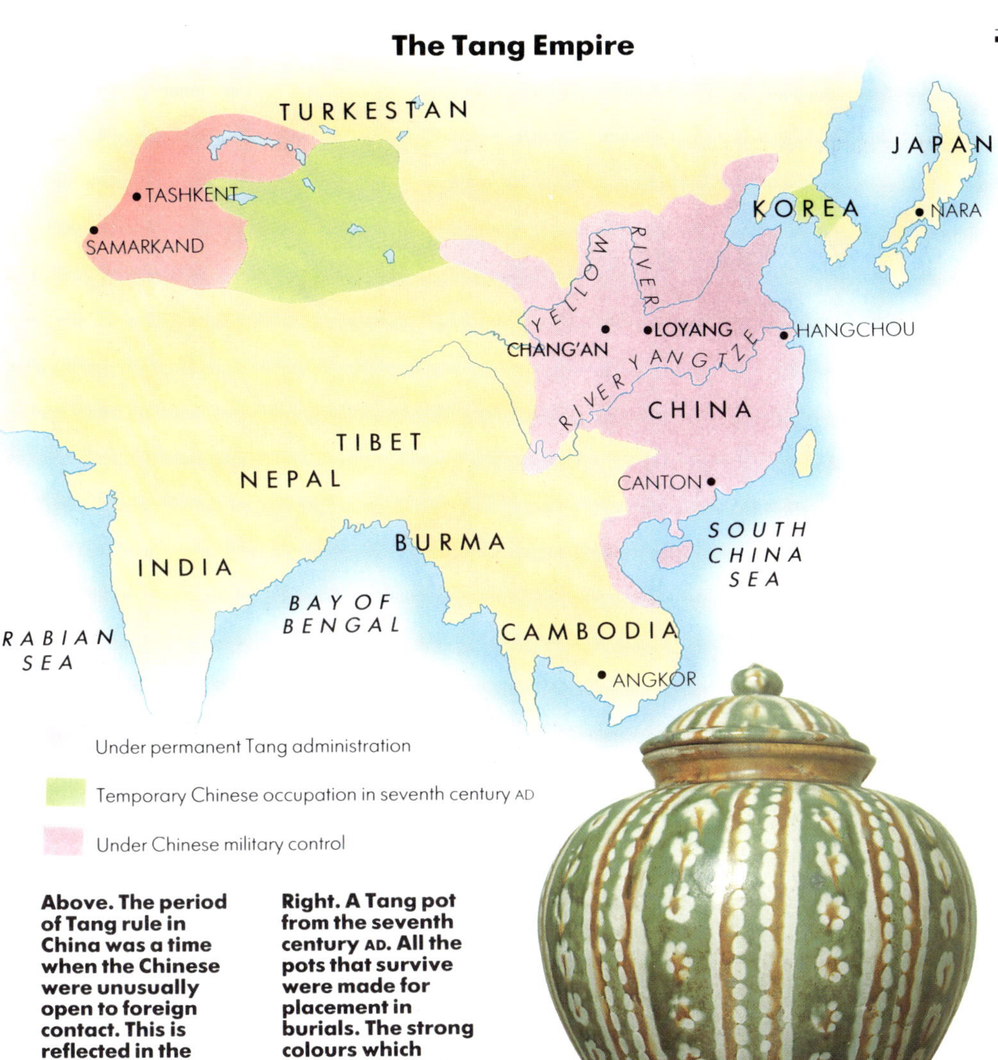

Above. The period of Tang rule in China was a time when the Chinese were unusually open to foreign contact. This is reflected in the extent to which Tang-influenced or controlled territory increased, as is shown in the map.

Right. A Tang pot from the seventh century AD. All the pots that survive were made for placement in burials. The strong colours which typically cover Tang pots repeat the tones and designs of textiles fashionable at the time.

Chinese Medicine

In ancient China, medical treatment was largely based on herbal remedies. The herb Artemesia Moxa (2) was used in moxibustion. This treatment involved burning the herb at points directly on the skin where the pain was felt. Many other herbs were used such as mint (1), which was believed to relieve headaches.

During the Tang Dynasty, a book known as *The Tang Book on Drugs and Herbs* was written. The information in it was used as the basis of the most respected book on the subject today.

Acupuncture was also developed by the ancient Chinese. Very thin needles are painlessly inserted into specific parts of the body to relieve a wide range of illnesses. The diagram above shows the heart meridian of the acupuncture system.

TRADE WITH THE OUTSIDE WORLD Throughout its long history, China has had periods of remaining shut off to other states, and periods of welcoming communication and trade with them. During this era, China was 'open' to the west and the south, and traded freely with other countries. Silk travelled west along the Silk Road, and spices, woods, gems, and fine pottery went west by sea via India to the Persian Gulf, Egypt and Africa.

In return came gold and silver and masterpieces of art. With the trade came foreign traders, including Arabs, Jews, Persians and *Nestorian* Christians from Central Asia. They made the Empire a centre of international trade, with their own living areas in the capital cities of Loyang and Chang'an, and in the ports of Canton and Hangchow. China was a great hive of activity during this period, and extremely cosmopolitan.

POTS AND PAINTINGS China's own crafts flourished too; underground tombs of the Tang period had beautifully painted walls, which show how magnificent the palaces must have been. Chinese pottery was very fine and highly prized by western customers.

This Tang *rhyton*, or drinking cup, dates from the seventh century AD. It features an animal's head and is decorated with relief carvings of musicians.

THE SILK ROAD

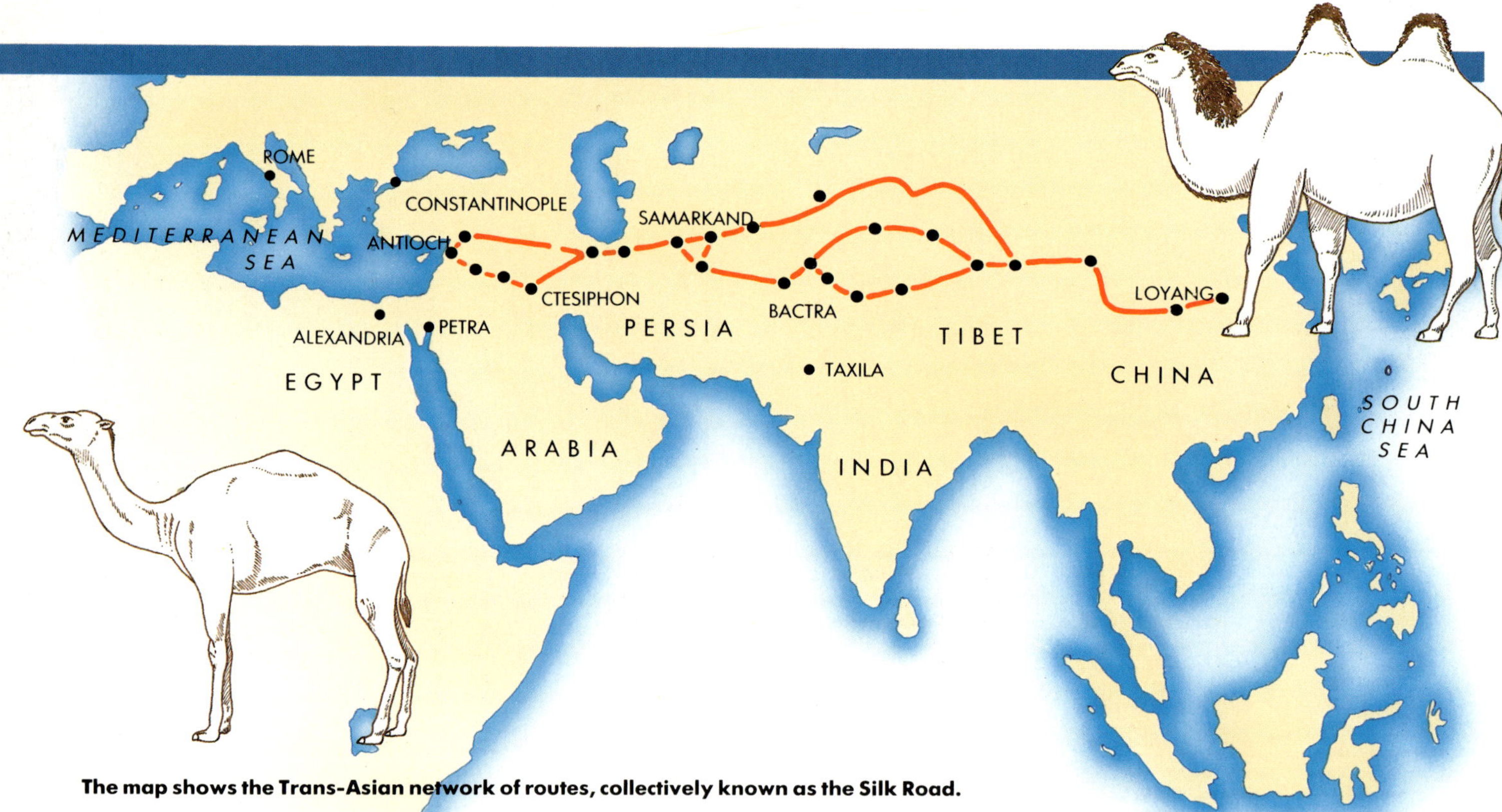

The map shows the Trans-Asian network of routes, collectively known as the Silk Road.

For many centuries the wonderful silk cloth that was made only in China had been brought thousands of miles to the Near East and Europe. The Romans had not been at all sure how it was made; they speculated that it came from a plant, but they were wrong.

After the fall of the Roman Empire, the demand for silk continued; the noble and royal families of the Arabs, Byzantines, Franks, Moors and Anglo-Saxons all delighted in the gossamer-like fabric.

THE SECRET OF SILK In the sixth century AD Persians came to the court of the Byzantine Emperor and Empress, Justinian and Theodora, and produced, from a hollow walking stick, the eggs of the silk worm. The Byzantines hatched them, and silk worms appeared as the answer to the puzzle. By unwinding the silken thread from the cocoons of these caterpillars, silk was made.

Soon the Byzantine silk works were weaving their own silk. But the finest, most luxurious, cloth still came from China.

OVER DESERTS AND MOUNTAINS The distance from the Great Wall of China to Antioch in Syria is more than 5000 kilometres, and the journey ranges over the deserts of Mongolia, the Pamir and Hindukush mountains, the high plateau of Iran and the rivers and deserts of Iraq. This was the overland route used for Chinese trade to Europe, known as the Silk Road. This was not a paved road like a motorway, but rather an overland track, dotted with countless caravans trudging all the way from China to Europe.

The route was formed out of a complicated chain of many links, some end-to-end and some side-by-side. Silk and other goods were shuttled from one city to the next, handled by dozens of different traders as one trader passed his commodities on to the next. It is unlikely that many traders from China ever saw Syria or Byzantium. But each trader would have had his share of rivers and deserts to cross and mountain passes to climb along the varied route.

RESTING PLACES A broad corridor of *caravanserais* (caravan depots) grew up where the caravans could stop for food and rest. These were like small walled towns, defended against attack and wild animals, and bustled with life.

THE SHIFTING ROUTES The exact route that any trader took depended on many things: the time of year was important since mountain passes might only be open in

The Heyday of the Silk Road

The first millennium AD had seen an explosion in urban development. Cities such as Chang'an and Alexandria may have had populations exceeding 500,000. These huge populations encouraged the growth of trade.

The heyday of the Silk Road was seen during the period of the Tang Dynasty in China (AD 618–907). Many remains of trade goods have been excavated along the routes. They show the great developments in art and culture which were achieved during this era.

Left. Itinerant merchants, like this Persian pedlar, travelled the Silk Road for many centuries.

Above. This fragment of silk embroidery dates from the third/fifth centuries AD. It was found on the Silk Road.

Below. The present-day ruins of Jiaohe which was once a bustling sixth-century Silk Road city. Cities such as Jiaohe grew very wealthy during the great days of the Silk Road because they controlled trade.

the summer, and deserts were easier to cross in the winter. Politics were important too; sometimes the invasions of Huns, Arabs, Persians, and Byzantines closed parts of the route. Sometimes local rulers imposed high taxes, and a different road would have to be found to avoid them.

THE SPICE ROUTE But there was a different way: a sea route started from China, swung around Malaya to India and continued on to the Persian Gulf, the Red Sea, Egypt and even down to the east coast of Africa.

When the monsoon winds were right, Arab traders would set out from China and make colossal journeys to carry silks, spices, precious stones and woods, and pottery, which would eventually reach the markets of Africa, Europe and Middle East. The sea route would be full of dangers, such as storms and pirates. However, its advantage over the Silk Road was that many more goods could be carried on a ship than on a camel. Both the Silk Road and the Spice Route were to endure through much of history as the most important routes of trade and communication between East and West.

JAPAN

When the Chinese Empire was strong, it sent out traders and ambassadors to its neighbours. They were sent to Korea, on the northeast frontier of China, and to Japan. In these lands Chinese practices and ideas mixed with the local cultures, sometimes resulting in brilliant civilizations.

SHINTO AND BUDDHA The traditional religion of Japan, *Shinto*, meaning the 'Way of the Gods', was concerned with spirits and gods of nature. These gods were worshipped at natural places such as springs, woods and rocks. But in AD 538 Koreans brought Buddhism to Japan; it had come a long way, from India via China and then Korea.

TEMPLES The emperors and noble families of Japan took to Buddhism enthusiastically, building palaces and temples in the Chinese style. The Japanese tradition was that a new palace, and a new royal temple, was built in honour of each new emperor. Thus Japan, even today, has a huge variety of large temples, each one a collection of finely built wooden structures clustered in a courtyard. Some, like the Horyuji temple shown here, have lasted for nearly 1500 years.

MONASTERIES The temples also served as monasteries. The monks who served the temples as priests lived in dormitories outside the courtyard. Inside the monastery was a main hall, filled with statues of the Buddha and Buddhist deities, which was used on ceremonial occasions. There was also a *sutra hall* where sacred books were kept, and a *pagoda*. This tall, many-roofed tower contained holy relics, often bones of the Buddha or a saint. Many pilgrims would travel to the monasteries to worship.

TOMBS Buddhism did not take over in every part of life in Japan. In some aspects the old ways lingered on, especially in death.

The proper Buddhist burial was cremation: the body was burned, the ashes put in a pot or a metal container, and eventually buried in the ground. But the old Japanese style was very different. Tombs were dug into the hillside like tunnels, or built of huge stones and buried under artificial hills. The bodies were placed inside, intact, and the entrance was blocked. Inside the walls of the tombs were sometimes painted, and pots, beads, buckles and other everyday objects placed with the body.

HOUSES AND PEOPLE In ordinary towns and villages the Japanese lived in wooden houses, simple versions of the great halls of the temples. Here they lived their lives as farmers, craftsmen and traders. They worshipped the old spirits of Shinto and the new gods of Buddhism.

The influence of China had improved their lives, but they were still free to live in their own culture and were not ruled by Chinese masters.

Key Dates in Early Japan

AD 258 or 318	'Emperor' Sujin, probably first chief of federated tribes under the Yamato
AD 300	Spread of wet-rice agriculture to whole of Japan, except Hokkaido
AD 475	Consolidation of Yamato state under horse-riding nobles
AD 538 or 552	Buddhism introduced into Japan from China
AD 607	First Horyuji Temple built
AD 670	First Horyuji Temple destroyed by fire
AD 708	Copper and silver coins officially minted
AD 710	Beginning of the Nara period. Japan becomes a centralized state based on the Chinese system of administration.

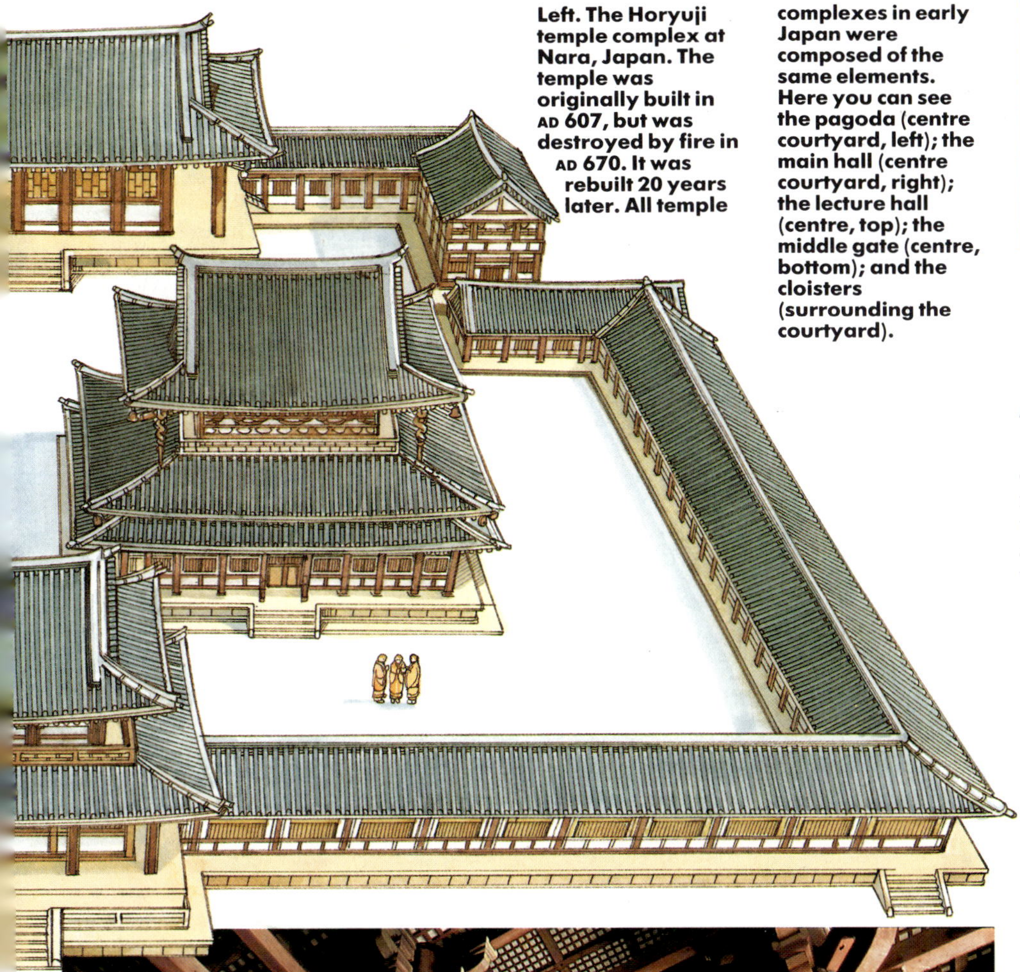

Left. The Horyuji temple complex at Nara, Japan. The temple was originally built in AD 607, but was destroyed by fire in AD 670. It was rebuilt 20 years later. All temple complexes in early Japan were composed of the same elements. Here you can see the pagoda (centre courtyard, left); the main hall (centre courtyard, right); the lecture hall (centre, top); the middle gate (centre, bottom); and the cloisters (surrounding the courtyard).

The main hall, called the Todaiji Temple, of the Nara temple complex houses this bronze Buddha figure, one of the largest in the world. Aristocratic Yamato women were asked to donate their fine bronze mirrors for recasting into this eighth century AD statue.

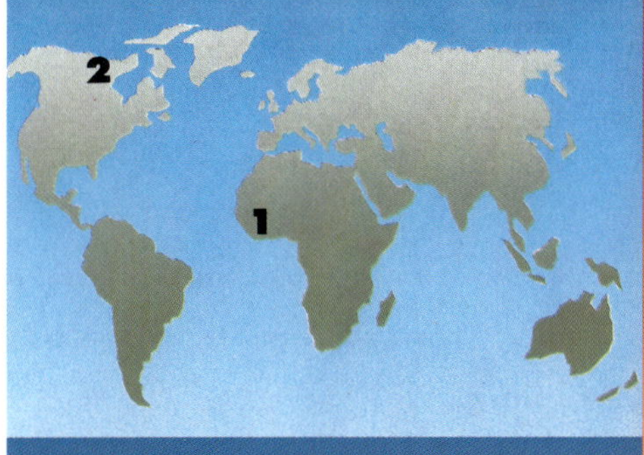

Japanese Buddhist Monks

The drawing below shows an early typical Japanese monk. Then, as now, the way of living adopted by a monk was harsh.

They want nothing for themselves and live with only what they actually need. They are dependent on people giving them food, but must not ask for it themselves.

Monks eat only one meal a day and this must be over before midday. This gives them the rest of the day for meditation, study, teaching, and practical tasks.

1 In Africa, in the eighth century AD, the Kingdom of Ife developed in the south of modern-day Nigeria. Ife was the capital city of the Yoruba people and is famous for the ritual brass heads that have been found there. Ironworking was also well developed at Ife. It was almost certainly an important centre for trade, and probably traded ivory and slaves with the African middlemen of the Sahara routes.

2 Around AD 800, the Dorset culture of the Inuit people of the Arctic thrived. This people made great advances in the development of the Inuit culture. Their settlements grew larger, and half-underground winter houses have been unearthed which would have held between two and three families. The people fished and hunted sea mammals and caribou with improved spears and harpoon-heads. In a short space of time, and for unclear reasons, this culture had completely disappeared by around AD 1000.

SETTLING THE PACIFIC

The inhabitants of Easter Island carved and erected a huge number of stone statues. All the statues on the island were pushed over face downwards in the late eighteenth and nineteenth centuries. But these at Ahu Akivi have been re-erected.

The East Indies and Pacific islands nearest to Australia, Micronesia and Melanesia, were settled very early. But between 2000–1000 BC a new people began to move eastwards through the settled islands. They had originally come from the coasts and islands of Southeast Asia, and by 1000 BC they had reached Samoa and Tonga, islands on the western edge of Polynesia, where archaeologists have found remains of their villages, with distinctive tools and pottery.

THE WIDE OCEAN Here they paused in their progress for more than 1000 years, and no wonder. Ahead of them lay the Pacific Ocean, 10,000 kilometres across, with islands scattered across it, some of them hundreds of kilometres apart. Exploration was dangerous and uncertain, but around AD 300 Polynesians began to spread east, and settled the main island groups, the Society Islands and the Marquesas Islands.

Imagine what the voyage must have been like. Men and women set out on journeys of 2000–3000 kilometres across the open sea in dug-out canoes containing their families and everything that was needed for a new life in a new land–seeds, plants, animals, tools–everything.

Polynesian Tools and Jewellery

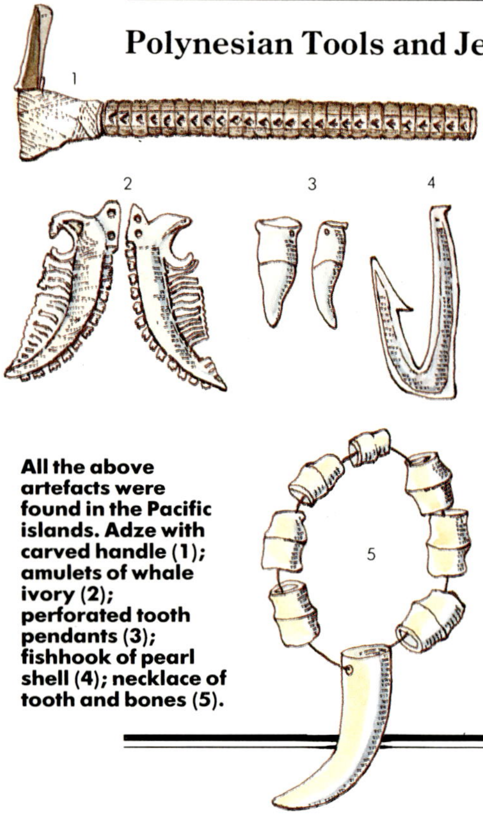

The early Polynesians abandoned the making of pottery in the first millennium AD, and metallurgy never reached the Pacific islands beyond western New Guinea.

Despite this, the archaeological remains which exist are rich and varied, and show us much about early Polynesian life. Most tools and jewellery were made from stone, bone, shell and whale ivory. Some of the carvings which survive are very ornate and show a high level of craftsmanship.

All the above artefacts were found in the Pacific islands. Adze with carved handle (1); amulets of whale ivory (2); perforated tooth pendants (3); fishhook of pearl shell (4); necklace of tooth and bones (5).

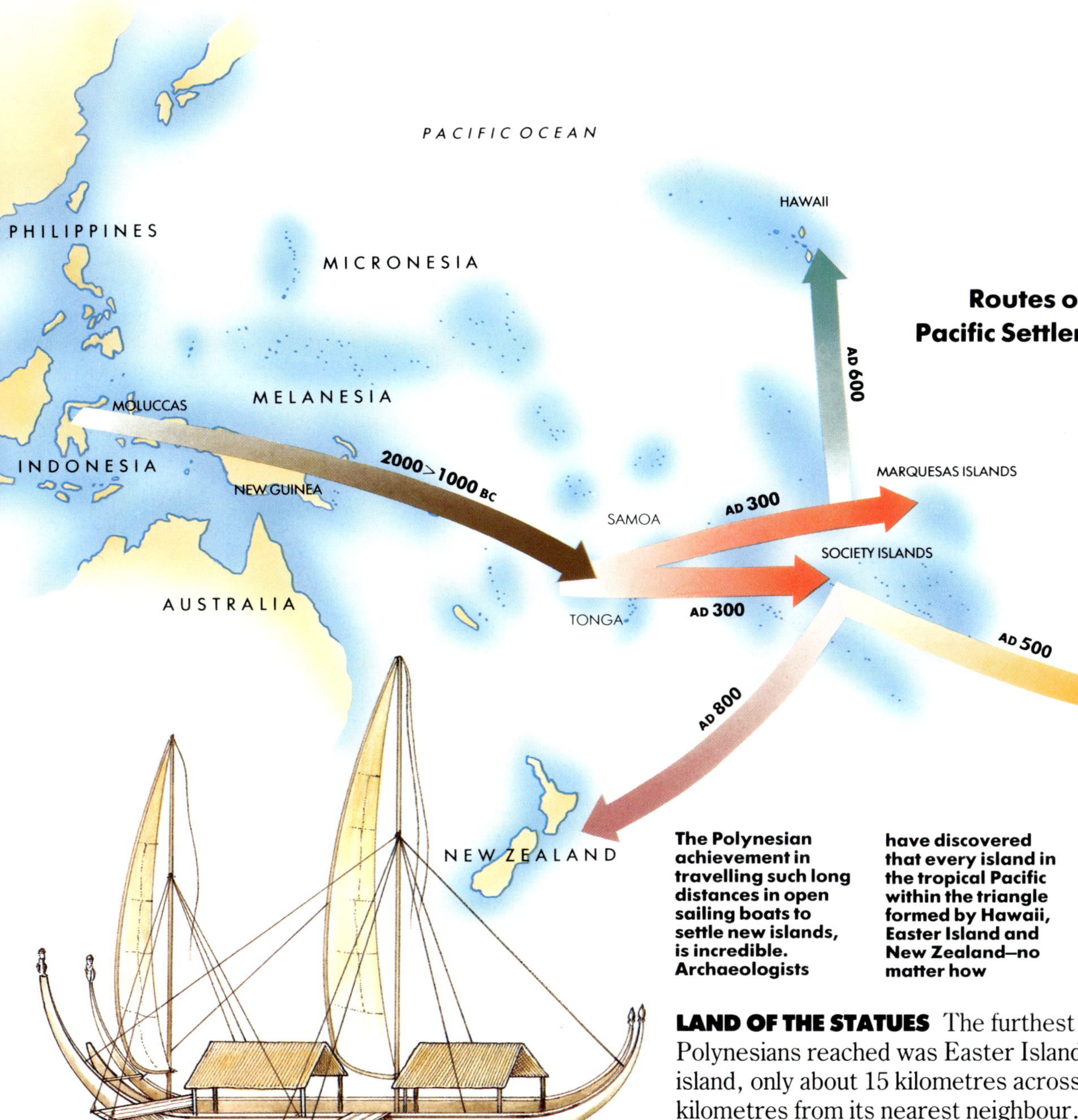

The Polynesian achievement in travelling such long distances in open sailing boats to settle new islands, is incredible. Archaeologists have discovered that every island in the tropical Pacific within the triangle formed by Hawaii, Easter Island and New Zealand–no matter how isolated–was reached at some time by Polynesian voyagers. This must stand as perhaps the greatest feat of exploration ever undertaken.

Above. The boats used by the Polynesians for their long voyages, possibly looked something like this reconstruction.

EASTER ISLAND AND HAWAII By AD 500 they had reached Easter Island, halfway to South America, and 100 years later they had reached the islands of Hawaii, far to the north. The distances they travelled were far in advance of any sea journeys undertaken by other peoples up to this point in history.

THE NEW HOMES On their new islands they grew yams, bananas, sweet potatoes, coconuts and breadfruit, and collected fish and shellfish from the sea. The rest of their meat came from the domestic animals that they had brought in their canoes–pigs, dogs, hens and rats. They built temples on stone platforms, and thatched wooden houses on land where building materials and food were easy to find.

LAND OF THE STATUES The furthest west that the Polynesians reached was Easter Island. It is a small island, only about 15 kilometres across and 2000 kilometres from its nearest neighbour. Here the intrepid explorers developed some extraordinary ideas. They built immense stone platforms, and on them they raised huge stone statues, up to 10 metres high and 80 tonnes in weight. For a people whose culture did not yet embrace the technology of metals and who had not developed the wheel, this was a colossal achievement.

THE COLD SOUTH The last great migration of the Polynesians was to the south, to the two islands of New Zealand, which they reached around AD 800 or 900. This was a different land to the rest; not a tropical paradise, but cooler and wetter.

Here the Polynesians, better known as *Maoris*, changed their way of life to suit the new environment. Most of their traditional crops died out, but sweet potatoes flourished, and sea food was plentiful. There were giant birds, called *moas*, which were hunted for meat in the forest. The Maoris had found a different sort of Pacific paradise.

AFRICA: SOUTH OF THE SAHARA

CHRISTIAN KINGDOMS When the Arabs spread so quickly across North Africa it was the Sahara Desert that stopped them spreading to the south, except in the case of Egypt. Here the rich valley of the Nile acts like a highway into the mountains of Sudan and Ethiopia. In the south of Sudan the Arabs were stopped by the kingdom of Nubia around Meroë; here were African Christians who had been converted by Byzantine missionaries in the 550s and 560s.

To the south of Nubia, and closer to the Red Sea was Axum, a kingdom which lived partly by trade across the Red Sea with Arabia. In fact, about 500 BC people from south Arabia had crossed over to Ethiopia, and this mixture of African and Arabian cultures produced a rich and exotic civilization. Axum is most famous for the huge stone *stelae*, or columns, set up over royal burials around AD 400. Soon after this, Greek and Syrian missionaries converted the people of Axum to Christianity, setting up a rival church to the Nubian one but one that still flourishes in Ethiopia today.

These kingdoms resisted the Islamic Arab expansion of the seventh century AD, but the trade routes of the Red Sea came under Arab control. Axum and Nubia were almost cut off from the outside world.

Right. This bronze casting of a human head comes from Igbo Ukwu in southeast Nigeria. The people of this culture produced some marvellous bronze statues, quite distinct in style from bronzes produced in other African states. This bronze dates from the ninth century AD.

Sub-Saharan Trade

Trade routes

This map shows the routes by which trade goods were carried across the Sahara and down the east coast. The cities founded on and around such routes developed the richest cultures.

GREAT GHANA On the other side of Africa another kingdom was growing. The Arabs called it Ghana, but it should not be confused with the country which we call Ghana today. The ancient kingdom was called Wagadu by its people and encompassed the region where Mali and Mauretania are situated today. To begin with it was a tribe of farmers in the savannah–the plains south of the Sahara Desert. But in the eighth and ninth centuries AD *Berber* merchants from North Africa crossed the Sahara with their camel *caravans*.

At Kumbi, on the southern edge of the Sahara, trade goods were unloaded from the desert camels and taken over by donkeys or human porters to be carried south over the savannah. In this way the city became rich on the trade. Gold from the mines of Bambuk, and ivory, skins and slaves were sold on to the cities of the Middle East. In return the Berbers brought copper to be made into ornaments, and salt. Before long Kumbi was a rich

Archaeological Remains at Igbo Ukwu

Left. A reconstruction of the burial at Igbo Ukwu.

Above. A view from above the burial pit, showing the positions in which the bones and artefacts were found.

Left. This bronze casting of an animal's head was found at Igbo Ukwu. Most of the bronzes found there are very elaborately decorated, even such everyday objects as pots, bowls and sword handles.

The Igbo Ukwu culture was only discovered relatively recently. A man was digging in his back garden for mud to build a new house. What he found were the remains of an ancient culture previously unheard of. Very little is known about the Igbo Ukwu people. From their remains it seems that they must have lived in a rich and sophisticated society which had surpluses to exchange for copper. Amongst the findings were beads from India, making it clear that these people engaged in long-distance trade.

The most remarkable find at Igbo Ukwu was the burial of a priest or ruler (see illustrations above). He was buried in a seated position in a wooden chamber along with his slaves. His foot was resting on an elephant tusk and a staff was placed in his right hand.

The bronzes left behind by these people are also remarkable. They are highly decorated and show an advanced technical skill, as well as a strong artistic sense.

city, with a royal palace and a special area of merchants' houses. It came to an end in the 11th century when Berbers from the desert invaded Ghana and converted it to Islam.

IGBO UKWU Further east, in the forests of Nigeria, the copper from the Sahara was being turned into wonderful ornaments for kings. At Igbo Ukwu an astonishing collection of bronze vessels and ornaments of the ninth century AD have been discovered. Close by was the burial of a man seated on a stool in all his finery.

1 Early in the AD 800s, the Vikings of Scandinavia began to expand into Russia. They seized parts of northern Russia in the AD 860s and founded the city of Novgorod. During the same period, the Vikings launched a series of attacks on England. Between AD 856–875 they conquered the Kingdoms of Mercia, Northumbria and East Anglia.

2 The Chola Dynasty became pre-eminent in India in the ninth century AD. The early part of their rule saw a great expansion in temple-building. During this period temples in the countryside became the social and economic centres of the community, and also acted as banks and schools. The Chola Dynasty came to an end in the twelfth century AD.

3 The Abbasid Caliphs took over as rulers of the Islamic world from AD 750. During their reign, architecture and the arts flourished and a new capital was founded at Baghdad in AD 766.

THE PEOPLE OF AMERICA: HUNTERS AND GARDENERS

Hunting the Buffalo

Though North American Indians hunted many animals, the buffalo was the most important. They used every bit of it for something. As soon as the animals had been killed, men, women and children joined in skinning and cutting up the carcasses.

Spoons (1) were made from horn. Stone hammers (2) were bound to their handles with *rawhide*. Skulls (3) were painted and used in religious festivals. Bone knives (4) and bone fleshing tools (5) were made from leg bones. *Parfleches* (6), envelopes used for carrying belongings, and cases (7) for storing war bonnets were made from rawhide. Hide was also decorated and used to make robes (8). Finally, the tail was used as a decoration on quillwork; this served as a tent ornament.

Some time in the last Ice Age, perhaps as long as 30,000 years ago, people first came to the vast continent of America.

OVER THE FROZEN WASTES The glaciers of the Arctic held so much of the world's water that the seas were 50 metres lower than they are now. What is now the Bering Strait, between Siberia and Alaska, was dry land.

Tundra stretched from Europe, through Asia, to America, and enormous herds of musk ox, bison, reindeer and horse roamed across it. Behind the herds were human hunters, and by following the herds they drifted into America. Soon they began to move south into warmer lands, through Canada into the United States and finally into South America. It was not a great migration; it was a very gradual process, tribes moving a little further each year and taking advantage of new hunting grounds. By 10,000 BC the whole of America, right down to Patagonia at the southernmost tip of the continent, was peopled by hunters.

THE LAND GROWS WARMER As the Ice Age died and the glaciers shrank, the environment changed. Forests spread over what had been endless tundra and deserts grew up where there had been forests.

The animals changed too; mammoth, horse and Arctic bison died out, to be replaced by deer, smaller bison and other species which were better adapted for the warmer climate. The hunters adapted too, and developed a new way of life.

HUNTERS TO FARMERS The first Americans brought domestic dogs with them, but it was many centuries before farming appeared in the continent. It was Central America and tropical South America where people started to grow their own food 7000–8000 years ago.

Some of the world's most important foods were cultivated here–potatoes, beans, marrows, peppers, sweet potatoes, and *maize*. Cotton was grown for cloth and some native animals were domesticated, such as the llama, macaw, turkey and guinea pig. The llama's wool and the meat of the guinea pig were particularly important in South America.

In North America farming, which in its earliest state was actually more like gardening, caught on slowly. By 2000 BC the idea of growing maize, beans and *squashes* had come in from Mexico, but hunting continued to be an important way of getting food. Villagers grew their crops in gardens at home while they hunted deer, rabbits and birds in the forests. The horse had died out, so all hunting was done on foot. One plant was grown which was no use at all for food or clothing–tobacco. Smoking was an important ritual, carried out at ceremonies and festivals.

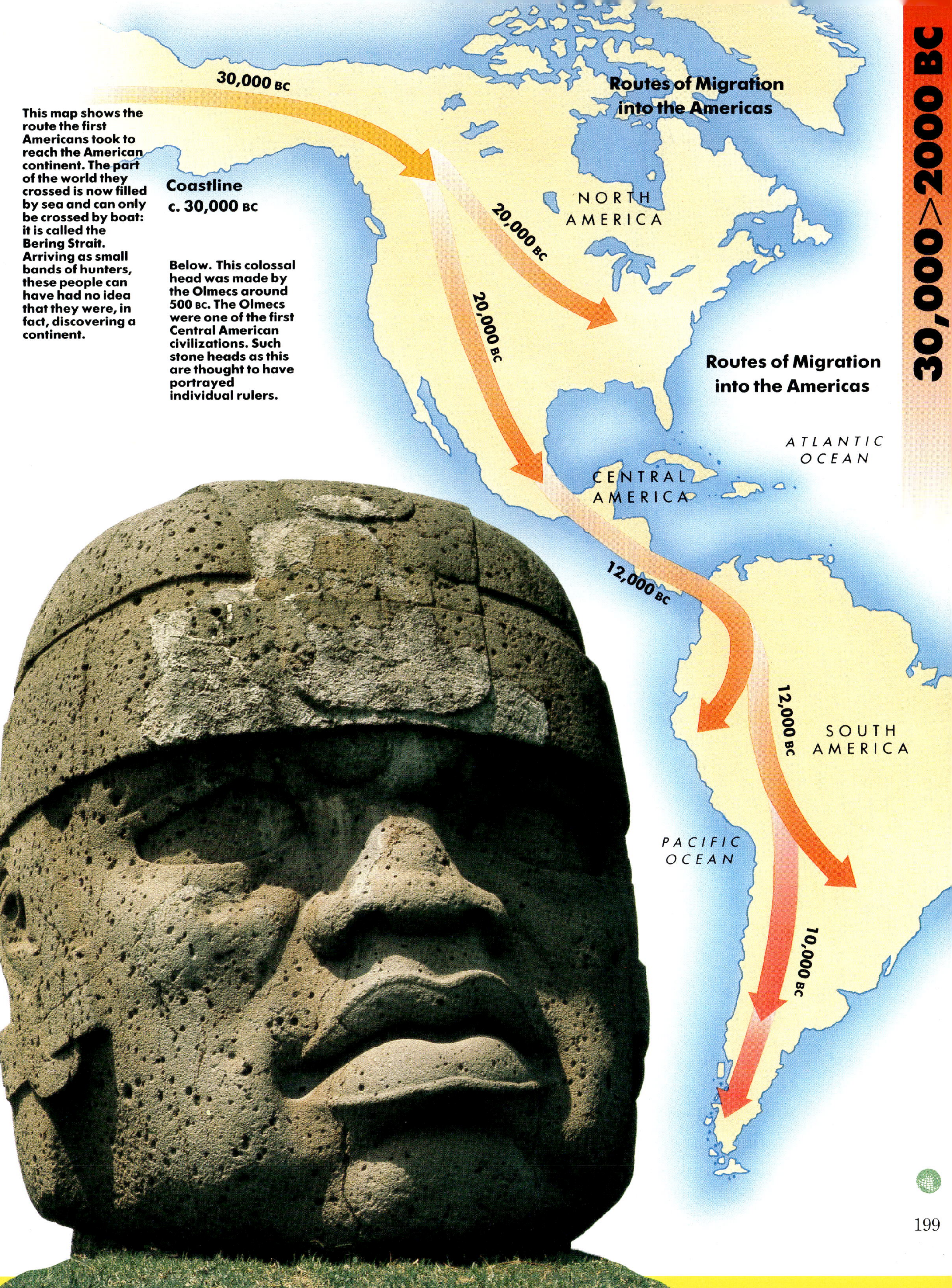

This map shows the route the first Americans took to reach the American continent. The part of the world they crossed is now filled by sea and can only be crossed by boat: it is called the Bering Strait. Arriving as small bands of hunters, these people can have had no idea that they were, in fact, discovering a continent.

Below. This colossal head was made by the Olmecs around 500 BC. The Olmecs were one of the first Central American civilizations. Such stone heads as this are thought to have portrayed individual rulers.

THE PEOPLE OF AMERICA: CITIES AND TEMPLES

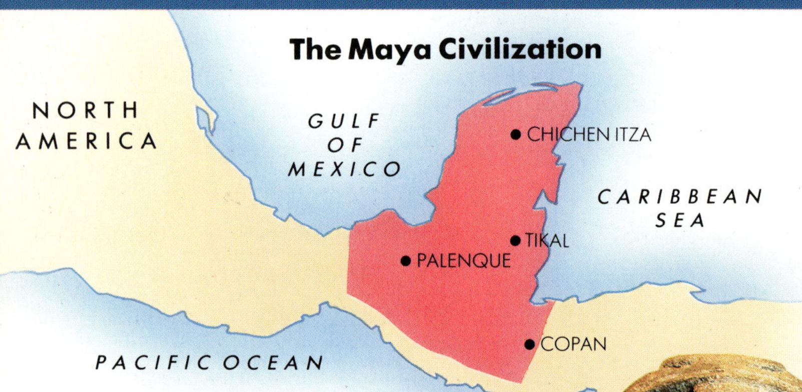

Above. Though the Mayan civilization covered a relatively small area, it probably developed the most advanced culture of the ancient American civilizations.

Right. This Mayan sculpture depicts a human face emerging from the jaws of an animal. You can see the animal's tongue hanging below the man's chin.

Even now, after many years of research, the beginning of cities and of civilization is still a mystery. Some ordinary farming villages grew into vast cities with thousands of inhabitants and specialist groups of citizens like priests, craftsmen and civil servants. This process happened at different periods in different parts of the world.

In the Americas, the first cities appeared in the jungles of Central America and on the mountains of Peru and Bolivia in South America, in about 1000 BC

THE OLMECS In Central America the first cities were built by a civilization called the Olmecs, between about 1000 BC and 400 BC. They were centred around stone temples where the Olmecs worshipped their jaguar gods. Why their cities died out we do not know, but there was a gap of about 400 years before the great cities of the Maya appeared.

Right. The Mayan city of Copan was one of the three or four main centres of the Classic Mayan civilization. Large architectural complexes such as this incorporated temples, palaces, plazas and ball courts. Such complexes formed the centres of Mayan cities, and were fundamental to their civilization.

MAYAN CITIES A Mayan city like Copan shown here was not the least like a modern one. There were no wheeled vehicles and the cities housed only relatively small populations. The heart of the city did not consist of shops or a market, but of squares, or plazas, surrounded by high stone pyramids. Unlike Egyptian pyramids, the Mayan constructions were not intended for burials, but served as huge platforms on which temples were built.

Between the pyramids citizens gathered for festivals, ceremonies and dancing, and to watch ceremonial ball games played in great stone-walled courtyards.

MAYAN ASTRONOMERS The houses of the city were scattered around the centre, still in uncleared jungle, but it was the plazas which were important. Here Mayan priests studied the sky and developed a sophisticated astronomical calendar. One of their hieroglyphic inscriptions records an astronomical conference held at Copan in AD 776.

TEMPLES OF TIHUANACO In the high Bolivian Andes, about 400 metres above sea level, is Tihuanaco, another great city of temples, courtyards and houses. Stone pillars and statues stand in courtyards decorated with carved human heads. Around the city 8000 hectares of land were farmed, irrigated by artificial water channels, to feed the potters, priests, metalworkers, weavers and administrators who lived in the great city.

NORTH AMERICA Many of the ideas from Mexican cities travelled north into the United States. Along the Mississippi River, square mounds of

The Mayan System of Numbers

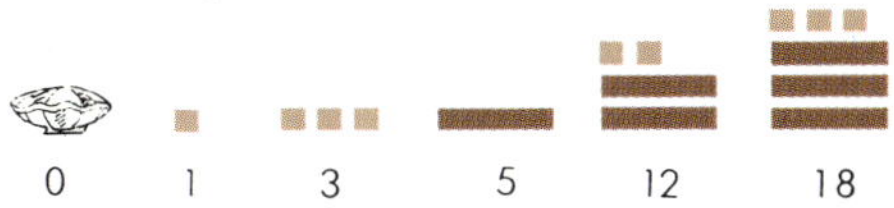

The Maya were the only truly literate civilization of the Americas. They devised a system of numbers, a calendar, and a writing system. They used three basic symbols for numbers: a shell for zero, a dot for one, and a bar for five.

Left. The dwellings at Mesa Verde in the southwest of the United States were built in the twelfth century AD by the Anasazi people. Of the many ruins, Cliff Palace, shown here, is the largest and most famous.
It contains over 400 rooms and is four storeys high in some places. The rooms were small with low ceilings. Some rooms seem to have been entered through the roof, by using ladders, rather than by doors. No-one is sure what the towers were used for at Cliff Palace. They could possibly have been defensive lookouts, or perhaps observatories for viewing the position of the sun.

earth with wooden temples appeared, which were very much like Mayan cities.

But most spectacular of all North American early towns are the towns in the deserts of the southwest of the United States. In Mesa Verde in Colorado, North American Indians built huge terraced houses in the shelter of the *mesa's* overhanging cliffs. These cliff dwellings housed hundreds of people. The people of Mesa Verde were farmers and traces of their fields can still be seen on top of the mesa.

Five hundred years before Columbus set foot in America, native Americans had achieved much that was equivalent to what their contemporaries had achieved in Europe.

New Empires and Cultures
TIME CHART

AD	BYZANTIUM/AFRICA	THE ISLAMIC WORLD	THE FAR EAST	AMERICA AND THE PACIFIC
320			Chandragupta founds Gupta Empire in north India	
330	Foundation of Constantinople (Byzantium)			
400	First towns appear in sub-Saharan Africa			Polynesians settle in the Pacific islands
440	Huns in Greece			
480			Gupta Empire overthrown	
500				Teotihuacan in Central America is sixth largest city in the world (population: 200,000)
527	Justinian becomes Emperor of Byzantium			
538	Silk worms brought to Constantinople			
550			Buddhism comes to Japan	
570		Muhammad born in Mecca		
589			Sui Dynasty begins in China	
622		The Hegira—Muhammad flees to Medina		
630		Muhammad captures Mecca	Tang Dynasty begins in China	
632		Muhammad dies		
642	Arabs conquer Egypt and spread into north Africa			
650		Persia invaded		All major island groups of the Pacific settled by Polynesians
660		Beginning of the Umayyad Dynasty		
700				The civilization of the Maya flourishes in Central America Domination of North American southwest by Mogollon, Hohokam and Anasazi cultures
710			Beginning of Nara period in Japan	
711		Invasion of Spain		
750		Muslims defeat Chinese army Umayyads overthrown by the Abbasid Dynasty. Capital of the Empire is moved from Damascus to Baghdad		
784			Beginning of the Heian period in Japan	
800	The civilization at Great Ghana in Africa flourishes		The Khmer Kingdom emerges in Cambodia	First use of the bow and arrow in the Mississippi valley
900	Civilization at Igbo Ukwu in Africa			Polynesians reach New Zealand
909		Fatimid Dynasty emerges in the Eastern Maghreb. Begins to compete with the Abbasids		
950				Toltecs rise to power in central Mexico
960			Sung Dynasty begins in China	
1050			Printing with moveable type invented in China	

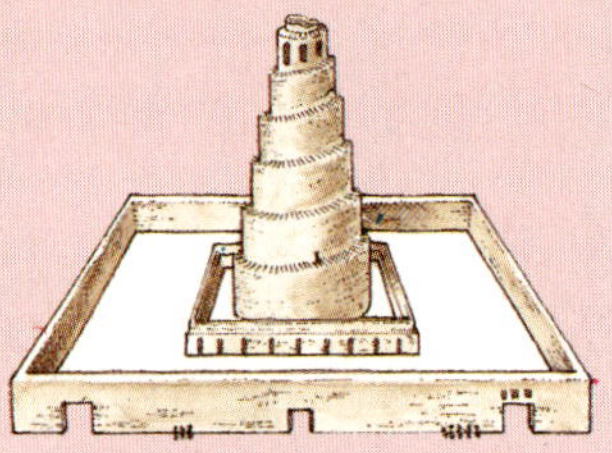

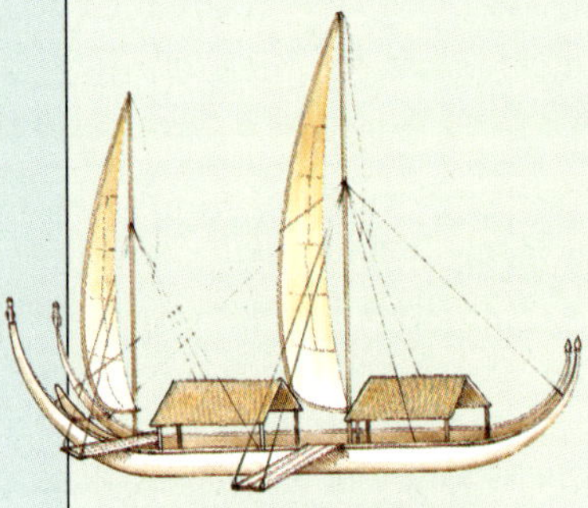

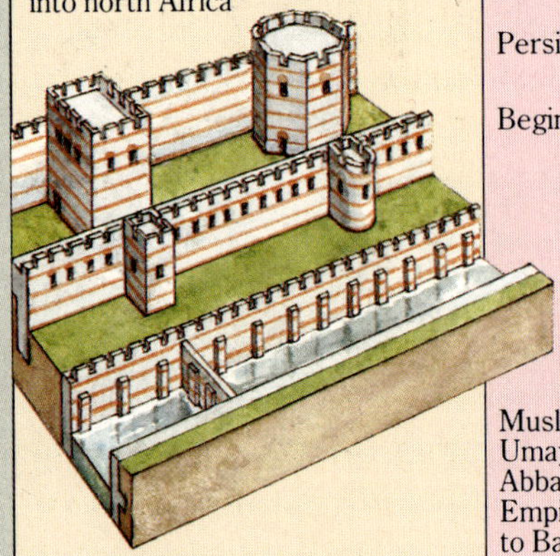

PART ONE

Three Great Civilizations

The next section looks at three great civilizations which flourished between AD 1100–1350. In western Europe, society was organized according to a *feudal system*; everyone, from the greatest noble to the lowliest peasant, was allowed to occupy their land only in return for paying some sort of rent or performing some sort of service. Nobles owed their feudal service (leading troops in battle) directly to the king; peasants owed theirs (doing farm work) to the nobleman or woman who had been granted the local great estate by the king. The Church was the other great force in western European civilization. Clergymen were the best educated people in Europe. They played an important part in government, as well as offering spiritual guidance and advice.

ISLAM In the medieval Muslim world, which stretched from southern Spain to the borders of China, law, government, art, literature and learning were all shaped by the teachings of the Islamic faith. People from many different backgrounds were linked together by this shared culture, and medieval Muslim achievements in mathematics, science and technology were admired and imitated around the world.

CHINA In the East, another brilliant and advanced civilization developed in Sung China, and influenced many of the neighbouring lands. Chinese technological discoveries, such as printing, gunpowder and paper money, were far in advance of anything known in the western world.

Chinese silks, porcelain, and spices were exported to Europe and the Muslim world, where they were highly prized. In this way, trade linked these three great medieval civilizations, and allowed their people, as well as their ideas and inventions, to make contact with one another.

POPULATION GROWTH AND PROSPERITY During the years 1100–1300, many countries in different parts of the world grew rich and prosperous. Populations increased, towns expanded, farming and trading became more profitable, and wealthy patrons paid for many beautiful buildings, paintings and other works of art.

EUROPE: COUNTRIES AND PEOPLES

Norman knights, from the Bayeux 'Tapestry', embroidered c.1100 by a group of noblewomen to record the Norman conquest of England in 1066. The tapestry shows the events leading up to the Norman invasion, and the decisive Battle of Hastings, in 'comic strip' form. It is over 70 metres long.

The 12th and 13th centuries are often called the 'High Middle Ages' in Europe. This is because they were a time of peace, growth and stability, compared to the restless and often violent years that had just passed.

During the years 700–1050, the peoples of Europe had lived through civil wars and *dynastic* disputes in France and Germany. They had faced invasions by *nomadic Magyar* tribes from the east, and by Muslim forces, based in Arabia and North Africa, from the south and west. Most damaging of all, they had suffered repeated pirate raids and savage attacks from roving bands of warriors–the Vikings of Scandinavia.

THE VIKINGS The last major Viking raid in Europe was the Norman attack on England in 1066. The Normans were Vikings, who had settled in Northern France. Under their leader, Duke William, Norman forces invaded and occupied England. The Norman language, customs, and ideas about government rapidly became mixed with local English traditions, and laid the foundations for the medieval civilization of England.

A NEW ERA But, by 1100, when this section begins, the centuries of pirate raids and large-scale invasions of Europe were almost over. In many European states, settled governments and freedom from outside attack led to a period of growth and expansion. Populations increased, new lands were cleared for farming, towns prospered, and trade and manufacturing industries became increasingly important. There was money to spare for building castles, churches, city walls and great cathedrals. Kings and government officials passed new laws and developed new ways to administer the countries they ruled.

THE BATTLES GO ON Even so, war and the disruption it brought to the lives of ordinary people had not completely vanished from Europe. In England and France, kings struggled to win new territory, or, sometimes, simply to stay in power. In Spain, Italy and southern France, local armies fought to recapture lands conquered by Muslim rulers.

The great Byzantine Empire in eastern Europe was constantly on the alert against attack by its great trading rivals, the Italian city-states of Venice and Genoa, or by Muslim forces from the Middle East.

And on the northeastern frontiers of Europe, the great Russian kingdom centred on the city of Kiev was repeatedly threatened by nomad invaders sweeping westwards across the plains of central Asia.

The countries of Europe, c.1100 AD, compared with a modern map of Europe. During the Middle Ages, wars, boundary disputes, quarrels over inheritance and marriage alliances all helped to shape the boundaries of European countries as we know them today.

Left. The Byzantine emperor John II Commenus, from a mosaic picture in the great church (now a mosque) of Santa Sophia in Constantinople (present-day Istanbul, in Turkey). He was a successful ruler, who made treaties with neighbouring Muslim states to protect the frontier lands of his empire, and so preserved its power.

Above. Viking longships were designed and built to carry passengers and cargo, as well as raiders across the stormy northern seas.

Key Viking Dates

c. 600–700	Growth of powerful Viking kingdoms in Scandinavia
793	First Viking raid on England
841	Vikings settle in Dublin, Ireland
911	Viking leader Rollo gains large territory in Normandy, France
982	Viking emperors settle in Greenland
c. 1000	Viking sailors cross the Atlantic Ocean and reach Newfoundland in Canada
1014–1035	Viking King Cnut the Great rules over an empire in Norway, Sweden, Denmark and England
1090	Normans invade and conquer Sicily, important centre of international trade
c.1100	Growth of separate, independent kingdoms of Norway, Sweden and Denmark. End of Viking raids

Left. Viking gravestone, from Gotland, Sweden, showing scenes from Viking mythology and a warship with a fully armed crew.

A LIVING FROM THE LAND

Peasants harvesting barley on their lord's land. They are using sickles, with sharp, curved blades to cut the straw. The man with the big stick is the lord's reeve, or overseer. He is giving orders and organizing the harvest work.

What was life like for the people who lived in Europe during the High Middle Ages? Most people worked on the land, growing food and rearing livestock. It was hard, dirty and heavy work, but essential if enough food was to be produced to feed Europe's growing population.

Men, women and, sometimes, children laboured in the fields, ploughing, sowing and harvesting corn; making hay to feed cattle and horses; gathering grapes to make wine; and picking apples and pears to provide welcome sweetness during the winter. Women made salty, pungent cheese from the milk provided by cows, sheep and goats. Fish were caught along the coast, and were preserved by salting, or hung outside to dry.

NEW TECHNOLOGY Power–to pull ploughs, carry loads, chop down trees or clear new lands–was provided by men and animals. There were few machines to help them, although some important inventions, such as windmills (for grinding corn) and water-powered *fulling mills* (used in making cloth), were developed at this time. Women kneaded bread, dug gardens, plucked chickens and skinned rabbits, churned milk, sheared sheep and spun wool, as well as looking after their homes, their husbands and their children.

HOUSES AND BUILDINGS Ordinary peoples' houses were made of strong, heavy timbers, sawn and shaped

A typical medieval village in northern Europe. The villagers' houses are grouped around the church. Each house had its own little garden, where vegetables were grown, and chickens and perhaps bees were kept. The largest house in the village belonged to the local lord. Unlike the villagers' homes, it had separate rooms for eating, sleeping and relaxing, and a proper chimney. Wealthy lords might have houses or castles in several villages. They travelled round from one house to another, leaving their staff of estate managers, farmhands and servants to manage everything while they were away. The villagers made their living by working in the fields surrounding the village. Land was often farmed in big *'open' fields*, rather than in small, separate, enclosed plots. It was easier to plough and to gather in the harvest that way. Each villager had several strips, divided by ditches, fences or boundary stones. They worked together in the fields; that way, everyone stood a chance of growing a good crop.

Population Levels

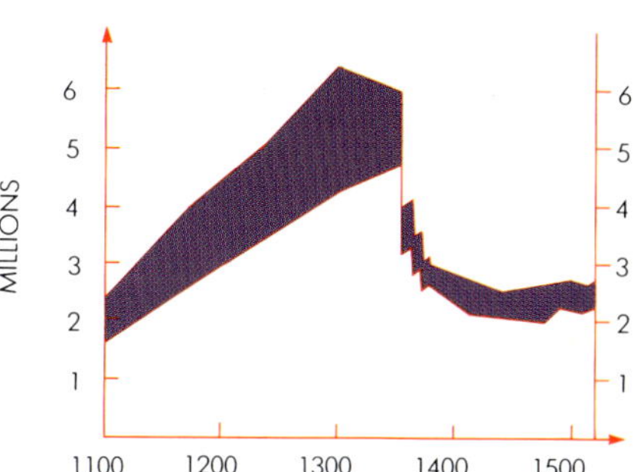

In comparison with the present-day, medieval population levels were very low. In AD 1000 the total population of Europe was around 38 or 39 million. (Today it is around 450 million.)

By the middle of the 14th century, the European population had almost doubled in size, to around 74 million. Plagues and famines then caused a dramatic fall, of perhaps 25 million, and the population did not regain its pre-plague size until the late 16th century.

The graph above details these changes for medieval England.

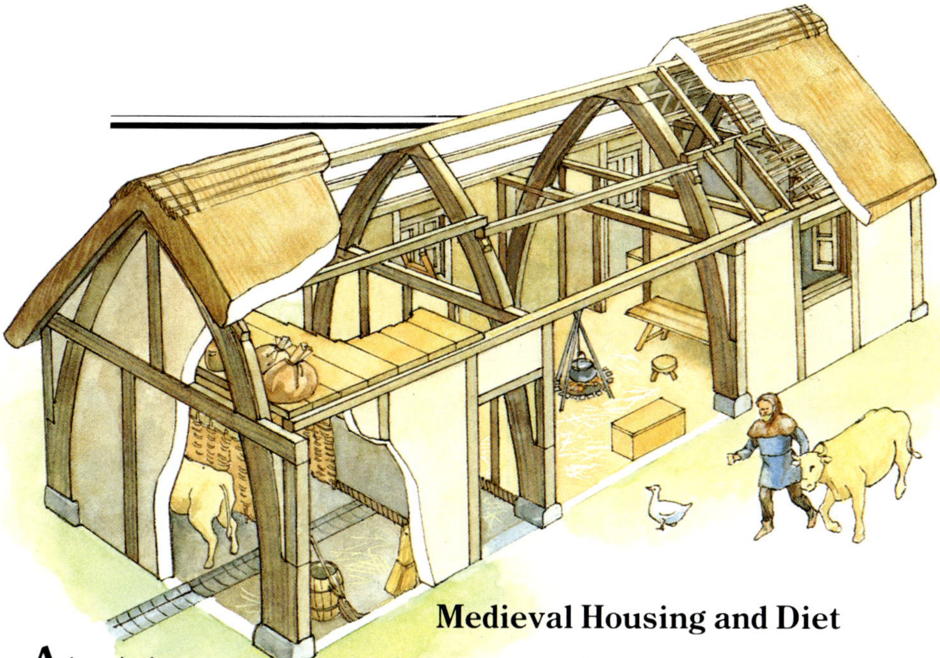

Medieval Housing and Diet

Above is shown a typical medieval village house. One end was used for eating and sleeping; the other was used as a barn, with stalls for cattle, and storage space for farm equipment and food.

The typical medieval diet in northern Europe consisted of bread, cheese, dried peas and beans (made into soup), cabbage, onions, garlic, apples, and pears, with watery ale to drink. Eggs, meat and fresh fish were luxuries.

In southern Europe, wine, soft fruit and olives provided welcome variety. When the harvest failed, or animals fell sick, people went hungry.

by hand, and fitted together with the help of friends and neighbours. The spaces between the timbers were filled with a sticky mass of clay, straw and horsehair, 'puddled' together by stirring and trampling underfoot. In places where timber was scarce, houses were made of rough stone, often with slate or turf for roofs.

SOCIAL STRUCTURE In many parts of Europe, ordinary people did not own their own plots of land. Instead, they occupied them as tenants of the local lord. They paid him rent (in money, produce, or by working a set number of days on his farm) for the right to live and work in 'their' houses and fields. Some people were also personally unfree. This meant that they were owned by the lord, in the same way that he owned horses and cattle. Unfree men and women could not marry, move house or travel without his permission, and, usually, without paying him a sizeable fee for the privilege.

THE RELIGIOUS WORLD

During the Middle Ages, Christian missionaries finally reached the far corners of Europe, and completed a process of conversion that had been going on for hundreds of years. It is hard to find out exactly what ordinary people believed. Probably many more people then than nowadays went to church regularly and said their prayers. They also gave money to build and decorate their local churches, and to support their local priests and religious charities.

But sometimes their Christian beliefs were mixed with the remains of old, *pagan* superstitions, and their understanding of the Church's religious teachings was rather confused.

THE ROLE OF THE CHURCH The Church was the most powerful institution in medieval Europe. Unlike kings and princes, it did not die, and could not easily be overthrown. Instead, it lasted from generation to generation. The head of the western Church was the Pope, who was Bishop of Rome. (Christians in Eastern Europe obeyed a different leader, based in Constantinople–present-day Istanbul).

The Pope ruled over a group of powerful Church officials in all the countries of Europe. There were frequent quarrels between the Pope and local rulers, when they disagreed over political issues, or on matters of Church business. In England, King Henry I gave orders for the English Archbishop Thomas Becket to be murdered, because Becket sided with the Pope and disobeyed the king.

THE WEALTH OF THE CHURCH The Church was also the biggest landowner in Europe. Wealthy, pious men and women gave land, houses, farms and vineyards to the

Above. Pope Urban II (1042–99) consecrates (blesses and pronounces sacred) the new church buildings at the great monastery of Cluny, in Burgundy, now part of France. You can see him on the left of the picture, wearing a golden robe. Cluny was rich, powerful and very influential in medieval Europe. One of its greatest abbots, St Benedict, introduced a new set of rules teaching monks and nuns how to live. These were widely copied and set a standard that lasted for many centuries.

Right. Nuns and priests walking in procession on their way to a church service. One nun is busy ringing the bells to summon everyone to prayer; you can see her pulling on the bell-ropes in the centre of the picture. The sacristan (responsible for all the holy objects in the nuns' church) carries her keys.

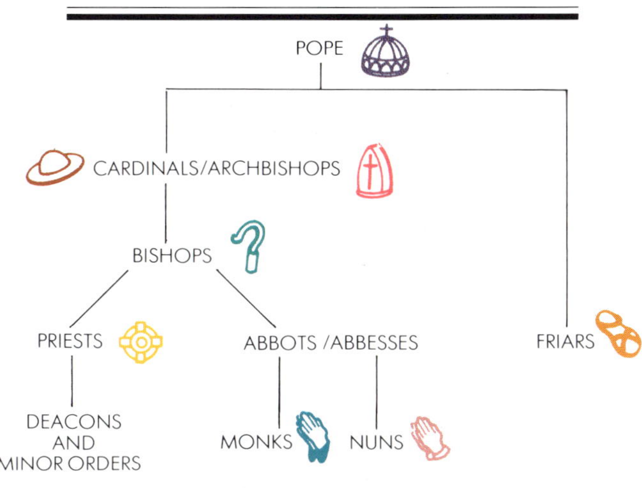

Hierarchy of the Medieval Church

The medieval church was a strict *hierarchy*. There were several different grades of clergy, with great differences of wealth and power among them. All clergymen began their career in the church as deacons and then became priests. A few progressed further to become bishops or archbishops, and a tiny minority might also be appointed cardinal and, eventually, Pope.

Church. They hoped that God would reward their generosity with a place in heaven. They also won fame and admiration among their fellow-Christians while they were still alive. Kings, queens and wealthy nobles competed with one another to build the most beautiful chapel, or the most noble church tower. They gave many rich and precious gifts to their local churches and cathedrals, and, in some cases, contributed large sums of money to pay for architects and craftsmen to design a whole new building in the latest, most fashionable style.

CHRISTIAN ART Many religious treasures have survived from the Middle Ages: gold and silver crosses, brilliant stained and painted glass, fine carvings and statues, *relics* of saints encased in jewel-studded boxes, sumptuous embroideries, and wonderfully decorated manuscripts containing Bible stories, hymns and prayers. These were produced by craftsmen in the towns, and also by monks and nuns, working in religious communities shut away from the world.

Left. Cathedrals are among the most beautiful and impressive buildings to survive from the medieval period. Architects experimented with daring and dramatic new structures, and invented ingenious new techniques to build, taller, lighter, more elegant designs.
A cathedral could take hundreds of years to build. Craftsmen working there had no power-tools to help them. Stones and woodwork had to be laboriously cut and shaped by hand. Roofs and spires were covered in tiles, or coated with heavy lead sheeting.
Inside, great care and attention was paid to cathedral decoration. Walls were painted with scenes from the Bible. Brilliant stained glass was installed, and elaborately decorated tiles covered the floors. Men and women embroidered robes and hangings in silk and gold thread, and gold and jewels were used to make crosses to stand on the altar.

GOVERNMENT, LAW AND LEARNING

The Church acted as an important centre of learning during the Middle Ages. Priests, monks and nuns studied and translated religious and philosophical texts; wrote books on religious topics; ran boarding schools for the children of wealthy parents; and acted as advisors to powerful men and women.

RELIGION AND EDUCATION Outside the enclosed world of monasteries and nunneries, students and teachers in all the great universities of Europe were enrolled in 'holy orders'. This meant that they had taken the first steps towards becoming a priest.

In fact, few of them took their religious careers any further. They went on, instead, to work as clerks, *scribes* and administrators for governments throughout Europe. Others became full-time scholars, seeking teaching jobs in schools and colleges, or worked as secretaries and private tutors in noble households.

THE CHANGE IN GOVERNMENT Kings and governments in Europe were becoming increasingly professional during the Middle Ages. In the past, rulers had relied on their loyal military commanders and on their household servants to carry out their orders. Now, educated men helped kings, nobles and local lords draft laws, keep accounts, collect taxes, compose important letters, conduct delicate negotiations, and discuss treaties and alliances between friendly nations. Kings also began to summon meetings of noblemen and representatives from the towns and the countryside to help them share the responsibility for decision-making, and to take the blame for unpopular measures such as higher taxes or harsh new laws.

THE ROLE OF KINGS Even with all these trained helpers, the personality and intelligence of each king was still tremendously important. He had to be able to understand national and international politics; to cope with the details of day-to-day administration; to know how to give orders that people would obey; and how to choose wise and prudent advisors. Most important of all, he had to win the trust, loyalty and affection of all his subjects. Often, the only way this could be done was by gifts and rewards.

Although the Church taught that kings were appointed by God, and that it was everyone's duty to obey them, a weak or foolish king found it difficult to gain support at home or allies abroad, and lived in constant fear of being overthrown.

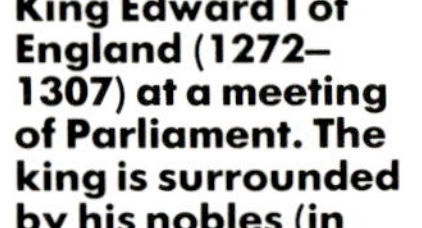

King Edward I of England (1272–1307) at a meeting of Parliament. The king is surrounded by his nobles (in scarlet robes) and by the bishops (wearing pointed hats, called mitres).

The First Universities in Europe

Medieval Education

Universities were founded throughout Europe in the Middle Ages. The earliest universities were in southern Europe, but by the end of the medieval period they had been established in northern European countries as well. Paris (France) and Bologna (Italy) were probably the most famous and respected universities; students flocked to study there from many lands.

By present-day standards, medieval universities taught a narrow range of topics: theology, law, medicine music and philosophy. Students prepared for their degrees by studying two groups of subjects: the *trivium* (which included linguistics, grammar and philosophy); and the *quadrivium*, which included mathematics, music and astronomy. Law and medicine were specialized extras. Most young people in medieval Europe did not go to school, let alone university. Parents taught poor children the practical skills they would need to earn a living; most medieval country people could not read or write, but these skills were sometimes learned by shopkeepers and other tradesmen living in towns.

Fourteenth-century carving from Italy, showing university students and their professor in a classroom. Italian universities were famous for their scholarship in medicine and law.

The Structure of Medieval Society

The most powerful person in any medieval society was the king or prince (or, very rarely a queen) who ruled the country.

Kings and princes relied on nobles to help them. They acted as war-leaders, governors of distant regions, and as senior government advisors. They were rewarded by kings with grants of land titles and other honours.

Knights were less wealthy and less powerful than the nobles, but played an important role, originally in war and later in local administration.

There was a small, but growing, professional group within medieval society – chiefly composed of lawyers and government administrators.

In towns, merchants and shopkeepers prospered.

But most men and women living in medieval Europe were poor, by modern standards. They occupied their land in return for money rent paid to the local landowner (a knight or noble), or in return for working on the landowner's farm. They also paid taxes – to the Church, to the king, and sometimes to the local lord. Some of these peasants were free; others were unfree. They 'belonged' to their lord, and could do little without his permission.

People without home, land or families to support them were at the bottom of medieval society. Beggars were a common sight, especially in towns.

5–10% KINGS, PRINCES, NOBLES, BISHOPS, ETC.
90–95% THE REST
5% THE VERY POOR

Structure of society in 1100

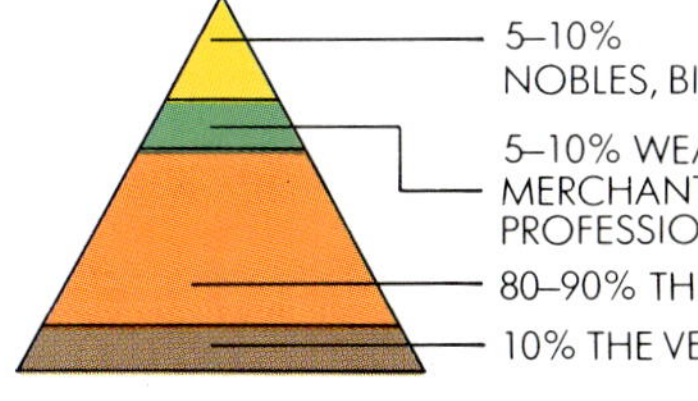

Structure of society in 1450

CHIVALRY: LOVE AND WAR

A Knight's Armour

Medieval knights rode into battle wearing armour to protect themselves from attack by swords and spears.

Chain mail was made from interlocking wire rings (see below) worn over a thick leather jerkin. Later, armour was made of solid metal plates joined together. It encased the wearer completely, but it was heavy and cumbersome.

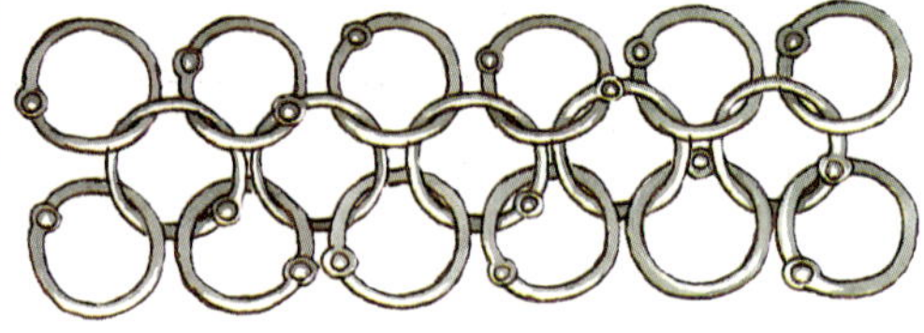

Left. The German nobleman, Heinrich von Anhalt (1170–1252) fighting with his companions at a tournament. Noble ladies look on while he prepares to 'unhorse' his opponent.

In medieval Europe, power was based on land ownership, and on the fighting men who could conquer and defend it. Medieval kings rewarded their faithful warriors, advisors and companions with gifts of land, as well as with titles and special privileges. These noblemen granted out smaller portions of their estates to their own followers, in return for a promise to fight alongside them when required.

In this way, men in the upper ranks of society became linked by ties of property and loyalty. The king could rely on his nobles to support him, otherwise he would take away their land. In turn, the nobles could rely (for the same reason) on a band of well armed followers, called *knights*, to accompany them in battle and assist them in local peace-keeping and *garrison* duties.

CHANGES IN THE MILITARY SYSTEM At first, the knights provided their own small private armies of ordinary soldiers. Foot-soldiers, armed with bows and arrows, were also recruited from among poor farm labourers, workers in towns, outlaws, petty criminals and even prisoners. But by 1300, rulers throughout Europe had begun to hire professional soldiers, who would fight for anyone who paid them. Some knights preferred to pay a sum of money, rather than provide troops or ride to war. This, along with tolls and taxes,

Castles were first built as military strongholds, and they continued to be important wartime fortresses throughout the Middle Ages. But, by the 14th century, they were beginning to develop into impressive family homes and centres of estate administration.

A large castle was like a town in miniature. It was surrounded by fields where food for the inhabitants was grown. Within the 'curtain' of its strong walls, there were: exercise yards for the castle garrison; a well to provide fresh water; a kitchen and bakery; various workshops; a blacksmith's forge; servants' housing; stables and barns; and perhaps even a pleasure garden where the castle ladies could stroll.

Right. Knights sometimes wore elaborate tunics over their armour, to display their heraldic coats of arms.

helped to pay for the costs of feeding and transporting the troops, and providing them with weapons.

THE IDEAL KNIGHT Even if some knights did not fight, the ties of loyalty between kings, great nobles and their knights were still very important. A code of behaviour grew up, embodying all the characteristics of the ideal knight. He should be bold and brave, yet gentle, considerate, wise and courteous. He should be a ruthless fighter, but also fond of music, poetry and polite society. Preferably, he should be inspired by the love of some beautiful lady, whom he worshipped from afar. He should be a good Christian, and follow the teachings of the Church. His manners should be perfect, his speech smooth and entertaining, his appearance manly, strong, energetic and elegant.

Understandably, this ideal knight did not really exist. But he is a familiar figure in many medieval songs and stories, and tells us a lot about the qualities that people valued at the time.

Chivalry, as this code of behaviour was called, applied to the upper classes only. Ordinary, rough soldiers were simply expected to shoot straight and obey orders.

EUROPE AT THE FRONTIERS

Christian armies loading troops and equipment onto a transport ship at a Mediterranean port, before sailing off to the Crusades. From a 14th century French manuscript.

We have seen that the 11th–13th centuries were a time of growth and stability within Europe. Even so, many European kings had to face opposition from powerful nobles within their kingdoms, or disputes with neighbouring countries over the possession of land. For example, Germany was shaken by civil wars during the period 1070–1120, and England and France quarrelled frequently over the ownership of lands in Aquitaine, a region in southern France.

FRONTIER BATTLES The situation was rather different for states on the frontiers of Europe. They were exposed to influences, and sometimes attacks, from non-European powers, whose languages, culture, and faith were often completely different from their own.

SPAIN These frontier contacts sometimes resulted in a rich new civilization. In southern Spain, which was governed by Muslim rulers for most of the Middle Ages, a well educated, multi-cultural and tolerant community developed.

Jews, Christians and Muslims lived peacefully side by side, and learned much from each others' traditions, skills and achievements.

But, inspired by their faith and by feelings of national pride, the Christian kings of northern Spain felt compelled to launch a series of attacks on the southern Muslim state which they felt was 'occupying' land that was rightfully theirs.

NORTHERN EUROPE On the northern frontiers of Europe, conquests disturbed local cultures. German forces advanced northwards and eastwards into lands occupied by the Slav peoples, in present-day Poland and Lithuania. German settlements were also established to the southeast, around the modern Czech Republic. German emperors tried to increase their power in Italy too.

THE CRUSADES Kings, knights and churchmen from all over Europe were involved in another series of invasions–the Crusades. During these wars, Christian troops attempted to capture the 'Holy Land', as they called the territory surrounding the city of Jerusalem (in present-day Israel and Jordan), from Muslim rulers.

The Crusades provide us with a good example of the typical medieval combination of high ideals, greed and brutal conduct. Undoubtedly, many soldiers joined the crusading armies because they wanted to see a Christian king ruling the land where Jesus had lived and died. But others hoped for the chance to win fame or rich plunder, or simply had a taste for adventure. The Christian troops disgraced themselves on several occasions by cruelty towards their Muslim enemies, and finally returned to Europe, defeated, in 1291.

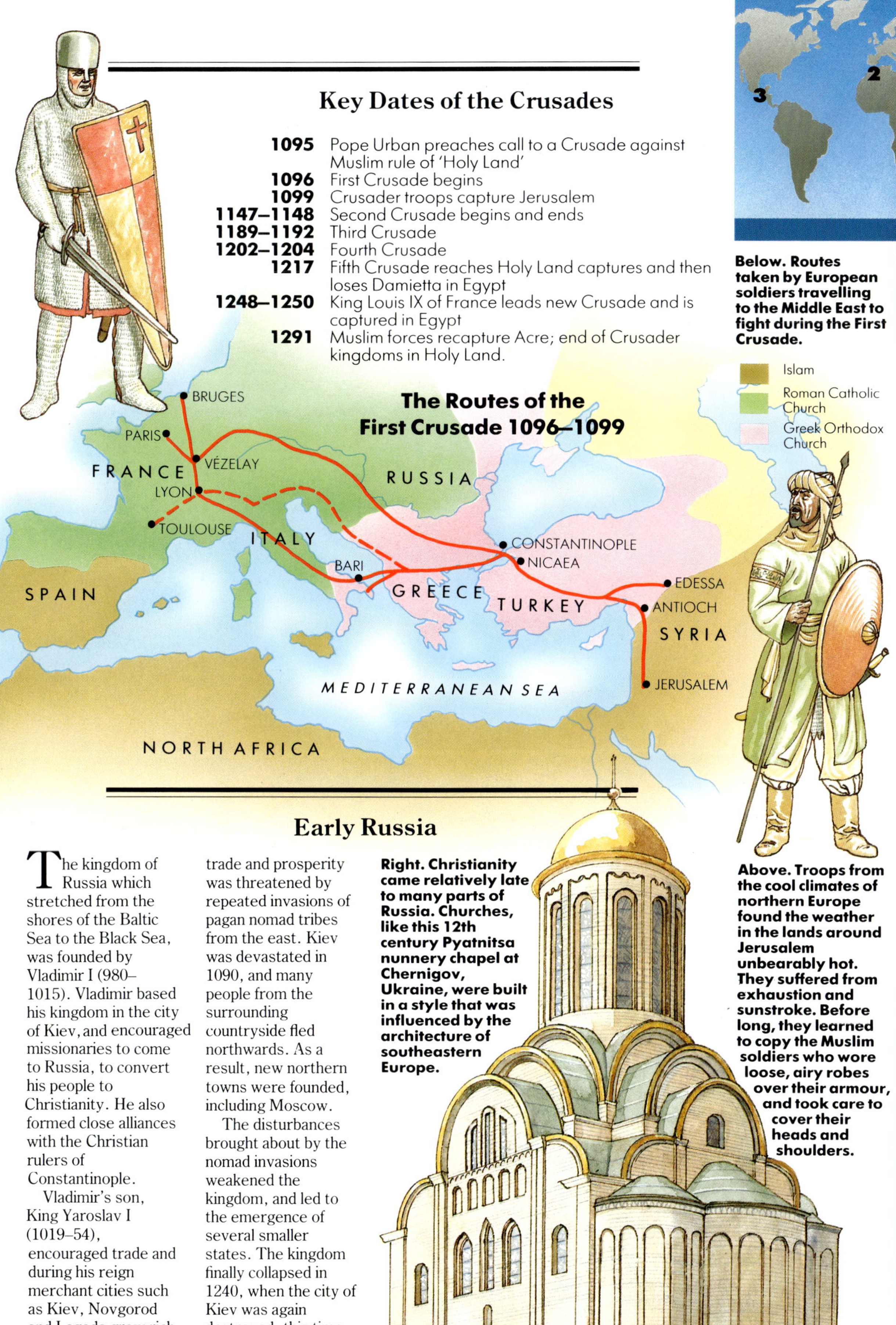

Key Dates of the Crusades

1095	Pope Urban preaches call to a Crusade against Muslim rule of 'Holy Land'
1096	First Crusade begins
1099	Crusader troops capture Jerusalem
1147–1148	Second Crusade begins and ends
1189–1192	Third Crusade
1202–1204	Fourth Crusade
1217	Fifth Crusade reaches Holy Land captures and then loses Damietta in Egypt
1248–1250	King Louis IX of France leads new Crusade and is captured in Egypt
1291	Muslim forces recapture Acre; end of Crusader kingdoms in Holy Land.

Below. Routes taken by European soldiers travelling to the Middle East to fight during the First Crusade.

Above. Troops from the cool climates of northern Europe found the weather in the lands around Jerusalem unbearably hot. They suffered from exhaustion and sunstroke. Before long, they learned to copy the Muslim soldiers who wore loose, airy robes over their armour, and took care to cover their heads and shoulders.

Early Russia

The kingdom of Russia which stretched from the shores of the Baltic Sea to the Black Sea, was founded by Vladimir I (980–1015). Vladimir based his kingdom in the city of Kiev, and encouraged missionaries to come to Russia, to convert his people to Christianity. He also formed close alliances with the Christian rulers of Constantinople.

Vladimir's son, King Yaroslav I (1019–54), encouraged trade and during his reign merchant cities such as Kiev, Novgorod and Lagoda grew rich. But in the years that followed, Russian trade and prosperity was threatened by repeated invasions of pagan nomad tribes from the east. Kiev was devastated in 1090, and many people from the surrounding countryside fled northwards. As a result, new northern towns were founded, including Moscow.

The disturbances brought about by the nomad invasions weakened the kingdom, and led to the emergence of several smaller states. The kingdom finally collapsed in 1240, when the city of Kiev was again destroyed, this time by Mongol invaders from central Asia.

Right. Christianity came relatively late to many parts of Russia. Churches, like this 12th century Pyatnitsa nunnery chapel at Chernigov, Ukraine, were built in a style that was influenced by the architecture of southeastern Europe.

1 Around 1000, a great settlement in southern Africa began to emerge, called Great Zimbabwe. The settlement was founded on trade, and remains of luxury goods from as far away as China have been found in the excavations.

2 The Muslim Almoravid Dynasty expanded its power and influence in north Africa and southern Spain at the end of the 11th century. Troops were sent across the Sahara Desert to conquer the rich West African kingdom of Ghana.

3 During the twelfth century, the Toltec civilization flourished in Central America. The Toltec capital city of Tula was founded in present-day Mexico.

4 Around 1126 the prosperous and very advanced civilization of Sung China came to be threatened by the invading Chin peoples from the north. The Chin people occupied about one-third of Sung territory, including the capital, Kaifeng. The Sung were therefore forced to create a new capital at Hangchow.

MANY PEOPLES, ONE FAITH

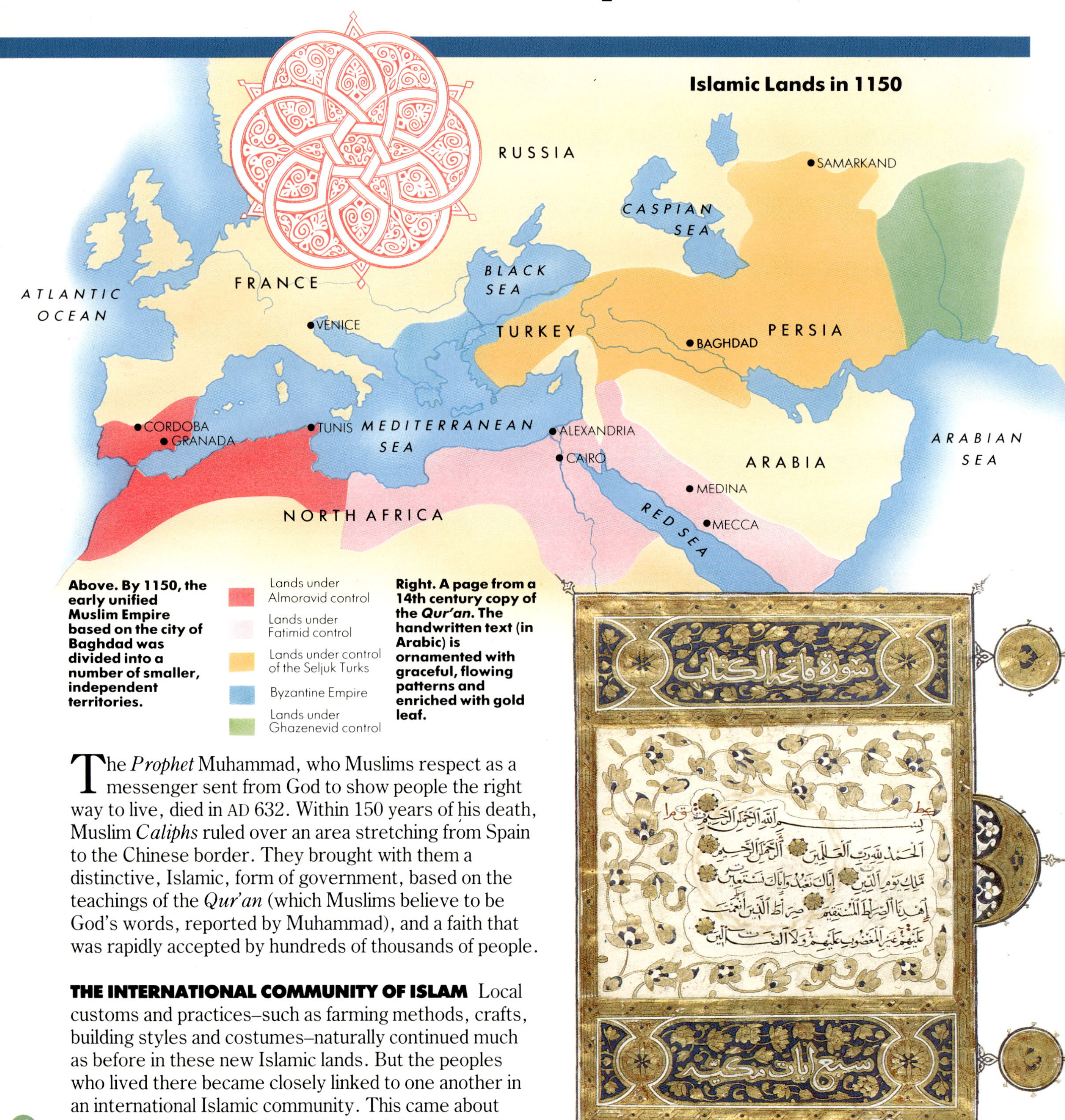

Above. By 1150, the early unified Muslim Empire based on the city of Baghdad was divided into a number of smaller, independent territories.

Right. A page from a 14th century copy of the *Qur'an*. The handwritten text (in Arabic) is ornamented with graceful, flowing patterns and enriched with gold leaf.

The *Prophet* Muhammad, who Muslims respect as a messenger sent from God to show people the right way to live, died in AD 632. Within 150 years of his death, Muslim *Caliphs* ruled over an area stretching from Spain to the Chinese border. They brought with them a distinctive, Islamic, form of government, based on the teachings of the *Qur'an* (which Muslims believe to be God's words, reported by Muhammad), and a faith that was rapidly accepted by hundreds of thousands of people.

THE INTERNATIONAL COMMUNITY OF ISLAM Local customs and practices–such as farming methods, crafts, building styles and costumes–naturally continued much as before in these new Islamic lands. But the peoples who lived there became closely linked to one another in an international Islamic community. This came about through their shared religion, through Islamic laws, and

Left. A group of Muslim travellers, pictured in a 13th century manuscript. Many medieval Muslim people were brave and adventurous travellers; merchants, explorers and geographers have all left accounts of their journeys. Other Muslim people travelled from all parts of the known world on pilgrimage to the holy city of Mecca in Arabia.

Above. Many beautiful buildings survive from medieval Muslim lands. This is the Court of the Lions in the Alhambra palace in Granada, southern Spain. It was built during the 13th and 14th centuries. Muslim palaces were famous for their lovely gardens and for the skill and delicacy with which they were built.

through the Arabic language (which was used for prayers and to write many documents).

Also, the friendships and business contacts Muslims made as they fulfilled their religious duty of going on pilgrimage to the holy city of Mecca encouraged close links. By the year 1100, western Muslim lands along the shores of the Mediterranean were increasingly being attacked. There were clashes between Muslim and Byzantine troops, as well. But whatever the problems faced by Muslim rulers in the west, their power remained secure in the 'Muslim heartlands' of Arabia, the Middle East, Iran and Iraq, North India and central Asia.

THE SELJUK TURKS Muslim power was further strengthened by the arrival, in the 10th and 11th centuries, of the Seljuk Turks. The Seljuks were a group of *nomadic* peoples from Central Asia. They settled in the Muslim lands, and took control of many countries. They soon became converted to the Islamic faith and formed a tough, trained fighting force, ready to defend their new-found faith and their newly conquered lands.

FURTHER EXPANSION The Islamic faith, and Islamic forms of government, continued to spread further round the world. Muslim states were established in the islands of the East Indies by 1300. In the 13th century, travellers to China noted that Muslim merchant communities could be found in many major cities there.

In Africa, Muslim travellers and traders journeyed southwards across the Sahara, bringing their faith to the peoples of Mali and the neighbouring kingdoms. Muslim seafarers introduced Islam to the mining and fishing communities along the East African coast, in present-day Ethiopia, Kenya and Tanzania.

ISLAMIC GOVERNMENT AND SOCIETY

Modern-day Muslim pilgrims making their way on foot around the Ka'ba, or 'House of Prayer' in Mecca, the spiritual centre of the Muslim world.

The characteristic Muslim form of government aimed to produce a truly Islamic society. In practice, this meant a society which was governed according to the rules laid down in the *Qur'an*, and which followed the example set by the Prophet Muhammad. But what was life really like for people living under Muslim rule?

First of all, it rather depended on whether you were a Muslim or not. For devout Muslims, living in a land which was meant, at least, to be governed according to the teachings of their faith was welcome.

Non-Muslims, especially Christians and Jews, were tolerated and sometimes even encouraged to settle in Muslim lands, and were free to practise their own religion. This was in striking contrast to much of Northern Europe, where religious minorities were often cruelly *persecuted*.

LEADERSHIP AND TECHNOLOGY Life for people in Muslim lands also depended on how faithfully rulers followed the teachings of Islam. The *Qur'an* encourages people to worship God, to work, to study, to be charitable and to live in peace. Not all Muslim leaders, however, proved capable or desirous of living up to these ideals.

Many Muslim rulers, though, did spend large amounts of money on projects designed to make life better for all citizens, whatever their religion. Irrigation schemes, safer roads, stronger bridges, clean water supplies and, when necessary, famine relief were provided. Muslim rulers and religious leaders also readily encouraged wealthy individuals to give generously to schools, hospitals, universities, mosques and libraries.

Left. Sixteenth-century ceramic tiles from Cairo, Egypt, showing the Ka'ba at the centre of the great mosque in Mecca. All Muslims hope one day to be able to make the pilgrimage to Mecca, but, for many people living in medieval times, this was not always possible. Other great Muslim cities like Cairo, Baghdad, Damascus and Timbuktu became important centres of trade and learning during the Middle Ages.

Above. Muslim horsemen, pictured galloping, from a 15th century manuscript. Medieval Muslim rulers were famous as patrons of scholarship and book production, and there were universities and libraries in many Muslim cities.

Below. In Persia (Iran), typically Muslim artistic styles mingled with local craft traditions to produce an elegant civilization. This 12th century Persian pottery bowl, with its fine-drawn decoration, shows a prince surrounded by his courtiers.

LIFE FOR ORDINARY PEOPLE For ordinary, uneducated people, the coming of Islam did not introduce great changes into their everyday lives, however much it changed their standards of behaviour towards one another, and their religious beliefs.

Muslim peasants continued to labour in the fields. Muslim craftsmen created beautiful carpets, pottery, glassware and metalwork in busy workshops. Muslim merchants and shopkeepers bought and sold their merchandise in noisy, crowded bazaars. Muslim women prepared food, cared for their families, brought up their children and worked as maids or domestic servants.

Like the ordinary people of Europe, Muslim country-dwellers and townspeople everywhere worked hard for their living.

MUSLIM ART AND LEARNING

The madrasa (Islamic college) of Ulug-Beg in Samarkand (present-day Uzbekistan), built during the 15th century.

Famous Medieval Muslim Scholars

The medieval Muslim world produced some very learned and influential scholars:

Ibn Rushd lived during the 12th century in Spain and North Africa. He was a lawyer and a judge, and wrote on philosophy, medicine, mathematics, law and theology.

Umar Khayyam lived in 12th century Iran. He is remembered today for his poetry, but was more famous during his lifetime for mathematical and astronomical discoveries.

Nasir Al-Din Tusi worked in Iran, under Mongol rule during the 13th century. He was an expert in geometry and astronomy, and founded a laboratory and observatory with the most precise scientific instruments yet discovered from the Middle Ages.

In many parts of the Muslim world, beautiful buildings, such as mosques, colleges and tombs, survive from the Middle Ages to remind us of the splendid achievements of Islamic civilization. In the same way that Muslim government was based on the Islamic faith, Muslim art and architecture was also strongly influenced by the teachings of the *Qur'an*, and by the simple, religious way of life followed by the Prophet Muhammad and the earliest Muslims.

ISLAMIC DESIGNS Local artistic styles and traditions also had an important part to play. Areas where people had developed particular skills, for example in weaving carpets or making pottery, continued to produce the goods for which they were famous, but in an Islamic way.

Islam forbids making pictures of any living creature whether a person or an animal. Thus, Muslim artists became very skilled at decorating all kinds of buildings and objects with beautiful geometric patterns and abstract designs. These beautiful Islamic objects were in great demand all over the medieval world. They have been found by archaeologists excavating sites as far apart as Scandinavia and China.

ADVANCES IN LEARNING The *Qur'an* encourages learning, and Muslim scholars were highly respected at home and abroad. They were especially famous for their discoveries in the sciences, in such fields as astronomy, mathematics, navigation, engineering, chemistry, geography and medicine.

They also preserved important scientific manuscripts surviving from the time of the Ancient Greeks. If they had not copied these ancient writings, and made accurate translations of them, a great deal of important knowledge would have been lost.

Both men and women studied, although most medieval Muslim women scholars concentrated on literature, philosophy, and religious studies. Some women religious thinkers and *mystics* were famous throughout the Muslim world.

EDUCATIONAL ESTABLISHMENTS Universities, colleges, observatories (for studying the stars) and schools were set up in many Muslim lands, often before similar institutions existed in Europe. One of the Muslim rulers of Baghdad built a special 'House of Learning', which combined a college for senior students from all over the Muslim world, a scientific observatory, and a well stocked library.

Muslim scholars were employed by many non-Muslim rulers who valued their skills. For example, King Roger of Sicily commissioned the Muslim geographer, Al-Idrisi, to compile a world map for him.

Muslim mathematicians and philosophers lectured to crowds of Christian students in Italy and Spain. One Spanish writer complained that the students were forgetting their own culture in their eagerness to listen to these great teachers. The writings of Muslim doctors, like Ibn Sina or al-Razi, were studied by scholars all over Europe, and did a great deal to improve the standards of medical care.

Right. Sometimes, Muslim artists did portray people in their work. This illustration comes from a manuscript produced in Baghdad in 1237. It shows Muslim scholars reading and discussing. They are seated in a library. You can see the books neatly stacked in pigeon-holes in a bookcase in the background of the picture.

Below. An Islamic bowl made in 1218 depicting an elephant with three riders.

Right. The Dome of the Rock, Jerusalem, is one of the earliest Muslim buildings to survive. It was completed in 691, just over 50 years after the death of the Prophet Muhammad. It is decorated with elaborate geometrical patterns.

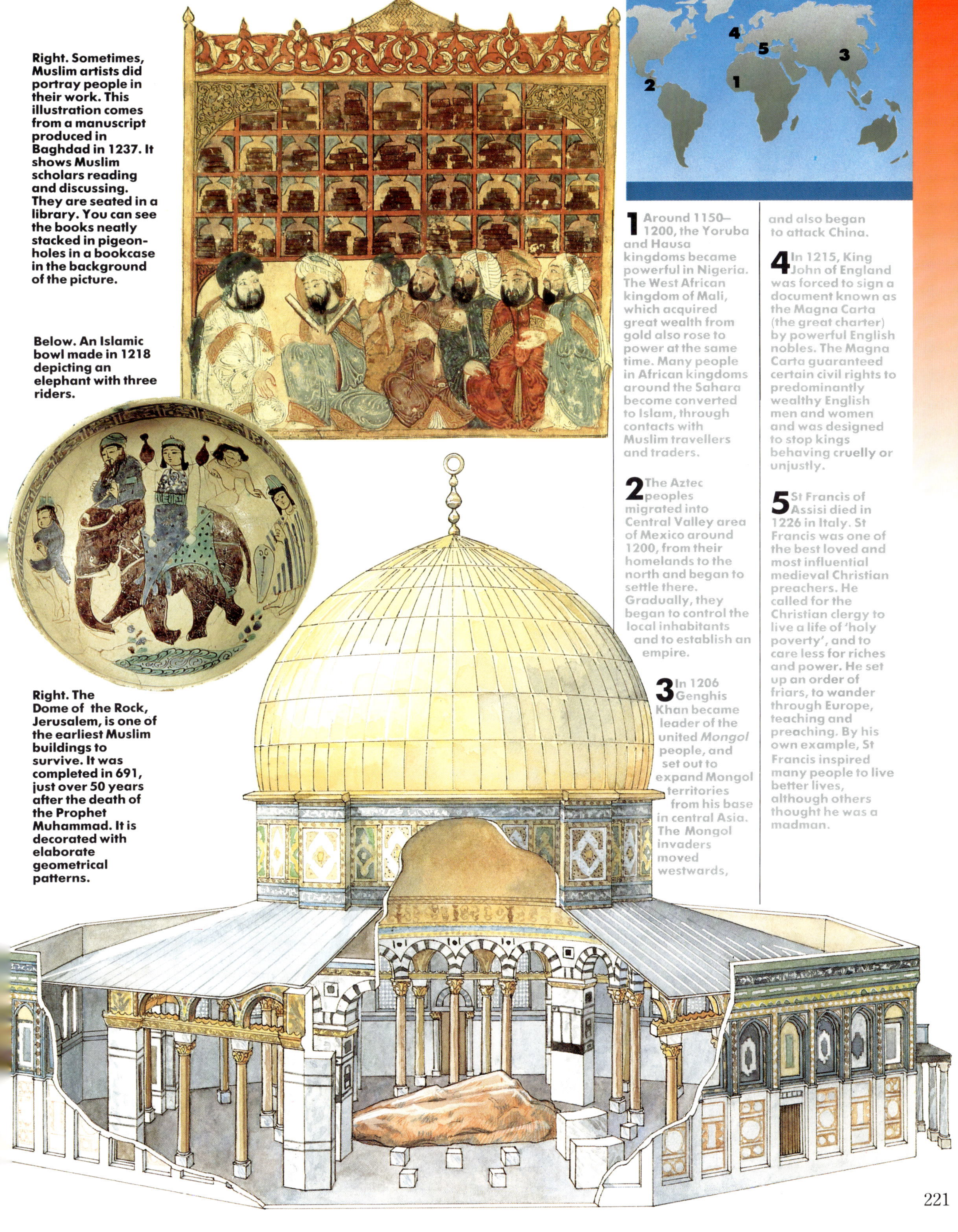

1 Around 1150–1200, the Yoruba and Hausa kingdoms became powerful in Nigeria. The West African kingdom of Mali, which acquired great wealth from gold also rose to power at the same time. Many people in African kingdoms around the Sahara become converted to Islam, through contacts with Muslim travellers and traders.

2 The Aztec peoples migrated into Central Valley area of Mexico around 1200, from their homelands to the north and began to settle there. Gradually, they began to control the local inhabitants and to establish an empire.

3 In 1206 Genghis Khan became leader of the united *Mongol* people, and set out to expand Mongol territories from his base in central Asia. The Mongol invaders moved westwards, and also began to attack China.

4 In 1215, King John of England was forced to sign a document known as the Magna Carta (the great charter) by powerful English nobles. The Magna Carta guaranteed certain civil rights to predominantly wealthy English men and women and was designed to stop kings behaving cruelly or unjustly.

5 St Francis of Assisi died in 1226 in Italy. St Francis was one of the best loved and most influential medieval Christian preachers. He called for the Christian clergy to live a life of 'holy poverty', and to care less for riches and power. He set up an order of friars, to wander through Europe, teaching and preaching. By his own example, St Francis inspired many people to live better lives, although others thought he was a madman.

THE SUNG EMPIRE: WEALTH AND GOOD GOVERNMENT

Above. Lands ruled by the Sung Dynasty during the 10th–12th centuries. The northern Sung lands were overrun by the invading Chin dynasty in 1126.

Right. A prosperous Sung couple comfortably seated at table, waited on by their four servants. Vivid tomb-paintings like this give us some idea what life was like in Sung China.

The civilization of medieval China astonished every western traveller who came into contact with it. The country and its people seemed amazingly prosperous, energetic, industrious and well governed.

CHINESE PROSPERITY Chinese cities were enormous by medieval standards. For example, Kaifeng, the capital of the Sung Empire, had over a quarter of a million inhabitants in 1120. In comparison, London and Paris housed only a few thousand citizens each. Chinese trade and industry was booming. Workshops and factories produced clothes, furnishings, household goods and porcelain for sale to customers at home and for export to the west, along with spices, drugs and tea.

THE DEVELOPMENT OF TECHNOLOGY The Chinese countryside was criss-crossed by a network of canals, used to transport heavy loads vast distances all over the empire. There were also thousands of irrigation ditches, which provided the water farmers needed to grow high yielding varieties of rice. These varieties were specially bred by Chinese scientists and gardeners to provide food for the rapidly increasing population.

THE SUNG SYSTEM OF GOVERNMENT Since 907, China had been ruled by the Sung *dynasty*. Like earlier Chinese rulers, the Sung emperors relied on a large number of officials to help them govern the country. In the past, most of these officials had come from wealthy upper-class families. They had been appointed to important posts because of their rank, rather than because of their skills and experience.

Under the Sung, the system of recruitment was changed. Young men who wanted a career in government had to take a difficult examination. If they passed, they were offered a job and a thorough training, no matter what their family background was. In this way, the Sung emperors made sure that their government was staffed

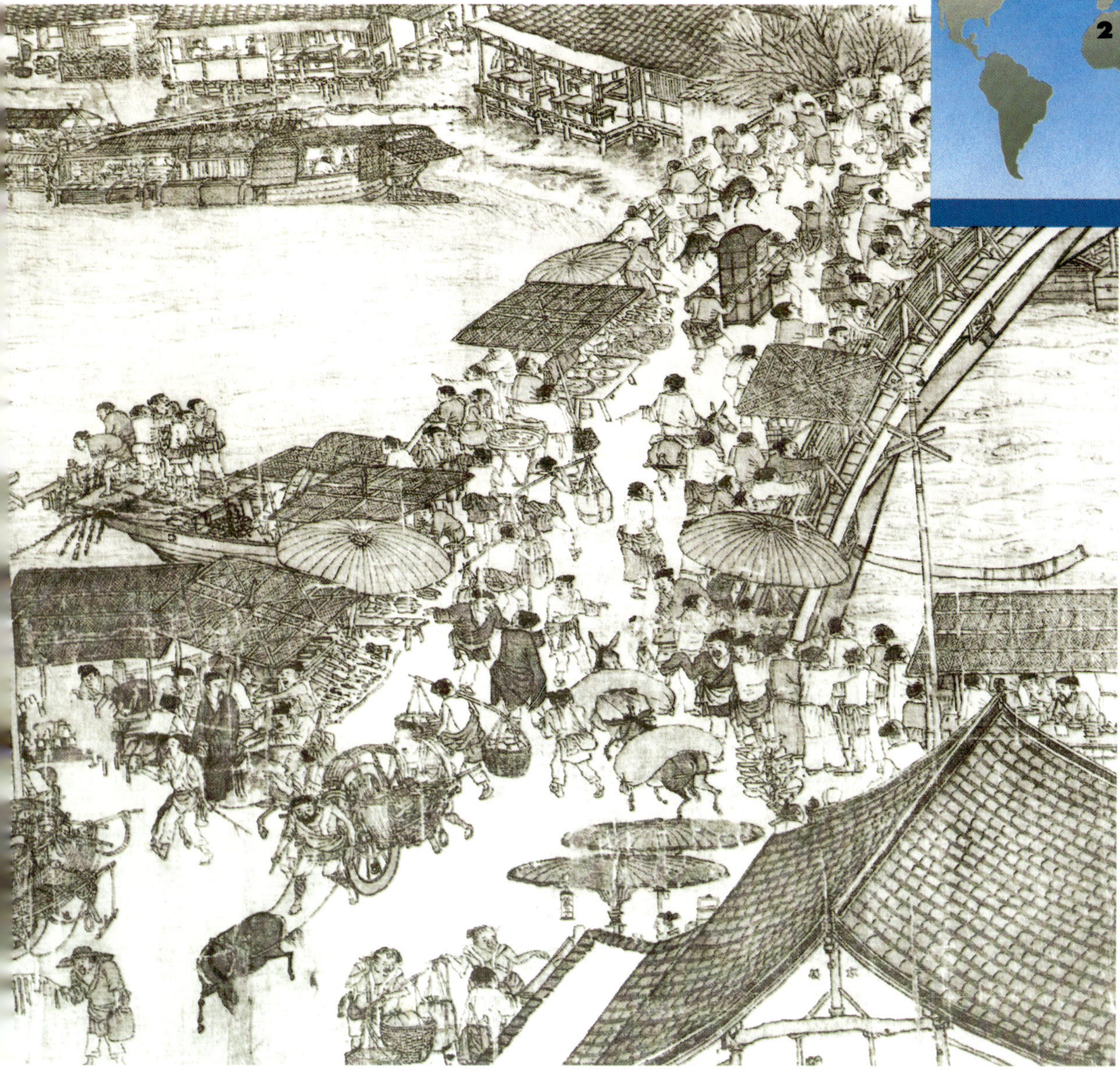

1 Around 1100 the first universities were founded in Europe, at Salerno, Bologna and Paris. This was also a great age of cathedral building in many European countries. Building work at Chartres cathedral, France, possibly the finest example of medieval *Gothic architecture*, began in 1154. Architects and craftsmen also designed many strong castles and forts. But in many ways, Europen technologies were less advanced at this time than the Chinese.

2 In 1175 Muhammad of Ghazni (in present-day Afghanistan) expanded his kingdom southwards and established the first Muslim empire in India. Muslim influence also expanded at this time in North Africa and the Middle East. In 1189 Saladin led Muslim forces to recapture the city of Jerusalem from Christian Crusaders.

Top. Detail from the Spring Festival Scroll, c.1120, showing a crowded bridge across the river in the Sung capital city of Kaifeng.

Above. An example of skilful Sung engineering, repaired and rebuilt in later centuries – canals and bridges in the walled city of Suzhou, China.

by the most able, intelligent and efficient men in the country. They also encouraged the Chinese people to believe that a career in public service was an honourable and worthwhile way of making a living.

CHINA INVADED All this meant that during the 11th and 12th centuries China was probably the wealthiest and best run state in the world. However, soon this would all change and the Sung emperors and their people began to face problems.

Northern China was invaded by the Liao people. The Sung therefore made an alliance with the Chin people, who lived nearby. The Chin helped to defeat the Liao invaders, but then turned to attack the Sung. By 1126, they had occupied about one-third of the Sung territory, including the capital city of Kaifeng. Quickly, the Sung emperors established a new capital at the important trading city of Hangchow, and life in the southern Sung lands returned almost to normal.

CHINA AND JAPAN: CULTURE AND CEREMONY

Japanese medieval temple architecture. This is the impressive gateway leading to the Todaiji Buddhist temple in the city of Nara. It was built during the 8th century.

The Sung emperors, and well educated people who ran their government, valued knowledge, scholarship and the arts very highly. To them, a 'civilized' man or woman was someone who enjoyed music, poetry, painting and philosophy, and could discuss them intelligently. If possible, they were meant to practise these arts as well. Several of the Sung emperors were skilled painters, *calligraphers* and poets, and they encouraged their *courtiers* and government officials to follow their example.

CODE OF BEHAVIOUR These 'civilized' people were expected to behave in a formal and delicate way. Life at the emperor's court was organized in a series of elaborate ceremonies; visitors had to obey a complicated code of polite behaviour and good manners. There was friendly rivalry among courtiers over who could write the most elegantly phrased letter, or compose the most fitting poem to celebrate a special day. For some people in Sung China, life itself became a work of art.

LIFE FOR THE RICH Wealthy families collected antiques and precious books, and purchased beautiful paintings by famous artists. Pictures of landscapes were especially liked. These rich patrons also gave money to set up new schools, or to support scholars researching into the relatively long history of Chinese culture, traditions and philosophy.

Above. Japanese houses were built with wide verandahs surrounding the rooms. Sliding screens divided off areas for eating and sleeping, and provided privacy for noble women who could not be seen in public. Furniture was simple, and low on the ground.

Left. Chinese porcelain was prized the world over. This three-legged vase, decorated with a pale green glaze called 'celadon', was made in the 12th century.

A reconstruction of what a typical 14th century Japanese court lady would have worn under her clothes. She wears a white silk kosode, a lined kimono, and hakama, full trousers of red silk. Up to 20 silk kimonos of different colours would have been worn on top.

MUSIC AND PLEASURE Among ordinary people, music and the theatre were very popular. At the end of a busy day, everyone enjoyed an outing to the parks, lakes and gardens that were built on the outskirts of the great Chinese cities.

In Hangchow, people could hire a boat and spend a pleasant evening drifting gently across the waters of the great West Lake, listening to music and eating delicious food.

Describing a visit to this spectacularly beautiful lake, Marco Polo (who visited China in the late 13th century) wrote that there was 'more refreshment and delectation (delight) than any other experience on earth'.

INFLUENCE ON JAPAN AND KOREA Chinese culture had a powerful influence on neighbouring countries, especially Korea and Japan. Chinese styles of architecture, painting, clothing and writing were admired and copied. A 'Pillow Book' (a sort of diary) written by a Japanese woman courtier has survived from the 10th century. The writer, called Sei Shonagun, frequently quotes Chinese poetry, traditional stories and philosophies, in order to demonstrate to her readers just how refined and civilized she is.

But before the end of the Sung period (around 1279), both Japan and Korea had broken free of Chinese influence, and had turned once more to developing their own national cultures and traditions.

CHINESE INVENTIONS AND DISCOVERIES

The wealthy, well educated, self-confident and energetic Chinese people who lived under the rule of the Sung Dynasty were active merchants and traders. They also sponsored a number of inventions which were far in advance of the technology known in other parts of the world during the Middle Ages.

MATHEMATICS, ASTRONOMY AND GEOGRAPHY We can group these medieval Chinese inventions and discoveries under several headings: mathematics and astronomy; medical science; weapons and civil engineering; and what we might today call 'information technology'.

To take some examples from each group, in mathematics Chinese scholars invented new, simple, ways of solving complicated mathematical tasks. They invented a counting board, which worked like a very simple computer. They also worked out a system for doing long division.

In astronomy and geography, Chinese scientists developed precision instruments to help them observe the moon and the stars, and also invented a sensitive machine to help predict earthquakes.

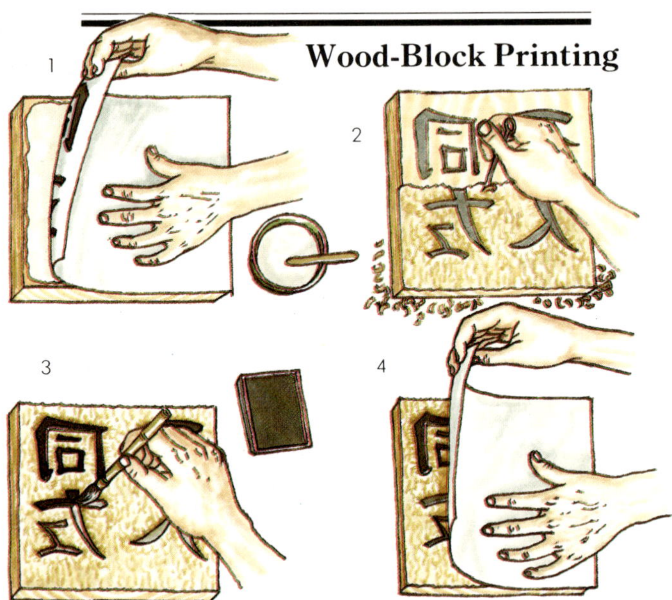

The drawings above illustrate the processes involved in wood-block printing.

1. Characters were drawn on paper. This was placed upside down on a wood block covered with rice paste, leaving a stain.
2. The paper was removed, and the wood around the stain was cut away.
3. This produced raised characters, which were then inked.
4. Clean paper was pressed onto the inked characters, producing a copy print.

MEDICINE In medical science, Chinese doctors developed the technique of acupuncture to control pain and relieve many other symptoms of disease. In addition, through their scientific *dissection* of corpses, they gathered a great deal of valuable knowledge about the human body and how it works. (In the west, the Church forbade the cutting up of dead bodies. It was considered disrespectful to God.)

MILITARY AND CIVIL ENGINEERING In military engineering, the Chinese invented gunpowder, flamethrowers, poison gas, cannons and tanks. More peacefully, Chinese engineers also invented machines to spin thread, weave cloth, and pump water to irrigate dry land. They extended the already vast system of canals, adding newly designed locks to enable heavily laden cargo ships to sail 'uphill'.

PRINTING To help the speedy spread of philosophical ideas and, later, practical information, Chinese technologists invented *wood-block printing* sometime during the ninth century. Paper money, which saved merchants from the trouble of carrying heavy loads of gold or silver on their travels, was in use in China by 1024.

THE DECLINE OF NEW INVENTIONS By 1500, the flow of new Chinese inventions and discoveries seems to have stopped. Why did this marvellous period of invention come to an end? Partly, the prosperity of the country was disrupted by war and invasion. Partly it was due to the rather repressive style of government adopted by the Ming Dynasty, which came to power in 1368. From 1330, the Chinese people were forbidden to carry weapons, and, after 1371, they were barred from travelling abroad. Scholars were encouraged to concentrate on *Confucian* philosophy, rather than on practical subjects like science and engineering.

But the revolutionary Chinese inventions were not lost or forgotten. Gradually, through contact with Muslim and other traders, Chinese ideas and inventions had been spreading to the west. Many of them, like printing and paper money, are still in use today.

This picture shows mulberry trees being planted by peasants. Mulberry leaves were essential for the Chinese silk industry – they provided food for silk-moth grubs. Silk had been a very early Chinese invention and methods of growing and cultivating developed considerably in order to keep up with demand.

Making Paper Money

Chinese paper was made from pulped fibres from a number of sources – mulberry bark, bamboo shoots and scraps of cloth (1). The bark was first softened (2) then mashed to a pulp (3). Thin layers were then laid over a wide mesh screen. When the layers of pulp were dry, they were removed from the screens, trimmed and pressed to make them as smooth as possible (4). Sheets of paper were printed, using the wood-block method or newer, moveable type. They were then cut into currency notes (5).

Key Dates of Sung and Ming China

907 Collapse of ruling Tang Dynasty, followed by over 50 years of civil war

c.979 Sung Dynasty takes control of large part of former Tang lands, except for regions in the north, which have formed breakaway kingdoms.

1126 The Chin people break their alliance with the Sung and invade Sung lands; Sung power now confined to southern China

1234 Mongol troops attack and overthrow Chin kingdom in northern China

1279 Mongol troops conquer southern (Sung) China. All of China now under foreign control

1340 Series of revolts against foreign rulers by Chinese people

1368 Rebel leader Chu Yuan-chang takes control of large area in southern China, proclaims himself Emperor and establishes new Ming Dynasty

1398 Chu Yuan-chang dies. Yung-lo, his successor as emperor, starts to build new Chinese capital city at Peking (Beijing)

1644 Ming Dynasty overthrown by new ruling family, the Manchu

LIVING IN TOWNS

In the Middle Ages it was unusual to live in a town. Most people, in most parts of the world, lived in the countryside. But the growth in population during the High Middle Ages and the expansion of trade and industry led to an increase in the size and number of towns.

RESOURCES FOR TOWNS Towns depended on the countryside. People living in farmsteads and villages produced food for the townspeople to eat, and raw materials used by craftsmen who lived there. They grew wool, flax, silk or cotton, depending on the local climate and soil, and supplied animal-based products such as leather, horn, bone, fur and feathers.

CENTRES OF TRADE People came to the towns to buy and sell. Some towns had originated as fortresses–safe places where people could shelter from attack–but even these soon developed into trading centres. Craftsmen set up their workshops in the towns, knowing that their goods would be seen and purchased by far more people than in isolated villages.

Professional people, such as lawyers, doctors and scribes, also came to live in the towns, where they knew their skills and services would be needed by many people. Shops and stalls selling food, clothes and household goods were opened to cater for the new town-dwellers. Some towns organized yearly fairs, where travelling merchants from many lands displayed their goods to customers who came from all around.

ROYAL APPROVAL Kings and princes encouraged the growth of towns in their countries. They knew that taxes and tolls levied on everything that was sold would mean extra income for them. They offered special protection to towns, and to merchants travelling to trade there.

DANGERS OF TOWN LIFE Life in towns was busy, and probably felt very exciting to a visitor used to a quieter life in the countryside. But towns could also be dangerous and unhealthy places to live. Criminals lurked in dark alleys; and diseases bred among the tightly packed shops and houses, and in the refuse cluttering the streets. In contrast, western travellers to Chinese and Muslim towns were greatly impressed by the gardens and orchards that surrounded them. They provided welcome fresh air, peace and relaxation for all the citizens.

Above. The town of Feurs, in the south of France, as it appeared in the early 16th century. The town walls and strong gates protect the inhabitants from enemy armies and from bands of local brigands. Within the walls, the houses are tightly packed together. The church stands in the centre of the town, with the houses of the most important citizens nearby. Outside the walls, there are fields, gardens, orchards and a monastery.

Above. This reconstruction of a street scene in a European medieval town shows many typical features of urban life: crowds, market stalls, shoppers and idle gossips, street musicians and entertainers, watchmen, heavily laden travellers, church-goers, and straying animals. What it cannot show is the noise, smoke and smells.

The Largest Medieval Cities

These maps show the location of the world's ten largest towns, in 1250 and in 1450. It is not surprising (see pages 222–7) to discover that the great Chinese cities head the list. European cities, like Venice and Paris, remained relatively small in medieval times. In 1250, Venice housed 90,000 people, and Paris 160,000. This is because most people in Europe made their living in the countryside from farming, rather than in towns, from trade or manufacturing.

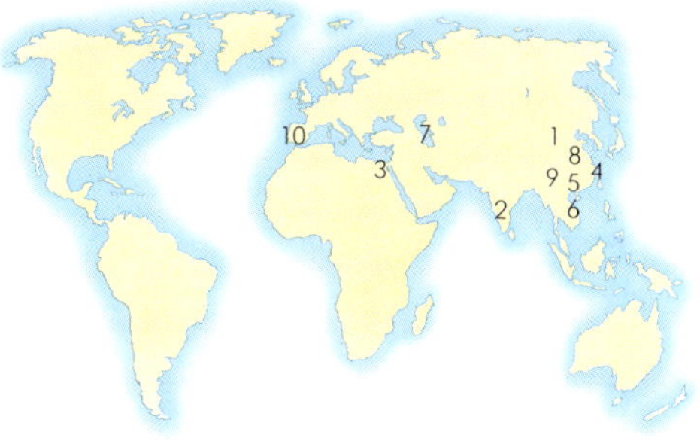

The 10 largest cities in 1250

1. Hangchow, 320,000
2. Cairo, 300,000
3. Canton, 250,000
4. Nanking, 250,000
5. Fez, 200,000
6. Kamakura, 200,000
7. Pagan, 180,000
8. Sian, 175,000
9. Paris, 160,000
10. Peking, 160,000

Other large cities at this time included:

Constantinople, 150,000
Baghdad, 100,000
Venice, 90,000
Seville, 90,000
Delhi, 80,000
Alexandria, 60,000

The 10 largest cities in 1450

1. Peking, 600,000
2. Vijayanagar, 455,000
3. Cairo, 450,000
4. Hangchow, 360,000
5. Nanking, 350,000
6. Canton, 300,000
7. Tabriz, 200,000
8. Soochow, 200,000
9. Mandu, 200,000
10. Granada, 165,000

Other large cities at this time included:

Samarkand, 100,000
Bruges, 95,000
Damascus, 85,000
London, 75,000
Chan-Chan, 70,000
Lisbon, 66,000

INTERNATIONAL TRADE

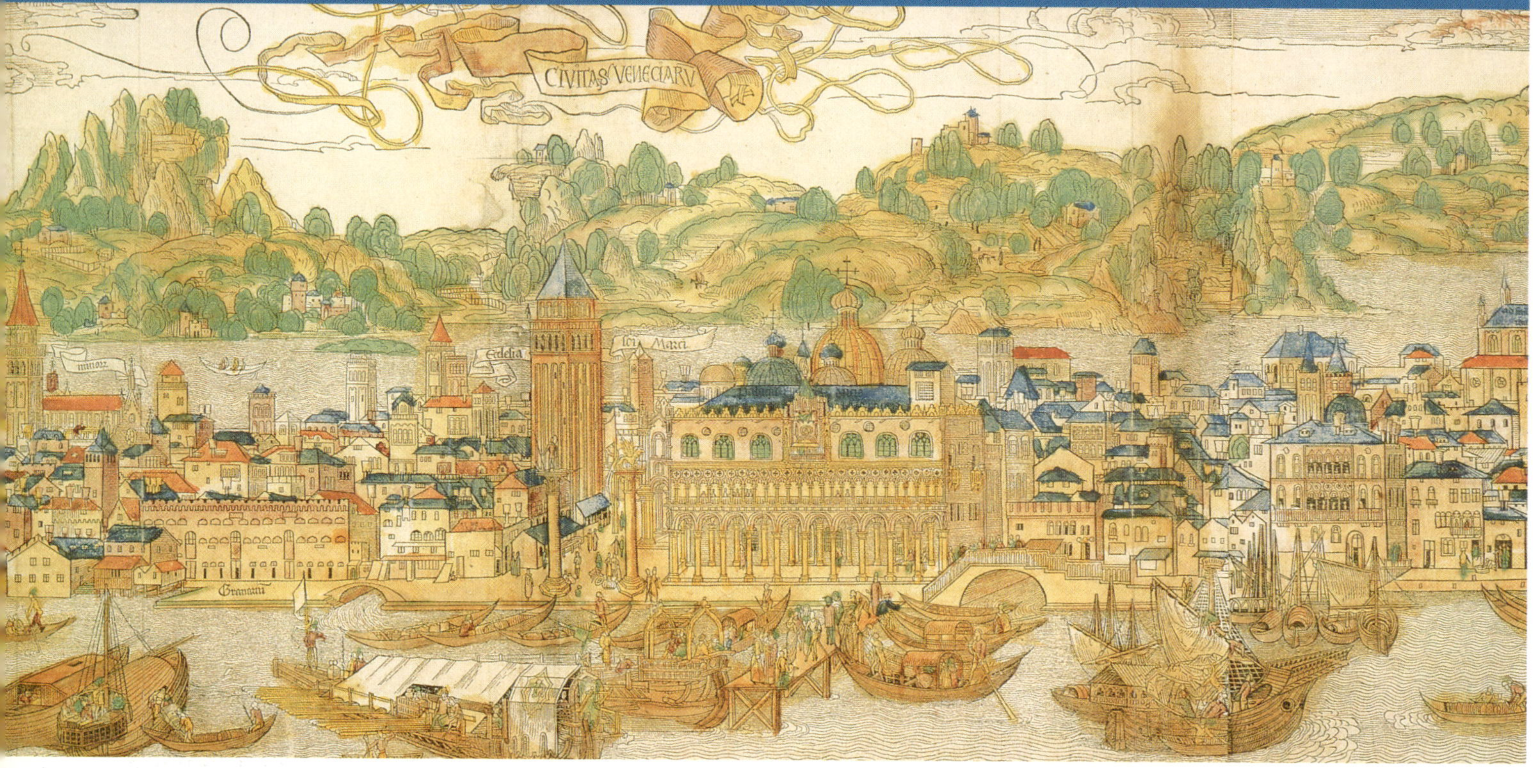

The waterfront at Venice in the late 15th century. Venice was the greatest port in medieval Europe, and a great meeting place for east-west trade.

International trade was well established long before the beginning of the Middle Ages. But the years 1100–1300 saw a great increase in the quantity of goods bought and sold, and in the amount of money made from trading. The growing population in many parts of the world meant that there was an increased demand for all kinds of goods.

BENEFITS OF TRADE FOR RICH AND POOR High prices for food led to high profits for landowners. They had money to spend on new buildings, and a whole host of luxury items. Ordinary people never had much money to spare for luxuries, but even they needed to buy basic necessities, such as new shoes, warm blankets, and sturdy cooking pots, from time to time. Everyday goods like these were made locally, but where did all the luxury goods come from? And how did they travel to markets halfway round the world?

THE LUXURY TRADE Jewellery and spices were the most valuable of all the goods traded. Spices were grown in India and the East Indies, and transported to eager customers in Europe and the Far East. Precious stones came from Burma and India; silk and porcelain (also cheap, *mass-produced* pottery) from China. The Islamic world produced glassware, metalware and carpets, while Northern Europe supplied fine woollen cloth, amber, furs, metalwork, gold and silverware.

TRADE ROUTES There were two major networks of international trade routes travelled by adventurous merchants from many lands, and many smaller trackways, as well. The 'Silk Road' led overland from European trading ports to the city of Hangchow on the east coast of China. The 'Spice Route' involved travellers in a long voyage by both sea and land. They set off from the Italian ports of Venice and Genoa to Alexandria in Egypt. From there they travelled overland, riding on horses or camels, to the Red Sea or the Persian Gulf. Finally they travelled by ship along the coasts of Arabia or East Africa, and across the ocean to India and the Spice Islands of the East Indies.

Journeys by either route were dangerous, unpredictable, and could take several years. Not many

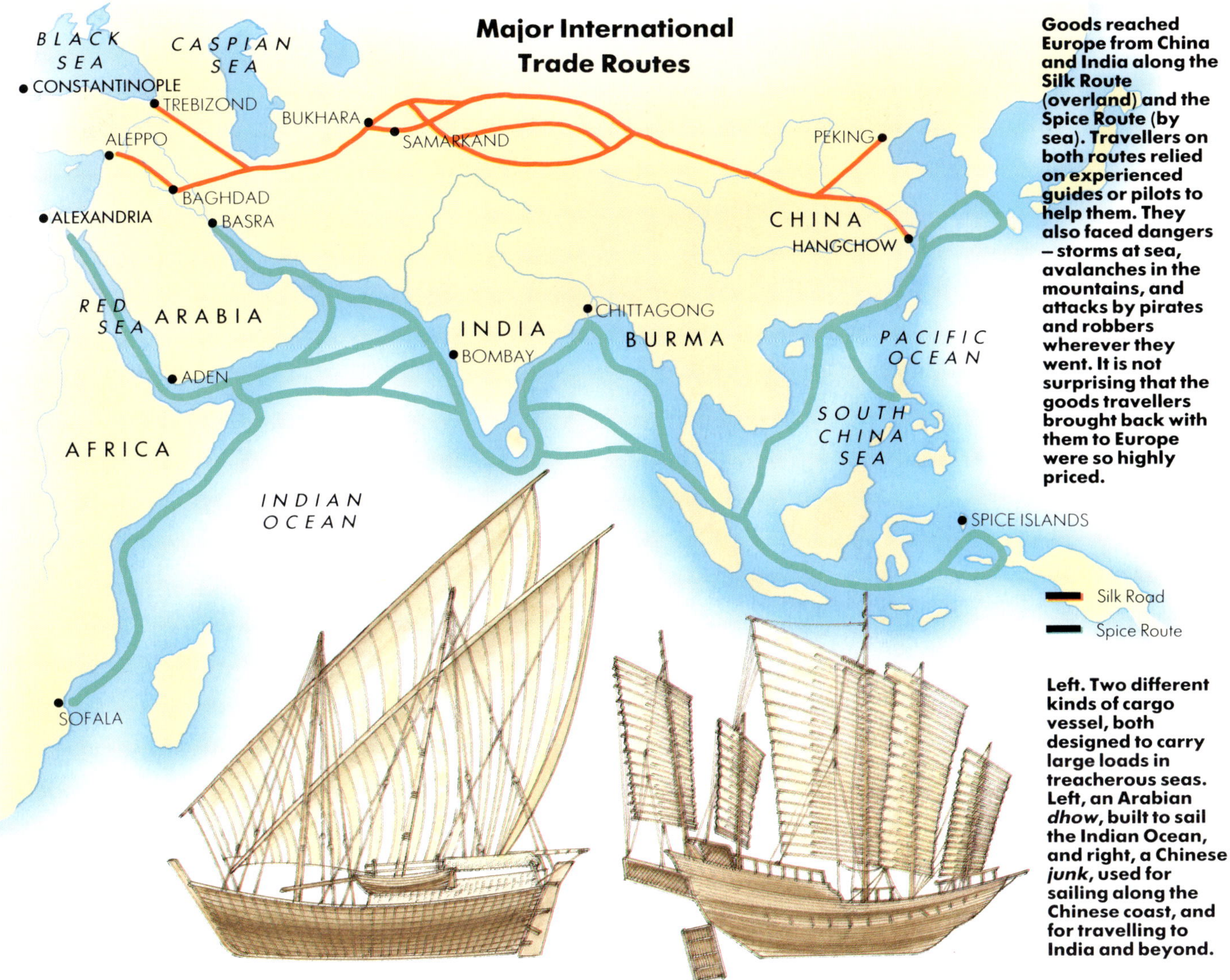

Goods reached Europe from China and India along the Silk Route (overland) and the Spice Route (by sea). Travellers on both routes relied on experienced guides or pilots to help them. They also faced dangers – storms at sea, avalanches in the mountains, and attacks by pirates and robbers wherever they went. It is not surprising that the goods travellers brought back with them to Europe were so highly priced.

Left. Two different kinds of cargo vessel, both designed to carry large loads in treacherous seas. Left, an Arabian *dhow*, built to sail the Indian Ocean, and right, a Chinese *junk*, used for sailing along the Chinese coast, and for travelling to India and beyond.

Medieval Trade

Below the modern historian, Sylvia Thrupp, describes a 15th century shopkeeper in the small English provincial town of Leicester. It shows how much international trade had developed by the end of the Middle Ages:

'This man was at the same time draper, haberdasher, jeweller, grocer, ironmonger, saddler and dealer in timber, furniture and hardware. Even this does not describe him adequately, for he had a small stock of wool, wool-fells (fleeces), and skins on his hands, and he could have offered you ready-made gowns in taffeta or silk, daggers, bowstrings, harpstrings, writing paper, materials for making ink, and seeds for the vegetable garden. His resources were greatest in the drapery department, which comprised twenty different kinds of British and imported cloth; he was also well stocked with small wares, notably purses of gold cloth, ribbons, children's stockings, silk coifs (headscarves) and kerchiefs for nuns.'

Money balance, used by merchants and bankers to weigh solid silver coins.

merchants travelled the whole distance themselves. Instead, they met other traders at well known market centres, like Samarkand and Bukhara in central Asia (present-day Uzbekistan), or Constantinople (Istanbul) and Trebizond, on the shores of the Black Sea. There they bought and sold valuable goods, and exchanged information about prices, opportunities for bargains and dangers along the route.

MONEY FOR TRADE GOODS Goods were sold for gold and silver coins (which could be weighed to find out their true value) or sometimes for precious stones. Marco Polo mentions sapphires and rubies sewn into the lining of his coat, to provide funds for emergencies. Italian merchant companies based in market towns began to operate as banks, issuing notes of credit (which worked rather like a modern credit card). They also loaned money to merchants.

Travellers to China commented on the fact that paper money was widely used among merchants there. But it was a long time before that Chinese invention was copied in the west.

MERCHANTS AND MERCHANDISE

If the risks of long-distance international trade were great, then so were the rewards. Shrewd, successful merchants were among the wealthiest people in many parts of the world. They even loaned money to kings and princes. During the 14th century, the kings of England borrowed huge sums to pay for the costs of their wars with France. Young men enthusiastically offered to work for great merchant families, in the hope that they would learn the secrets of how to make money.

TRICKS OF THE TRADE In fact, there were no great secrets to learn. Medieval merchants made their profits because of the scarcity value, and, usually, the high quality, of the goods they offered for sale. Spices, silks, jewels and perfumes were very expensive to buy, but they were essential purchases for any noble or wealthy family which wanted to have social standing.

Medieval people–in many lands–were very conscious

Above. Bankers and money-lenders played an important part in medieval trade. Here, we can see medieval bankers counting their stock of gold coins, and locking them safely away in a strong wooden chest.

Left. Travellers in many Middle Eastern and Asian lands had to pass through wild, empty countryside, far from the nearest town, or village. They stayed at *caravanserais*, like the one shown in this reconstruction drawing. Caravanserais were rest-houses, which provided rooms and food for weary travellers, as well as fodder and shelter for their animals. There was also the opportunity to meet other merchants and travellers, and to gather information about the route that lay ahead. Some caravanserais were provided with bath-houses, which must have been very welcome after days or weeks without the chance to wash.

of appearances. A nobleman and his wife knew they must dress as well as other nobles, or risk losing the respect of people around them. It was also their duty to offer hospitality and entertainment to important people, to keep their friendship and, perhaps, to seek their protection and goodwill. Merchants could therefore charge high prices for their produce, because they knew that people simply had to buy them.

ACCOUNT-KEEPING Successful merchants also kept a close watch on how their business was operating. We know from several surviving letters written by merchants that they worried constantly about prices, arrangements for shipping goods, the dangers of damage or theft, and about lazy employees in their shops and offices. During the Middle Ages, improved systems of keeping accounts were developed, which made it easier for merchants to calculate the profits and expenses on any transaction.

'When the traveller leaves Kerman (in Iran), he rides for 7 days along a very uninviting road . . . For 3 days he finds no running water, or as good as none. What water there is is brackish and green as meadow grass.' MARCO POLO

THE SOCIAL WORLD OF MERCHANTS Great merchant families made use of social contacts and arranged marriages between their children to improve business prospects. They knew, also, that generous gifts to charities in their home towns would make people think well of them. They were careful not to offend local rulers and officials, in whatever country of the world they happened to be. They did not want to languish in some foreign prison, or have their goods seized.

Often, merchants played an active part in politics in their native cities. They became town councillors, or advisers to the government. In such positions they could make sure that all new laws that were passed increased their chances of making a profit.

Left. Muslim travellers, seated on camels, arrive in a Middle Eastern village. In the background, you can see the mosque, with its dome and minaret. Inside the village houses, the local people are working and talking. A shepherd girl is spinning thread, and watching over her goats who have come to drink at the pond. Scenes like this must have been familiar to many medieval travelling merchants.

Above. Merchants in Europe sold their goods at markets and fairs. One of the most important international fairs was the Lendit fair at Paris, held every year shortly before Easter. This 15th century manuscript shows the Bishop pf Paris (centre) blessing merchants who are busy setting up their stalls. Many have arranged their goods under curved, tent-like covers, made of canvas stretched over wooden frames.

Three Great Civilizations

TIME CHART

	EUROPE	MUSLIM WORLD	CHINA AND THE EAST	REST OF WORLD
AD				
969		Muslim power established in Egypt; city of Cairo founded		
979			Sung Dynasty re-unites Chinese lands	
1000			'Golden Age' of Chinese painting and porcelain	Vikings land in North America, Beginnings of settlement at Great Zimbabwe, Africa
1019	First Russian Kingdom prospers under King Yaroslav I			
1045			Printing with moveable type invented in China	
1055		Seljuks take control of government in Baghdad		
1066	Norman Conquest of England			
1071		Seljuks defeat Byzantine armies at Battle of Manzikert. Byzantine Empire now in danger		
1095	Pope Urban encourages the sending of the First Crusade			
1096>1291		Fighting between Muslim troops and Crusader armies in the lands around Jerusalem		
1100	First universities founded in Europe			Toltec civilization powerful in Central America
1125	German peoples expand their settlement into eastern Europe			
1126			Sung Chinese lands invaded by Chin peoples from the north	
1150			Great Hindu temple of Angkor Wat built in Cambodia	Yoruba states rise to power in Nigeria
1150>1250	Flowering of noble culture celebrating knighthood and chivalry			
1170			Powerful kingdom of Srivijaya flourishes in Java and East Indies	
1175		Muhammad of Ghazni founds first Muslim Empire in India		
1193			Zen Buddhist philosophy established in Japan	
1200				Kingdom of Mali (West Africa) flourishes. Aztec peoples migrate to Mexico
1215	Magna Carta signed; shows kings' powers can be controlled by the people			
1300				Benin kings establish empire in Nigeria

PART TWO

Crisis and Change

After 1300, living conditions in many parts of world changed dramatically. Famines, wars, invasions and, worst of all, plague, swept across Europe and many parts of Asia, bringing death and destruction.

THE BLACK DEATH Plague, in particular, had a disastrous psychological effect. People became anxious and depressed. They feared that the world might be coming to an end, or that they were being punished by God for their sins. In Europe, 15th-century preachers suggested that children were killed by the plague because they disobeyed their parents: '*it may be that for vengeance of this sin of un-worshipping and despising their fathers and mothers, God slayeth children by pestilence [plague], as you see every day . . .*'.

The next section looks at these catastrophes, and examines their effects. It also shows how these disasters were followed by a slow period of recovery, until, by about 1500, life was almost 'back to normal'.

RECOVERY However, the series of disasters had left their mark. The world in 1500 was a very different place from the world 200 years earlier. Old beliefs had been shaken, new governments had seized power, and different ways of fighting, farming and manufacturing had been introduced. In some countries, economic recovery had brought with it a sense of excitement and possibility, and a wish to explore, question and make discoveries.

In 15th-century Italy, the movement known as the *Renaissance* (re-birth) led to great changes in learning, philosophy and the arts. In Germany, the invention of printing allowed these new ideas to be spread throughout Europe much faster than before.

TRAVEL AND EXPLORATION In the Muslim world, intrepid travellers like Ibn Battuta covered vast distances, recording and commenting on all the sights they had seen. Chinese voyagers journeyed westwards to India and beyond, while European sailors and adventurers sailed southwards along the west coast of Africa to try and discover new routes to the East.

The most important of these late-medieval discoveries was the accidental landing in America by European explorers in the late 15th century. Although it is incorrect to think of either North or South America as empty, undeveloped land, the realization that there was a vast area of the earth's surface that no-one in Europe or Africa had previously known about had an enormous impact on people living in Europe at the time.

At the same time as many countries and civilizations were recovering from the 14th century crises, they were also developing a whole new way of looking at the world.

TENSIONS IN EUROPE

Religious Discontent in Europe

By the end of the Middle Ages, many priests, religious scholars and ordinary people had become dissatisfied with the conduct of the Catholic Church. The 14th century saw a number of political scandals within the Church (including, for a time, two rival popes) which lessened people's respect for the Church as an institution.

Religious protest took several forms. Some people stayed away from church, others set up illegal, 'alternative' congregations, or circulated forbidden translations of the Bible and other religious books. Their main criticisms and demands were as follows:

- Church government should be reformed.
- There should be better control of Churchmen's personal behaviour.
- The Bible should be translated into European languages, which everyone could understand, rather than remain in Latin.
- There should be more participation by ordinary people in Church services, and these should be said in everyday languages, rather than in Latin.
- Corrupt practices should be abolished. For example, the selling of 'indulgences' (pardons for sins) for money should be banned.
- There should be freedom to discuss matters of belief without fear of punishment.

Left. There was also discontent among priests and their congregations during the late Middle Ages. Martin Luther (1483–1546), the German Protestant reformer, came at the end of a long tradition of demands for reform within the Catholic Church.

In many ways, European society during the Middle Ages was never far from disaster. War, disease, drought, floods and fire could devastate an entire village or town. Thus, although the years 1100–1300 were times of growth and prosperity for many parts of Europe, there were also tensions, difficulties and dangers lying in wait.

AGRICULTURAL CRISIS There were problems connected with farming. As the population increased, new lands had been cleared and planted with crops. Some historians think that by 1300 all the suitable land in Western Europe had been taken into cultivation, and there was no more room for expansion. Other historians have suggested that, by 1300, the population of Europe had already grown too large for the land available. In years when harvest yields were below average, there would not be enough food to go round.

There were widespread famines in Europe between 1315 and 1320, caused by a series of very wet summers which caused crops to rot in the fields and animals to sicken and die. The world climate began to change at this time; winters grew longer and summers were shorter and cooler. The period from the 14th–17th centuries is sometimes known as the 'Little Ice Age'.

SOCIAL PROBLEMS There were also problems with the way that medieval European society was organized. Kings found it increasingly difficult to rule their countries without the cooperation of their subjects. This could not always be guaranteed. Thoughtless, cruel or incompetent kings faced rebellion and disorder. During the 15th century, English kings were deposed by powerful nobles four times.

Ordinary people also felt bitter and angry. They resented the enormous differences in wealth between the nobles and themselves. In particular, they hated being unfree. Throughout the 14th and 15th centuries, kings in Europe faced open revolt by groups of peasants and by workers in towns. The reasons for each local disturbance differed, though many stemmed from arguments over taxes, land or rent.

Although none of these rebellions succeeded in overthrowing a national government, they helped to weaken landlords' control over the people who worked on their estates. By 1600, except in Eastern Europe, most of the people living in the countryside were free.

INTERNATIONAL PROBLEMS Late-medieval (1300–1500) societies were also disrupted by wars between nations, struggles among rival political groups, and by religious discontent. Many people disliked the power and magnificence of important church leaders. Then in the late 1340s, a new disaster struck which was to have a drastic and lasting effect on the population. The *Black Death* arrived in Europe.

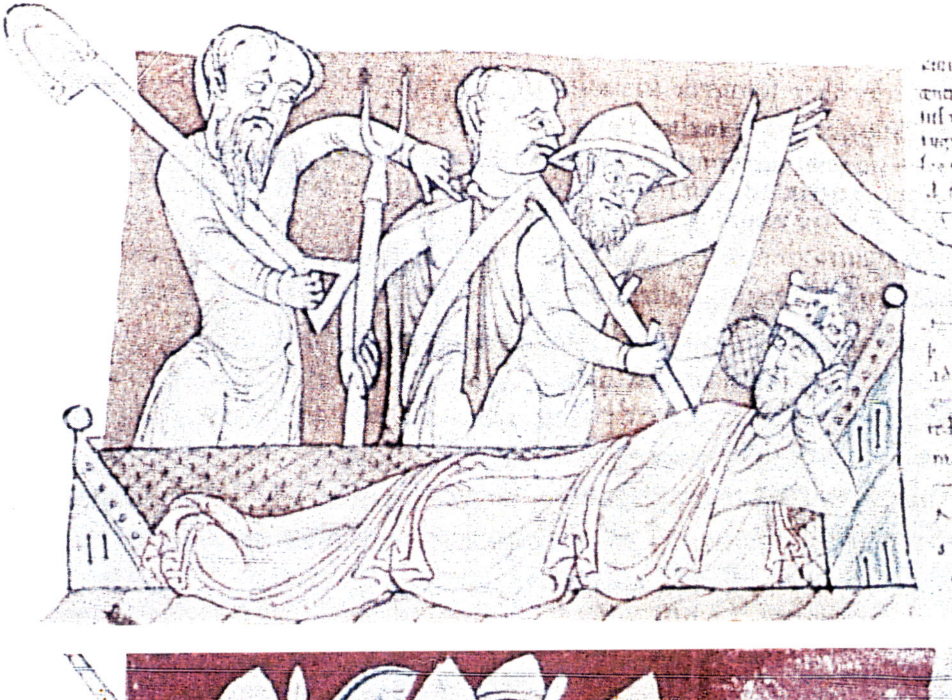

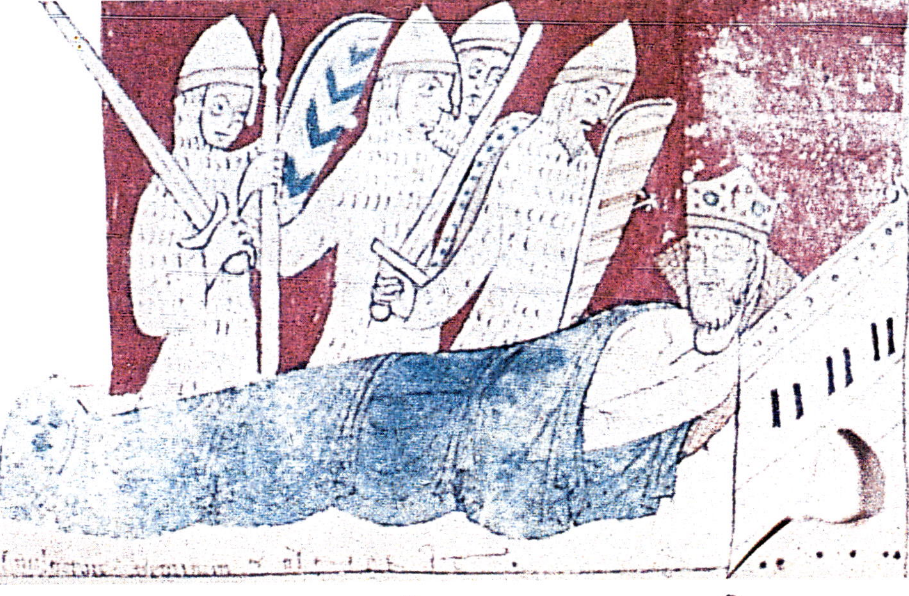

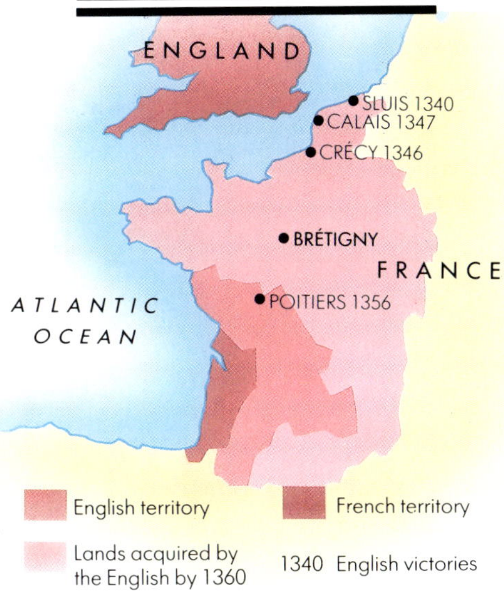

The Hundred Years War

The war was fought between England and France over the claim by the English kings to be rulers of the southwestern part of France, and their refusal to accept the King of France as their feudal lord. Instead, they regarded themselves as equals, and in 1328 and again in 1337, King Edward III of England went so far as to claim the French crown for himself by right of inheritance. This led to open conflict, and the war between England and France continued, with pauses and interruptions, for over 100 years, from 1337–1453.

England and France were at war for many years during the 14th and 15th centuries over the English king's claim to rule Aquitaine. This map shows the lands claimed by the English kings, and the sites of some of the most important battles fought between the opposing armies.

Left. These three pictures from a 13th century manuscript portray scenes from a dream that King Henry II of England (1153–89) is supposed to have had. In fact, they represent every medieval king's nightmare. They show the three most likely causes of trouble within a medieval European kingdom. The top picture shows discontent among the ordinary people. Armed with their farming tools, spades and pitchforks, they have brought copies of the documents on which their rents and labour services are recorded by their lords, to protest to the king about the unfairness of their position. The second picture shows fully armed knights – on whom the king depended for the defence of his country – turning to attack their royal master. The third picture shows bishops and monks – who played a valuable part in the king's government and administration – arguing with the king, instead of carrying out his orders.

THE BLACK DEATH

Above. Plague victims, suddenly struck down. From a 15th century German woodcut.

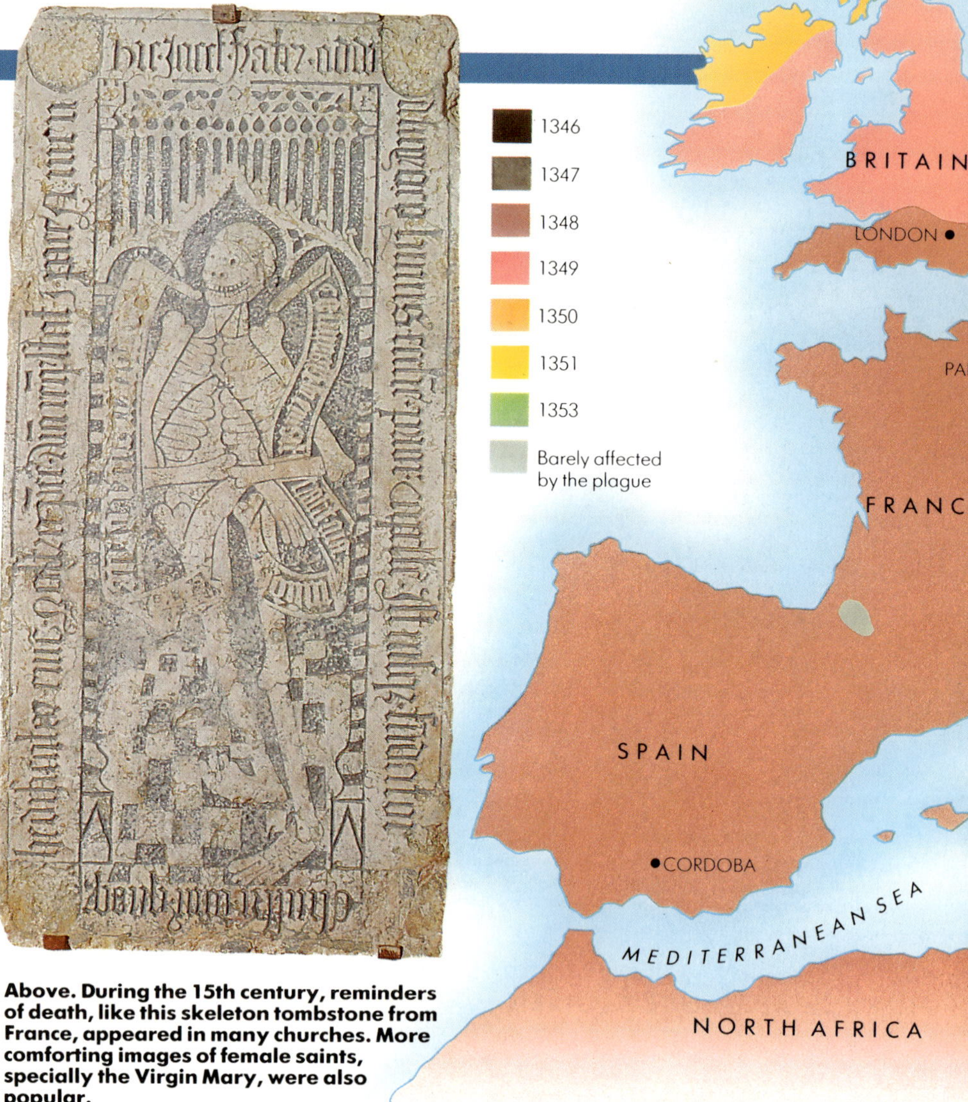

Above. During the 15th century, reminders of death, like this skeleton tombstone from France, appeared in many churches. More comforting images of female saints, specially the Virgin Mary, were also popular.

The Black Death killed millions– suddenly, swiftly and terribly. Its symptoms were particularly unpleasant: huge, painful swellings, like boils, appeared in the victims' necks, armpits and groins, oozing blood and pus. The sufferer developed a high fever, became delirious, and usually died within 48 hours.

Medieval medicine was powerless to cure the disease, although many strange and wonderful remedies were tried. People also hoped to protect themselves by carrying magic *amulets*, or reciting charms. Priests led weeping processions of *penitents*, beating themselves and praying for deliverance. Some people, more practically minded, washed themselves in herb-scented vinegar, which did, in fact, have powerful antiseptic properties.

HOW THE PLAGUE SPREAD What was this deadly disease? Most historians think that it was a variety of bubonic plague, a serious *bacterial* infection that can prove fatal even today. The plague bacteria were carried in the saliva of blood-sucking fleas, who themselves caught the infection by feeding off plague-ridden rats. When the fleas bit people, the bacteria entered the human bloodstream, where they multiplied rapidly.

A few people were strong enough to fight off the disease, but, as we have seen, most succumbed within a very short space of time.

THE COURSE OF THE PLAGUE The plague arrived in Europe in 1347. It spread westwards from the plains of central Asia, where there was a 'reservoir' of the disease. It soon devastated the entire continent. The Black Death caused tremendous loss of life in the Middle East, North Africa and northern India, as well. Nobody knows exactly how many people perished, but modern estimates suggest that at least a third, and perhaps as many as a half, of the total population died.

Deaths were concentrated in areas where people lived close together, especially in towns. The greater density of population made it easier for the disease-carrying rats and fleas to spread. But no-one really knew

The Spread of the Black Death

The Black Death spread westwards to Europe and the Middle East from its homeland in central Asia. Only a few remote and sparsely-populated areas, such as the highlands of Scotland, escaped. This map shows how rapidly the plague spread, travelling on infected rats in the holds of cargo ships, and then on infected fleas hopping from person to person. Medieval people did not understand how the plague was carried. They thought that strong smells, such as perfumed pomanders or *nosegays*, would drive away the evil plague 'vapours'. But, coincidentally, some medieval housewives may have helped keep disease away from their homes by killing fleas, which nobody liked anyway. Medieval books on housekeeping contain many recipes designed to kill fleas, flies and other insect pests.

1 The outbreak of plague in Asia and Far East occurred in 1341. Even though there was widespread loss of life, Chinese rulers went ahead with their plans to expand Chinese territory overseas. In 1349, the first Chinese settlement in Singapore was established.

2 During the 1370s, the great Hindu kingdom of Vijayanagar in India grew more powerful. It controlled the very profitable spice and cotton trades, and ruled over a large, densely populated territory. Travellers there reported that it was vast (over 11 kilometres across), strong, and full of beautiful buildings. There were marble palaces, cooling streams and marvellous gardens. In the north of India, the Muslim Sultanate of Delhi was also rich and powerful. The Sultan held court in great state, and rode in procession with elephants, trumpets and drums.

When a flea bit an infected rat, it sucked in plague bacteria from the rat's bloodstream. When the flea moved on from rat to human, it injected a minute quantity of rat blood, still carrying the plague bacteria, into the human bloodstream. Infected humans could also spread bacteria by coughing and sneezing.

where the plague would next make its deadly attack.

THE CHURCH AND THE PLAGUE Today we understand that the plague is caused by a type of bacteria, but people living (and dying) in the 14th century did not realize this. The fear of death was all around, and even the survivors had to live with horrible memories of suffering and bereavement. Some medieval people saw the plague as another natural disaster, like an earthquake or a flood. Many left their homes and workshops and fled to the remote countryside, hoping to escape infection.

Others shared the Church's view that it was a punishment sent by God, as a result of their wickedness. They gave money to pay for statues, crosses and new church buildings, or commissioned vivid paintings of the torments that awaited sinners in Hell.

THE MONGOL ADVANCE

The Mongol siege of Baghdad in 1258, from a 13th century Persian manuscript. Even though its power had begun to decline, it was still a major disaster when Mongol troops attacked Baghdad, as part of their campaign to conquer the Middle East. This picture shows the high brick walls and tall watch-towers defending the city, and the splendid buildings crowded within the walls. The Mongol troops, with their tents and horses, are camped outside. They are using a giant catapult to try and smash their way through one of the gates. When the Mongol army finally did make their way into the city, they caused death and destruction. Although medieval casualty figures cannot always be trusted, one contemporary chronicler reported that over 400,000 people were killed.

The Black Death brought disease and desolation to a large part of the medieval world. But for people living in India, China, central Asia and the Middle East, it was not the first major disaster to strike their lands. For a long period during the 13th century, whole nations had lived in the fear of *Mongol* attack.

THE ORIGIN OF THE MONGOLS The Mongols were a nomadic people who originated in the harsh *steppe* country of central Asia. They roamed over the vast plains which stretched from Mongolia to the borders of Hungary, seeking good grazing for their flocks and herds. During past centuries they had clashed with more settled civilizations. Most of the time, however, they fought among themselves, since there was fierce rivalry between the different Mongol clans.

GENGHIS KHAN In 1206 the Mongol people became united under one leader, Genghis Khan, and set out to conquer the world. Genghis Khan's ambition was to become 'prince of all that lies between the oceans' (that is, the Pacific and the Atlantic). He very nearly succeeded in his aim. At the time of his death, he was ruler of the largest land-based empire the world had ever seen.

THE COURSE OF THE MONGOL ATTACK First the Mongols looked to the East. At this time China was divided into two hostile dynasties: the Chin in the north and the Sung in the south. In 1211 the Mongols invaded the Sung Empire, and they captured the most important northern city of Peking (Beijing) in 1215. Next they moved westwards, to attack the Muslim kingdom of

Left. Genghis Khan (1206–1227) sitting in his richly decorated tent. He is surrounded by courtiers, including his sons Jochi and Ogedei. The yak tails flying outside the doorway were a traditional Mongol symbol of authority. From a 13th century Persian manuscript painting.

Mongol Military Techniques

All Mongol soldiers were well equipped with bows and arrows, and well supplied with fast, easily-manoeuvrable horses. They could cover up to 160 kilometres a day.

They used traps and false ambushes to cause panic among enemy troops, or to lure them to destruction. And they imposed a reign of terror on all the lands they captured. Anyone who dared fight against them was mercilessly killed.

Below. Mongol invasions during the 13th and early 14th centuries. Mongol troops poured westwards across the desolate central Asian plains, towards the rich trading cities of the Middle East.

'[The Mongols] are more numerous than ants or locusts . . . detachment after detachment arrived, each like a billowing sea.'
JUVAINI, A PERSIAN HISTORIAN

Kwarazim (now part of Uzbekistan). They captured the great trading city of Bukhara in 1220, and burnt it to the ground. Over 30,000 inhabitants were brutally murdered.

The Mongols took few prisoners, preferring to slaughter anyone who opposed them. This cruelty shocked medieval chroniclers, who described the Mongols as bloodthirsty monsters, lacking all human feelings and delighting in death and destruction.

Genghis Khan died in 1227. His son, Ogedei, who ruled after him, first conquered the Chin people in northern China, and then turned to attack Europe. Mongol armies advanced into Russia, where they destroyed the capital city of Kiev in 1240 and continued westwards into Hungary. Ogedei died in 1241, and his army retreated. Europe had a lucky escape.

CHINA AND THE MIDDLE EAST The Mongol rulers after Ogedei preferred to concentrate their attacks on the Sung Empire in China, and on the Muslim lands of the Middle East. The Muslim capital of Baghdad was attacked in 1258, and, for a time, it looked as if the Muslim holy cities of Mecca and Medina in Arabia would also be captured.

But once again, the Mongol forces retreated. Soon, another invasion was planned, but the Mongol troops were heavily defeated by a Muslim army at the battle of Ain Jalut (in present-day Israel) in 1260.

After more than 50 years of terror and bloodshed, the Mongol threat to Islam had disappeared. China was not so fortunate. The Sung people fought valiantly against repeated Mongol invasions, but were finally defeated.

THE RESULTS OF THE MONGOL INVASIONS

Genghis Khan with his descendants, including Babur, who founded a new ruling dynasty in India.

Key Dates of the Mongol Invasions

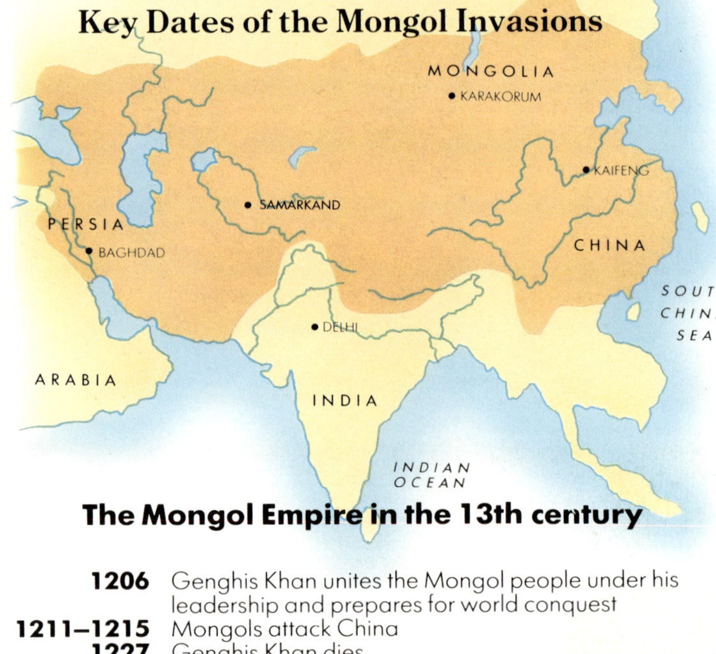

The Mongol Empire in the 13th century

1206 Genghis Khan unites the Mongol people under his leadership and prepares for world conquest
1211–1215 Mongols attack China
1227 Genghis Khan dies
1229 Ogedei Khan proclaimed new Mongol leader
1234 Ogedei's generals capture northern China
1240 Russian capital city of Kiev captured
1258 Important Muslim city, Baghdad, captured
1260 Kublai elected Great Khan
1279 Mongol troops overthrow Chinese Southern Sung Dynasty
1294 Kublai Khan dies; Mongol power declines
1336–1405 Mongol power temporarily revives under Timur. After Timur's death, the era of Mongol danger is over.

Although *Mongol* armies vanished from western lands, Mongol conquests in the east continued. Sung China was overrun in 1279 by an army led by Kublai Khan, who ruled from 1260 to 1294. Kublai Khan was less bloodthirsty than some of his ancestors. He was intelligent, curious and interested in philosophy. But he still went to war. He sent two separate battle fleets to try and capture Japan, in 1274 and 1281, but they were both defeated. The Japanese said that the gods had sent a 'divine wind' from heaven to drive the Mongols away.

THE ACHIEVEMENTS OF KUBLAI KHAN Kublai Khan used the riches from his Chinese conquests to pay for a mighty army. He did not destroy the rich Chinese trading cities, but exploited their wealth and enjoyed the comfortable lifestyle they offered. Marco Polo, who worked for Kublai Khan and admired him, called him 'the most powerful man since Adam'. But Kublai Khan's empire did not last long after his death. By the 1360s Chinese rebels had overthrown their Mongol conquerors and established a new ruling dynasty, the Ming, who governed the Chinese people for the next 300 years.

EFFECTS OF THE MONGOL INVASIONS In the short term, the nations which Mongol armies attacked suffered terribly. Hundreds of thousands of people were killed. The Muslim historian, Ibn al-Athis, reckoned that it was the greatest disaster humanity ever had to endure. Prosperous cities, full of fine houses and graceful mosques were destroyed. Many rare books, works of art, scientific instruments and precious jewels were smashed or looted. Fields and orchards lay neglected and full of weeds; the men and women who worked in them fled in terror as they heard of the Mongol approach.

In the long term, the Mongols achieved very little of

The Career of Genghis Khan

In 1206 Temujin, a Mongol prince, was proclaimed leader of all the Mongol peoples at a great assembly. He went on to take the name Genghis Khan, which means 'Prince of all that lies between the oceans'. He devoted the rest of his life to conquest, death and destruction.

He died in 1227 in China 'without regrets'. His body was carried from China to his homeland in Mongolia with great ceremony. Every living creature met by the funeral procession was killed so that it might serve Genghis Khan in the next world.

Left. Genghis Khan's funeral procession which carried his body from China, where he died, aged 73, to his ancestral homeland in Mongolia.

Tomb of the Mongol leader, Timur, in Samarkand. Timur became a Muslim; his tomb is built in an Islamic style.

lasting importance. But, in spite of their appetite for death and destruction, they did manage to bring peace, of a sort, to many parts of Asia for over 100 years. Once lands were under Mongol control, feuds between local chieftains which made overland travel so dangerous for merchants came to an end.

THE MONGOLS UNDER TIMUR The 'Mongol Peace' vanished soon after the collapse of Mongol power in China. But the threat of Mongol attacks did not completely disappear for another 100 years. Under their leader Timur (sometimes known as Tamburlane), Mongol armies clashed with Muslim forces in Turkey. Timur had the defeated Muslim commander, Sultan Bayezid, paraded round his court in a cage.

But Timur, although savage, was different from earlier Mongol leaders. He abandoned the tribal beliefs and the *nomadic* way of life of his ancestors. He became a Muslim, and seems to have appreciated life in towns. He rebuilt his capital city of Samarkand with many beautiful mosques, elegant tombs and lovely gardens.

EUROPE: PROSPERITY RENEWED

The *Black Death*, and the repeated outbreaks of *plague* during the 14th and 15th centuries, had an unexpected side effect. Many of the survivors grew richer. How did this happen?

CHANGES IN WORKING CONDITIONS At first, farming, trade and industry all suffered as the plague devastated towns and villages. But soon, merchants, craftsmen and farm labourers were back at work. There were, however, important differences from life in the old days. Before the Black Death, there had been plenty of workmen available. Some historians even think there were too many workers, and that some were unemployed. This meant that wages were low, and working conditions were poor. Masters in the towns and in the countryside knew that they could always find men and women desperate for work.

The plague changed all that. Since so many people had died, workers were now in short supply. Wages rose, and workmen felt free to move from job to job, seeking better pay. At the same time, prices of basic necessities, like food and fuel, fell lower. The smaller population meant that there was less demand for them. With higher wages, and a

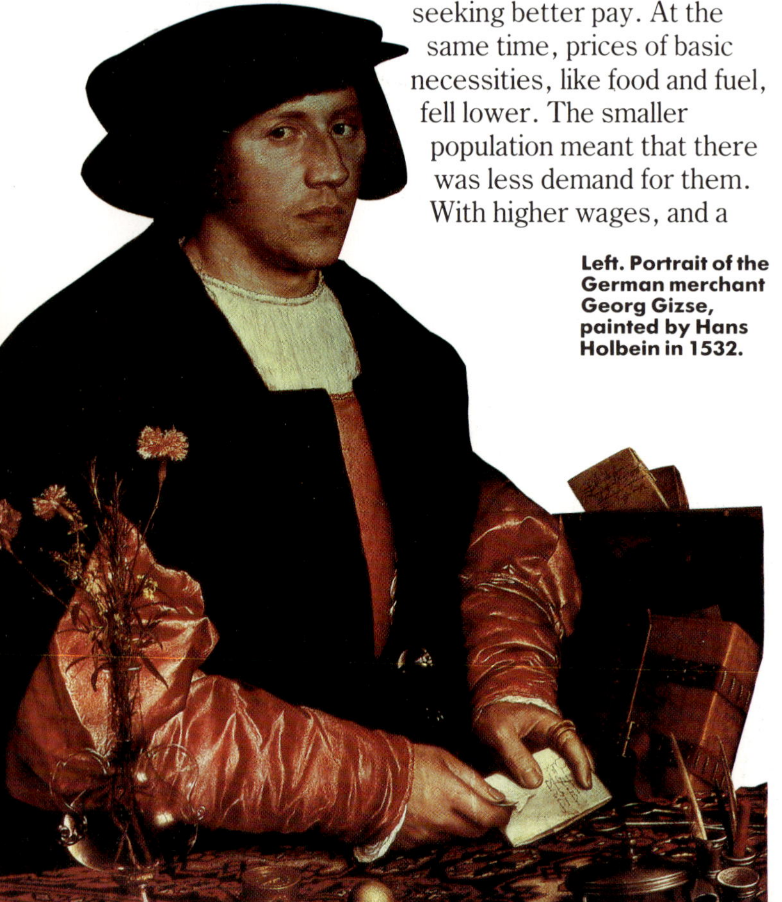

Left. Portrait of the German merchant Georg Gizse, painted by Hans Holbein in 1532.

Merchant cities in northern Europe grew rich on the profits of trade. In particular, ports along the shores of the Baltic and the North Sea flourished and prospered. Many, like King's Lynn in eastern England, or Bruges in Belgium, spent money on fine new buildings. This photograph of Rothenburg, in northern Germany, shows substantial merchant houses of the type built during the later Middle Ages.

Europe After the Plague

After the Black Death had disappeared, many people tried to reason why it had occurred. Fifteenth century preachers thought that the repeated attacks of plague (which killed mostly young people, who had not developed a resistance to the plague bacteria) were sent from God to punish disobedient children. Here are the reasonings of one preacher:

'it may be that [for] vengeance of this sin of un-worshipping and despising of fathers and mothers, God slayeth children by pestilence, as you see every day, for in the old law, children that were rebels and unbuxom to their fathers and mothers were punished by death . . .'

lower cost of living, workers now had money left over to spend.

Some bought or rented bigger houses or more land; others chose to purchase better quality food, or finer clothes. Governments passed laws to try and stop this, feeling that rich foods and fashionable clothes were only fit for nobles. But they were not very successful.

PROSPERITY How did all this affect other members of society? Merchants and craftsmen welcomed the extra money that workers had to spend. And, as their businesses expanded, they, too, made more money. As the number of people in Europe gradually increased, merchants and craftsmen prospered still further, and took on more workmen to help them produce more goods.

HARD TIMES FOR LANDLORDS Almost the only people in medieval Europe who did not grow more wealthy as a result of the plague were landlords. If they wanted workers to harvest their crops, they had to pay high wages. But they knew that the corn they took to market would not fetch a very high price. Their profits were disappearing. What could they do?

Some landlords leased their fields to farmers in return for a low income. Some let fields return to woodland or waste. Others, especially in England, gave up growing corn and raised sheep instead. Wool still fetched a good price, and sheep needed few workers to look after them. Harsh landlords tried to force people who rented houses and plots of land to do all their farm work for them, as they had during the 11th and 12th centuries. But workers simply left these lords' estates, and found a better place to live elsewhere.

Merchant Cities

Another confident civic building – the Town Hall at Bruges, in Belgium, built during the 15th and early 16th centuries.

Towns and cities in northern Europe, especially in Belgium and northern France, grew rich on the profits of buying and selling. The most prosperous towns were connected with the cloth trade. They made their money by importing fleeces and yarns, then weaving, dying and finishing fine woollen fabrics. Rural areas, like the Cotswold hills of England, where sheep were raised to produce high quality fleeces, also grew rich.

The picture was not so rosy for some southern European cities. Plagues, wars and bad debts all led to a slowing down of trade within the Mediterranean area. Although individual merchant families managed to make good profits throughout the economic depression, other businesses in Italy and southern France found their profits decreasing.

Right. A reconstruction drawing of the magnificent market hall at Bruges in Belgium, built during the 15th century to bring honour and prestige to the town. It is topped by a spectacular tower, built in a flamboyant Gothic style.

THE RENAISSANCE

Even though many parts of Europe prospered during the later 14th and 15th centuries, many people must still have been miserable and frightened. Most families knew someone who had died of the plague. Worse still, nobody really understand how the disease spread, and so people lived in the constant fear that soon it might be their turn to die.

As a result, many religious brotherhoods and sisterhoods were formed. Many beautiful paintings, statues, prayer books and other works of art on religious subjects were given to churches. Wandering preachers thundered out their message to packed congregations, urging them to abandon their sinful lives.

THE BEGINNING OF THE RENAISSANCE However, at the same time as all this intense religious activity, a new, confident and non-religious way of looking at the world was emerging. The *Renaissance* (it means 'Re-birth'), as this movement was called, began as a collection of artistic and philosophical ideas. They first became popular in Italy, but were soon discussed by artists and scholars all over Europe.

A NEW LOOK AT THE WORLD Renaissance painters, sculptors, teachers and thinkers combined a keen interest in the remains of ancient Greek and Roman culture with the wish to create something totally new. They abandoned the old medieval styles of painting and writing. Instead, they tried to show the world with scientific accuracy. They studied the human body, plants, rocks and animals, and experimented with new ways of drawing, so that they could reproduce 'real' landscapes and 'real' people in their pictures. They examined ancient statues and carvings, to learn from the skills of artists who had lived hundreds of years ago.

THE IMPORTANCE OF PRINTING Renaissance scholars also studied Greek and Roman texts, and translated, edited and printed them so that the ideas they contained could become widely understood. Printing, which was invented in Germany during the 15th century (although a similar system had been known in China for many years), was very important in spreading Renaissance ideas throughout Europe. Many Renaissance artists and philosophers lived as Christians. But for others, the newly available Greek and Roman ideas, and their own observations from nature, led them to challenge the teachings of the Church. Some were even prepared to die for their beliefs.

Italian City States in the 13th and 14th Centuries

Italy was not a unified country at the time of the Renaissance. Instead, it was divided into many smaller city states, usually consisting of a busy town and the fields and farms surrounding it. Some of these city states were rich and powerful, like the great ports of Venice and Genoa. Others were small and impoverished. Wars were frequent among the Italian states.

PATRONAGE Who paid for all this artistic and scholarly activity? Wealthy patrons demanded new buildings, paintings, sculptures and books, all produced in the Renaissance style. Kings, nobles and city governments competed with one another to employ the most skilful artists, and the most intelligent philosophers. Powerful men and women became interested in Renaissance ideas, and in discussing what made the ideal Renaissance society.

The Renaissance changed Europe in very many ways.

Left. Roman art, from the second century BC. A carved marble tomb, showing a mythological scene.

Below. Renaissance art, imitating Roman designs. A carving by the Italian artist, Luca della Robbia, in Florence Cathedral, c. 1438. Della Robbia has used a pagan style over 1500 years old to decorate a 'new' Christian building.

Key Figures of the Italian Renaissance

Filippo Brunelleschi (1377–1446) was an architect who studied Ancient Roman buildings and sculpture. He built the dome of Florence cathedral in classical Roman style.

Piero della Francesca (1420–1492) perfected the art of perspective drawing. This was an important Renaissance technique which enabled painters to depict space accurately and realistically in their works.

Marsilio Ficino (1433–1499) was a Renaissance *humanist* who studied the writings of Ancient Greek and Roman philosophers. He believed that human achievements, rather than God's will, could bring about a 'golden age' of peace, beauty and goodwill.

Sandro Botticelli (1444–1510) was a painter who combined traditional Christian religious subjects with Renaissance humanist ideas. The style of his paintings was greatly influenced by Ancient Greek and Roman art.

Leonardo da Vinci (1452–1519) was a painter, scientist, military engineer and inventor. He studied human anatomy and the world of nature, and portrayed them accurately in his works. He designed many extraordinary machines, including a submarine and a helicopter.

Niccolo Machiavelli (1469–1527) was a writer on politics, who offered advice to Italian Renaissance princes. He is famous for suggesting that, in politics, 'the end justifies the means'. That is, any methods, however unpleasant or unlawful, should be considered when planning effective political action.

Michelangelo Buonarotti (1475–1564) was a painter, sculptor and poet and is famous for his paintings decorating the ceiling of the Sistine Chapel, in Rome. His work displays his belief in the nobility, beauty, freedom and power of humanity.

Left. Two figure-studies by Renaissance artists: Michelangelo's statue of David and an anatomical drawing by Leonardo.

Left. An engraving of Michelangelo. He was one of the greatest artists of the Renaissance.

Above. A self portrait by Leonardo da Vinci. He was one of the most extraordinary and talented figures of the Renaissance.

Raphael (1483–1520) was a painter who combined portrayals of traditional Christian subjects with a typically Renaissance realistic technique based on Ancient Greek and Roman models.

Galileo Galilei (1564–1642) was a scientist and professor at the University of Padua. He dared to claim that the earth and the planets orbited round the sun, in defiance of the Church's teaching.

RESTORING ISLAM: THE OTTOMAN EMPIRE

A French 15th century view of the city of Constantinople. The artist, who had obviously never been there, pictured it as a western European city.

At the same time as the Renaissance was taking place in Europe, there was revival and recovery in the Muslim world as well. Some parts of the old Muslim empire–Egypt, Syria, Spain and North Africa–had escaped the Mongol invasions, and survived as peaceful centres of the Muslim way of life. As we saw on page 241, the Muslim holy cities of Mecca and Medina had also been saved from destruction.

In all these places, Muslim scholars, scientists and philosophers continued the Muslim tradition of learning and discovery. In the towns, Muslim craftsmen continued to produce splendid objects in metal, pottery and glass.

But the political strength of the great Muslim Empire, which was already weakened and threatened by rival sultanates in many parts of the Muslim world, had been destroyed for ever by the Mongol invasions. By the middle of the 14th century, however, a new Muslim world power–the Ottoman Empire–was beginning to emerge.

UTHMAN As the Mongols retreated, their authority had been replaced by a number of small Muslim states. One of these states was led by Uthman (which became 'Ottoman' in medieval English), a Turkish chieftain who lived from 1281–1324. During his lifetime, Uthman led Muslim troops on campaigns to capture the territories that surrounded his little kingdom.

OTTOMAN EXPANSION The sultans who ruled after Uthman continued this policy of expansion. In 1326 Ottoman troops captured the important Byzantine city of Bursa, close to the Black Sea, which became the Ottoman capital. By 1400, the Ottomans controlled a huge area. In 1453, they captured the Byzantine capital city of Constantinople (Istanbul). This brought an end to the Byzantine Empire, and caused a ripple of fear to run across Europe. Where would the Ottomans attack next?

Ottoman conquests continued throughout the 15th and 16th centuries. Under one of their most famous leaders, Sultan Suleiman the Magnificent, the Ottomans advanced eastwards, to capture the old Muslim capital of Baghdad. In the west, they controlled the lands known today as Bulgaria, Greece, Albania, Serbia, Croatia, Bosnia and Hungary. By 1520, they also controlled the once-powerful Muslim states of Egypt and Syria, as well as Mecca, Medina and the wealthy trading port of Aden in Arabia.

THE OTTOMAN SYSTEM OF GOVERNMENT Like earlier Muslim governments, the Ottomans treated conquered peoples fairly and well. They employed the most capable people they could find–whatever their faith–to help them run their empire. They also used Christian troops, the *Janissaries*, to help them fight their battles. They recruited clever Christian boys to serve in their administration. Also like earlier Muslim rulers, the Ottoman sultans spent a great deal of money on encouraging the arts. Many grand and beautiful mosques were built on the orders of Ottoman rulers.

Below. The Ottoman empire in 1566. The empire had been greatly expanded during the brilliant reign of Sultan Suleiman the Magnificent (1520–1566). Now it covered over 2.6 million square km, and was a major world power.

1 The Italian Renaissance was at its height from 1400–1500. Important new developments occurred in painting, sulpture, architecture and science. Also, the first printed book in Europe was produced in 1445, by Johannes Gutenberg, in Germany. Painters of the 'Northern Renaissance', like Memling, van Eyck and Holbein, were active in Belgium, northern France and England. There was a final flowering of Gothic architecture: Cologne Cathedral, and King's College Chapel, Cambridge, were built during this period.

2 From 1470–1520, the Inca peoples in South America conquered the neighbouring Chimu kingdom and began to establish an empire. The Aztec Empire was very powerful in Mexico. These empires were soon to end; in 1492 Christopher Columbus crossed the Atlantic Ocean and made probably the first European contact with American peoples for almost 500 years.

Above. Muslim astronomers studying the stars, and geographers studying a globe, from a 16th century Persian manuscript.

Right. The Ottoman leader, Sultan Mehmet II 'the Conqueror', who ruled the Ottoman Empire from 1451– 1481.

CHINA AND JAPAN: CONSTRUCTION AND DESTRUCTION

The most successful Chinese rebel leader against the Mongols was Chu Yuan-chang (1328–1398). He became the first emperor of the new Ming dynasty. The Ming emperors quickly began the task of reconstruction after the Mongol invasions. New canals and irrigation ditches were dug; the ancient Great Wall of China (originally designed to protect the country against Mongol attacks) was strengthened and repaired; and the war-torn city of Peking was rebuilt. The Ming emperors made it their new capital, and constructed a huge, secret palace (the 'Forbidden City'), to be a home for themselves, their families, and the royal court.

NEW WARS The Chinese emperors soon had to fight to defend their new freedom. Mongol troops launched repeated attacks from the north, and pirate raids became an increasing danger to ships and coastal cities in the south. There were wars, too, when some of the more ambitious Ming emperors tried to conquer new territories. Chu's son, the Emperor Yung-lo, tried

The *Samurai*'s elaborate costume was designed to display his warrior status and to protect him in battle. In medieval Japan, everyday activities, like washing and dressing, could become surrounded by elaborate ritual in royal or noble homes.

This extract comes from the 'Pillow Book of Sei Shonagun' and shows how highly developed simple ceremonies had become. It was written by a female courtier who lived in a Japanese imperial palace during the 10th century. She is describing an early morning scene:

'Now the attendants brought water . . . As I recall there were altogether six attendants – two young maids and four servants of lower rank . . . The young attendants looked very pretty in their loose, cherry-coloured coats; I enjoyed watching them take the basin of water from the servants . . . [The ladies in waiting, who were also taking part in the ceremony] wore divided skirts of green and shaded material, Chinese jackets, waistband ribbons and shoulder sashes; their faces were heavily powdered. The servants passed them what was needed for the washing and I was pleased to see how everything was done with proper ceremony in the Chinese style.'

The diagrams above show the many garments that made up the Samurai's battle dress. The ritual of arming could take a long time because he first bathed and perfumed himself so that if he died he would smell sweet.

unsuccessfully to capture Vietnam, and sent huge fleets to demand tribute from rulers in Southeast Asia, India and Sri Lanka.

LIFE IN THE COUNTRYSIDE For ordinary people in the Chinese countryside, life was still hard work, although the new canals and irrigation schemes helped to increase rice production. Chinese peasants had some machines to help them, unlike farmworkers in western lands. Foot-powered threshing machines, for example, made the task of separating grains of rice from the stalk very much easier.

INCREASES IN PRODUCTION Since the population was increasing rapidly, there was a constant need to clear more land for farming, and to grow bigger and better crops. Farm workers who grew tea and tended silkworms were also kept busy, meeting the demands of foreign customers who were eager to buy these Chinese products. In factory areas, pottery was mass produced; cheaper, basic goods for everyday use at home and abroad, and fine, fragile wares for the luxury trade.

JAPAN: THE WARRING STATES Japan was never invaded by the Mongols, and remained independent throughout the period from 1100–1500. But the years 1350–1600 were a time of unrest and disorder, often known as the Warring States Period. Rival groups of noblemen, each with their own highly trained private army, struggled to gain control of the country.

In spite of these wars, Japanese culture–especially religious thought–flourished and developed at this time. Most Japanese people followed the *Buddhist* faith. During the 12th and 13th centuries, one particular branch of Buddhism–known as *Zen*–became very popular, especially among the noble warriors and their troops.

Beautifully finished pottery was made in specialist centres throughout the country during this period. Solemn, polite, careful ceremonies, based on everyday actions like making tea, but also containing a religious or philosophical meaning, became an important part of upper-class Japanese life at this time.

Above. The Great Wall of China, begun in AD 221 and extended and rebuilt by the Ming emperors. It also provided a powerful symbol of the wealth and resources of the new Ming Empire. The wall runs for over 24,000 kilometres through rugged countryside, from the Pacific coastline to the deserts and plains of central Asia. There are guardhouses and watchtowers at regular intervals, so that soldiers stationed at the wall could give early warning of an enemy approach.

Above. The Golden Pavilion, or Kinkaku-ji, Japan, built as a country-house and monastery by the Japanese *Shogun* Askikaga Yoshimitsu in 1397. The pavilion is surrounded by beautiful gardens and looks over a peaceful lake.

Right. Emperor Chu Yuan-chang, founder of the Ming Dynasty. He was born into a peasant family and won fame as a war-leader.

VOYAGES TO THE INDIES

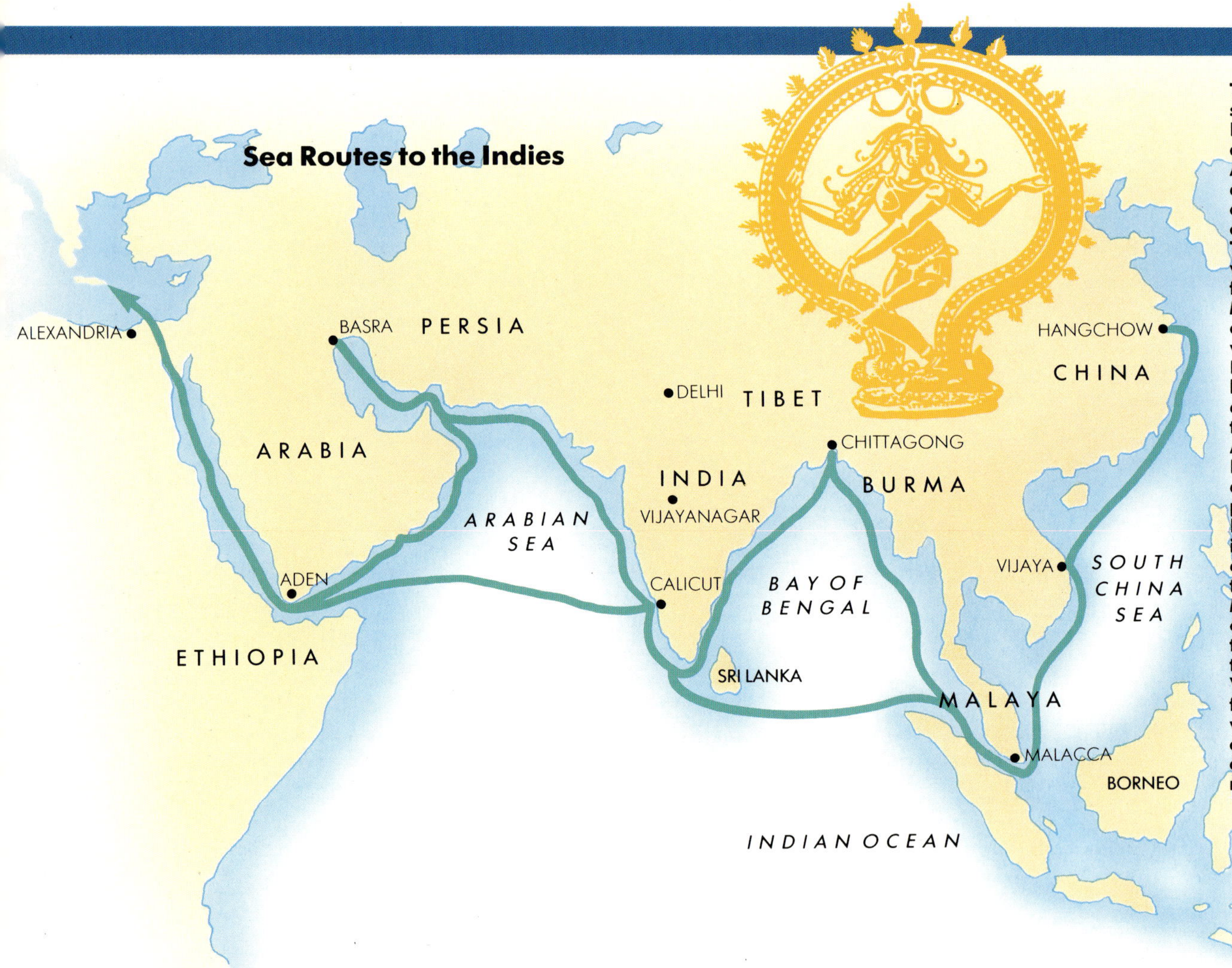

Sea Routes to the Indies

The map shows the sea-routes between Europe and the East during the Middle Ages. Ships sailed along the Chinese coast to the islands of the East Indies. There, they traded with merchants from India or the Middle East, who carried their goods westwards to Europe. One route led up the Red Sea, and then overland, to the great port of Alexandria, in Egypt. An alternative route passed through the Persian Gulf to the important trading city of Basra, and then overland to the Mediterranean coast. Goods were then sent by sea to the Italian ports of Venice and Genoa, from where they were carried overland to countries in northern Europe.

Some of the most important medieval sea routes were centred on the Indian Ocean, the Bay of Bengal, and the South China Sea. Sailors used seasonal winds (the monsoons) to carry them from Arabia and East Africa to India, Sri Lanka and the islands of the East Indies. When the winds changed, as they did after a few months, they sailed home again, loaded with cargo from distant ports. What were these eastern lands like, and why did sailors risk their lives to get there?

INDIA From the 10th century, most of northwestern India had been ruled by Muslim princes. Among the most famous of these was Muhammad of Ghazni (998–1003), who, like so many Muslim rulers, encouraged poets, scholars, artists and scientists to come to his court. Another powerful Muslim kingdom in India was the Sultanate of Delhi, which was established in 1206.

In earlier years, India had been the home of a brilliant

Eastern Spices

Medieval people liked to use eastern spices to flavour their food. Here is a 15th century recipe for cooking beefsteak or venison:

'Take venison or beef, slice it and fry it until it is brown; then take vinegar and a little *verjus* and a little wine, and add ground pepper and powdered ginger, cook together to make a sauce; when it is ready to serve, scatter powdered cinnamon on top.'

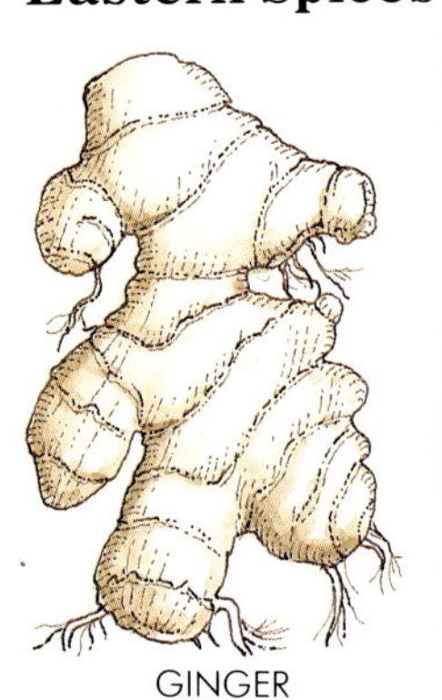

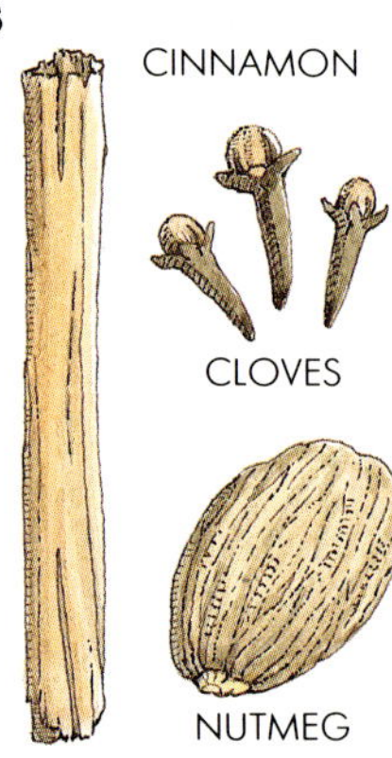

Above are shown some of the spices brought back from the East.

Right. An impressive temple chariot, carved in stone, and decorated with statues of Hindu gods and goddesses. From the ruined Vitthala temple in the great Indian city of Vijayanagar.

Left. Part of the magnificent temple buildings at Madura, southern India, dating from the 10th century. Each side of the building is covered with elaborate carvings, showing scenes from Hindu religious epics.

Right. A procession of warriors, war-horses and elephants from a carved stone frieze in the Hazara Rama (king's private temple) in the Indian city of Vijayanagar.

Hindu civilization, ruled over by the Gupta kings. Scientists working then made important discoveries, and Indian philosophers were so famous that Chinese scholars travelled vast distances to talk with them. But by 1100, the Gupta Empire had collapsed. Southern India (along with present-day Burma, Thailand, Cambodia, Malaysia, Indonesia and the islands of the East Indies) was divided into small, independent kingdoms. They were linked by shared religious traditions (Hindu and Buddhist) and busy international trade.

TRADE GOODS FROM THE EAST In these lands, ordinary peoples' lives were based on farming and producing goods for sale. Many of these were valuable. Cotton, perfume, pearls, rubies, medicines, dyestuffs and elephants came from India. Malaysia exported tin and timber; the islands, especially Java and Sumatra, grew pepper and spices. Hardwood trees were cut from forests in Burma and Thailand.

Over the years, some of these trading kingdoms grew rich and expanded, while others declined. All of them left behind wonderful temples and shrines– monuments to their peoples' beliefs and to the wealth of the kings who built them.

THE VIJAYANAGAR EMPIRE Towards the end of the Middle Ages, a new and powerful Hindu empire began to rule over southern India, and to control the profitable spice and cotton trades. Travellers reported that its capital city, Vijayanagar, had half a million inhabitants, was 11 kilometres wide, and was surrounded by seven city walls, one inside the other. The mighty Vijayanagar Empire, however, had a relatively short life and only lasted until 1565, when it was overthrown by armies from north India.

SOUTH OF THE SAHARA

A page from the *Catalan Atlas*, produced for King Charles V of France in 1375. This extract shows Mansa Musa, ruler of the wealthy African kingdom of Mali, holding a gold coin.

During the Middle Ages, Africa was the home of a number of wealthy and thriving civilizations. In several different parts of the continent, powerful kings ruled over busy, prosperous communities. In the northwest of Africa, the kings of Mali were world-famous for the fabulous treasure they owned, as well as for the fairness and justice of their rule. They gained their wealth from the rich goldfields in and around their lands.

TRADE Merchants from Europe and the Middle East made the long camel trek across the dry, empty Sahara Desert to bring back trade goods. They also made dangerous voyages along the west African coast to trade with these prosperous kingdoms, and to bring back gold and other treasure. They returned telling elaborate, exaggerated travellers' tales, full of unlikely incidents and improbable detail.

ISLAMIC INFLUENCE Many of these western kingdoms had been converted to Islam. Some of the impressive Islamic buildings–mosques, colleges and tombs–dating from this period still survive today, despite damage by centuries of harsh tropical weather. The city of Timbuktu in present-day Mali became a centre of Islamic learning, attracting scholars from the wide expanse of Africa south of the Sahara.

GREAT ZIMBABWE In the southeastern part of the continent, there was another flourishing civilization, also based on gold, centred on the fortress-city of Great Zimbabwe. Elsewhere in eastern Africa, people mined iron ore and produced other valuable commodities, such as salt, leather, ivory and dried fish. They traded these goods with Arab merchants, who sailed along the east coast of Africa to the countries known today as Kenya, Tanzania and Mozambique.

There was also a profitable trade in slaves, who were employed as domestic servants throughout the Middle East. Today slavery is not tolerated, but it was widespread in many parts of the world (including southern Europe) during the Middle Ages.

EVIDENCE FOR THE AFRICAN LIFESTYLE There are few written sources describing the lives of many of the peoples living on the African continent during the Middle Ages. But archaeological evidence has revealed to us that they had developed a way of life that was remarkably well adapted to their surroundings. Sometimes they grew crops, sometimes they lived off travelling flocks and herds, depending on the soil and climatic conditions.

Surviving examples of African art also tell us that these peoples had a complex and sophisticated system of beliefs. This involved ancestral spirits, the forces of nature (such as wind and weather), sacred places, animals, trees or objects. This period also saw a number of major changes in the 'human landscape' of Africa, as various groups and peoples left their homelands and migrated towards new and more productive territory.

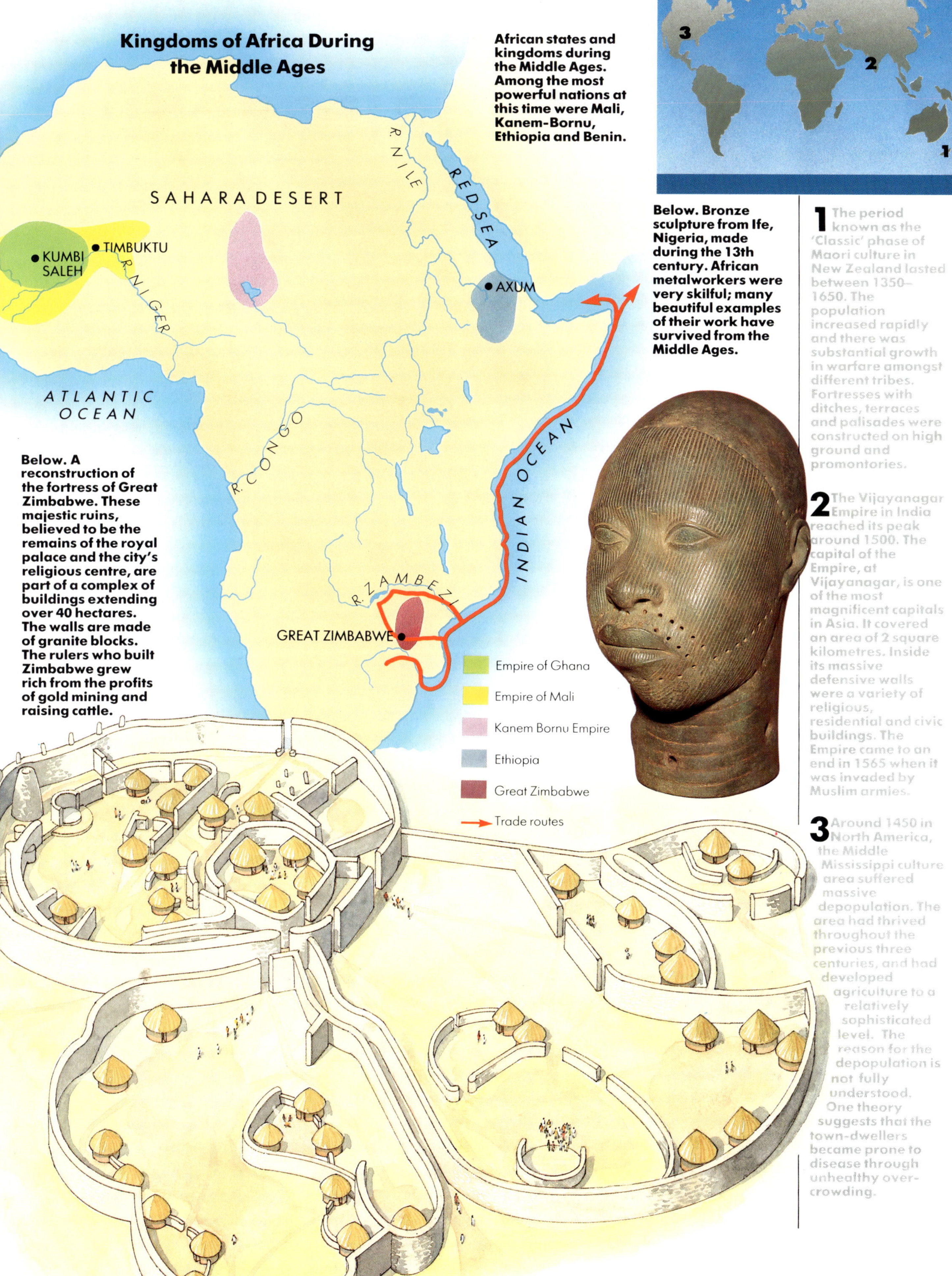

African states and kingdoms during the Middle Ages. Among the most powerful nations at this time were Mali, Kanem-Bornu, Ethiopia and Benin.

Below. Bronze sculpture from Ife, Nigeria, made during the 13th century. African metalworkers were very skilful; many beautiful examples of their work have survived from the Middle Ages.

Below. A reconstruction of the fortress of Great Zimbabwe. These majestic ruins, believed to be the remains of the royal palace and the city's religious centre, are part of a complex of buildings extending over 40 hectares. The walls are made of granite blocks. The rulers who built Zimbabwe grew rich from the profits of gold mining and raising cattle.

1 The period known as the 'Classic' phase of Maori culture in New Zealand lasted between 1350–1650. The population increased rapidly and there was substantial growth in warfare amongst different tribes. Fortresses with ditches, terraces and palisades were constructed on high ground and promontories.

2 The Vijayanagar Empire in India reached its peak around 1500. The capital of the Empire, at Vijayanagar, is one of the most magnificent capitals in Asia. It covered an area of 2 square kilometres. Inside its massive defensive walls were a variety of religious, residential and civic buildings. The Empire came to an end in 1565 when it was invaded by Muslim armies.

3 Around 1450 in North America, the Middle Mississippi culture area suffered massive depopulation. The area had thrived throughout the previous three centuries, and had developed agriculture to a relatively sophisticated level. The reason for the depopulation is not fully understood. One theory suggests that the town-dwellers became prone to disease through unhealthy over-crowding.

NORTH AMERICA AND THE CARIBBEAN

Totem poles from the village of Kispiox, British Columbia, in Canada. The carvings show magical creatures, and scenes from family history.

Several flourishing civilizations occupied the vast landmass of North America during the Middle Ages. Archaeologists have estimated that there were over 100 different languages spoken there round about 1500. All these different peoples did not live in isolation. Small groups joined together under the protection of a strong local leader, or were conquered and controlled by a powerful empire. Other 'families' of peoples were linked by a common ancestry, or by shared religious beliefs and traditions.

TRADE ROUTES Long-distance trade routes crossed the country, enabling goods and raw materials from one region to be exchanged for local produce from another. Trading contacts also helped new ideas and inventions in farming, warfare and craft techniques to spread over a wide area.

EVIDENCE OF THE AMERICAN PAST Few of these early Americans left any written records, but many of the objects they manufactured–buildings, *earthworks*, pottery, textiles, metalwork and jewellery–have survived until today. In recent years, archaeologists have also used a number of scientific techniques to discover more about the early American people. Fragments of wood, the contents of rubbish pits, shrivelled grains and seeds, ruined storehouses and burial mounds have revealed what people ate, what animals they farmed or hunted, what crops they grew and what clothes they wore.

The early European explorers regarded the native Americans as little more than savages, but the archaeological remains tell a different story. They reveal that early American societies were well organized, very skilled and often wealthy. They also show that the American people had developed a number of different ways of life, all designed to make the best use of the soils, climate and vegetation of the region in which they lived.

ANCIENT CITIES Among the most impressive remains dating from the Middle Ages in America are the great walled cities of the Chaco people, who lived in the southwest between 950–1300. The Mississippi people, who lived in the river valleys of the southeast, also built huge cities. During the 11th–13th centuries, their capital city, Cahokia, had about 10,000 inhabitants, and was larger than either London or Paris. Mississippi farmers developed an intensive system of cropping based on corn, beans and *squash*. These provided a well balanced vegetarian diet for the city population.

In the northeast, coastal peoples lived in wealthy village communities organized around fishing, hunting and trapping. They built strong wooden houses decorated with magnificent carvings. Further inland, in the great plains, villages were defended by deep moats, strong walls and stockades. Houses were large, and provided shelter and protection for several families living together. In each village, deep pits were dug to store grain for food during the cold winter months.

THE CARIBBEAN In the far south, the islands of the Caribbean were inhabited by the Arawak and Carib peoples. They were fishers and farmers, growing plentiful crops of tropical plants, especially *manioc* (for flour), pineapples, peanuts, beans and peppers. They wove cotton cloth, moulded fine pottery and little clay statues, and were famous for their skill at making musical instruments.

Peoples of North America and the Caribbean c.1500

The map shows the distribution of the peoples of North and Central America in 1500. Civilizations in all parts of the Americas, including the Caribbean, developed in isolation from cultures in Africa, Europe and Asia, which were linked by travel and trade. Crops, animals, religions and languages were all very different from those in the 'other half' of the world. Even within the North American landmass, cultures and lifestyles developed differently. This was largely due to the wide variation in climate, vegetation and soils.

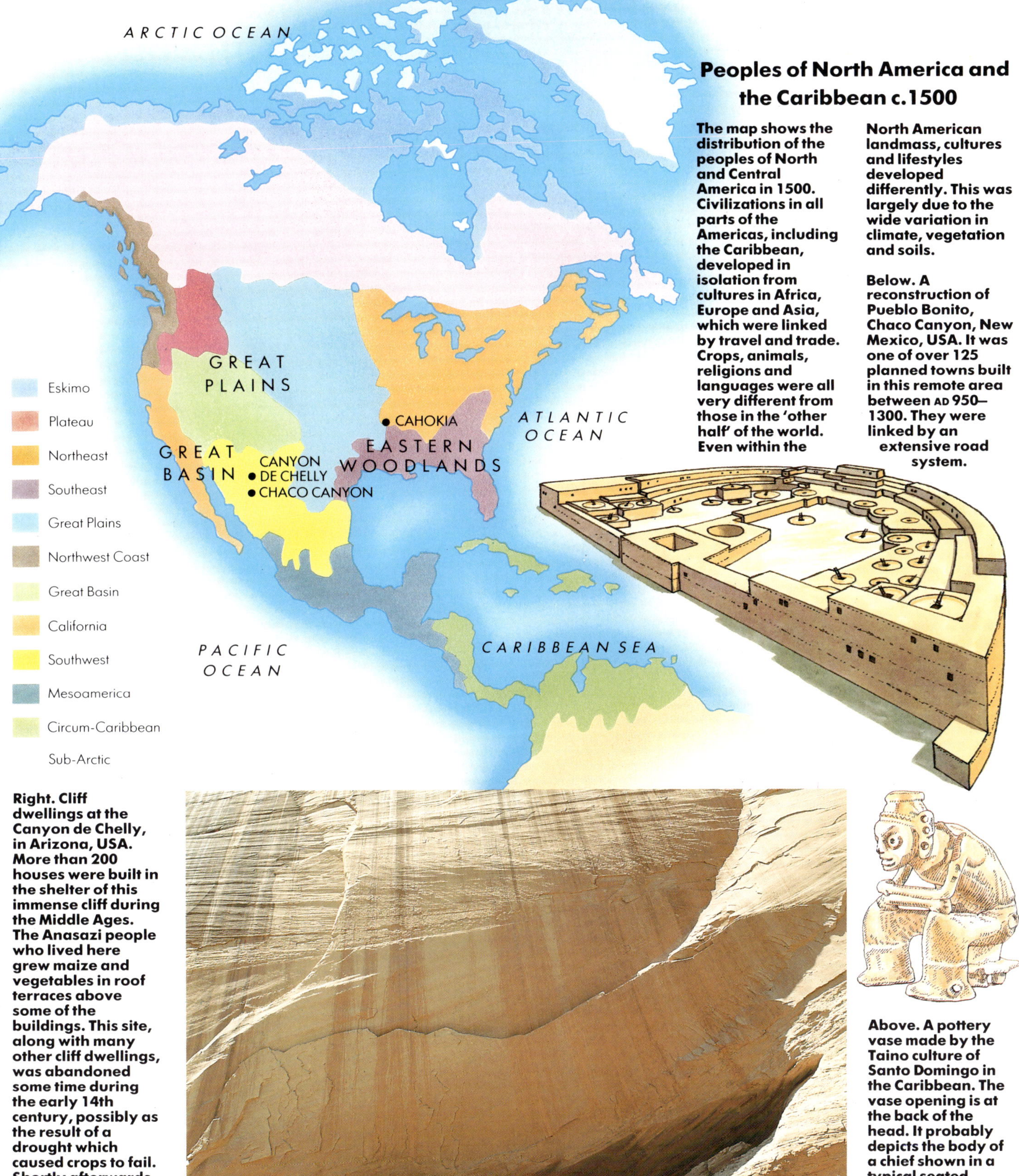

Below. A reconstruction of Pueblo Bonito, Chaco Canyon, New Mexico, USA. It was one of over 125 planned towns built in this remote area between AD 950–1300. They were linked by an extensive road system.

Right. Cliff dwellings at the Canyon de Chelly, in Arizona, USA. More than 200 houses were built in the shelter of this immense cliff during the Middle Ages. The Anasazi people who lived here grew maize and vegetables in roof terraces above some of the buildings. This site, along with many other cliff dwellings, was abandoned some time during the early 14th century, possibly as the result of a drought which caused crops to fail. Shortly afterwards, the area was invaded by nomadic peoples, including the Apache. This brought the Anasazi settled, farming, lifestyle to an end.

Above. A pottery vase made by the Taino culture of Santo Domingo in the Caribbean. The vase opening is at the back of the head. It probably depicts the body of a chief shown in a typical seated burial position. Small pottery objects like this have been found in several sites throughout the Caribbean.

AZTECS AND INCAS

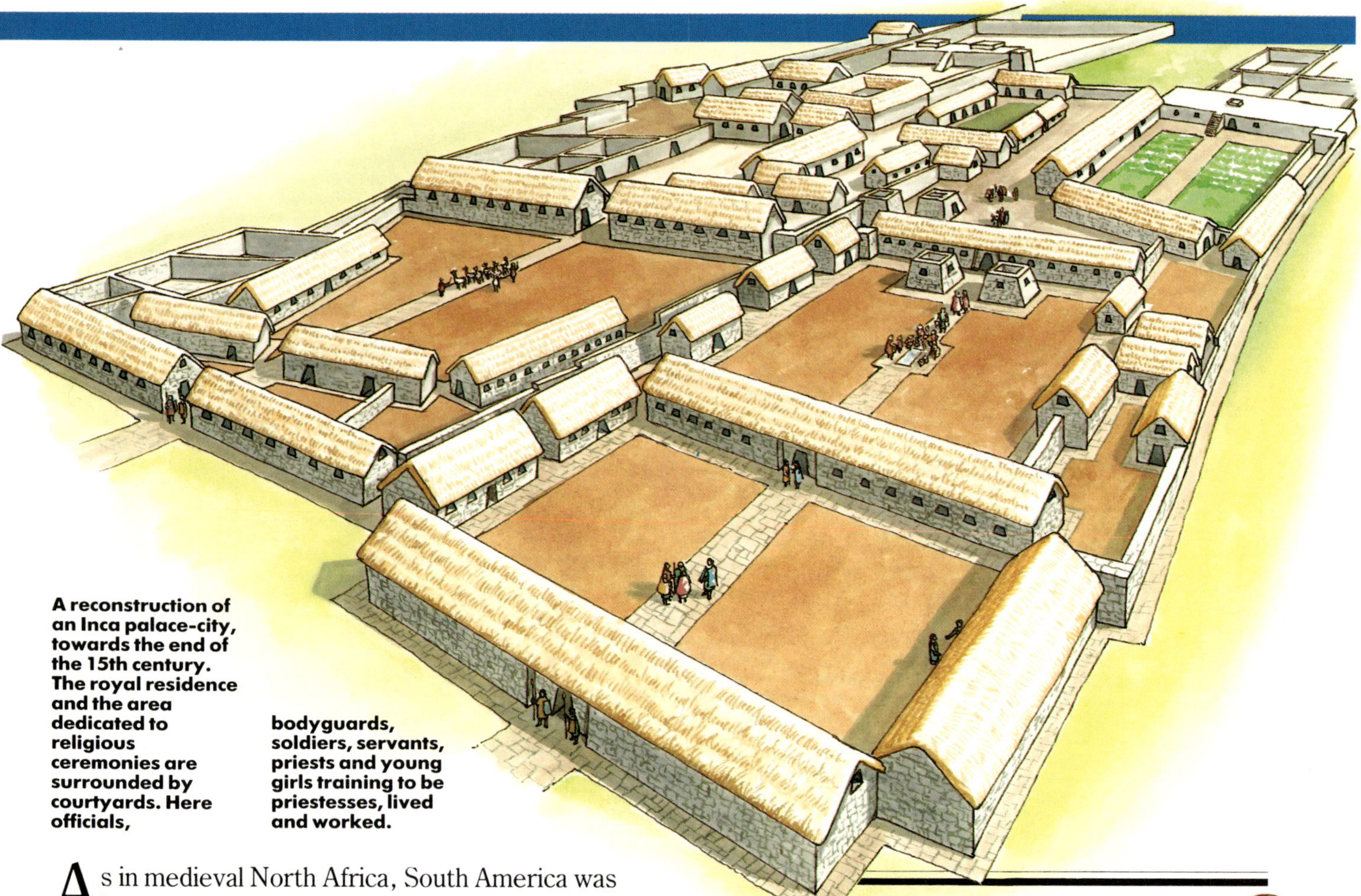

A reconstruction of an Inca palace-city, towards the end of the 15th century. The royal residence and the area dedicated to religious ceremonies are surrounded by courtyards. Here officials, bodyguards, soldiers, servants, priests and young girls training to be priestesses, lived and worked.

As in medieval North Africa, South America was inhabited by groups of small, tribal communities. In addition, however, for many centuries and in many areas, the tribal peoples had been brought under the control of powerful empires. Kings and priests living in great cities ruled over the surrounding lands, and demanded taxes or tribute from all the local inhabitants.

THE EMPIRES In the later Middle Ages the two most powerful peoples in Central and South America were the Aztecs and the Incas. The Aztecs ruled over an empire based in present-day Mexico. The Incas controlled a long stretch of territory along the west coast, from present-day Bolivia to the far south of Peru. The Aztec and Inca Empires were rich, terrifying and very powerful. But they were both destroyed by the arrival of European soldiers during the first half of the sixteenth century.

The Aztecs seized power during the 14th century, replacing earlier Mexican civilizations–the Toltec, Oxaca and Mixtec–but continuing many of their traditions and beliefs. Aztec society was highly organized and strictly

Key Dates

c.1200	Aztec peoples arrive in Mexico from the north
1350–1475	Aztec Empire established
Pre–1400	Inca peoples established as one of many small groups living in Andes Mountains
1428	Aztecs take control of whole valley area of central Mexico
1476	Incas conquer powerful neighbouring Chimu kingdom
1521	Cortes takes control of all Mexico. End of Aztec power
1533	Pizarro captures Inca capital city of Cuzco,and controls Peru, Bolivia and Ecuador. End of Inca power

Right. Pottery figure of an Inca warrior, from the northern part of the Inca Empire.

The Aztec and Inca Empires

Right. The Aztec and Inca Empires were both established in harsh, hostile lands. The Aztecs settled on the marshy shores of a vast inland lagoon, surrounded by mountains and hot, dry scrubland. The Inca Empire stretched for over 6500 km along the coastline of South America. Close inland were the high, cold, remote Andes Mountains. For both the Aztec and Inca peoples, transport and communications were always difficult, especially since wheeled vehicles were unknown in the Americas at this time.

Crafts and Agriculture of the Aztecs and Incas

Above. Examples of some of the fine craftsmanship produced by the Aztecs and Incas.

People living in these great South American empires were skilled workers. Men made pottery, carved stone and produced marvellous gold jewellery, ornamented with precious stones. Women wove brightly coloured cloth with intricate patterns.

They used wool from llamas and vicunas, feathers from hummingbirds, and dyes made from tropical plants and insects. South American farmers also made skilful use of local resources. They built terraces on steep mountain slopes, so they could grow *maize* and potatoes, and constructed irrigation channels to bring water to semi-desert lands.

Tenochtitlan, the capital city of the Aztecs, was supplied with food from 'floating gardens'– carefully tended marshland where plentiful crops of beans, peppers and *squash* were grown.

controlled. Trade, farming and craft-working flourished, and magnificent cities and monuments were built. But the emperor and his officials were feared and hated by many of the ordinary people whom the Aztecs conquered. Some historians have even suggested that the ordinary Aztec people welcomed the European soldiers who came in the 16th century as liberators, who would set themfree.

AZTEC SOCIETY AND BELIEFS Like many South American societies, the Aztec civilization was based on war. Battles were necessary to provide a steady stream of captives to be killed as sacrifices to the gods. The Aztecs believed that if they stopped offering human blood and hearts to the gods, then the sun would stop shining, and crops and people would die.

INCA SOCIETY AND BELIEFS The Incas took control— though for less than one century—in Peru during the early 15th century. They conquered the neighbouring Chimu Empire, which had ruled a large territory around its capital city of Chan-Chan in the north of the country.

Like the Aztecs, the Incas demanded complete obedience from the people they ruled. They also imposed heavy taxes. Inca tax-collectors took two-thirds of all crops grown, in return for providing food and shelter for anyone who became too sick or old to look after themselves. The state also started vast construction projects, such as the great city at Cuzco, which were enormously expensive, and employed hundreds of thousands of workmen.

ROUTES OF COMMUNICATION Inca officials kept detailed records of taxes and other administrative matters on *qipus*–carefully knotted string. These qipus show that the Inca Empire was highly organized, with a large army and many government servants. There was also a network of government roads linking distant parts of the empire. Messengers hurried along with urgent orders, and armies marched with bands of protesting captives on their way to forced resettlement in regions far from their homes. Ordinary people were not allowed to travel on these roads without a special permit.

TRAVELLERS AND EXPLORERS

Medieval people were great travellers, even though journeys were slow, uncomfortable and exhausting.

MODES OF TRANSPORT Ordinary people plodded wearily on foot, or jogged and jolted along on horses and camels. Wealthy people could afford well upholstered carts, but these frequently got stuck or were overturned in the deep ruts and potholes which scarred the surfaces of many medieval roads. The most comfortable way to travel was probably by litter–an enclosed 'cabin' slung on poles between two or four horses–but this was usually reserved for royal ladies, or clergymen.

DANGERS OF TRAVEL Medieval travellers faced danger, as well as discomfort, along the way. Attacks by highway robbers, pirates and bandits were common. Shipwrecks, landslides, floods, bitter cold and searing heat all caused loss of life. It was hardly surprising that people came to believe that particularly desolate stretches of countryside, like the Gobi Desert in China, were haunted by evil spirits, lying in wait to lure unwary travellers to a certain death.

REASONS FOR TRAVEL Why, then, did medieval people travel? First, to make money. We have already seen how merchants covered vast distances, by land and sea, to bring valuable goods from China and India to markets in the Middle East and Europe.

Some medieval people travelled in search of food. For example, fishermen from northern Europe made the long and dangerous journey to the icy Arctic waters off Norway to bring back huge catches of cod. These were dried and salted for use in winter.

The Travels of Ibn Battuta

EUROPE
CONSTANTINOPLE
PEKING
BAGHDAD
ASIA
ALEXANDRIA
FEZ
DELHI
CHITTAGONG
AGADEZ
TIMBUKTU
ADEN
CALICUT
AFRICA
SUMATRA
INDIAN OCEAN

Ibn Battuta was born in North Africa around 1300. He trained as a lawyer, but spent most of his life in adventurous travel. We know about his exploits because he dictated his memoirs to a secretary in 1363, and copies of this book have survived. As you can see from the map, he travelled an extraordinary distance during his lifetime.

The dangers of travel by sea. A shipwreck, dramatically illustrated in a 14th century Italian manuscript.

The Voyages of Cheng Ho

ASIA
DAMASCUS
NANKING
ASABON
CHITTAGONG
ADEN
SRI LANKA
SUMATRA
BORNEO
INDIAN OCEAN
JAVA

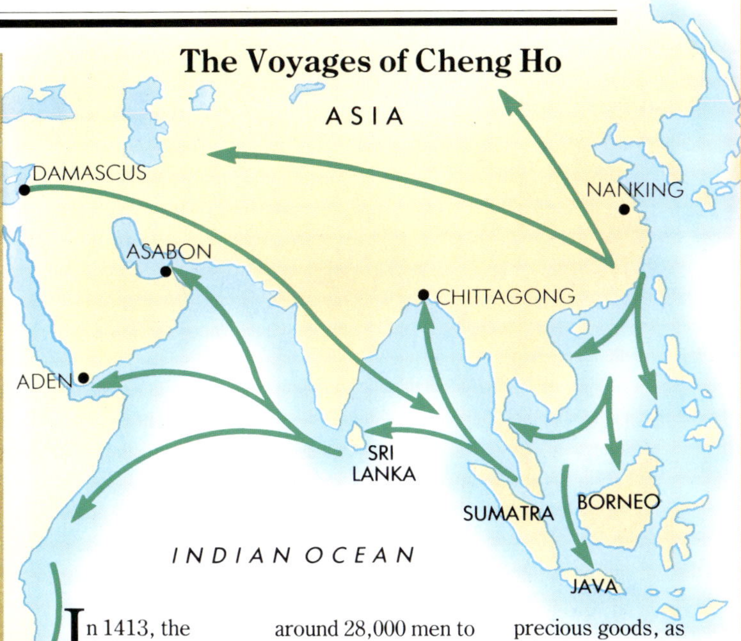

In 1413, the Chinese Emperor, Yung Lo, sent 63 large ships carrying around 28,000 men to lands west of China. These expeditions were commanded by a Chinese Muslim, called Cheng Ho, a brave and skilful sailor.

They brought back all kinds of rare and precious goods, as gifts from nations hoping not to offend the powerful Emperor. In 1411, even the king of Sri Lanka travelled to China with Cheng Ho to pay his respects at the Emperor's court

Left. This picture shows just one of the rare 'goods' that Cheng Ho brought to China – the giraffe.

The farming and fishing communities of Polynesia also travelled long distances. They sailed in fragile boats across the vast Pacific Ocean to found new settlements on fertile volcanic islands.

Religion was a third reason why people travelled during the Middle Ages. Believers from many different faiths went on *pilgrimages* to holy places all over the world. Muslims visited Mecca. Christians travelled to Jerusalem, Rome and the shrines of various saints throughout Europe. In India and the surroundings lands, Hindu and Buddhist pilgrims travelled to pray at temples, or to listen to holy men and religious teachers.

All these pilgrims, whatever their religion, saw their journeys as a time for thinking about God and the right way to live. In addition, for many people a pilgrimage was also a long, exciting and enjoyable holiday.

Left. An illustration from *Sir John Mandeville's Travels*. This was a popular (but largely fictitious) book describing several adventurous journeys. It was written in the 14th century, and translated into many European languages. This scene shows a mysterious group of philosophers, who, according to Mandeville's book, lived on the top of Mount Athos, in Greece.

VOYAGES OF DISCOVERY Some medieval travellers needed no excuse for their journeys. Like people who go on holiday today, they simply wanted to see the world and to escape from everyday routine. In every country, villagers flocked to nearby towns to enjoy markets and fairs, or to take part in festivals. A few brave, daring, and, usually, wealthy invididuals made longer journeys, spurred on by curiosity and by the wish to discover all they could about distant lands.

We know about some of these travellers because records of their amazing journeys have survived. Marco Polo (who travelled through China), Ibn Fadlan (who journeyed overland from Baghdad to the Viking kingdoms of Russia and Scandinavia), Ibn Battuta (a Muslim from North Africa who spent 20 years travelling in Asia and India) and Cheng Ho (a Chinese explorer who made daring voyages through the South China Seas) all left descriptions of their adventures, full of fascinating details about the lands and peoples they visited.

SAILORS AND SCHOLARS

Exploration during the late 15th and 16th centuries led to great advances in geographical knowledge. The large map (left), printed in 1486, shows the medieval European view of the world. America is unknown, Africa is strangely shaped, and India is very small. The smaller map (below), drawn in 1587, shows how much had been learned in just over 100 years.

During the Middle Ages, most people had only a very hazy understanding of geography. Even the great medieval travellers, like Marco Polo or Ibn Battuta, were often rather confused about exactly where the countries they visited lay in relation to one another.

GEOGRAPHICAL DISCOVERIES There were two groups of people in medieval times who did, however, know a great deal about the earth's surface. These were sailors and scholars. Geographers, mathematicians and astronomers made calculations and performed experiments to discover more accurate ways of measuring time and distance.

By the time Marco Polo set out on his travels in the late 13th century, leading scholars were convinced that the earth was round, and not flat, as earlier people had believed. But they still had no clear idea of the shape and size of the different continents, nor of how much of the globe was covered by dry land, and how much by the sea.

THE SCIENCE OF NAVIGATION Unlike the scholars, most sailors could not read and write, but they studied coastlines, tides, currents, winds and weather. By the 15th century, the book-learning of the scholars and the sailors' practical skills began to be combined. European rulers, like Prince Henry 'the Navigator' of Portugal, encouraged travel and exploration. Prince Henry even set up a training college for would-be adventurers.

There was a financial reason for this government interest in travel, as well. Wars in Asia, and the capture of Constantinople (Istanbul) by Muslim troops in 1453, disrupted overland trade with the east. People began to wonder whether they could find a sea route to India which would mean that they did not have to rely on overland travel.

In the late 15th century Portuguese sailors set off to explore west Africa, and to see what lay beyond. This was, for them, a brave and risky venture. Some old-

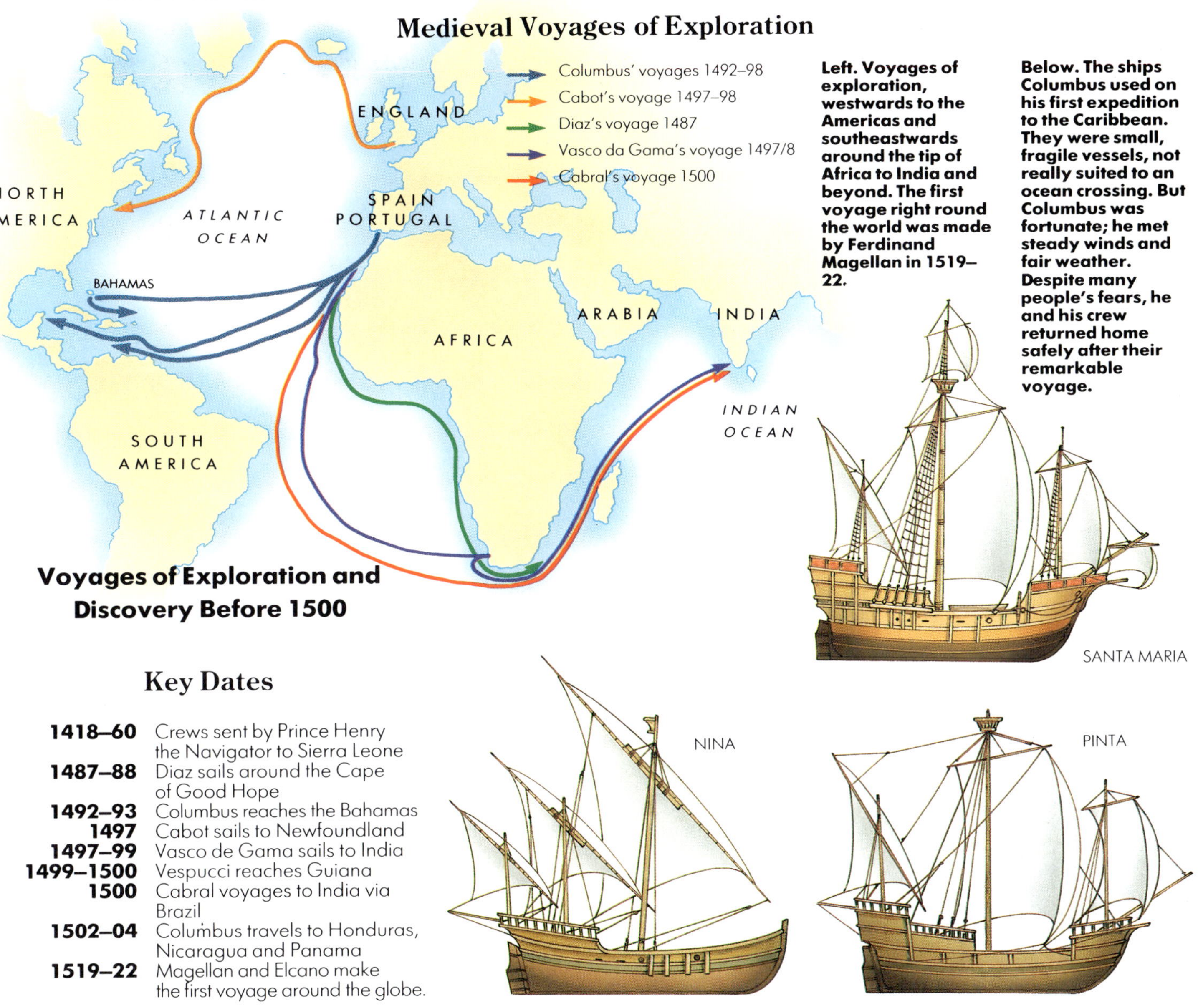

Voyages of Exploration and Discovery Before 1500

Left. Voyages of exploration, westwards to the Americas and southeastwards around the tip of Africa to India and beyond. The first voyage right round the world was made by Ferdinand Magellan in 1519–22.

Below. The ships Columbus used on his first expedition to the Caribbean. They were small, fragile vessels, not really suited to an ocean crossing. But Columbus was fortunate; he met steady winds and fair weather. Despite many people's fears, he and his crew returned home safely after their remarkable voyage.

Key Dates

1418–60 Crews sent by Prince Henry the Navigator to Sierra Leone
1487–88 Diaz sails around the Cape of Good Hope
1492–93 Columbus reaches the Bahamas
1497 Cabot sails to Newfoundland
1497–99 Vasco de Gama sails to India
1499–1500 Vespucci reaches Guiana
1500 Cabral voyages to India via Brazil
1502–04 Columbus travels to Honduras, Nicaragua and Panama
1519–22 Magellan and Elcano make the first voyage around the globe.

fashioned scholars warned that they would be burned up in seas of fire, or swallowed by terrible monsters, if they travelled too far south.

JOURNEYS TO INDIA In 1498, a fleet led by Vasco da Gama landed triumphantly in western India, and returned home safely to Portugal. But the eastward route to India proved to be very long, and very costly.

A few sailors began to wonder whether they could reach the eastern lands by travelling westwards. They had heard strange rumours about floating islands and mysterious shapes on the horizon. In the late 14th century, the Vivaldi brothers sailed westwards, but vanished without trace. Perhaps the old geographers, like Ptolemey, were right, and the dry lands of the world were ringed by an endless ocean, where travellers could drift forever, lost and without hope?

CHRISTOPHER COLUMBUS A young and rather inexperienced sailor, named Christopher Columbus, was determined to prove these theories wrong. He was certain he could reach India by travelling west, and that his journey would be quicker than da Gama's eastward route. Columbus spent many years trying to raise money to buy ships.

At last, in 1492, he set sail and, after a smooth and easy voyage, he sighted land. Eagerly, he searched the shore for the fabulous riches of the East described by Marco Polo and other travellers to China. But all he found were fragile thatched huts, and timid, friendly people, dressed simply in cotton cloth ornamented with shells and feathers. Was this really the fabulous East?

THE NEW WORLD

When Columbus first sighted land, he recorded in his journal that he had arrived in Japan. For the rest of his life, Columbus maintained that he had reached the Far East, and never gave up hope of finding rich stores of gold and jewels.

Today we know that the land where he first came ashore was one of the Bahamas Islands, off the coast of Florida, USA. Columbus may not have sailed to the Indies, but he had, by chance, arrived on the edge of a vast 'new' continent, which no-one in Europe had imagined to exist.

AMERICA The explorers who came after him named this unknown land America, after Amerigo Vespucci, who travelled there in 1499. But to many Europeans, throughout the sixteenth and seventeenth centuries, it became, simply, the 'New World'. Of course, as we have seen on pages 256–9, this land was not 'new' at all. It was inhabited by a number of different peoples, who had developed skilled and well organized civilizations.

In addition, although they did not know it, Columbus and the other late-medieval explorers were not the first Europeans to travel there. Round about the year 1000, Viking sailors had established settlements on the northeast coast, in present-day Canada. And recently discovered cave paintings in the Caribbean suggest that either the Vivaldi brothers (see page 263) did reach America, only to perish on the homeward voyage, or that West African peoples had also made the crossing from their homes on the other side of the Atlantic Ocean.

Metals from South America

The Spanish explorers and conquerors of South America greedily plundered their newly acquired lands. Many Aztec and Inca treasures were looted, and local peoples were cruelly made to work like slaves in the rich South American mines. The Spaniards brought back vast amounts of silver, gold and precious stones to Europe. Most of the silver was minted into coins. These imports of silver caused rapid price inflation in Europe, particularly Spain.

Inca statue (made of solid silver) of a man holding a set of pan pipes, a typical Andean instrument.

Stone jaguar, from a temple in the Maya-Toltec city of Chichen Itza. The Mayas and Toltecs were the most powerful peoples in Central America before the Aztecs came to power.

THE EUROPEAN INVASION OF AMERICA The years following Columbus' arrival in the Americas were unhappy ones. The Europeans, armed with powerful weapons, and able to travel swiftly on horseback, quickly overpowered the local peoples. They also exploited them in their search for gold, jewels and other exotic treasures. The Aztec and Inca leaders were hunted down and killed.

European weapons and, worse still, infectious diseases, such as measles and smallpox, soon wiped out a large number of native Americans. A few missionary priests had the courage to try and stop the heartless destruction of the *New World* civilizations and their peoples. But the damage had been done. European governors were appointed, and the New World was turned into a profitable *colonial* empire, whose main purpose was to supply gold, silver and other valuable goods to the monarchs of Spain and Portugal.

THE INFLUENCE OF AMERICA Although cruelly exploited, the 'New World' and its people did have a powerful effect on the countries of Europe. Many new crops, which before grew only in America, were imported, and soon became part of everyday life. New ideas, words and technologies were described in the reports brought back by travellers.

Most important of all, the maps had to be redrawn. Columbus and his discoveries had–for sailors and scholars throughout Europe–literally changed the world.

Above. European scholars, kings, princes and fortune hunters were all fascinated by travellers' descriptions of the landscape and peoples of America. Many expeditions set out to explore the territory, most spurred on by greed for treasure and gold. This map of South America was produced in France around 1550. It shows how much of the continent had become known to Europeans in a very short time.

Right. Gold mask, probably used to cover the face of a mummified corpse, from Colombia, South America. Severed heads and masks, sometimes in the form of skeleton faces, have been found at many sites in South America. They are mostly very finely made, using gold, silver and precious stones.

New Foods from the Americas

European travellers brought several new plants and animals back with them from the Americas. These unknown species aroused great interest and sometimes suspicion. For many years, they remained expensive luxuries, although eventually some, like the potato (11) and the tomato (3), became widely grown in many lands around the world.

Among the other important plants from America were red and black kidney beans (10), marrows and pumpkins (sometimes called squashes) (1), maize, sunflowers (2), cocoa beans (used to make chocolate) (6), red and green peppers (5), pineapples (12) and tobacco (4). Sweet potatoes (9) and cactus (7, 8) were introduced into southern Europe. In spite of their name, turkeys (13) also came from the west, not from eastern lands.

All the above vegetables, fruits and animals were new to Europeans in the 16th century.

Crisis and Change

TIME CHART

AD	EUROPE	MUSLIM WORLD	CHINA AND THE EAST	REST OF WORLD
1206		Mongol invasions westwards begin		
1234			Mongols destroy Chin Empire	
1275			Marco Polo arrives in China; works for Kublai Khan	
1299		Ottoman Turks start to grow powerful; lead Muslim world towards recovery		
1315	Famines, caused by bad weather and perhaps overpopulation			
1337	Hundred Years War begins between England and France			
1341			Black Death epidemic starts in Asia	
1346		Black Death kills thousands in Middle East		
1347>9	Black Death kills about one third of the total population			
1368			Ming Dynasty takes control of China from Mongols Vijayanagar Empire becomes powerful in south India	
1377		Death of Ibn Battuta, famous Muslim traveller and explorer		
1400				Malacca (in East Indies) established as great international trading centre
1400>1550	Italian Renaissance; 'rebirth' of culture			
1405			Chinese travellers explore westwards	
1415				Portuguese capture Ceuta, north Africa; it becomes base for colonial expansion
1428	Joan of Arc leads French armies in Hundred Years War			
1430				Great stone palace-city built at Zimbabwe
1445	First book printed in Europe			
1453		Ottoman Turks capture Constantinople; end of Byzantine Empire		
1470				Inca Empire expands in Peru
1478	Ivan the Terrible, Tsar (king) of Russia, finally expels Mongols from his lands			
1492				Columbus crosses the Atlantic
1497				British explorer John Cabot sails across North Atlantic to Newfoundland
1498			Vasco da Gama makes first voyage to India from Europe	
1519				Cortes begins conquest of Aztec Empire
1520>1566		Reign of Sultan Suleiman the Magnificent		
1532				Pizarro begins conquest of Inca Empire

Conflicts in Europe

The years from 1500 to 1650 mark the change from the Middle Ages to the Europe we know today. The changes did not come suddenly in 1500, however. Some things had already started to alter before then, while others were much the same by 1650. For example, many people still died as a result of warfare, famine and disease, just as they had done in the Middle Ages. Many children died before their first birthday and few people lived to be 70.

Most people still lived and worked in the country, but by 1500 towns were growing in size. This was partly because the population had finally got back to the level it had reached before the *Black Death* struck in 1347–48, and had then started to increase. As a result, there was not enough land for everyone and so some people went to seek a living in towns.

EUROPEAN KINGDOMS Another change was the rise of powerful monarchs in Spain, France and England. These monarchs set up governments to rule over a whole country, instead of just a part of it. The boundaries of some kingdoms were different from today, however. For example, the kings and queens of England ruled over Wales and Ireland, as well as over Calais in France until 1558. Scotland had its own ruler, but the Netherlands was governed by the Spanish monarch, who also ruled Portugal from 1580 to 1640. Italy was divided into many small states and kingdoms. Because many of these were rich, the French and Spanish both tried to conquer them and make them part of their empires.

Germany was divided into small states and was part of the *Holy Roman Empire*, which included modern-day Austria, parts of northern Italy and Hungary. It was usually ruled by the Habsburg family.

ART AND RELIGION The greatest change in this period was in people's outlook on life, as a result of the Renaissance, which had started in Italy in the fourteenth century. People became more interested in the world about them. Artists painted portraits and landscapes, as well as religious subjects. Sculptors carved life-like statues. Other people studied things scientifically, instead of just accepting what they were told.

As these new ideas spread, some people began to question the teachings of the Church. This led to serious conflict, which lasted throughout the period. By 1650 many people had died for their beliefs and many others had fled overseas to escape *persecution*.

THE REFORMATION

Desiderius Erasmus and Thomas More

Erasmus (1466–1536), one of the most influential scholars of the Renaissance period, was born in Rotterdam. He studied and taught all over Europe, including France, England, Italy and Switzerland.

In 1516 Erasmus made the first translation of the New Testament from Greek into Latin, which won him the support of many critics of the Roman Catholic Church.

Erasmus was opposed to the power of the priests and to the corruption within the Church. He gave some support to Martin Luther, but he remained a Roman Catholic priest all his life.

Above. Sir Thomas More.

Right. Desiderius Erasmus.

Sir Thomas More (1477–1535), an English lawyer and scholar, was one of Henry VIII's advisors. He became Chancellor in 1529, but resigned in protest in 1532 when the king declared himself head of the English Church. In 1535 he was beheaded for treason after false evidence was used against him.

His most famous work was a book called *Utopia*, which was about an ideal social and political system.

As new ideas about life and religion spread across Europe, some people began to want to reform the Catholic Church, because they thought it had grown too powerful and too greedy. They also thought it had moved away from its spiritual work and was more concerned with worldly matters, such as making money. For example, some popes gave important jobs within the Church to their friends and relations in exchange for expensive gifts. Others also made money by accepting payments for letting priests have more than one *parish*, or allowing bishops to have more than one *diocese*, even though this was against the rules of the Church. Money was also made by selling indulgences. These were certificates from the pope that people could buy from travelling salesmen, which they believed would release them from doing a *penance* for their sins.

MARTIN LUTHER One person who objected to the sale of indulgences was Martin Luther (1483–1546), a German priest who lived in Wittenberg. He believed that a person could only be saved through faith in God and not through good deeds on earth or by giving money to the Church. He felt so strongly about this that in 1517 he made out a list of things he thought were wrong with the Church and nailed it to the door of the church in Wittenberg.

Luther thought his list would lead to a debate among clergymen, which in turn would lead to reforms within the Church. Instead he found himself accused of *heresy*. When he refused to take back what he had said, the pope *excommunicated* him. By this time, however, his ideas were gaining support in northern Germany and Switzerland. At first his followers were called *Lutherans*. They became known as *Protestants* in 1529 when some of them went to the Diet (meeting) of Speyer and protested against restrictions on their teachings.

Hampton Court Palace

Hampton Court was built for Cardinal Wolsey, who entered Henry VIII's service in 1509 and became Bishop of Lincoln and then Archbishop of York. He became a cardinal in 1515 and took advantage of this to make a huge fortune.

Wolsey gave Hampton Court to Henry VIII in the 1520s. He also tried to persuade the pope to allow Henry to divorce Catherine of Aragon. When he failed, he fell from power and died on his way to face trial in London.

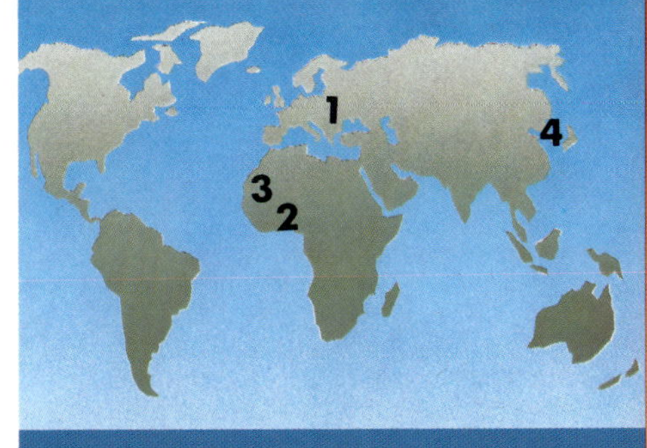

Left. Around the time of the Reformation, there were many paintings, woodcut pictures and pamphlets which mocked some of the beliefs of the Roman Catholic Church. This is part of one of these paintings. It shows nuns, monks and priests trying to bite a loaf of bread as it swings from a rope in a tree. The artist was Hieronymus Bosch.

1 The Safavid Dynasty was founded in Persia (now Iran) by Shah Ismail in 1500. He established Shiism as the state religion and ruled until his death in 1524. Persia had a time of great prosperity between 1587 and 1629, then its fortunes started to decline. The Safavid Dynasty lasted until 1736.

2 In 1546 the people of the Songhai Empire destroyed the Mali Empire. In 1591 their own empire was destroyed by the Moroccans.

3 After the battle of Al Kasr al Kebir in 1578, the Moroccans destroyed the power of the Portuguese in the north-west of Africa.

4 In 1592–3 and 1597–8, the Japanese invaded Korea. On both occasions they were driven out by the Chinese.

ULRICH ZWINGLI One of Luther's earliest supporters was Ulrich Zwingli (1484–1531), a clergyman who started the Reformation in Switzerland in 1519 with his preaching in Zurich. He was more extreme in his views than Luther, and in 1524 he abolished the Catholic Mass (church service) in Zurich. This led to civil war in Switzerland, as some *cantons* wanted to remain Catholic instead of joining Zwingli's reformed cantons. The Catholics were eventually defeated, but not before Zwingli had been killed in battle.

JOHN CALVIN Another early leader of the Reformation was John Calvin (1509–1564), a Frenchman who had studied law and theology. In 1536 he went to Basle in Switzerland, where he published a book called *The Institutes of the Christian Religion*. In this book he set out his views on religion, which later influenced John Knox (1514–1572), the Scottish theologian who led the Reformation in Scotland in the mid-sixteenth century.

DISAGREEMENTS BETWEEN PROTESTANTS
Although both Luther and Calvin agreed that the Church needed to be reformed, they disagreed on other points. This led to a split among the Protestants, with some following Luther and others following Calvin.

Above. A portrait of Martin Luther, the German priest who started the Reformation.

Left. The French theologian, John Calvin.

THE SPREAD OF PROTESTANTISM

Catholic churches, like this cathedral in Florence, Italy, shown above, were very ornate. Inside, the walls were decorated with religious paintings. Protestant churches such as the one on the right were usually plain. There were no stained glass windows or statues.

Martin Luther's intentions to reform the Catholic Church led instead to the founding of Protestantism. Its followers rejected the leadership of the pope and many of the teachings of the Catholic Church. They built plain churches and concentrated on the teachings of the Bible and on preaching, rather than on the *holy sacraments*. They also stopped using Latin in their services and instead used the language of the country they were in so that everyone could understand what was being said.

NORTHERN EUROPE These new ideas soon became popular in northern Europe. By 1529, King Gustavus I (1523–1560) had made Lutheranism the religion of Sweden and Finland. In 1536 the king of Denmark made Lutheranism the religion of his country and of Norway, which he also ruled over.

In other countries, however, the changes were less straightforward. Although many of the people in the seven northern provinces of the Netherlands followed the teachings of Calvin, their country was ruled by the king of Spain, who was a Catholic. His attempts at suppressing Protestantism led to a revolt which started in 1568. Eleven years later, the seven provinces declared their independence from Spain, but Spain did not recognize this until 1648.

FRANCE Calvin's followers also had problems in France, where they were known as *Huguenots*. As their numbers grew, there was rivalry between their leaders and members of the influential Guise family, who were Roman Catholics. This rivalry led to a series of civil wars, known as the Wars of Religion, which started in 1562 and lasted until 1598, when Henry of Navarre became king of France and gave the Huguenots their religious freedom.

ENGLAND UNDER HENRY VIII In England the break with the Roman Catholic Church came as a result of a quarrel between Henry VIII (1509–1547) and Pope Clement VII (1523–1534). The king decided he wanted to divorce his wife, Catherine of Aragon, because she had not given him the son he wanted. He had to ask the pope for permission to do this and Clement refused to agree. Henry then decided to set up a new Church which would be under his control and which would allow him to divorce Catherine and marry Anne Boleyn. The new Church was not very much different from the Roman Catholic Church. Henry still thought of himself as a Catholic, but in the late 1530s he closed all the monasteries and convents and sold their land.

EDWARD VI After Henry was succeeded by his young son, Edward VI (1547–1553), the Church in England became much more Protestant. Statues and pictures were removed from churches and wall-paintings were covered with whitewash. Priests were allowed to marry and the heresy laws were abolished. In 1549 the first *Book of Common Prayer* was published.

The Spread of Protestantism

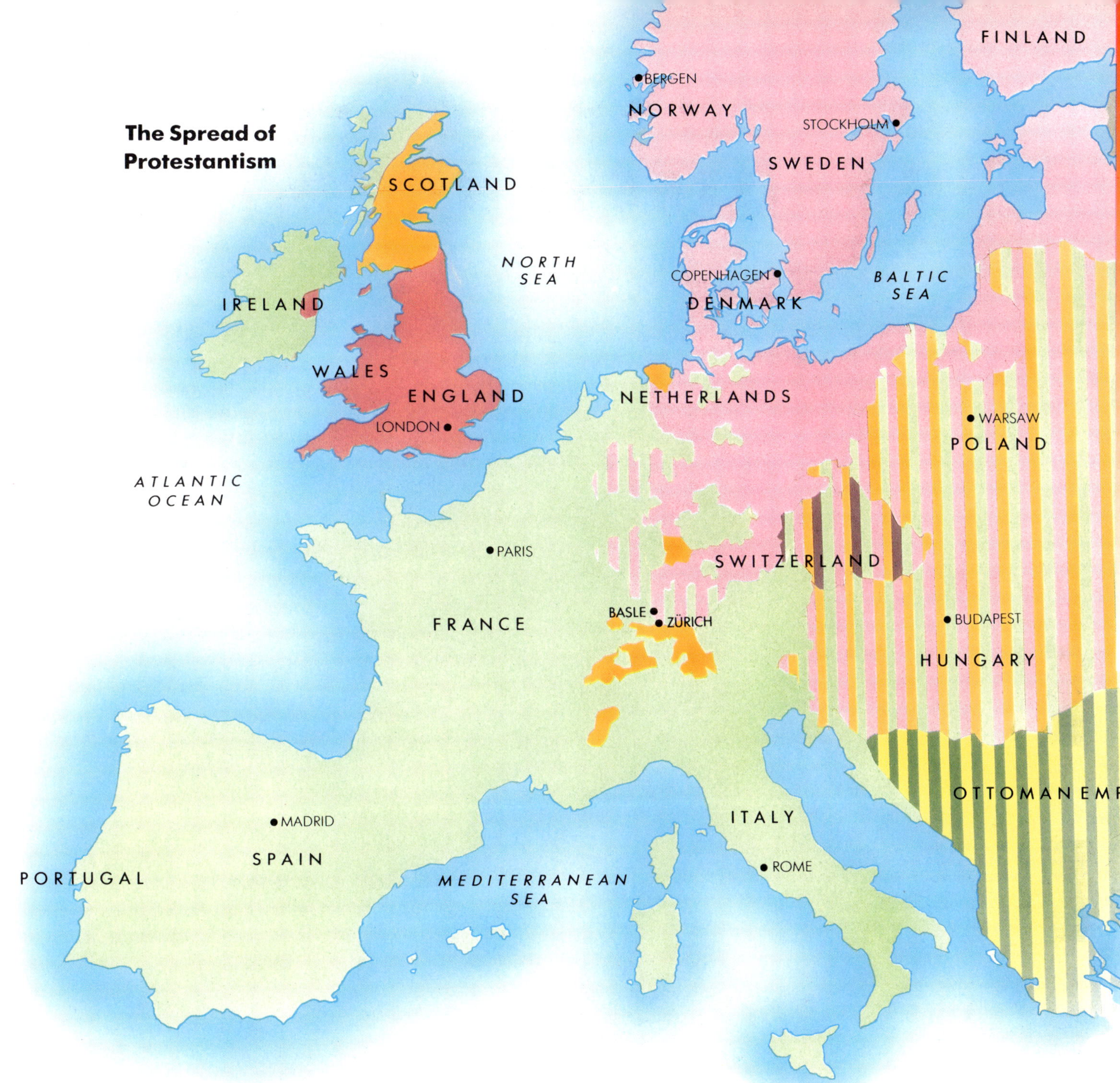

FINLAND
BERGEN
NORWAY
STOCKHOLM
SWEDEN
SCOTLAND
NORTH SEA
IRELAND
COPENHAGEN
DENMARK
BALTIC SEA
WALES
ENGLAND
LONDON
NETHERLANDS
WARSAW
POLAND
ATLANTIC OCEAN
PARIS
SWITZERLAND
BASLE
ZÜRICH
FRANCE
BUDAPEST
HUNGARY
OTTOMAN EMPIRE
ITALY
MADRID
SPAIN
PORTUGAL
ROME
MEDITERRANEAN SEA

Right. The St Bartholomew's Day Massacre took place in Paris in 1572. Catherine de Medici, the mother of King Charles IX, encouraged the Catholic Guise family to shoot Coligny, a leading Protestant. Coligny was only wounded, but Catherine was afraid that the Huguenots would attack the palace in revenge. She persuaded her son to agree to the massacre of about 3000 Hugenots.

Above. Europe was soon divided by religion. In general, countries to the north became Protestant, while those to the south remained Roman Catholic. The main problems arose in the countries where the rulers were Catholics but a large number of the people wanted to be Protestants. This was especially true in some north German states which belonged to the Holy Roman Empire. This led to the Thirty Years' War.

Roman Catholic
Lutheran
Calvinist
Hussite
Orthodox
Muslim
Anglican

THE COUNTER-REFORMATION

The Inquisition

Pope Gregory IX set up the *Inquisition* in 1231 to fight heresy. When it accused people of heresy, it used torture to make them confess. Those who confessed had to do a penance or pay a fine, while those who refused to confess were put in prison or executed by burning.

In 1478, the Inquisition was revived in Spain and used against Jews and Muslims. It became known as the Spanish Inquisition. After the Reformation, it was used against Protestants in Spain and later in the Netherlands.

Later, Pope Paul III set up the Roman Inquisition to try and stop heresy and the spread of Protestantism. One of its victims was the astronomer Galileo, who spent the last years of his life as a prisoner in his own house for saying that the earth moved round the sun.

Left. People who were condemned to death by the Inquisition were executed in public. Often several of them were burnt at once in the main square of a town. Special stands were constructed so that the crowds could see what was happening. The Spanish called these burnings an *Auto-de-Fé*, or Act of Faith.

Throughout the fifteenth century various people had tried to reform the Catholic Church, but they had not had much success. The Church had been too powerful and any signs of heresy or *dissent* had been stamped out. Once the Protestants rejected the pope's leadership, however, the Catholic Church realized that it had to look seriously at reforming itself. In 1522 Pope Adrian VI admitted that there was much wrong with the Church, but he died before he could make any changes.

Adrian VI was followed by Clement VII and, while he was pope, Rome was attacked and looted by troops of the Holy Roman Empire. Many people were killed and much damage was done to the city, its art treasures and its religious buildings. This attack was in 1527 and many Catholics saw it as a symbol of the collapse of the old Church. Nothing was done until 1534, however, when Paul III succeeded Clement VII as pope.

POPE PAUL III Realizing that the Church was in a crisis, Paul III (1534–1549) determined to try and solve its many problems. He started by encouraging the preaching

This reconstruction shows the Vatican in Rome. The popes have lived there since 1377, but it has been expanded many times since that date. It now has over 4000 rooms, including five museums and a library. The most famous room is probably the Sistine Chapel, which was built at the end of the fifteenth century and has a ceiling painted by Michelangelo. As well as being the residence of the pope, the Vatican is also the administrative centre for the Roman Catholic Church throughout the world. Since 1505 it has been guarded by its own private army called the Swiss Guard.

Left. Ignatius Loyola was born into a wealthy Spanish family in 1491. He started his career as a soldier, but after he was wounded in battle he became interested in religion. Loyola became a priest in 1534. He planned to preach to the Muslims, but Pope Paul III persuaded him to help the Catholic Church in its struggle against the Protestants.

Above. Mary I of England became known as 'Bloody Mary' because of her persecution of Protestants. She was a devout woman who believed Protestantism was heresy.

and *missionary work* of the Capuchins, an order of friars which had been founded in Italy in 1525.

In 1540 he gave his approval to the Society of Jesus, or Jesuits, which Ignatius Loyola had founded in 1534 to spread the Catholic faith. As well as being missionaries, the Jesuits also set up schools and colleges. In countries where there were Protestants as well as Catholics, the Jesuits accepted children of both religions into their schools in the hope of converting the Protestants back to Catholicism.

THE COUNCIL OF TRENT Encouraged by the Holy Roman Emperor, Charles V (see p. 276), Paul III called the Council of Trent in 1545 to decide how the Catholic Church should be reformed. This Council met three times between 1545 and 1563 and made many important decisions. These included the setting up of colleges, or seminaries, so that priests could be better trained; a rule that bishops should live in their dioceses; and a rule that priests, nuns and monks should keep to their vows of poverty. The Council also agreed with the old beliefs of the Catholic Church, such as the importance of the holy sacraments, and *salvation* through good deeds on earth.

MARY I OF ENGLAND Charles V encouraged the Counter-Reformation still further in 1554 with the marriage of his son, Philip, the future king of Spain (see p. 277), to Mary I of England (1553–1558). Mary was the Catholic daughter of Henry VIII and Catherine of Aragon, who had made England into a Catholic country again when she became queen. She brought back the laws of heresy and soon began persecuting Protestants. Many fled abroad, but about 300 were burnt for their beliefs.

Philip left Mary when she had not given birth to a child after they had been married for 14 months, but he still was able to persuade her to join with Spain in a war against France in 1557. As a result England lost Calais. Mary's subjects never forgave her for this and few were sorry when she died.

THE GROWTH OF PURITANISM

When Elizabeth I (1558–1603) came to the throne after the death of her half-sister Mary, she made England into a Protestant country once more. Although she was only 25 years old when she became queen, Elizabeth already knew of the problems which could be caused by extreme religious views. She also knew that she had to reunite the country under her rule and get rid of the deep divisions caused by Mary's reign. She did this partly by giving the new Church of England features of both the Protestant and the Catholic Churches, saying that she wanted to create a 'middle way'. For example, there were still bishops, but now they were chosen by the queen and not by the pope. Churches were kept fairly plain, but priests still wore robes, called *vestments*, during the services.

THE FIRST PURITANS Most people accepted this new Church of England, but there were some who thought that it was not Protestant enough. Many of these people had lived in *exile* during Mary's reign and, influenced by the ideas of Calvin (see p. 269), did not approve of bishops. They wanted to get rid of the priests' vestments and anything else that was left over from the old Catholic religion. They believed that this would purify the Church and, because of this belief, they became known as *Puritans*. As the number of Puritans grew, some became Members of Parliament and others became clergymen within the Church of England, thinking that holding these positions would help them to change the Church. In 1583, however, John Whitgift, the Archbishop of Canterbury, managed to make the Puritan clergymen leave the Church. In spite of this, the Puritan movement continued for the rest of Elizabeth's reign.

THE REIGN OF JAMES I Elizabeth I had no children and so when she died the throne of England passed to her nearest relation. This was her cousin, King James VI of Scotland, the son of Mary, Queen of Scots (1542–1567), who had been executed for treason by Elizabeth in 1587, 20 years after she had been deposed from the Scottish throne.

Mary's son became King James I of England (1603–1625). He persecuted Catholics and, although he met with the Puritans in 1604, he refused to give in to any of their demands, apart from authorizing a new translation of the Bible. For many Puritans this was not enough and some of them thought of leaving England and starting a new life.

THE PILGRIM FATHERS By 1606 some Puritans had decided to set up their own *congregations*, which were separate from the Church.

These congregations were illegal and the people who belonged to them were known as Separatists. In 1607 the members of one congregation in Scrooby in Nottinghamshire tried to flee to Amsterdam to avoid arrest. This first attempt failed, but in 1609 they returned to the Netherlands and settled in Leiden. In 1620, however, the Separatists decided to try and set up an English *colony* in America. A group of them set sail on a ship called the *Mayflower* in September 1620 and reached America 65 days later (see p. 326).

TOWARDS CIVIL WAR The problems with the Puritans grew worse in the reign of James's son, Charles I (1625–1649). Many more Puritans became Members of Parliament and, as their views clashed with his, Charles tried to rule without Parliament. This failed and in 1642 the two sides declared war (see page 282).

Puritans' Lifestyle

Puritans wanted to live plainly and quietly. They dressed in a simple way. They worked hard, but set Sunday aside as a day of prayer. Puritans had little time for pleasure and tried to ban old customs such as dancing around the Maypole. When Oliver Cromwell became Lord Protector of England in 1653, he even abolished Christmas.

Above. Some of the English Protestants who had settled in the Netherlands leaving Delft on their way to join the *Mayflower*.

Punishment of Witches

If people who were tried for witchcraft said they were innocent, they were tortured until they confessed, then they were killed. These tortures included being stretched on a rack, being ducked in a pond, and being forced to swallow large amounts of water.

Sometimes people accused of witchcraft were thrown into deep water. If they swam out they were guilty, and were hanged or burned at the stake. Those who were innocent drowned.

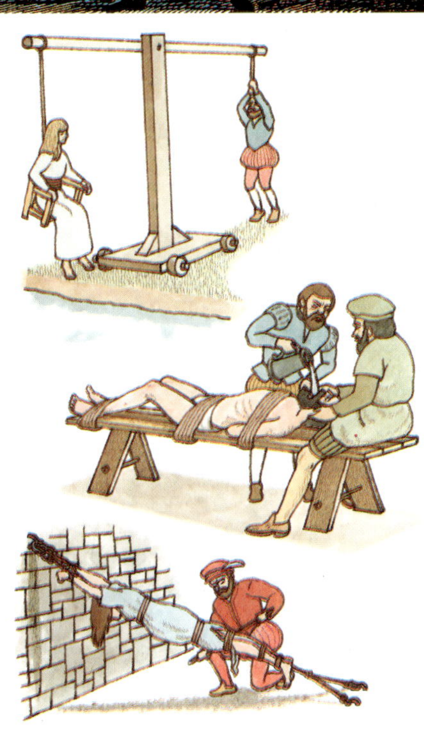

Left. This is a reconstruction of the *Mayflower*, the ship in which the Pilgrim Fathers went to America. They had to take all their provisions with them, including food and fresh water for the journey, plus food for when they arrived. There were no refrigerators and so all the meat had to be smoked or salted to stop it going bad. They also took tools to cut down trees and build cabins to live in, tools for farming and guns so that they could go hunting and defend themselves if necessary.

THE RISE AND FALL OF SPAIN

Spain's rise to power began in the late fifteenth century during the reign of Ferdinand (1479–1516) and Isabella (1479–1504). Their marriage had united the two ancient kingdoms of Castile and Aragon and later they brought Granada and Navarre under their rule as well. Their daughter, Catherine of Aragon, married the English king, Henry VIII (see p. 270). Another daughter, Joanna the Mad, married Philip, Duke of Burgundy, who was the son of Maximilian of Austria, the Holy Roman Emperor. Philip's lands included the Netherlands, where he and Joanna lived and where their son, Charles, was born in 1500.

WAR AGAINST FRANCE When Duke Philip died in 1506, Charles became the ruler of the Netherlands. In 1516 he inherited Spain from Ferdinand and in 1519 he inherited the Holy Roman Empire from Maximilian. King Francis I of France (1515–1547) and Pope Leo X (1513–1521) both objected to this, as they thought it would make Charles too powerful, but in spite of their protests he was crowned as Emperor Charles V in 1520.

This marked the beginning of a struggle for power between France and Spain which was not finally settled until 1659, although the two countries were not at war all the time. They were at war for most of Charles's reign, however, as both tried to gain power in Italy, which at that time was divided into many *city-states*.

WAR AGAINST THE PROTESTANTS After the Reformation (see p. 268), Charles also had to face the problem of a growing number of Protestants in Germany and in parts of the Netherlands. He hoped to convert them back to Catholicism, but instead the German princes formed a military *alliance* against him, called the Schmalkaldic League. In 1546 Charles V went to war against it. His armies defeated those of the League the

Right. A painting, titled 'El Espolio', by Domenikos Theotokopoulos. He was known as El Greco, or 'the Greek'. He trained as an artist in Venice and later lived in Toledo in Spain.

Below. Charles I of Spain inherited the kingdom of Spain from his grandfather, Ferdinand, in 1516. Four years later he also became Emperor Charles V of the Holy Roman Empire.

Above. A fiesta in the Plaza Mayor in Madrid in around 1600. Madrid was a small town until Philip II made it the capital of Spain in 1561. He planned it carefully, with wide streets and large squares such as this one. Madrid became a centre for art and literature as well as a centre of government. By 1600 the rich lived in large houses, but most people lived in slums.

following year, but in 1551 two of the German Protestant rulers joined forces with Henry II of France (1547–1559) and made Charles accept their demands.

PHILIP II By 1554 Charles was getting old and tired and so he decided to hand the throne of the Netherlands to his son, Philip. Two years later he also gave Philip the kingdom of Spain and its overseas possessions. Charles then gave the Holy Roman Empire to his own brother, Ferdinand, before retiring to a monastery where he died in 1558.

SPAIN'S GOLDEN AGE Spain reached the height of its power in Philip's reign. In 1559 he signed the Peace of Cateau-Cambrésis, which ended the wars with France over Italy and gave Spain control of Milan, Naples, Sardinia and Sicily. He made Madrid into his capital in 1561. Art and literature flourished. In 1580 Philip took over Portugal and united it with Spain.

SPAIN'S DECLINE Philip's obsession with stamping out heresy led him into costly wars. He intervened in the French Wars of Religion against the Huguenots (see p. 270). He also hoped to turn England and the United Provinces of the Netherlands back to Catholicism and in 1588 he launched his Armada, a great fleet of ships, against them (see p. 278). When he died in 1598, Spain's economy was ruined and the country was almost bankrupt.

Annexation of Portugal

In 1578 King Sebastian of Portugal was killed in battle in Morocco. He had no heirs to succeed him, so a temporary monarchy was set up with Cardinal Henry as king. Cardinal Henry asked the pope to allow him to marry in the hope of starting a new line of Portuguese monarchs, but he died in 1580 before this could happen. Philip II of Spain then claimed the Portuguese throne as he was Sebastian's uncle and nearest relative.

Dynastic Inheritances of Charles V

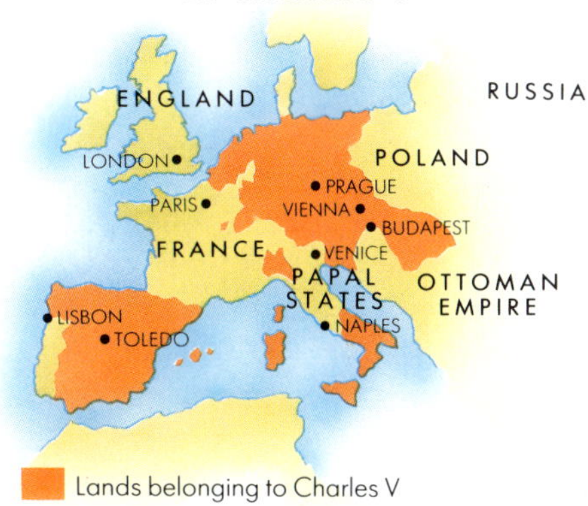

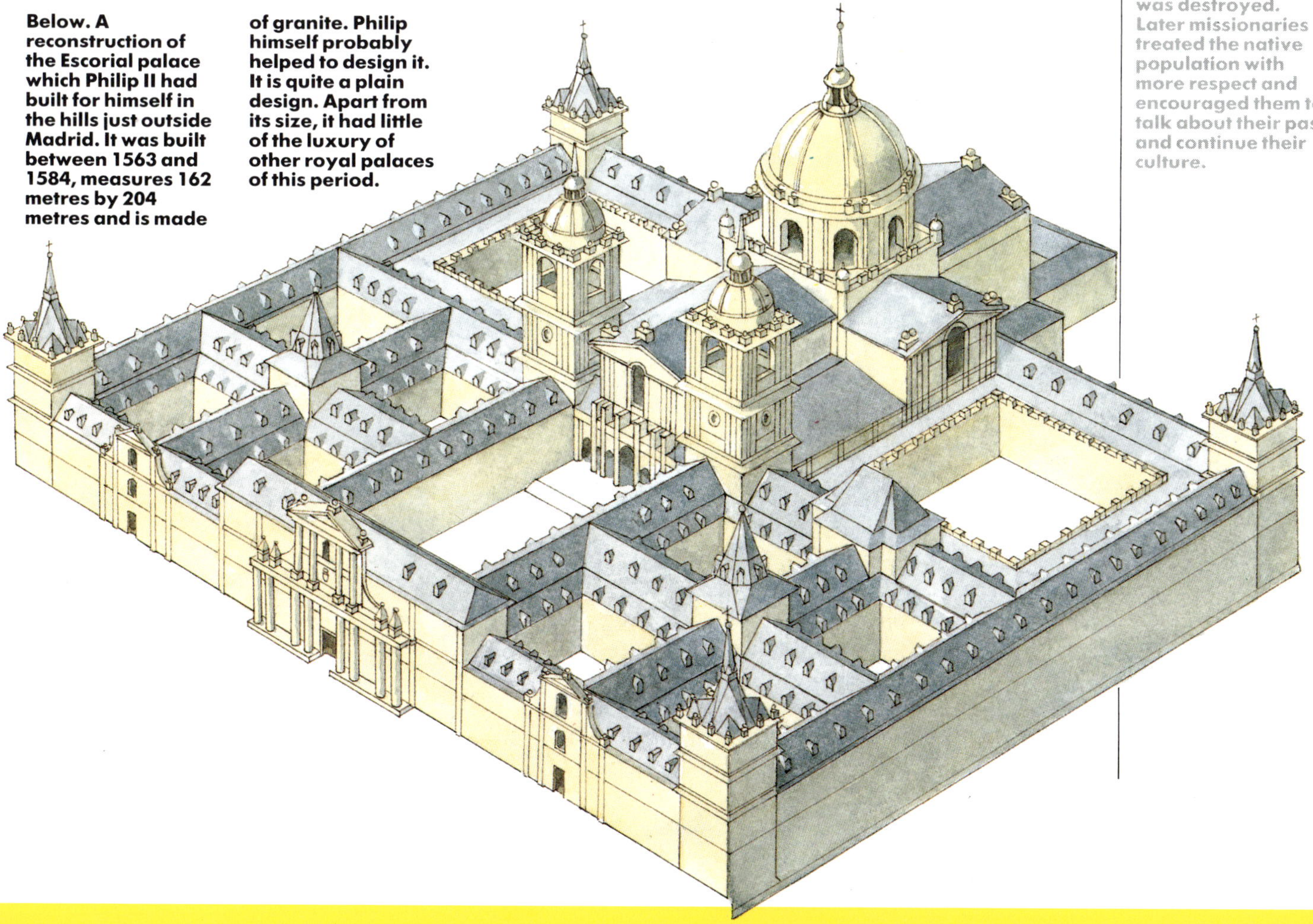

1 In India, Nanak founded the Sikh religion in 1519. He was born in Lahore in 1469 and brought up as a Hindu. He travelled widely in India, visiting both Hindu and Muslim centres. He finally settled in Kartarpur, where he attracted a large number of followers. His new religion combined ideas from both the Hindu and the Muslim faiths.

2 After the Spanish conquest of the Aztecs in Mexico, missionaries set out from Spain to convert the survivors to Roman Catholicism. At first this was often done by force and everything relating to the old religions was destroyed. Later missionaries treated the native population with more respect and encouraged them to talk about their past and continue their culture.

Below. A reconstruction of the Escorial palace which Philip II had built for himself in the hills just outside Madrid. It was built between 1563 and 1584, measures 162 metres by 204 metres and is made of granite. Philip himself probably helped to design it. It is quite a plain design. Apart from its size, it had little of the luxury of other royal palaces of this period.

THE SPANISH ARMADA

The Route of the Armada

Left. At this time ships were made of wood and so fire was always a danger, especially if the ships were close together. A fire could easily spread among them.

Above. This map shows the route taken by the Spanish Armada after it left Lisbon on 30 May 1588, up to when it returned home in the autumn of that year.

In the early sixteenth century, Spain and England were allies, but by the 1580s they were enemies. One reason for this was the difference in their religions. Philip II of Spain wanted England to remain a Catholic country after the death of his wife, Mary I, in 1558. When it did not, he supported Mary, Queen of Scots, in her claim to the English throne. Elizabeth I of England had Mary executed in 1587 and also supported the Netherlands in its struggle for independence from Spain. Meanwhile, English ships were also attacking and robbing Spanish treasure ships returning from America. Philip decided to settle all these problems by force and made plans to invade England.

THE INVASION PLAN Philip had an army of around 20,000 men in Spain and another of about 30,000 men in the Netherlands. He thought that the armies together would be able to invade England. He planned to send his army from Spain to the Netherlands on a fleet of ships which became known as the Spanish Armada.

PREPARING THE FLEET Philip needed a great many ships to transport so many men. He also needed warships to defend them from an English attack at sea, and large supplies of weapons and food. Early in 1587 he started to gather all these things together at Lisbon in Portugal, and at Seville and Cadiz in Spain.

THE ATTACK ON CADIZ In May 1587, Philip's plans suffered a great setback when the English sea captain, Sir Francis Drake, raided Cadiz. In the attack Drake and his men destroyed many ships and some of the warehouses where the supplies of weapons and food were stored. This incident became known as 'The Singeing of the King of Spain's Beard'.

SETTING SAIL The 130 ships of the Armada finally left Lisbon on 30 May 1588. They had been delayed by bad weather and there were more storms as they sailed northwards. On 19 June they had to stop at Corunna for repairs and more supplies. Only 50 ships could get into the harbour and the rest were scattered when another storm blew up that night. It took a month for the Armada to regroup and get ready to sail again.

THE BATTLE The Armada was seen off Cornwall on 29 July and the next day the English fleet sailed out of Plymouth to meet it. The first shots were fired on

Above. Philip II.

Right. The English fleet was much smaller than the Armada, but it had better ships. They were smaller and faster and had heavier guns. Also, their sailors knew the area better.

Above. Sir Francis Drake.

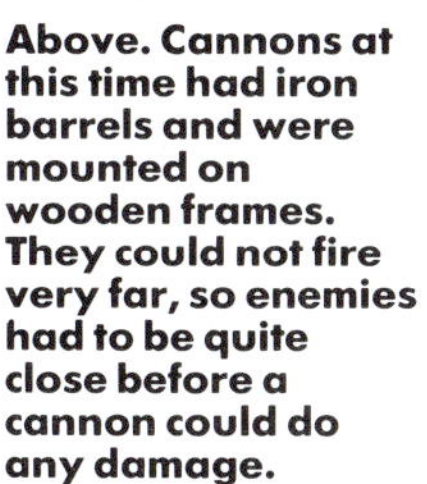

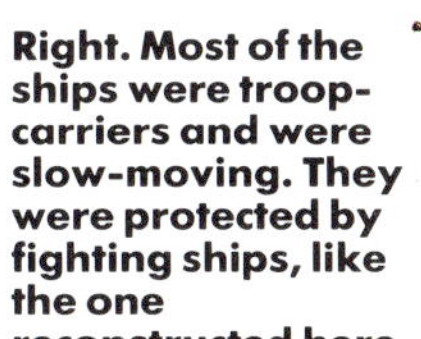

Above. Cannons at this time had iron barrels and were mounted on wooden frames. They could not fire very far, so enemies had to be quite close before a cannon could do any damage.

Right. Most of the ships were troop-carriers and were slow-moving. They were protected by fighting ships, like the one reconstructed here.

How England Prepared for War

England had been expecting a Spanish invasion, but Elizabeth I was reluctant to spend money on defending the country. The English army fighting the Spanish in the Netherlands had not been paid for months, and there was no army at home. However, Sir John Hawkins persuaded the queen to strengthen the navy.

A system of beacons was also set up on all the hilltops in England, from Cornwall to York. Their fires were lit to warn everyone when the Armada was sighted off the English coast.

31 July, but at first neither side did much damage to the other.

On 1 August the Armada formed into a crescent shape, which was difficult to attack. It headed for Calais, France, near to where it hoped to meet the Spanish soldiers from the Netherlands. The English fleet followed and at midnight on 7 August attacked the Armada with eight *fire ships* while it was at anchor. The Spanish captains panicked and many headed for the open sea. The next day the English fleet took advantage of this by attacking the scattered ships off Gravelines.

THE ARMADA DEFEATED The English ships were easier to manoeuvre than the Spanish ones and their sailors were more used to the English Channel. They sailed in between the Spanish ships and fired cannons at them from close range. Many Spanish ships were damaged, one sank and two ran aground. Then the wind changed, forcing the Armada into the North Sea.

The English fleet followed as far as Scotland, before it ran out of ammunition. The Armada then sailed right round Scotland and along the west coast of Ireland to get back to Spain. The weather was stormy and fewer than half of the ships managed to return home.

1 Christopher Columbus sailed to the West Indies in 1492 and claimed the islands where he landed for Spain. This was the start of the Spanish conquest of Central and South America. It is estimated that before the conquest the native population was around 25,000,000. By 1580, it was no more than 1,900,000 as a result of ill-treatment, malnutrition and disease spread by the Europeans.

2 In 1545 the Spaniards discovered silver in Peru and Mexico. They forced the native people to work in the mines, but shipped all the silver back to Spain.

3 In 1571 Spain claimed a group of islands and named them the Philippines after Philip II. This gave them a share of the spice trade which had previously been dominated by the Portuguese.

THE THIRTY YEARS' WAR

The religious and political conflicts which had divided Europe since the Reformation (see p. 268) came to a head in the Thirty Years' War. This started in 1618 when Protestant noblemen in Bohemia (in the modern-day Czech Republic) threw two of their Catholic governors out of one of the windows of a castle in Prague. The noblemen then chose the Protestant Frederick as the next king of Bohemia. Less than a year after Frederick was crowned, however, Ferdinand II became Holy Roman Emperor (1619–1637). Ferdinand wanted to convert his whole empire back to Catholicism. He started by attacking Bohemia.

THE BOHEMIAN WAR, 1618–1627 The Bohemians did not get the help they expected from the Protestant countries of Europe and so in 1620 Ferdinand's army entered Bohemia. It defeated Frederick's army outside Prague and marched triumphantly into the city, while Frederick and his family fled to the Netherlands. Ferdinand's victory was so complete that by 1627 Catholicism was the only religion allowed in Bohemia.

DENMARK JOINS THE WAR, 1625–1629 The Thirty Years' War soon spread to other parts of the empire and involved other countries too. Spain took the side of the Holy Roman Empire and in 1621 fighting broke out between the Spanish and the Dutch in the Rhineland. The Spanish army was the more successful and so in 1625 the Dutch asked Denmark and England for help. The Danes did most of the fighting, but by 1629 they had been defeated. England withdrew from the war and Denmark agreed not to interfere in German affairs again.

SWEDEN JOINS THE WAR, 1630–1634 After the defeat of Denmark, King Gustavus Adolphus of Sweden (1611–1632), 'the Lion of the North', felt that the Protestant religion was in danger. Swedish trade was also threatened by the plans of the Spanish Prime Minister, Olivares, to expand Spanish power to the Baltic Sea. These threats led Gustavus to go to war against Spain and the Holy Roman Empire in 1630.

At first the Swedes were successful, defeating the Imperial army at Breitenfeld in 1631. The Swedish army stayed in Germany and in November 1632 won another victory at Lützen.

Gustavus was killed in this battle and his chancellor, Oxenstierna, took command. He was less successful than the king, however, and in September 1634 his army was defeated by the armies of Spain and the Holy Roman Empire at Nordlingen and Sweden withdrew from the war.

Left. Gustavus Adolphus, king of Sweden 1611–1632. He was a great soldier and also made reforms in education and administration.

Above. Angry Protestants in the state of Bohemia throwing two of their Catholic governors out of a window of a castle in Prague in 1618. This became known as the Defenestration of Prague. It led to the start of the Thirty Years' War.

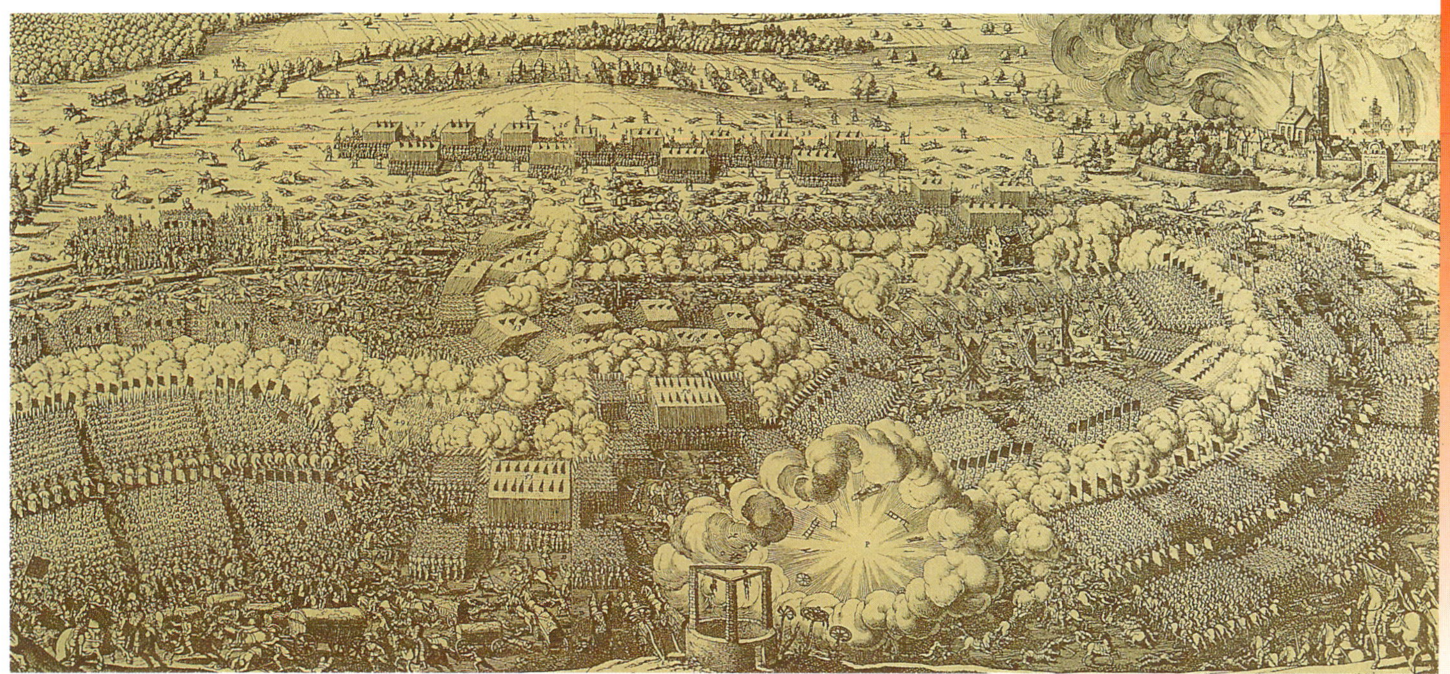

Right. This map shows how the Thirty Years' War affected the civilian population. In areas where the fighting was heaviest, some small towns and villages lost more than 50 per cent of their inhabitants. Some people simply moved away to a different area, but many died when their towns were besieged or set on fire. Even more died as a result of diseases such as plague and typhus which were spread by the soldiers.

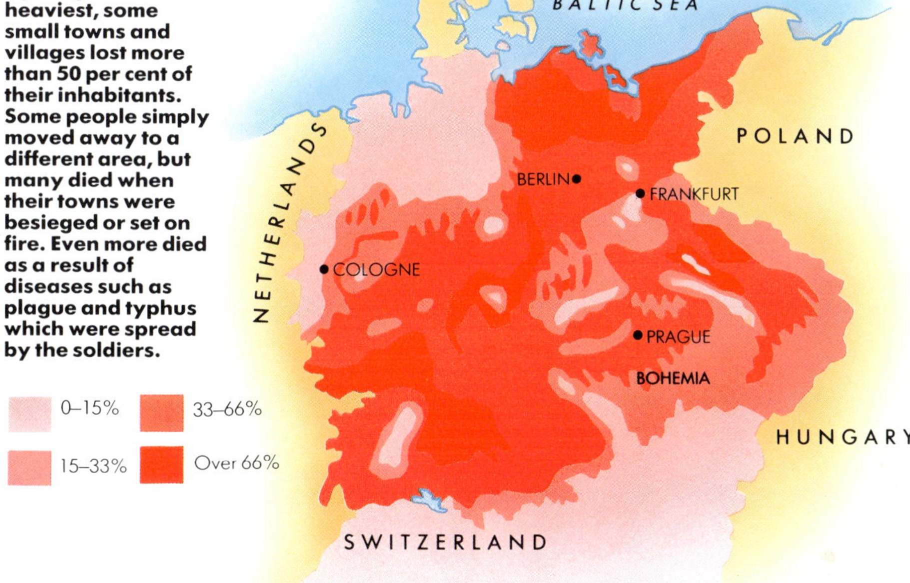

Above. The Battle of Lützen, November 1632. Gustavus Adolphus was killed in the fighting, but his army went on to win the battle.

Above. Cardinal Richelieu, who helped to make France more powerful than Spain.

Treaty of Westphalia

Under this treaty, the Holy Roman Empire lost much of its power. German states such as Saxony, Brandenburg and Prussia became separate countries.

Sweden was given land on the south shore of the Baltic Sea, and France gained Alsace, together with the cities of Metz, Toul and Verdun. The United Provinces of the Netherlands, which had been in revolt against their Spanish rulers since 1568, finally became independent, as did Switzerland.

THE FRENCH PHASE OF THE WAR, 1635–1648 In 1635 the French minister Richelieu decided to take his country into the war against Spain and the Holy Roman Empire. As France was also a mainly Catholic country, this action meant that religion was no longer an important aspect of the war. Instead it had become a continuation of the old conflict between the Habsburgs, who ruled Spain and the Holy Roman Empire, and the Bourbons, who ruled France.

In 1636 part of the Spanish army almost reached Paris, but from 1637 the French and their Protestant allies began to defeat the Spanish. After the French victory at Rocroi in 1643 Olivares fell from power, but another five years passed before there was peace.

THE TREATY OF WESTPHALIA, 1648 The Thirty Years' War was brought to an end by the Treaty of Westphalia in 1648. This treaty gave independence and religious freedom to the United Provinces of the Netherlands, to the Swiss cantons, and to many of the German states which had been part of the Holy Roman Empire. It did not bring peace between the Bourbons and the Habsburgs, however, and the struggle for power between France and Spain continued until 1659.

THE ENGLISH CIVIL WAR

As this picture shows, the execution of King Charles I took place in the open air and attracted a large crowd of people.

The conflict between the king and the Puritans in Parliament led to civil war in the reign of Charles I (1625–1649). One reason for this was Charles himself. He believed he was king by *Divine Right* and represented God on earth. This convinced him that he was always right and so he only took Parliament's advice when he wanted to. If Parliament disagreed with him, he dismissed it and ruled on his own. As he was always short of money, however, he had to keep calling Parliament back in order to obtain more money through taxation, because he could not legally raise taxes without the agreement of Parliament.

THE KING RULES WITHOUT PARLIAMENT Charles' most serious attempt at ruling without Parliament started in 1629. With the help of three ministers, he found ways of raising money without taxation. By 1635 his financial problems were over, so long as England did not become involved in any wars.

REBELLION IN SCOTLAND Charles ruled both England and Scotland, but the two countries had separate governments. Although both countries were Protestant, the Scottish Church had developed along different lines from the English Church. In 1637 Charles tried to make the people of Scotland use the *English Prayer Book*. They refused and in 1639 they raised an army against him. Charles could not afford to fight a war and so in April 1640 he had to call another Parliament.

THE TENSION INCREASES This Parliament was dismissed after three weeks. Charles was still short of money, so he had to call Parliament again in November, but it seemed impossible to resolve the differences between its Puritan members and the king. Then in October 1641 Charles made peace with the Scots. Before he could dismiss Parliament again, rebellion broke out in Ireland. The Puritans would only give him the money to deal with this rebellion if he allowed Parliament to elect the chief officers of the kingdom. Charles refused and in January 1642 he tried to arrest five Members of Parliament in the House of Commons. He did not succeed, but this act made war unavoidable.

THE COUNTRY AT WAR The first Civil War started on 22 August 1642 and lasted for four years. In that time, fighting took place in many parts of the country. In some places there were pitched battles, as at Edgehill and Marston Moor. In other places towns or castles were besieged. When this happened, normal life was disrupted

Main Battles and Sieges during the Civil War

Above. The main battles and sieges of the Civil War. Nearly every part of the country was involved at some time between 1642 and 1646. There were many little skirmishes as well as the major battles shown here.

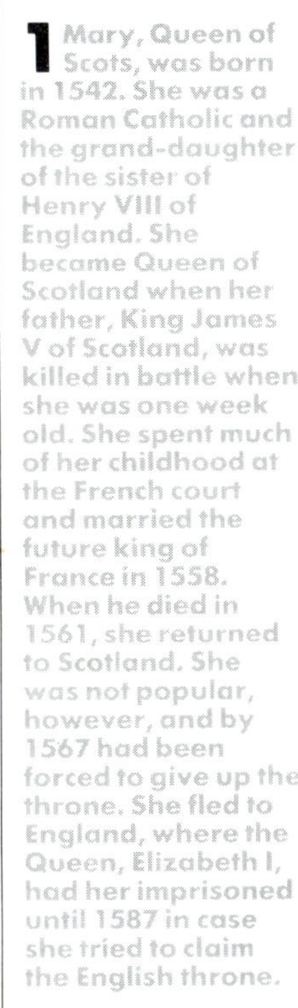

Above left. A Royalist, or cavalier, soldier wore his hair long and curling. On the right is a typical Parliamentarian soldier, also known as a Roundhead because of his short hairstyle. He wore plainer clothes too.

Above. A portrait of the Parliamentarian leader, Oliver Cromwell.

and many people suffered whether they were soldiers or civilians.

No particular group of people supported either side and even families were sometimes divided, with some family members supporting the king and others supporting Parliament. In 1646, however, the Parliamentarian army under Oliver Cromwell (1599–1658) defeated the Royalists and the king was taken prisoner. The first Civil War was over.

THE DEATH OF THE KING Even in prison Charles carried on scheming. He planned a second Civil War, which started in the summer of 1648, but his armies were soon defeated. His actions proved he could not be trusted and on 20 January 1649 he was accused of treason and tried before Parliament. He was found guilty and executed on 30 January.

The second Civil War continued until 1651, when Cromwell defeated the army of the dead king's son, who was also called Charles. England was ruled without a monarch until 1660, with Cromwell ruling alone without an elected Parliament from 1653 until his death in 1658, when he was succeeded by his son Richard. Two years later, Charles I's son returned from France and became King Charles II.

The Execution of Charles I

Charles I spent his last night at Whitehall Palace, where he had held many lavish entertainments during his reign. A special scaffold had been built outside the banqueting hall and at 2 o'clock in the afternoon Charles stepped on to it from an open window.

It was a bitterly cold day and so Charles wore two shirts so that he would not shiver and seem frightened in front of the large crowd which had gathered to watch. On the scaffold with him were three shorthand writers who took down his last words. Then he put his head on the block and the executioner cut it off with one blow.

1 Mary, Queen of Scots, was born in 1542. She was a Roman Catholic and the grand-daughter of the sister of Henry VIII of England. She became Queen of Scotland when her father, King James V of Scotland, was killed in battle when she was one week old. She spent much of her childhood at the French court and married the future king of France in 1558. When he died in 1561, she returned to Scotland. She was not popular, however, and by 1567 had been forced to give up the throne. She fled to England, where the Queen, Elizabeth I, had her imprisoned until 1587 in case she tried to claim the English throne.

2 In the 1580s Sir Walter Raleigh made the first attempts at founding English colonies in North America, but none of them succeeded.

CHANGES IN LAND WARFARE

Although castles were a good means of protection in the Middle Ages, this picture of Raglan castle in Wales shows that stone walls were no defence against gunpowder.

Between 1500 and 1650 there were many changes in the way battles were fought on land and in the effect they had on the people involved. One reason for this was the increasing use of gunpowder, which made new weapons possible and at the same time meant that castles and fortified houses became useless as a means of defence.

Another reason was the rise of powerful rulers, first of all in France, Spain and England, and later in countries like Sweden and the Netherlands. These monarchs had armies of their own and so, unlike the medieval kings, they did not have to rely on help from private armies raised by rich noblemen in times of crisis.

THE SIZE OF ARMIES At this time, armies were usually quite small. An army of 30,000 men was almost certain to outnumber its enemy, as a force of even 20,000 was thought to be large. When the French fought against the Spanish in Germany in the Thirty Years' War in the early seventeenth century (see page 280), their largest army only numbered 14,000 men. This meant that most battles were on a fairly small scale.

TACTICS AND DISCIPLINE In the sixteenth century most armies were badly organized and badly disciplined. They did very little drill or practice and often ignored commands on the battlefield.

Gustavus Adolphus of Sweden (see p. 280) was one of the first to organize his armies so that they could fight well. In the Thirty Years' War he split them into groups of 500 so that everyone in each group knew what was happening. He also changed the way that battles were fought. At the opening of a battle, he used his *musketeers* and gunners with mobile field-guns to shoot down the *pike-men* at the front of the enemy lines. Then he charged through with the *cavalry* to mow down as many of the enemy as possible with the weight of the attack. He also ignored the traditional battle season, which only lasted through the summer, and was prepared to go on fighting throughout the winter.

DISEASE AND INJURY If a soldier in this period was injured, he was far more likely to die of an infection in his wounds than from the wounds themselves. This was because military camps were very unhygienic and nobody understood the need to keep a wound clean. There were no proper army hospitals or trained nurses to look after those who were injured or sick.

A soldier was also more likely to die from disease than be killed in battle. No-one knew how to stop diseases from spreading, and sometimes more than half an army could be wiped out by diseases like plague, typhus and malaria. For example, in 1625 the Duke of Buckingham left England with an army of 12,000 men to fight against the Spanish army in the Netherlands. They had only reached Calais on the French coast when plague broke out and killed 9000 of them. The rest returned home without having fired a shot.

CIVILIAN SUFFERING Wars on land affected the civilian population as well as the armies. If a town was attacked or besieged by an enemy, many of its buildings might be destroyed. Its trade might be disrupted and some of its inhabitants might die of starvation.

People in the countryside did not fare much better. Armies destroyed crops, either accidentally during the course of a battle, or on purpose to stop them falling into enemy hands. Some of the worst civilian suffering of all happened in the Thirty Years' War, which lasted from 1618 to 1648.

Above. Typical soldiers from the sixteenth century rarely wore any sort of a uniform and were not very well organized. They carried a variety of weapons. Some went on foot and some on horseback.

Above. Soldiers in the countryside were not always content just to take crops that were growing in the fields. They often also broke into the farmhouses and attacked the people in them before stealing food and supplies.

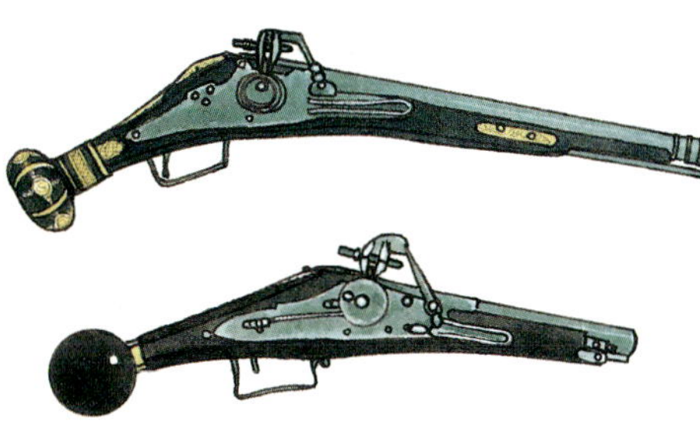

Left. Gunpowder was used for handguns as well as for cannons. The guns could only fire one shot before they needed reloading. They were not always reliable and could easily explode, injuring the user instead of his enemy.

More Disciplined Armies

By 1650, armies were becoming more organized. In the Thirty Years' War, Gustavus Adolphus of Sweden had a disciplined army whose soldiers knew who was in command and what they were supposed to be doing.

Oliver Cromwell brought similar ideas to the New Model Army in the English Civil War. His soldiers could be fined for swearing or being drunk. This discipline and organization helped them to win.

LIVING IN THE COUNTRY

Most people still lived and worked in the countryside, as they had done in the Middle Ages. However, in much of Europe the countryside was slowly changing as the old feudal system disappeared. Many peasants now paid a money rent for their land, instead of having to work for their landlord for two or three days each week. This meant they could work on their own land every day, and this extra work often led to an improvement in the crops and animals they produced. The pattern of land-holding changed, too, as the old *open fields* were reorganized into individual farms. The exception to most of this was France, where the feudal system lasted until the late eighteenth century.

Owners of châteaux like this one at Chaumont in France were very wealthy and often owned more than one large estate. Most of them spent their money on their own houses and pleasure, rather than doing anything to improve their land and the way it was farmed. The peasants who lived on the estates were little better than slaves.

FARMING FOR CASH Many farmers now started to grow more crops than they needed, and to sell the surplus. What they grew depended on where they lived. In southern Europe they grew grapes for wine, and mulberry bushes to feed the silk worms for the expanding silk industry. In colder areas farmers grew flax for the linen industry and also plants to make dyes.

An increasing population meant that more woollen cloth was needed to clothe everybody and so sheep farming was very profitable. In England some landlords evicted their tenants and used the land for sheep farming. This became so great a problem that in 1534 Henry VIII passed a law forbidding anybody to keep more than 2000 sheep.

TIMES OF FAMINE Even though there were improvements in farming, the farmers still could not always produce enough food for everybody. Sometimes diseases killed whole flocks of sheep and cattle, and in northern Europe grain crops such as wheat and barley failed in cold or wet summers. In southern Europe the crops failed when the spring was too dry.

When this happened, some people died of hunger. Many more were weakened by *malnutrition* and then died of diseases such as plague and smallpox. The famines often led to riots, especially where rich people could afford to buy food from another area and poor people could not.

This painting, by the Flemish artist Pieter Brueghel, shows both men and women helping in the fields with the haymaking, while others are carrying baskets of freshly-picked fruit and vegetables on their heads. Although agriculture in general was much better organized than it had been in medieval times, most work had to be done by hand. At busy times many people were needed on the farms, but in the winter there was very little work for them to do.

RECLAIMING THE LAND People began to look for ways of making more land available for farming. Most of the forests had already been cleared, but there were still many marshy areas which could be used if they were drained. The pioneers in this work were the Dutch. If an area was below sea-level, they drained it by digging *dykes* around it and pumping the water out into them. Tide-gates, or barriers, built across the dykes then closed automatically when the tide rose and so stopped the water flooding the land.

Charles I of England employed a Dutch engineer, called Vermuyden, to drain much of the land in East Anglia. This upset many local people who had caught fish and water birds on the marshes for a living. These people later turned firmly against the king during the English Civil War (see pp. 282–3).

NOT ENOUGH LAND FOR EVERYBODY By 1500 the population of Europe was back to the size it had been before the Black Death struck in 1347–48. As it started to increase, there was no longer enough land for everyone in the countryside to make a living from farming. Some solved the problem by combining farming with small-scale industry, such as weaving cloth. Many more left the countryside altogether and went to seek their living in a town or city.

As the feudal system disappeared and farming methods became more scientific, the landscape of Europe began to change. Individual farms appeared, surrounded by their own fields and barns. New boundaries were marked out with hedges or walls and in some areas windmills were built to pump the water from low-lying land and make it suitable for farming.

LIVING IN TOWNS

At the beginning of the sixteenth century most European towns were still quite small by modern standards. Even the capital cities like London, Paris and Lisbon counted their populations in thousands and not millions.

THE TOWNS EXPAND Most towns started to grow in this period, partly because the number of births was larger than the number of deaths. People were also moving in from the countryside to find jobs. Those who did, settled down, married and had children to add to the population. The rest joined the growing number of beggars and homeless people, as there was not enough work for everyone. Governments thought that beggars were a threat to the community and passed laws to make life as difficult as possible for them.

THE GREAT FIRE RISK Town streets were usually very narrow and had houses on both sides. Many houses were three or four storeys high and each floor jutted out over the one below it. This meant that by the fourth floor, the houses at opposite sides of the street almost touched. This was a great fire risk, as most of the houses were built completely of wood and some also had thatched roofs. If a fire started, whole streets could be destroyed. Because of this, important buildings such as *guild halls* and churches were usually made from stone or brick, which made them less likely to catch fire.

HEALTH AND HYGIENE The overcrowded houses and narrow streets were both health risks. People threw their rubbish into the streets and left it to rot, which attracted rats and other vermin that spread diseases. There were few drains and so pools of stagnant water often gathered in the streets.

Where there were drains and sewers, they were often left open. Nobody understood where diseases came from and so the dirty water was often allowed to flow back into the drinking-water supply, leading to outbreaks of disease, especially during hot summers. The streets were not lit at night and therefore people were also in great danger of being mugged or murdered if they went out after dark.

Shakespeare and the Theatre

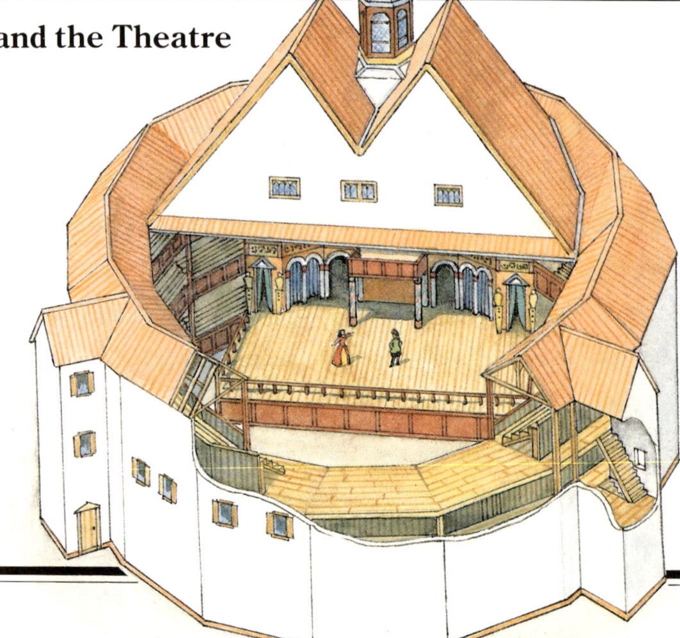

In 1564 William Shakespeare, the English playwright, was born at Stratford-on-Avon. He was the son of a wealthy tradesman and in 1582 he married a local woman, Anne Hathaway, with whom he had three children. Shortly after this, he left for London where he joined the leading theatrical company as an actor. By 1589 he had written his first play and 10 years later he was a shareholder in the newly-built Globe Theatre in Southwark, on the south bank of the River Thames in London.

Up to this time, many plays had been performed in the courtyards of inns and taverns and this was reflected in the design of the Globe. The stage was in the middle of the circular building. Richer members of the audience sat in galleries all around the stage, while the poorer ones stood in the open area near it.

Although theatre-going was very popular in England, the Puritans thought it was not very respectable. All the theatres were closed when Oliver Cromwell came to power.

Most towns at this time were quite small, but very busy. There were often entertainers, like the man and his dancing bear in this picture. Most shopping was done in the open, often from market stalls. Instead of glass windows, shops had wooden shutters which were used as counters by day and covered the window at night.

FASHIONABLE SOCIETY Despite the risks involved in living there, it was fashionable for rich people from the country to have a town house at this time. They often spent the whole winter there. They were more likely to hear the latest news in town and find out about any political intrigues. There was also more entertainment to keep them amused through the winter months.

ENTERTAINMENT Some of the entertainments of this period seem very cruel to us today. For example, people enjoyed watching bear-baiting and cock-fighting. They also enjoyed watching public executions. There were plenty of these as people could be hanged for a great many crimes, including theft or vandalism.

Theatre-going was also popular and there were many street entertainers such as jugglers, acrobats, musicians and men with dancing bears. They travelled from town to town to perform and to entertain people.

The Shambles in York, England, was the street where the butchers had their shops in the sixteenth century. At one point it is so narrow that people can shake hands across the street from the top storeys of the houses.

THE BEGINNING OF INDUSTRY

The discovery of how to produce cast iron made it possible to manufacture large objects such as cylinders and gun-barrels, like the ones shown in this picture.

During the sixteenth and seventeenth centuries, industry was beginning to expand in many parts of Europe. It was also becoming better organized. It was still on a very small scale compared with industry today, however. There were very few factories. Instead, most of the work was carried out in people's homes, especially in country districts where farms were not large enough to support a whole family. To earn extra money, the people in these areas worked at such jobs as spinning yarn, weaving cloth and making small metal goods, like iron nails or links for chains. This often involved the whole family, including children as young as four or five.

TEXTILES Cloth-making probably employed more people than any other industry at this time. Most of them worked in their own homes making woollen cloth. The women used a spinning-wheel to turn the raw wool into yarn, which the men wove into cloth on a handloom made mostly of wood. This work was slow, as it took eight women to spin enough yarn for one man to produce one length of cloth.

When the cloth came off the loom, it was taken to the nearest *fulling-mill* to be washed. It might also be dyed. While the cloth was still wet, it was put on a *tenter-frame* in the open air. This helped to stretch the cloth to the required length and width as it dried.

England dominated the cloth trade in the sixteenth century, but its position was challenged by the Netherlands in the seventeenth century. Linen cloth was produced throughout Europe, while silk was produced in France and Italy. By 1650 cotton had been introduced from India and soon became an important textile.

IRON-MAKING For iron ore to turn into metal it has to be smelted. At the beginning of this period, the smelting was done in a *bloomery*, which was little more than a partly enclosed fire, and only produced a few kilograms of iron at a time. The iron contained many impurities, most of which had to be hammered out by a skilled smith.

In the middle of the sixteenth century the first blast furnaces came into use. These were stone structures that could smelt about a tonne of iron at a time in a charcoal fire which was totally enclosed. At first, when the furnace was tapped, the molten iron ran out into moulds shaped like a sow and her piglets, so it was called pig iron. Later, different shapes of moulds were used to cast the iron directly into objects such as cannons and cylinders. It then became known as cast iron.

THE IMPORTANCE OF COAL Coal-mining was also growing in importance, especially in England. The main coalfield was in Northumberland and Durham. Coal from there was carried by sea to London and to other parts of Europe. Much of it was for domestic fires in towns and cities where the local supplies of firewood had been used up. On the banks of the River Tyne, coal was used to heat large pans of sea-water to make salt and to heat furnaces to produce glass.

By the end of this period, coal was also being used to supply heat for several other industries, such as brick-making, brewing and pottery. However, it was not used successfully in the iron industry until the early eighteenth century.

Right. The main industrial areas in Europe during this period. In general, areas with good farming land had very little industry. In areas where the land was not good, many families relied on industries such as cloth manufacture, mining and iron-making to provide them with work.

Trade and Industry in the Sixteenth Century

Major textile areas

Major metallurgical areas

Below. A forge needed iron ore, a good supply of wood for the furnace and water to drive the waterwheel. This wheel worked the bellows for the fire and the trip-hammers to hammer the iron.

The Woollen Industry

Many people worked in the woollen industry during this period. Several specialized processes were needed to turn the raw wool into cloth. Most of them had to be done by hand.

The fleeces sheared from the sheep's backs were often tangled, so people had to comb them before the wool was smooth enough to spin into yarn. After being combed, the yarn was still harsh and greasy, so once the cloth was woven, it was taken to a fulling-mill. Here the workers washed out the grease and pounded the cloth to make the threads firm and fluffy.

When the cloth was dry, another group of people cropped the fluff with shears to give it a smooth surface. The cloth was then straightened and pressed.

Above. Women used spinning wheels to make wool into yarn.

Above. Men wove the yarn into cloth on looms made mostly of wood. The shuttle was thrown across by hand.

Above. A picture from a book called *De Re Metallica*, by a German called Georgius Agricola, which was published in 1556. It was the first textbook on metal-mining, and was written in Latin and illustrated with many woodcut pictures like this one. Despite his scientific approach to his subject, Agricola was as superstitious as many other people of his time. He warned his readers about the demons that were to be found in some mines.

TRADE AND FINANCE

Above. Sixteenth century Antwerp was a very busy town. As well as being a centre of European trade, it was also an important money market and industrial centre. Its population grew from 50,000 in 1500 to 100,000 in 1550.

Although industry was only carried out on a small scale for most of the sixteenth and early seventeenth centuries, it still needed raw materials to make things from and markets to sell the goods when they were completed. This buying and selling was usually conducted by merchants. During the late Middle Ages most of them had been based in Italy, in cities such as Venice, Genoa, Naples and Milan. By 1500, however, other European countries were also becoming important centres of trade. These new centres were to the north and west of Italy and by 1650 they had moved, via Switzerland and Germany, to the Netherlands and Britain.

Left. This is a reconstruction of a typical market-hall. The market officials had their offices upstairs, from where they could see that everything was running smoothly. People who could not afford their own stalls sold their goods in the open area beneath the offices, while richer traders set up their stalls in the market-place.

FAIRS AND MARKETS Much of the trade at this time was carried out at international fairs. One of the largest in the sixteenth century was at Frankfurt in Germany. Here all sorts of goods from many parts of the world were bought and sold. Other markets concentrated on just one product, like woollen cloth, lace or precious metals. Merchants who bought goods at these fairs and markets usually sold them on to shopkeepers to sell to the public in towns and large villages. The merchants also sold to chapmen—travelling salesmen who went to remote areas, taking with them a selection of small goods, such as ribbons, buttons and laces, to sell to the people living there.

THE MERCHANT ADVENTURERS In 1407 an English company called the Merchant Adventurers was founded

Above. This painting by Quentin Massys shows an early sixteenth century Netherlands banker and his wife working together and counting their money. Their clothes are practical and simple and neither of them is wearing any jewellery. This simplicity, together with a fair amount of equality between men and women in trade and finance, helped to make the Netherlands successful as a trading nation. By the time of the Revolt of the Netherlands against Spain, Amsterdam had overtaken Antwerp as the most important trading centre of northern Europe. It imported, exported and manufactured goods, as well as providing banking and other financial services.

Hans Fugger founded the family's business after moving to Augsburg (Germany) in 1367. Its prosperity reached its height in the sixteenth century, led by Jakob Fugger. By that time, the Fuggers controlled the mining of gold, silver and copper in much of central Europe. They had contacts in Venice and Portugal and dominated the port of Antwerp. In the 1530s they had a branch in Chile and by 1587 they also had links with India.

to control the export of woollen cloth from England to Europe. It soon became very powerful. From 1446 to 1567 the company had its centre at Antwerp. The centre then moved to Hamburg in Germany for 13 years before moving back to the Netherlands.

The most important rivals of the Merchant Adventurers were the traders of the Hanseatic League, which was an association of trading towns in northern Germany. This rivalry often led to trade wars between the two companies and, although they were both still trading in 1650, both companies were dissolved shortly afterwards.

THE RISE OF THE NETHERLANDS As it was quite close to England by sea and had access by rivers to much of continental Europe, the Netherlands was in an ideal position to become a great trading nation. By the middle of the sixteenth century Amsterdam had become its main trading centre, handling both goods and finance. This success in trading was one of the reasons which led the United Provinces of the Netherlands to declare their independence from Spain in 1579, although the Spanish did not accept their independence till 1648.

THE FUGGER FAMILY Several families made a fortune out of manufacturing and trading at this time. Some went on to start early forms of banks, lending money to monarchs and statesmen as well as to other businessmen and merchants. One of the best-known was the Fugger family from Germany, whose business was founded by Hans Fugger, a weaver, in the late fourteenth century. By the sixteenth century his grandson, Jakob Fugger, had also gained mining interests in Europe and acted as the pope's banker. In 1519 he used his money and influence to back Charles V's election as Holy Roman Emperor (see p. 276).

After Jakob's death, the family fortunes declined. One of its members, Anton Fugger, went *bankrupt* in 1550 and caused financial chaos in parts of Europe. Despite this, the business kept going for another 100 years and was not dissolved until the middle of the seventeenth century.

EDUCATION AND SCIENCE

As a result of the Renaissance, many more people in the sixteenth century wanted to be educated. They wanted to learn ancient languages, such as Greek and Latin, and to study subjects like mathematics and law, as well as religion and *philosophy*. Because of this growing interest in education, many new universities were founded in the sixteenth century and many old ones expanded.

GOING TO UNIVERSITY University education was only for the sons of the rich. Girls were not allowed to study there at all and poor people could not afford to. The son of a rich family might go to university when he was only 10 years old, however. He might study at one university for a year or so and then move on to another. Most of the teaching was done in Latin and so an English boy could study in France, Germany or Italy without learning any

Above. The university at Heidelberg in Germany was founded in 1386. It was one of the many European universities which expanded during the sixteenth century.

Above. Leonardo da Vinci (1452–1519) trained as an artist in Florence, but was also an engineer, designer and scientist. He was interested in anatomy, botany and geology, and worked in France as well as Italy.

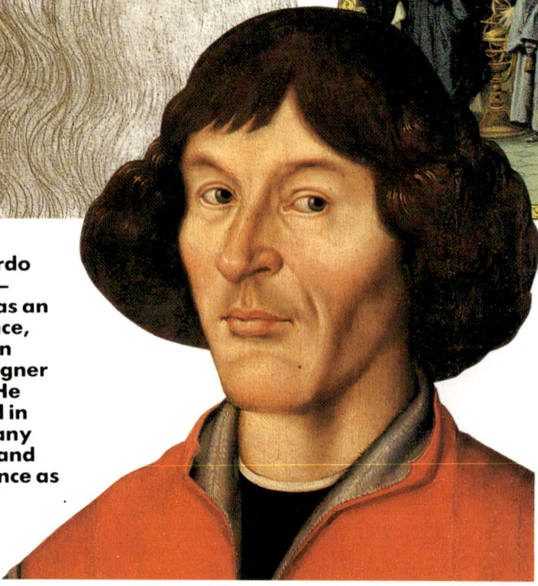

Left. Copernicus studied mathematics and music at Cracow and Bologna. He then began to calculate the positions of the planets and thought this would be easier if he pretended that the earth moved around the sun. Then he realized that this was what actually happened.

Above. At this time the Roman Catholic Church taught that the earth was the centre of the universe and that the sun, the planets and the stars revolved around it. Copernicus proved this was wrong, but the Church condemned his findings. In 1632 Galileo published a book called *Dialogue on Two World Systems*, which looked at the two different views of the universe and supported Copernicus's view. As a result, he was accused of heresy. This picture shows one of his appearances before the Inquisition in Rome in 1633.

modern foreign languages.

In the early sixteenth century, it was also possible to go through university without learning to read or write. This was because there were very few books. The teacher usually had the only copy. He read out loud from it and his students had to learn his words by heart. The examinations were oral, not written, and so some students graduated without ever writing a word.

EDUCATION FOR THE NOT-SO-RICH The sons of merchants, tradespeople and small landowners usually went to *grammar schools* in the towns where they lived. There they learnt Latin grammar, scripture and a little arithmetic. Girls were taught at home. They learnt needlework, dancing and how to look after the house.

In contrast, poor children never went to school at all. Instead, they helped their parents in the home or at work from the moment they were old enough to be useful.

THE GROWTH OF SCIENCE Many Renaissance scholars studied the works of the ancient Greeks and Romans. From them they learnt to observe what was happening in the natural world, instead of just accepting what they were told. They carried out scientific experiments and studied plants and animals, as well as human beings.

THE CLASH WITH THE CHURCH This new interest in science brought some people into conflict with the teachings of the Church. One of the first to realize this was Nicolaus Copernicus (1473–1543), a Polish *astronomer* who was also a priest in Germany. His calculations proved that the earth revolved around the sun. This was the opposite of what the Church taught, however, and so Copernicus dared not publish his work until the year he died. His theory was later supported by the work of the Italian scientist, Galilei Galileo (1564–1642).

When the Church heard of this, Galileo was accused of *heresy*. Under pressure from the *Inquisition* in 1632, he had to take back his views. He was at first put in prison, and was then placed under house arrest until his death.

DISCOVERIES AND INVENTIONS Despite threats from the Church, the scientists continued their experiments. The English physician, William Harvey (1578–1657), published his findings on the circulation of blood in the body, while the Dutch physicist, Cornelius Drebbel, built the first working submarine. Other inventions from this time include the barometer, the dredger, the telescope and the watch.

Medicine and Surgery

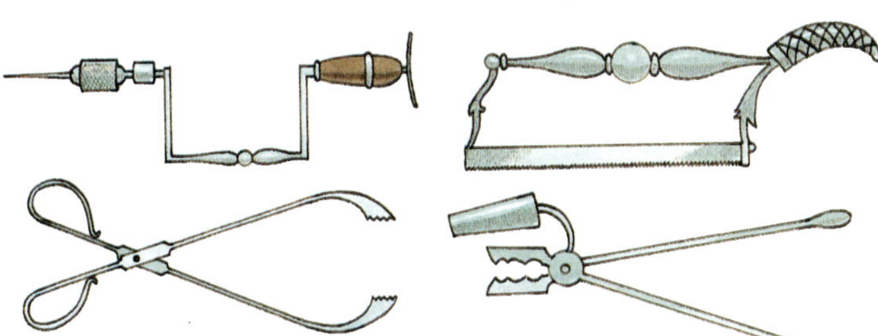

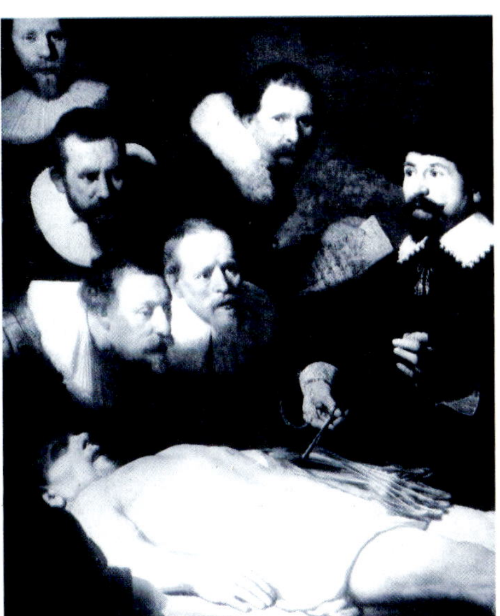

In the sixteenth century, nobody knew much about the human body or about diseases. Some medicines were made from herbs, but others used substances that did more harm than good.

Operations were carried out by barber-surgeons who had few qualifications. Using primitive instruments (some of which are shown above) and no painkillers, they did everything from pulling out teeth to chopping off poisoned legs.

Right. These are reconstructions of some inventions from this period. Peter Hele, or Henlein, invented the watch (2) in 1510 in Germany. He found that if he wound up a strip of springy wire, it would try and straighten itself and this energy could be used as the driving force for a watch. Then came the long-case clock (3), in which the spring was wound up with weights on a chain, and more complicated clockwork (5), used to drive big clocks on churches and other buildings. Lippershey and Jansen made the first microscope (6) in the Netherlands in the 1590s. Lippershey also made the first telescope (1) in 1608. In 1643 Torricelli invented a simple barometer (4), while he was trying to make a suction pump to raise water up for more than 10 metres.

THE SPREAD OF IDEAS

Above. This is Gutenberg's 42-line Bible. Each page had two columns of text and each column was 42 lines long. Before printing was invented, books were written out by hand, like the one shown on the left. Monks did much of this work and it could take months to produce a book.

Travelling from one place to another was difficult in the sixteenth century. Most roads were so bad that people who had to use them travelled on horseback or on foot, rather than in wheeled vehicles. Merchants used strings of *packhorses* to transport many of their goods, while heavy loads went by boat on rivers and lakes whenever possible. In spite of these problems, many people managed to travel long distances.

IDEAS SPREAD BY WORD OF MOUTH Pilgrims, nuns and clergymen made journeys to Rome and other religious centres. Merchants travelled to trading centres like Antwerp and Amsterdam in the Netherlands, and to the cities of northern Italy. Teachers went from one university to another and monarchs sent royal messengers to all parts of their kingdoms. As the old *feudal system* began to disappear in many parts of Europe, country people were able to travel outside their villages without asking for permission. When they bought or sold goods at local markets and fairs, they talked to the people they met. They discussed new ideas and what was going on in the world about them, just as the merchants and *pilgrims* did with the people they met on their travels. When they got home, they told their families and friends about what they had seen and heard and so the ideas passed on from one place to another without having to be written down.

PRINTED BOOKS For those who could read, the increasing use of printing made the spread of ideas much simpler. Although some books had been printed before the middle of the fifteenth century, they had been very rare and expensive. This was because a whole page of type at a time had to be cut or engraved into a block of wood or metal, and so the block could only be used for that one page.

A German printer called Johann Gutenberg (*c.* 1400–1468), however, invented a system of printing which used movable type. In this system, a page of type was made up of individual letters which were each cut into a separate piece of metal. When that page had been printed, the type could be rearranged and used for another page. Gutenberg's first printed book appeared in 1455.

PRINTING AND SCIENCE Gutenberg's invention was soon copied in other European countries. This encouraged people to write about their scientific discoveries and during the sixteenth century books were published on subjects such as agriculture, geology, geography, surgery, anatomy, zoology and botany. Other people published plays, poetry and books about travel.

POLITICS AND RELIGION As printing became more widely used, many books and pamphlets on politics and religion were published. These helped to change the way people thought about life and sometimes led to conflict with the state as well as with the Church. Many Bibles were also printed in this period. At first they were all in Latin, as this was the language used by the Roman Catholic Church. After the *Reformation* (see pp. 268–9), however, Bibles for Protestants were translated into the language of the country where they were going to be read.

Key Dates in the Development of Printing

c.105 Tsai Lun invents paper in China.

700s Chinese prisoners pass the knowledge on to Arabs; it eventually reaches Europe.

c.1045 Pi Sheng, a Chinese printer, makes the first movable type, using a separate piece of clay for each character. Because the Chinese language has so many characters, it is easier to print a page at a time from a block of wood.

1370–1400 Europeans discover how to print with wooden blocks. A paper-mill is set up in the German states.

1430s Gutenberg starts printing with movable type.

1476 William Caxton sets up first printing press in England.

1539 First printing shop in North America set up in Mexico City.

1639 Stephen Daye and his son set up a printing press in Cambridge, Massachusetts— the first in the American colonies.

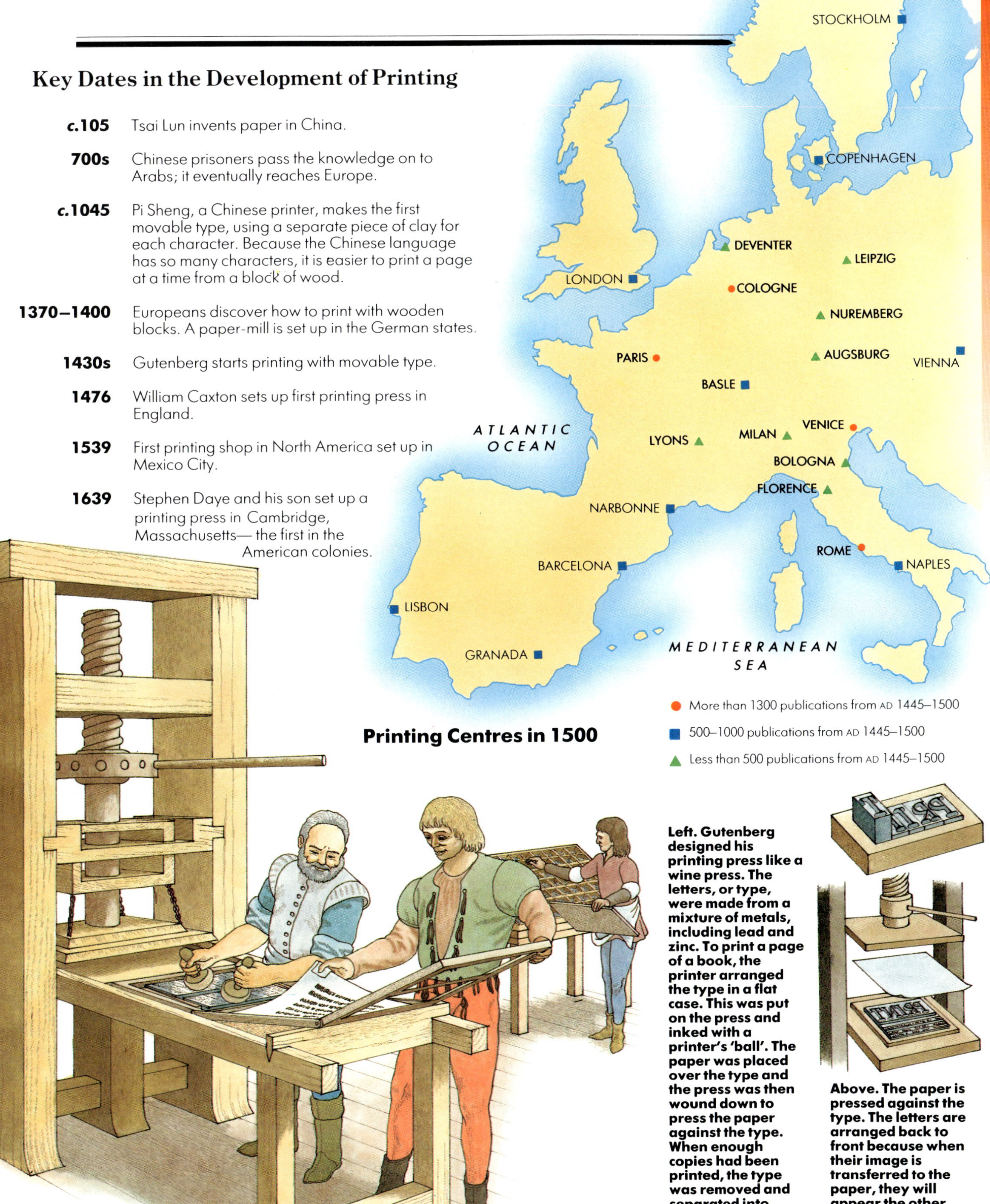

Printing Centres in 1500

● More than 1300 publications from AD 1445–1500

■ 500–1000 publications from AD 1445–1500

▲ Less than 500 publications from AD 1445–1500

Left. Gutenberg designed his printing press like a wine press. The letters, or type, were made from a mixture of metals, including lead and zinc. To print a page of a book, the printer arranged the type in a flat case. This was put on the press and inked with a printer's 'ball'. The paper was placed over the type and the press was then wound down to press the paper against the type. When enough copies had been printed, the type was removed and separated into individual letters.

Above. The paper is pressed against the type. The letters are arranged back to front because when their image is transferred to the paper, they will appear the other way round.

Conflicts in Europe
TIME CHART

	FRANCE AND SPAIN	BRITAIN	REST OF EUROPE
AD			
1500		Wynken de Worde sets up his printing press in Fleet Street, London. This street will be a centre of publishing for almost 500 years	
1517			Martin Luther starts the Reformation in Wittenberg, Germany
1519			Death of Leonardo da Vinci, one of the most important artists of the Renaissance
1520	King Charles I of Spain is crowned Emperor Charles V of the Holy Roman Empire. War breaks out between Spain and France		
1523		The first manual on farming is published	
1534		King Henry VIII breaks with the pope. He sets up a church in England with himself as the head	Ignatius Loyola founds the Society of Jesus—the Jesuits
1543			Nicolaus Copernicus, a Polish astronomer, publishes his theory that the earth moves around the sun
1545			First meeting of the Council of Trent to decide on how to reform the Catholic Church
1547			Michelangelo becomes chief architect of St Peter's in Rome
1554		The future King Philip II of Spain marries Queen Mary I of England	
1558	England loses Calais to the French		
1559	The Peace of Cateau-Cambrésis brings a temporary halt to the conflict between France and Spain		
1560	Death of Henry II of France. His widow, Catherine de Medici, acts as regent until 1574	The first Puritans appear in England	
1561	Philip II of Spain makes Madrid his capital. Construction starts on the palace of El Escorial		
1564		Birth of William Shakespeare, the playwright	
1562>1598	The Wars of Religion are waged in France		
1568	The start of the revolt by Dutch Protestants against the rule of Philip II of Spain		
1577			Peter Paul Rubens is born in Westphalia. He was to become the greatest Baroque artist
1588	Philip II launches the 'Invincible Armada' against England		
1603		James VI of Scotland becomes James I of England on the death of Elizabeth I	
1605	In Spain the novelist Miguel de Cervantes publishes Part One of *Don Quixote*		
1609			Lippershey, a Dutch scientist, designs a telescope
1618>1648			The Thirty Years' War
1620		A group of Puritans leaves England to avoid persecution and sets up a colony in America	
1629	Cardinal Richelieu becomes Chief Minister to Louis XIII of France		
1642		The English Civil War starts	
1649		King Charles I is executed. England is ruled by a Protector for the next 11 years	

Opening up the World

As the Europeans escaped from the narrow views of the Middle Ages, they began to show an interest in the world beyond their own boundaries. Part of this interest was simply curiosity and a desire for more knowledge, but there were other, more important reasons behind the great voyages of discovery in the late fifteenth and early sixteenth centuries.

TRADE The most important reason was the search for new trading routes to the Far East, where luxury goods such as spices and rich materials like brocades came from. Before 1453 these goods had come overland to the markets of the Byzantine Empire, based at Constantinople (modern-day Istanbul), and were then transported to markets further west by merchants who sailed the Mediterranean. In 1453, however, the Ottoman Turks conquered Constantinople and made it the centre of a Muslim empire which controlled all the overland routes to the Far East. This gave them a *monopoly* on the spice trade, which the Europeans wanted to break.

In their search for new routes, the European explorers came across some lands which were sparsely populated. This was especially true in North America, where the native population was quite small and spread out. To people who felt oppressed or restricted by life in Europe, these places offered the chance to start a new life and many people went to the New World to escape religious persecution in Europe.

After the Counter-Reformation (see pp. 272–3), many Catholic missionaries also set out for other parts of the world. They hoped to find other Christians, as well as to convert people from other beliefs which they regarded as *heathen*.

DIFFERENT LANDS The world the Europeans found was different from what they had expected. Except for Russia, there were either very few Christians, or none at all. Some countries, such as China, had a more advanced civilization than Europe and so were not impressed by these new visitors.

Other people were still living in the Stone Age, without the benefit of the horse, the wheel or metal tools. This included all the Indians of the Americas, and yet the Inca Empire of South America looked after the old, the young and the sick in a way which Europe would not equal for over 400 years.

The first modern explorers sailed from Portugal and Spain. They were soon joined by the English, the French and the Dutch. By 1650, these countries had sent explorers right around the world and had begun to divide it into new empires for themselves.

THE FIRST WAVE OF EUROPEAN EXPLORATION

In the last quarter of the fifteenth century European explorers began to look for new ways of travelling to India and the Far East, so that they could deal directly with the producers of spices and other luxury items. In the past these goods had either been sent overland to Byzantine markets, or had come from India via the Red Sea and Alexandria. Now, however, both these routes were in the hands of the Muslims, who were thought of as enemies by the Catholic monarchs of Spain and Portugal. Because of this, both kingdoms were willing to support expeditions to find new routes.

THE PORTUGUESE EXPLORERS From the early fifteenth century onwards, the Portuguese had been sailing further and further south along the coast of Africa in search of gold, spices and slaves. In 1487 Bartolomeu Dias sailed round the Cape of Good Hope and into the Indian Ocean before turning back. Vasco da Gama followed his route and reached Calicut in India in 1498. In 1500, Pedro Alvarez Cabral left Lisbon to make the same journey as Vasco da Gama. On the way he landed by chance on the coast of Brazil and claimed it for Portugal, before going on to India.

THE SPANISH EXPLORERS By the late fifteenth century most Europeans knew that the earth was round, not flat, and in 1492 an Italian sailor called Christopher Columbus (*c.* 1451–1506) convinced the king and queen of Spain that Asia could be reached by sailing westwards from Europe. He left Spain with three ships on 3 August that year and, after reaching the Canary Islands on 6 September, he next made landfall on 12 October at San Salvador in the Bahamas. Having over-estimated the size of Asia and under-estimated the size of the earth, Columbus was convinced he had reached India. He still thought this when he died in 1506, even though by that time he had made three more voyages to the New World and claimed all the places where he landed for Spain.

Spanish explorers followed his route to become the first Europeans to set foot on other islands in the West Indies, the mainland of South America and Mexico, and parts of North America.

OTHER EUROPEAN EXPLORERS While the Spanish sailed west and the Portuguese sailed southeast, other Europeans looked for a northwest passage to Asia and then for a northeast one. In 1497 John Cabot and his crew became probably the first Europeans to see Newfoundland since the Vikings had been there in the eleventh century, while in 1553 Willoughby and Chancellor sailed round the North Cape and reached Archangel in Russia. Jacques Cartier (see p. 327) journeyed from France to Canada three times between 1534 and 1541 and explored the east coast and the St Lawrence River. A new sea-route to Asia was never found, but several countries were newly opened up for settlement and trade.

NAVIGATION The ships that the explorers used were only small and were often at the mercy of the wind and the currents. To find their way, they had to rely on a compass and on observations, made with a *sea-astrolabe*,

Tools of Navigation

The explorers of this period had only very simple equipment to help them navigate. The simplest of all was the compass, which would always point to magnetic north and allowed them to work out which direction they were sailing in.

To find out where they were, sailors had to find their latitude by using an astrolabe and charts that showed the positions of the stars in relation to the earth. They could find their approximate longitude by calculating how fast the ship was travelling in an hour and multiplying this by the number of hours which had passed since they left a known point.

Above. Using a cross-staff, a sailor could work out how far north or south he was by checking the position of the stars.

Above. This astrolabe was used to measure the height of the midday sun.

Above. A compass like this one told the sailor which direction he was sailing in.

Preparing for a Journey

Above. Jacques Cartier visited Canada between 1534 and 1541. Left, John Cabot went to Newfoundland in 1497. Right, Christopher Columbus landed in the Bahamas in 1492.

Exploration Routes 1497–1644

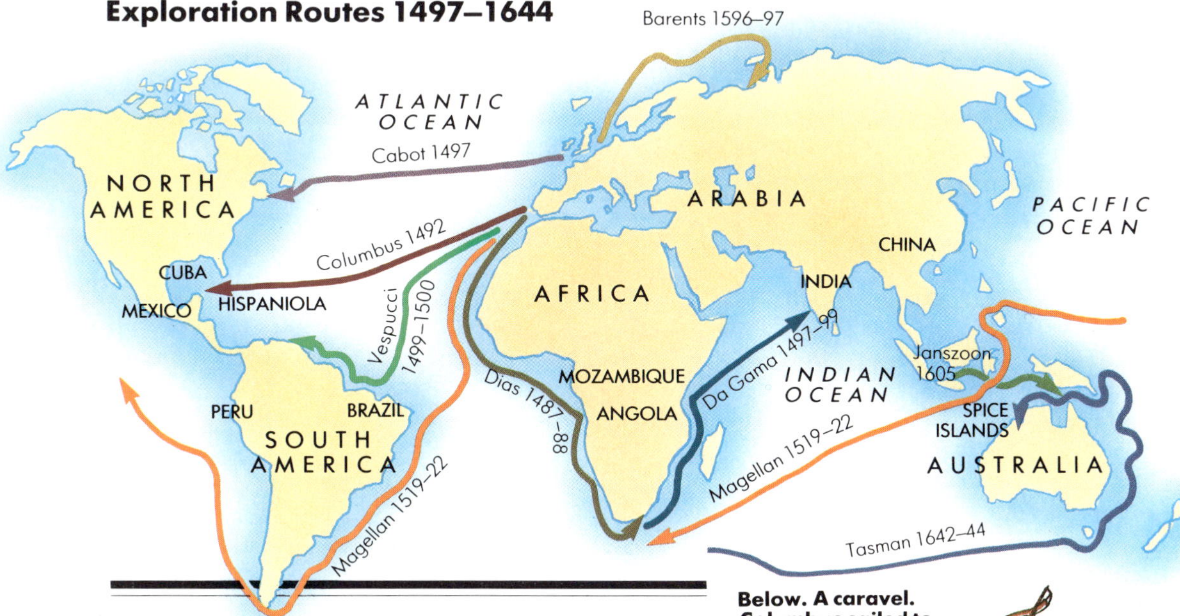

Left. This map shows some of the routes followed by European explorers between 1487 and 1553.

Before he could sail, an explorer had to raise money to buy ships and supplies. These included as much food and fresh water as possible, as nobody knew when the ship might reach another port. For the crew, he had to find good sailors who were also very brave and prepared to be away from home for as long as two or three years.

The explorer himself prepared by studying whatever charts and written accounts were available. Often, however, he and his men would be the first Europeans to try the route and so there was nothing to guide him.

of the height of the sun above the horizon at midday or the position of the Pole Star at dusk. With the help of mathematical tables, the sailor could then work out his *latitude*. He could only make a rough estimate of his *longitude*, however, based on the distance he had sailed in a given time. If the sky was clouded over for any length of time, the calculations could not be made accurately and ships often missed their intended destinations. For example, the *Pilgrim Fathers* (p. 326) reached Cape Cod when they were trying to get to Virginia. Another group heading for Virginia found themselves instead in Bermuda when they were shipwrecked there.

Below. A caravel. Columbus sailed to America in a ship like this.

INTERNATIONAL TRADE

Overseas Trade 1600–1700

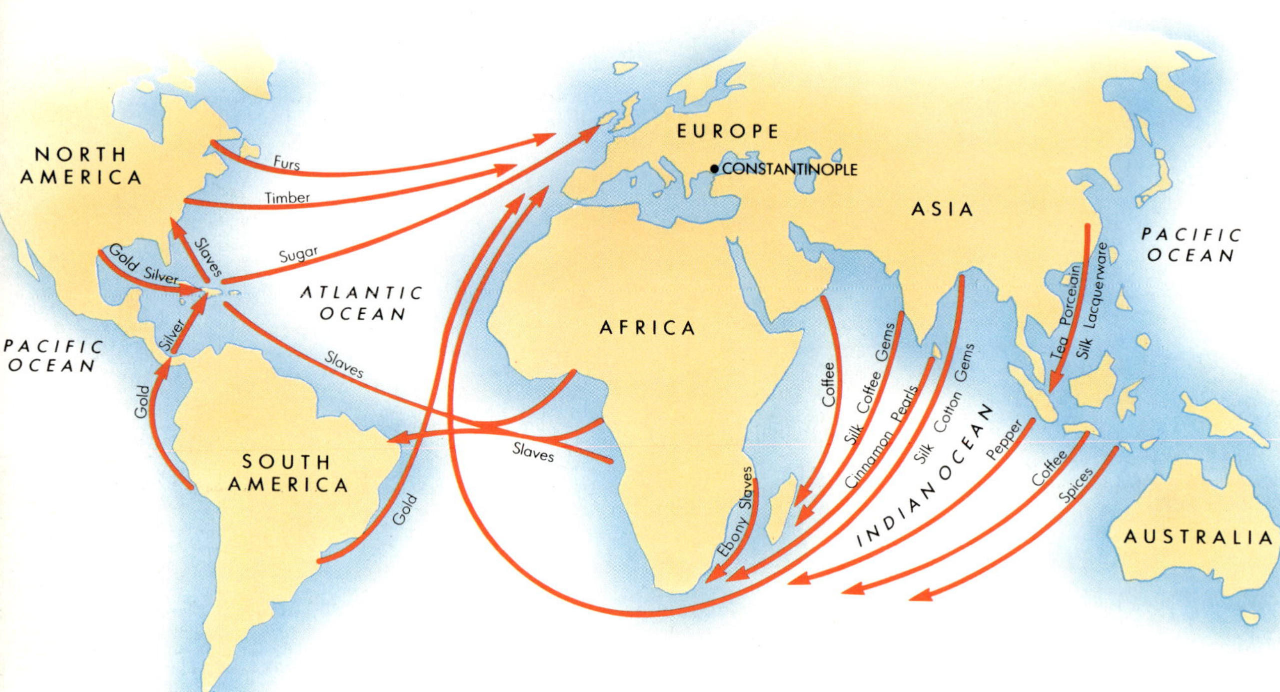

International trade was well established by 1500. Silks and brocades came overland from China to the Mediterranean coast and then into Europe. On the east coast of Africa, Arabian merchants traded with India, China and the African countries. European countries traded with each other, and also obtained spices and luxury goods from India and the Far East. When the Ottomans took control of the spice trade, Europeans began to look for routes to trade directly with spice-producing countries. Once they found these routes, trade began to change and by 1650 the Europeans were starting to control it.

By the sixteenth century the countries of Europe needed a two-way trade with the rest of the world. As well as wanting to import spices and luxury goods, they also wished to find markets for their own products. This became even more important as the century went on and European industry expanded to produce more goods than were needed at home. Overseas markets had to be found where these goods could be sold for money or traded for something which Europe could not produce.

WHY EUROPE NEEDED SPICES During this period many cattle were killed for meat at the beginning of autumn because the farmers did not have enough foodstuffs to feed all the herd through the winter. There were no refrigerators and so often meat had started to go bad before it was eaten. The only way to keep it fit to eat for any length of time was by salting it, but so much salt had to be used that the meat tasted of nothing else. To make it taste better, people added spices such as pepper, ginger and cinnamon when they were cooking the meat.

When the Europeans visited the New World, they found many plants which they had never seen before, including bananas, pineapples, coconuts, maize and tobacco. They also found tomatoes and potatoes, which they took back to Europe with them. At first they grew potato plants for decoration only, but later they became a very important food crop in several European countries.

THE SPICE TRADE As spices only grew in hot countries, they had to be transported over long distances. Each

Left. The Spanish controlled the production of cochineal. It was used as a red dye and came from the dried bodies of insects that lived on a cactus in Mexico.

Below. In 1576 Ivan IV of Russia sent these merchants and noblemen to Austria. They took furs with them in the hope of setting up trading links between the two countries.

European Exports

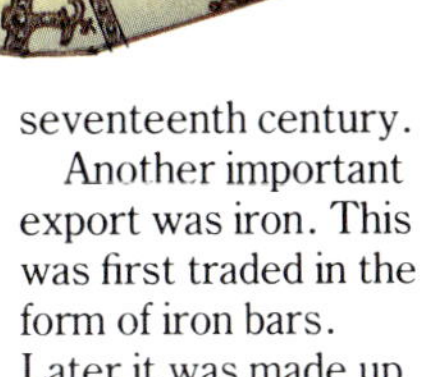

Woollen cloth was the main European export in this period. At first it was quite thick to suit colder climates. As trade increased with warmer countries, people tried finer yarns to make less bulky cloth. This was perfected in the seventeenth century.

Another important export was iron. This was first traded in the form of iron bars. Later it was made up into different items before it was exported, as this meant that the Europeans could make more profit from it.

merchant who handled them wanted to make a profit, and when that was added to the cost of bringing the spices to Europe they became very expensive. When the Portuguese reached India, they were able to buy some of these spices directly. This cut their costs and also encouraged them to sail on to find the Moluccas, or Spice Islands (now part of Indonesia). The king of Portugal then claimed a monopoly on the spice trade. This did not last very long, however, as other European explorers found different routes to the Spice Islands and India and also began to trade directly with them.

LUXURY GOODS AND NECESSITIES Besides spices, the European traders were also looking for other luxury goods. For instance, as their own continent became more and more cultivated, there were fewer wild animals to be hunted for their skins. As rich people still wanted furs, these had to be brought from overseas. When Richard Chancellor went to Russia in 1553 and set up the Muscovy Company, the fur trade was one of the things he was most interested in. Similarly, when Samuel de Champlain explored Canada in 1608 he started a trade in furs for France (see p. 327).

The Europeans were also interested in obtaining brocades and tea from China, silks and printed cottons from India, and unusual foods, such as pineapples, from the New World.

Not all trade was in luxury goods, however. As Europe used up all its own tall trees for building houses and ships, timber began to be imported from America. Harvest failure was always a possibility in Europe, too, and so grain was sometimes imported to be sold at a high price in times of famine.

THE THREATS TO TRADE Trading with countries overseas was always a risky business. Apart from the constant threat of wars, storms and shipwrecks, there was also a danger from pirates who might capture the ship and steal its cargo. Because of all these risks, wise merchants invested their money in several different ships and each ship had a number of owners. Thus, if the ship and its cargo did not reach their planned destination, the loss was spread among several merchants and they were all able to carry on trading. Despite the risks, some merchants became very rich and were able to buy large town houses and even country estates.

COLONIZING DISTANT LANDS

The Portuguese built Fort Jesus near Mombasa in Kenya in the late sixteenth century to protect their trading routes to East Africa and India.

When the Europeans began their voyages of discovery in the late fifteenth century, they were looking for new trade routes. As they found these, they began setting up permanent trading posts in the countries they were trading with, and they soon grew into European colonies. In many countries the traders from Portugal and Spain were soon followed by missionaries, who hoped to convert the local populations to Catholicism. In some countries the colonies outgrew their original purpose and Europeans who were not traders moved to live there.

COLONIES THAT FAILED Not all the attempts at building colonies were successful. In some countries the Europeans were turned out and the frontiers were closed against them. This happened in Japan, even though the Europeans had been welcomed there at first. In China the situation was even worse because the Chinese thought the Europeans had nothing to offer them and looked on their methods of trading as a form of piracy. By the 1550s, they allowed Portuguese traders onto the waterfront at Macao, but would not let them go any further.

AFRICA The Europeans had more success in Africa, where the Portuguese set up some of the earliest trading colonies along the coast. By 1600 there were Portuguese colonies at Luanda on the west coast, and at Butua, Matapa, Mozambique, Kilwe, Mombasa and Malindi on the east, but the interior of the continent remained a mystery.

THE SPANISH IN AMERICA The Spaniards soon realized the wealth of the new lands they had reached and set about exploiting them to the full. In the West Indies they took the land from the Arawak and Carib Indians (see pp. 328–9), who were there when the Spaniards arrived, and turned the Indians into slaves. They did the same to the Aztecs in Mexico and the Incas in South America (see pp. 322–3).

TREASURES FROM AMERICA The Aztecs and the Incas did not use metal for making tools. They did use vast amounts of both gold and silver for making ornaments and statues, however. When the Spaniards found this, they melted all these down into ingots and shipped them back to Spain. There the precious metals were used to pay for the wars being fought against other European powers and also to buy other goods in Europe to trade with the New World. When this supply of gold and silver ran out, the Spaniards discovered silver at various sites in Mexico and South America. They forced the Indians to mine these sites and, when most of the Indians had died from diseases and ill-treatment, the Spaniards replaced them with slaves from Africa.

THE EUROPEANS IN NORTH AMERICA The colonization of North America happened later than that of South America and Mexico. Although Verrazzano sailed along the east coast of North America in 1524 and Cartier explored the St Lawrence River in 1536, both claiming these lands for France, no serious attempts at colonizing were made until the 1580s.

At this point an English explorer, Sir Walter Raleigh, tried to establish some English colonies in an area he called Virginia, but none of them survived. A more successful attempt was made in 1607 when Jamestown was founded and this encouraged other settlers to follow. These settlers had a little more respect for the American Indians than the Spanish had, but they still forced the native peoples off the land which had been theirs for generations. Many Indians also died from diseases brought to America by the Europeans.

Right. Jamestown was the first successful English colony in America, but the early years were very difficult for the settlers. The climate and soil were wrong for the seeds they brought with them. Many people died of famine and disease. Then one of their leaders discovered how to grow maize and grind it into flour. Another man found out how to grow tobacco and this was traded in England in return for farm tools and other essential goods.

Problems of Colonization

When people first started to try and colonize the land which Sir Walter Raleigh had called Virginia, they ran into many problems.

At the end of a long and often dangerous sea journey, they had to try and make homes for themselves in unknown territory before the winter set in. They had to clear the land of trees and make them into houses and furniture. They also had to find a reliable water supply and try to gather or grow enough food to last until the spring, as the ships they had arrived on were not big enough to allow them to bring many supplies from England.

All these efforts failed, and many of the early colonists died in America from a combination of the cold weather, disease and malnutrition.

European Possessions c. 1650

NORTH AMERICA
JAMESTOWN
ATLANTIC OCEAN
TENOCHTITLAN
SOUTH AMERICA
LIMA
RIO DE JANEIRO
EUROPE
ASIA
AFRICA
PACIFIC OCEAN
INDIAN OCEAN
GOA
MALINDI
MOMBASA
LUANDA
KILWE
MOZAMBIQUE
JAVA

Portuguese
Spanish
British
French
Dutch

Above. Some of the places that were colonized by Europeans in the sixteenth and seventeenth centuries. Many colonies were set up for trade. Others were set up as places for people from Europe to settle as farmers and merchants. This usually involved taking land from the native peoples and destroying a way of life they had followed for centuries.

Right. Sir Walter Raleigh.

Right. This woodcarving shows a plan of the Dutch trading colony in Nagasaki harbour in Japan. Dutch merchants started trading with the Japanese in 1567 and at first they were welcomed. However, in the early seventeenth century the Japanese wanted to end all contact with foreigners. All Europeans were banished, apart from a few Dutch merchants. Even they had to keep to this one small island.

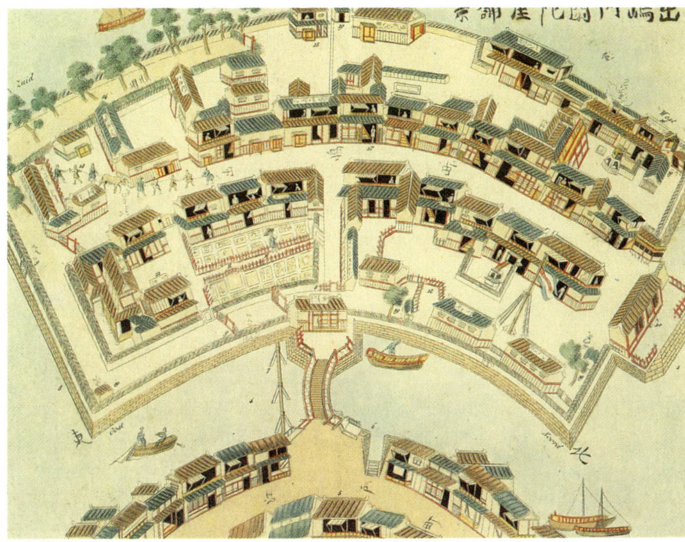

EXPLORING THE PACIFIC OCEAN

Above. The Portuguese navigator, Ferdinand Magellan, using an astrolabe on board his ship. Because most artists had no idea of what lived in the oceans, they added creatures like mermen and sirens to their pictures.

The greatest problem for adventurers wanting to explore the Pacific Ocean was the lack of an accurate method of navigation. The astrolabe and the *quadrant* worked well enough for finding the way to a large area of land, but were not much use in the Pacific Ocean where there were so many small islands. One of these islands might be sighted on one voyage and then not seen again for many years, as they could not be marked accurately on a chart. Because of this, no serious attempts were made to explore the ocean itself until the middle of the seventeenth century, although it was crossed several times by navigators looking for a southwest route to the Spice Islands. The Spanish conquistadors also sailed north and south across the Pacific along the coast of America.

FERDINAND MAGELLAN The Portuguese navigator Ferdinand Magellan (*c.* 1480–1521) gave the Pacific Ocean its name. He also led the first expedition to sail right around the world. Magellan was supported by the king of Spain, who gave him a fleet of five ships to go in search of a western route to the East Indies. He left Seville in September 1519 and reached the Pacific Ocean in November 1520. After 98 days' sailing, he arrived in the Philippines. Soon afterwards, Magellan was killed in a local dispute and Juan Sebastian del Cano took command. He crossed the Indian Ocean, visited Mozambique and arrived back in Seville with just one ship in September 1522. He and his crew had circumnavigated the world. Their route was later followed by others, including Sir Francis Drake from England.

THE PHILIPPINES Although Magellan reached the Philippines in 1521, they were not conquered by Spain until 1571. Even then the Spanish influence was mainly on the coast, and Muslims, called 'Moros' by the Spaniards, kept them off the islands of Mindanao and Sulu. The Philippines became a trading centre, with Chinese *junks* carrying porcelain and silks to Manila to be traded for silver from Mexico.

THE DUTCH EAST INDIA COMPANY Because of their struggle for independence from Spain, the Dutch were forbidden to trade for spices in Lisbon. They therefore decided to break the Portuguese and Spanish monopoly by trading directly with the spice-producing countries, and in 1602 they set up the Dutch East India Company to do this. In 1619 the Dutch founded the town of Batavia in Indonesia, taking control of that country and calling it the East Indies.

TERRA AUSTRALIS Many people believed there was a large continent in the South Pacific or Indian Ocean to balance those in the northern hemisphere and prevent the world falling over. The Dutch explorer Willem Janszoon actually landed on the northeast tip of Australia in 1605–6, when some members of his crew were killed by the first Aboriginals ever seen by Europeans. Other

The Peoples of Australia and New Zealand

Australia and New Zealand were both inhabited at the time of the first European visits. In Australia, the people known as Aboriginals had probably been there for many thousands of years. They lived in different tribes, which each had its own language.

The Aboriginals were great artists and painted pictures on bark, on the ground and on the walls of caves. They led a mainly nomadic life, hunting, fishing and gathering berries.

Below. This sixteenth century Maori bone box was made to hold the bones of the child of a chieftain.

The Maori had probably come to New Zealand from Polynesia in the ninth century AD.

Maori society was very warlike and boys were taught martial arts from an early age. The Maori were also very skilled woodcarvers. The clubs that they used for fighting were very elaborate.

Above. A view of Batavia on the island of Java in what is now Indonesia. In the early seventeenth century it was the headquarters of the Dutch East India Company and a base from where the Dutch could protect their hold on the spice trade.

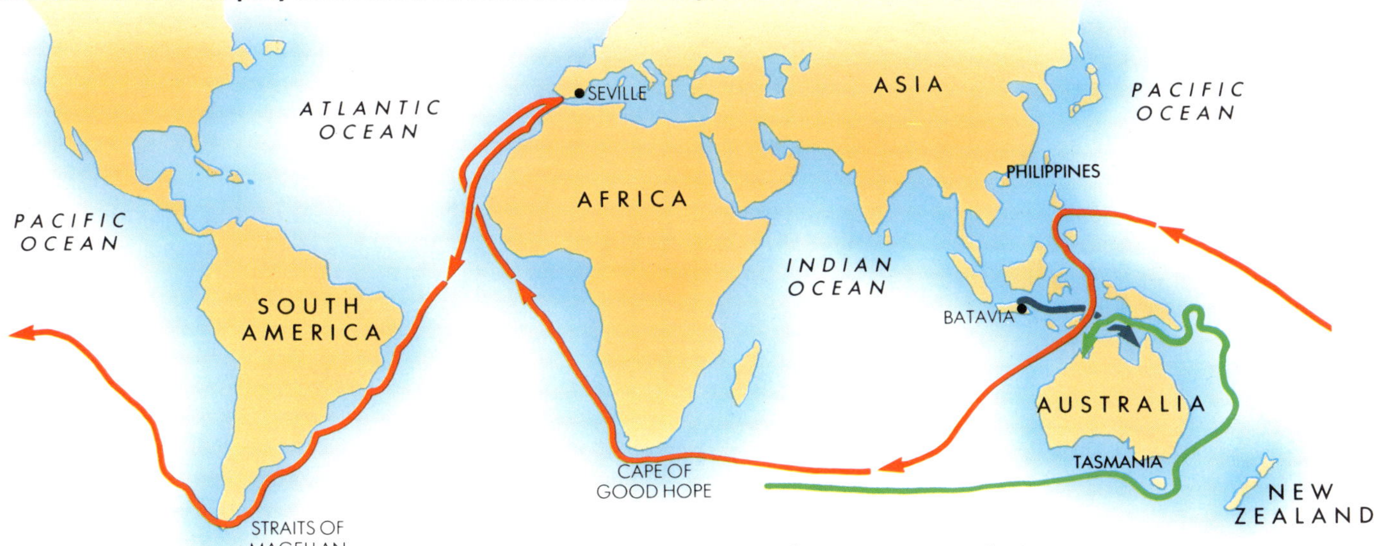

Pacific Voyages of Discovery

Above. The most northerly route on this map is the one followed by Ferdinand Magellan and Juan Sebastian del Cano after they left Seville in 1519 to sail around the world. The other routes are those followed by Tasman when he set out from Batavia to explore the south Pacific, and by Janszoon when he sailed to Australia.

Dutch explorers sighted or landed at points on the northern and western coasts of Australia over the next 20 years, but the land they saw was thought to be too poor to be the continent they were looking for. They expected this new continent to contain great riches.

TASMAN'S VOYAGES In 1642 Anthony van Dieman, the governor-general of Batavia, commissioned Abel Tasman (1603–1659) to explore the South Pacific. Tasman sailed further south than Janszoon had done and saw Tasmania, which he called Van Dieman's Land, and New Zealand. His journey home took him to Tonga and Fiji. On his second voyage, in 1644, he sailed along the north coast of Australia. It was still thought to be a poor place, and no attempts at colonization were made.

Left. The Dutch sailor, Abel Tasman. His voyages proved that Australia was not joined to the islands of the Dutch East Indies. However, people still believed that there was another continent to be discovered in the south.

TOWARDS OVERSEAS EMPIRES

An engraving of an indigo factory in the West Indies. Indigo was a plant which grew well there. It was used as a dark blue dye by the European textile industry.

At the end of the fifteenth century, Portugal and Spain were the dominant powers in Europe. They were also the most interested in sponsoring long-distance voyages to discover new routes to India and the spice-producing countries. During the sixteenth century, however, strong rulers came to power in England and in France, and the Netherlands declared its independence from Spain. This led to conflict within Europe as different rulers tried to dominate the continent. The conflict was then repeated overseas as England, France and the Netherlands joined in the search for new routes and new lands.

THE LINE OF DEMARCATION In 1493 the pope realized that the Portuguese and Spanish voyages might lead to trouble between the two countries. To avoid this, he drew an imaginary 'Line of Demarcation' around the world, running from north to south through a point which was 563 kilometres to the west of the Azores and the Cape Verde Islands. It touched the east coast of South America, before continuing around the world. Spain could claim land to the west of this line and Portugal could claim land to the east.

THE TREATY OF TORDESILLAS Neither Spain nor Portugal was completely satisfied with the Line of Demarcation and so in 1494 they agreed to change it. By the Treaty of Tordesillas, the line was moved to a point 2084 kilometres west of the Cape Verde Islands. This was later to give Portugal territory in eastern Brazil, even though that country was not known to the Europeans until 1500.

THE TREATY OF SARAGOSSA The Line of Demarcation gave Portugal the right to claim the Philippines. Spain recognized this right in the Treaty of Saragossa, which was drawn up to set a new line to the east of the Moluccas (Spice Islands). In later treaties between the two countries, Portugal gave up its claim to the Philippines in return for the whole of Brazil.

NEW CLAIMS TO TERRITORY England, France and the Netherlands ignored the Line of Demarcation and other claims made by Spain and Portugal and started to claim land and trading rights for themselves. By 1600, all three countries had established colonies in the West Indies and in North America. The English and the French traded with India, while the Dutch controlled the East Indies.

The colony of New Amsterdam was founded by the Dutch on Manhattan Island in America in 1624. When the British captured it in 1664, the name was changed to New York.

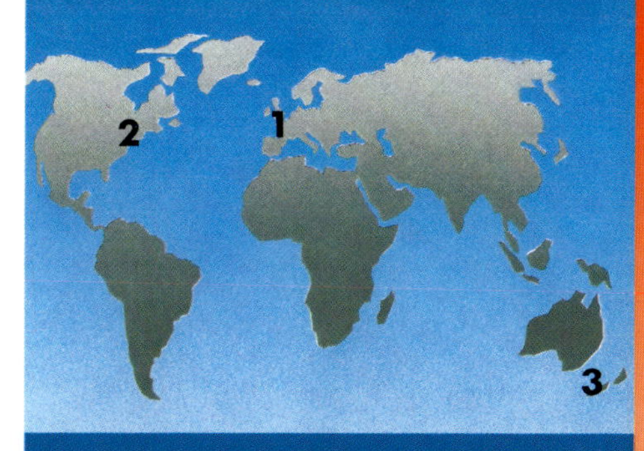

Left. A view of Bombay harbour in India in the seventeenth century. Portugal controlled the town from 1534 to 1661. It was then given to the king of England as part of the dowry of the Portuguese princess, Catherine of Braganza, who married Charles II.

1 Throughout this period, much of Europe was troubled by war, and by outbreaks of plague and other illnesses. There were also occasional famines when the crops failed or were destroyed by armies.

2 Harvard University was founded in Cambridge, Massachusetts, in 1636. It was the first university in what is now the USA, but there was already a university in Mexico, founded in 1551.

3 In 1642 Abel Tasman became the first European to see New Zealand. It was inhabited by Maoris, who had probably migrated there from Polynesia in the ninth century. They lived mainly in the North Island in large, fortified villages of wooden houses. Most of them were farmers. Some were also woodcarvers of great skill.

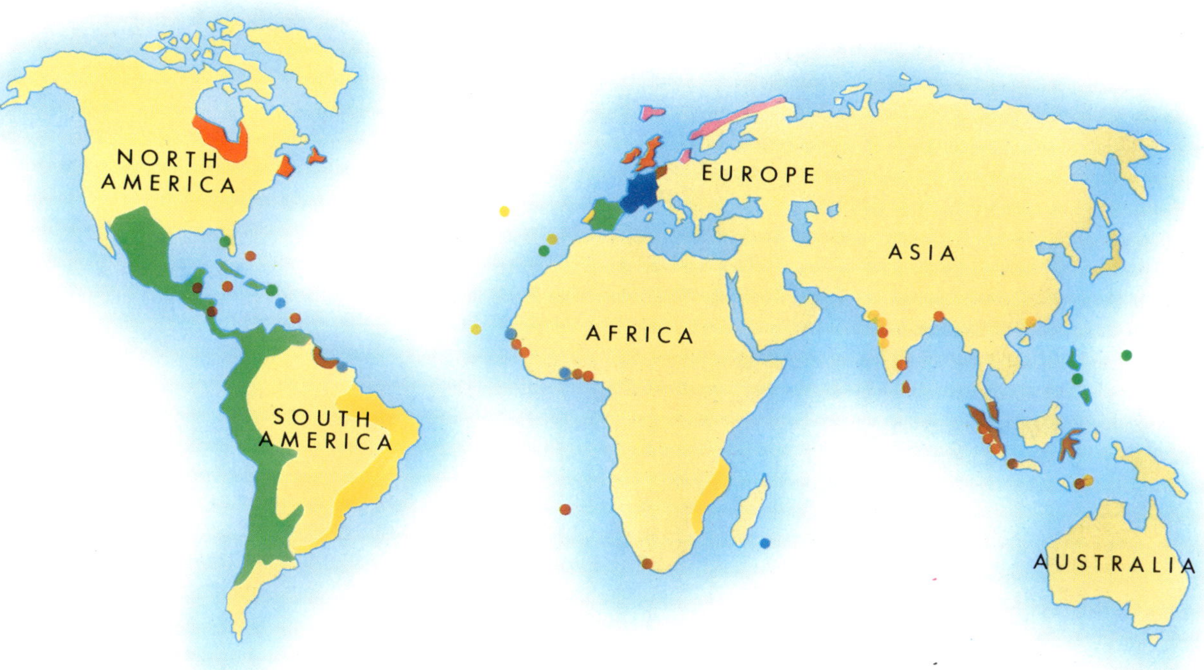

THE NEW BALANCE OF POWER The overseas discoveries encouraged economic growth in Europe. New markets were found, as well as new sources of raw materials such as cotton, sugar and tobacco. These were especially important to England, France and the Netherlands, all of which had growing industries.

In contrast, Portugal still relied solely on trade and Spain depended on silver from its American colonies to pay for manufactured goods from the rest of Europe. As a result, the power of Spain and Portugal gradually declined, while England, France and the Netherlands became richer and more dominant. By 1650 the balance of power within Europe had shifted towards these three countries, while the importance of their territories overseas was beginning to reflect the same distribution of power.

Above. This map shows how the European powers had begun to divide the world up between themselves by the middle of the seventeenth century. England, France and the Netherlands ignored the imaginary lines which had divided the world between Portugal and Spain. They began to set up trading links and colonies of their own. Using raw materials from the colonies to supply their growing industries at home, England, France and the Netherlands became more important as Spain and Portugal declined.

Spanish possessions
Portuguese possessions
British possessions
French possessions
Dutch possessions
Danish possessions

THE OTTOMAN EMPIRE

In 1453 the Ottoman Turks, led by Mehmet II (1451–1481) captured the Byzantine capital of Constantinople and made it into the centre of a Muslim empire. By 1500 this empire included the whole of Turkey, Greece and the Crimea. Although it was a Muslim empire, its rulers, or sultans, were tolerant of other religions, so long as their followers paid a *tribute* either in money or in men. The *Orthodox Christians* who had lived in the Byzantine Empire knew that the Catholics would never be so tolerant of them and so they paid their tribute and often fought alongside the Muslims against the Holy Roman Empire.

THE SULTAN'S PERSONAL SLAVES To make sure that all the members of his armed forces and his government stayed faithful to him, Mehmet II decided to make them all into his personal slaves. These included many Christian youths from the Balkans who were brought to Constantinople as part of the Christian tribute and converted to Islam for a lifetime of service to the sultan. Some of them joined the Janissary corps, which was the part of the army whose job was to protect the sultan. Others were given a good education and became government officers and civil servants. After Mehmet's death in 1481 the system continued under his successors.

Left. Suleiman the Magnificent was better known in the Ottoman Empire as Suleiman the Lawgiver, because of his legal and administrative reforms.

THE EMPIRE EXPANDS Selim I (1512–1520) started a new period of expansion. Between 1516 and 1517 he doubled the size of the territory under his control by adding Egypt, Algeria, Syria and Palestine to it.

After Selim's death, the empire passed to his son, Suleiman, and the expansion continued. Budapest fell to the Ottomans after the Battle of Mohacs in 1526, and much of Hungary was added to the empire some years later. Suleiman's army went on to capture Armenia and parts of Persia (modern-day Iraq) and Croatia. It also besieged Vienna, the capital of the Holy Roman Empire, but failed to capture the city.

THE GOLDEN AGE OF SULEIMAN The Ottoman Empire gained great wealth through trade, because of its position at the crossroads of some of the busiest trade routes between Asia and Europe. In its markets there were goods such as woollen cloth from England, silk from Persia, porcelain from China and

The Ottoman Empire

CRIMEA
BUDAPEST
BLACK SEA
GREECE
CONSTANTINOPLE
TURKEY
PERSIA
ALGERIA
MEDITERRANEAN SEA
SYRIA
EGYPT
RED SEA

Above. By 1645, the Ottoman Empire had expanded so far that its rulers controlled land in three continents.

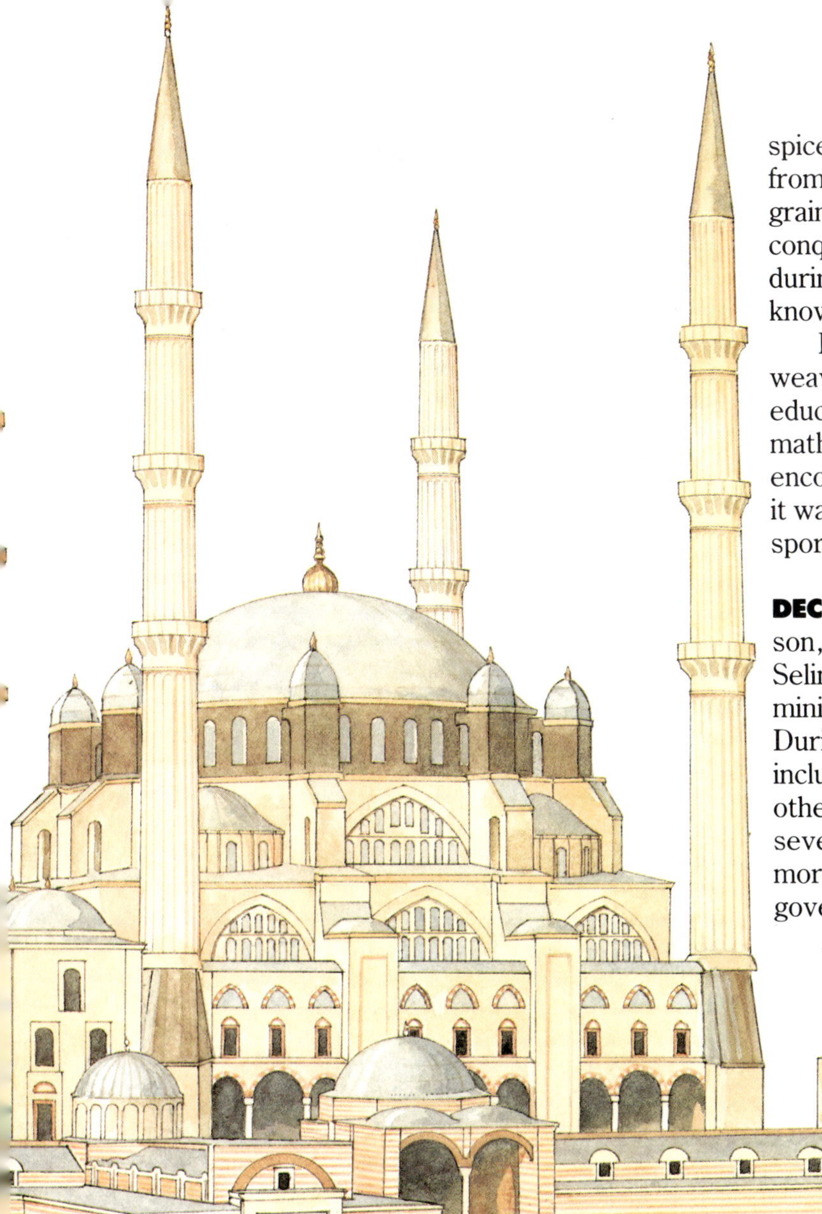

spices from India and the Far East. Wealth also came from farming, as the empire was a great producer of grain. This wealth, together with the newly conquered lands, led to a Golden Age for the empire during the reign of Suleiman I (1520–1566), who was known as 'the Magnificent'.

In the arts, literature, architecture, carpet-weaving and tile-making flourished. Although education emphasized religious studies, mathematicians and astronomers were also encouraged, while medicine was more advanced than it was in Europe at this time. People also enjoyed sports such as archery and wrestling.

DECLINING POWER Suleiman was succeeded by his son, Selim II (1566–1574). Unlike his father, however, Selim was content to lead a life of leisure and let his ministers and generals run the empire on his behalf. During his reign, the Ottoman Empire expanded to include Cyprus, but its decline had already started. No other sultan had Suleiman's ability and so, in the seventeenth century, the ministers and generals grew more and more powerful, which created problems in the government.

At the same time, trade became less important as the Europeans found new trade routes to India and the Far East and began to deal with these countries directly, saving time and money, instead of going through the lands of the Ottoman Empire. The great source of its wealth, trade, began to dwindle, though it remained a great centre of learning.

Above. As the Islamic faith spread through the empire, Ottoman architects designed many new mosques like this one, with domed roofs and slender minarets.

Right. Selim II tried to gain control over the whole of the Mediterranean, so the Holy Roman Empire and Spain, together with some Italian states, sent a combined fleet to attack the Ottoman navy. The two sides joined battle on 7 October 1571 off the town of Lepanto in the Gulf of Corinth, Greece. The Ottoman navy was defeated and is said to have lost at least 20,000 men.

Below. Suleiman encouraged the arts and crafts in his empire. Craftsmen wove beautiful carpets from wool on handlooms and made patterned tiles to decorate the walls of houses. They also made large storage jars like this one.

THE EMERGENCE OF RUSSIA

After Constantinople was captured by the Ottoman Empire in 1453, Moscow became the new center of the Orthodox religion. Tsar Ivan III (1462–1505) married the niece of the last Byzantine emperor in 1472 and took as his emblem the Byzantine emblem of a double-headed eagle. He was responsible for the creation of a new Russian state, declaring himself independent from the *Tartars* who had been overlords of Russia for almost 250 years. Ivan III expanded his territory to include Novgorod and other cities, making Moscow his capital and rebuilding its *Kremlin*, which had been badly damaged by two fires in the 1460s.

IVAN THE TERRIBLE Ivan III was succeeded by his son, Vasili III (1505–1533), who was in turn succeeded by his three-year-old son,

Right. St. Basil's Cathedral in Moscow was built between 1554 and 1560 after Ivan IV's victories in Kazan and Astrakhan. It was designed by two Russians called Posnik and Barma. The cathedral was originally dedicated to the Virgin Mary, but became known as St. Basil's after Basil, a Russian saint, was buried there in the reign of Ivan IV's son, Fyodor.

Above. By the end of Ivan III's reign, the territory ruled from Moscow included Pskov and Novgorod. Ivan IV wanted to expand still further to give Russia access to the Baltic Sea. This led to an unsuccessful war against Poland and Lithuania and in 1584 the port of Archangel was built on the White Sea coast instead. Towards the end of Ivan IV's reign, the territory also started to expand to the east as the exploration of Siberia began. By 1649 the Russians had access to the Pacific Ocean.

Ivan IV (1533–1584). This young king was crowned tsar of Russia in 1547 and by 1555 had reformed the legal system and local government. His territories increased when his armies took Kazan and Astrakhan from the Tartars, while his influence grew when he set up trading connections with England.

However, Ivan IV had had a harsh upbringing and this turned him into a brutal man. From 1560 onwards he had thousands of people executed and in 1581 he killed his eldest son in a fit of rage. This earned him the name of "Ivan the Terrible." After his death, he was succeeded by his second son, Fyodor (1584–1598).

BORIS GODUNOV AND THE TIME OF TROUBLES Boris Godunov (1598–1605) rose to power in the reign of Ivan IV. He was regent for Fyodor until the latter died in 1598. As Fyodor had no children and his younger brother Dmitri had died before him, Boris Godunov was elected tsar.

The Time of Troubles began after Boris Godunov's death, when the so-called False Dmitri claimed the throne, saying that he was the son of Ivan IV. He was backed by Poland. He was killed in 1606, but a second False Dmitri claimed the throne two years later. This claimant was murdered in 1610, but a third False Dmitri appeared between 1611 and 1612. The Time of Troubles finally ended when Michael Romanov was elected tsar in 1613.

THE FIRST ROMANOV Michael Romanov (1613–1645) was a weak ruler and relied heavily on his father, who was the head of the Russian Church. In spite of this weakness, Michael ruled Russia for 32 years and started a *dynasty* which lasted for 300 years. *Serfdom* increased during his reign and the Cossacks began to lose some of their independence.

THE COSSACKS The Cossacks were descended from the Tartars and from escaped serfs. They were expert horsemen and lived in independent communities in southwest Russia. They received special privileges from the Russian rulers in exchange for military sevice.

THE SETTLEMENT OF SIBERIA A Cossack called Yermak captured the town of Sibir from the Tartars in 1581. This victory gave the name Siberia to the whole region between the Ural Mountains and the Pacific. Other Russians followed and by 1600 they had founded a settlement at Tobolsk. They then traveled east along the great rivers, defeating the native tribes as they went.

In 1649 the Russians reached the Pacific, then turned south to Lake Baikal, founding the town of Irkutsk in 1651. The fur trade made Siberia important and the defeated tribes had to pay a tribute in furs to the Russian government. Once Siberia had been opened up, many peasants went there to escape from serfdom.

Above. This picture shows Russians travelling in sledges known as troikas. They used these sleds to travel long distances.

Russian Peasantry

The peasants in Russia lived as serfs, or slaves, on the estates of wealthy noblemen. They had no rights and few possessions. Their homes were often flimsy and gave little protection against the icy cold winters. In times of famine many of them died of illnesses brought on by hunger. This was especially true when the crops failed between 1601 and 1603. Thousands died, while others turned to robbery and cannibalism in order to survive.

In the unrest after the death of Boris Godunov, however, many serfs escaped to make new lives for themselves in Siberia.

Right. Ivan the Terrible was an intelligent man who wrote well and composed prayers and music for the Church. He encouraged art and literature and the use of printing in his country. He married six times; three wives died, two were divorced and one outlived him.

THE MOGUL EMPIRE OF INDIA

At the end of the fifteenth century, Babur (1495–1530), a descendant of the Mongol leader Genghis Khan, became the ruler of Fergana in Turkestan. He hoped to reconquer his ancestors' kingdom of Samarkand, but failed, turning his attention instead to Afghanistan and capturing Kabul. From there he raided India and in 1526 he led his troops down the Khyber Pass and onto the plains of India. He defeated and killed the sultan of Delhi in battle, and the following year he defeated the Rajputs in a battle near Agra. Although the Rajputs were the best soldiers in India, Babur was able to defeat them as they rode into battle on elephants, while his men were mounted on swift-moving horses. After this victory, he soon took control of the whole of northern India and became the first ruler of an empire which was to last, in some form, until 1857.

Above. The Taj Mahal at Agra is probably the most famous building in India. It was built for Mumtaz-i-Mahal, wife of the Mogul Emperor Shah Jahan, and they are both buried here. It took more than 20,000 workmen 22 years to construct the building, which is made of pure white marble, inlaid with precious stones. Shah Jahan was the grandson of Akbar but, unlike his grandfather, he was a ruthless ruler.

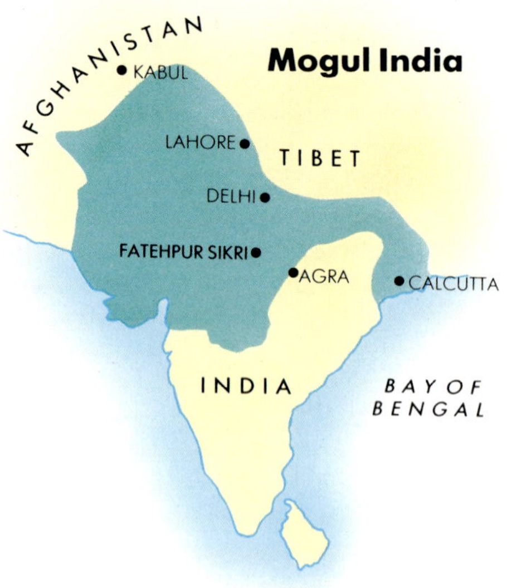

Above. The Mogul Empire. It was founded by Babur, who began by raiding India from his base in Afghanistan and later took control of the north of the country. By the time Babur's grandson, Akbar, became emperor, the empire stretched as far south as central India.

THE EARLY YEARS OF THE MOGUL DYNASTY The empire which Babur founded was known as the Mogul Empire. Its survival in the early years was uncertain, for when Babur died, his son, Humayun (1530–1556), was at first unable to hold the throne. After 10 years of fighting, Humayan was driven out of India and into Persia (Iran).

Below. Emperor Jahangir (1605–1627) looking at a portrait of his father, Akbar. Jahangir was a wise and just ruler who expanded the Mogul Empire and encouraged sports and the arts. He also encouraged trade with Britain through the East India Company.

Above. Part of the city of Fatehpur Sikri in Uttar Pradesh in northern India. It was built for Emperor Akbar in a mixture of Hindu and Muslim styles of architecture. It is now deserted, but from 1569 to 1585 it was the capital of the Mogul Empire.

Right. As these dagger handles show, craftsmen of the Mogul Empire were skilled at working with jade, gold and precious stones. Others painted pictures, especially miniatures showing scenes from court life, legends and history.

In 1555 he started to reconquer his empire, but before he achieved very much he died in an accident, leaving his 14 year-old son, Akbar, to fight for the throne.

REGAINING THE EMPIRE When Akbar (1556–1605) came to the throne of Hindustan, the whole of India was in a state of civil war as Hindus and Muslims struggled for power. Because Akbar was so young, his mother and her courtiers ruled for him for four years, then he determined to rule for himself and started out to recover the territory that had been lost. By the time of his death he had achieved this and more, leaving an empire which stretched from the Hindu Kush Mountains in the north to the Godavari River in central India.

THE WISDOM OF AKBAR Because Akbar realized that there would be no peace in his empire while there were differences between the Muslims and the Hindus, he decided to treat both religions equally. Although he was a Muslim himself, he married a Hindu princess. Akbar was also prepared to listen to the beliefs of others and allowed the Jesuit missionaries into India. He set up a system of law which gave Muslims and Hindus the right to be tried according to their own customs. He also changed the method of tax collection, so that the peasants knew in advance how much they ought to pay and were therefore less likely to be robbed by dishonest tax collectors.

Although Akbar could neither read nor write, he encouraged literature and painting, as well as architecture, and he held a brilliant court in his capital city of Agra. He also had a city at Fatehpur Sikri built for him in a combination of Muslim and Hindu styles of architecture.

THE FIRST EUROPEANS IN INDIA India was a land with many riches. It produced gold and jewels, as well as beautifully printed cloths like cottons and muslins. It also grew many of the spices which the Europeans wanted, including pepper, cinnamon and ginger.

The Portuguese were the first Europeans to come to India in search of these products, but they were soon followed by the English and the Dutch, all of whom set up trading colonies. In 1600 the British East India Company was founded and, as the power of the Mogul emperors began to wane in the early eighteenth century, this company started to affect every aspect of life in India.

THE MING DYNASTY OF CHINA

Left. Chinese landscape artists painted what they thought was important, instead of exact copies of real scenes.

Above. The Chinese empire during the Ming Dynasty. It was cut off by high mountains, deserts and oceans. Its emperors distrusted foreigners. Traders found it very difficult to do business in China at this time.

The Ming Dynasty was at the height of its power in the sixteenth century. It was founded in 1368 by Chu Yuan-chang, who freed his country from the control of the *Mongols*. He and his successors brought a period of stability and prosperity to their country, but, in reaction to the period of Mongol rule, the Ming emperors looked down on anything that was foreign. Because of this, the European traders who visited China in the sixteenth century were treated as inferiors and their activities were compared to piracy.

The missionaries who followed the traders did not fare much better, as the Chinese already had well-established religions of their own. Some people were Taoists and some were Buddhists, but the majority followed the teachings of Confucius.

CONFUCIUS Confucius (*c.* 551–478 BC) was a Chinese philosopher who believed that people were born good and that they had a moral duty to each other. He thought sincerity, fearlessness, wisdom and compassion were important. He also thought that people should know their place in society and be content with it. Confucius made strict rules about this. Everyone, from the poorest peasant to the emperor himself, was expected to conform to these rules and to live in harmony with nature. These ideas were known as Confucianism and belief in them helped the Ming emperors to be successful.

CHINESE SOCIETY The Confucianist ideal was a mainly agricultural population living under an educated *bureaucracy* which in turn was guided by a wise and compassionate emperor. For two centuries the Ming Dynasty managed to achieve this ideal.

The government

encouraged irrigation schemes which allowed the rice to be harvested twice a year. It also encouraged the growth of cash crops such as cotton and tea. It paved roads, built bridges, and enlarged the canal system to avoid a long stretch of dangerous coastline.

These schemes and many others were paid for by taxes which were collected by many hundreds of government officials, called *mandarins*. These men reached their positions by passing examinations and not by inheriting them from their fathers.

ARTS AND CRAFTS IN MING CHINA This period of peace and prosperity led to a flowering of arts and crafts in China. Encouraged by the emperors, some artists made beautifully painted and glazed porcelain. Others wove silk brocades or produced elaborate *lacquerwork* boxes and screens. Printing reached high standards and many people painted pictures. At first these were mainly of birds and flowers, but later landscape painting also became popular.

THE COLLAPSE OF THE MING DYNASTY Early in the seventeenth century, the Ming Dynasty began to weaken. Sending the Ming armies to defeat the Japanese in Korea in 1592 and 1597 proved very costly and after this came a peasant rising in western China and a famine in the north. In Beijing (Peking) officials struggled with each other to gain power, and also raised taxes while leaving the army unpaid. At the same time, the emperors became mainly interested in their own power and wealth.

THE RISE OF THE MANCHUS As the Ming Dynasty declined, the tribes of Manchuria in northeast China united under a chief called Nurchachi. In 1618 the Manchus over-ran the Ming province of Liaotung. Nurchachi died in 1626, but his successors soon took control of northern China and set up a new dynasty.

Chinese Dress

During the Ming Dynasty, the clothes that people wore reflected their place in society. There were strict rules about every item, from the hat to the shoes.

For example, only the most important government officials could wear crimson silk robes decorated with dragons. Less important officials wore robes decorated with birds or with animals, depending on whether they worked with civilians or the army. The position of the decorations also showed the wearer's importance.

Above. A high-ranking Chinese official. His silk gown was embroidered with silk threads. This, together with his very long fingernails, shows he did not have to do any manual work.

1 The Spanish capture the Philippines to increase their share of the spice market.

2 The Pilgrim Fathers set sail in 1620 to start a new life, as the Ming dynasty comes to an end.

3 Portuguese sailors visit Japan. They are the first Europeans to arrive. They eventually start a colony in Nagasaki.

A reconstruction of the Forbidden City of Peking (Beijing) in the Ming Dynasty. Peking, the capital of Ming China, was made up of two walled cities. The Inner City, which had been the capital of Mongol China, was surrounded by a stone wall 15 metres high, 18 metres thick and 7 kilometres long on each side. To the south was the Outer City, with walls 8 kilometres long. Within the Inner City was the Imperial City, surrounded by red walls. The Forbidden City got its name because everyone except the emperor, his family and his closest advisers was forbidden to go in.

JAPAN AND THE SHOGUNS

At the beginning of the sixteenth century Japan was a feudal state, ruled by an emperor. Each feudal lord had his own private army of warriors known as *samurai*, and these armies were often involved in local wars against each other.

The economy of the country was based on agriculture and rice was the most important crop. Improvements in irrigation meant that it could be harvested twice a year. There was also some mining for copper and silver, but craftsmen and workers in industry were thought to have a lowly status when compared with other groups of people such as farmers and military men. Japan's nearest neighbour was China and trade between the two countries was encouraged.

Right. This pagoda, or temple, shows the strong Chinese influence on Japanese architecture. It seems more solidly built than many in China, but it is made largely of wood and its many tiled roofs with dragon decorations are very much like those on Chinese buildings from the same period. The colours are also similar to the ones that were used in China.

Left. Japan is a series of islands, separated from the mainland of Asia by the sea. For centuries the Chinese were the only people from outside to visit Japan. They set up trading links and had a great influence on Japanese architecture and religion. The first Europeans reached Japan in 1543. They were welcomed at first, but in less than a century Japan had isolated itself from the rest of the world once more and nearly all links with foreigners were cut.

THE EMPEROR AND THE SHOGUN Legend has it that the first emperor of Japan was Jimmu, who ruled in around 660 BC, and that all the emperors who followed were descended from him. At first the country was ruled by powerful emperors. However, from the twelfth century onwards the emperors became sacred, shadowy figures, often living in monasteries, and the real power was in the hands of a nobleman known as the shogun.

THE FIRST EUROPEANS In 1543 a party of Portuguese sailors became the first people from Europe to visit Japan. Six years later Francis Xavier, a Spanish priest, arrived and began to convert some of the Japanese to Roman Catholicism. This encouraged more missionaries to come from Spain and Portugal and traders came with them. At the start of the seventeenth century, other traders came from England and from the Netherlands.

HIDEYOSHI AS SHOGUN In 1585 Hideyoshi became the shogun. He was a great warrior and planned to build a large Japanese empire which would include China. In 1592 and 1597 his armies got as far as Korea, but both times they failed to conquer it.

THE TOKUGAWA SHOGUNATE In 1603 Ieyasu became the shogun. He was from the Tokugawa family, which was to rule Japan for the next 250 years. Ieyasu was a wise statesman who had been Hideyoshi's chief deputy in eastern Japan. Under his rule, the warfare between the local samurai bands was brought to an end and a time of peace and prosperity began. He achieved this by dividing the country into about 250 regions called domains. Each domain was led by a *daimyo*, who controlled the samurai and had to swear allegiance to the Tokugawa shogunate.

KEEPING LAW AND ORDER During the early years of the Tokugawa shogunate, Japan became isolated from the rest of the world once more. Ieyasu was afraid that the missionaries from Europe might bring armies with them to conquer Japan, and so he and the shoguns who followed him decided to rid Japan of Christianity. The missionaries had to leave and the Japanese converts had to give up their religion or be killed.

The Tokugawa shoguns also thought that the only way to keep law and order within Japan was by ending contact with the rest of the world. In the 1630s almost all ties with other nations were cut. Only the Dutch were allowed to keep one small trading station in the harbour at Nagasaki. All other foreigners had to leave and Japanese people who were abroad at the time were not allowed to return home. By 1650 Japan's isolation was complete.

Ieyusa's Capital at Edo

Towards the end of the sixteenth century, Edo was a small fishing village of about 100 houses built around a castle. Then in 1590 Hideyoshi gave the castle to Tokugawa Ieyusa, along with a large amount of land in the area.

Ieyasu made Edo into his principal castle and, when he became shogun, Edo became his administrative centre. He had land reclaimed from the sea, drained marshes and diverted the river to make room for the new city which spread out like a spider's web around the castle.

About 80,000 samurai moved to Edo and all the daimyos had to have a house there and spend some of their time in it. By 1613 the population was estimated to be 150,000. It included craftsmen, merchants and commoners.

Above. Tokugawa Ieyasu, who founded the Tokugawa shogunate. He kept a strict control over all the other noble families in Japan. He also encouraged agriculture and Confucianism.

Left. Japanese society at this time was very strict and rigid. Manners and etiquette were very formal and it was thought better to be dead than to lose respect or honour. Within society, military men were the most important group, followed by farmers, then craftsmen and industrial workers. Women were treated almost as decorations. As you can see from this picture, their clothes were very impractical. Their wide sleeves made it almost impossible for them to do any work, while their flowing gowns and high shoes made it hard for them to walk. All the pins and combs in their hair made it difficult for women even to move their heads.

THE EMPIRES OF AFRICA

The continent of Africa at this time was made up of many different peoples, cultures, kingdoms and empires. Many of the empires were based on long-distance trading across the deserts and grasslands. The goods which were traded included gold, salt and ivory. People captured in war or by raiding parties in the south were sold as slaves in the north, while others were sold as slaves to India and Arabia. Those empires which touched the coasts of Africa became known to European traders during this period. The Europeans were not interested in the interior of Africa, however, and most of it remained a mystery to them until they explored it in the nineteenth century.

The Songhai Empire of West Africa

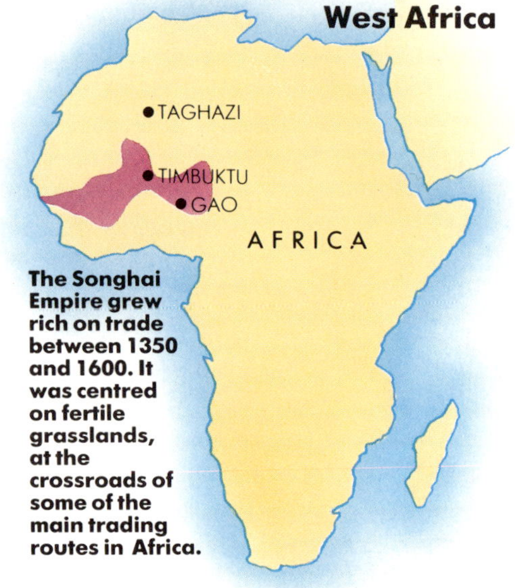

The Songhai Empire grew rich on trade between 1350 and 1600. It was centred on fertile grasslands, at the crossroads of some of the main trading routes in Africa.

THE ISLAMIC INFLUENCE The north and east of Africa had been under Islamic influence from the late seventh century AD. The Friday Mosque at Kairouan in Tunisia was founded in 670 and Islam spread west from there through Algeria and into Morocco. The religion also spread south across the Sahara Desert and reached trading centres such as Timbuktu, Gao and Jenne by the eleventh century. Islam was also important along the east coast of Africa, which was nearest to Arabia. The adoption of the Islamic religion and way of life brought a long period of stability to many parts of Africa. It also encouraged trade between Africa and the rest of the Islamic world.

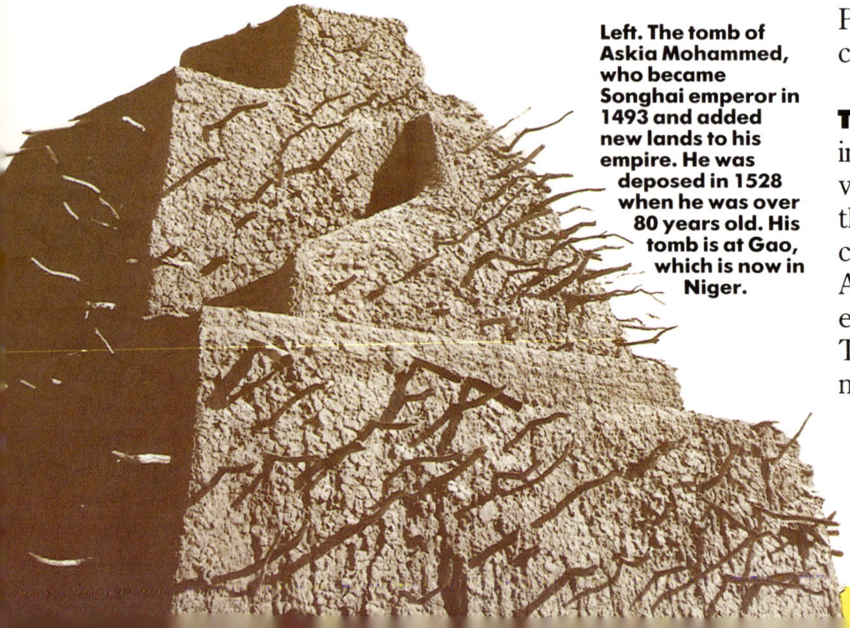

Left. The tomb of Askia Mohammed, who became Songhai emperor in 1493 and added new lands to his empire. He was deposed in 1528 when he was over 80 years old. His tomb is at Gao, which is now in Niger.

THE SUDANESE EMPIRES The vast grasslands of Africa which lay to the south of the Sahara Desert were known as the Sudan. From medieval times they were dominated by a series of empires whose wealth was built up on trade.

Between about 1350 and 1600 the most important of these was the Songhai Empire, which stretched from the coast of West Africa to the shores of Lake Chad. Its two main trading centres were the cities of Gao and Timbuktu, where gold from the forest lands to the south was exchanged for salt from Taghazi in the desert to the north. Cotton goods, copper, slaves and even dried seafish were also traded. The goods were carried on horseback or camel, depending on whether they were crossing the grasslands or the desert. The Songhai Empire started to collapse in 1591 when it was invaded by Moroccans from the north.

THE EAST COAST Many ports and city-states on the east coast of Africa had grown important through trade. As they were on the Indian Ocean they had links with Arabia, India and even China. Their main exports were metals (including gold, copper and iron), ivory, tortoiseshell and a small number of slaves. These were exchanged for cotton and beads from India, luxury items such as silks and brocades, and porcelain from China. From 1500 onwards, these cities were taken over by Portuguese traders and the pattern of trade was changed.

THE SLAVE TRADE There had always been a slave trade in Africa, but until the sixteenth century it had been on a very small scale. After the Europeans began to settle in the Americas in the sixteenth century, that started to change. The Europeans found the climate of the Americas too hot for them to work in and so they enslaved the native Indians to do the work for them. Then, as a mixture of ill-treatment and disease killed most of the Indians, increasing numbers of Africans were transported to the Americas to take their places in the mines and on the plantations.

Above. Timbuktu, a major city in the Songhai Empire. In the early sixteenth century it was described as a city of learning. The king was said to have an army of 3000 cavalry. The city had many magistrates, learned doctors and religious men, as well as a big market for the sale of books. It was a centre of Islamic culture and its mosque is now the oldest in West Africa. Its wealth was built on trade, but it started to decline after it was invaded by the Moroccans in 1591.

Below. The ruins of one of the castles built by King Fasilidas at Gondar in Ethiopia. He ruled from 1632 to 1665 and Gondar was his capital.

1 In 1497 John Cabot landed in Newfoundland. He was probably the first European to go there since the Vikings.

2 Between 1554 and 1556 the Ottoman Turks expanded their empire by conquering the coast of North Africa.

3 Until the 1580s the calendar used in Europe was the Julian calendar, introduced by Julius Caesar in 46 BC. This was based on a year which was 11 minutes and 14 seconds longer than the time the earth actually takes to orbit the sun, so by the 1580s the calendar was wrong by 10 days. Pope Gregory corrected this in 1582 by making 5 October into 15 October. Roman Catholic countries adopted this Gregorian calendar straight away. Many Protestant countries did not change until 1700, and Britain waited until 1752.

Arts and Crafts of the Songhai Empire

The people of the Songhai Empire were skilled metal-workers. Gold and copper were brought to the trading centres of Gao and Timbuktu. Here the craftsmen mixed copper with tin to make bronze, which they made into intricately patterned bowls and cups, jewellery and ornaments. Sometimes they added a thin layer of gold, called gilt.

Some potters produced realistic human statues and heads, others made patterned tiles for decoration. Other craft-workers included cotton weavers who made fine cloth for export.

Woodcarvings from the Songhai Empire. Some carvers made realistic statues like the one in the middle. Others carved shapes which followed the natural lines of the wood they were using.

CENTRAL AND SOUTH AMERICAN EMPIRES

This Aztec knife was probably used at special ceremonies. It has a stone blade because the Aztecs did not know how to make metal into tools.

Prior to European landings in the 'new world' in the sixteenth century, several highly developed societies thrived in the swamps, jungles and mountains of Central and South America. Perhaps the most highly developed of all early American societies, however, were the Aztecs of Central America and the Incas of the high Andes Mountains in modern-day Peru.

THE AZTECS The people known as Aztecs arrived in Mexico in the twelfth century, and settled on an island in Lake Texcoco. By the fourteenth century, through a process of land reclamation, they had made their island much bigger and had built a flourishing city there called Tenochtitlan. In the early sixteenth century there were probably around 150,000 people living there.

Aztec society was highly militaristic. A large, well-equipped professional army was maintained which was dedicated to conquering new territory and acquiring *tribute*. Gold, cotton, turquoise, feathers, food and a whole host of other commodities were sent as tribute to Tenochtitlan. These were all itemized on detailed tribute lists, many of which still survive.

HUMAN SACRIFICES The most significant of all tributes was a huge number of human beings, all of whom were destined for sacrifice in Tenochtitlan. The Aztecs believed that the offering of human sacrifices was the only way to please their sun god, Huitzilopochtli. Most sacrifices involved cutting out the heart of the victim whilst he or she was stretched out on a stone slab before the temple of the god. The scale of human sacrifice was enormous. At the consecration of a new temple in Tenochtitlan in 1487, as many as 20,000 men and women were ritually murdered over four days.

Left. Humans being sacrificed at Tenochtitlan. The priest killed them in a way that made their hearts spring out as he cut them.

Above. The Aztecs valued the feathers of brightly-coloured birds and accepted them as tribute from people they had conquered. The feathers were used to decorate objects such as this ceremonial shield.

Left. A page from the *Codex Mondeza*, a book which describes the life of the Aztec people.

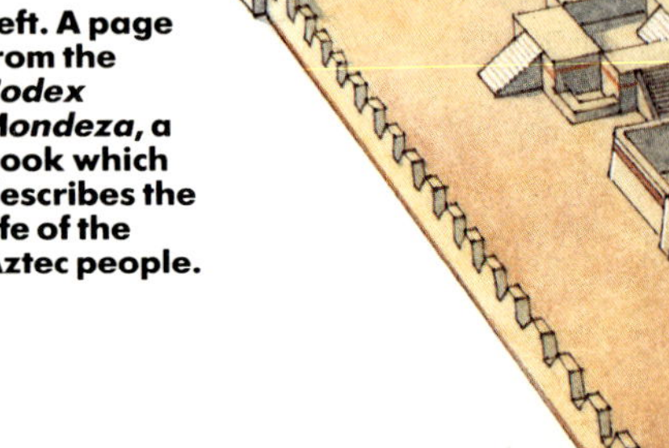

The Aztec and Inca Empires

Right. The Aztec and Inca empires when the Spanish came. The main Aztec city was Tenochtitlan in the middle of Lake Texcoco. The Spanish burnt it down and built Mexico City in its place. The Inca Empire was bigger than the Aztec one. Its capital was Cuzco. Most of the Inca cities were destroyed, but Machu Picchu survived because it was hard to find.

Below. A reconstruction of the centre of the Aztec capital of Tenochtitlan. It was built on an island and was connected to the mainland by long bridges. The temples of the sun and rain gods were at the top of the large pyramid. Prisoners were sacrificed here to keep the gods happy.

MONTEZUMA The Aztecs chose a new emperor in 1502. He was to be the last Aztec emperor; his name was Montezuma (1502–1520). He became a ruthless leader and proclaimed himself the equal of the gods. His reign was a turbulent period of crop failures, local revolts and demands for increased tribute. By the time the Europeans arrived in 1519, the Aztec Empire was in considerable disarray.

THE INCAS Around the time the Aztecs first settled in Mexico, the Inca family was coming to power in Cuzco in modern-day Peru. The political structure of Inca society was headed by the 'Sapa Inca', who was believed to be descended from the sun.

The ascent of Pachacuti Inca to the throne as the Sapa Inca in 1438 began a period of massive increase of Inca power. By 1476, the empire stretched for 6500 kilometres along the Andes Mountain range. This huge growth was made possible through an extremely thorough social and political organization. State control of labour and resources maintained a well-trained army, and provided the workforce and materials necessary to carry out huge civil engineering projects. Some 14,500 kilometres of paved roads, bridges and tunnels linked all parts of the empire to Cuzco, the capital city.

RIVALS TO THE THRONE Inca society, however, ultimately depended on the ability of the Sapa Inca in power. In 1525 two rival claimants to the throne arose, Huascar and Atahuallpa. This marked the beginning of a bloody civil war. The beginning of this war coincided with the arrival of Europeans in South America, weakening the empire and making the Incas easy prey to the strangers' weapons and diseases.

AMERICA: CONTACTS WITH SPAIN AND PORTUGAL

By the end of the fifteenth century the monarchs of both Portugal and Spain wanted to expand their territories and gain new wealth for themselves and their countries. They hoped to do this by opening up new trade routes to the east, but instead they came across America. After conquering the islands of the West Indies, they sent expeditions to the mainland, going first to Mexico, then to South America and finally to California, Arizona and New Mexico.

CORTES AND THE AZTECS Hernando Cortes (1485–1547) was born in Spain and went to Hispaniola in the West Indies when he was a young man. From there he took part in the conquest of Cuba and in 1518 was chosen to lead an expedition to Mexico with about 500 Spanish soldiers and about 300 Indians who had become their allies. He also took firearms and cannons, as well as mastiff dogs and 16 horses, none of which the Aztecs had ever seen before.

When Cortes arrived at Tenochtitlan, the Aztec Emperor Montezuma (p. 323) thought he was the god Quetzalcoatl and did not resist when Cortes captured him and started to rule in his place. When Cortes returned to the coast, however, the Aztecs rebelled and he went back with his army to try to put the rebellion down. Montezuma was killed in the fighting and Cortes retreated to the coast again.

The following year Cortes returned once more to Tenochtitlan and this time destroyed it and perhaps 100,000 of its people. The rest were made into slaves. Spanish settlers took the land, and all the Aztec treasures were melted down into gold ingots and shipped back to Spain.

THE FOUNDATION OF NEW SPAIN As well as the Aztec Empire, the Spanish also conquered the territory which had belonged to the Maya and the Toltecs. In 1535 all this land became the Vice-Royalty of New Spain, governed by Antonio de Mendoza, who encouraged economic development of the area and set up the first printing press in the New World. California, Arizona and New Mexico were added to New Spain later.

PIZARRO AND THE INCAS Like Cortes, Francisco Pizarro (*c.* 1478–1541) was born in Spain but went to America as a young man. In 1513 he accompanied Balbao on an expedition across Panama to the Pacific and later settled there. In partnership with a soldier called Almagro, he went exploring the west coast of South America. On their travels, they heard of the rich Inca

Left. This map shows the lands in America which were conquered by the Spanish and Portuguese. The Spanish treated the local peoples cruelly, until a Spanish bishop wrote an account of what was happening in Mexico. The king of Spain passed laws to protect them, but the laws were not very successful.

Far left. Francisco Pizarro. In 1541 he was murdered by Almagro's followers.

Above. Montezuma's ambassadors bringing Aztec treasures for Hernando Cortes.

The Legend of El Dorado

The Spanish conquistadors spent a lot of time looking for the legendary kingdom of El Dorado, or the Golden Man, which they thought was full of gold.

The legend probably came from the Muisca people in the northern Andes. When a new king came to the throne there, he made an offering to the gods at Lake Guatavita. His body was covered with gold dust and he and his courtiers went at night to the middle of the lake on a raft. The courtiers threw gold objects into the lake and the king dived in after them. As he did so, the gold dust washed from his body and sank into the water.

By the time the Spaniards heard the legend, the Muisca had already been defeated. Their gold had been melted down and sent to Spain.

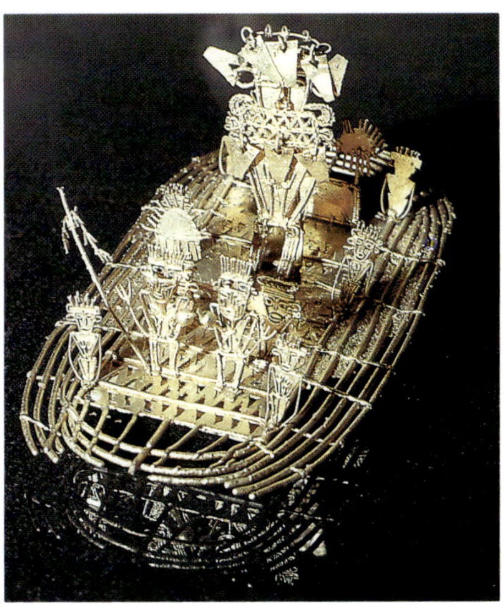

Few gold treasures survive from before the Spanish conquest of Central and South America. The Inca mask above probably represents the sun. The tunjo (raft) on the left was made by the Muisca and represents the raft from the El Dorado ceremony. The gold puma on the right is from the Mochica period in Peru, between the fourth and the ninth centuries AD. The puma has a human face decorating its tongue and double-headed serpents on its body.

Empire and in 1528 Pizarro returned to Spain to obtain permission to conquer the empire and become its governor. He set out in 1530 and after two unsuccessful attempts landed on the coast of Peru.

Pizarro found the empire in the midst of a civil war between Huascar, the rightful Sapa Inca, and Atahuallpa, his half-brother (see p. 323). The Europeans took advantage of the situation and, after Atahuallpa had Huascar killed, the Spanish executed Atahuallpa and set up the young Manco as ruler, although the Spanish had the real power. Pizarro and his men then seized the lands of the Incas, stole their treasures and forced the Indians into slavery.

THE PORTUGUESE IN BRAZIL Portuguese explorers landed on the coast of what is now Brazil in 1500, while they were looking for a new route to India. They claimed the land for Portugal, but at first very little was done about it as the country was not thought to have many resources other than some dye-woods. After a revolt of slaves on the African island of São Tomé in the 1570s, however, the Portuguese decided to move their sugar plantations from there to Brazil. This encouraged the slave trade and also made Brazil suddenly seem attractive to other European powers.

The silver mines at Potosi, Bolivia, where the Spaniards used local people as slaves to remove over 18,000 tonnes of silver ore. The mines were worked out in the seventeenth century.

AMERICA: THE PILGRIM FATHERS

While the Spanish and Portuguese journeyed to Central and South America, and to the southern part of North America, other Europeans started to explore the north-east coast. Most of them were looking for a possible northwest passage to Asia, and it was only when they failed to find one that they started thinking about colonization.

THE FOUNDATION OF VIRGINIA In 1583 Humphrey Gilbert claimed Newfoundland for England. When he was drowned in a storm, his half-brother, Sir Walter Raleigh (1552–1618) took up his idea of setting up colonies in America. He thought this would help to solve the problems of over-population and unemployment in England and also encourage trade between the two countries. Between 1584 and 1589, Raleigh sent out six expeditions to start a colony in a place he called Virginia at the suggestion of Queen Elizabeth I. These all failed, but in 1607 the Virginia Company was set up and the first successful colony was established at Jamestown. The company hoped to make quick profits through the discovery of gold mines, or from producing wine and silk. In this they were unsuccessful, but in 1612 one of the settlers started to grow tobacco and this led to prosperity for the colony.

THE ARRIVAL OF THE PILGRIM FATHERS The Pilgrim Fathers is the name given to the group of 102 Puritans who left England on the *Mayflower* in September 1620. They planned to go to Virginia, but their ship took them further north and they landed at Cape Cod in November. They decided to stay in that area and searched for a site to settle in. On 11 December they arrived at Plymouth, where they built huts and a meeting house. They elected John Carver as their first governor and befriended the local Indians.

During that first winter, however, nearly half the colony died as a result of the severe weather and a lack of

Early Settlement in North America

The first European colonies in north-east America were along the coast. Some settlers went there to make money, but many went because they were persecuted for their religious beliefs at home. These groups included Roman Catholics, as well as very strict Puritans like the Pilgrim Fathers. Many Puritans were very intolerant of people who did not share their beliefs. This led to people with less strict views setting up separate colonies.

food. The rest were only saved when the ship *Fortune* arrived with food and other necessities. The *Fortune* also brought more settlers and so the colony managed to survive.

EXPANSION Once the Pilgrim Fathers were settled in Plymouth, other Puritans decided to follow them. They were given a grant of land and formed themselves into the Massachusetts Bay Company. The first group left England in 1630 and by 1640 there were over 14,000 Puritans in Massachusetts. They were intolerant of non-Puritans, however, and this led to the founding of more liberal colonies such as Rhode Island.

Meanwhile, Lord Baltimore, a Catholic, was also granted some land, which he called Maryland, in North America. He encouraged his fellow Catholics to move there. Although they were few in number, they enjoyed the equal rights and religious freedom which they had been denied in England.

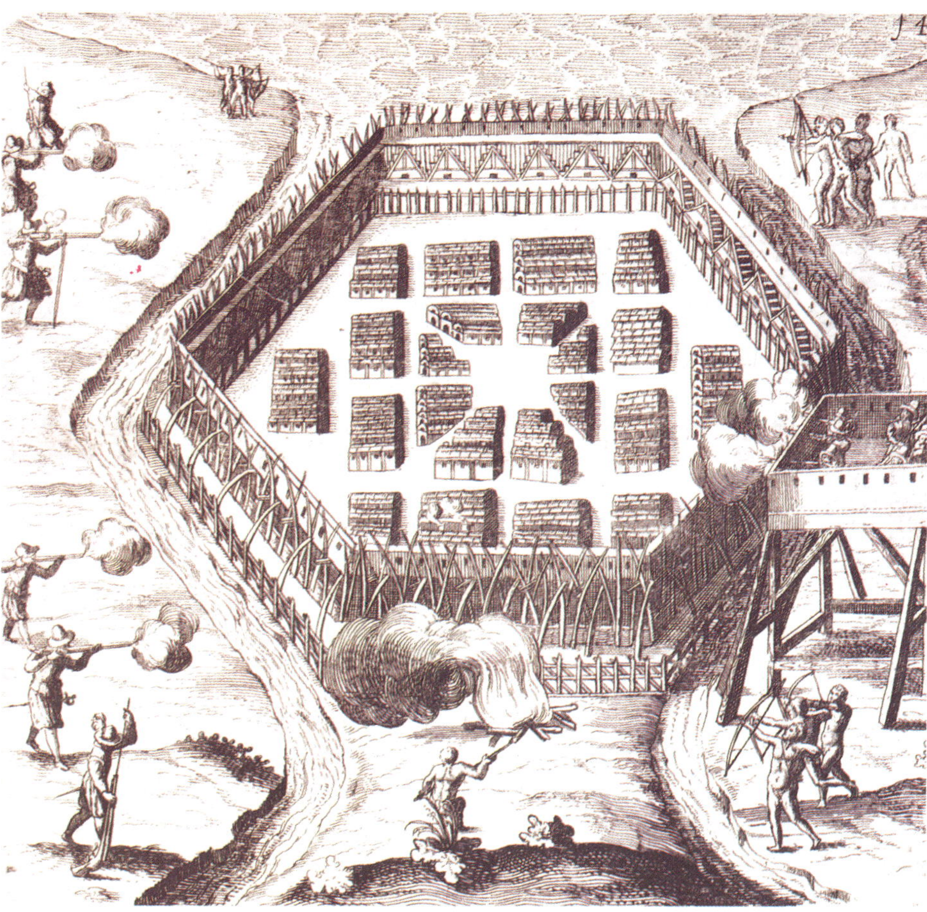

Above. Onandago Fort was set up in Quebec by Samuel de Champlain.

THE FRENCH SETTLEMENT IN CANADA A French navigator called Jacques Cartier (1494–1557) made three voyages to Canada between 1534 and 1541. On his second journey, he sailed up the St Lawrence River with the help of two Indians, while on the third he set out to look for a mythical place called Saguenay. This expedition was a failure, but it gave France a claim to land in Canada.

Little was done about this claim until 1608, when the explorer Samuel de Champlain (1567–1635) founded the town that was to become the city of Quebec and started to organize the fur trade between France and Canada. He also formed an alliance between France and the Huron and Algonquin Indians against the Iroquois Indians. Very few French people were tempted to go to Canada at this time and the number of European settlers in this area remained small until after 1650.

A reconstruction of one of the early colonies. When the settlers landed on the coast, they looked for a site with a good supply of fresh water. Then they cleared the land by cutting down the trees, to give them firewood and building material for their houses, barns and fences. The fences protected the houses and gardens from wild animals. Each settlement usually had a large building to use as a meeting house and centre for the community. This was often built inside a high fence, or stockade, to protect it against Indian attacks.

THE WEST INDIES

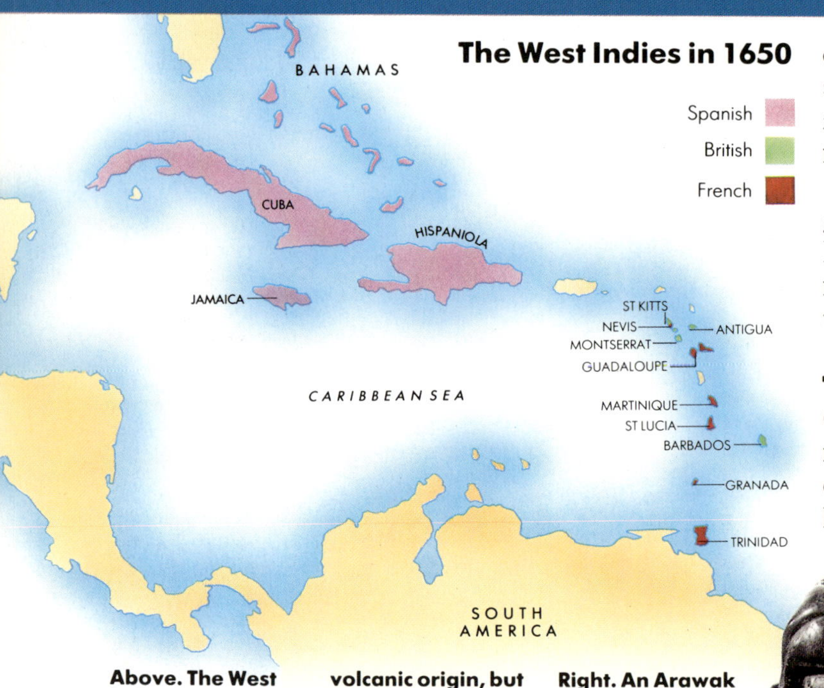

Above. The West Indies is a series of islands which stretches for over 2400 kilometres, from Florida to Venezuela. Most of the islands are of volcanic origin, but some are made largely of coral. The Spanish were the first to set up colonies there, followed by the English and French.

Right. An Arawak zemi, carved from wood, representing one of the spirits which were worshipped by the Arawaks before the Europeans arrived.

On 12 October 1492 Christopher Columbus sighted what came to be known as the New World. He thought it was Asia, but instead it was an island in the Bahamas which he named San Salvador. He claimed it for Spain and went on to visit Cuba and Hispaniola. On later journeys he and his crew became the first Europeans to sight Jamaica, Trinidad, Honduras and Costa Rica and, although these places were inhabited by people he called Indians, Columbus claimed them all for Spain.

THE ARAWAK INDIANS The first Indians Columbus saw when he arrived in the West Indies were the Arawaks. They were farmers whose main crops were maize (corn), cotton and root crops called yams and manioc. They also grew tobacco. The Arawaks lived in large villages of as many as 3000 people in 1000 houses. According to the Spanish, their society was divided into noblemen, commoners and slaves. Their religion was based on the worship of a number of spirits called 'zemis' and they made figures of these out of stone, wood and clay. Each person owned at least one zemi, which was kept in the house and had to be offered food.

The Arawaks were a peace-loving people. They had gone to live in the Greater Antilles when the Carib Indians had migrated from the mainland and driven them from their homes in the Lesser Antilles not long before the arrival of the Spanish.

THE CARIB INDIANS In contrast to the Arawaks, the Carib Indians' chief interest was war. They were expert navigators and went raiding over long distances in large, dug-out canoes. When they captured other people, they killed the men and ate their flesh, but kept the women as slave-wives. On the islands they lived in small, independent villages, but had no leaders except in times of war. They lived by growing plants such as manioc and by hunting a range of animals for food. The weapons that the Carib used included javelins, clubs and arrows tipped with poison.

THE SPANISH SETTLERS The first Europeans to colonize the West Indies were the Spanish. They settled down and lived as farmers on the larger islands, where they grew tobacco on small farms and used the native peoples of the area as slave labour. Because these people had never mixed with Europeans before, they had no resistance to the new diseases which the Spanish brought with them from Europe. By the middle of the sixteenth century so many Indians had died from diseases such as smallpox, and also from ill-treatment, that the Spanish settlers started to buy slaves from West Africa, who were made to work on their plantations.

OTHER EUROPEANS The Spanish were not the only Europeans to colonize islands in the West Indies. Thomas Warner, an Englishman, sighted the island of St Kitts in 1622 and by 1625 it had both an English

Left. This picture shows a sugar cane factory. The cane was cut, bundled up and taken to a press which was driven by a waterwheel. The press squeezed the juice out of the cane. The juice was then boiled in cauldrons until the water evaporated and left the sugar crystals behind.

Below. In the late sixteenth century, English sailors were still able to trade with some of the native people of the West Indies. A hundred years later, both the Arawaks and the Caribs had almost disappeared.

Right. Christopher Columbus visited Hispaniola in 1492 and claimed it for Spain. The native people tried to resist the Spanish, but they only had bows and arrows and spears against guns. By 1496 the Spanish had colonized Hispaniola and about 100,000 of its native population had died of disease, violence or starvation.

The Manioc Plant

Manioc was an important food crop in the West Indies. It had to be processed before it was eaten, as its roots were poisonous. The outer covering was peeled off and the rest was grated into a pulp. The juice was squeezed out and simmered, leaving a syrup which became the base for a stew. The remaining pulp was made into flour.

and a French settlement. From there the English went on to Nevis, Montserrat and Barbados, while the French went to Guadaloupe, Martinique and St Lucia. The Dutch claimed Curaçao, Aruba and St Eustatius, but these were mainly used as trading posts.

THE SLAVE TRADE The Europeans had hoped to find treasure in the West Indies. However, all they found were pearls and a small amount of gold. Then in the middle of the seventeenth century they began to grow sugar-cane in the islands. Large sugar plantations replaced the small tobacco farms and the slave trade began in earnest. Ships set out from Europe to West Africa carrying cargoes of beads and blankets. These were exchanged for slaves, who were in turn shipped to the West Indies. There the slaves were exchanged for sugar, which was taken back to be sold in Europe, before the ships went back to Africa for more slaves. The slaves were transported in the most primitive conditions. They were chained to the decks and they were so cramped that they could not stand up. Many died on the voyages to the West Indies.

Opening up the World

TIME CHART

AD	THE AMERICAS	INDIA, CHINA AND JAPAN	AFRICA	REST OF THE WORLD
1500	Cabral lands briefly in Brazil and claims it for Portugal		Cabral and his ships call at Mozambique and Malindi	
1517			The Ottomans conquer Egypt	
1520				Magellan sails around South America and into the Pacific Suleiman the Magnificent becomes Ottoman emperor
1522	Hernando Cortes defeats the Aztecs in Mexico			
1526		Babur founds the Mogul Dynasty in India		
1528			Askia Muham, the Songhai emperor, is deposed	
1532	Francisco Pizarro defeats the Incas in Peru			
1533				Ivan IV becomes Tsar of Russia
1535	The lands of the Aztecs, Maya and Toltecs become the Vice-Royalty of New Spain			
1543		Portuguese sailors are the first Europeans to visit Japan		
1562			The English sea-captain, John Hawkins, makes a slaving voyage to Sierra Leone.	
1571				The Spanish capture the Philippines The Ottomans are defeated at the Battle of Lepanto
1581				The Russian settlement of Siberia begins
1591			The Songhai Empire is invaded by the Moroccans	
1593			The Portuguese start to build Fort Jesus at Mombasa	
1600		The British East India Company is set up to trade with India		
1602		The Dutch East India Company is formed to trade in spices and other goods from the Far East		
1603		The start of the Tokugawa shogunate in Japan		
1605>1613				The Time of Troubles in Russia
1607	Jamestown is founded by the Virginia Company			
1608	Samuel Champlain founds Quebec			
1619				The Dutch found the colony of Batavia in Indonesia
1620	The Pilgrim Fathers sail from England to America			
1642				Abel Tasman sails to Tasmania and New Zealand
1644		The Ming Dynasty of China is defeated by the Manchus		Abel Tasman sails along the north coast of Australia

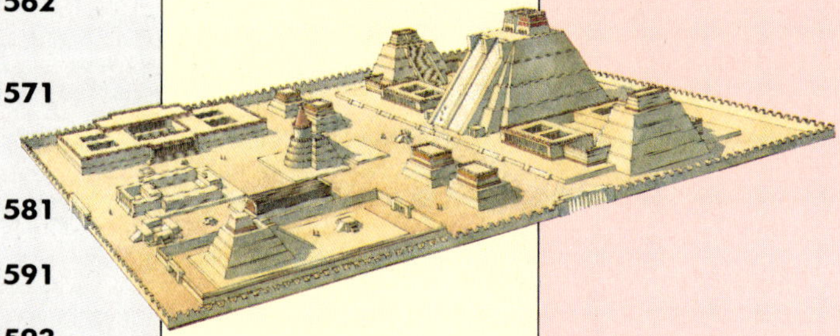

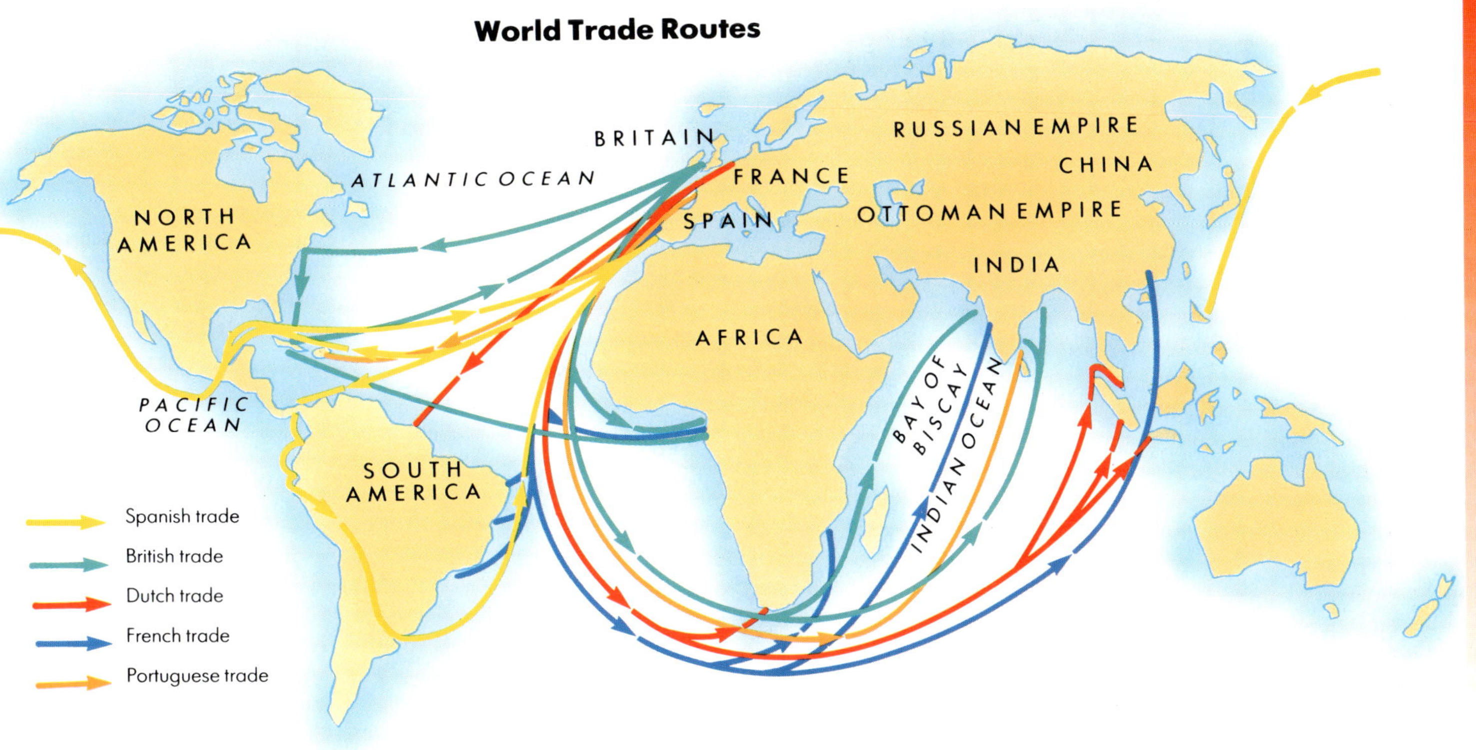

Changes in Europe

The European voyages of discovery in the fifteenth and sixteenth centuries were not the first journeys that people had made across the oceans. We know that the Vikings had sailed from Europe to America several hundred years earlier. Others had travelled across the Pacific Ocean on rafts from the western coast of South America. New Zealand had been reached by the Maoris from Pacific islands by the ninth century AD. The Aleuts and the Inuits had crossed the Bering Strait from Siberia to North America about 12,000 years ago. There are probably many other sea voyages that people made in the long-distant past about which we have no clues as yet.

However many voyages there may have been, none of them had the instant impact that the European voyages of discovery had in the sixteenth century.

OPENING UP THE WORLD Suddenly the world was opening up as it never had before. By 1650 there were sea routes to the Far East, to Africa and to the Americas, so that all sorts of goods could be brought to Europe. The voyages were risky and often ships were lost at sea, but the risk was worth it for the gains that were made. Trade was no longer confined largely to the Mediterranean Sea and around the coasts of lands like China, Japan, the East Indies, India and Africa. In 1650, trade was on the edge of becoming global. By 1800, it was global.

At first Spain and Portugal dominated the scene. Then they were challenged by the Netherlands, France and Britain—powerful countries with good ocean ports.

THE WORLD OUTSIDE EUROPE Meanwhile, life went on in the rest of the world as it had for thousands of years. China and India had their own high levels of civilization and culture, stretching back for hundreds of years. Many of the societies which we call 'primitive' lived in harmony with nature, as people did not see themselves as separate from nature. There is a story about an Australian Aboriginal who, in trying to explain this, sat beneath a tree and painted a line up his body and then continued to paint the line up the tree. He and the tree were part of the same life and energy of the world.

The Europeans, however, had little respect for any culture that was different to their own. As the search to expand trade and influence turned to colonial settlement, especially after 1800, the Europeans tried to impose their way of life on the peoples they dominated.

EUROPE IN 1650

A group of French Huguenot refugees landing at Dover in southern England in 1685. After the Edict of Nantes was passed as a law in France, Huguenots (Protestants) were not allowed to practise their religion there.

Europe was just emerging from nearly half a century of a war in which there had been huge casualties. Divisions over religion had been a major cause of the persecutions and fighting since the *Reformation* in the early sixteenth century (see p. 268). Catholics and Protestants had fought each other and had claimed that each was in the right and was following the one true religion of Christ. By the middle of the seventeenth century, many religious refugees had been forced to leave their countries and find a home elsewhere.

The *Huguenots*, for instance, were French Protestants who had been persecuted in Catholic France. Many moved to England and to the northern Netherlands. They were great weavers and in both countries they helped to bring about the rise of the cloth industries. Other Protestant refugees went to Switzerland and contributed to the growing craft industries there. The *Pilgrim Fathers* were a group of over 100 men and women who did not feel that England gave them enough freedom to practise their religion. They sailed to North America in 1620 to found a new colony on the east coast (see p. 326).

POPULATION GROWTH The restlessness was not only due to religious persecution. The population of Europe had risen dramatically in the sixteenth century and, by 1650, much of Europe no longer grew enough food to feed its population. This was a very serious situation. Spain had been a great power, but by the seventeenth century it was in decline. Part of the reason for this was that farming did not keep pace with the population. Spain was taking huge amounts of gold and silver from the mines in South America, but people cannot eat gold and silver. Spain had to use this money to buy food, such as wheat from Poland. It was becoming obvious that the gold and silver had not made Spain rich. Instead, these precious metals were passing through the country to pay for all the goods the Spanish needed, but did not grow or make.

CHANGES IN AGRICULTURE The growing population all over Europe was a key factor in everything that happened in the world between 1650 and 1800. For instance, the European explorers had brought the potato back from South America at the end of the sixteenth century and had found it grew well in Europe. If you plant a field with potatoes, you can feed four times the number of people than if you plant the field with wheat. The potato, together with huge imports of wheat from Poland, helped to feed the population of Europe, and encouraged it to grow.

Apart from new foods, new ways of farming to grow more food were also needed. This led to the Agricultural Revolution. The need to make things to sell for money that would buy food was a factor in the coming Industrial Revolution. Iron ore was found in places like Britain, so people there could make machines of iron to sell to other places and then use the money to buy food.

THE URGE TO EXPAND If this was all that was needed, Europe might have remained trading within its own boundaries. But the explorers had already shown that there was a world outside. They had shown that it was possible to sail anywhere. They had shown that marvellous foods, cloth, porcelain and jewels could be brought back to Europe to make life better and more interesting for those Europeans rich enough to pay for them. The prospect was irresistible.

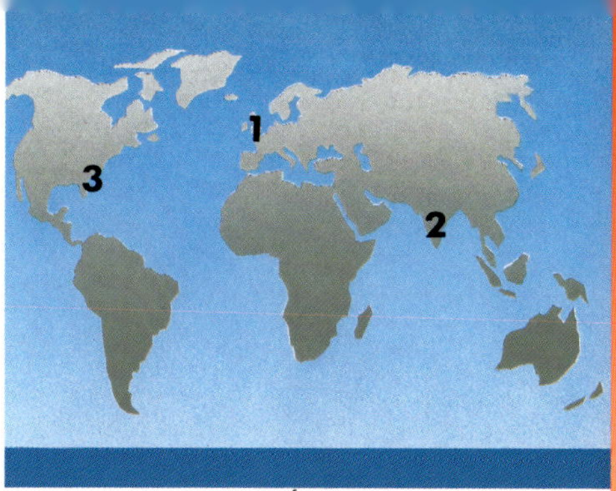

European Expansion 1500–1775

1500

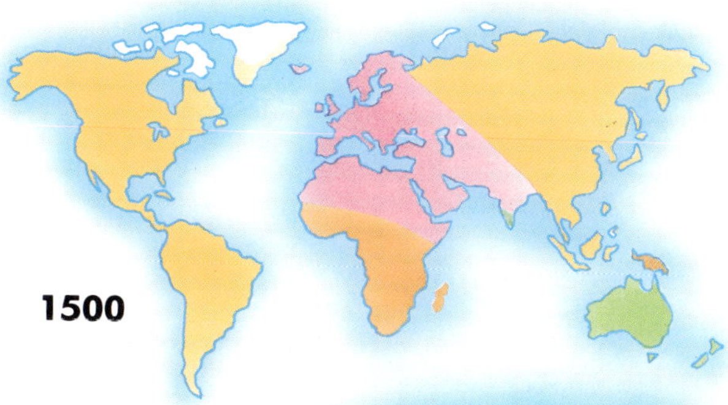

1775

Asiatic/Indian
Caucasian
Black-Australian
Black-African

NORTH AMERICA
SOUTH AMERICA
EUROPE
AFRICA
ASIA
AUSTRALIA

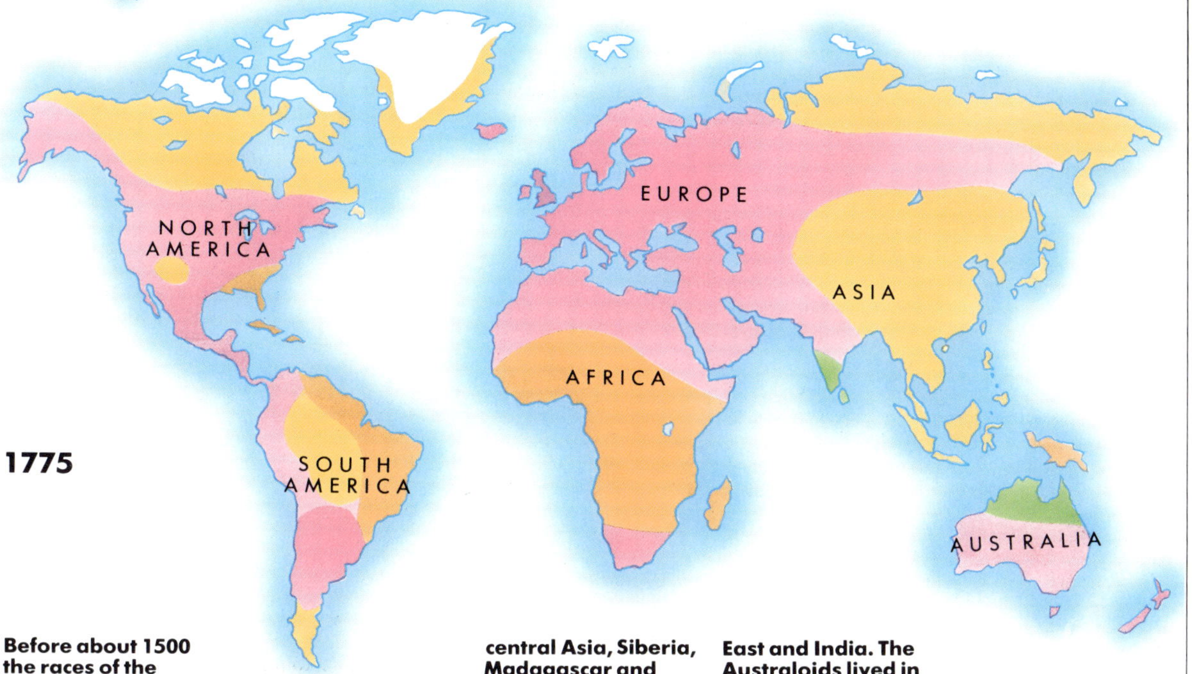

Before about 1500 the races of the world were largely separate, living in their own areas. The Negroids were mostly in Africa, south of the Sahara Desert. The Mongoloids were in central Asia, Siberia, Madagascar and the Americas. The Caucasoids were in Europe, North Africa, the Middle East and India. The Australoids lived in Australia and India.

By 1775 the races were spreading around the world.

World Population Figures

In AD 1 the world's population was about 300 million. By AD 1650 it had reached 600 million and by 1800 it was 1000 million. At first the population level grew slowly—between AD 1000 and 1750 it rose by about one tenth of 1 per cent a year. Many babies were born, but only about half of them lived to the age of five. Famines and epidemics kept the rate of growth very slow.

From AD 1750 the world's population grew rapidly. This was particularly so in Europe and North America. The huge rises in population, however, came after 1800.

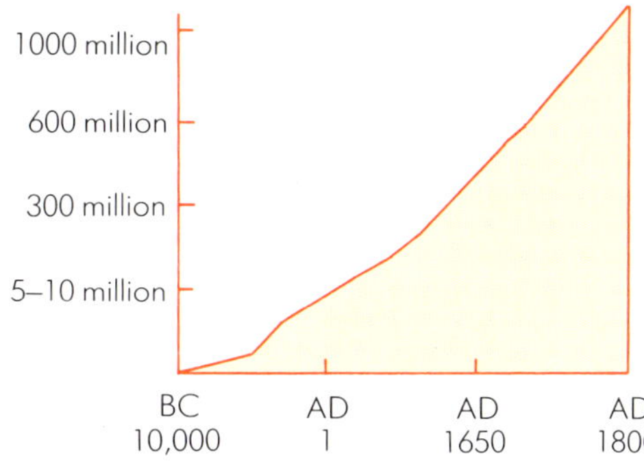

Not only did numbers rise but the races of the world became more mixed after 1650. Europeans moved into the Americas and Australia. Africans moved to the Americas. Chinese, Indians and Russians moved to new areas as well.

Eastern Imports

European ships brought back spices from the East, such as nutmeg and pepper, to flavour the dull, bland (and sometimes not very fresh) winter foods of Europe. Fine porcelain came from China, along with silk that was much softer to wear than rough woollen cloth. Jars like this one were so precious that they often had silver rims to prevent chipping.

1 In 1642 civil war broke out between King Charles I and Parliament in Britain. In 1645, Parliament's New Model Army crushed the king's forces at the Battle of Naseby. Charles escaped to Scotland but was 'sold' to Parliament for £400,000. In 1649 he was executed and England was declared a Commonwealth. In 1651 Cromwell, leading the Parliamentary forces, defeated the new king, Charles II, at Worcester. Charles fled to France. In 1660 he was invited back to England to be king again. This was known as the Restoration.

2 In 1669 the Moghul Emperor Aurangzeb banned the Hindu religion and ordered all the non-Islamic schools and temples to be destroyed. Because of this there was more and more unrest in his empire. This led to the break-up of the Moghul Empire in 1707.

3 The Europeans were exploring and settling North America at this time. In 1664 the British gave the name New York to the town then called New Amsterdam. In 1673 French explorers reached the headwaters of the Mississippi River, and eight years later a Frenchman called La Salle explored the whole length of the Mississippi River. In 1683, the first German immigrants settled in America.

DIVISIONS OF SOCIETY IN EUROPE

Left. Sir Roger de Coverly, a rich landowner in England, going to church. The people around are tenants farming land on his estates. They are dressed in their best clothes and show great respect to him.

Above. A well dressed Russian noble man and a serf.

In 1650, Europe was still in many ways a *feudal* society. Nobles no longer held land from their king or queen in return for raising an army of knights and going to fight for them; instead they now owned their land themselves. But in most other ways the nobles behaved in a feudal way. From Russia to Spain, they expected to be the close advisers of their king or queen. They expected the highest positions in governments and in the army. In some countries, like France, only members of the nobility were allowed the highest jobs. In most countries the nobles lived for most of the year on their estates. Some were good managers, but they all expected their peasants to work their land in a way that seems like slavery to us.

SERFDOM The situation varied across Europe, and there was a general difference between eastern and western Europe. In eastern Europe the *serfs*, who had to work on the land, had become less free. From 1593, in Russia, serfs were no longer allowed the two weeks a year of free movement that they had previously been

Feudalism

Up to the Middle Ages, European nobles had held their land from the king. The king owned all the land of a country (often because he had conquered it in war), but he could not farm it and run it all alone. He would allow his friends and fighting companions to farm and run large areas of land for him. They did not own the land. They held it in return for swearing loyalty to the king and serving him in the army or government. This was called feudalism.

Protestant Europe in 1650

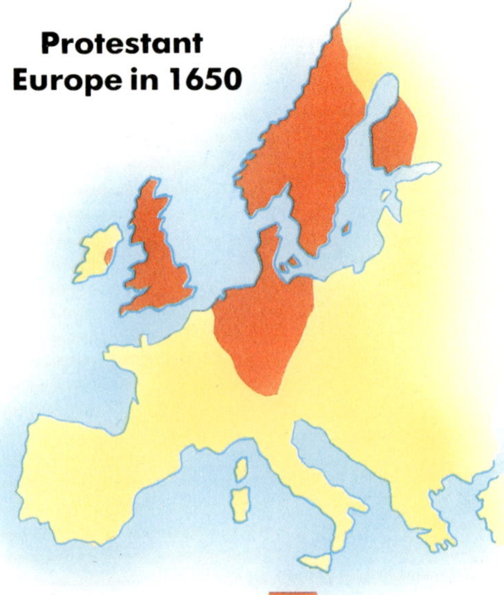

By 1550 nearly 40% of the population of Europe belonged to some sort of Protestant religion. By 1650 this figure had fallen to about 20%. The two largest countries that were won back to Catholicism were France and Poland.

Monarchs, Parliament and Society

Kings and queens (left), were still very powerful in most of Europe, particularly in France, Prussia, Austria and Russia.

The Catholic and Protestant Churches relied on the monarch and Parliament for support.

In some countries, particularly Britain and the Netherlands, Parliament's power was growing.

Merchants and bankers became more important as trade developed. They usually supported Parliament.

Well-established landowners often supported the monarch, while recent landowners usually did not.

The influential Members of Parliament were lawyers, because they were skilled in discussions.

The army often supported Parliament. During the English Civil War (1642–1649) Cromwell led an army against the king.

The poorest people in society were shut out from power. Those in the countryside had to work for the landowners, while those in the towns worked for the merchants, bankers, lawyers and so on.

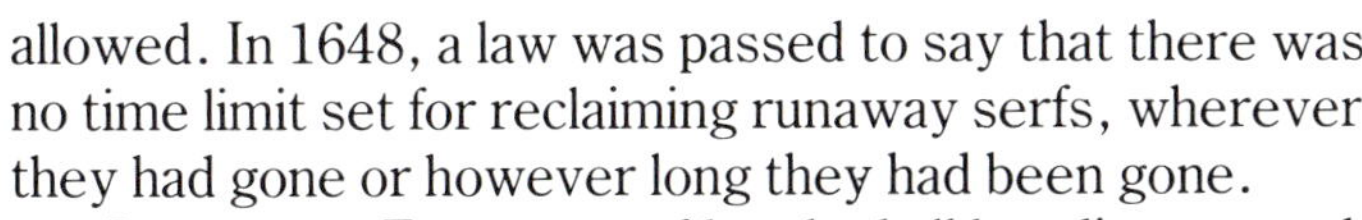

Above. A painting of the inside of a farmhouse by Jan Brueghel (1568–1625). How many people and animals are in the kitchen? How many activities are going on?

Left. Cardinal Richelieu (1585–1642) was a bishop by the time he was 21. At 39 he was the chief minister of the royal household and was virtually the ruler of France. He made the king's government very strong.

allowed. In 1648, a law was passed to say that there was no time limit set for reclaiming runaway serfs, wherever they had gone or however long they had been gone.

In western Europe, serfdom had all but disappeared. This did not mean that peasants working on the land in these countries were better off. In France they were bowed down with taxes. In the German states, a great deal of land had been ruined during the fighting in the Thirty Years' War (see p. 280), which had ended in 1648. However poor the peasants, the nobles made sure they had plenty of money with which to build their houses, hunt and dress well.

THE CLERGY The clergy were another large section of society in seventeenth and eighteenth century Europe. Whether Catholic or Protestant, bishops and lesser clergymen represented the Church in their countries. The clergy were meant to look after the spiritual needs of all the people. In return, the people were expected to pay a tithe (tenth) of their income to support the clergyman who lived locally. This was yet one more burden on the poor. It was one that became more unpopular as people began to resent the amount of land the Church owned and the fact that many clergy did not do their jobs very well. In France, cardinals, such as Richelieu in the seventeenth century, were also politicians. In Germany, some bishops lived like princes. In England, by the eighteenth century, some clergymen were going fox-hunting and living the life of idle gentlemen.

THE THIRD ESTATE The nobles and clergy were known during this period as the *First and Second Estates*. The *Third Estate* was the commoners. This included merchants, lawyers, farmers and so on—in fact, everyone who was not noble or in the Church.

These were the divisions that existed in most of Europe in 1650. They were not found in Switzerland or in the new Dutch Republic. Neither of these countries had a king or a nobility. On the whole the ordinary people there—the Third Estate—were much freer to take part in the government of the country.

FARMING THE LAND

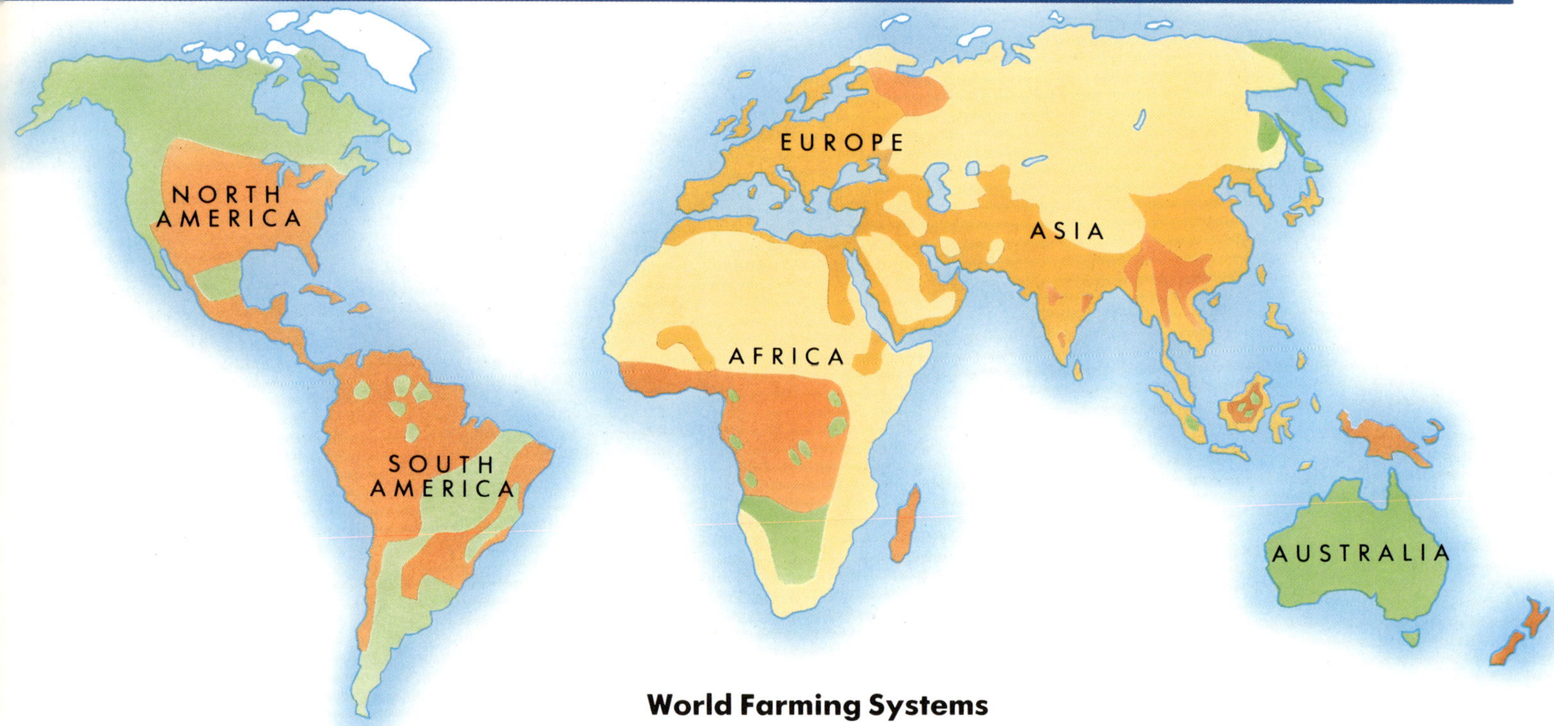

World Farming Systems

Most people in the world at this time spent their lives looking for or producing their own food, as there was little industry. The map above shows the different types of farming in different parts of the world.

The majority of people in Europe lived off the land. In 1650, over three-quarters of the world's land surface was occupied by *hunter-gatherers* or by *herdsmen*. Only about one-quarter of the land was under the plough. However, ploughing and farming land produced far more food than the other ways of life did. This one-quarter of the world's land surface was probably producing enough food for three-quarters of the world's population.

FARMING AREAS Most of the land being ploughed and farmed was located in an area running from China, through India, to the Middle East and Europe. A small part of Russia and North Africa was also included in this farming land.

Nowadays, in developed countries, we can import food from other countries and we can preserve food by many methods, such as refrigeration. This means that what we eat does not vary a great deal throughout the year. Nor do we worry if crops such as wheat or oranges fail in one area because of bad weather, as we can always buy these foods from another area. However, this was not so in 1650, when most people in the world had to produce their food themselves. In good years there would be a little over to sell to the small numbers of people who lived in towns.

TYPES OF FARM In Europe, most farmers had small areas of land, each averaging between two and 10 hectares. Sometimes this land was not all in one place, but was scattered in small strips of land around the village. Usually only an orchard or vegetable garden was right next to the farmer's small cottage. Each farmer and family might produce about 20 per cent more than they ate, kept for seed for next year or used to make clothes. The rest was sold at local markets.

What crops were grown and what animals were kept depended on the climate. In northwest Europe, wheat, barley, oats, rye, milk, cheese, butter, eggs and timber were important. Further south, some wheat and other grains like barley, millet and sorghum were grown, together with fruits, olives, wine, rice and sugar.

THE YEARLY PATTERN Whatever the crops, the work of all farmers, from Scotland to China, depended on the seasons and the climate. In Europe, in spring, the

Farming in North America

By 1690 farming settlements were scattered along the eastern coast of North America.

At first the settlers brought their tools, animals and seed for growing crops with them from Europe. But they found the land was not very fertile and the seeds that were suitable for the short north European summers did not grow well in North America. They adapted their crops and learned from the native Amerindians to grow crops such as maize, soya beans, pumpkins and sunflowers. These foods were new to the settlers, as they did not grow in Europe.

Below. Countrywomen on their way to market.

Farmers' wives traditionally looked after the poultry and cows. Often they took the eggs, hens, butter or cheese to market in the local town and kept the profits they made as their own money.

Below. Tools of the period as shown in an illustrated book.

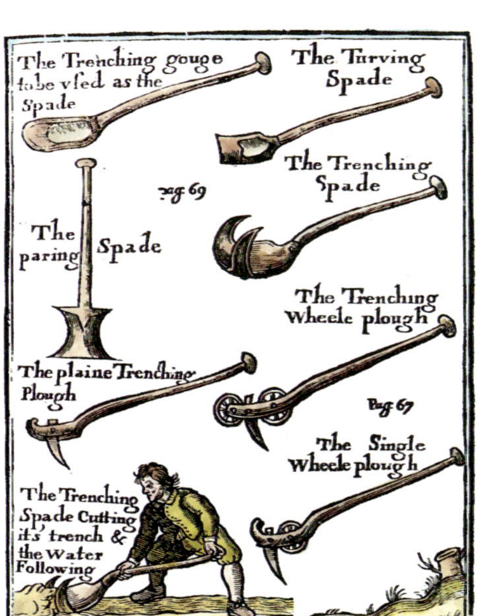

A countrywoman carrying birds to market. Before the days of refrigerators, many animals were sold live to keep them fresh.

farmers ploughed and sowed seeds and turned their animals out to graze in the fields. In summer, they weeded, cut the hay and tended the animals. Early autumn was the busiest time, because crops had to be harvested. Wheat had to be cut, stacked and stored. In the south, grapes were picked, crushed and made into wine. Fruit was picked and preserved.

Lastly, in the cold north of Europe, winter meant that the grass stopped growing. Therefore, only enough animals were kept through the winter to start breeding from when spring came. Slaughtering and salting down the meat was the last autumn ritual of the harvest. There was a good feast and then, all over north Europe, men and women settled down to a quiet winter, keeping warm and trying to make the food last till spring. The cows that had been saved had to be fed on hay (dried grass). When that ran out, the children gathered holly for them to eat. Sometimes in the spring the cows and sheep were so weak they had to be carried to the fields.

In the vast areas of northern China, a similar yearly routine went on. In hotter lands, the routine varied according to the rainy season rather than the cold.

Everywhere in the farming world, if the crops failed hundreds of thousands of people starved.

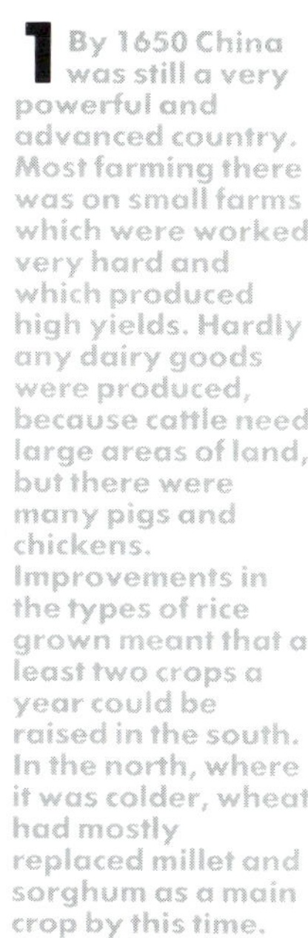

1 By 1650 China was still a very powerful and advanced country. Most farming there was on small farms which were worked very hard and which produced high yields. Hardly any dairy goods were produced, because cattle need large areas of land, but there were many pigs and chickens. Improvements in the types of rice grown meant that at least two crops a year could be raised in the south. In the north, where it was colder, wheat had mostly replaced millet and sorghum as a main crop by this time.

2 In India, like China, most farmers grew enough to feed themselves, with some surpluses to use for trade. Rice was grown in the south and wheat in the north. As with China, spices such as pepper and ginger were grown for export. India was also a source of sugar at this time; later, western Europe started to get sugar from plantations in the West Indies and a little from beet grown in Europe.

3 In Australia, the Aboriginals were almost entirely hunter-gatherers, as they had been for thousands of years. Aboriginals near the coast gathered shellfish and fished in the rivers and sea. Further inland they ate a great variety of plants and animals.

THE AGRICULTURAL REVOLUTION

Two main changes took place in farming in Europe between 1650 and 1800. One was that new crops were grown. Most of these came from the Americas and they included maize and potatoes, which began to be widely grown in Europe and even reached as far as China. These new crops meant that more people could be fed.

WAYS OF FARMING The second change, in ways of farming, was called the Agricultural Revolution. Changes made during this period made farming more efficient, so that more food could be grown to feed the increasing population.

The Dutch started *reclaiming land* from lakes and from the sea, using windmills to drive pumps to drain the water away. By 1715, they had reclaimed 147,531 hectares. The British used the Dutch methods to drain many square kilometres of land in eastern England, which became rich farmland.

Dutch Land Reclamation

NORTH SEA
ZUDERZEE
AMSTERDAM
NETHERLANDS

land reclaimed before 1600

land reclaimed between 1600 and 1800

Left. Map showing how the Dutch reclaimed land that was below sea level. They used windmills to pump the water from the low-lying land into canals.

Windmills

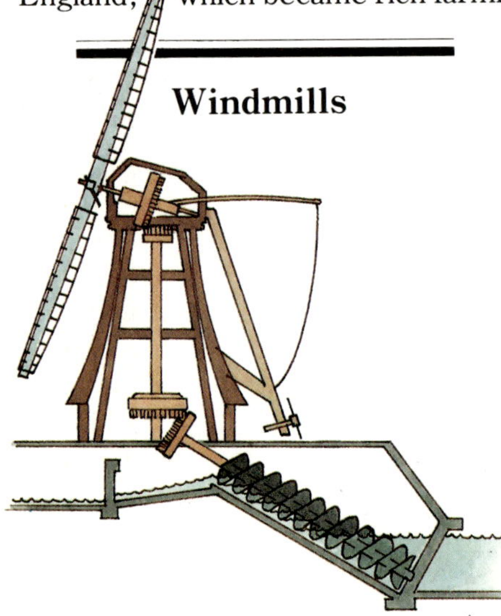

A windmill has sails or blades mounted on arms connected to machinery inside. The machinery could be big circular stones to grind corn, or an Archimedes screw (as shown in the picture) for raising water. The Dutch drained the land that lay below sea level in this way. The sails had to face the wind, so the whole windmill (or the top of it, to which the sails were attached) had to be moved round when the wind direction changed. Until 1750 this was done by hand. Then a fantail was invented which helped 'blow' it round.

But these methods were expensive in manpower and money, so every centimetre of reclaimed land had to be used. The old way of farming was to leave one field *fallow* (resting) every third year, so that it would not become drained of nourishment. To the land-hungry Dutch this was a waste of land. They worked out a system of *crop rotation*, growing a different type of crop on the same field each year. Each crop took different chemicals and minerals from the soil.

Because of crop rotation, the amount of land that could be farmed increased by one-third—a large jump. However, these methods were slow to spread, although Belgium copied the Dutch, and wealthy farmers in Britain took up the new ideas with enthusiasm.

MACHINERY New machines for cultivating the land were invented in the eighteenth century. One of these was Jethro Tull's seed drill. Previously, three-quarters of the seed might be lost when it was thrown on to the bare field, as the wind blew some away, or some fell on stony ground where it could not grow. The seed drill dug a hole, the seed trickled in and then the hole was covered with earth.

Once seeds were sown in rows it was also easier to weed between them. Another new machine was a horse hoe, which used a horse to pull several hoes, so that several rows of seeds could be weeded at once.

New farming magazines appeared. Farmers read them and learnt about new methods of manuring and caring for their land. Arthur Young wrote in 1768:

'Around Bridgend there are many farms which consist of very light land, and yet no turnips are sown. One farmer from England, sowed two acres, and was at great pains to hoe them well; the neighbours ridiculed him and really thought him mad; but were surprised to see what a great crop he gained.'

IMPROVEMENTS IN ANIMAL BREEDING Another great improvement was in animal breeding. Robert Bakewell, who was born at Dishley in Leicestershire in 1725, was just one of many pioneers of new methods in this area during the eighteenth century. In 1700, the average British cow weighed about 170 kilograms. By breeding the biggest, fattest cows with the biggest, fattest bulls, the weight of the average cow had reached 360 kilograms by 1800.

Thus, despite its rising population, Europe could be fed. By 1700, the Netherlands was exporting 90 per cent of its cheese. Denmark sent 80,000 cattle a year to Germany. By 1750, about 17 per cent of Britain's exports were food. The changes in farming in northwest Europe were paying off.

Left. Jethro Tull's seed drill. Notice the hoppers (boxes) that held the seed. Rakes covered the seed and also sowed it in rows, making it easier to weed between crops. Crop rotation meant sowing a different crop in a field each year. In the first year wheat might be grown; the second year, clover; the third year, barley; and the fourth year, turnips. Each crop took different chemicals from the soil. Some crops like legumes (peas, beans, etc.) put nitrates back into the soil.

Above right. A Lincolnshire bull painted by George Stubbs. Many rich farmers at this time commissioned artists to paint their prize animals. The artists always painted them as large and fat as possible to please their owners.

Key Dates for Agricultural Developments

end 1600s	Four-course rotation established in Norfolk Drainage of fens in England Enclosure of farmland in Germany
early 1700s	Rotherham plough (like modern plough) first used in Netherlands and Britain Jethro Tull invents seed drill and horse hoe in Britain
1760–1820	Peak time of enclosure of open land in England
1770–1790	First machines introduced for chopping turnips, winnowing and threshing
1783	First factory to make ploughs set up in England

TOWN LIFE IN THE SEVENTEENTH CENTURY

Because the population of the world rose in the sixteenth century, more and more people lived in towns. The Chinese had long had a flourishing town life, with cities of over a million people. By 1650, cities in Europe were beginning to grow large too.

DISEASE One problem with large towns was disease, because people lived close together. There were always diseases like typhoid and others caught from dirty water supplies. For instance, in London, all the sewage ran out into rivers such as the Fleet and the Tyburn, which then joined up with the River Thames. Many Londoners went to the Thames for their drinking water and could catch diseases from the sewage in it.

Another disease that ravaged Europe for several hundred years was the *plague*, which last appeared in Britain in 1665. The Bill of Mortality for London in that year lists 68,596 dead of the plague. The usual death toll was about 25,000 a year.

THE GREAT FIRE Fire was another large problem in towns. In 1666 came the Great Fire of London. After a long, dry summer, a baker's oven caught light one night in September and a strong wind soon had the fire raging through the city. The streets were narrow and the buildings were made of wood. In a few days over half the city of London, including St Paul's Cathedral, was burnt to the ground. People searched among the ashes for lost belongings, a fortnight after the fire had gone out, the cinders still burned the soles of their shoes. Medieval and Tudor London had gone.

THE NEW LONDON The new city was to be built of brick and stone. Many people made grand plans for wide, straight roads, but in the end people clung to the plots of land they owned, so the new houses occupied the same spaces as the old. This meant the streets of London were as narrow as ever.

PARIS London was not the only European city to suffer plague, fires and population growth. Paris, with a population of 400,000, was the largest city in Europe in the seventeenth century, partly because successive kings encouraged rebuilding. For instance, the wooden bridges of Paris were rebuilt in stone. The kings leased plots of land to individuals on condition that the person built according to an agreed plan.

Above. A painting of the Great Fire of London in 1666. The old St Paul's Cathedral is in the centre.

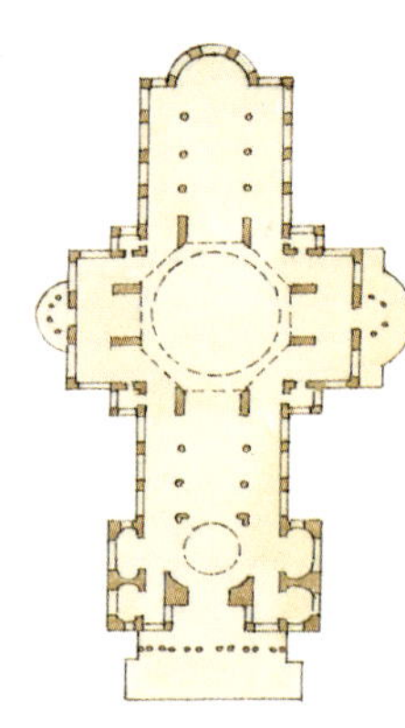

In this way they tried to plan the way in which Paris grew. There were new designs available for houses.

A TOWN HOUSE A town house might be four storeys high. A rich husband and wife each had a separate set of rooms, consisting of a reception room and a bedroom. One or two small rooms, called closets, opened out from the bedroom. These could be dressing rooms, studies or primitive lavatories. Separate bathrooms were rare before 1670. A large tub-like bath would be brought into the bedroom and placed before the fire. Then hot water was carried up the stairs by servants to fill the bath.

Other rooms in the house included a kitchen, dining room and general reception rooms. The senior servants and children slept on the top floors, while the lesser servants slept in the attics, or over the stables which were attached to the house.

The Growth of Towns 1500–1700

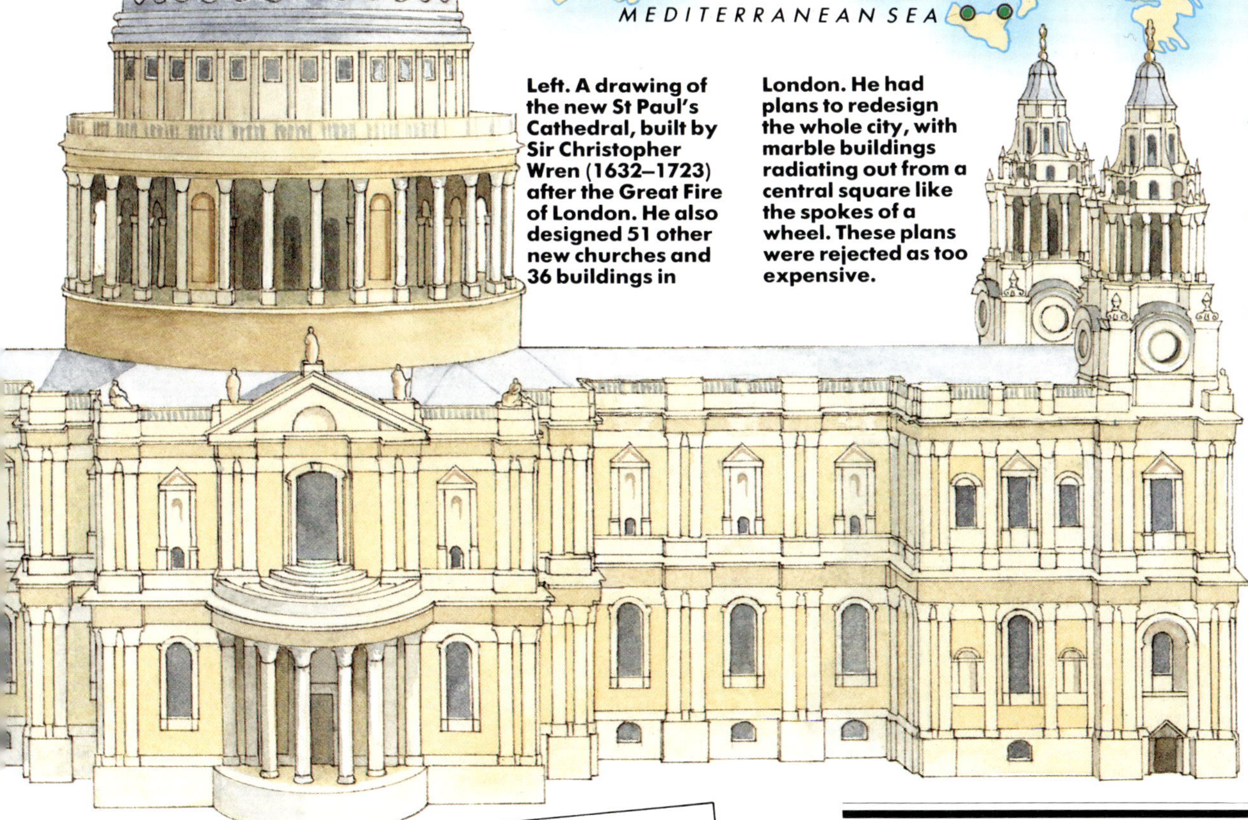

Left. A drawing of the new St Paul's Cathedral, built by Sir Christopher Wren (1632–1723) after the Great Fire of London. He also designed 51 other new churches and 36 buildings in London. He had plans to redesign the whole city, with marble buildings radiating out from a central square like the spokes of a wheel. These plans were rejected as too expensive.

Towns of more than 30,000 people throughout the period

Towns of more than 30,000 people in the seventeenth century

Towns of more than 30,000 people in the eighteenth century

Above. A map of Europe in the eighteenth century, showing centres of trade and industry. Italy and Spain were already less important than they had been. Britain, the Netherlands, France and Sweden were becoming more developed.

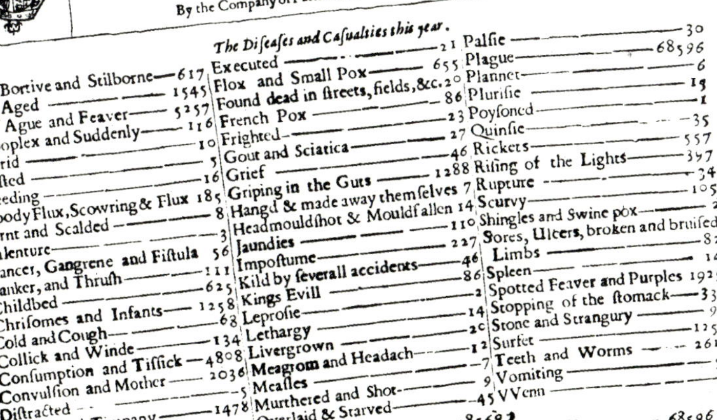

A generall Bill for this present year, ending the 19 of *December* 1665. according to the Report made to the KINGS most Excellent Majesty.
By the Company of Parish Clerks of *London*, &c.

The Diseases and Casualties this year.

Bortive and Stilborne—617
Aged—1545
Ague and Feaver—5257
poplex and Suddenly—116
drid—10
asted—5
eeding—16
loody Flux, Scowring & Flux 185
urnt and Scalded—8
Calenture—3
Cancer, Gangrene and Fistula 56
Canker, and Thrush—111
Childbed—625
Chrisomes and Infants—1258
Cold and Cough—68
Collick and Winde—134
Consumption and Tissick—4808
Convulsion and Mother—2036
Distracted—5
Dropsie and Timpany—1478
Drowned—50

Executed—21
Flox and Small Pox—655
Found dead in streets, fields, &c. 20
French Pox—86
Frighted—23
Gout and Sciatica—27
Grief—46
Griping in the Guts—1288
Hangd & made away themselves 7
Headmouldshot & Mouldfallen 14
Jaundies—110
Impostume—227
Kild by severall accidents—46
Kings Evill—86
Leprosie—2
Lethargy—14
Livergrown—20
Meagrom and Headach—12
Measles—7
Murthered and Shot—9
Overlaid & Starved—45

Palsie—30
Plague—68596
Plannet—6
Plurisie—15
Poysoned—1
Quinsie—35
Rickets—557
Rising of the Lights—397
Rupture—34
Scurvy—105
Shingles and Swine pox—2
Sores, Ulcers, broken and bruised Limbs—82
Spleen—14
Spotted Feaver and Purples 1929
Stopping of the stomack—332
Stone and Strangury—98
Surfet—1251
Teeth and Worms—2614
Vomiting—51
Wenn—8

Christned { Males—5114, Females—4853, In all—9967 }
Buried { Males—48569, Females—48737, In all—97306 } Of the Plague—68596

Increased in the Burials in the 130 Parishes and at the Pest-house this year—79009
the 130 Parishes and at the Pest-house this year—68590

Left. The Bill of Mortality for London in 1665. What did most people die of?

Deadly Diseases

People in Europe, Asia and Africa had had contact with each other for thousands of years. The populations had developed some immunity to the many different diseases that spread from one area to another, even in densely populated towns. However, people in America, Australia and the Pacific Islands had not met the Old World illnesses.

The Amerindian population of Mexico may have been about 30 million before the European conquest in the mid-sixteenth century. Within 100 years it was 3 million. Nine out of every 10 Amerindians had died. Many were deliberately killed, but many more died of Old World diseases such as smallpox, measles, bubonic plague, influenza, tuberculosis, malaria and yellow fever.

TOWN LIFE IN THE EIGHTEENTH CENTURY

Below. The main thoroughfares in Amsterdam were canals. There were roads lined by trees on both sides of each canal. The gables at the top of the houses were very elaborate. A person could change the style of a house by rebuilding its gables to keep up with the fashion.

Left. Amsterdam was built on peaty soil. This ground had supported the wooden houses of the Middle Ages. However, the Dutch in the seventeenth century wanted to build stone houses that lasted longer. They had to be supported by piles driven down about 10 metres to reach firm, sandy sub-soil.

By the eighteenth century the nobles were not the only people who could afford town houses. Increasingly, merchants who were making money from the growing world trade could also afford fine houses in the towns.

AMSTERDAM One of the greatest centres of this trade was Amsterdam. The Dutch were quite a new nation, who had broken away from Spain in 1579 to become an independent Protestant country, although Spain did not recognize their independence till 1648. Because their land had few natural resources, the Dutch had relied on trade for their livelihood for a long time. They were hardworking and ingenious, and were excellent ship-builders and merchants. By 1700, they were the richest people in Europe. Merchants of the Dutch East India Company imported such luxuries as silk, porcelain, tea, spices and sunshades from the Far East.

HOUSES IN AMSTERDAM The rich Dutch merchants wanted good brick or stone houses like the rich

Left. The inside of a Dutch merchant's house. Goods could be stored in the cellar or winched up to the roof. In this house logs and peat for fires are stored in one top room and the laundry is done in the other. (Other families might have used the rooms as extra bedrooms.) Below is a reception room and a bedroom. On the ground floor is the kitchen with a peat fire. The high-ceilinged room next to it was often the merchant's office. This one has been split into lower and upper rooms.

Above. An engraving by William Hogarth (1697–1764). He specialized in pictures which tell a story. This one is called 'Gin Lane'. It tells of the horrors of gin-drinking. Gin shops advertised that you could be 'Drunk for a penny, dead drunk for two pence; straw to lie in, free'. Gin-drinking caused most problems in London between about 1700 and 1750. Then the government put a tax on it and the greater expense meant less gin was drunk. What signs in the picture show that Hogarth thought gin-drinking was dangerous?

Dress Styles

The dresses of rich women were made of silk and lace. For most of this period they were worn over hoops of various widths and shapes.

Wigs were very popular for both men and women. There were many different sorts—full-bottomed wigs, bagwigs, Ramillies wigs (with a long plait and black ribbons), bob wigs and tall, elaborate, individually styled wigs for women. These styles could be very complicated and were sometimes kept in place for weeks, causing itching scalps.

Wig powder was first used in 1703 and white was the most fashionable colour. At the height of the powdered wig fashion (1760–1776), blue, violet and dove-pink powders were also used.

everywhere in Europe, but there was a problem. Amsterdam is built on a peaty marsh. The medieval wooden houses were light, while the new brick houses had to be built on piles driven 10 metres deep, down to the hard sub-soil. The foundations were often as expensive as the house, but the Dutch were not put off by this. They built rows of tall, brick houses along the canals, which were the roads of Amsterdam.

Often the front room of the town house was a shop or office. The merchant stored goods in the cellar, or had them winched up to the attic (which was drier). Dutch housewives were very house-proud. The mistress of the house usually did the housework and shopping herself, with the help of a maid. There were fewer servants in the Netherlands than anywhere else in Europe.

VENICE The other city of Europe that was built around a network of canals was Venice. Although it had once been a powerful trading centre, by the eighteenth century Venice was a beautiful but declining city. Stuck in a corner of the Mediterranean, it was not in a good position to capture the new trade with the Americas, Africa and the Far East.

LONDON Because it was in an ideal position for trading, London grew rich in the eighteenth century as Britain's trading trebled between 1700 and 1775. People made fortunes in such trades as sugar and tea, and merchants used their wealth to build fine town houses on new land outside the old city of London.

ENTERTAINMENTS In France, the German states and Italy, the nobles dominated the social scene. In Britain, rich merchants and nobles mixed together more often.

The rich enjoyed dancing, music and gambling. There were a number of gentlemen's clubs where you could gamble as much as 50 guineas on each throw of the dice. (A guinea was £1.05.) Balls and assemblies were popular for dancing, and rich parents used these opportunities to choose husbands for their daughters. London and Bath were full of rich young ladies during the season (April to July) known as the Marriage Market.

THE ABSOLUTE MONARCHS OF FRANCE AND PRUSSIA

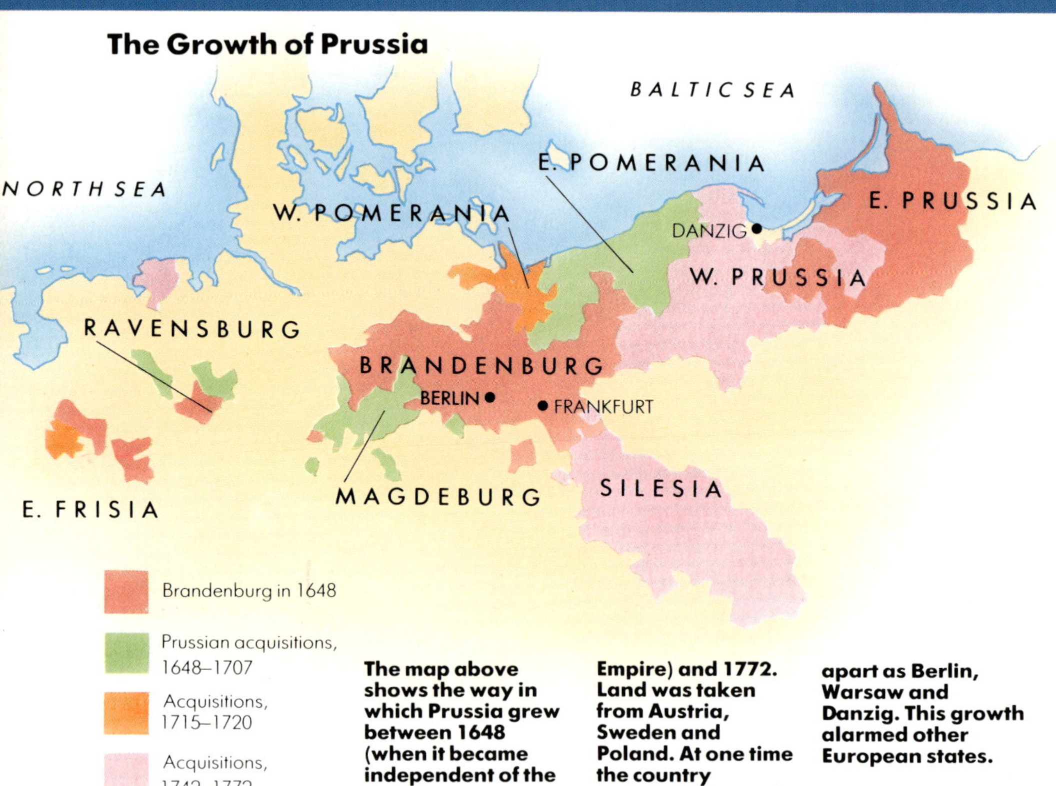

The map above shows the way in which Prussia grew between 1648 (when it became independent of the Holy Roman Empire) and 1772. Land was taken from Austria, Sweden and Poland. At one time the country included cities as far apart as Berlin, Warsaw and Danzig. This growth alarmed other European states.

By 1650, Europe was a continent of emerging *nation states*. Each one was competing for power and land. During this period a series of *absolute rulers* appeared in many European states. Absolute rulers were those who held all the power for themselves, instead of sharing it with other groups within the state, such as the nobility.

LOUIS XIV (1643–1715) The first and greatest example of an absolute ruler was Louis XIV of France.

Louis inherited the throne of France when he was five years old. Throughout his childhood, there were continual arguments between his mother, who ruled on his behalf, and the council of nobles, who wanted a share of power. When Louis was old enough, therefore, he disbanded the council and said that he would be the only power in the land. He used the words: *'L'état c'est moi'* ('I am the state').

The young king chose his own advisers and met them every morning to decide everything that should be done, working 12 hours a day for the rest of his long reign.

VERSAILLES Louis not only worked hard, he wanted to be the most magnificent and powerful king ever. To this end, he built a huge palace at Versailles, 23 kilometres west of Paris, to house his court, nobles and government. The king became known as the Sun King because of the brilliance of his court.

FOREIGN AFFAIRS Louis XIV's aim in foreign affairs was to increase French power, and following this policy meant that from 1667 until 1713 he was almost constantly at war with other European powers. When he was 64 years old, he declared war on Spain, trying to win the Spanish throne for his grandson, Philip. The War of the Spanish Succession lasted for 11 years and bankrupted France. Despite the constant fighting, Louis gained nothing for France.

FREDERICK THE GREAT (1740–1786) Frederick II of Prussia was another great absolute king. He, too, worked long hours and he called himself 'the first servant of the state'.

Like Louis, he embarked on a number of wars to gain land and power for Prussia. When the Austrian Emperor Charles VI died in 1740, Frederick immediately invaded and conquered Silesia, the part of the Austrian Empire nearest to Prussia. Determined to keep it, he attacked the new empress, Maria Theresa. He had inherited a very efficient and well-organized army from his father and, leading his own troops into battle, he very soon forced Maria Theresa to agree that he could keep the land.

In the years that followed, Frederick was often fighting. Sometimes he was successful, sometimes his armies were cut to pieces, and at one time Berlin itself (the capital of Prussia) was occupied by enemy troops.

His power was absolute within Prussia but, unlike Louis, Frederick did have the interests of his people

Left. The first stage of Louis XIV's building at Versailles. The architect was Le Vau and the garden designer was Le Notre. In 1678, Louis spent a quarter of the French budget enlarging the new palace. He built two wings, each one the size of the original palace.

Education and Improvements

As with many absolute rulers at this time, Frederick II only wanted better education for the middle classes who would be useful in the civil service. He supported the founding of new schools and a new school-leaving examination, called the Abitur, that boys had to pass before going to university. (Girls were not expected to be educated.)

He encouraged new farming methods. He bred cows, sheep and horses and lent the best male animals to landowners so that they could improve their own stock. He supported the enclosing of the big, open fields and the use of fertilizer.

at heart. For instance, he encouraged agriculture, having the Oberbruch marshes drained and turned into farmland. He also abolished torture and the *censorship* of newspapers.

Frederick encouraged science and education and made the government of Prussia very efficient. When he died, at the age of 74 years, he left behind a strong country and one that was about twice the size that it had been when he came to the throne.

DIFFERENCES BETWEEN FREDERICK AND LOUIS

Frederick II doubled the size of his country, kept Prussia free from debts and was tolerant in religion. The great French thinker, Voltaire, corresponded with Frederick and addressed him as 'Your Humanity'. Louis XIV, on the other hand, was famous for banning all religions, except Roman Catholicism, and for closing all their churches. He left huge debts and did not succeed in greatly enlarging France.

PETER THE GREAT AND RUSSIA

Peter the Great and the Serfs

Under Peter the Great the serfs became even less free. He brought in a new tax called the 'soul tax', to be paid by every male peasant of working age. Each local lord was responsible for collecting the tax from his own serfs. A serf could be moved, sold or exchanged by his master.

Catherine the Great wanted to change this. But she could not, because it was so much a part of the way that farming and the economy were run. The only hope for a badly treated serf was to run away to the borders of the Russian Empire, where it was so wild that he might not be found.

Although Russia bordered on to Europe, it remained very isolated. One of the reasons for this was that Russia was cut off from trading with Europe, or with anywhere else. For most of the year, its northern sea border was ice-bound. Sweden and Poland blocked the western border. The Turks blocked the southern border. To the east lay deserts and mountains and then China, which was not keen to trade abroad.

PETER THE GREAT (1696–1725) From 1639 on, Russia expanded rapidly (see map). Peter the Great, who became tsar in 1696 at the age of 24, went on a tour of Europe in 1697–98 and saw that Russia was lagging behind. Peter did not just visit kings, he also met scientists like Sir Isaac Newton in England and Leeuwenhoek in Holland. His greatest passion was for ships and he even worked (in disguise) as an ordinary shipwright in the Dutch East India Company's shipyards in Amsterdam, humping timber and sawing wood. He took trips on every sort of ship he could, from warships to whalers.

After his return to Russia to put down a rebellion, Peter set about bringing Russian ship-building and industry up to European standards. However, his admirers in Europe were alarmed to hear how he had supervised the torture and execution of leaders of the rebellion. In this his attitude was a long way from that of Frederick II of Prussia (see p. 344).

IMPROVING RUSSIA In the next 25 years, Peter turned the Russian army, which had been defeated by Sweden, Poland and Turkey, into an up-to-date force. He led it to victory over Sweden in 1721 and gained the provinces of Estonia and Livonia, including a port in the west (called Riga) that was not ice-bound for most of the year.

Peter also built up the Russian navy and made the iron industry as good as any in Europe. He saw clearly, as Frederick the Great did, that he had to make his country more wealthy by improving its farming and

The Winter Palace in St Petersburg was built by Peter the Great and enlarged for his daughter, the Empress Elizabeth (1741–1762).

Map showing the growth of Russia in the seventeenth and eighteenth centuries. Trade was one reason for Russia wanting to expand. Russia needed to have overland and sea routes to Europe so that it could trade. Thus Peter the Great fought Sweden for the states on the Baltic Sea and Catherine the Great fought the Turks for land by the Black Sea. In the east, Russia gained more and more land until it reached the Pacific Ocean.

industries. Only in this way could Russia become a great power.

THE PEOPLE OF RUSSIA Unlike Frederick, Peter was not interested in the welfare of his people. The Russian peasants were *serfs*, practically slaves, and remained so until 1861. They worked for Russian nobles who had almost life and death powers over them.

ST PETERSBURG Like Louis XIV of France (see p. 344), Peter the Great wanted a grand centre of government to reflect his power, so he built the city of St Petersburg at the mouth of the Neva River. So many people died in making the foundations that it is said to be built on bones.

Catherine the Great became empress after her husband Peter died.

CATHERINE THE GREAT (1762–1796) Catherine II, known as Catherine the Great, continued the work of Tsar Peter. She gained land by the Black Sea that included the port of Odessa, giving Russia a port in the south for trading with southern Europe.

At home, Catherine favoured better treatment for serfs, but the Russian nobles were too powerful for her to act. Unlike Louis XIV of France, she could not break their power and many Russians continued to be treated as slaves.

THE WEAKNESS OF TURKEY AND POLAND IN EUROPE

Left. A map showing the Ottoman Turkish Empire and its steady decrease in size.

Right. Janissaries were slaves, usually Christians who had been converted to Islam. They served the Turkish sultan as a powerful army against outside enemies and against rebellious Turkish nobles. Janissaries were important and well treated but at this time they were not allowed to pass on their jobs to their sons, although this changed over the centuries.

The Turkish Ottoman Empire had been a great and powerful empire under Suleiman the Magnificent (1520–1566). However, by the seventeenth century the empire was being weakened by problems within its various territories, while it was also being challenged from outside by the countries surrounding it.

WEAKNESS OF THE TURKISH EMPIRE After the reign of Suleiman the Magnificent there were a number of weak (and one or two near idiotic) sultans. Added to this, the empire had been built on war. Its elite soldiers were the *janissaries*, who were brought up to be fighting men and became restless if there was no war. By the seventeenth century Turkey was unable to gain any more land, for the countries around it were too strong, and this prospect of a peaceful, stable empire did not suit the janissaries. They were also discontented because they were badly paid, as Turkey was suffering from rising prices, or *inflation*, so that their wages could not be increased. The silver that flooded in from the Americas in the sixteenth and seventeenth centuries caused inflation all over Europe, and the increasingly weak Turkish Empire was badly affected. To make this problem worse, everyone in the empire had to pay more and more taxes, because all the wars against Persia (Iran) and Austria in the late sixteenth century had cost the sultan so much money.

Right. Sultan Mehmet IV (1648–1687) was more interested in hunting than in running the government.

THE SIEGE OF VIENNA (1683) Because the Ottoman Empire was a warlike society, one way to prevent rebellions among the soldiers was to send them off to fight a war.

The painting above shows the raising of the siege of Vienna by German and Polish armies on 12 September 1683.

Mehmet IV, who had become sultan in 1648, decided to occupy his army, please people in the empire with a victory and perhaps gain some land by attacking Vienna in Austria. Vienna was only 150 kilometres from the Turkish frontiers in Europe. Mehmet thought that even if the Turkish army could not hold the city, the army could plunder it and bring the goods home.

The Austrians held out against the Turkish siege for some weeks. Then help came in the form of an army of Germans and Poles led by John Sobieski, the king of Poland (1674–1696). The Turks, who were tired from weeks of besieging Vienna, were outnumbered and defeated and so went home.

This defeat in Austria marked a turning point for Turkey in Europe. Over the course of the next 100 years, Turkey lost a great deal more land to both Austria and Russia.

The Partitions of Poland

Left. The growth of Russia on one side, Prussia on another and Austria in the south threatened Poland. Although it fought to stay independent, battles against Sweden finally weakened Poland. Russia, Austria and Prussia took its land.

POLAND Turkey was not the only loser. In the seventeenth century Poland came under attack from Sweden on one of its borders, from the increasingly powerful Russia on the other, and also from Prussia.

Russian armies were based in Poland and Russian ships used Polish ports without permission. Catherine II of Russia (see p. 347) made sure she had the king she wanted on the Polish throne. Finally, at the end of the eighteenth century, Poland's territory was divided between Prussia, Russia and Austria.

TURKEY AND RUSSIA Alarmed by the growing Russian strength the Turks attacked Russia in 1768. But Turkey had been left behind in developments in warfare, so the well-equipped Russians marched into the Turkish Empire and their navy destroyed the Turkish fleet in the Mediterranean. It looked as if the Turkish Empire might collapse altogether.

THE FRENCH COURT AND THE ARTS IN EUROPE

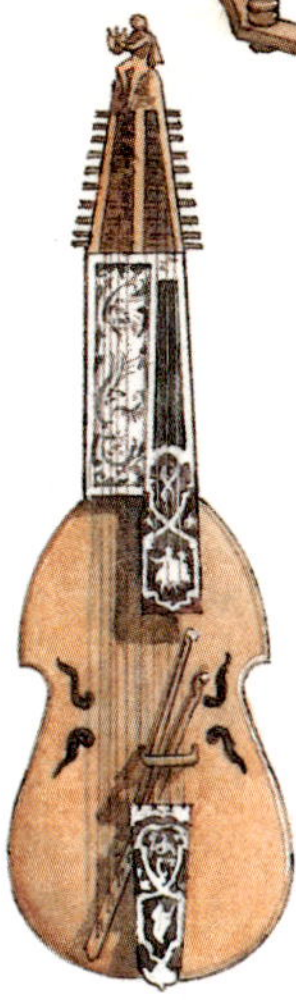

The picture on the left shows a concert at the court of the prince-bishop of Liège (in present-day Belgium). Musical instruments at this time were often highly decorated. The harpsichord, shown above, was a forerunner of the piano. The baryton, pictured on the left, was played with a bow, like a cello, but its strings could also be plucked by the musician's fingers.

The rich nobles of France in the seventeenth and eighteenth centuries led the most luxurious, civilized and glamorous lives of anyone in Europe at that time. They were not allowed to work in trade or industry; instead, they lived on the rent from all the land they owned, and did not have to pay taxes.

Louis XIV built the palace of Versailles (see p. 344) to house his court, nobles and government. Anyone who was anyone had to be seen at Versailles. The nobles drove there from Paris in their carriages and the huge gilded halls were filled with beautifully dressed people. Louis encouraged his nobles to spend extravagantly, so that they would not have enough money or time to plot rebellions.

The court became a centre for musicians and for artists, so it was always crowded. Louis loved dancing—ballet as we know it started at this time. The whole court used to take part in the ballets (not very strenuously) and the king often took the leading parts.

LOUIS XV (1715–1774) Louis XIV's grandson, Louis XV, who came to the throne in 1715 at the age of five, grew up to be quite different. He was a shy man. He kept up the ceremonies such as the levée and the couchée (the daily public ceremonies of the king rising and of going to bed at night), but when the last noble courtier had gone, Louis got out of bed, put on his dressing-gown and returned to his private rooms for supper and a game of cards with close friends.

THE SALONS Fashionable Parisians copied this more relaxed way of living. Entertaining in salons was usually presided over by the lady of the house and consisted of conversation and the exchange of ideas. One of the most

Above. The most famous room in the Palace of Versailles is the Galerie de Glaces (Hall of Mirrors). It was designed by Hardouin-Mansart. The size, and the lavish use of marble, painted ceilings and mirrors, all give the room an overwhelming grandeur.

Eastern Influences

As the Europeans explored other parts of the world, so they brought back artistic ideas. French settees in this period had legs carved like Egyptian sphinxes.

Wealthy British and French people bought Persian and Indian rugs. The patterns on Chinese porcelain and wallpaper influenced the designs on European tableware and on walls. Cabinets and screens were made of Far Eastern lacquerware.

Wolfgang Amadeus Mozart (1756–1791)

Mozart could play the harpsichord when he was three, and before he was five he was composing music. At the age of six he was giving concerts all over Europe. He grew up playing the piano and violin, conducting at concerts, teaching the harpsichord and piano, and writing music and operas for money.

When Mozart was 31 his father died, leaving him heavily in debt. He was under great stress, constantly overworked, and suffered from ill-health. He died in 1791 at the age of 35.

Despite his early death, Mozart's life was not a waste, as he wrote 150 pieces of music as well as his 12 complete operas. These include *The Marriage of Figaro*, *Don Giovanni* and *The Magic Flute*. For many music lovers, he is the finest classical composer who ever lived.

famous of these hostesses was Madame de Staël, who lived in the late eighteenth century. Some *salons* were very intellectual. Nobles like the Duc de Choiseul mixed with *philosophers*, scientists and writers such as Voltaire, Montesquieu and Rousseau. These gatherings fostered the spirit of free-thinking and enquiry and led to criticism of religion and absolute monarchs. This was one factor that led to the French Revolution (see pp. 372–3).

MUSIC Singing was a favourite entertainment for many people, although only the rich of Europe went to the opera. Italy led the field with comic and serious operas. Other forms of music were popular too. Powerful princes kept their own orchestras. Joseph Haydn was Kapellmeister (chief musician) to Prince Esterhazy in Hungary. He produced operas, masses and other music which was listened to by everyone who came to the prince's court. Haydn's music was liked so much that he was showered with invitations to perform all over Europe.

The Austrian composer, Mozart, worked in a more freelance way, playing, conducting and composing all over Europe until he died at the age of 35 in 1791. He was not the only musician to travel; for instance, although Handel came from Germany he composed music in England for theatres and for public ceremonies. There were many opportunities to earn a living if you were a gifted musician.

PAINTING Other forms of art also flourished in this period. Styles of painting varied from the Italian, Antonio Canaletto, who painted several grand pictures of Venice and London, to the homely paintings of the Dutch artist, Jan Vermeer.

THE ENLIGHTENMENT

In the medieval and early modern times, people had been ruled by beliefs in God and also by superstition, but by 1650 there was a new system of ideas. It was called Reason. This did not mean that religion or superstition died out; instead people, led by the great scientists and *philosophers*, began more and more to look for reasons *why* things happened. This search for reason and order in the universe grew out of the explorations which had opened up the world. For instance, no one could believe that the world was flat any more. What else might be untrue? A whole new way of looking at this large, spherical planet of ours, and at humankind's place on it, had to be found.

VOLTAIRE AND ROUSSEAU Different thinkers approached the problem of making sense of the world in different ways. The French philosopher, François-Marie Voltaire (1694–1778), criticized the Church and the governments of the time, saying that they were superstitious and did not allow people to think for themselves. He believed that people had a right to think in whichever way they liked, as long as they did not force their ideas on to others. Voltaire is famous for saying: *'I disapprove of what you say, but I will defend to the death your right to say it.'*

Jean-Jacques Rousseau (1712–1778) wrote plays, operas and articles in encyclopaedias. He became interested in so-called 'primitive' people and began to wonder if the civilization he lived in was such a good idea. His most famous book, called *The Social Contract*, begins: *'People are born free but are everywhere in chains.'* Rousseau goes on to say that human beings will win freedom and happiness only if they re-learn the ways of the *'noble savage'*, because 'primitive' people are not greedy. They do not try to get more possessions or power than they need.

KANT Immanuel Kant (1724–1804) was a great German thinker who was influenced by the writings of Rousseau and Sir Isaac Newton (see p. 354). As Newton looked for order and laws that governed the way the universe worked, so Kant looked for laws that governed the way human beings lived. He believed that the special ability of human beings was to think and reason. He wrote many books and is famous for his golden rule for living a good life—people should behave as though every action they take will, in future, be made a general rule for everyone to obey.

THE REASON FOR REASON All the great philosophers thought that everything in the world could be done better if there was order and reason. This led to a desire for justice, because in a well-run world there should not be suffering and unfairness. These ideas reached a peak in the American Declaration of Independence (see p. 370) and in the French Revolution (see p. 372).

In this way the ideas of the *Enlightenment* influenced the lives of ordinary people all over the world, although it took some time for many of the changes to happen.

In a completely different way, the desire for order and reason, together with the rise of scientific thinking, shaped the way that medicine came to be practised in the Western world, and that affected everybody and made them healthier and longer lived.

The first lecture at Madame Geoffrin's salon in Paris in 1750. Rousseau and Diderot are in the audience.

Mary Wollstonecraft

Left. Voltaire made his name writing plays. He wrote a book called ***Letters on the English***, comparing British freedom with French lack of freedom. Because of this he was forced to flee to Switzerland.

Above. Immanuel Kant was interested in mathematics and politics as well as philosophy. His best known book is the ***Critique of Pure Reason***, where he argues that only ideas are real.

Wollstonecraft was a teacher, writer, publisher and translator. She believed that girls should be as well educated as boys. She also wanted to make life better for ordinary people and took a great interest in the French Revolution. When people attacked the revolutionaries, saying that it was against God's laws to rebel against their king Wollstonecraft wrote a book in reply called *Vindication of the Rights of Man*. She asked what else the revolutionaries could do when the rich people treated them so badly. Many people read her book.

Wollstonecraft's next book, called *Vindication of the Rights of Women*, claimed that women were equal to men.

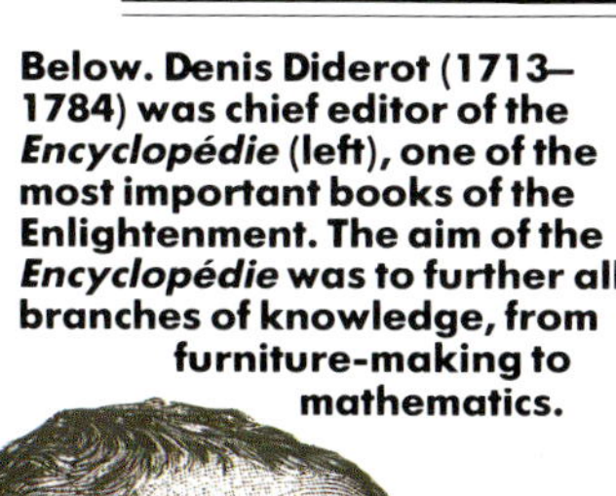

Left. Jean-Jacques Rousseau began his career writing plays, operas and encyclopaedia articles. His work led him to find out about so-called 'primitive' peoples. From this he moved on to think about the ways in which people are ruled.

Dr Samuel Johnson (1709–84)

Johnson was probably the most famous writer in England in the eighteenth century. He is well known today for his *Complete Dictionary of the English Language*, which was supposed to contain every word used in England at the time it was written, together with its correct spelling and meaning.

It took Johnson and his eight assistants seven years to complete the dictionary. It was the first one of its kind, for all other dictionaries had previously only included words that were hard to spell, not every word in the language. Johnson's dictionary included 43,500 words.

Below. Denis Diderot (1713–1784) was chief editor of the *Encyclopédie* (left), one of the most important books of the Enlightenment. The aim of the *Encyclopédie* was to further all branches of knowledge, from furniture-making to mathematics.

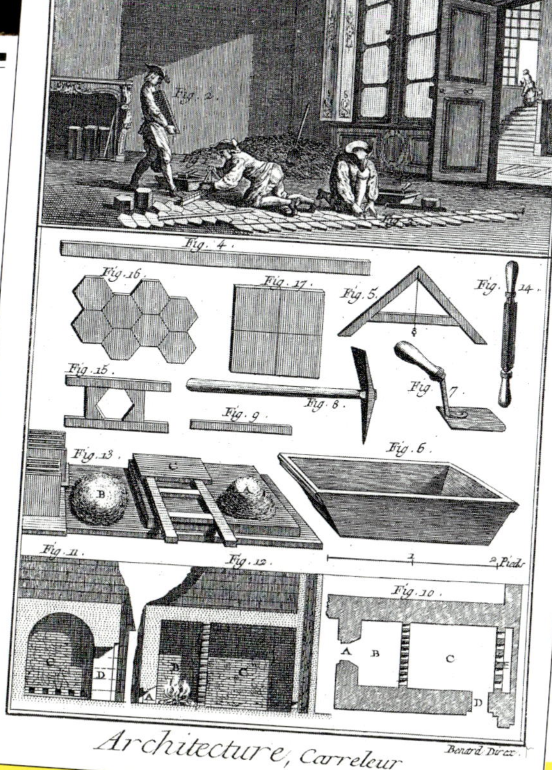

THE RISE OF SCIENTIFIC THINKING

The period 1650 to 1800 was a time of great scientific advances. In the Middle Ages learning had been in the hands of the Church. This had often prevented any sort of study that might go against the teaching of the Catholic Church. With the European *Renaissance* of the fifteenth and sixteenth centuries, people began to look at different areas of learning. Men and women were interested in finding out what the great ancient civilizations of Greece and Rome had written about the way in which the world worked. From this they went on to study the world we live in and to try to find out more about it. The *Reformation* in sixteenth-century Europe carried on the work of the Renaissance in breaking the power of the Church as the only authority over people's beliefs and thoughts. By the seventeenth century people were freer to explore all sorts of new ways of looking at things.

SIR ISAAC NEWTON (1642–1727) One of the greatest scientific thinkers of the seventeenth century was Sir Isaac Newton. When he was young he read the work of the French mathematician René Descartes (1596–1650). He could not agree with what Descartes wrote about light, so he decided to do some experiments himself.

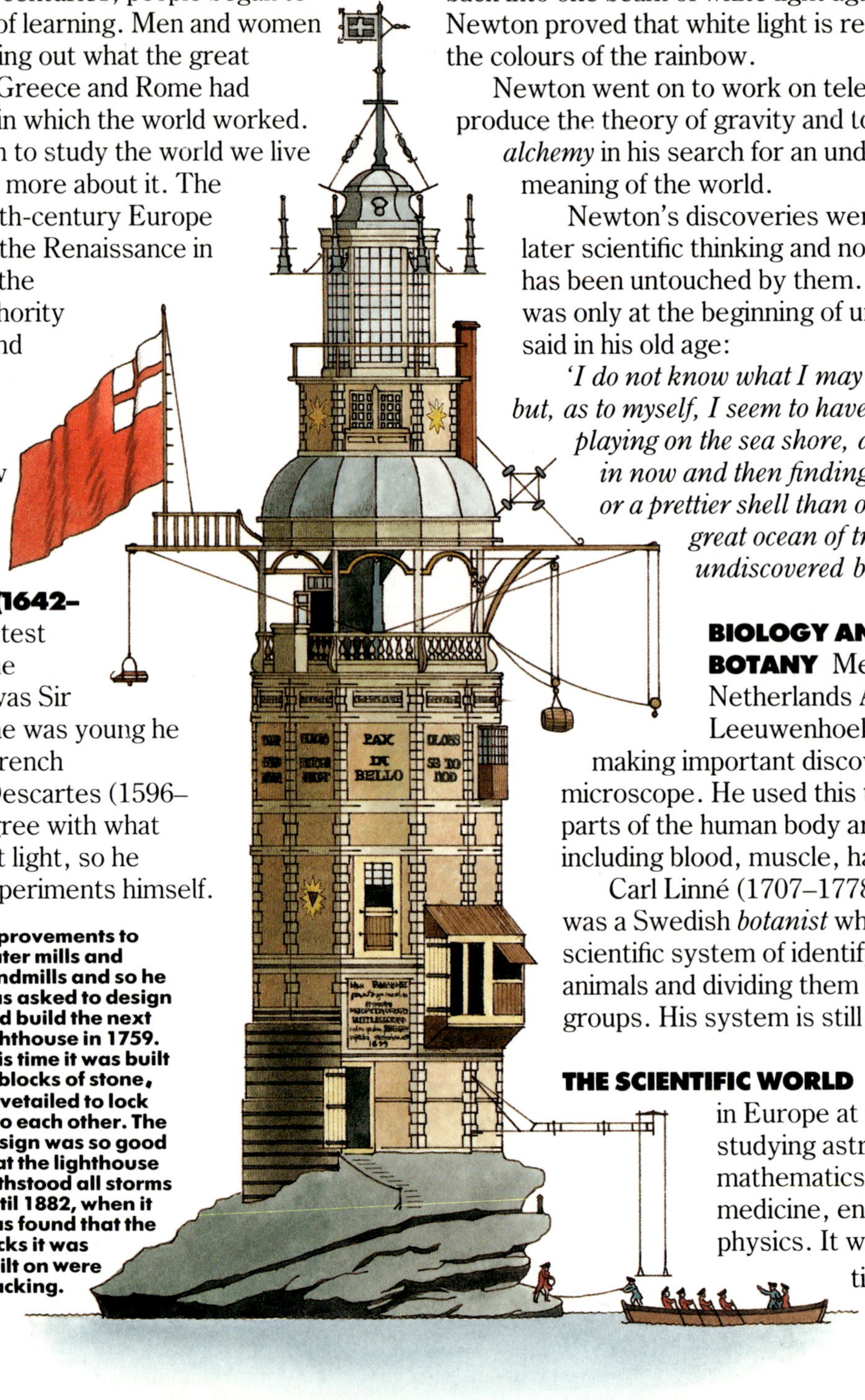

Right. The Eddystone Lighthouse was built on rocks in the English Channel near Plymouth. The first one was built of wood and was swept away in a storm in 1703. The second lighthouse was burnt down in 1755. By this time trading in ships was so important to Britain that a new and better design was needed. John Smeaton had already made improvements to water mills and windmills and so he was asked to design and build the next lighthouse in 1759. This time it was built of blocks of stone, dovetailed to lock into each other. The design was so good that the lighthouse withstood all storms until 1882, when it was found that the rocks it was built on were cracking.

Like Descartes and others, he used a glass object called a *prism* to break up a beam of light into a *spectrum* (the seven colours of the rainbow). He then went further than Descartes by placing another prism, upside down, behind the first one, to make the beams of coloured light form back into one beam of white light again. In this way Newton proved that white light is really made up of the colours of the rainbow.

Newton went on to work on telescopes, to produce the theory of gravity and to dabble in *alchemy* in his search for an understanding of the meaning of the world.

Newton's discoveries were the basis of all later scientific thinking and no scientist or thinker has been untouched by them. But he knew he was only at the beginning of understanding. He said in his old age:

'I do not know what I may seem to the world, but, as to myself, I seem to have been only like a boy playing on the sea shore, and diverting myself in now and then finding a smoother pebble or a prettier shell than ordinary, whilst the great ocean of truth lay all undiscovered before me.'

BIOLOGY AND BOTANY Meanwhile, in the Netherlands Anton van Leeuwenhoek (1632–1723) was making important discoveries with the microscope. He used this to find out how parts of the human body are made up, including blood, muscle, hair and skin.

Carl Linné (1707–1778), or Linnaeus, was a Swedish *botanist* who worked out a scientific system of identifying plants and animals and dividing them into different groups. His system is still used today.

THE SCIENTIFIC WORLD Other scientists in Europe at this time were studying astronomy, mathematics, chemistry, medicine, engineering and physics. It was an exciting time.

Some Discoveries between 1650 and 1700

Above. Anton van Leeuwenhoek.

1665 Robert Hooke, of England, uses an early microscope to look at a piece of cork and becomes the first person to see cells
1666 Newton forms his theory of gravity
1669 Hennig Brand of Hamburg in Germany isolates the element phosphorous
1675 Dutch scientist, Anton van Leeuwenhoek, improves the microscope so that it can magnify an object 200 times and discovers microscopic organisms
1690 Papin, a French engineer, invents a pump with a piston driven by steam
1698 Hunckwitz produces the first phosphorous matches

Some Discoveries between 1700 and 1800

1715 German physicist, Gabriel Fahrenheit, introduces the mercury thermometer
1731 John Hadley invents an early type of sextant, used to measure the angle above the horizon of the sun or the stars, and so help sailors to find their position at sea.
1742 Celsius invents the centigrade thermometer in Sweden
1746 American writer, scientist and politician, Benjamin Franklin, begins his researches into electricity which prove that it causes lightning
1753 Carl Linnaeus, a Swedish botanist, publishes his new system for grouping plants

Above. This chronometer, designed by John Harrison, kept very accurate time and helped sailors to fix their longitude.

1761 Mikhail Lomonosov, the founder of Moscow University, discovers that the planet Venus has an atmosphere
1765 James Watt improves Thomas Newcomen's pumping engine
1774 Joseph Priestley, a British scientist, discovers oxygen and Karl Scheele, a Swedish scientist, discovers chlorine
1783 The Montgolfier brothers, of France, make the first hot air balloon ascent
1786 British astronomer Sir William Herschel forms the theory of the shape of a galaxy
1789 An Italian, Luigi Galvani, experiments on the muscular contractions of dead frogs
1790 French scientist Antoine Lavoisier produces the first table of chemical elements

Below. Isaac Newton took his degree at Cambridge University in 1665. Within months the university was closed because of the plague and Newton went home to live with his mother. He worked on theories about splitting light and about the law of gravity.

Above. Newton's first reflecting telescope. He used mirrors to overcome the lack of good quality glass lenses.

Above. The old Royal Observatory, Greenwich, England. It was built in 1675 to carry out research into ways of improving navigation.

THE ART OF WAR

Europe developed the art and equipment of warfare to a high degree in the seventeenth and eighteenth centuries. One reason for this was the change in the organization of armies.

PERMANENT ARMIES Almost constant warfare in the 100 years before 1650 had left parts of Europe, such as the German states, devastated. It had also become obvious that permanent armies were useful, as previously armies were only raised when wars broke out.

By 1650, France was the leading military power in Europe. Its kings, particularly Louis XIV (see p. 344) and his ministers, realized that a strong army would keep France powerful. However, if France began to set up a large army, then every other monarch in Europe also had to keep a large army. This was a seventeenth century arms race.

THE SIZE OF ARMIES In 1610, France's army was made up of about 20,000 soldiers; in 1650, there were 150,000; during the eighteenth century this number rose to 250,000 and more in time of war. In the same way, Sweden's army was 15,000-strong in 1590 and 100,000 in 1700.

Above. The Battle of Culloden, 1746. Bonnie Prince Charlie (1720–1788) came to Scotland to proclaim his father, James Stuart, the true king of Britain. He gathered an army and marched south to Derby before turning back to Scotland and being defeated at Culloden.

In the seventeenth century a soldier on horseback wore much the same armour as a pikeman (far left), who went on foot. He had a helmet, breastplate, backplate and some protection for the thighs. The musketeer (left) was the first soldier to do without armour, for with his musket and gunpowder he had enough to carry without it.

The Development of Navies

In many countries, there were merchants who hired ships to sail long or short distances to buy and sell goods. Europeans in particular built large ships and sailed great distances to trade. They needed to protect their ships from pirates who might attack and steal their goods, so often their *merchant ships* were armed.

Special sailing ships were built by countries like the Netherlands, France, Spain and Britain. These were warships, built to fight battles at sea and protect their countries' interests, defend their trade and help to build empires.

At this time, the warships were armed with cannons along the side of the ship; the cannons were fired through open portholes.

Matchlocks and Flintlocks

Matchlock muskets were developed in Europe in the fifteenth century. Although they were an important development from the days of fighting with swords and pikes alone, they were not completely satisfactory.

Flintlocks, which replaced matchlocks in the seventeenth century, remained in use for the next 200 years.

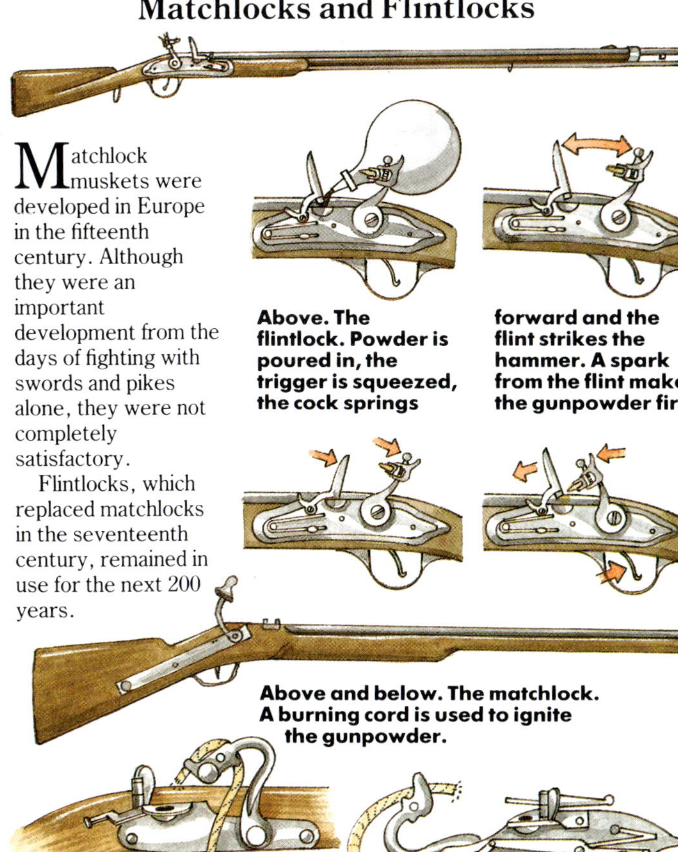

Above. The flintlock. Powder is poured in, the trigger is squeezed, the cock springs forward and the flint strikes the hammer. A spark from the flint makes the gunpowder fire.

Above and below. The matchlock. A burning cord is used to ignite the gunpowder.

GUNS Perhaps the greatest breakthrough on the battlefield was the development of a new type of early gun, the flintlock musket.

With the old matchlock musket, a *musketeer* (soldier who used the gun) had to pour loose gunpowder into the weapon and then detonate it with a smouldering cord. It was very slow to load and could easily misfire. The new flintlock meant that the gunpowder (which came in measured paper cartridges) was ignited by a spark from the flint. This usually worked reliably and in all weathers. Loading was much faster, so there was far more firepower available on the battlefield.

More firepower meant the end of armour on the battlefield. Once bayonets were fixed to the barrels of the muskets, not so many *pike-men* were needed to keep off *cavalry* attacks. Within a short space of time more soldiers were armed with guns than with anything else.

PROFESSIONAL ARMIES Armies gradually became more professional. Better weapons needed better soldiers. It was no use recruiting peasants in times of war, giving them complicated guns and then expecting them to be good soldiers. More and more soldiers were now employed full-time. They drilled and trained. They were given uniforms, weapons and, in some countries, even health-care and pensions. All this meant that large government departments grew up to clothe, arm, control and feed the armies. The monarchs were strong enough to take the control of regiments of soldiers away from the nobles, who had previously been in charge. The nobles remained as officers and still did some recruiting, but the army was now the army of the monarch.

PRUSSIA Frederick William I of Prussia (1713–1740) built up a well-equipped, disciplined army. It was his pride and joy. He had scouts sent all over Europe to find the tallest young men (they did not have to be Prussian) to serve in his army. If they could not be persuaded to join, he was not above kidnapping them. The problem was that he did not like risking any of them in fighting. His son, Frederick the Great (see p. 344), was more practical. He improved the training of soldiers and set about conquering more land to make Prussia the most powerful of the many German states.

NAVIES Similar widescale changes took place in the navies. The British navy grew in size, professionalism and firepower and led to British dominance at sea.

THE COMING OF INDUSTRY: COAL AND IRON

Above. Newcomen's engine was used to pump water out of mines. The boiler at the bottom right heated the water to make steam, which rose into the cylinder. A jet of cold water was injected into the cylinder. The steam condensed. As it became cooler, it took up less room than the steam had and so a vacuum was created. The piston dropped down, pulling down the arch head on the big wooden beam, which lifted the water.

The foundations of present-day European industry were laid in the eighteenth century with the development of new machinery and processes that is known as the Industrial Revolution. Although these new developments soon spread all over Europe, it was in Britain that most of them originated.

BRITAIN AND THE INDUSTRIAL REVOLUTION In 1700, Britain had large reserves of coal and plenty of iron ore. However, that alone does not make an industrial revolution. Britain had other advantages too. The first was that the country had been united for a long time. Monarchs came and went, but the government carried on through Parliament. This provided a stable background in which business could flourish.

Another advantage was that Britain was an island, so the wars that raged throughout Europe in the sixteenth and seventeenth centuries did not touch its countryside. These wars were devastating in places like the German states, where large amounts of land were laid to waste.

Yet another advantage was that during the eighteenth century Britain was expanding overseas and gaining a great deal of money from trade, so that some British people had the capital (money) to invest in new ideas such as canal-building, cotton factories and steam engineering.

In some ways the country that seemed to have the most advantages, however, was China. China was a united, stable empire with (like Britain) many skilled workers in agricultural and structural engineering. The difference between Britain and China seems have been their different attitudes. The British belonged to Europe. They had taken part in world explorations. They were among the pioneers of scientific thinking. They were part of the outward-looking, progressive and wealth-seeking European climate of the eighteenth century. The Chinese, on the other hand, saw themselves as the Middle Kingdom—the centre of the world. They did not need the rest of the world.

So the small, united, peaceful and relatively rich land of Britain experienced the first industrial revolution, soon to be followed by other countries and eventually by a great deal of the world.

NEW DEVELOPMENTS This industrial revolution was made possible by new discoveries in science and engineering. For instance, Abraham Darby (1677–1717) pioneered the use of coked coal to smelt iron ore. For the first time good quality iron could be produced. Large quantities of high-quality iron were needed to make the new machines and steam engines that men like Thomas Newcomen (1663–1729) and James Watt (1736–1819) were inventing, while large quantities of coal were needed to power them.

WOOL AND COTTON INDUSTRIES At first the steam engine was stationary. It was used to pump water out of the deep mines. Then people realized that it could be used to drive machines. For instance, previously the mills that wove wool had to be sited by fast-flowing rivers

Left. Wrought iron is strong and supple. It was popular in the eighteenth century for things like balcony railings outside town houses. One common pattern was called 'heart and honeysuckle'.

The staircase above and fireplace below are made of wrought iron.

1 In 1756 a factory was built at Sèvres in northern France to make porcelain. This followed the factory at Meissen in eastern Germany earlier in the century. At last the Europeans had discovered for themselves the Chinese secret of making the very fine china called porcelain.

2 The Chinese did not want the Europeans to gain too much influence in their country. In 1757 they insisted that all foreign ships that wanted to trade with China, had to be restricted to the port of Canton.

3 The Portuguese unified their South American empire in 1776. It was to be ruled from Rio de Janiero (in present-day Brazil).

4 In 1770 James Bruce became the first white person to journey along the Blue Nile to where it joined the White Nile.

Left. The iron bridge at Coalbrookdale, Shropshire, in England was the first iron bridge in the world. The iron ribs of the arches are 67 metres long.

Below. The Coalbrookdale Ironworks in the eighteenth century. Steam engines drove the bellows that kept the ironworks going day and night.

Children being let down a coal mine. They worked long hours, pulling tubs of coal, crawling on hands and knees along underground passages. Six-year-olds sat for hours in the dark to open the doors as the tubs were pulled along. In 1842, Britain forbade women and children under the age of 10 to work underground.

so that the water could power the machines. By the late eighteenth century this was no longer so. Woollen mills and the newer cotton mills could be built anywhere if the power source was a steam engine rather than water.

This led to the building of cotton mills in Lancashire. They were near the coal fields, so it was easy to bring coal to the steam engines in the mills, and they were also near the ports of Liverpool and Manchester, where cotton was brought in from India, Egypt and America and from where the finished cotton cloth was exported all over the world. All these developments meant that Britain's industry, trade and wealth were able to grow enormously.

THE COMING OF INDUSTRY: COTTON AND TRANSPORT

In 1650, wool and flax were the main raw materials that were used to make clothes in Britain. Small amounts of silk from China and cotton from India were imported for rich people.

By the eighteenth century, however, printed cotton cloth (calico) from India was becoming so popular in Britain that the government banned its import. This was to protect the small but growing British cotton industry in Manchester. At this time the cotton mills only made crude copies of the Indian calicoes, but as the eighteenth century progressed the quality of their cloth improved. More and more people wanted dresses, shirts and so on made out of cotton, because they were lighter to wear and easier to wash than woollen clothes.

Left. A Spinning Jenny. The cotton fibres were combed out in the wooden 'bed'. They were then picked up by one of the many spindles on the spinning wheel.

Below. A working mill. Until the invention of steam-powered machines at the end of the eighteenth century, factories and mills were built near fast-flowing rivers. The water turned a waterwheel, which provided the power for all the machines. You can see the large waterwheel in the centre of this picture. Notice all the women working. The man in the top hat is overseeing the work.

Above. The Portland Vase is a Roman vase made of glass with white figures on it. The figures are slightly raised, and stand out from the surface of the vase. This gave Wedgwood the idea of making his blue pottery with raised white figures on it.

The Dangers of Highwaymen

Highwaymen were a menace on the roads during this period. Some famous robbers in Britain were Moll Cutpurse, who held up coaches dressed as a man, and Dick Turpin, who was finally hanged in 1739.

Stage coaches were held up so often that in 1784 a new service was tried out between London and Bath. It was called the Mail Coach and it was accompanied by an armed guard. Soon there were mail coaches running from London to all the cities in Britain.

The Growth of Canals

The first efforts to improve water transport were attempts to widen, deepen and straighten rivers, to allow boats to get further inland. This helped trade because more heavy goods could be carried by water, as packhorses could only carry fairly small loads.

Straightening rivers was so successful that people decided to build artificial rivers. They were called canals. By the end of the eighteenth century there were canals all over Britain.

JAMES HARGREAVES, RICHARD ARKWRIGHT AND THE MULE The people who span the long threads from the raw cotton could not work fast enough to keep up with the increased demand. To overcome this problem, James Hargreaves (1720–1778) invented the *Spinning Jenny*, a machine which span eight threads at once.

Shortly afterwards, Richard Arkwright (1732–1792) pioneered the *water-frame*. This brought great changes. It was too heavy to be turned by hand and so it was driven by a water-wheel. This meant that, instead of working at home, spinners now went to work in mills that were built beside rivers. These were some of the earliest factories, which changed people's working lives beyond recognition.

Then, in the 1780s, Samuel Crompton (1753–1827) invented another new machine, called the *mule*, which could spin cotton threads as fine as any from India, and far more cheaply.

MANCHESTER AND COTTON The next change in the production of cotton came when the steam engine was used for power instead of the water-wheel. Now that mills did not have to be built by rivers, they appeared all over Manchester, not far from the port of Liverpool, where raw cotton arrived in huge bales from Turkey and India. Soon the cotton imported from these countries was not enough to supply all the mills, and so Britain turned to the *New World*. Cotton grew well in the southern states of North America, where plantation owners began to grow great quantities of cotton, using their slaves to grow and then pick the cotton. This cotton was shipped to Liverpool and sent from there by canal to Manchester.

CANALS AND ROADS In the second half of the eighteenth century, the Duke of Bridgewater built the first canal, 68 kilometres long, to link his coal mines with Manchester. It had cost him £2 a tonne to transport his coal by road, but now, by canal, it cost only 50p a tonne. Because he saved so much money in this way, the duke could afford to sell his coal more cheaply than other mine-owners could, and so more people bought his coal. Other mine-owners followed his example and soon canals were being built all over Britain.

Josiah Wedgwood (1730–1795), the famous pottery manufacturer, used canals to transport his pottery from the Midlands to London. This was cheaper than sending it by road and also meant that the pottery was less likely to break.

Roads were improved, too. In 1658, it took 96 hours to travel from London to Exeter, while in 1784 the new Royal Mail coach could do it in 32 hours.

Britain now had everything that was needed for full industrial take-off—*raw materials* (coal, iron, cotton), power (water, steam) and transport (canals, roads). Soon steam would be applied to transport and the huge industrial expansion of the nineteenth century would begin.

Changes in Europe

TIME CHART

AD	BRITAIN	FRANCE	RUSSIA	REST OF EUROPE
1656				Completion of the building of St Peter's in Rome
1660	Foundation of the Royal Society in London			
1660>1700		Classical period of French literature: Molière, Racine, Corneille		
1662		Louis XIV begins building Versailles		
1666	Great Fire of London kills over 60,000	Foundation of Académie Française in Paris		
1683				Turkish siege of Vienna
1687	Isaac Newton's *Principia* published			
1696			Peter the Great takes full control in Russia	
1700		Great period of European Enlightenment begins: Voltaire, Diderot, Hume, etc.		Great age of German Baroque music begins: Bach, Handel, Buxtehude, etc.
1701	Jethro Tull invents horsedrawn drill to plant seeds in rows			
1703			Foundation of the city of St Petersburg	
1709	Abraham Darby discovers coke-smelting technique to produce pig-iron		Peter the Great defeats the Swedes at the battle of Poltava	
1710	Christopher Wren's St Paul's Cathedral is completed			Meissen porcelain industry is established in Saxony
1719			Jesuits expelled from Russia	
1724			Scientific Academy set up in St Petersburg	
1725			Death of Peter the Great	Prague Opera House is established (Czech Republic)
1742				Celsius invents the centigrade thermometer
1743		French explorers reach the foothills of the Rocky Mountains in North America		
1747	Samuel Johnson plans the first dictionary of the English language			
1757	The first modern British canal is constructed in Lancashire			
1764	James Hargreaves invents the Spinning Jenny			Mozart produces his first symphony at the age of eight
1765	James Watt refines the steam engine			
1781			Siberian highway is begun	
1783		Montgolfier brothers make the first balloon ascent	Russia annexes Crimea	
1789		French Revolution begins		
1790				Great age of European orchestral music: Haydn, Beethoven, Mozart, etc.
1791			Russia gains Black Sea steppes from Turkey	
1799		Napoleon becomes First Consul		

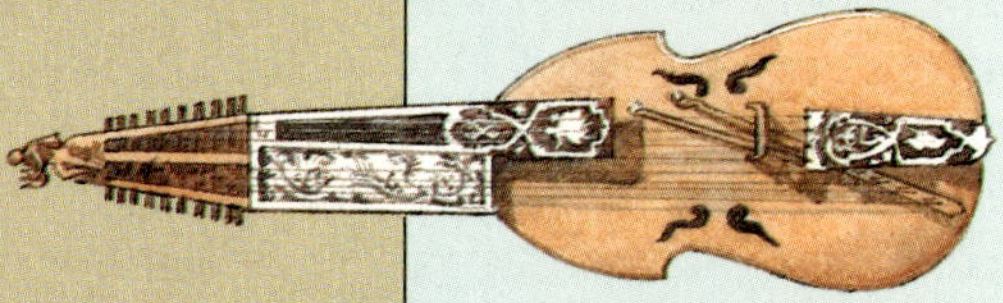

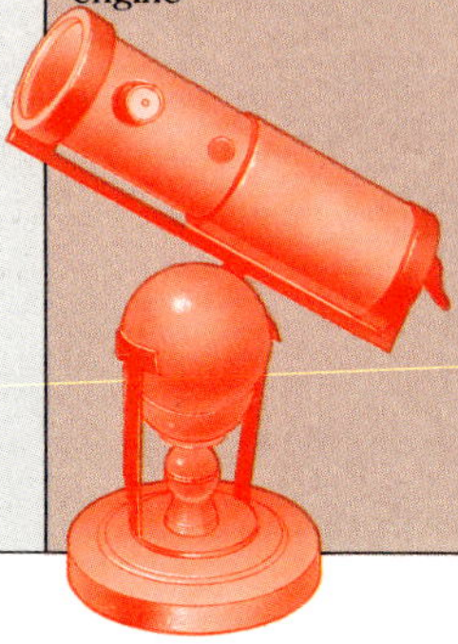

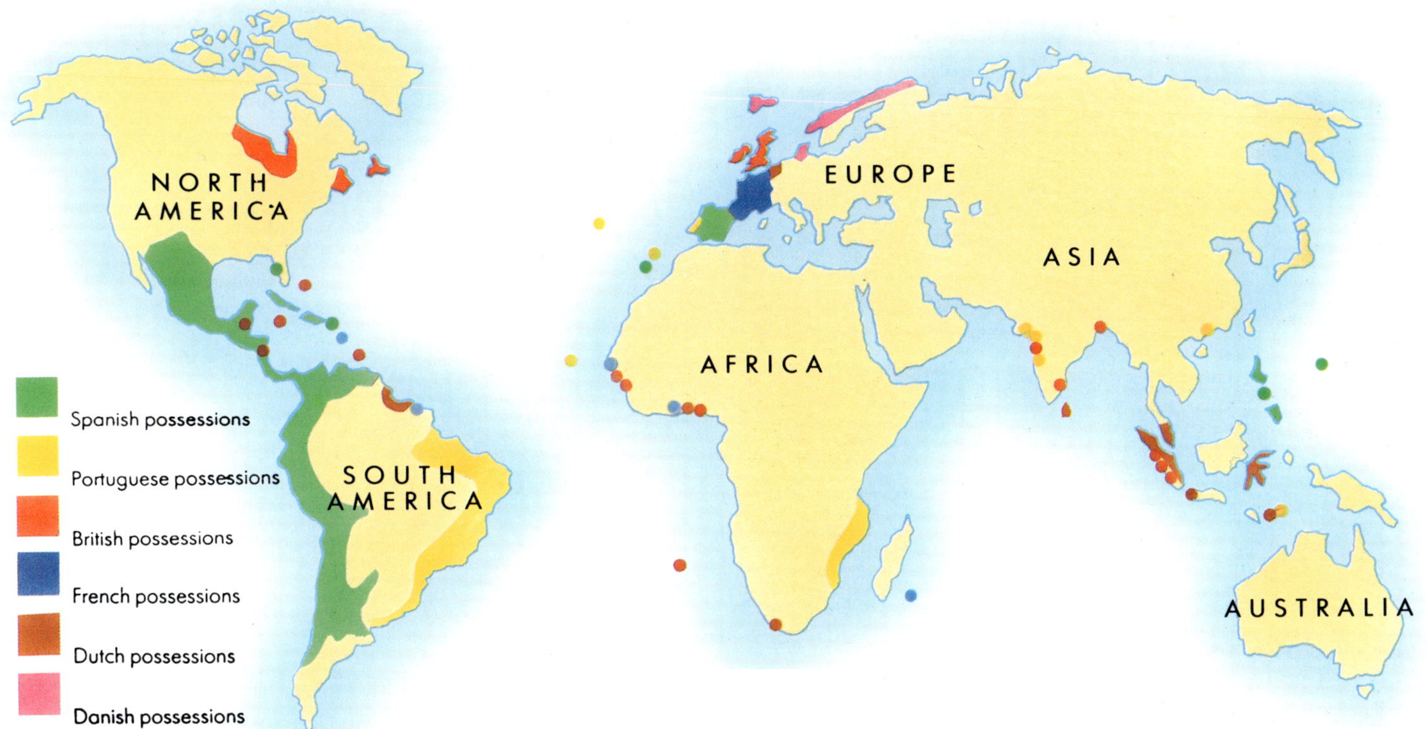

Revolution and Empire

Until the seventeenth century the world, on the whole, had pressed in on Europe. From 1650 on, Europe pressed out on the world. China had been the most civilized, advanced and densely populated country in the world in 1500. By 1650, however, the Chinese were losing interest in the outside world and in new things. The Europeans, on the other hand, were looking outwards from Europe. The first wave of explorations was over and the time of European trade and settlement was beginning.

GLOBAL TRADE European ships sailed to the East Indies, India, the West Indies, Africa and North and South America. They traded in everything, from spices to slaves, from silver to sugar, setting up trading posts around the world. The Dutch had trading posts in the East Indies, the Portuguese in Africa, the British and French in India. Different races of people, and different animals and plants, were spreading around the globe. This was to have far-reaching effects.

SETTLEMENT After trade came settlement. In the Americas the native populations declined by about 90 per cent, due firstly to the violence of the new settlers towards them, and secondly to new diseases that the settlers brought with them. The native American peoples were replaced by white Europeans, black Africans and some mixed races. This was to be the most significant world change in the distribution of races, taking place over two or three centuries. By the nineteenth century, trade and settlement had an overwhelming effect on every human life on earth.

At the same time, Eurasian animals such as horses, cows and sheep were introduced to the Americas, while plants like the potato and maize were introduced from the Americas to Eurasia. These changes, too, affected people's lives dramatically.

THE DESIRE FOR TRADE The hunter-gatherer societies had everything they wanted. Many of them were *nomadic* or semi-nomadic. If you are always on the move, then possessions are a burden. Only when people settled down to farm and stay in one place did they discover the need for chairs and tables, for bowls, beds, sheets, changes of clothes, pictures, ornaments and so on. Trade grew up from the desire to own things. Someone else living a kilometre away or 1000 kilometres away always seemed to have something that was very desirable.

In this way trade grew up everywhere and more and more ships plied back and forth across the oceans of the world.

THE THIRTEEN COLONIES OF NORTH AMERICA

By the seventeenth century, European settlers in the Americas had defeated the native Americans and the British had emerged in control of the eastern seaboard of North America.

The 13 British colonies hugged the east coast, stretching inland only for about 240 kilometres. For a long time, any further expansion was prevented by the mountains to the west, beyond which lay lands unexplored by white people, where the *Amerindian* peoples had lived for thousands of years. The European settlers wanted this land, and there were bound to be clashes as the new farmers cut down forests for timber and to make fields, because these were the forests where the Amerindians hunted.

The Thirteen Colonies

NEW HAMPSHIRE
MASSACHUSETTS
NEW YORK
RHODE ISLAND
CONNECTICUT
NEW JERSEY
PENNSYLVANIA
MARYLAND
DELAWARE
VIRGINIA
FRENCH LOUISIANA
N. CAROLINA
S. CAROLINA
ATLANTIC OCEAN
GEORGIA
SPANISH FLORIDA

Above. Map showing the thirteen colonies in North America in the eighteenth century.

LIFE IN THE COLONIES In 1690, about 200,000 settlers lived in the 13 colonies. Although most of them were British settlers (many Scottish and Irish), there were also Swedish, Dutch and German people, together with French Huguenots who had fled from persecution in Catholic France.

A large number of religious English people had settled in the part of America that became known as New England. They wanted to live and worship God in a simple and pure way and because of this they were often known as *Puritans*. Their wooden houses were clustered round village greens, and each village had a meeting house for worship and where people could meet to discuss community affairs. The settlers wanted a just and free society for everyone, with people meeting together to decide how best to run the community. They were very strict about religious matters, but otherwise they wanted people to be equal and free in this new land. Near to the village green there was a house for the minister, and perhaps also a small school house where all the children would go. The settlers themselves lived by farming, fishing and trading in furs and timber.

Further south, in Maryland,

The scene above shows William Penn, who founded Pennsylvania, making a treaty with the Indians.

most of the settlers were Catholic. Neighbouring Pennsylvania was founded by *Quakers*, who were also religious people who wanted to live simply. They were hardworking people who farmed and tried to live in peace with the local Indians.

In the southernmost parts of North America, religion was not so predominant. The land here was good for farming crops like tobacco and cotton. Since there was a demand for both these products in Europe, trading settlements soon grew up along the coasts.

THE NEW CITIES The city of Philadelphia was founded in 1681 and by 1750 it was the busiest port in America. Baltimore was slower to grow. In 1752, it had only 25 houses and 200 people, but in the next 50 years it became a huge centre for exporting wheat and for shipping. Goods were sent from ports like these to Europe and to the West Indies.

BRITAIN, SPAIN AND FRANCE By the early eighteenth century, there were around 900,000 British settlers in North America. There were also about 5000 Spanish and 50,000 French settlers in colonies founded by Spain and France. The Spanish were not interested in expanding their colonies in Mexico, Florida and California, but it was a different matter with the French.

Left. A New England town from this period. Each house was made of a wooden frame covered with overlapping wooden planks and had a big, brick chimney built in the centre. The roofs were covered with shingles (tiles) made of pinewood. Most houses had a cellar to keep food cool in the hot summers and protect stores from frost in the hard, cold winters.

THE FRENCH AND BRITISH IN NORTH AMERICA

Above. A view of the British army taking Quebec in October 1759. The British soldiers are seen disembarking and climbing up the cliff to fight the French.

By the early eighteenth century, there were 50,000 French settlers in North America, who had gained a vast amount of land on the other side of the mountains from the British colonies in New England. The French lived mostly as hunters and fur traders, on friendly terms with the Amerindians, because there were not enough French settlers to make much difference to the local people's way of life. The British, on the other hand, having a much larger colony of 900,000 people, wanted to cross the mountains to gain more land. When they did this they clashed not only with the Amerindians, but with the French as well, who built a line of forts to stop the British advancing.

The French not only wanted to stop the British colony expanding, they wanted to expand too, looking towards the sea and the possibility of attacking the British along the river towards New York. So, in turn, the British built forts to stop them. From the late seventeenth century onwards, war in Europe between France and Britain was reflected by almost continuous warfare between the French and British settlers in North America.

WASHINGTON AND BRADDOCK The first clash came in 1754, when the British colony of Virginia felt threatened by a strong French fort on the Ohio River. Virginia only had a *militia* (part-time army), but a tall, confident, 21 year-old militia officer called George Washington (see above) persuaded the governor of Virginia to send him with 159 men against the French fort. Although he captured the fort, Washington had to surrender it later.

The next year an army of British soldiers, led by

George Washington (1732–99)

When Washington was 11 years old, his father died and his step-brother brought him up. After this brother died, Washington ran the family estates. When he was in his 20s he led soldiers for the British against the French who were attacking the colonies.

Washington represented his fellow landowners in the Virginia parliament, and when trouble flared up between the British and the American colonists he was given the job of recruiting and leading an army made up of farmhands and craftsmen. This amateur army kept the British forces occupied until the French joined the Americans in 1778 and forced the British to surrender at Yorktown in 1781. Washington was the first president of the new independent states of America, from 1789 to 1797.

Above. The map on the left shows the way in which the European powers had laid claim to lands in America by 1713. On the right, the second map shows how British claims had grown by 1763.

Left. A French Canadian in the mid-eighteenth century. Many of the French who settled in Canada became hunters and trappers. They hunted animals such as the beaver whose fur was popular in Europe, particularly for hats. They learnt many skills from the Indians, including the use of snow shoes to travel across the deep winter snow. The French Canadians also had the advantage of having guns.

Key Dates in the British-French Dispute

- **1750** British-French commission fails to agree boundaries
- **1753** George Washington is sent on mission to tell the French not to confront the British
- **1754** British troops sent to expel French
- **1755** French and Indian war against Britain
- **1756** French drive British from the Great Lakes. The opening of the Seven Years War
- **1758** British take Louisburg
- **1759** Spain joins France in war against Britain
- **1759** British take Quebec
- **1760** British win control of the St Lawrence River and gain Montreal
- **1761** British dominate West Indies
- **1762** Britain declares war on Spain and takes more West Indian islands
- **1763** Peace of Paris between Britain, France and Spain ends the Seven Years War.

General Braddock, was easily defeated by the French. Braddock himself was mortally wounded. The French went over to the attack, taking all the British forts guarding the way to New York, and it looked as if nothing could stop them.

THE SEVEN YEARS WAR However, the war in America was only one part of the larger conflict between the French and British for world power. Because this conflict stretched all over the world, the role played by their ships and navies was very important.

In 1756, the Seven Years War diverted the French towards fighting in Europe. The British seized their chance. British ships controlled the sea routes across the Atlantic Ocean and did not allow French ships to reach America. This meant that the French forts were starved of soldiers, food and ammunition.

The British took Louisburg in Canada in 1758 and moved on Quebec next. General Wolfe was put in charge of the British army. He sailed up the St Lawrence River with a few thousand soldiers, who entered Quebec secretly in the night and defeated the French army. In 1760 the British captured Montreal too.

THE PEACE OF PARIS, 1763 This treaty ended the Seven Years War and was a great defeat for France. Britain gained all the French possessions east of the Mississippi River, except New Orleans, while the territory to the west was granted to Spain. Britain also gained Florida from the Spanish (although this was returned 18 years later) and, on the other side of the world, made gains from the French in India, giving up some West Indian islands in return.

THE BOSTON TEA PARTY

The painting above shows the Boston Tea Party. Some of the colonists disguised themselves as Indians and threw the tea overboard in protest against British taxes.

Soon after the British had defeated the French in the Seven Years' War, they were in trouble with their own North American colonists. By 1770, there were about two million people living in the 13 colonies. Large ports, like Boston and New York, were growing rich on trading.

Moreover, as the eighteenth century wore on the colonies developed in their own ways. They were governed by the British king's governor and council, but power really lay with the elected assemblies in the colonies themselves. They ran their own affairs 5000 kilometres away from Britain. They prospered and made most of the manufactured goods they needed. They were fast becoming Americans.

NAVIGATION LAWS The colonists resented the British Navigation Laws, which protected British trade and ship-building. For instance, the colonies were only allowed to trade with Britain and all goods had to be carried in British ships.

STAMP DUTY On the other hand, the British had used their army to fight off the French. They felt it was only fair that the colonists should pay some money in taxes towards the cost of defending the colonies, and so they decided to raise taxes by means of a stamp duty, a tax on legal documents. The colonists were furious. They claimed the stamp duty was illegal, saying that the very reason that British people were freer than most other peoples in Europe was they they could not be taxed unless it had been agreed in Parliament, whose Members were elected by at least some of the British population. The Americans said that they had not voted for any Members of Parliament in London, so how could those Members put taxes on them? There was such a protest that the British repealed the stamp duty.

Key Dates leading to the Declaration of Independence

1765 The Stamp Act
1766 Repeal of the Stamp Act
1770 New taxes on items such as tea lead to unrest and to British soldiers killing four colonists
1773 Boston Tea Party
1775 Concord raid and battle at Lexington
Heavy British losses at Bunker Hill
1776 American Declaration of Independence

Left. The *Spirit of '76*, the American Revolution painting by A.M. Willard. The picture shows the revolutionaries carrying the flag of the 13 colonies, who now called themselves 'states'. In the blue square there is one white star for each new state. Since 1776 many states have joined the United States and each time another white star has been added to the flag.

1 The Quebec Act guaranteed Roman Catholics freedom to worship in Canada. This angered the Puritans in New England.

2 The Treaty of Kuchuk Kainardji ended the Russo-Turkish War. Russia gained ports on the Black Sea from Turkey and also the right to represent the Greek Orthodox Church in Turkey.

3 Britain forbade cotton-making machinery made in that country to be exported anywhere in the world. This was to prevent the cotton industries of other countries developing into rivals of the British cotton industry.

4 The Austrian doctor, Franz Anton Mesmer, first used hypnosis for health purposes in Vienna.

Paul Revere (1735–1818) was one of the Boston leaders of the revolt against the British. He took part in the Boston Tea Party. When the revolt began, the British set out to seize the American military stores at Concord, Massachusetts. Revere learned of the plan and on 18 April 1775 he galloped through the night waking the people, so that when the British approached Concord the next day there were armed men to meet them. The story is told in a poem by the American poet, Longfellow, in *Paul Revere's Ride*.

THE BOSTON TEA PARTY Instead, the British said duties (taxes) must be paid on goods such as tea. The colonists did not like this either and the British sent soldiers to keep order in Boston. Tempers went from bad to worse. In 1773, a group of 150 colonists boarded three ships in Boston Harbor and threw all the tea overboard. The British put Boston under a military governor, General Gage, and closed the port of Boston until the colonists paid a fine.

From this time on, the colonists and the British were moving towards an open conflict. The Americans did not see this as a revolution. Rather, they thought the British were acting like illegal tyrants. Most Americans had no wish at this time to break away and become an independent country, they just wished to be free to grow and prosper in their own way. Some people in Britain sympathized with the Americans, as the thinkers of the Enlightenment (see page 352) had made people aware of the rights of others. These rights did not include slaves or women, but at least the idea was a beginning of thoughts about freedom and democracy. However, the British government stood firm. If the colonists were allowed to get away with it this time, then they could defy Britain over anything. Each side decided to stand firm.

THE AMERICAN DECLARATION OF INDEPENDENCE

Map showing the lands of the new United States of America in 1783 and the lands in North and Central America that were claimed by the European powers. Much of the Spanish lands north of Mexico were passed to France in the 1790s and were sold to the United States in 1803.

In July 1775, representatives from all 13 rebel colonies met at Philadelphia and asked George Washington (see p. 366) to take command of the Patriot army. After this, fighting between the British and the colonists dragged on. The following year the representatives met again and on 4th July they agreed to adopt the Declaration of Independence.

This Declaration was drafted by Thomas Jefferson (1743–1826) and others. It explained simply the American complaints against George III, the king of Britain. Then it went on to describe the sort of government the Americans wanted to set up, which was much influenced by the ideas of the Enlightenment (see p. 352).

EQUALITY The Declaration said that all men were created equal. Governments were set up to make sure that ordinary people could live safely, freely and happily. If they failed to protect this freedom, the ordinary people had the right to throw out the government and set up a new one. The British, however, had no intention of accepting such a document.

THE WAR OF INDEPENDENCE It was one thing to declare independence, another to break free of the British. In 1775, when the American War of Independence began, there were 8500 British soldiers in America; by 1781, there were over 48,000. They were professional, disciplined soldiers. The American militia, however, were part-time soldiers, keen to fight, but also keen to go back to their farms to get the harvest in.

WASHINGTON George Washington was commander of the new American Continental Army. At its best, it numbered about 20,000 men in 1777, but numbers went up and down as men signed up for a few months and then went home.

Over the next few years, despite some British victories, Washington trained and disciplined his men. While they shaped into an efficient army, the British faced more and more difficulties. All their guns, horses and food had to be brought 5000 kilometres across the Atlantic Ocean from Britain. Often the army leaders were not very good. One of the British generals was 'Gentleman' Johnny Burgoyne, who was more interested

The New Constitution

The 13 colonies had worked together to fight the British, but Washington and others realized that the new states would be stronger if they made a formal agreement to act together. For instance, it had been very difficult to get all 13 to pay taxes to pay for the soldiers. In another war this might be disastrous.

A new constitution was drawn up and the people in each of the 13 states were asked to vote to agree to it. In some states the voting was very close. In Virginia, 89 were for the constitution and 79 against.

The new constitution used the British idea of protecting the individual person by dividing up the powers of the state, so that no single person (e.g. the president) or group of people (e.g. the judges) would be so powerful that they could become absolute rulers. There was to be a president, two legislative houses (sets of people voted in to make laws) and an independent group of judges who could not be told what to do by the legislative houses.

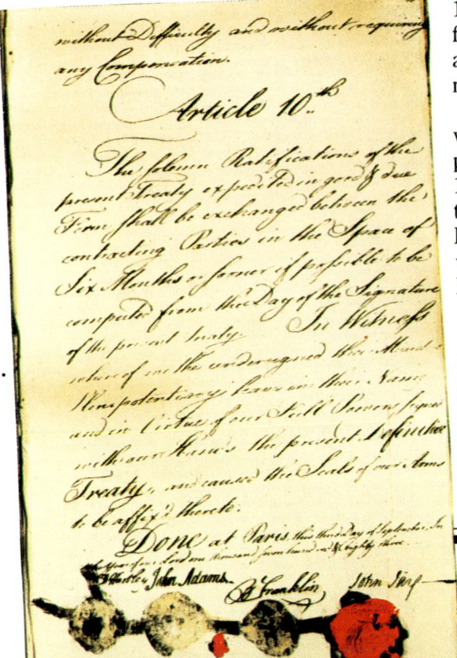

without Difficulty and without requiring any Compensation.

Article 10th

The solemn Ratifications of the present Treaty expedited in good & due Form shall be exchanged between the contracting Parties in the Space of Six Months or sooner if possible to be computed from the Day of the Signature of the present Treaty. In Witness whereof we the undersigned their Ministers Plenipotentiary have in their Name and in Virtue of our Full Powers signed with our Hands the present Definitive Treaty, and caused the Seals of our Arms to be affix'd thereto.

Done at Paris, this third Day of September

John Adams. B Franklin John Jay

Left. One of the Articles of the Treaty of Paris signed between the British and Americans to end the war.

Key People apart from Washington

Left. The British forces led by Cornwallis surrendering to Washington and the French at Yorktown. In 1783 Washington entered New York and the British finally recognized the independence of the 13 states. The rest of the British soldiers went home.

Right. Alexander Hamilton (*c.* 1755–1804) started work at the age of 11 in a counting house in New York. He fought against the British in the War of Independence. He later trained as a lawyer and was Secretary of the Treasury after independence, helping to build a strong central government for the new United States.

Below. John Adams (1735–1826), a lawyer, helped to draw up the Declaration of Independence. He was the second president of the US and the first to live in the White House.

Left. Benjamin Franklin (1706–90) was an inventor, writer and thinker. In 1776 he joined with Jefferson and others to draft the Declaration of Independence. After the war, he helped to draft the new constitution for the United States.

Above. Thomas Jefferson (1743–1826) was a lawyer and politician who helped to draft the Declaration of Independence. He was an ambassador in Europe during the War of Independence.

Jefferson was later president of the United States of America from 1800 to 1808.

in the cases of champagne he had brought with him than in leading his men in battle. He was forced to surrender to the Americans at the Battle of Saratoga in 1777.

BENJAMIN FRANKLIN AND THE FRENCH The war continued. Then Benjamin Franklin (1706–1790), a clever American diplomat, persuaded the French that the Americans would win. The French, seeing a chance to get back some of the land they had lost to Britain after the Seven Years' War (p. 367), entered the war on the side of the colonists. By 1781, Spain and the Netherlands had joined in as well, also against Britain, and the small colonial war had become a world war. The combined navies of France, Spain and the Netherlands made it even more difficult for food and guns to reach the British soldiers in America.

THE END OF THE WAR The end came suddenly. Washington gathered an army of 16,000 American and French soldiers and hemmed in the British army at Yorktown in Virginia. The British General Cornwallis surrendered. In 1783 Britain was thoroughly defeated and signed a treaty at Versailles in France agreeing that America was now independent.

The soldier pictured furthest to the left is an American soldier from George Washington's army. Next to him, to the right of the picture, is a British soldier.

Above. The flag of the newly independent 13 states. Each star and red and white stripe represents a state. As more states joined, so more stars were added to the flag, but the number of stripes remained the same to represent the original 13.

THE FRENCH REVOLUTION

By 1789, France was a collection of provinces which had been brought together as one country. Each had its own customs, styles of clothing and even laws. Louis XIV (see p. 344) had been a very strong king and had held all the provinces together. The next two kings were weak and, under their kingship, the problems of an old-fashioned country began to show.

CLERGY, PEASANTS AND NOBLES The adult population of France in the late eighteenth century was about 25 million. Only one million of these were nobles and clergy, but the clergy alone owned one-fifth of all the land in France. Most of the rest was owned by the nobles or the king.

The peasants worked from dawn to dusk on land owned by their local lord. Taxes to the king were high as a result of the wars that France had fought in the seventeenth and eighteenth centuries, and because of the extravagance of Louis XIV and Louis XV. In addition, all peasants had to pay a tithe (tenth) of what they earned to the clergy. The nobles and clergy, on the other hand,

Above. The storming of the Bastille on 14 July 1789. The French revolutionaries saw the Bastille as a great symbol of the king and the government.

Left. A French general from the king's army stands furthest to the left. Next to him is a soldier of the Revolution, called a *sans culotte* because he wore trousers instead of knee breeches.

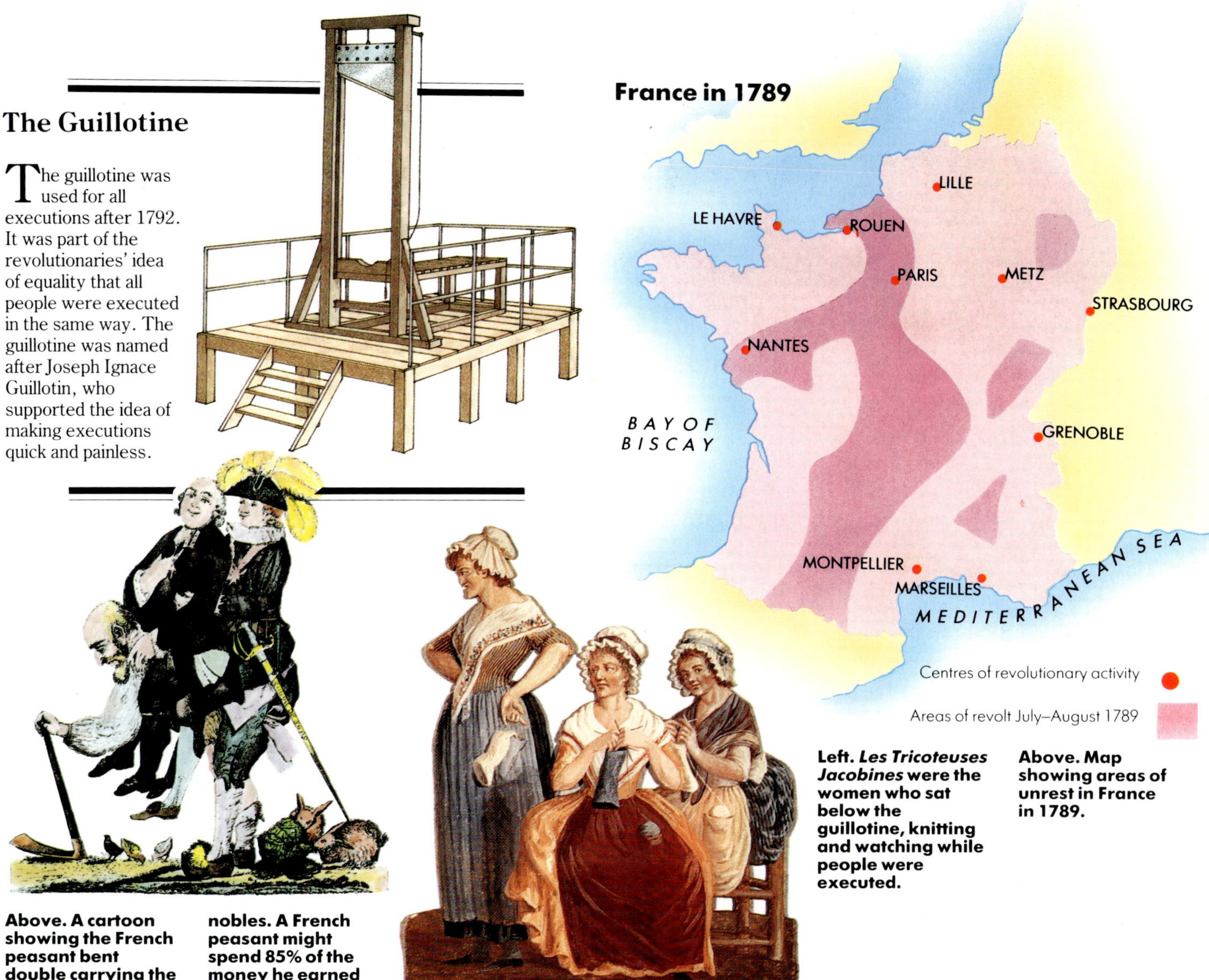

The Guillotine

The guillotine was used for all executions after 1792. It was part of the revolutionaries' idea of equality that all people were executed in the same way. The guillotine was named after Joseph Ignace Guillotin, who supported the idea of making executions quick and painless.

Above. A cartoon showing the French peasant bent double carrying the Church and the nobles. A French peasant might spend 85% of the money he earned on taxes.

Left. *Les Tricoteuses Jacobines* were the women who sat below the guillotine, knitting and watching while people were executed.

Above. Map showing areas of unrest in France in 1789.

paid no taxes at all, even though they were the ones who could afford to do so.

The thinkers of the Enlightenment (see p. 352), like Rousseau, pointed to the unfairness of this. Such ideas of freedom fashioned the American Declaration of Independence (see p. 370) and altered the thinking of many middle-class people in France (who, like the peasants, also had to pay taxes). They were angry, too, that only the nobles could have the best jobs in the army, the navy and the government.

THE ESTATES GENERAL All these problems came to a head in 1789. French soldiers had fought for the Americans' freedom against the British in the War of Independence and had then returned to France, where the complete lack of freedom was obvious. Bad harvests in 1788 had led to widespread hunger and on top of this the king (Louis XVI, 1774–1792) had no money to pay the army, the navy, or the cost of running Versailles and running the country.

Louis decided to call the Estates General to ask them to pay taxes. The Estates General, the nearest thing to *Parliament* in France, had not been called since 1614. It consisted of nobles, clergy and about 600 commoners (mostly middle-class merchants, bankers, lawyers and so on). For the first time, the king now asked the nobles and clergy to pay taxes. They were horrified.

Meanwhile, the commoners (known as the *Third Estate*) suggested that the payment of taxes to the king should allow them to have a say in the running of the country. The result was an uproar. Louis would not hear of such a thing. He locked the Estates General out of the hall they were meeting in at Versailles. They stormed out and met on the tennis court to discuss their complaints.

THE STORMING OF THE BASTILLE Matters went from bad to worse. On 14 July, a mob of poor people stormed the *Bastille*, a royal fortress in Paris. To the Parisians it stood for all the power of the king, the nobles and the clergy. After the Bastille had fallen to the rioters, other riots followed all over France.

FRANCE: ROBESPIERRE TO NAPOLEON

In the summer of 1789 the Estates General re-formed itself as a National Assembly and got down to business, calling for a less powerful monarchy. Louis XVI would not agree, so he was arrested and brought to Paris. Time dragged on, but the king still would not agree to limiting his power. Finally, the mob stormed the palace of the Tuileries, where Louis was living, and fear of the mob helped persuade the National Assembly to put the king on trial and send him to the *guillotine* in 1793.

THE REPUBLIC Protests by moderate people were ignored. France was now ruled by a Committee of Public Safety and justice was carried out by a Revolutionary Tribunal. The extreme revolutionaries who wanted complete change were called *Jacobins*. (They even renamed the first year of the republic, 1792, as Year One.)

ROBESPIERRE (1758–1794) The Jacobins' leader was the pitiless Maximilien Robespierre, a clever lawyer and judge who had joined the Estates General at the age of 31 and who believed passionately in the rights of ordinary people. In Robespierre's view, it was only a rotten society and the work of evil men that stopped ordinary people from being perfect, so it was necessary to kill all the evil people.

Now the guillotine rose and fell day after day. The enemies of the people (at first only the rich) were destroyed one by one, starting with the widowed queen, Marie Antoinette, then the Duc of Orléans, then nobles and clergy. After this Robespierre hunted down the more moderate people who had previously supported him, like Danton, and their wives and families. Then he turned on rival Jacobins. Robespierre saw evil men and women everywhere.

To oppose the 'Terror', as it was called, was a crime. For a year, all France lived in fear. About 500,000 people were arrested and 17,000 were guillotined. Finally, the frightened colleagues of Robespierre turned on him and he too was guillotined.

THE RISE OF NAPOLEON At first many people in Europe were pleased that the revolution was making the French more free. But other monarchs were alarmed because the French guillotined their monarch and nobles and declared they would support revolutions in other countries. By 1793, Austria, Prussia, Britain, Spain and the Netherlands were all at war with France.

Many of the army officers had fled from France to avoid the guillotine and the soldiers who were left were poorly equipped, although they were very loyal to France. An officer called Napoleon Bonaparte (1769–1821) took control. His first military success was at Toulon, where he defeated an army of rebel Frenchmen, the British and Spanish. From then on Napoleon seemed invincible.

THE DIRECTORY After the fall of Robespierre, the government was taken over by five men called the Directory. They supported Napoleon in his campaigns against the Austrians. In 1798, he set sail for Egypt to defeat the Turks and capture the British route to India. Although he did not succeed in this, Napoleon returned to France, overthrew the Directory and, with two others, became a consul of France. He became emperor in 1804.

The Jacobins

The Jacobins gained their name because they met in Paris in what used to be a Dominican (or Jacobin) convent. Their aim was to protect the gains of the French Revolution. They were the most powerful group in the government from mid-1793 to mid-1794, although many moderate people left the Club over the question of getting rid of the king.

There were probably about 500,000 members of Jacobin clubs at one time, but after the fall of their leader, Robespierre, the Jacobin clubs virtually closed down.

Above. Jacobin clubs in France between 1789 and 1791.

Right. Maximilien Robespierre.

Napoleon I (1769–1821)

Napoleon was born on the island of Corsica, which belonged to France. When he was 15 years old, he went to study at the military school in Paris. In 1793 he was in charge of the artillery at Toulon against the British and Spanish. He stormed the town and was made a general.

After that Napoleon fell out of favour and was so poor he had to sell his watch and books to survive. He was recalled in 1795, when he defended Paris against rebels and avoided civil war. He led the French army to defeat the Austrians and invade Egypt, and became First Consul of France in 1799. Later he became emperor.

Above. Map showing how large Napoleon's empire was and the places where his major battles took place. By 1812, he controlled most of Western Europe.

Top. A painting showing the Battle of Aboukir Bay (Egypt) in 1798.

Right. Napoleon Bonaparte, painted by Jacques Louis David. He is shown going forward to conquest. His army is in the background.

MANCHU CHINA

The wealth of China was based on farming. The fertile valleys of the Chang Jiang (Yangtze) and Huang He (Yellow) Rivers produced crops of rice, wheat and vegetables that fed China's vast population, which reached 100 million in 1650. However, one year in every five was reckoned to be a disaster, due either to drought or to flooding of the great river basins. Loss of the food crops led to starvation and often to rebellion.

THE MANCHUS In the seventeenth century, there were a number of food crises and rebellions in China. The Manchu people in the north saw their chance, surging southward, capturing the capital city of Beijing (Peking) and taking control of most of China by 1652.

The Manchus were not Chinese. In fact they never made up more than 2 per cent of the population of China. They kept themselves separate and did not inter-marry with the Chinese. However, they took over all the Chinese ways of ruling, with the Manchu emperors using the enormous and efficient Chinese civil service to run the empire.

CHINESE SELF-SUFFICIENCY The Chinese always considered themselves at the centre of the world, regarding those who lived beyond the boundaries of China as 'barbarians'. Although trade did exist (more at some periods of history than at others) between the west and China, the Chinese had never been very impressed with what the west could offer. In return for their beautiful silks, porcelain and *lacquerware*, all the Chinese wanted from the west was silver or gold. They had everything else that they wanted.

Since farming was considered the most important

Left. Map of China showing the major cities.

Canton harbour, a busy Chinese port.

job, China was largely self-sufficient in food (able to grow enough to support its population). Barges loaded with rice, salt, sugar and tea sailed from south China, along the Grand Canal to Beijing. The rivers bustled with trade. China produced enough iron, silk, hemp, bamboo (used for pipes, tubes, bridges and so on), leather and wood for the needs of its farming people.

THE EUROPEANS As the eighteenth century wore on, it became more difficult for the Chinese to ignore the Europeans. The Emperor Ch'ien-lung (1736–1796) insisted that European traders should be allowed to call at only one port, Guangzhou (Canton). From there it was up to the Chinese to transport the goods to the emperor. Ch'ien-lung had his own view of these goods, looking on them as gifts from the European 'barbarians'. The Europeans, however, expected him to buy them. Moreover, they wanted to sell their goods all over China.

LORD MACARTNEY AND THE EMPEROR In 1792, the British sent Lord Macartney as the first ambassador to China. He took with him a hot air balloon; scientific instruments, such as telescopes, microscopes and sextants; clocks and watches, and air guns. The 83 year-old Emperor Ch'ien-lung was delighted. Macartney also presented a letter from King George III of Britain (1760–1820), asking the emperor for several things, including permission for British merchants to call at all Chinese ports. The emperor ignored the request.

Despite China's wish to remain separate from the rest of the world, the Europeans were becoming richer and more powerful. Within 50 years they were strong enough to force the Chinese to trade with them.

Emperor Kangxi (1661–1722)

Right. An embroidered court robe made of silk. Below. A decorated porcelain plate.

Above. These animal figures have been carved out of jade.

Kangxi became emperor at the age of seven. When he was 15 he took control. He defeated the three powerful warlords in the south of China before conquering Taiwan, parts of Russia, Outer Mongolia and Tibet.

He was also a great administrator, and set up projects to repair the Grand Canal and the flood control works on the Yellow River.

Kangxi loved studying. A European Jesuit missionary called Ferdinand Verbiest taught him geometry and became responsible for cannon production in China. The emperor's liking for the Jesuits encouraged other missionaries, but they were not tolerant of the Chinese. This led to all missionaries except the Jesuits being ordered to leave the country.

JAPAN DURING THE TOKUGAWA SHOGUNATE

Kabuki Theatre

This was a popular form of Japanese drama, with spectacular stage sets and costumes. It consisted of music, mime and dance. All the parts were played by men. Traditionally, the actors and audiences used to talk to each other. The plays went on all day and people came and went according to which scenes or plays they wanted to see.

By 1650, the Japanese, like the Chinese, had lost interest in the Europeans. They rejected both the European religion of Christianity and European trade.

TRADE In the seventeenth century, the only Europeans who were allowed to come to Japan were the Dutch. However, they could only send one ship a year, and they had to stay on the tiny island of Deshima in Nagasaki Harbour. The Japanese continued to trade with China and Korea, but the Japanese people themselves were forbidden by their government to travel abroad. (Death was the penalty for travelling abroad—if you were foolish enough to return!) To make sure that Japanese people stayed at home, the government forbade the building of any large ships. They felt threatened by the Europeans.

THE TOKUGAWA SHOGUNS All this could be done because the government in Japan was very strong. The emperor of Japan was simply a figurehead and the real power lay with the *shoguns*, the military leaders. In 1603, one family of shoguns, called the Tokugawa, had established its power over the others. From this time on there was only one shogun in Japan. All the others were now called *daimyos*. They ruled their own lands but they recognized the Tokugawa shogun as their leader. To make sure they were loyal, the shogun ordered them to spend every other year at his capital, Edo (which is now Tokyo). There he could keep an eye on them and ensure that they did not become too powerful in their home lands.

This system of government lasted well into the nineteenth century. Japan prospered. Trade with China, Korea, the East Indies and Russia grew. Main roads were built to link all the big towns and ports of Japan.

SOCIETY Japanese society became more rigid, however. There were four levels: the most important men were warriors; next came merchants; then craftsmen, and lastly, peasant farmers. No Japanese person could think of changing his or her level. The son of a peasant could not train as a craftsman. Even the warriors (*samurai*) could not change masters and go to serve another daimyo.

CONTROL By 1650, the penalty for being a Christian was death and so Christianity virtually disappeared from Japan. Then the Tokugawa shogun decided to get rid of guns, another European influence that had been brought to Japan in the sixteenth century. The daimyos had been fascinated by these guns. Not only did they buy them, their swordsmiths quickly learned how to make them. The Tokugawa shogun decided to turn the clock back.

He did not want the daimyos forming their own armies of samurai warriors armed with guns, so he granted fewer and fewer licences to gunsmiths until all the samurai were once more armed only with swords and had no guns at all.

Since Japan was peaceful during this period of history, there was very little for the samurai to do. Many started to work as administrators in the government rather than have nothing to do.

Japan seemed deliberately backward to the outside world, but in fact it was a well-organized, artistic and prosperous country. Three of the 10 biggest cities in the world in 1750 were in Japan. Tokyo was the largest Japanese city, with half a million inhabitants.

The picture above, painted by an anonymous Japanese artist, shows the execution of Jesuit priests in 1622. Christians were persecuted in Japan during the seventeenth century.

Right. The shogun, Tokugawa Ieyasu (1542–1616). He founded the dynasty of shoguns who ruled Japan from 1603 until 1868.

Above. Map of Japan showing the major cities.

MOGUL AND MARATHA INDIA

The Mogul emperors ruled a large part of India from the early sixteenth century to about 1750. Their religion was *Islam* and they were known as Muslims. The most famous Mogul emperor was Akbar, who reigned from 1556 to 1605. He brought about many reforms, such as the end of the enslavement of prisoners of war. More importantly for the future of India, he insisted on religious toleration. Prisoners of war and their women and children were not to be forced to become

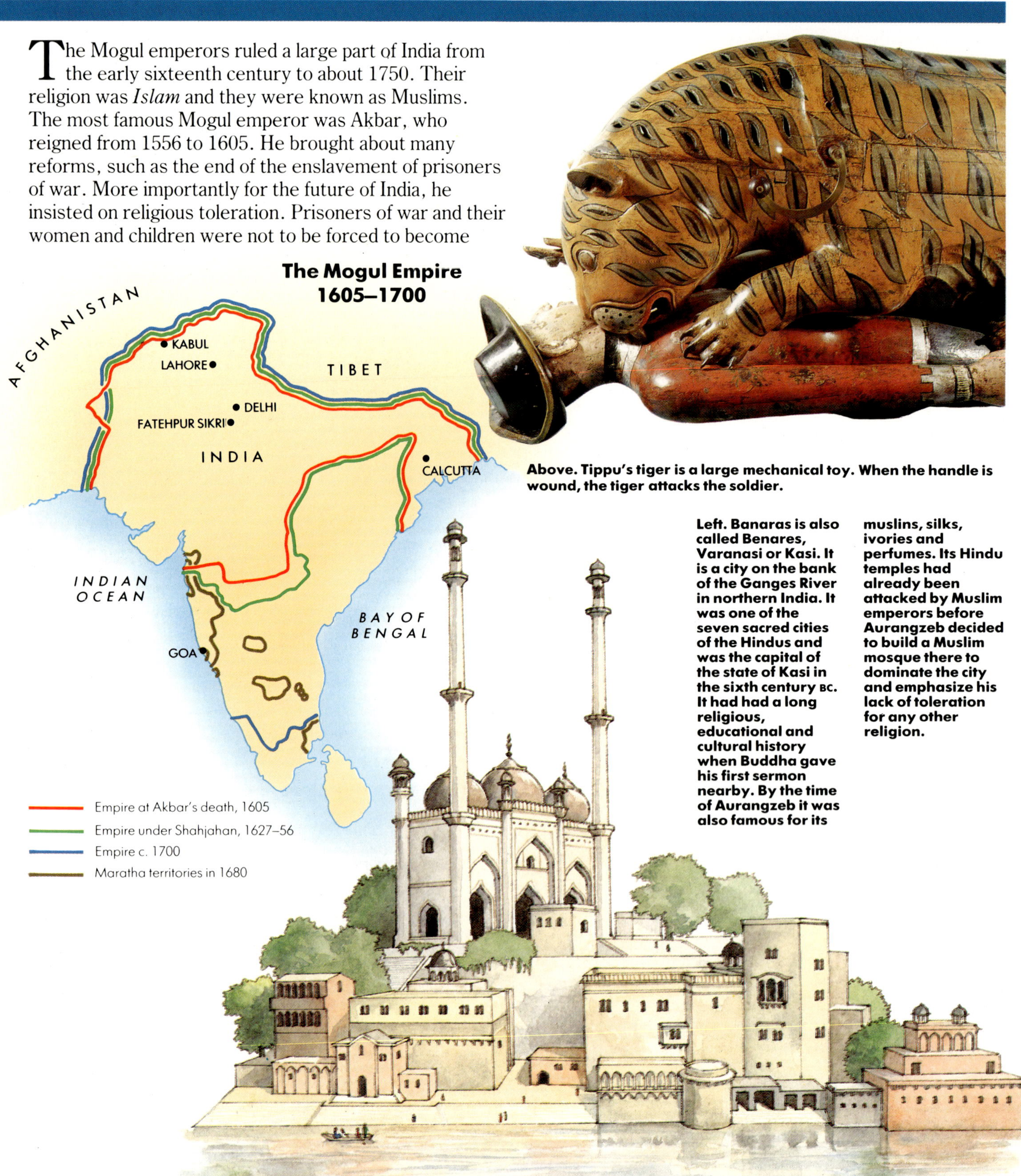

Above. Tippu's tiger is a large mechanical toy. When the handle is wound, the tiger attacks the soldier.

Left. Banaras is also called Benares, Varanasi or Kasi. It is a city on the bank of the Ganges River in northern India. It was one of the seven sacred cities of the Hindus and was the capital of the state of Kasi in the sixth century BC. It had had a long religious, educational and cultural history when Buddha gave his first sermon nearby. By the time of Aurangzeb it was also famous for its muslins, silks, ivories and perfumes. Its Hindu temples had already been attacked by Muslim emperors before Aurangzeb decided to build a Muslim mosque there to dominate the city and emphasize his lack of toleration for any other religion.

Muslims. *Hindus* were not to be made to change their religion either. Akbar worked to make India into a united country with one official language but toleration for other languages and beliefs. He passed on a strong country to his successors, many of whom were clever rulers. However, they were frequently faced with rebellions, often led by their own sons, and this weakened the empire.

SIVAJI AND THE MARATHAS As the Mogul Empire weakened in the seventeenth century, another centre of power arose further south. This was founded by Sivaji, leader of the *Marathas*, who wanted to conquer more land at about the same time that Emperor Aurangzeb (1658–1707) came to the Mogul throne.

The two men signed a treaty in 1665 in which Sivaji agreed to surrender to the Moguls 23 out of the 35 forts that he had conquered from another Indian prince. He also agreed to acknowledge the power of the Moguls. In return, Aurangzeb supported him in claiming many of the prince's lands.

Above. Aurangzeb, the Mogul emperor from 1658 to 1707. His name means 'ornament of the throne'.

When Sivaji visited Aurangzeb, he did not like the patronizing way he was treated at the Mogul court. He flew into a rage and fainted. Aurangzeb did not trust Sivaji, but he was afraid that Sivaji's followers might join with enemies of the Moguls and depose him. He put Sivaji under house arrest in comfortable surroundings. Sivaji, however, is reputed to have made his escape in a fruit basket.

Sivaji continued to fight and conquer other lands. He built up a strong army and, seeing trouble from Europe, developed a navy as well.

THE ATTRACTION OF INDIA The Europeans were attracted by the wealth of India. Its main exports were precious stones (including diamonds, rubies, sapphires and pearls), cotton textiles (such as calico), sugar, pepper, ivory and a dye called indigo. The Europeans were fascinated by such exotic riches. The Portuguese already had small trading stations on the coast of India, and they were now followed by the Dutch and the British.

Above. An East India Company trading station in Bengal, 1665. These stations, often called factories, were big warehouses and were built like fortresses. European traders and their families lived inside them.

CLIVE OF INDIA

Robert Clive

Clive went to India as a clerk in the East India Company, but soon became a soldier. He went on to lead British troops to defeat Indian and French forces and establish British rule in India.

In the picture on the left, Emperor Sha Alam hands Clive an edict that gives the Company the right to collect revenues from Bengal, Bihar and Orissa.

Clive returned to Britain in 1767. His rule in India had made him unpopular and he killed himself in 1774.

Both Britain and France, together with other European powers, had started to set up trading stations in India from the middle of the seventeenth century. As in other parts of the world during this period, the British and the French were strong rivals in trade.

The chance for France to gain the upper hand over the British in India came in 1748. Two princes of Indian states claimed a strip of land called the Carnatic, on the east coast of India, where the French and the British both had trading stations. The French supported one prince, called Chanda. The British supported the other, Mohammed Ali.

ROBERT CLIVE (1725–1774) The British trading activities in India at this time were run by the British East India Company, which sent an army of 500 men to help Mohammed Ali. This army, led by Robert Clive, captured Carnatic and then held out for 53 days when it was besieged by an army 20 times larger. The fighting dragged on, but eventually Mohammed Ali was made ruler of the area. He favoured the British, who gained more trade through his friendship.

THE BLACK HOLE OF CALCUTTA, 1756 Both the French and the British had trading stations in Bengal, the state ruled by Suraj-ud-Daulah, who favoured the French. In a dispute with the British over an enemy of Suraj's whom they were sheltering, he attacked the British trading station of Fort William. After a fight, 145 British survivors surrendered. Suraj locked them in a cell measuring six by five metres. Without water and with only two, small, barred windows, the prisoners struggled for air through the hot tropical night. When the door was opened in the morning, 123 people had died of suffocation or had been trampled to death. This incident made the British furious.

THE BATTLE OF PLASSEY, 1757 Clive, with an army of 3000, pursued Suraj. Camping overnight at the village of Plassey, they awoke in the morning to face a semi-circle of 60,000 of Suraj's soldiers. However, with the help of an

Left. Mohammed Ali, the Indian prince whom the British supported.

Indian Arts and Crafts

Mogul India was famous for carpets, glassware and paintings. The carpets were made of fine wool that was often mistaken for silk. Glassware was made by craftsmen who painted designs onto coloured glass.

Many paintings were done for book illustrations, showing birds and animals, court scenes and stories from history.

Left. An official of the British East India Company living in great style and splendour in India. Notice the English portraits but the Indian furnishings.

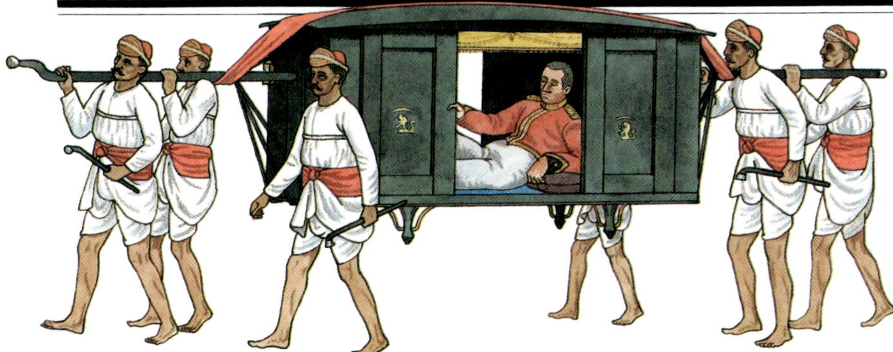

Left. An official of the Company being carried in a litter by Indian servants.

Indian general, Mir Jaffir, who had deserted from Suraj, Clive's army won the Battle of Plassey.

THE IMPORTANCE OF PLASSEY TO THE BRITISH The Battle of Plassey gained an area of land for Britain the size of England and Wales. Mir Jaffir was made ruler of all Bengal, but the British had the real power. From then until the mid-twentieth century, the British were dominant in India.

Up to 1750 the economic effects of the British in India were small, However, once they gained control of Bengal after the Battle of Plassey, they became much more powerful. Some British merchants made huge fortunes and many came back to Britain to spend them. They were known as *nabobs*. People like Clive, and later Warren Hastings, tried to reform the British East India Company and the British government had some control over it after the India Act of 1784. Despite this, the British in India were still making fortunes in the early part of the nineteenth century. Although some Europeans went to India as *missionaries* or to work as administrators, it was trade and the money to be made from it that were the most important reasons why the British, like other Europeans, were interested in India at this time.

The Growth of British Power in India

Above. Map showing India in the eighteenth century and the growth of British power up to 1805. Most areas they controlled were in the south, along the east coast and on the northern border. The Marathas were the only rival to British power by 1805.

1 In 1760, China reached its greatest size under the Ch'ing dynasty. It took in Manchuria, Mongolia, Tibet, Korea, Taiwan and Eastern Turkestan as well as Inner China.

2 In 1762, Jean-Jacques Rousseau of France, one of the leading figures of the Enlightenment, wrote *The Social Contract*. This said that governments should act for the good of the people they governed and should give them justice and equality.

3 In 1768, James Cook of Britain began his exploration of the Pacific Ocean, coming across many places, including New Zealand and Australia, that Europeans had known little or nothing about before.

4 In 1776, the 13 colonies in North America declared their independence from Britain. This was the beginning of the end of Britain's first empire.

5 In 1789, revolution broke out in France. This led to the execution of King Louis XVI and the setting up of a revolutionary government which was eventually taken over by Napoleon Bonaparte.

AFRICA AND THE SLAVE TRADE

The Slaves

In the late 1500s, a few thousand slaves were transported from Africa to the New World every year. The figure peaked (50,000–100,000 a year) in the eighteenth century.

Altogether, 10 million slaves were recorded as landing alive in the New World, with two million dying during the voyages. The real figures for deaths may have been much higher.

Left. A ship carrying slaves. The slaves were chained together in rows on shelves only half a metre apart. They could not sit up or move freely.

Above. Map showing the Triangular Trade between Britain, West Africa, the West Indies, North America and Britain.

For centuries most of North Africa was dominated by Arabs, who traded with the Mediterranean countries to the north as well as with kingdoms such as Ghana and Mali in West Africa, south of the Sahara Desert. The trade was in goods like copper, horses and salt from the north, and in ivory, gold and slaves from the West African kingdoms.

Most people in East Africa were farmers. They had little to do with the people on the coast, where a great deal of trade had taken place for centuries. Trading centred on coastal towns like Mombasa (now in Kenya), which had a population of about 10,000 by 1500. Many traders were Arabs, or of mixed Arab and African descent, and trading ships went as far afield as China.

The huge areas in the centre of Africa were largely untouched by Europeans until after 1800. However, the growth of the slave trade greatly affected the people who lived on the coast, as well as many people who lived inland and were captured and sold as slaves. Slavery was not new to places like West Africa. The kings of that area had sold captured prisoners into slavery for centuries.

THE EUROPEANS Parts of North Africa, trading stations down the coasts of West and East Africa, and the Dutch settlement in South Africa, were the only footholds that the Europeans had in Africa by 1800. Yet Europeans

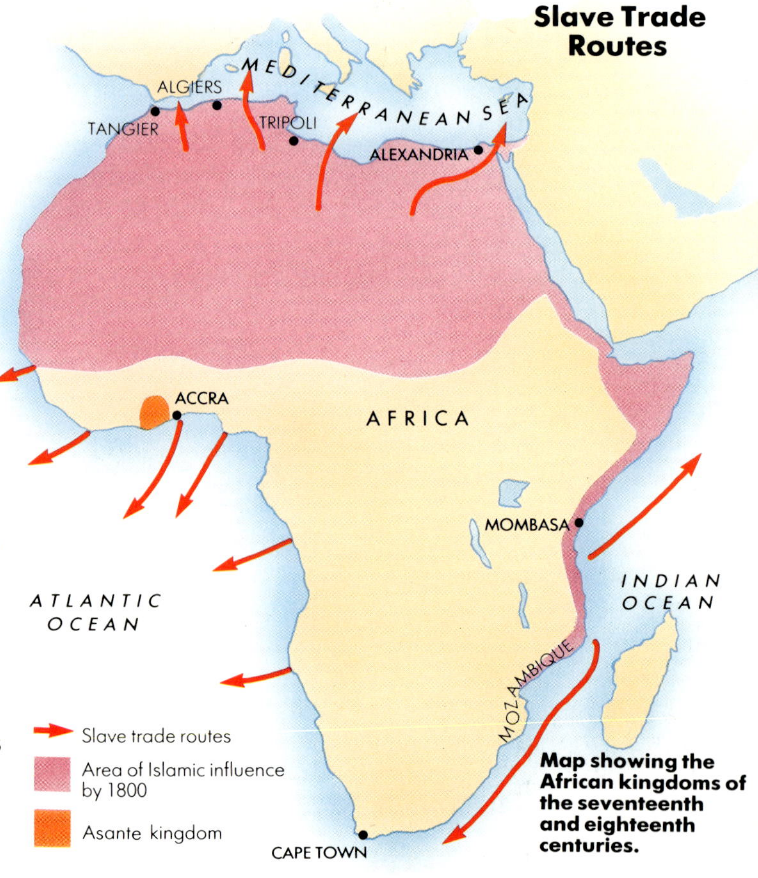

Map showing the African kingdoms of the seventeenth and eighteenth centuries.

1650>1700

The Kingdom of Asante

In the 1670s Osei Tutu founded the kingdom of Asante as a loose confederation. Chiefs paid him tribute taxes collected from their villages and the profits from their gold fields. They provided soldiers for a confederation army led by Osei Tutu.

By 1750 the Asante controlled most of the gold fields and most of modern Ghana. This made the Asante kings very wealthy. Most of the gold mines were worked by slave labour. The gold was used to buy cloth, metal, European firearms and salt from the many traders who passed through the area.

Above. This comb was used as part of a burial ritual. When it was found, it had a crust of lime, egg and millet on it. These were the foods given to the spirits.

Left. A mask representing the head of an enemy. It was probably attached to a stool.

Above. Breast ornament of the Asantehene, or king of the Asante. Other ornaments included bracelets, headbands and necklaces made of finely worked gold. The king's base or capital was near Kumasi, a great trading centre.

were already affecting the future of the continent by taking people from there to work on the new plantations and in the mines of the Americas. This was slavery on a greater scale than Africa had ever known.

Sugar-cane plantations were set up in the West Indies and were followed by cotton and tobacco plantations in the southern part of North America, and by sugar and coffee plantations in Brazil. All these plantations needed large numbers of people to work them. The native Amerindians were almost wiped out by European disease and violence. European slaves (mostly convicts) were too few in number and quickly died of tropical disease. So the Europeans turned to Africa for slaves.

THE TRIANGULAR TRADE By 1650, the British and French had joined the Dutch in the slave trade. Merchants loaded ships with cotton cloth, beads, alcohol and cheap guns and sailed to Africa, where they traded these goods for young black men and women. Then they set sail for the Americas. In America, the slaves were traded (for two or three times the price paid for them) for items like sugar, rum, raw cotton, coffee and tobacco. The merchants then sailed back to Europe to sell these goods, having made a good profit.

THE SLAVES During this period of history, there were many wars between different African tribes. The tribe that had won often sold the prisoners it had taken to dealers. These dealers in turn sold the slaves to European traders, who chained and packed them naked into special slave ships for the journey to America. Up to a third died on each voyage, and were thrown overboard.

Once in the Americas, the Africans were sold as livestock. Some never recovered from the trauma of their capture and voyage. With no hope of seeing their home again, a third of the slaves died within three years of their arrival. Few of the rest survived the hard labour on the plantations for more than 10 years.

THE DUTCH AND SOUTH AFRICA

The Dutch governor of the Cape Colony in South Africa on his farm. Compare the architecture of the house with the Dutch houses on page 342.

The area of land that came to be known as South Africa was not an empty land when the Dutch first landed there in the seventeenth century. There were many different tribes and peoples living there, including hunter-gatherer societies and tribes which farmed cattle and sheep. These tribes traded among themselves. For instance, the Khoisan obtained their copper and iron from the Batswana to the north of them, trading the metals that they did not use with the Xhosa in exchange for tobacco. Trade spread right across the region.

The most important group as far as the white settlers were concerned was the Khoisan. About 50,000 of these cattle and sheep farmers lived in the south of Africa in the seventeenth century.

CAPE TOWN The first Dutch sailors who landed in South Africa were on their way to the Dutch colonies in the East Indies. They needed fresh meat, vegetables and water, because they were only part of the way through this long voyage, and they bought these goods from the Khoisan. As more and more Dutch ships stopped at the Cape, the sailors wanted more and more food. If they could not persuade the Khoisan to sell to them, they sometimes seized their animals. Then the Dutch decided it would be easier to set up their own farms round Cape Town, so that they could grow their own food to supply their sailors.

SETTLEMENT Dutch people came out to South Africa to settle on farms within 100 kilometres of Cape Town. They grew wheat and fruit and became known as *Boers* ('boer' is the Dutch word for farmer). In 1685, French Protestants, known as Huguenots, began to be persecuted in France by Louis XIV (see p. 344) and some came to settle in South Africa. They were expert wine-makers and were soon growing vines and farming.

LABOUR Slavery was introduced in 1658. The Boers found that the local tribes were too independent to work on the Dutch farms, preferring to follow their own ways of life. So the Dutch brought in slaves from places such as West Africa and Malaysia.

ISOLATION AND RELIGION As the population of European settlers grew and all the land around Cape Town was settled, the Boers trekked northeast to found new farms. The climate here was drier, so they raised sheep and cattle instead of growing wheat and fruit.

The Boers lived on huge farms, cut off from the civilized life of Cape Town. They developed their own language, called Afrikaans, which was a simpler form of Dutch and included many African words.

The settlers had brought with them a very strict form of Christianity, called *Calvinism* after John Calvin (see p. 269), and they found justification for owning slaves in the Old Testament. In practical terms, it seemed the only way to run the big farms they had.

The further the Dutch spread out from Cape Town, the more they threatened the ways of life of the native peoples of southern Africa. Clashes between the Boers, the Khoisan and different *Bantu* people started before 1800, but the real trouble came later. The hunter-gatherers were either pushed further away from the fertile land, into areas like the Kalahari Desert, or they had to work for the Boers.

The Khoisan and the Dutch

In the mid-seventeenth century, about 50,000 members of the Khoisan tribes lived in the area behind what became Cape Town. At first they welcomed trade with the Dutch, but as more and more white people came their land was threatened. Arguments led to the first Khoi-Dutch war in 1659. Although the Khoisan tribes united and drove back the Dutch, they could not capture the Dutch fort and eventually had to give up.

Afterwards there was a meeting of Khoisan and Dutch leaders. A Dutchman called Van Riebeeck recorded in his diary:

'They spoke for a long time about our taking every day more of the land which had belonged to them from all ages. They also asked whether, if they were to come to Holland, they would be permitted to act in a similar manner.'

At the end of the meeting, the Dutch leaders said that the Khoisan had lost their land in war, and therefore could not expect to get it back.

From this time on the Khoisan were in retreat. They had three choices: to fight the Dutch, to move further north, or to become servants of the Dutch farmers.

Above. Khoisan people trading with Dutch sailors.

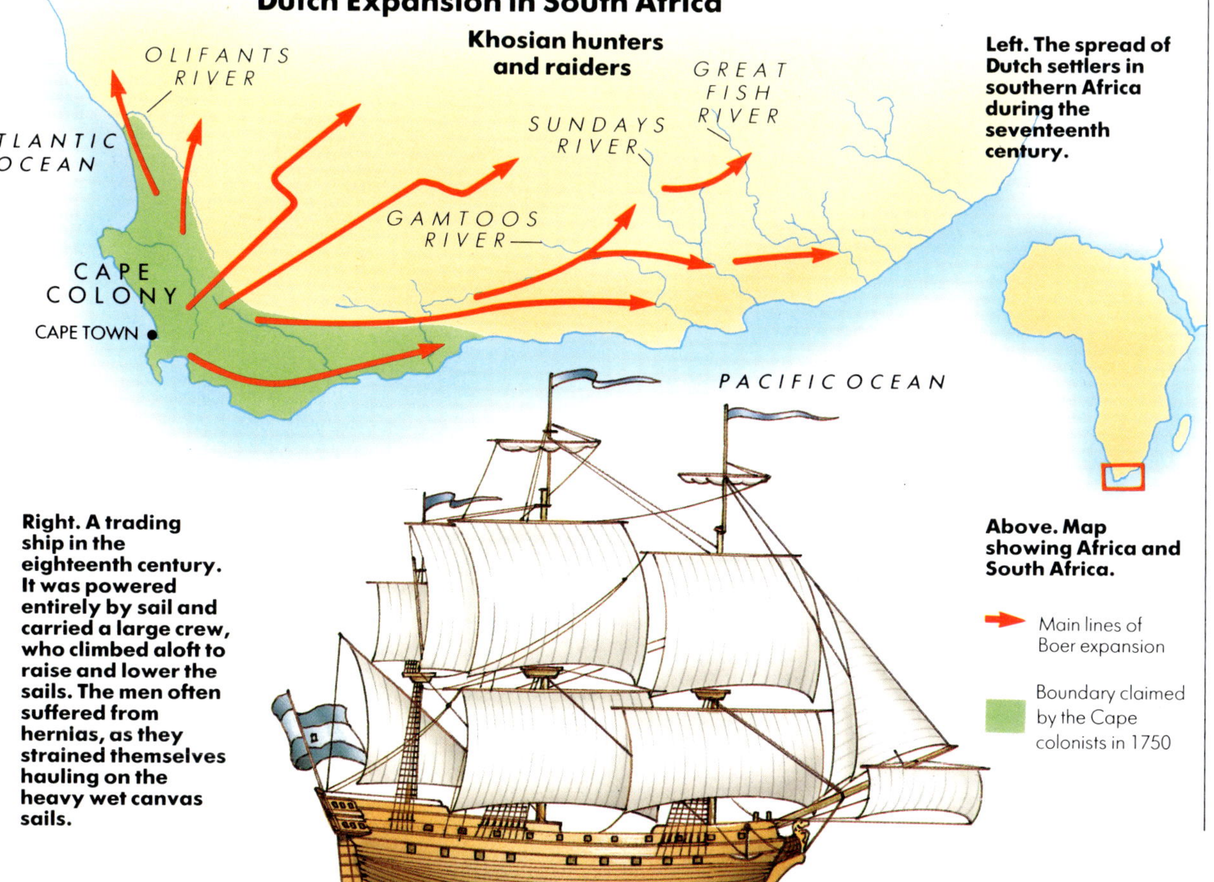

Left. The spread of Dutch settlers in southern Africa during the seventeenth century.

Above. Map showing Africa and South Africa.

Right. A trading ship in the eighteenth century. It was powered entirely by sail and carried a large crew, who climbed aloft to raise and lower the sails. The men often suffered from hernias, as they strained themselves hauling on the heavy wet canvas sails.

1 In North Africa, which included Algeria and Egypt, the Ottoman Turks had established an empire by 1500. Arab influence in North Africa remained very strong and throughout the period 1650 to 1800 it extended southwards, through trade in items such as gold and slaves.

2 In West Africa, the sixteenth century had seen the rise of the highly developed states of Benin and Oyo. By the eighteenth century, the more powerful states were Dahomey and Asante on the Gold Coast.

3 In East Africa, Arab influence extended down the coast almost to South Africa. In the interior, however, Ethiopia and other states continued to control their own affairs.

4 Central Africa was largely untouched by outside influences by 1800. Tribes here lived off the land, trading some goods, such as copper, when required.

5 The Russian tsar, Peter the Great, began to build the city of St Petersburg in 1703. It became the capital of Russia.

6 Dutch settlers in the East Indies began growing coffee there in 1711. Soon there were large coffee plantations and by 1723 about 6 million kilograms were being produced each year.

ABORIGINAL AUSTRALIANS

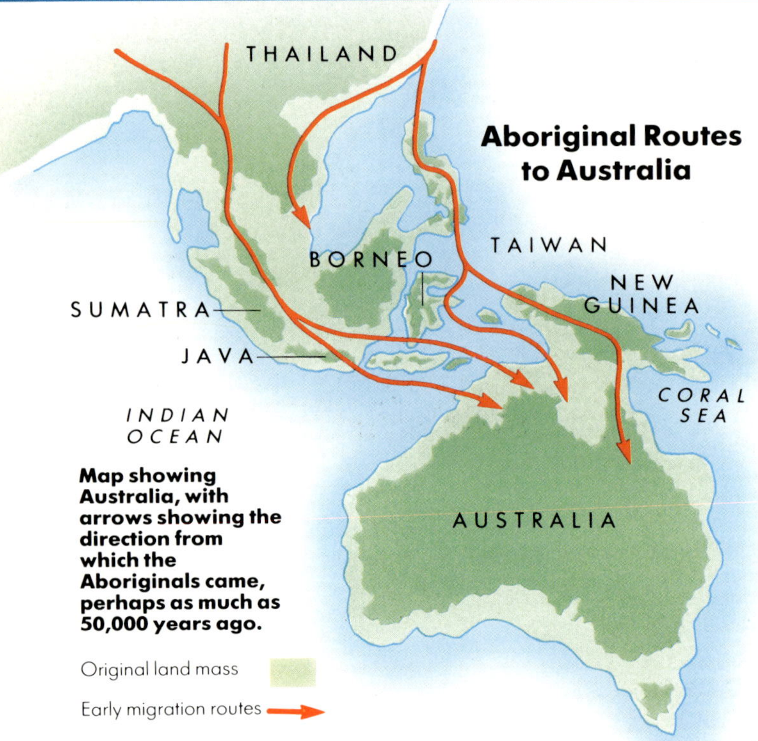

Map showing Australia, with arrows showing the direction from which the Aboriginals came, perhaps as much as 50,000 years ago.

The first people to live in Australia came from Asia, possibly as much as 50,000 years ago. They probably journeyed from one island to the next in canoes or rafts. These people were the discoverers and colonizers of Australia.

HUNTER-GATHERERS At the point in history at which people settled in Australia, all the people on earth were nomadic hunter-gatherers. As time wore on, most people changed from living as nomads to being settled farmers. However, this did not happen in Australia because of the general lack of water and resources throughout the land. Thus, most Aboriginals continued as nomads and had to live in balance with the food and water available during each season. Groups of men, women and children adapted to what was available in each area, whether the land was rich or arid. People lived in small groups throughout Australia. They differed from each other in their physical appearance, language, beliefs, traditions and cultures.

Fighting between the British and Aboriginals in the early nineteenth century.

TRADE AND RELIGION About 3000 years ago, some Aboriginal tribes began to travel long distances to trade ornaments and other goods with other tribes. In areas that were better for farming, such as the swamp regions of inland Victoria, there were settled villages where as many as 700 people lived.

Ritual life was extremely important to the Aboriginals. Ceremonial gatherings took place on sacred sites, such as the painted rock shelters associated with the idea of dreamtime, which is a mythical golden age of the past. Hundreds of people came from miles away to gather for short periods at such occasions. These ceremonies were often associated with the harvest of special foods, such as the cycad nut or the bogong moth.

By the time that Europeans arrived in Australia, the Aboriginals had successfully adapted to the often difficult environment of their country. They ate many different kinds of plant and animal food, from the witchetty grub to the kangaroo, from oysters to flying foxes, and from turtle eggs to the roots of daisy yams.

THE COMING OF THE EUROPEANS Australia was first sighted by a European—the Dutch explorer Willem Janszoon—in 1605. Abel Tasman, another Dutchman,

Above. Uluru (Ayers Rock) was and is a sacred place to Aboriginals.

Left. An Aboriginal picture of the 'lightning man', Obiri Rock.

Above. An Aboriginal bark painting of a kangaroo.

The Aboriginal Dreamtime

In Aboriginal belief, long ago the world was only a flat emptiness. Then the Ancestors or Beings came out of the earth and made the hills and valleys, the rivers, lakes, springs, trees, plants and animals. The Aboriginals' name for this time of creation is the Dreamtime.

When they had finished their work of creating the world, the Ancestors sank back into the earth, but their spirit is still in the world—in the rocks and trees and all around.

Usually the Ancestors were in human form, but they could take the shapes of animals if they wished to. The Aboriginals give the Ancestors many names, some of which mean 'dream'.

Each of the many Aboriginal tribal groups had (and still has) sacred places. Uluru (Ayers Rock) in the middle of Australia is the sacred place of two groups of the Pitjantjara tribe. These sacred places are where the Ancestors lived, hunted and performed ceremonies to show the way that the Aboriginals are to live their lives. There are many pictures at the sacred places that illustrate the doings of the Ancestors.

sighted Tasmania in 1642 and sailed right along the northern and part of the western coasts of Australia in 1644. However, Australia remained undisturbed until the British Admiralty sent Captain James Cook to explore the continent. He claimed it for the British in 1770. From 1788 Britain sent convicts to serve their prison sentences in Australia. Many of them stayed on in the country when their sentences were over. Other settlers gradually began to arrive too.

Soon after the European arrival, the number of Aboriginals fell sharply. It has been estimated that there were 300,000 Aboriginals in 1770; by 1900, the population amounted to about 66,000. Many died from bullets and many more from the strange European diseases, such as tuberculosis. The rest had lost their land and their sacred places. It was not their home any longer. The Aboriginals became despondent and thc death rate rose dramatically. The European colonists, however, grew rich and their numbers increased.

Left. The Aboriginals built shelters out of whatever materials were available. Often these were wood, twigs and leaves. Shelters could be semi-permanent, depending on how much a tribe moved around in search of food. More permanent villages were built in areas that were rich in food supplies, like the swamp regions of inland Victoria.

MAORI NEW ZEALAND

Above. A drawing of a Maori *pa* or fortress.

People from Polynesia sailed to New Zealand around AD 800–900. They were already farmers and settled down to grow yams, sweet potatoes and taro on North Island. However, the colder climate of South Island made farming impossible there, so on that island small groups of nomads lived by fishing and gathering native plants. The people who settled in New Zealand were called Maoris.

THE MOAS Over time, the number of people in the warmer northern regions of North Island grew quite large. They hunted flightless birds, called *moas*, which were easy prey. The moa was extremely important to the Maoris. It was a large bird, possibly bigger than an ostrich. Its flesh was used for food, its bones were carved into tools and ornaments, and the shells of its enormous eggs were used as containers for carrying water. As time passed, however, the moa became extinct and the Maoris became more dependent on farming.

MAORI WARFARE As tribes grew larger, they needed more land to grow food, and fights over land became

Tattooing

The way in which the Maoris tattooed themselves was more like carving. They used tiny chisels to carve intricate patterns into the skin. It was very painful. Men had more tattooing on their faces than women did. Tattooing was done all over the body, sometimes including the thighs and buttocks as well.

There is no-one alive today tattooed in this way. The last man tattooed like this died 50 years ago, but there are still a few old people with tattooing on parts of their faces.

Right. A map of New Zealand showing where *pa* were built. Most settlements were around the coast and more people settled in North Island, where the climate was better for farming.

Above. The old tohunga, or wise man, is in a *tapu*, or sacred state. He cannot touch cooked food, so the boy is feeding him.

Right. A carved lintel showing the skill and detail of Maori work. Compare this style with the picture of the face on the page opposite.

Right. The moa was an enormous bird which could not fly. It was related to the ostrich but was much larger; some were three metres (compare the size of the chicken next to it). Once the Maoris arrived and started to hunt them, moas quickly became extinct.

common. The Maoris built fortresses, called *pa*, with terraces, ditches and palisades, on the sides of extinct volcanoes, on fairly flat land and even on swampy ground. As time went on, tribes of Maoris built more and more large *pa* and their defences became stronger. Accounts from the eighteenth century describe houses and storehouses around central open spaces, called marae, and sometimes even plots of land on which to grow vegetables inside the walls of the fortresses.

The men taught Maori martial arts to the boys from an early age. Their weapons were designed for hand-to-hand fighting and were used for stabbing, thrusting or clubbing. War was usually caused by arguments over land and property, but the honour (mana) of the tribe also had to be guarded against insults of all kinds and any such insults were avenged. Feuds could continue for generations. There were also periods of peace when enemy tribes might join forces to fight a third enemy.

RELIGION OF THE MAORIS Religion was an important part of daily life; an important belief was *tapu*. This means 'sacred' or 'forbidden'—the same as the word 'taboo'. Certain places, objects, activities or even people might be *tapu*. They had to be avoided altogether or treated with great care, under the direction of a tohunga—a sort of priest or wiseman. Otherwise, the Maoris believed that terrible misfortunes would happen to them. Though this may seem superstitious, this religious attitude to life also acted as a way of making sure that people behaved well. If someone failed to observe a *tapu* restriction, the tohunga soon made sure that they were punished in some way.

THE COMING OF THE EUROPEANS A Dutchman, named Abel Tasman, visited New Zealand in 1642, but it was not until the arrival of Captain James Cook in 1769 that real contact was made with the Europeans. Along with materials, such as iron, cloth and pottery, that the Maoris thought were wonderful, the Europeans also brought diseases which the Maoris had never known and to which they had no natural immunity.

The first Europeans to live in New Zealand were a rough crowd—escaped convicts from Australia, seamen from visiting whaling and trading ships, and a few adventurers. Many of the Maori died and their way of life changed forever.

THE UNTOUCHED WORLD

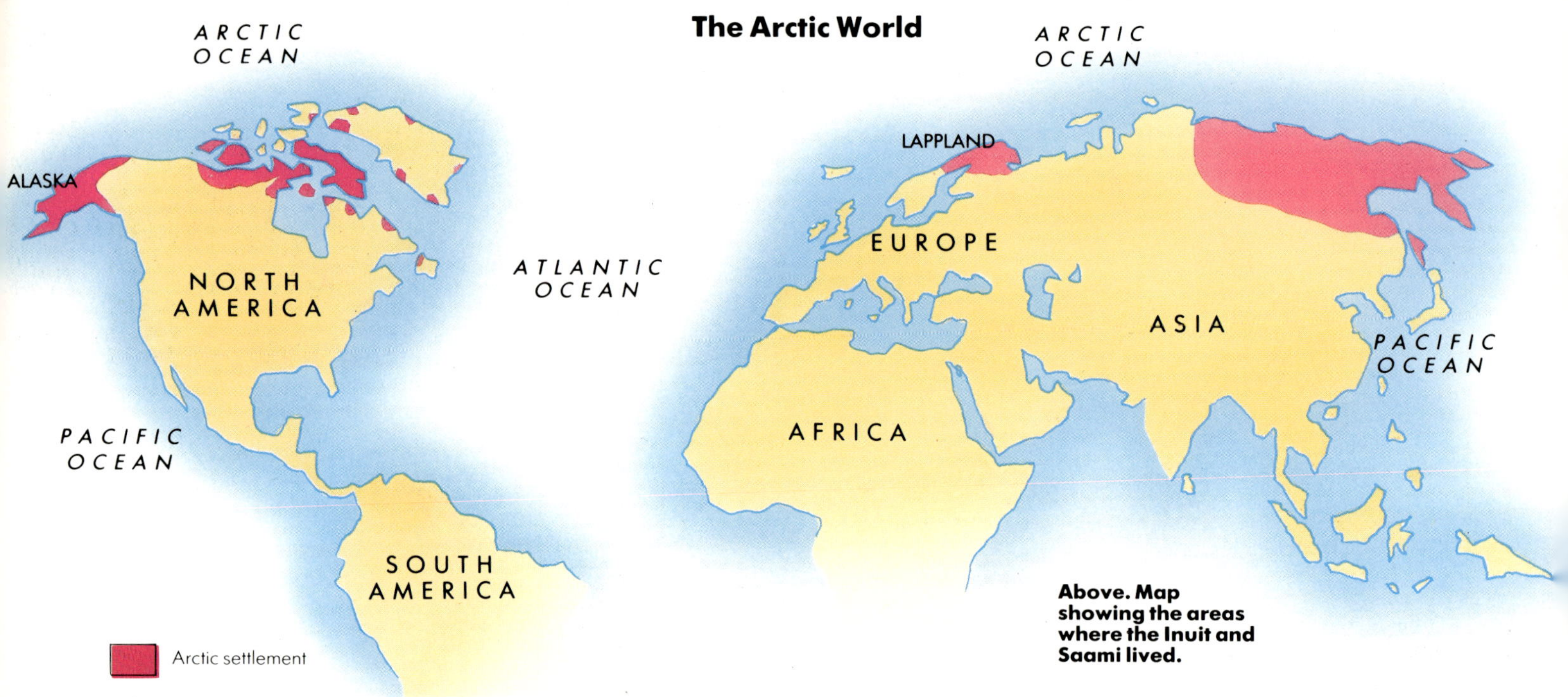

The Arctic World

Arctic settlement

Above. Map showing the areas where the Inuit and Saami lived.

Captain John Ross meeting Inuit people in the early nineteenth century. This is the first recorded meeting of white people with Inuit.

By 1800, almost every part of the world had been touched by the arrival of the Europeans. The voyages of exploration and discovery from the late fifteenth century to the seventeenth century had uncovered whole new worlds for the Europeans. The cultures of the South and North American Indians, various African tribes, the Aboriginals of Australia and the Maoris of New Zealand had been revealed in exotic places which must have been beyond many Europeans' imaginations.

TRADE AT ANY COST At this time in history, Europeans embarked on voyages of exploration in order to increase their trading opportunities. When they arrived in 'new' lands, their main interest was to find out what goods these lands could provide to be shipped back to Europe. The Europeans strengthened their claim on a new trading post by colonizing it. In this process, little thought was given to, or interest shown in, the cultures that they came across, and almost every such culture suffered through contact with the Europeans. The rapid depletion in numbers of all *indigenous* cultures was a great price to pay for European expansion.

THE ARCTIC WORLD The only cultures to remain untouched during this process were those of the Saami and Inuit (Eskimos) of the Arctic. From c. 10,000 BC, people who seem to have originated in central Asia migrated across the Bering land bridge into Arctic America. These were the ancestors of the Inuit. A similar development took place in Europe, where hunting groups moved from the east, south and west into Lappland—an area that covers northern Norway, Sweden, Finland and the Kola peninsula of Russia. The Inuit of America and the Saami of Lappland were separate groups, but there were many similarities in their cultures.

Inuit Dwellings

The polar Inuit people spent the winter in houses called igdlus. The shape of the igdlu and the sleeping platform inside it were cut into the ground. The walls and roof were made of rock slabs. The top of the roof was turfed and a window made of seal-gut was put in.

Blubber lamps inside gave heat and light and made it so warm that people did not need to wear many clothes.

There was not much space. The men mended tools and sledges. The women made clothes from animal skins. Everyone in the family slept on a sleeping platform covered with rugs.

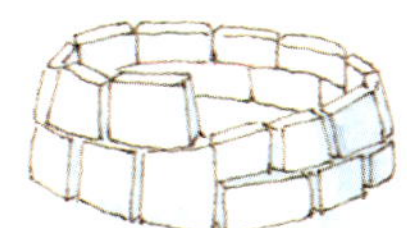

Right. Igdlus of a more permanent kind were made from rock slabs dug into the earth. They were covered with turf to insulate them against the freezing temperatures.

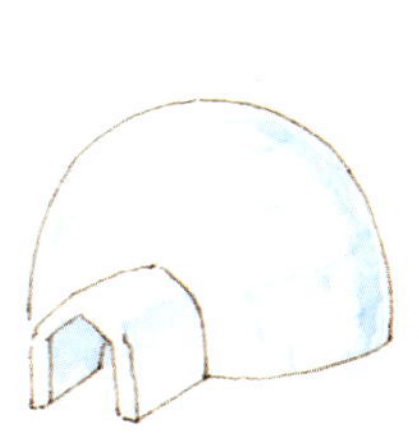

Above. Igdlus made of snow blocks were mostly used during winter travel. A husband and wife could make one in a few hours.

THE SAAMI The Saami lived by hunting, fowling and fishing. Elk and bear were frequently hunted and later reindeer were herded and used to pull sledges.

Shamanism was the main Saami religion and in this religion the bear was regarded as sacred. The Saami had a cult in which the animal was killed, the meat was eaten and the bones were buried with the skull at the top. Animal sacrifices were also carried out next to unusual trees and stones.

From the sixteenth century onwards, the Saami used portable tents, known as Kåta, to live in. The Kåta was divided into two sections: the sleeping area at the front, and the sacred kitchen and hearth at the back.

THE INUIT The early Inuit usually lived in flimsy hide tents. By the time of the Dorset culture (AD 800–1000), however, their settlements had grown larger. They built houses which were partly underground and which could hold up to three families each.

A later culture, the Thule of Alaska (AD 1000–1600), had a successful economy in which whaling played a large part. They used dog sledges, boats and kayaks and had a settled lifestyle with well-insulated winter homes. Around AD 1100, the Thule expanded eastwards and spread over a territory ranging from the east Siberian coast to Greenland. They were the ancestors of the modern-day Inuit (Eskimo).

THE EUROPEANS The first European to come across the Inuit was a British man, Captain John Ross. He met a party of Thule Inuit in 1818 when he was leading an expedition searching for a northwest passage to India and the East. European expansion had reached the last untouched culture and was soon to have a devastating effect on the lifestyle of the Inuit.

Inuit Religion

Shamanism is important in the religious life of the Inuits. A 'shaman' is a person in the tribe who can heal the sick and communicate with the spirits. Often he is chosen because he is different from other people—he might have more teeth or an extra finger. The shaman frequently has the ability to go into a state of ecstasy.

Very often the shaman is not only a healer and central figure of ceremonies but is much respected and may become a leader.

Below. An Inuit mask representing the spirit of the Moon.

Revolution and Empire

TIME CHART

AD	CHINA AND JAPAN	THE AMERICAS	INDIA	AFRICA AND AUSTRALASIA
1652				Foundation of Cape Colony by the Dutch in South Africa
1653			The Taj Mahal in Agra is completed	
1658			Aurangzeb ascends the throne of the Mogul Empire	
1659				The French found a trading station on the Senegal coast
1662				Destruction of the Kongo Kingdom by the Portuguese
1664		New Amsterdam (New York) taken by the British	French East India Company is founded	
1674			Sivaji creates the Hindu Maratha Kingdom	
1688>1703	The regime of the Tokugawa Shoguns in Japan reaches a peak			
1690			Foundation of Calcutta by the English	
1693		Gold discovered in Brazil		
1697	Chinese occupy Outer Mongolia			
1699>1702		Start of French colonization of Louisiana		
1700			The Punjab becomes a Sikh state	Creation of the Dyula Kingdom of Kong (Côte d'Ivoire). Rise of Asante power on the Gold Coast (Ghana) of West Africa.
1707			Death of Aurangzeb. Mogul Empire begins to decline	
1716>1751	Reign of the Japanese shogun Tokugawa Yoshimune			
1730				Revival of the Borno Empire of Central Sudan
1731	Chinese occupy Tibet			
1736>1796	The reign of Ch'ing Emperor Ch'ien-lung			
1756>1763		Seven Years' War between the French and British		
1757			Battle of Plassey. Robert Clive defeats the Indian troops of the Nawab of Bengal	
1761			Capture of Pondicherry. British destroy French power in India	
1764>1765		American colonists protest over British-imposed stamp duties		
1770				Captain James Cook claims Australia for Britain
1773		The Boston Tea Party.		
1775	China's population is 264 million			
1775>1783		American War of Independence		
1776		The Declaration of Independence		
1788				Foundation of New South Wales in Australia as a convict settlement
1789		George Washington becomes the first US president		

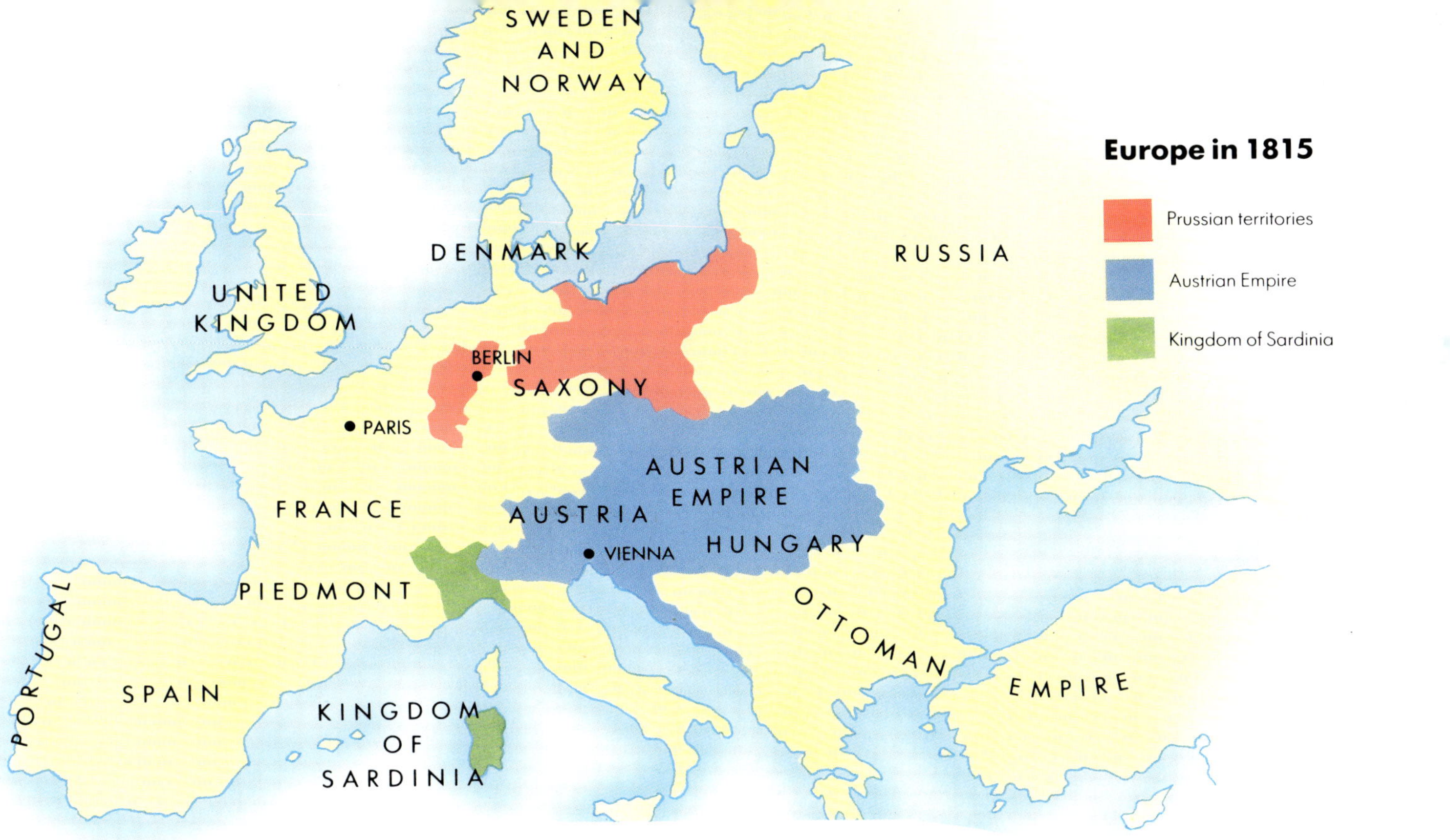

Europe in 1815

Prussian territories
Austrian Empire
Kingdom of Sardinia

SWEDEN AND NORWAY
DENMARK
RUSSIA
UNITED KINGDOM
BERLIN
SAXONY
PARIS
AUSTRIAN EMPIRE
FRANCE
AUSTRIA
VIENNA
HUNGARY
PIEDMONT
OTTOMAN EMPIRE
PORTUGAL
SPAIN
KINGDOM OF SARDINIA

The Old World

In 1792 the French had set out to conquer Europe. The wars that followed, known as the Napoleonic Wars, lasted more than 20 years and finally ended at the Battle of Waterloo in June 1815, when Austria, Britain, Prussia and Russia defeated the French. Afterwards, the European leaders held a long series of meetings in Vienna in Austria to work out a peace settlement. This series of meetings is known as the Congress of Vienna.

MAKING PEACE The Napoleonic Wars had been long and costly. The victors were determined that there would never be another war like them and they decided to divide Europe up so that no single country was strong enough to make war on the others as France had done. The Congress took no notice of what the people of Europe themselves wanted, which later led to trouble when the people of some of the smaller states fought for independence. But in one way the Congress was successful, for it was 100 years before another major war broke out in Europe.

RICH AND POOR The Congress of Vienna was a celebration as well as a conference. There were great banquets, balls and parties and the statesmen enjoyed themselves.

But life was not so good for the ordinary people of Europe. Thousands of soldiers returning from the wars found it hard to get jobs. During the wars, many people had made their living by making or selling all kinds of war materials, from cannons to uniforms, and when peace came they lost their jobs, too. Many other families had fled from their homes during the 20 years of battles and now had nowhere to live. In some countries, the war had ruined farmland and food was scarce.

THE THREAT OF REVOLUTION So behind the peace agreement and the celebrations there were many problems. Before the Napoleonic Wars, the French Revolution (see p. 372) had toppled King Louis XVI (1774–1793), and other European rulers were terrified that there might be revolution in their own countries. The gap between rich and poor had been one of the causes of the French Revolution, and throughout Europe the gap was still there.

Yet, very gradually, another revolution had begun, although it was not the kind that rulers feared. This was the Industrial Revolution, which marked the change from farming to manufacturing as the main source of work and wealth. By 1900, the 'old world' of Europe had become a group of industrial nations and industry had spread to the world's other continents.

Changes in Society
POVERTY AND PROTEST

Most wars cause more problems than they solve. The Napoleonic Wars between France and the rest of Europe were no different. When they were over, most of the people of Europe were living in misery.

War was not the only reason for their poverty. Another was that the number of people in Europe had almost doubled in the previous 100 years. People lived longer and had larger families. More children survived illness and grew up to become parents in their turn. This meant that more families were trying to make a living from the same amount of land.

RICH AND POOR Poor country families could not help noticing the difference between their lives and the lives of the landowners in their grand houses. Things were no better in the cities. Factory-owners and merchants lived in luxury while the people whose work made them wealthy had poor homes, poor pay and often not enough to eat. For many families there was no work at all and no money to live on. They had to go begging in the streets.

GOVERNMENTS How could things be changed? Ordinary people had no votes, so they could not bring about changes by voting for a different government. The French Revolution of 1789 was long over, but the ideas that had sparked it off lived on and spread. People wanted more say in how their countries were run. They wanted a share in the wealth of the rich. Countries that were part of foreign empires wanted their own rulers.

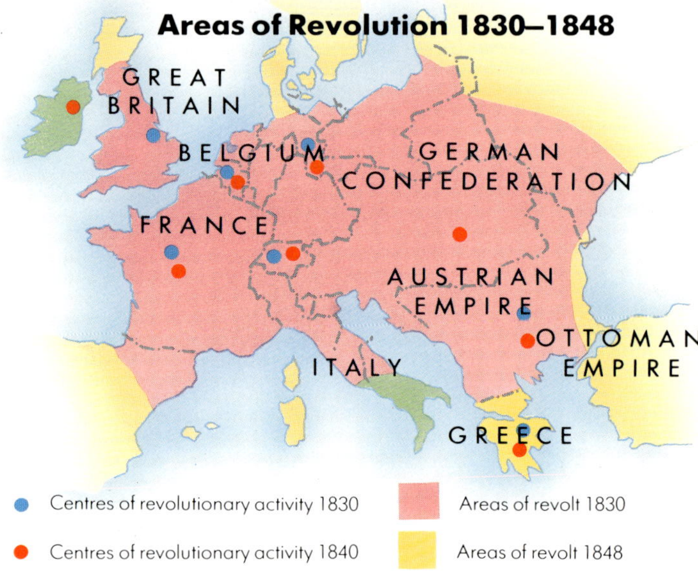

In 1830 and 1848, the spirit of revolt spread from France through Europe. In 1848 it even reached the repressive regimes of Russia and the Ottoman Empire.

In Germany and Italy there was another problem. Each was made up of numbers of small states, some poor and some rich. Many Germans wanted *unification*—the joining of the German states into one Germany. Many Italians felt the same about Italy.

Some of the people of Austria wanted exactly the opposite. Austria was one country made up of many races with different languages and ways of life. Each of these groups wanted to govern themselves.

Napoleon, seen here at the head of his troops, had aimed to make the whole of Europe a French empire. When he was finally defeated, statesmen had to re-draw the map.

The Communist Manifesto

In 1848 two German writers published a book which was to change the way people thought about government. Karl Marx (1818–1883) and Frederick Engels (1820–1895) called their book *The Communist Manifesto*.

Marx and Engels believed that the time was coming when the people who did the work would rule. Statesmen and the rich owners of industries and land would be overthrown, and the workers would elect their own leaders. In 1848, it seemed for a while as if they might be right.

The Wars with France 1792–1815

1792 April: France declared war on Austria

1793 January: King Louis XVI executed. Britain and Spain unite war against France.

1799 Frightened by French successes in the war, Austria, Britain, Russia and Turkey joined forces. They were called the Allies

1802 Napoleon planned the invasion of Britain.

1805 The British navy defeated the French fleet at the Battle of Trafalgar, but the French army defeated the Austrians and Russians at Austerlitz

1812 Napoleon's army reached Moscow before being forced to retreat from Russia

1814 The Allies invaded France and forced Napoleon to abdicate as emperor

1815 Napoleon, imprisoned on the island of Elba, escaped and gathered a new army to fight the Allies. He was finally beaten at the Battle of Waterloo in June

REVOLUTION In 1830 and again in 1848, all these feelings boiled up into revolution in many parts of Europe. Monarchs and statesmen were frightened. They sent troops to attack the rioters and rebels, killing them or putting them in prison. The governments of other countries often helped these rulers, because they were afraid that if revolution succeeded in one country, it would spread to others.

The 1848 revolutions began in Paris when troops fired into a crowd of demonstrators. When news of this spread, there were riots in Austria, Italy and parts of Germany. In some places, revolution brought changes, but these made very little real difference to most people. The revolutionaries had no experience of power and started quarrelling among themselves. Life continued as before, with the rich getting richer and the poor staying poor.

But ideas do not die. Writers and speakers went on saying that things must change and that all people, not just the rich, should decide how their country should be ruled. The struggle for *democracy*—votes for everyone and government by the people—had begun.

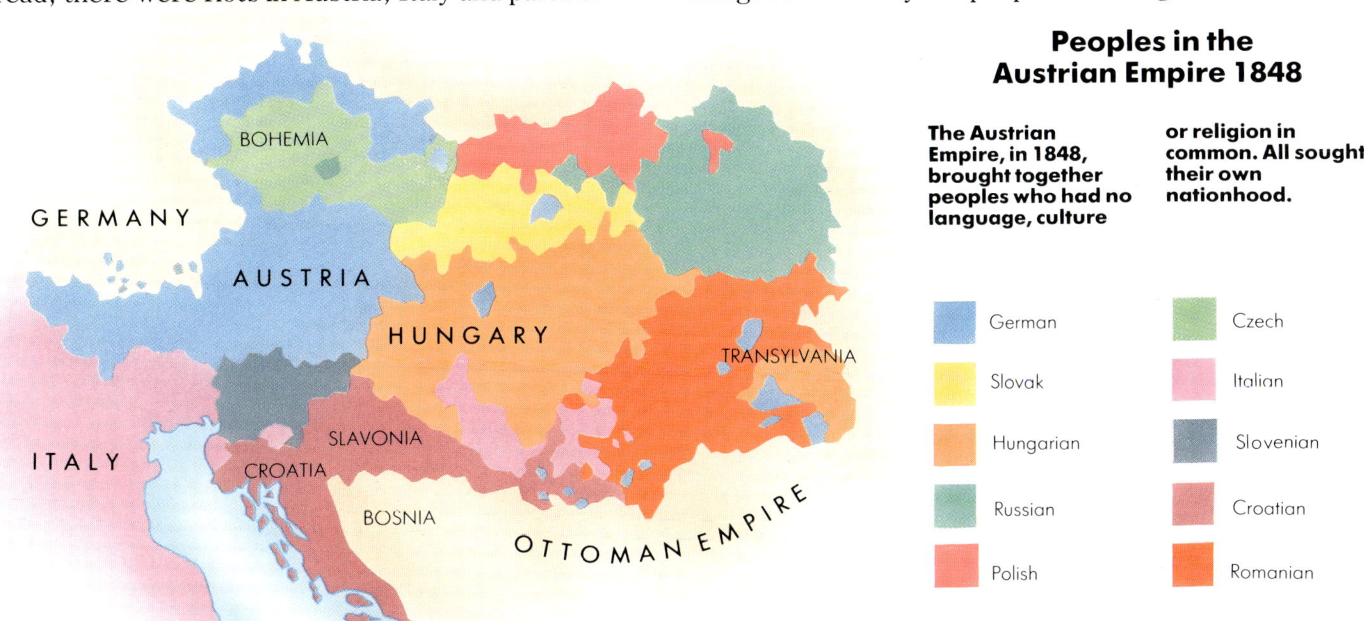

Peoples in the Austrian Empire 1848

The Austrian Empire, in 1848, brought together peoples who had no language, culture or religion in common. All sought their own nationhood.

THE INDUSTRIAL REVOLUTION

Before the Industrial Revolution, most things were made using human energy. Cotton and woollen thread were spun on spinning-wheels which were turned by hand or foot. Thread was woven into cloth on *looms* operated in the same way. Blacksmiths used hammers to beat iron into tools. Wood was cut with hand-saws.

The Industrial Revolution began gradually, late in the seventeenth century, when machines were invented to spin and weave cotton. At first these machines were driven by water power, but after about 1800 steam engines were used to make them work.

The Industrial Revolution began to develop in Britain and spread quite rapidly to the coal-mining areas of north-western Europe over the next few years.

FACTORY LIFE By 1830 most cotton goods made in Britain were made in factories. Other countries followed Britain's lead and by 1850 Belgium, France, Germany, Italy and the United States of America were catching up. Meanwhile, many other industries—such as wool spinning and weaving, iron-making, brick-making, pottery and brewing—also began to start factory production using steam power.

Factory work meant a new kind of life for millions of people. Instead of working on their own or in small groups, they now worked alongside hundreds of other people. They could take a rest or a meal only when the factory-owners said so. The working day was very long, sometimes 12 hours or more. Many factory workers were children, some as young as five or six years old. Four-year-olds were employed in some of Germany's linen mills.

There were two reasons for employing such young children. One was that they could be paid very low wages; the other was that they were small enough to crawl into machines that were still running. In the weaving industry, 'piecing' was one of the jobs given to small children. When threads broke in the loom, the children had to climb in and join the threads together again. Every day they risked terrible injury or death.

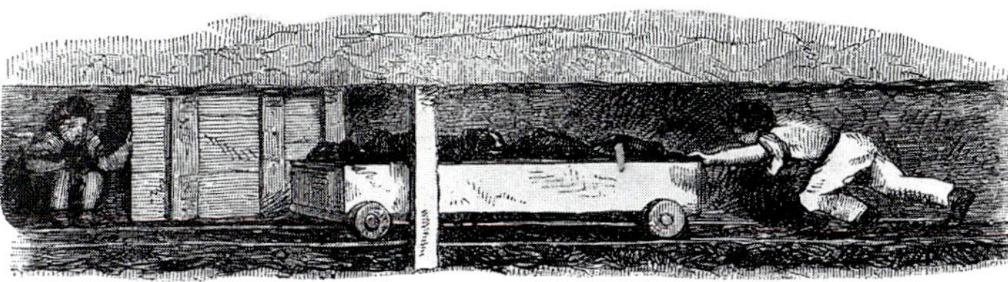

Left. Factory workers toiled in smoke, noise, grime and constant danger. This was the scene in a German iron-foundry in 1875.

Above. Until 1842, young children were employed in British coal mines.

Left. The Davy lamp detected gas, but led to the sinking of deeper pits.

THE DEMAND FOR COAL Steam engines were fuelled by coal. As the number of factories grew, so more coal was needed. Again, Britain led the development here and in 1830 it produced four-fifths of the world's coal. Much of it was sent to Europe to fuel the factories there. To find more coal, miners had to sink deeper and deeper pits. This was possible because steam engines could drive the lifts that carried the miners and the coal between the coal-face and the surface. But in deep mines there was a greater danger of rock-falls, flooding or poisonous, explosive gas. During the nineteenth century, about 1000 British miners were killed and over 150,000 seriously injured each year. In the early years of the Industrial Revolution, many of these were women and children.

MAKING WORK SAFER From about 1830, there were moves in some countries to make work in factories and mines safer. Working hours became shorter and there were laws to prevent young children being employed. But there were not enough inspectors to make sure that the law was being obeyed, and parents usually needed the wages that their children brought home.

Children at Work

Elizabeth Bentley started work in a cotton mill in 1815 when she was six years old. The work was dreadfully hard and the factory owners gave no thought to the safety of their employees or the conditions under which they worked. This is the story she told:

'I worked from five or six in the morning till seven or nine at night. I had forty minutes for a meal at noon. At any other time, we had to eat or drink as we worked. If we got tired, the overlooker [man in charge] *beat us with a strap. Sometimes we could not see each other for dust.'*

Above. Hand-loom weavers were thrown out of work by faster, cheaper factory weaving.

Below. The spinning wheel could not compete with the spinning machines in the factories.

THE COMING OF THE RAILWAYS

On 27 September 1825 there was great excitement in the towns of Stockton and Darlington in north-east England. Everyone had the day off work and crowds gathered along the railway line that had been built between the two towns.

Soon, cheering could be heard along the line. Then a locomotive puffed into view, pulling more than 20 open wagons filled with passengers. They were the first passengers in the world to travel on a steam train.

By 1875, railway travel for the rich had a touch of luxury. This Pullman car echoed the saloon of a Victorian country house with its plush furniture and decor. Servants were on call at the touch of a bell.

THE RAILWAY AGE The Stockton to Darlington Railway was built mainly to carry coal from the mines at Darlington to the port at Stockton. But it showed that railways had a future for carrying passengers too. Soon, plans were made for more railways both in Britain and in other countries. America's first railway, the South Carolina Railroad, opened in 1830. The first French line was built in 1832 and Germany, Belgium, Russia and Italy followed. The Railway Age had begun. By the 1870s, all the main cities in Europe and in the eastern states of America were linked by rail.

The great advantage of rail transport was its speed. In the early nineteenth century, travelling by road, on horseback or in horse-drawn vehicles, was slow and uncomfortable. The fastest stage-coaches could only travel at 16 kilometres an hour and it took 18 hours to cover the 300 kilometres from London to Manchester.

The first train from Stockton to Darlington reached over 24 kilometres an hour and railway journeys at twice that speed were soon usual. In 1838 the rail journey from London to Manchester took only 12 hours and within a few years it was even quicker.

RAILWAYS AND TRADE Railways made it possible for people to travel further to work, to visit friends and go on holiday. But it was the goods that were carried by trains that made most difference to people's lives. Carrying goods by rail was very much faster and cheaper than sending them by road or canal, so manufacturers built their factories near railway stations to take advantage of this. Towns near railways grew rapidly, for heavy goods such as bricks and coal could be carried there easily and cheaply. Milk, eggs and other fresh food could also be taken overnight from country towns to the cities.

There was another important result of railway-building. It used up huge amounts of iron and steel, and this led to the growth of the iron and steel industries in European countries and in the United States of America.

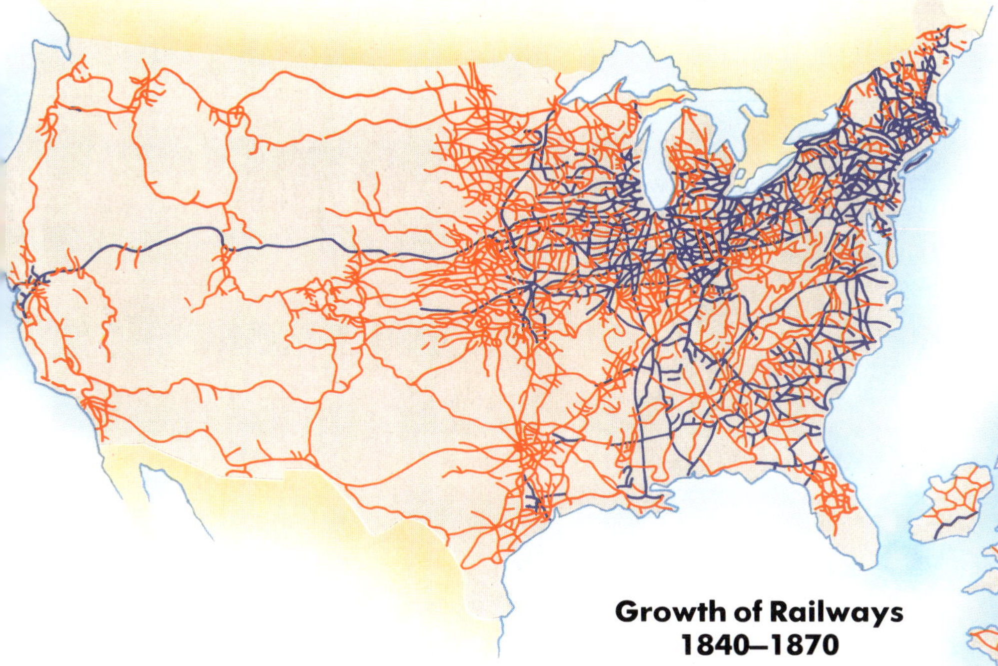

1840 to 1870 was the great age of railway expansion. Below. The map shows the extent of railway development in Europe. Kilometres of track in 1870 were 21,700 in Britain, 16,800 in France, 28,000 in Germany.

Left. The American rail network was also spreading rapidly across the continent. In 1870 there were 82,000 kilometres of track across the United States.

Growth of Railways 1840–1870

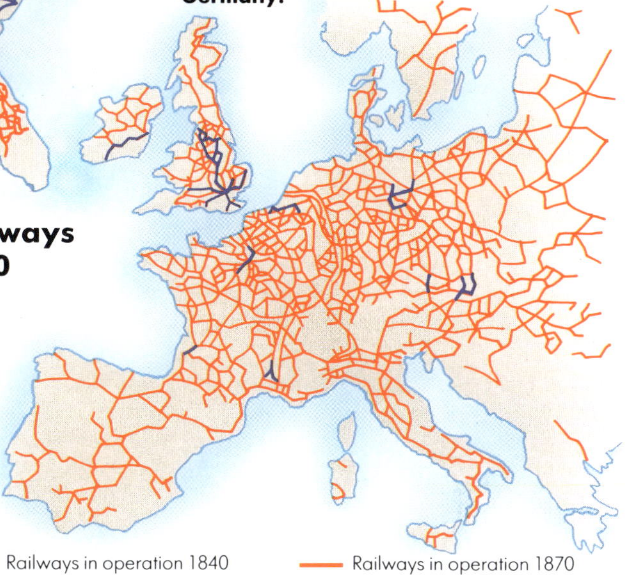

Railways in operation 1840

Railways in operation 1870

Above. The *General* races against the *Texas*.

The General – Texas Chase

Railways were soon found useful for moving troops and equipment in wartime.

In the American Civil War of 1861–65 (see page 422) there was a famous chase between two locomotives, the *General* and the *Texas*, driven by opposing sides. The plan was for the *General* to use explosives to blow up the line behind it, but the *Texas* kept so close that this was impossible. After a chase at a speed of 100 kilometres per hour, the *General* ran out of fuel and its crew was captured.

RAILWAYS AND COMMUNICATIONS The railways also brought a revolution in communications. As early as 1838, the governments of both Britain and the USA recognized railways as official carriers of the mail. Newspapers also began to be distributed by rail, which meant that copies could be carried overnight to places hundreds of kilometres from where they were printed.

The railways were also among the first users of telegraphy, which was invented in the 1840s (see page 68). In some countries, including Britain, the railway telegraph was used as a postal service to carry and deliver urgent messages in country areas.

The opening of the Stockton to Darlington Railway on 27 September 1825, the first railway in the world to carry passengers and goods. The train was headed by George Stephenson's *Locomotive Engine No 1*. The flag carried by the man in front bore the motto in Latin, 'Through private danger to the public good'. The violent jolting of the train may have made passengers reflect on these words! In 1829, Stephenson won the £500 prize in a competition to decide which locomotive would be used on the new Liverpool to Manchester line. His famous *Rocket* reached speeds of 56 kilometres per hour.

MANUFACTURERS AND MARKETS

Bales of raw cotton are loaded at Savannah, Georgia, for shipment to the mills of Europe.

After the Industrial Revolution began (see pp. 398–9), factories made goods in larger numbers than ever before. This meant that they needed good supplies of *raw materials* such as cotton or iron to turn into manufactured products, and they also needed more customers to buy their products. Many raw materials came from abroad, and manufactured goods were sent abroad in exchange for them.

TRADING AROUND THE WORLD The Industrial Revolution brought a huge increase in trade between countries. We can see how this happened by taking just one industry as an example. British inventions had made the British cotton industry the world leader. Cotton cannot be grown in Britain, so British mills needed raw cotton from overseas to make into thread and then into cloth. Most of it came from America and India. Cotton cloth, and clothes made from it, were then sent abroad to be sold. So the cotton industry, as well as giving jobs to British factory workers, provided work for British ships and sailors to collect the raw cotton from abroad and then take the finished goods overseas again.

TRADE ACROSS THE WORLD
Countries depended more and more on one another for trade and a disturbance in one country could affect a trading partner thousands of kilometres away. For example, during the Napoleonic Wars of 1792 to 1815 (see p. 397), the British and French navies interfered with each other's merchant ships, which affected world trade. The USA suffered most and this led to war between the USA and Britain from 1812 to 1814.

The war was not a very serious conflict, but it put a stop to American overseas trade and led to high unemployment and many businesses going *bankrupt* in America. It also caused distress in the British cotton industry because the war interrupted supplies of raw American cotton.

THE TRADING ROUNDABOUT Other industries grew in the same way as cotton, by importing raw materials from overseas and exporting goods manufactured from them. By 1850, half of the wool used in British mills came from Australia. Jute from India was turned into canvas goods. Iron and other metal ores all poured into Europe to be made into manufactured goods for export. European industrial machinery was used to produce even more raw materials in other countries, and so trade went on. Trade and industry were like the horses on a roundabout, speeding round faster and faster.

When the trade roundabout was spinning fast, manufacturers made good profits and workers earned good pay. But sometimes the roundabout slowed down or stopped. If more goods were produced than could be sold, prices had to be cut, which in turn cut profits and pay. At other times, a poor harvest overseas could lead to a shortage of raw materials for the factories. For the first time in history, people's lives could be affected by something that happened on the other side of the world.

Business deals were made in 'exchanges' which specialized in particular goods. Left. The Corn Exchange in London. There, samples would be inspected and prices agreed.

1 The Industrial Revolution began in Britain but soon spread to France and Germany. At first, Britain tried to hold on to its lead by banning the export of machinery such as textile looms, but this was ended in 1843. Coal was the basic fuel for industry. World coal production increased by at least 60 per cent every ten years between 1830 and 1880. Britain was the largest producer, turning out 86 million tonnes in 1860, compared with Germany's 21 and France's 10. Much of Britain's coal was exported to Europe.

2 The development of industry created a need for capital and a means of spreading the risk for investors. In Britain and France, and later in Germany, the principle of *limited liability* made investment less risky, and limited liability companies became the usual way of financing new enterprises.

Britain and France

In 1830, the world's two main trading nations were Britain and France. Britain's main imports — items brought in from abroad — were raw cotton, sugar, grains and tea. Its chief exports — those it sold overseas — were cotton and woollen thread and cloth, linen and cutlery.

France's principal imports were cotton, sugar, silk and animal skins.

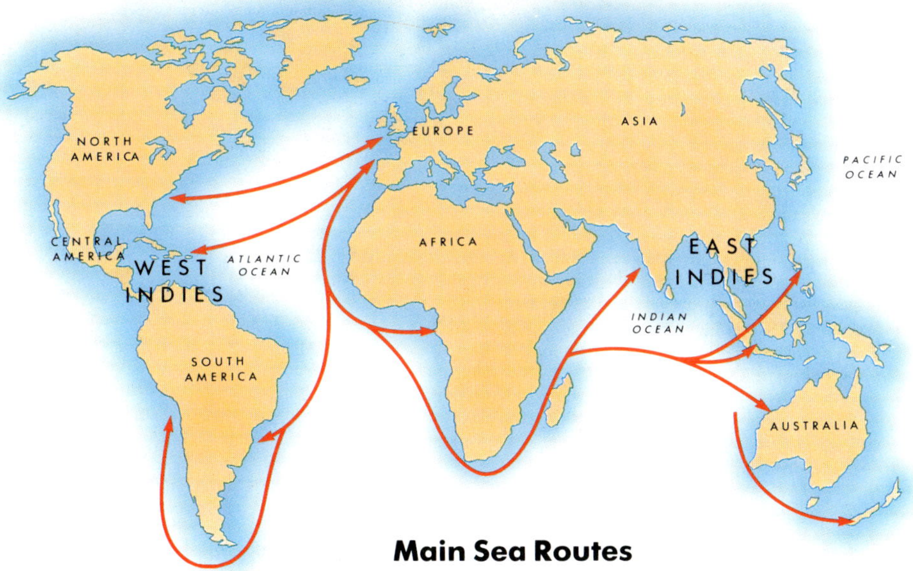

Main Sea Routes

Above. The world's main sea trading routes in the mid-nineteenth century, before the opening of the Suez Canal in 1869 which greatly shortened voyages between Europe and the East.

Right. War broke out in 1812 between Britain and the USA over British attempts to prevent American ships trading in Europe. The battle of New Orleans was the last engagement of the war, which almost ruined the British cotton industry by cutting off supplies of raw materials.

LIFE IN THE CITIES

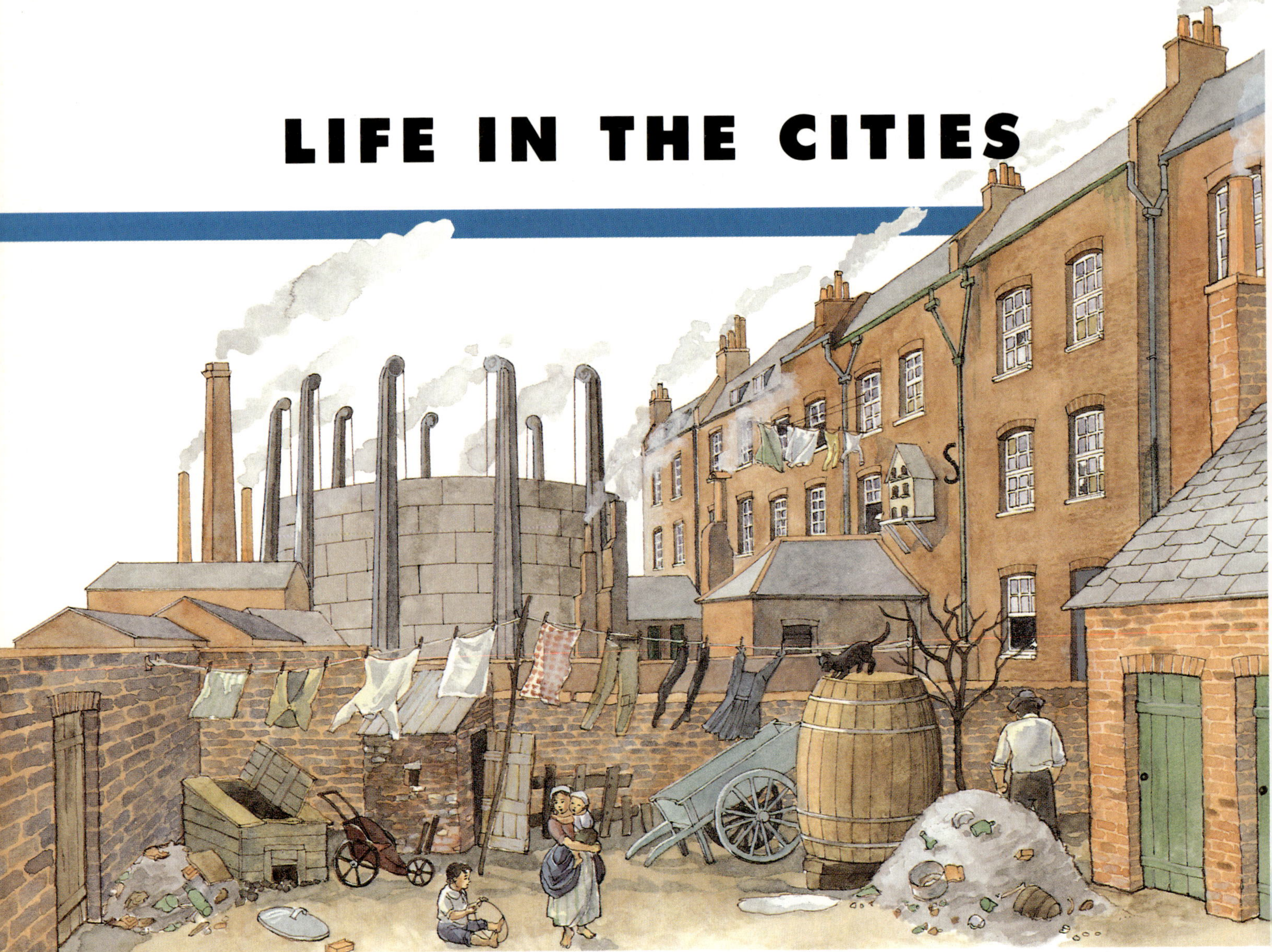

Typical housing in an industrial city. Each floor of these tenements would be occupied by a separate family. Their communal wash-houses and lavatories were outside in the yard.

What was life like for factory workers in the growing industrial cities in Europe and North America?

HOUSING PROBLEMS Life was not very pleasant. The industrial cities grew very quickly. In 1851 the population of Bradford, the centre of the British woollen industry, was four times what it had been in 1801. The American weaving city of Philadelphia, Pennsylvania, trebled its size during the same 50 years. Families who had come from the country to work in the factories were desperate for somewhere to live. A builder would buy a plot of land and try to cram as many homes as possible on to it, often building on damp, marshy land that was no use for anything else. Many houses were built '*back-to-back*' so that there was only one wall between two rows of houses.

Most homes were 'two up, two down'—that is, there were two rooms (a kitchen and a living-room) downstairs and two bedrooms upstairs. Families were large, often with 10 or more children, so several children often had to share one bedroom and even one bed. Water came from a pump at the end of each row of houses. Several families shared a wash-house and lavatory. In some cities builders put up blocks of *tenements*, which were two-roomed apartments built several storeys high.

The smell was terrible. There were no sewers to carry away dirty water and human waste, which simply drained away in the streets. There was no collection of rubbish, so this, too, was left to rot. Some families even kept their rubbish in their homes until they could stand the smell no longer! Rats, mice, flies, bugs and other vermin lived freely in the streets and houses.

DANGER AT WORK At work, there were other risks to health. Industries such as pottery, iron and brick-making produced *pollution* of all kinds. Smoke, dust and poisonous fumes belched out of factory chimneys. There was no control over the disposal of waste produced by

Above. Industrial cities grew so rapidly that many families had to crowd into single rooms with little furniture and no proper cooking or sanitary facilities. Left. New industrial housing was often built 'back to back' to save space and materials. Shared lavatories for the whole terrace were built at the end of each row.

Many of Emile Zola's novels attacked the squalor of life in industrial France.

Charles Dickens began his working life in a factory and knew industry at first hand.

Above. How the rich lived. Increasingly in the nineteenth century, the source of their wealth was industry. The hunger for coal and iron ore made fortunes for many landowners. Disraeli, the Prime Minister, commented that Britain had become two nations, rich and poor.

factories, so it often seeped into the ground and poisoned water supplies.

It is not surprising that when sickness broke out in the cities, it spread rapidly. Few factory workers could afford doctors, so they tried to cure their illnesses with cheap, useless medicines.

THE GREAT CHOLERA EPIDEMICS In the 1820s a dreadful disease spread throughout Asia and Europe from India. It was cholera. No-one knew how it spread, but by 1830 it had reached Russia and by 1831 had arrived in Germany, France and Britain. From Europe it travelled by ship to North America.

There was no cure. If you caught cholera, you would almost certainly die within a few days. In Russia in 1830, one in 20 people died of the disease, in Poland one in 30. In Belgium, the Netherlands and Britain, cholera killed about one person in every 130. In 1848 and 1854, the disease broke out again.

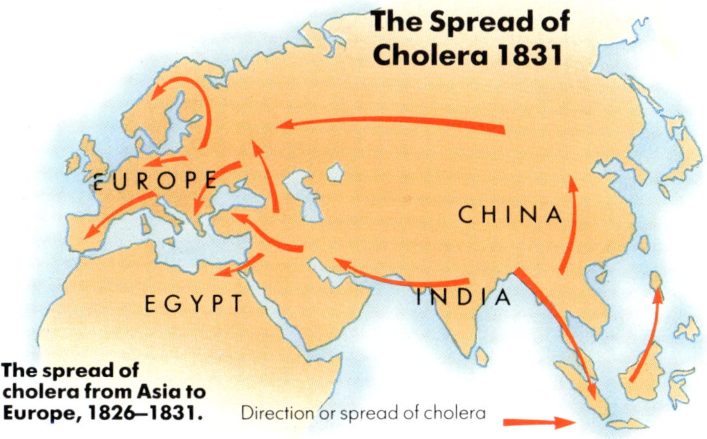

The spread of cholera from Asia to Europe, 1826–1831.

Cholera was only one of the diseases spread by infected water, open drains and overcrowded homes. Other illnesses were caused by working conditions and pollution in the factories. People who lived in the industrial cities of the nineteenth century faced an unhealthy life and an early death.

THE PROTESTERS

A cartoon of the 'Peterloo Massacre' in Manchester in 1819. A peaceful protest was broken up by mounted troops and eleven protesters were killed.

The Industrial Revolution (see pp. 398–9) changed the lives of millions of people, but for most of them change did not mean improvement. Although manufacturers, mine and ship-owners, railway builders and merchants made fortunes, there were few rewards for the people who worked for them. Their work had created a new kind of society, but they had no say in how it was to be run. In most countries, government was in the hands of small groups of powerful people. An exception was the United States of America, which had a form of democracy (for white men only) from 1801. In some countries such as Russia, the ruler had absolute power and no-one could question what he or she did.

STUDENTS AND CRAFTSPEOPLE In every country there were people who were determined that something must be done to improve life for the workers. Their aim was democracy—government by the people. In Germany, France and Italy, students held meetings and produced newspapers demanding democracy. Students were among the leaders of the revolutions of 1830 and 1848 (see p. 397). The Communists Marx and Engels worked out their first political ideas at university.

In Britain, students had to be more careful in what they said or wrote because if they upset the universities, they would be told to leave. This meant that in Britain the protesters tended to be craftspeople like weavers and printers. Some formed a society called the Chartists, which wanted all adult men to have the vote so that ordinary people would be represented in *Parliament*. But they never gained enough supporters to bring about any change.

CONTROLLING IDEAS
Governments and their armies were too strong for the revolutionaries, as the events of 1830 and 1848 showed. Governments also did all they could to stop the spread of new ideas. In 1819 the German states agreed to *censor* magazines and newspapers, ban political meetings and keep a check on anyone with 'dangerous' opinions. In Italy, the leaders of protest movements were forced to go abroad to escape punishment, and until 1847 newspapers were censored.

In Britain, *trade unions*—groups of workers joining together to demand better pay or working conditions—were banned until 1824. Even 10 years later, six British farm-workers were sent to a prison camp in Australia because they tried to form a union. Another way of controlling ideas in Britain was the heavy tax on newspapers that was the law till 1855. This meant that only the rich could afford them, so newspapers only printed news that the rich wanted to read.

THE UNDERGROUND PRESS These restrictions held back the movement for reform, but they did not completely stop it. In most European countries there were presses operating 'underground', meaning that they secretly printed illegal newspapers, pamphlets and books despite the risk of police raids and imprisonment.

Slowly, governments came to see that it was better to accept some reforms than to risk revolution and bloodshed. All Frenchmen were given the vote in 1851 and Britain gave votes to an increasing number of men as time went on.

Voices of Protest

Guiseppe Mazzini (1805–1872) planned to make his career in law, but after leaving Genoa University he founded an organization called 'Young Italy' whose aim was to unite all the Italian states under a *republican* government. 'Young Italy' was involved in the revolutions of 1830 and 1848, but Mazzini himself spent much of his life in *exile*. He lived to see Italy unified — but under a king and not as a republic.

Louis Kossuth (1802–1894) was a journalist who led a movement in Hungary which wanted democratic reform and freedom from Austrian control. He was imprisoned for what he wrote, but after he was released he continued to write pamphlets which were either illegally printed or copied out by hand. In 1847 Kossuth was elected to the Hungarian parliament and he became a leader of the 1848 Hungarian revolt. This failed, and he spent the rest of his long life in exile.

Above. German cavalry ride against protesters. Right. Italian patriot Guiseppe Mazzini. Far right. British Chartist leader Feargus O'Connor.

Feargus O'Connor (1794–1855) became leader of the Chartist movement in Britain. The Chartists wanted all men to be able to vote in a *secret ballot* at annual elections to Parliament. They organized three *petitions*, in 1839, 1842 and 1848, which contained these and other demands. O'Connor was a brilliant speaker and ran a Chartist newspaper called *The Northern Star*. But when he died the Chartist movement died with him.

Left. Producing an underground newspaper in a German cellar. Police raids meant that many such papers were short-lived, but they would often be started up again in new hiding-places.

Literature of Dissent

1791 Tom Paine's *The Rights of Man*

1840 Guiseppe Mazzini's *The Duties of Man*
1848 *The Communist Manifesto*
1859 John Stuart Mill's *On Liberty*
1867 Karl Marx's *Capital*

CRISIS IN THE COUNTRYSIDE

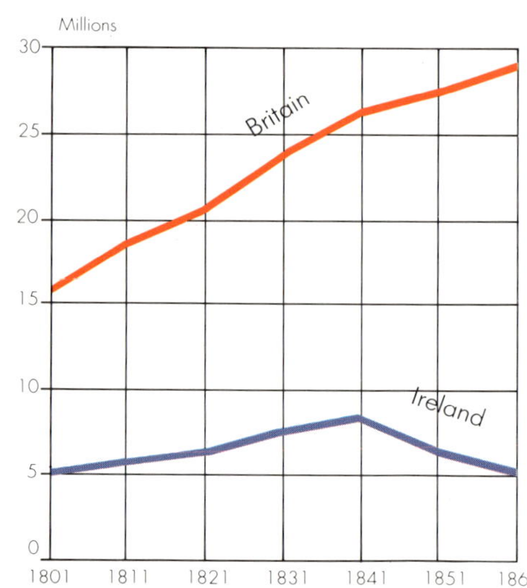

Left. Starving families seek food and shelter at an Irish workhouse in 1846. So many people needed help that the workhouses could not cope with the demand and people were turned away to die in the streets.

Above. This graph of the population of the British Isles from 1801 to 1861 shows how the Great Famine hit Ireland. Even today, the Irish population has not returned to its 1861 level.

Until about 1830, the main industry in Europe and North America, and in the rest of the world, was farming. Most people lived and worked in small farming communities. Their work was hard and their pay was poor, they ate simple food and lived in cramped, often damp houses. Life was not easy for farm-workers, but they were able to survive. The most prosperous farm-workers in Europe were the French. Many had their own small plots of land for crops and could keep animals on pasture which was shared with others.

MOVING TO THE CITIES At the time of the Industrial Revolution (see pp. 398–9), all this began to change. Farm machinery was too expensive for small farm-owners in France to buy. In other countries, the use of farm machinery meant that fewer farm-workers were needed. If farm-workers lost their jobs, they also lost their houses, which were owned by the farmers. There was no pay for people who were out of work. All they could do was to move somewhere else to look for work.

Throughout the nineteenth century there was a great movement of people from the country to the towns, where the new factories could provide jobs and homes were available nearby. It was usually the younger and fitter families who moved. Old people, the sick, the disabled and the very poor who could not afford to move were left behind in the countryside. For them, life became even harder. They had to take any work they could find, for any wage the farmers would pay. Farmers often gave work to women and children, who were paid less than men.

THE GREAT FAMINE Then, in 1845, there was another blow. The main food of country people in many parts of Europe was potatoes. In 1845, a disease called blight attacked the potato crop, turning the potatoes black and rotten. Food became desperately short. The famine was worst in Ireland, where almost one million Irish people

Above. This idealized view of an Irish croft may have been true to life before 1845. Things changed after the famine, however, and many families starved to death.

Right. Before the invention of the threshing machine, threshing corn with a flail provided work for farm labourers through the winter.

Left. The threshing machines robbed the men of weeks of work because they could do the job more quickly and with fewer workers.

The Threshing Machine

The increasing use of machinery in farming meant less work for families who stayed in the countryside. The first important development was the threshing machine, which separated grain from the straw. This was invented by a Scotsman called Andrew Meikle in 1786 and by the early nineteenth century it was widely used.

Previously, threshing had been done by hand, using flails to beat the corn on the threshing-floor of the barn, and farm-workers had relied on this work in the winter to provide them with jobs when other work was scarce. Now the threshing machine, which was driven by horses or water at first and later by steam, did in a few days the work that used to occupy many workers for months. The result was that there was very little work available after the harvest, and in those days the rule was: 'No work, no pay'.

starved to death over the next two years. But the picture was similar all over Europe, especially in Germany. Despite the numbers who had moved to the towns, there were still too many people trying to make a living from the land.

FEEDING EUROPE The Great Famine of the 1840s was really part of a much wider problem. Since the eighteenth century, the population of Europe had been growing. In 1830 it was about 230 million, almost twice what it had been 100 years earlier. Farm machinery had increased the production of food, but not enough to feed the extra numbers of people. In the early part of the nineteenth century, many people feared that Europe would face starvation in a few years' time.

There were two possible answers to the problem. One was for some of the people in Europe to move to other parts of the world. The other was for Europe to find new sources of food. Both of these things happened.

1 Population figures for Europe's major cities show how they were a magnet for people from the countryside. Between 1801 and 1851 the populations of Berlin and St Petersburg increased by over 140 per cent, London by 127 per cent, and Paris and Vienna by over 80 per cent.

2 Europe was not the only part of the world with a rapidly increasing population. There are no fully reliable world population figures for the nineteenth century, but it has been estimated that between 1845 and 1914 the number increased from 1,009 millions to 1,900 millions. This huge increase brought problems to many societies. In Africa, for example, tribes were forced to find – or fight for – new land to feed their growing numbers as their own land became degraded by over-cultivation.

RUSSIA: THE SLEEPING GIANT

In 1800, the world was changing fast. War was altering the boundaries of European countries. The United States of America, which had only just been founded, was growing in power and wealth. Australia and New Zealand were about to be developed by settlers from Europe. But between Europe and Asia lay a sleeping giant which was still part of the old world of the Middle Ages. This was Russia.

AN UNCHANGING SOCIETY Russia did not have an elected government. It was ruled by an emperor called the tsar, with an army of officials to carry out his orders.

The agricultural and industrial revolutions in western Europe had passed Russia by. About half of its population were still *serfs*. They were the property of the person who owned the land on which they lived and worked. Russia had expanded its control to the east as far as the Pacific Ocean, but there were not enough people to settle in this huge area and the Russians knew nothing of the technology needed to develop it. So the occupation of central Asia required a large army to fight constant battles against the tribes of the region.

Russia's problems were made worse by the cruelty, violence and even madness of the tsars. Tsar Paul I (1796–1801) refused to take advice from his officials and combined cruelty at home with disastrous policies abroad. He was finally murdered and his son Alexander (1801–1825), who had taken part in the murder plot, took over.

In 1812 the French army invaded Russia and reached as far as Moscow before being defeated. After the final defeat of France in 1815 (see p. 397), Tsar Alexander

Russian Empire in Asia to 1900

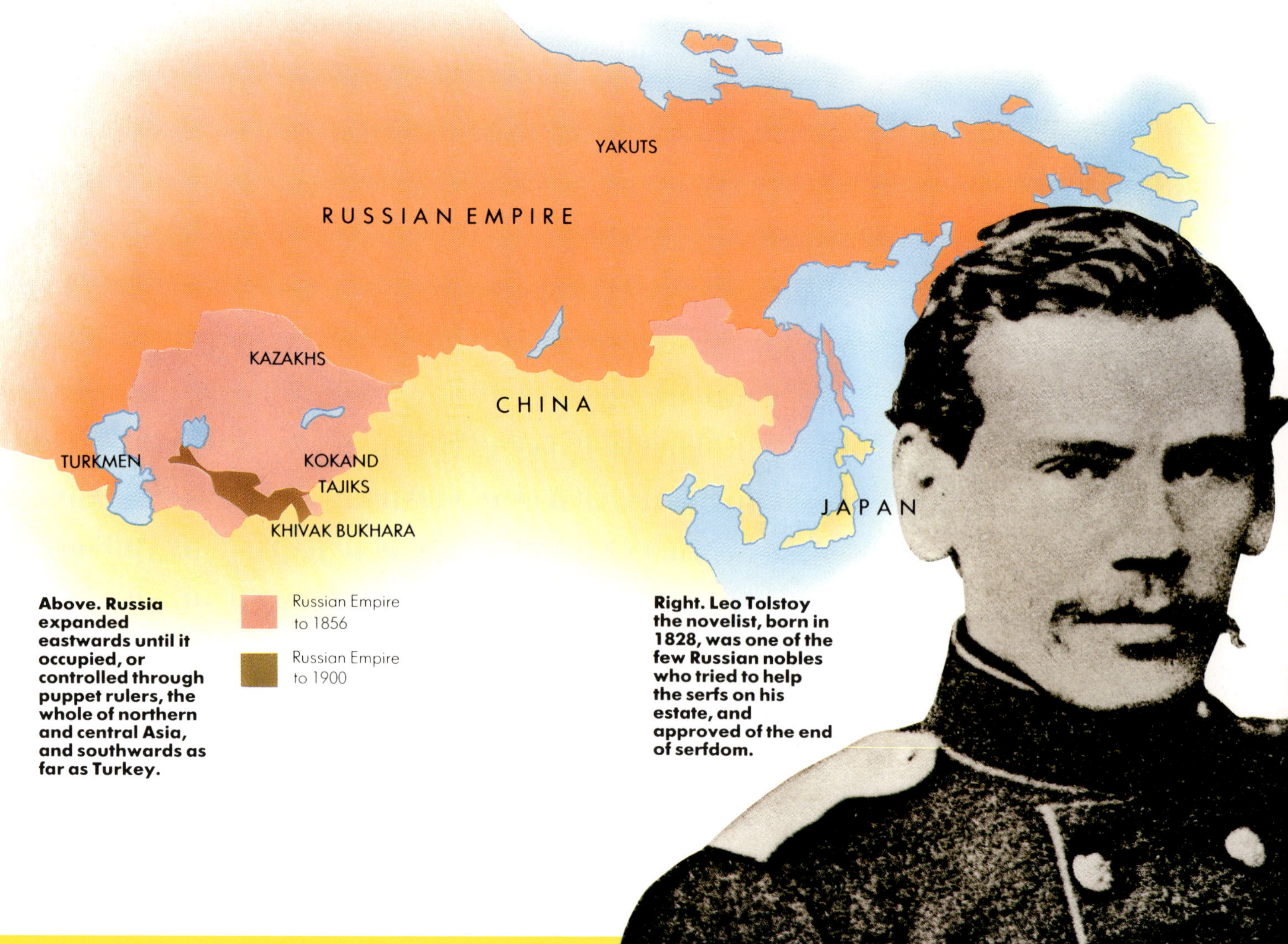

Above. Russia expanded eastwards until it occupied, or controlled through puppet rulers, the whole of northern and central Asia, and southwards as far as Turkey.

Right. Leo Tolstoy the novelist, born in 1828, was one of the few Russian nobles who tried to help the serfs on his estate, and approved of the end of serfdom.

lived in fear of revolution and any talk of reform was forbidden. He set up a network of spies and secret police to report on any threat to his rule.

Alexander was succeeded by his brother Nicholas I (1825–1855), who trusted no-one. It was said that he made himself do with as little sleep as possible so that he would not be murdered in his bed. He had been trained as a soldier and believed in strict military discipline for everyone, soldiers and civilians.

THE CRIMEAN WAR One of Russia's problems was that it had very limited access to the sea, which prevented it from playing a full part in world trade. The ports on its northern coast froze up in winter and could not be used. Russians had always wanted to be able to reach the Mediterranean, but Turkey was in the way.

Tsar Nicholas's plan to take over Turkey led to the Crimean War in 1854, in which Britain and France joined to defend Turkey. The war ended in 1856 with Russia defeated, but by that time Nicholas I had died.

NEW REFORMS The next tsar, Alexander II (1855–1881), saw that reform was needed if Russia was to catch up with the rest of the world. He began by freeing the serfs, who were then able to move from the land to the cities. This in turn made it possible for Russian industry to develop and forced farmers to adopt more modern methods of agriculture, using machinery. The sleeping giant began to awaken.

Ill-fed, ill-housed and treated like beasts of burden, Russian serfs lived lives of unremitting hard work and misery.

Left. Tsar Alexander II reads his proclamation abolishing serfdom in 1861. This was one of his many reforms which brought Russia closer to the modern world. He also improved education, administration and military organization. People resented his autocratic rule, however, and he was eventually assassinated.

The Trans Siberian Railway 1890

Right. British forces fighting in the Crimea went through terrible suffering from injury and disease. Their plight inspired Florence Nightingale (in the centre) to take a team of volunteer nurses to set up proper hospitals in Turkey and to devote the rest of her life to nursing.

The Exploration of Siberia

Russia had no need to go overseas to find an empire. To the east lay the huge undeveloped land of Siberia, which was rich in resources such as timber, furs and minerals. Explorers from Russia had travelled in Siberia since the seventeenth century, and more recently a chain of forts had been set up to police the area. But there were too few people in Siberia to develop its resources and because most of its rivers ran north to the frozen Arctic they could only be used for a few summer months.

Until the building of the Trans-Siberian Railway at the end of the nineteenth century, Siberia's resources were hardly touched.

BUILDING EMPIRES

Hudson's Bay, in northern Canada, in the early nineteenth century. The Hudson's Bay Company controlled all trade in fur from the Atlantic to the Pacific.

Soon after Europeans had made their voyages of discovery to distant parts of the world in the fifteenth and sixteenth centuries, they began to take over these lands for themselves. By 1800 the British, French, Spanish, Portuguese and Dutch all had empires overseas.

THE BRITISH EMPIRE By the 1820s Britain had by far the largest empire, with the strongest navy in the world to protect trade and travellers going to and from its colonies. In 1783, Britain had lost its American colonies in the American War of Independence (see p. 370), but it still had Canada. In 1788 the British also claimed Australia as their territory.

After the defeat of France in 1815 (see p. 397), Britain took over Cape Colony in South Africa from the Dutch, and French islands in the Caribbean too. India was ruled by the British, too, and there was also a scattering of small British islands across the South Atlantic and the Indian oceans. In 1840 New Zealand was added to the British Empire.

But although this empire looked huge on a map of the world, most of the countries it included had small populations and much of the land had not been explored by Europeans. It was not until the middle of the nineteenth century that the vast territories of Canada and Australia began to be settled and developed by large numbers of Europeans.

Emiliano Zapata was an Indian farmer in Mexico who led his people in a struggle to recover their land.

European Empires in 1870

CANADA
PACIFIC OCEAN
ATLANTIC OCEAN
BRITISH HONDURAS
CUBA
BRITISH GUIANA
DUTCH GUIANA
FRENCH GUIANA
PORTUGUESE GUINEA
SENEGAL
GAMBIA
SIERRA LEONE
GOLD COAST
NIGERIA
ALGERIA
ASCENSION ISLAND
ST HELENA
SPANISH GUINEA
GABON
OBOCK
SEYCHELLES
MOZAMBIQUE
MAURITIUS
REUNION
CAPE COLONY
NATAL
INDIAN OCEAN
INDIA
CEYLON
CHINA
MACAO
HONG KONG
SUMATRA
BORNEO
AUSTRALIA
NEW ZEALAND

Above. The extent of the main European empires in 1870. The Spanish, French and Portuguese empires were in decline, and in 1870 neither Germany nor Italy had begun their programmes of expansion.

British
French
Spanish
Portuguese

Growth of the British Empire 1760–1860

1763 Britain took Canada away from French control.
1767 British troops defeated the French in India and gradually expanded the area controlled by Britain
1788 The first British convict settlement was set up in Australia, soon followed by settlers who were not convicts
1795 British troops occupied the Cape of Good Hope at the southern tip of Africa
1808 Sierra Leone, in West Africa, became a British colony
1815 By the Treaty of Vienna, Britain gained the Cape (South Africa), Ceylon (Sri Lanka), Mauritius, Malta and the French possessions in the Caribbean
1829 Britain claimed the whole of Australia as part of the Empire
1830 The Gold Coast (Ghana) came under British 'protection'
1840 New Zealand became part of the British Empire
1842 Britain occupied Hong Kong
1843 The Gambia, in West Africa, became a British colony
1860 Lagos (Nigeria) became part of the Empire

SPAIN AND PORTUGAL The second largest empire in 1800 was Spain's, which extended from Mexico to the southern tip of South America. But this was soon to come to an end. One by one, Mexico and the South American states fought for their independence. By 1824 the once-powerful Spanish Empire only contained Cuba and Puerto Rico.

Brazil had never been part of the Spanish Empire, but belonged to Portugal. It became independent in 1820, leaving Portugal with only a few colonies such as Goa in India.

Empire travel made Europe aware of other cultures. Left. A decorated figure from Papua New Guinea. Above. An African stool carved from solid wood.

CHANGING ATTITUDES TO EMPIRES There are two ways of building an empire. One is to take over and rule a country that already has a large population and a settled government. This is what had happened in India. The other is to lay claim to a land where few people live, say that the country is 'empty' and send settlers to live there.

In 1815, Britain had no intention of expanding its empire. Many Britons thought that overseas colonies were a nuisance. The American War of Independence had been a costly blow, while holding on to India involved keeping a large and expensive army there, as well as naval forces to protect the trading routes. It was hard to see how an empire could help Britain's wealth.

This attitude changed as the Industrial Revolution got under way (see pp. 398–9). Colonies could provide cheap raw materials for British factories and, once settlers had arrived in those colonies, new markets for manufactured goods as well. At the same time, the empire offered homes and work for Britain's increasing population. So, from about 1840 onwards, the British began to take an interest in expanding their empire. This was to lead them into conflict later in the century with other European countries which had the same idea.

THE BRITISH IN INDIA

"NEW CROWNS FOR OLD ONES!"

Above. Reinforcements arrive to relieve Lucknow, where the British had been surrounded by 60,000 Indians. This marked the end of the 1857 Indian Mutiny.

Above right. A cartoonist comments on British attitudes, represented by Queen Victoria, to India.

Right. Life for British families living in India was one of luxury. Here, boar hunters take a break for lunch.

The first European traders to reach India were the Portuguese in 1498. They were followed by Dutch, French and British expeditions. The Portuguese and Dutch were interested in India only as a trading post, but the French and British had grander ideas. By 1767 the British had defeated the French and had begun to take over all of India. British India included the areas which are now the separate countries of Pakistan and Bangladesh.

THE EAST INDIA COMPANY British control of India was in the hands of the East India Company, which had been set up in 1600. The company had its own army, with British officers and mostly Indian troops. By the end of the eighteenth century the company had become so powerful that the British government became alarmed and sent several regiments of the regular British army to India to share the company's power.

India was a long way away from Britain and communications were slow. The commanders of the company and British armies could do more or less as they liked, setting themselves up as rulers of large areas. They interfered with the *Hindu* and Muslim religions of India and tried to make the local people follow European ways and ideas. They spent money on roads, ports and industry—but this was for the benefit of trade, not to help the Indian people. The British officers lived well and enjoyed hunting large animals and other sports. They treated India as if it was a vast estate providing them with wealth and an unlimited supply of servants.

MUTINY OR REBELLION? Indian resentment of the British grew until it exploded into violence in 1857. This began in the army, when Indian troops in Bengal in northern India refused to obey the orders of their British officers. British historians still call this the period of the Indian *Mutiny*, but to Indian historians it was the 'Great Rebellion' or 'The Great War of Independence'. For the next year there were outbreaks of violence all over northern India. British soldiers and their families were

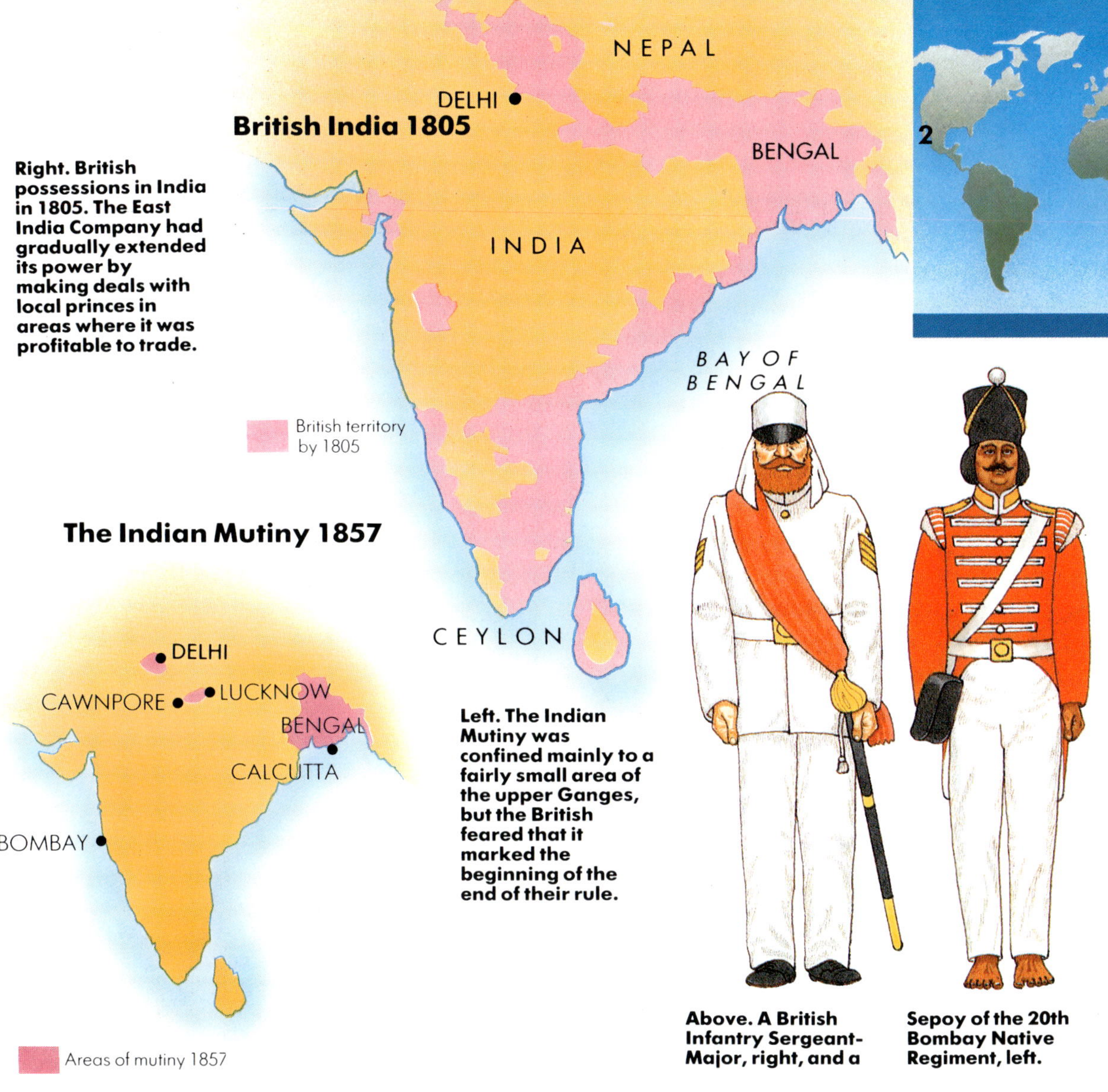

Right. British possessions in India in 1805. The East India Company had gradually extended its power by making deals with local princes in areas where it was profitable to trade.

Left. The Indian Mutiny was confined mainly to a fairly small area of the upper Ganges, but the British feared that it marked the beginning of the end of their rule.

Above. A British Infantry Sergeant-Major, right, and a Sepoy of the 20th Bombay Native Regiment, left.

The Indian Mutiny 1857–1858

10 May 1857	At Meerut, 85 sepoys imprisoned. Others mutiny and march to Delhi
11 May 1857	Sepoys capture Delhi
4 June 1857	Sepoys at Cawnpore mutiny
24 June 1857	British at Cawnpore surrender. Rebels kill the troops and take the women and children prisoner
30 June 1857	British besieged at Lucknow
16 July 1857	British retake Cawnpore, find that their women and children have been murdered
14 Sept. 1857	British recapture Delhi
16 March 1858	Rebels at Lucknow defeated
19 June 1858	Rebel army defeated at Gwalior

attacked and murdered by the rebels. The worst violence was at Cawnpore, where over 600 British troops were murdered after they had surrendered, and the rebels then turned on their wives and children.

The British, afraid that they might lose control of India altogether, behaved just as violently in return. The rebels were ruthlessly hunted down, and by July 1858 the Mutiny had been quelled. India would have to wait for another 90 years before it gained its independence from Britain.

AFTER THE MUTINY The Mutiny had shaken the British, who now decided that the government would rule India directly, instead of through the East India Company. The army was strengthened and a new Indian Civil Service, with British staff, was set up to run the country. The system set up after 1858 lasted until India became independent in 1947.

Under direct British rule, India became the 'jewel in the crown' of the British Empire, with good transport and successful industries. But almost all the benefits went to Britain, and the Indians became more and more resentful of the occupation of their country by a foreign army.

1 Apart from its importance as a source of raw materials and a market for finished goods, India was important to the shipping trade. Its importance increased after the introduction of steamships in the mid-19th century. Steamships travelling to the Far East and Australasia needed bunkering stations, where they took on supplies of coal, and Bombay was well-placed for this. After the opening of the Suez Canal in 1869 ships heading east found India even more convenient for bunkering.

2 Mexico is the largest of the Central American countries. In 1821 it became independent of Spain, which had colonized Mexico for 300 years, but there was an attempted Spanish invasion eight years later. From 1846–48 Mexico was at war with the United States. Defeat was followed by the loss of more than half Mexico's territory to the United States. In 1863 the French invaded and there was a war which lasted four years.

THE GREAT MIGRATIONS

Above. A familiar dockside scene in nineteenth century Britain, as relatives say goodbye to their emigrating loved ones. Many families decided to go to America to find work.

Left. Conditions on the emigrant ships were far from comfortable.

In 1850, Britain controlled large areas of the world where the population was small compared to the size of the land. These areas included Canada, the whole of Australia away from the coast, and New Zealand.

The countries of the British Empire were not the only ones which seemed to offer opportunities to European settlers hungry for land to farm. There were vast areas of the United States of America which seemed almost unoccupied compared to overcrowded Europe. In South America, the countries that had won their independence from Spain also welcomed newcomers from Europe.

A FLOOD OF EMIGRANTS A steady trickle of *emigrants* leaving Europe for North and South America, Australia and New Zealand began before 1846, but after that the trickle quickly grew into a flood. The emigrants included many thousands of Irish and German families who had escaped the Great Famine (see pp. 408–9) and were hoping to start a new life in the USA.

In North America, many of these people found work and homes in the growing industrial cities of the east. Others took the trail westwards to begin farming there. Like the emigrants to Australia and New Zealand, they sent home news of cheap—sometimes free—land, good crops and healthy living.

Many organizations offered to lend emigrants the fare for the journey, which they could pay back from their first earnings in their new country. Even so, it was a big decision to make. The fare from Britain to New Zealand, for example, was £18 for an adult, which was almost a year's wages for a farm-worker. The fare for a child was £10, so two adults and three children (a small family in those days) needed more than £60 to get there.

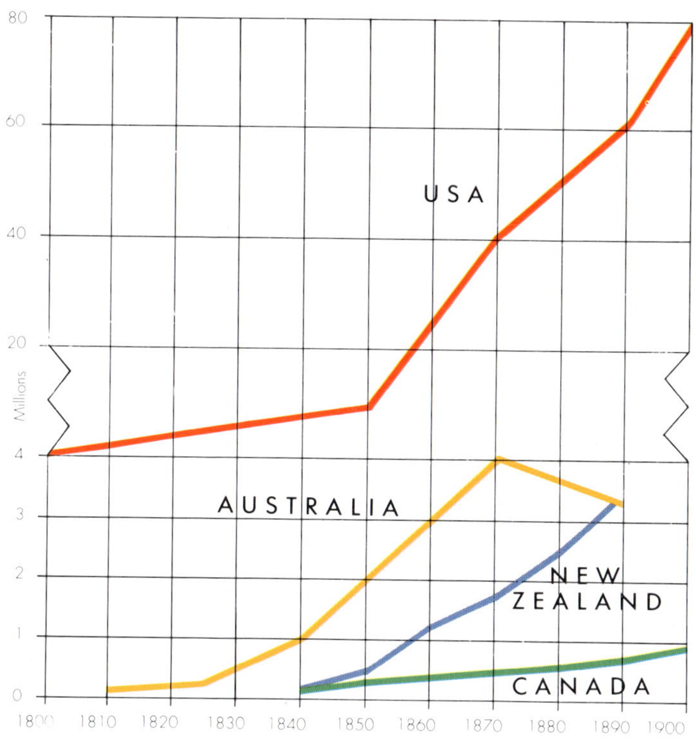

Above. This graph showing the destinations of emigrants from Britain between 1800 and 1900 reveals a changing pattern, with Canada gaining in popularity after 1890. This followed the completion of the Canadian Pacific Railway in 1885 which opened up the interior.

Above. Emigration was put forward as a cure for poverty – but the really poor had no money for the fare.

Left. A view of Vancouver Harbour in 1876, just before it began to develop.

DANGEROUS VOYAGES Some of the ships used for emigrants had previously been used as slave-ships, and conditions were almost as cramped as they had been for slaves. The voyage from Britain to New Zealand took 80 days. In the year 1847 alone, 17,000 emigrants to Canada died of 'ship's fever' (typhus) either during or after the journey.

Once they had arrived in their new country, the farming emigrants had to 'break in' the land, using only hand-tools to make farmland out of scrub or bush. Many gave up the idea of having their own farms and went to work for the larger farmers instead. But others succeeded and became large farmers themselves.

An advertisement inviting immigrants to settle in California.

THE DESERTED VILLAGE The people of Bodney in Norfolk in eastern England were part of this great adventure. In 1855 the Oakley family, including five children, set out for Tasmania. Two years later the minister of the village's Methodist chapel organized a group of about 50 people—almost the whole village—to follow them. Most of the adults who went were young people in their 20s and 30s. Only the old and the sick were left behind.

When they arrived in Tasmania, they settled in an area which became known as 'Norfolk Creek'. Some families built up large farms. Others gave up farming and went off in search of gold, which had just been found in Tasmania. Their home village of Bodney gradually became deserted and almost disappeared, but for the people who got away there was new life and new hope.

THE AMERICAN WEST

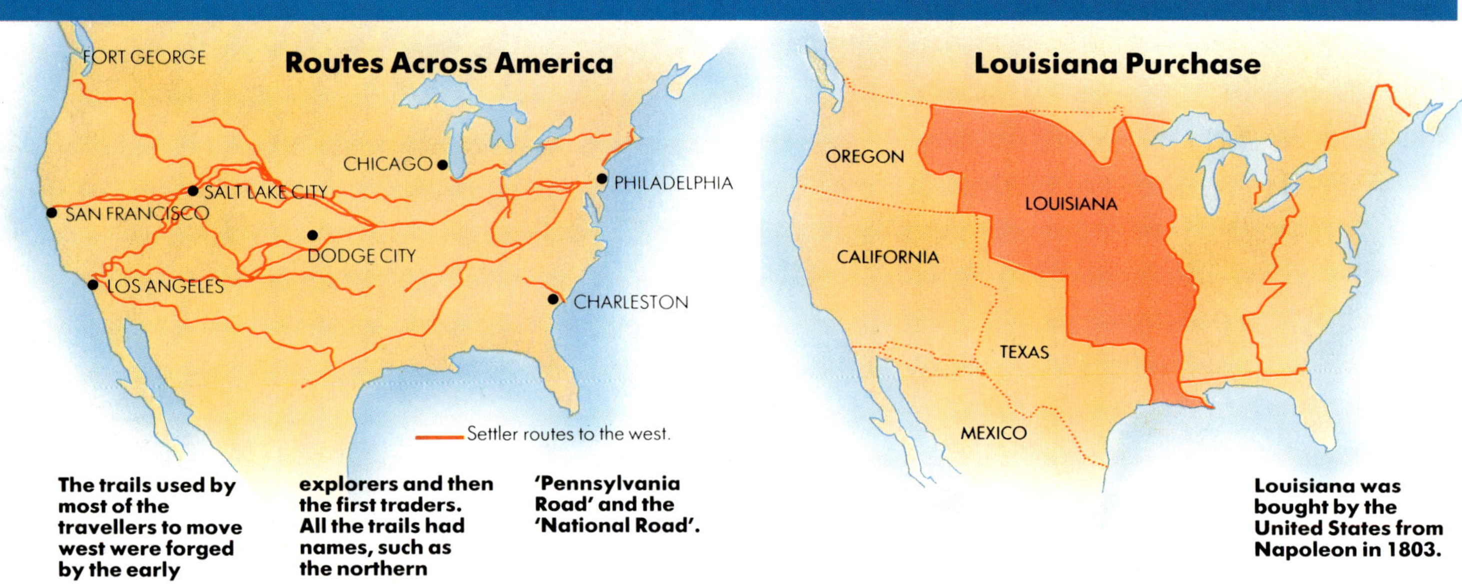

The trails used by most of the travellers to move west were forged by the early explorers and then the first traders. All the trails had names, such as the northern 'Pennsylvania Road' and the 'National Road'.

Louisiana was bought by the United States from Napoleon in 1803.

The first Europeans to settle in North America made their new homes in the eastern states. Few people travelled west of the Mississippi River or the Great Lakes. But as more travellers ventured westwards, they brought back news of good farming country. From about 1820 onwards, thousands of families decided to go west to seek their fortunes. They settled in the western states of the United States and Canada.

WAGON TRAINS For safety, families travelled together in wagon trains. There were dozens of ox-drawn covered wagons in each train, led by a captain who had made the journey before. The *pioneers* had to take everything with them—food, clothes, bedding, tools, even furniture. There were no shops where they were going.

The journey west took several months, for wagon trains travelled slowly. They kept to fixed trails, but there were no roads or even tracks. It could take a day to travel 15 kilometres or cross a river. If a wheel broke, the whole train had to stop until it was mended. At night, the captain chose a place to camp and the men moved the wagons into a circle while the women cooked a meal over camp fires. Then the men took turns to watch for wild animals or attacking Indians while the others slept.

PIONEER LIFE Once the settlers had found a place to farm, life was no easier. First they had to make a clearing in the forest and build their homes out of the timber from the trees they had cut. They they had to dig up the tree

The California Gold Rush

News of the discovery of gold brought over 80,000 people to California in 1849 alone. They came over land along the pioneer trail or by sea round Cape Horn. At one time, there were 500 ships in San Francisco Bay whose crews had deserted to go and search for gold.

Most of the miners had come to California without their families. There was nothing to do except work and drink. The result was that California became the most lawless of the American states for many years.

Left. The movement of settlers to the American West was not good news for the indigenous Amerindian population, whose land was simply taken from them. They were treated as having no rights whatsoever and when they protested, they were mercilessly hunted down.

Right. The bison, too, was a victim of the pioneers. While the Indians had only hunted it to provide for their immediate needs, the new settlers hunted it almost to extinction.

roots to clear the land before they could plough it. There was no time or energy to do anything but work, except when winter snow drove the families indoors. In the early days there were no towns and there were few chances for people to get together. There were no doctors or hospitals, no teachers or schools. The pioneers' lives centred round their own families and they rarely saw anyone else.

The pioneers thought that the land was theirs to take—but it was not. The native Americans, or Amerindians, were there already. At first, the local people were willing to share with the settlers, but many of the pioneers treated the Amerindians like animals and hunted them down, so the local people fought back. Sometimes they attacked the wagon trains. Sometimes they waited until the pioneers were settled in their lonely farms and then they attacked. In the end the pioneers won, but the story of the destruction of the Amerindian nation is one of the most terrible in American history.

GOLD FEVER In 1848 came exciting news from California, in the west. Gold had been discovered. The next year, thousands of families set out on the California trail. Most prospectors searching for gold were unlucky, although the 'Gold Rush' of 1849 brought fortunes to a few people. But the 'Forty-niners', as they were called, had opened up the trail to California and thousands more families followed them to settle on the Pacific coast.

The pioneers depended entirely on themselves and their families for food and shelter. As soon as their gruelling journey was over, they had to set about building a home and clearing the land. They had to bring all their equipment (right) with them. This included cooking utensils, furniture and farming implements as well as the few clothes and household items they possessed.

ENDING THE SLAVE TRADE

Anti-slave trade engraving from 1790.

In 1800, millions of people in North and South America and the West Indies were slaves. They or their parents or grandparents had been hunted and captured in West Africa, packed into ships like cattle and then brought to be sold in the markets of the *New World*. From there, they were taken to work in places such as the tobacco, rice, sugar or cotton *plantations* in the southern states of the United States of America. In South America, slaves were put to work in the gold and silver mines. Slaves were also kept by the Dutch in South Africa and the Dutch East Indies, as well as by other countries.

NOTHING OF THEIR OWN French, British and Spanish settlers in the American continents had introduced slavery there early in the seventeenth century. By 1850 there were about four million slaves in the southern USA alone. There were a few kindly slave-owners, but most worked their slaves hard, driving them on with whips and punishing them cruelly for minor offences.

Slaves and their families belonged to their owners. So did a slave's home and all their possessions. Owners encouraged the women to have children to increase the number of slaves they owned. They hunted down and tortured any slaves who escaped.

THE MIDDLE PASSAGE Slavery made the fortunes of many European ship-owners. They sailed to Africa with cargoes of goods to exchange with tribal chiefs in return for slaves. The second part of the voyage was called the Middle Passage and it took the slaves across the Atlantic Ocean to the Americas. On the return journey the ships would carry cotton or tobacco from America to Europe. Many European ports, including Liverpool and Bristol in Britain and Nantes in France, owed their wealth to this three-way trade.

Conditions on the slave ships were terrible. Slaves were packed tightly together, fastened in their places with iron chains. Many died on the voyage. Sometimes the sick were thrown overboard when they were still alive to prevent the spread of disease.

BANNING SLAVERY During the eighteenth century, protests had begun in Europe against this trade in human beings. One by one, European countries with overseas *colonies* banned the trade. Denmark was first, in 1802. The French, Dutch, Portuguese, Swedes and British followed, but slaves who were already in the colonies were not set free until later. It was 1838 before the British Empire freed all its slaves. This left just one major nation with large numbers of slaves—the USA. There, the cotton farmers of

Above. A slave auction in Virginia, 1861.
Left. Slaves began their journey to America in Africa, where they were sold to European traders by tribal chiefs. The traders treated the Africans as a commodity, not as fellow human beings.

The Abolitionists

William Wilberforce (1759–1833) was the leader of the movement to abolish slavery in the British Empire. He was elected to Parliament in 1780 and began his campaign soon after that. Britain was involved in slavery in two ways. Not only did slaves do most of the work in the British colonies, but British ships and crews also played a leading part in the slave trade with other countries, especially the USA.

Wilberforce devoted much of his life to fighting slavery, but progress was slow. In 1807 a law was passed banning the slave trade in the British Empire, but there were 750,000 slaves already living there who were not freed. Finally in 1833, the year of Wilberforce's death, all the slaves in Britain were set free and five years later the slaves in British colonies were freed too.

Harriet Beecher Stowe (1811–1896) was brought up in Cincinatti, Ohio in the USA. There was no slavery in Ohio, but slaves from the neighbouring state of Kentucky often escaped across the Ohio River. In 1852, Beecher Stowe published *Uncle Tom's Cabin*, a story that told of the terrible conditions under which slaves lived and worked. Her book persuaded thousands of Americans that slavery should be abolished and when it was published in Europe it encouraged European opposition to American slavery.

Right. Harriet Beecher Stowe. Below. William Wilberforce.

the southern states depended on slave labour to plant, pick and harvest the crop.

As long as there was a demand for slaves in North America, some ship-owners were willing to risk supplying that demand. A 'pirate' slave trade continued, despite anti-slavery patrols by the ships of European navies. Treatment of the slaves was worse than ever. At least two slave captains threw hundreds of slaves overboard when they sighted patrol boats. The only way of ending the Atlantic slave trade for ever was to abolish slavery in the United States. This did not happen until 1865.

Slaves picking cotton in the southern US. Planters lived in grand style, for which slaves were essential. Some owners were very cruel, others treated their slaves kindly.

THE UNITED STATES DIVIDED

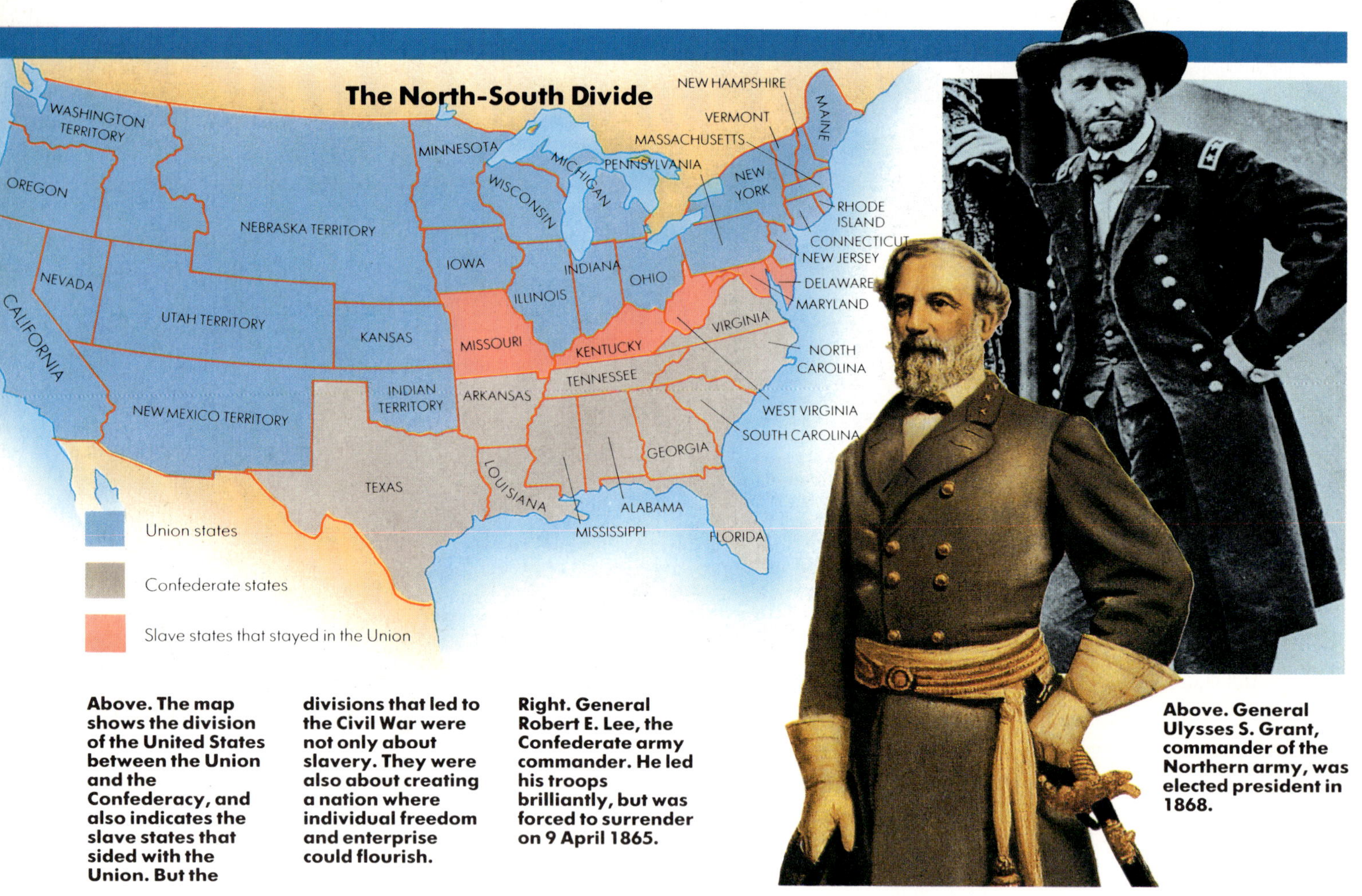

Above. The map shows the division of the United States between the Union and the Confederacy, and also indicates the slave states that sided with the Union. But the divisions that led to the Civil War were not only about slavery. They were also about creating a nation where individual freedom and enterprise could flourish.

Right. General Robert E. Lee, the Confederate army commander. He led his troops brilliantly, but was forced to surrender on 9 April 1865.

Above. General Ulysses S. Grant, commander of the Northern army, was elected president in 1868.

Since the United States had become independent from Britain in 1783, the northern and southern states had been gradually drawing apart. The north was a land of small farms and growing industrial cities, whose people held on to the ideal of freedom that had been brought to America with the *Pilgrim Fathers* in the early seventeenth century. In the south, states like Virginia and Georgia depended mainly on cotton, which was grown on large farms by rich landowners using slave labour. But slavery was only one of the causes of the American Civil War which broke out in 1861.

NORTH AND SOUTH Although the United States had been founded in 1790, the truth was that it was two nations: north and south. The north wanted change and progress. The south wanted life to go on as it was. The Constitution signed in 1790 had spoken of justice and liberty. How could this be, people in the north asked, while there were four million slaves in the south?

UNION AND CONFEDERACY By 1850, more than half the American states had banned slavery. In 1860 Abraham Lincoln, who was opposed to slavery, was elected President of the United States. It seemed to the southern states that if they stayed in the Union of states their way of life was doomed. In 1861, 11 southern states broke away and formed their own union, which they called the Confederacy. This was the signal for the outbreak of war with the 23 states of the north.

Was there to be one United States of America, or two groups of states always quarrelling with each other? That was the question behind the Civil War. It took four years of bitter fighting to decide. At first, the southern army had better leadership and won several battles. But in July 1863, at Gettysburg in Pennsylvania, the Confederate forces were forced to retreat and this was the turning point of the war. From then on the Union army, led by General Grant, was the more successful force on the battlefield. At last, in April 1865, General

Richmond, Virginia, was the Confederate capital. On 9 April 1865, with Northern troops approaching, the people evacuated the city and set fire to it.

Farming and Industry in the USA

Right. Before the Civil War, industrial development in the United States was confined almost entirely to the northern states, where essential raw materials such as coal were available.

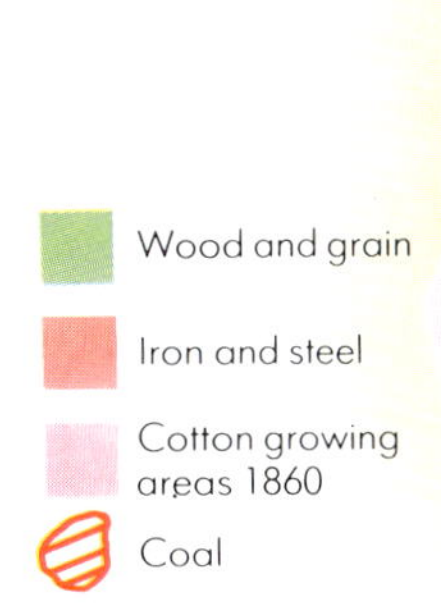

The American Civil War 1861–1865

Right. Union and Confederate (far right) troops. The Union army had a black troop which the Confederates did not. They were also better armed than their southern opponents.

Left. The major battlefields of the American Civil War.

Above. The rival flags: top, the flag of the Confederacy, and below, that of the Union.

Abraham Lincoln 1809–1865

Abraham Lincoln spent only about a year at school, but he taught himself to read and write. He had several low-paid jobs and then studied to become a lawyer.

By 1847 he had been elected to the House of Representatives and in 1858 he became a senator. Lincoln believed that the division between the northern and southern states would destroy the Union. This was the basis of his presidential campaign.

After the Civil War, Lincoln pledged himself to 'bind up the nation's wounds'. But on 14 April 1865 he was shot at the theatre. He died the next day.

Lee's Confederate army was forced to surrender.

The war was over, but the cost had been terrible. Over half a million people—about one in 50 people in the USA—had been killed, two-thirds of them by disease caused by the conditions of war. And even after peace had come, bitterness between the north and the south continued for many years.

FREEING THE SLAVES In the middle of the Civil War, President Lincoln signed a proclamation freeing all the slaves in the USA. When the war was over, freedom from slavery and equal rights for all races were written into the United States Constitution. But this did not mean that the troubles of the blacks in the south were over. When the northern troops went home, the south went back to its old ways. Although slavery had been abolished, the blacks in the south still did not have equal rights and it was another 100 years before *discrimination* against them began to break down.

REVOLUTIONS AND EVOLUTION

In Victorian Britain, social classes were clearly distinguished by their clothes.

At the beginning of the nineteenth century, when people in the West thought of 'civilization' they meant Western civilization, based in Europe and carried by European settlers to areas such as North America. Western thinking was dominated by Christianity and the belief that Genesis, the first book of the Bible, was a complete and literal record of the creation of the world. Europeans knew of other civilizations, such as those of *Islam* and *Hinduism*, but they thought of these as *pagan* and inferior.

The Christian churches, both Protestant and Catholic, influenced every aspect of life in Europe. They taught that monarchs, nobles, landowners and employers had been chosen by God to occupy their positions and power. A verse of a hymn sung in English churches put it like this:

The rich man in his castle,
The poor man at his gate,
God made them high or lowly
And ordered their estate.

It was almost impossible to escape from the influence of the churches. They controlled most universities and schools and the entry to most professions. For governments wanting to retain their power, Christian teaching was very convenient. Who had the right to question or criticize rulers who had been chosen by God?

Above. Samuel Wilberforce was the Bishop of Oxford in 1845. He attacked Darwin's views and wanted to see the Church have more power over the everyday life of people.

Right. William Blake's visionary 'Book of Job', one of a series of paintings with Biblical themes that he produced throughout his life. He also wrote, illustrated, printed and published his own poems.

How Ideas Spread

One reason why ideas spread more quickly in the nineteenth century was that steam power made printing much faster and cheaper. The first steam presses were used in 1814 to print *The Times* newspaper in London.

Later printing became even cheaper after new inventions such as presses which printed on reels of paper instead of separate sheets.

For those who could not read, books and newspapers were read aloud in public. For the first time, ordinary people could hear different views, not just those of their priest.

The rotary press, printing on reels rather than sheets of paper, speeded up the spreading of news and made newspapers cheaper.

REVOLUTIONARY CHALLENGE The French Revolution of 1789 had challenged these ideas with its demands for freedom and equality. On the other side of the Atlantic Ocean, the same demands had led the American states to fight for independence from Britain. But European governments did not want new ideas. They wanted things to go on as before. Then, in 1859, a book was published in London that would change the whole way of thinking in the West.

DARWIN'S BOMBSHELL The book was *The Origin of Species,* written by Charles Darwin (1809–1882). Darwin was a British scientist who had travelled widely and studied the development of plant and animal species. From his studies, he had worked out the Theory of Evolution. This said that the Earth and its plant and animal life had developed slowly over millions of years and had not, as many people believed from the Bible, been created in exactly six days.

Darwin's ideas did not change everyone's way of thinking at once. But he convinced most scientists—and scientists, with the improvements they had brought about in medicine and the standard of living, were very popular in the nineteenth century. For many years the churches attacked Darwin fiercely, because he had produced an explanation of human creation that cast doubt on the basic ideas behind Western Christian culture.

THE MELTING POT Darwin's book was just one example of the way Western ideas were changing. Another change was the attitude of people towards their rulers. Almost all countries were ruled by monarchs. But was this necessary? The United States of America, for example, managed very well without a monarch and it gave the people a greater say in how the country was run.

Other people asked why it was that the poor were poor. Were they made that way, or had they simply not had the opportunities and education that the rich had had?

Slowly but surely, in the nineteenth century the ideas which had previously been the foundation of Western civilization were going into the melting pot and new ideas and attitudes were being formed.

Right. Dawes Point, Sydney, one of the *Beagle*'s landfalls on Charles Darwin's voyage of discovery.
Below. Darwin in 1840, aged 31, four years after his return. He spent the next 20 years developing his theory of evolution.

The Voyage of the Beagle

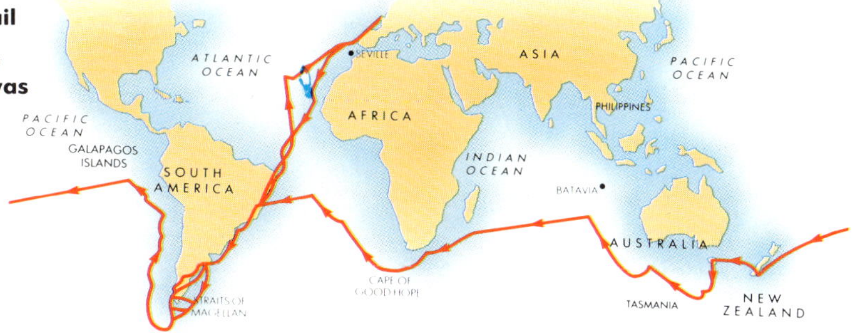

The *Beagle* set sail westwards from Britain in the last days of 1831. It was to be a five-year voyage.

The Old World
TIME CHART

AD	EUROPE	NORTH AND SOUTH AMERICA	REST OF WORLD
1789	Outbreak of the French Revolution	George Washington becomes the first president of the United States of America	
1792>1815	Napoleonic Wars		
1811>1824		Spain's former colonies in Central and South America achieve independence as separate states, except for the islands of Cuba and Puerto Rico	
1812	French army invades Russia and is defeated outside Moscow		
1815	Congress of Vienna		Britain adds Cape Colony, South Africa, to its empire
1819	First steamship crossing of the Atlantic by the Savannah		
1820		Brazil becomes independent from Portugal	
1825	Opening of the Stockton and Darlington Railway in Britain Nicholas I becomes tsar of Russia		
1829			Britain claims the whole of Australia
1830	Revolution in France Revolts in Belgium, Italy and Poland Cholera spreads from Asia to Russia	America's first railway, the South Carolina Railway, opens	
1837	Victoria becomes queen of Britain		
1838			All slaves in the British Empire set free
1839			First British settlers land in New Zealand
1840			New Zealand added to the British Empire
1845>1846	The Great Famine		
1848	Revolution in France Revolts in parts of Italy, Germany and the Austrian Empire *The Communist Manifesto* published The Chartist campaign for democracy in Britain fails		
1849		California Gold Rush	
1854>1856	The Crimean War		
1855	Tsar Nicholas I dies		
1856	Tsar Alexander II takes control		
1857>1858			The Indian Mutiny
1859	*The Origin of Species* published		
1860		Abraham Lincoln becomes president of the USA	
1861>1865		The American Civil War	
1865		Slavery abolished in the USA	

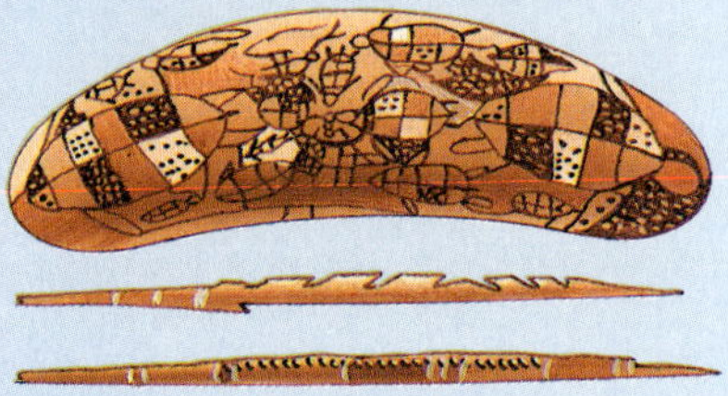

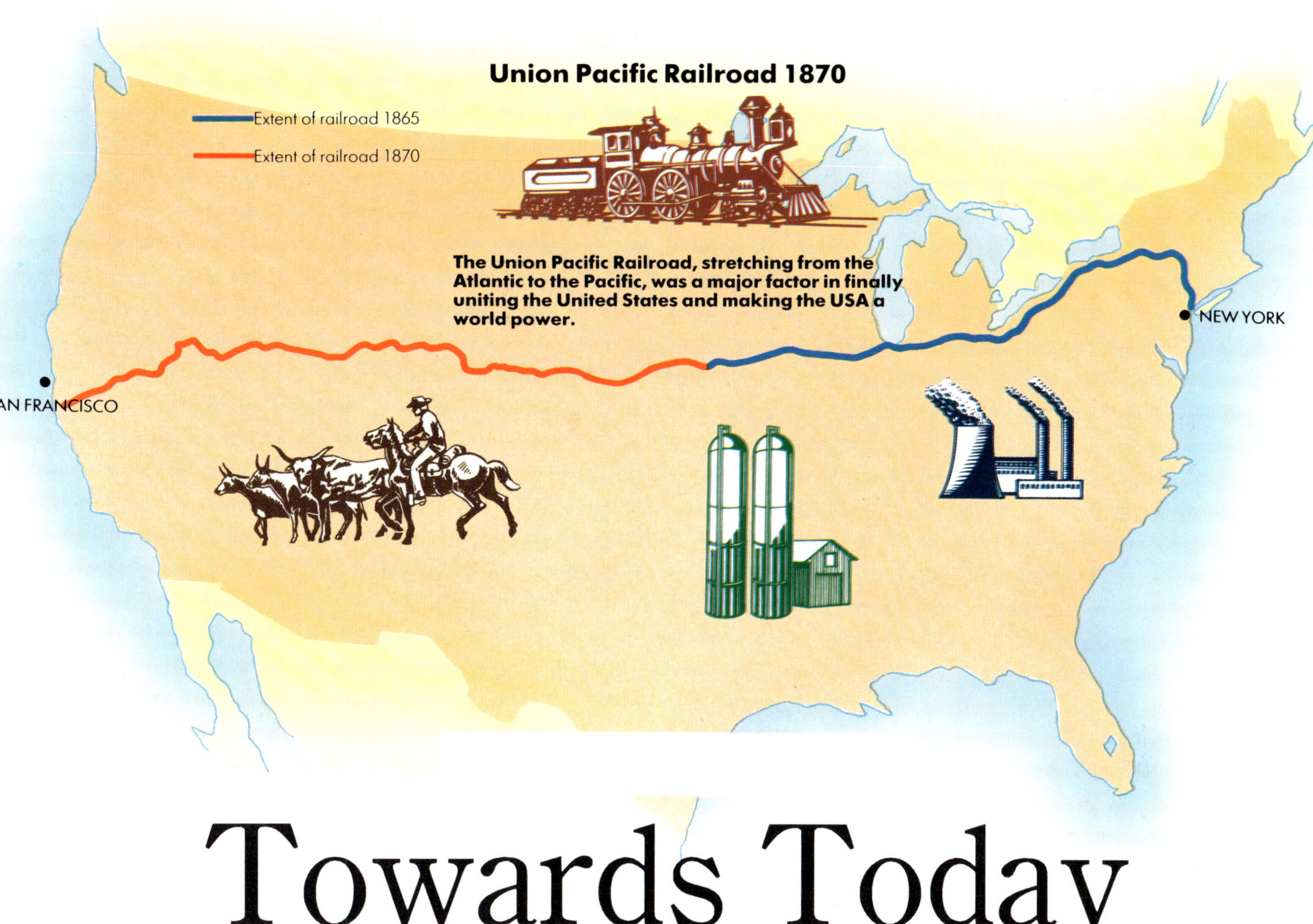

The Union Pacific Railroad, stretching from the Atlantic to the Pacific, was a major factor in finally uniting the United States and making the USA a world power.

Towards Today

The second half of the nineteenth century saw great changes in the power of different countries, both in Europe—which had played a leading role in political and technological developments for so many centuries—and in the wider world.

FROM THE ATLANTIC TO THE PACIFIC In 1865 in the United States of America, work began on a major engineering project, building a railway linking the Atlantic and Pacific coasts. The Union Pacific Company employed a workforce of former Civil War soldiers and Irish *immigrants* to extend its railway line from Omaha, Nebraska in the east, over the Rocky Mountains. Meanwhile, the Chinese labourers of the Central Pacific line set out to meet them from California in the west.

The two lines met at Promontory Point, near the Great Salt Lake in Utah, on 10 May 1869. For the first time, passengers could travel by rail from one side of North America to the other.

GROWTH OF THE USA It was an important moment for the United States, and for the world. The American Civil War (see pp. 422–3) was over. The USA was ready to become a major world power. The new railway would speed up farming development and transport meat and grain from the farms to the cities and ports. It would help Americans to feel that they belonged to one vast country.

Within 20 years the USA had become the world's largest supplier of grain, meat and steel. The country also took the lead in many of the inventions of the second half of the nineteenth century.

Up to now, almost all of America's immigrants had come from Europe. Now, America could look across the Pacific as well as the Atlantic. It stood between the world's two great oceans. In the first half of the nineteenth century, the Atlantic had been the world's great sea highway for passengers and cargoes. In the second half, the Pacific was opened up in the same way.

THE SHRINKING WORLD Meanwhile, faster communications were drawing the rest of the world closer. The late nineteenth century was the age of the steam train and the steamship. In 1872 the French writer Jules Verne published his book *Around the World in Eighty Days*. It was an adventure story, but it contained an important message: faster travel made the world seem smaller and what was happening in the rest of the world was important to everyone.

CHANGING THE MAP OF EUROPE

The map of Europe in the middle of the nineteenth century looked similar in many ways to that of today, with two important differences. Where today's map shows Italy and Germany as two large countries, on the older map there was a mass of small states. Two of the most important changes in Europe between 1851 and 1871 happened when these states were grouped into the two nations of Italy and Germany.

ITALY UNITES The 1848 revolution in Italy (see page 397) was a protest against being ruled by foreign governments. Austria occupied the northern Italian states, the Spanish controlled the southern half of the country and the pope ruled a group of states in the centre. The only independent part of Italy was Piedmont, made up of the north-western state of Piedmont and the island of Sardinia. The 1848 revolution failed to bring any change, but from 1852 onwards Piedmont set out to unite Italy into one nation.

War with Austria in 1859 led to unity between Piedmont and some of its neighbours. In 1860 a rebellion in the south united these to most of the rest of Italy except for the state of Rome, which was controlled by the pope. Finally, in 1870, the pope agreed to hand over all of Rome except for the Vatican City, the small area round St Peter's Cathedral. At last, after much fighting and bloodshed, Italy was one united country.

The years after Italian unification were disappointing. The very poor southern states were jealous of the prosperity of the north. It seemed to the south that the government's main aim was to make the north even richer.

ONE GERMANY Just as one state, Piedmont, led the unification of Italy, so the largest German state, Prussia, took the lead there. After 1815, Austria ruled about a quarter of what is now Germany. Prussia ruled an area of much the same size. The rest of Germany was made up

The Nation-Builders

Count Camillo Cavour (1810–1861) believed that Italy should be united as a monarchy and not a republic. He was born in Piedmont, which was controlled by Austria. In 1847, he founded a newspaper called *Il Risorgimento* to put forward his views. He became prime minister of Piedmont in 1852 and was able to follow his campaign to drive the Austrians out of northern Italy.

Count Otto von Bismarck (1815–1898) was a Prussian from a wealthy background. After studying, he served as an ambassador for Prussia then became prime minister in 1861. He was determined that Germany should unite under Prussian leadership and go on to become a world power.

Wars with Austria in 1866 and France in 1870 showed Europe the power of the Prussian army, which Bismarck had built up.

Left. Count Camillo Cavour Sardinian statesman who led the movement for Italian unification.

The Unification of Italy 1859–1870

LOMBARDY
TYROL
TRIESTE
VENETIA
SAVOY
PARMA
PIEDMONT
MODENA
FLORENCE
TUSCANY
PAPAL STATES
KINGDOM OF SARDINIA
CORSICA
SARDINIA
KINGDOM OF THE TWO SICILIES

Kingdom of Sardinia

Left. The movement for the unification of Italy began in Piedmont and spread southwards towards the Mediterranean. Venice and Rome were the last states to give way, leaving only Vatican City outside the united Italy.

The Unification of Germany

SCHLESWIG
HOLSTEIN
EAST PRUSSIA
HANOVER
HOLLAND
PRUSSIA
BERLIN
RUSSIAN EMPIRE
WESTPHALIA
HESSE-NASSAU
BELGIUM
SILESIA
PRAGUE
BAVARIA
AUSTRIAN EMPIRE
BADEN
WURTENBURG
SWITZERLAND

Above. Germany, made up of a collection of tiny states, needed unity to combat the large nations that surrounded it. It was this threat that led Prussia to lead the fight for a united Germany.

Prussia 1815
Lands acquired by Prussia to 1867
German Empire 1871

of about 40 small states which were under Austrian control.

In 1866 Prussia defeated Austria after a war that lasted seven weeks. Prussia then took over control of most of the small German states in the north and set up links with the southern states. But the thought of a large united Germany alarmed France, and war between Prussia and France broke out in 1870. The French army was no match for the skilled and well-equipped Prussian troops, however, and by January 1871 France had surrendered.

Now that France was defeated, Prussia could complete its plan for a united Germany. It humiliated France still further by choosing the Palace of Versailles near Paris as the place where Wilhelm I, King of Prussia, was proclaimed Kaiser (emperor) of all Germany.

GERMAN STRENGTH Almost at once, Germany became a leading power in western Europe. But French bitterness and shame at its defeat did not fade and Britain also soon became worried by Germany's growing strength. In the last 30 years of the nineteenth century, these tensions increased. They were eventually to spill over in the First World War of 1914 to 1918.

Left. A scene of waste and destruction in the centre of Paris during the Prussian siege of the city in 1870–1871. The French were no match for the efficient Prussians and surrendered after 131 days.

Above. On the way to Italian unity, 1860. The revolutionary leader Garibaldi hands over to Victor Emanuel II, King of Sardinia, the land he has conquered in central Italy.

THE WEST COMES TO CHINA

To most Europeans at the start of the nineteenth century, China was a mysterious, unknown country on the other side of the world. For centuries, European traders had been travelling there to buy silk, porcelain and tea. But contacts with Europe had not changed the Chinese. They had their own civilization, which was far older than Europe's. They thought of Westerners as 'barbarians'.

A cartoon from a propaganda book, published in 1891, urging the Chinese to make war on Westerners and resist Western influence. The Chinese resented the fact that many European powers, including Britain, and Russia, had set up trading posts on Chinese territory which were exempted from Chinese law.

THE OPIUM WARS In the eighteenth century, merchants began to bring the drug opium into China to pay for Chinese goods. By the 1830s, opium was doing so much harm to Chinese society that the emperor of China ordered European and American traders to stop supplying it. This led to war. In 1839 British forces landed at Chinese ports and threatened to move inland unless the emperor allowed traders to operate freely. He agreed, but war broke out again in 1856. By 1860 Europe, America and Japan were all allowed to trade in Chinese ports. Meanwhile, in 1842 Britain had taken over the port of Hong Kong as part of the British Empire.

Traders were not the only visitors from the West. Christian *missionaries* also poured into China. They aimed to convert the Chinese *Buddhists*, whom they regarded as *heathen*, to Christianity, whether they wanted to be converted or not. After slavery was abolished in the United States of America (see page 423), the Americans looked to Chinese workers as a source of cheap labour. Thousands were bribed or kidnapped to go to the USA and elsewhere, where they were treated as little more than slaves.

China was not prepared for the agression of the West. The ruling Manchu family said that the Chinese should hold on to their old values and way of life, which had served them well before the Europeans

The Manchu Family

The Manchu family, or *dynasty*, had ruled China since 1644. They were warriors from Manchuria in the north, who ruled harshly and expanded the Chinese Empire.

The Manchus saw no reason to change the traditional Chinese way of life. China had a huge population, so there seemed no reason to replace cheap manual labour with expensive machines. But the opium traders and missionaries brought Western ideas, one of which was that it was wrong for the wealthy to live in luxury while the peasants often starved to death, an idea that helped to create dissatisfaction.

In 1861 Emperor Hsien Feng died, leaving a son who was still only a child. Hsien Feng's widow, Ci Xi, took over. She put most of her effort into outwitting any ministers who opposed her instead of developing the country. In 1890, for example, she cancelled plans to modernize the navy because she had quarrelled with the admirals and spent the money on rebuilding her Summer Palace in Beijing. As a result, Japan defeated them five years later.

Ci Xi lived until 1908, but by then the Manchus had lost power and the scene was set for the revolution four years later.

China under Foreign Control

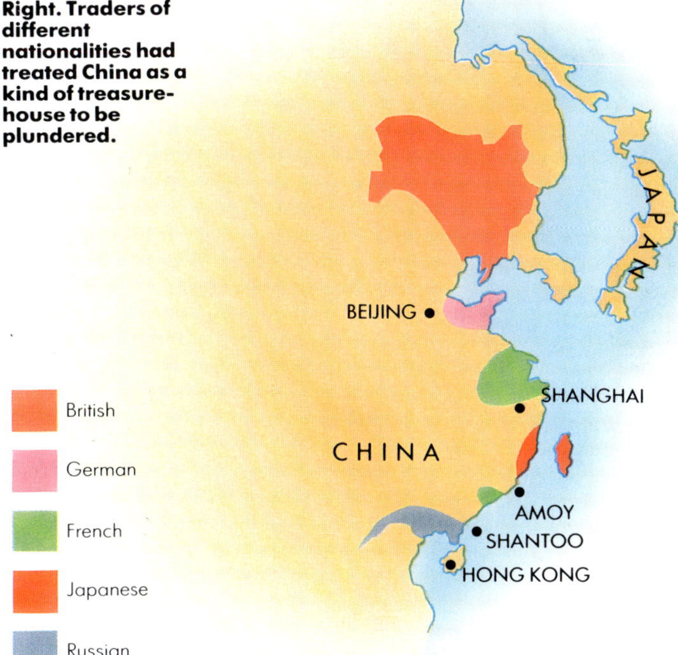

Right. Traders of different nationalities had treated China as a kind of treasure-house to be plundered.

These women musicians represent Chinese cultural values which were under threat from the West.

arrived. Others argued that China must bring itself up to date with Western inventions such as modern weapons, industries, steamships and railways. If this was done, they said, China would be powerful enough to drive the foreigners out of their land.

YEAR OF REBELLION In the years following the Opium Wars the argument flared up into a series of rebellions. The most serious was the Taiping Rebellion, which began in 1850. The Taiping rebels wanted reforms based on Western Christian ideas. For 14 years they fought their way through the most heavily populated part of China, capturing city after city. They were finally defeated by an army led by American and British *mercenaries*.

Several other countries took advantage of China's weakness. Russia took over an area of northern China. France defeated China in a war in 1885, and in 1895 Japan forced China to hand over land and trading rights.

THE BOXER RISING A drought in 1899 led to famine. When the government did nothing to help, another rebellion, known as the Boxer Rising, broke out. Its leaders called for the Manchu family to be overthrown and for all foreigners to be 'destroyed'. At first the rebels were successful, but they were defeated in 1900 by a force of foreign troops.

Although the Boxer Rising failed, it was clear that the Manchu dynasty could no longer govern China properly. Twelve years later it was forced to hand over power to a new government.

The West Gate of Peking, now known as Beijing, China's capital city. The splendour of the imperial city contrasts with the very basic buildings of the farmers on the other side of the river.

JAPAN'S LEAP FORWARD

A Japanese artist's impression of the arrival of the United States navy's 'black ships' in 1853.

Japan, like China (see pp. 430–1), was another Far Eastern country which was cut off from the rest of the world until the middle of the nineteenth century. It was even more isolated than China. There was no foreign trade, no foreign visitors were allowed to enter the country and no Japanese were allowed to leave.

Japan had an emperor, but the real ruler was the *shogun*, the commander of the army. He controlled the land and the roads and even how the Japanese dressed. His rule was enforced by warriors called *samurai*.

THE BLACK SHIPS Japan's isolation ended suddenly. In July 1853, four United States warships sailed into Tokyo Bay. Two were steamships, and when the Japanese saw black smoke pouring from the funnels they called them 'the black ships'. The ships brought a message for the emperor: he must open his ports to American ships; if he did not, a larger American force would be sent.

Next year, the Americans were back again, this time with 10 ships and a force of 2000 men. The emperor was forced to agree to let American trading ships call, and soon Japanese ports were open to ships from all nations.

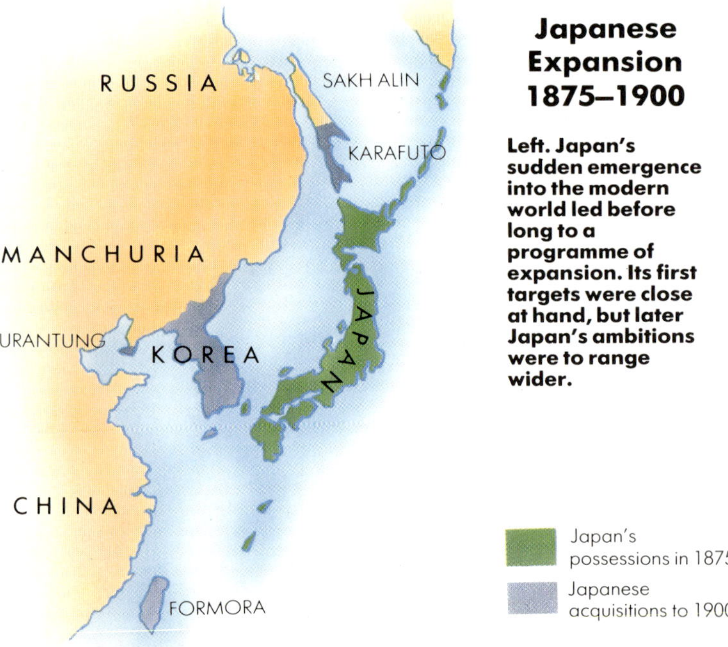

Japanese Expansion 1875–1900

Left. Japan's sudden emergence into the modern world led before long to a programme of expansion. Its first targets were close at hand, but later Japan's ambitions were to range wider.

THE SHOGUN'S REACTION The emperor's decision upset the shogun, who encouraged the samurai to attack foreigners. When three British men were murdered in

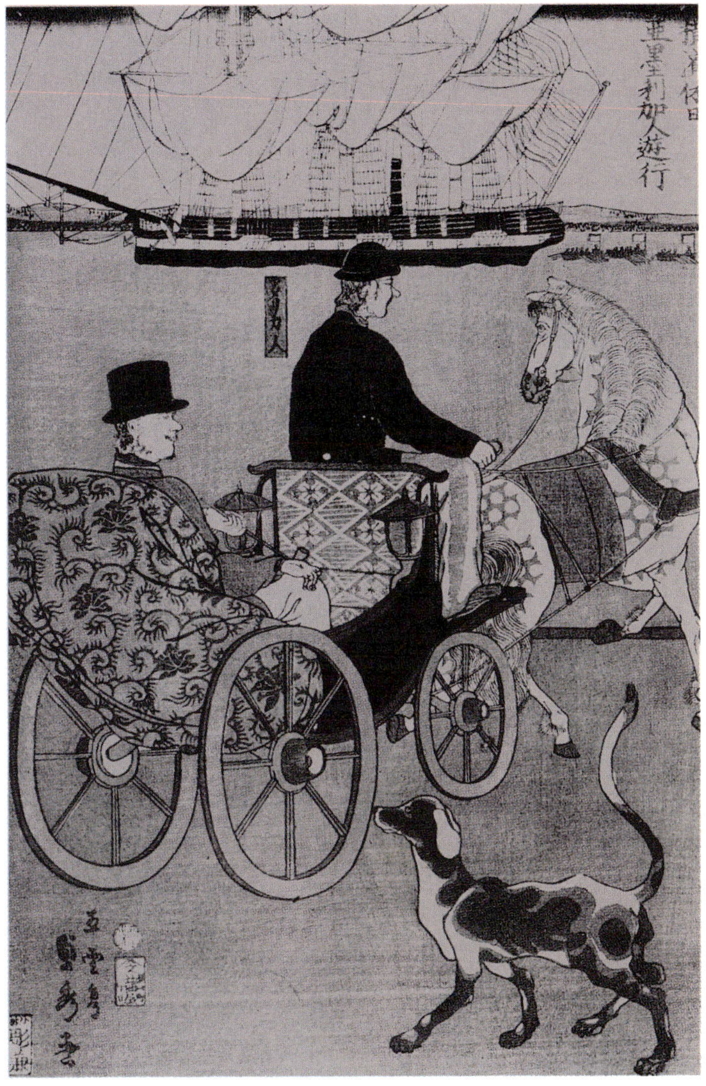

Far left. An American visitor takes a pleasure trip round Yokohama.

Left. Traditional Japanese dress in the late nineteenth century: a farm worker and a lady of fashion.

Below. 'The Great Wave of Kanagawa' by the Japanese artist Katsushika Hokusai, who died in 1849. His work influenced many late nineteenth-century European painters.

1862 and the shogun refused to punish the murderers, British ships attacked the city of Kagoshima. In 1863 a Japanese force fired on Dutch, French and American merchant ships and a fleet of 16 warships was sent to destroy it. The message was clear: Western nations were not going to let the shogun interfere with trade.

The shogun had feared that contact with the West would make the Japanese want more freedom and prosperity for themselves, and he was right. In 1865 civil war broke out and after three years' fighting the shogun was defeated.

The New Japan

1854 Trading treaty signed with the USA
1865 Civil war between traditionalists and reformers
1867 Accession of Emperor Mutsuhito, who was to introduce *Meiji* ('enlightened government').
1872 Introduction of Western-style education, policing, justice and banking. Japan's first railway opened
1889 Parliamentary government introduced, but the emperor had the right to reverse its decisions

MODERNIZING JAPAN From then on, the Japanese attitude to the West suddenly changed. British engineers were invited to build Japan's first railway, which opened in 1872. The ban on Japanese travel abroad was lifted, and British and American advisers were brought in to help to organize post and telegraph services.

In 1871 a group of learned Japanese men was sent abroad to learn about Western civilization. They were away for nearly two years, visiting the United States and Europe. They studied everything in great detail and when they returned they were full of news about what they had seen, from cameras to steam engines and from schools to post offices.

Japan at once started a programme of modernization which was to continue over the next 60 years. Its aim was to make Japan a world power which was respected by other nations. But it was not long before the new, more confident Japan began to look dangerous. In 1894 it launched its first modern foreign war, against the Chinese in Korea. Ten years after that, the new Japanese navy was strong enough to sink or capture the entire Russian fleet in the Russo-Japanese War.

SOUTH AFRICA AND THE BOERS

With so many European countries building up their empires overseas during the nineteenth century, their interests sometimes clashed. One place where this happened was in South Africa—with tragic results.

RIVALS FOR THE CAPE The Dutch had first settled at the Cape of Good Hope in 1650, mainly to provide a harbour for Dutch ships on their way to and from the East Indies. But some Dutch settlers went inland and started farming. They became known as *Boers*, from the Dutch word for 'farmer'.

After the Congress of Vienna in 1815 (see page 7) the Cape became a British colony. Britain wanted it for the same reason as the Dutch, to use it as a staging post for ships going to the East. British settlers began to arrive at the Cape; soon there were 4000 of them and it was decided that the language of the area should be English. This was bad enough for the Dutch settlers, but there was worse to come. In 1838 slavery was banned throughout the British Empire and the Dutch were ordered to free their slaves.

THE GREAT TREK Many Boers strongly disliked being ruled by Britain and decided to travel north to areas beyond British control. This movement north, called the Great Trek, began in 1834 and went on until 1839. About 14,000 Boers took part. The land they reached was occupied by the Zulu and Matabele tribes. The Boers, with their better

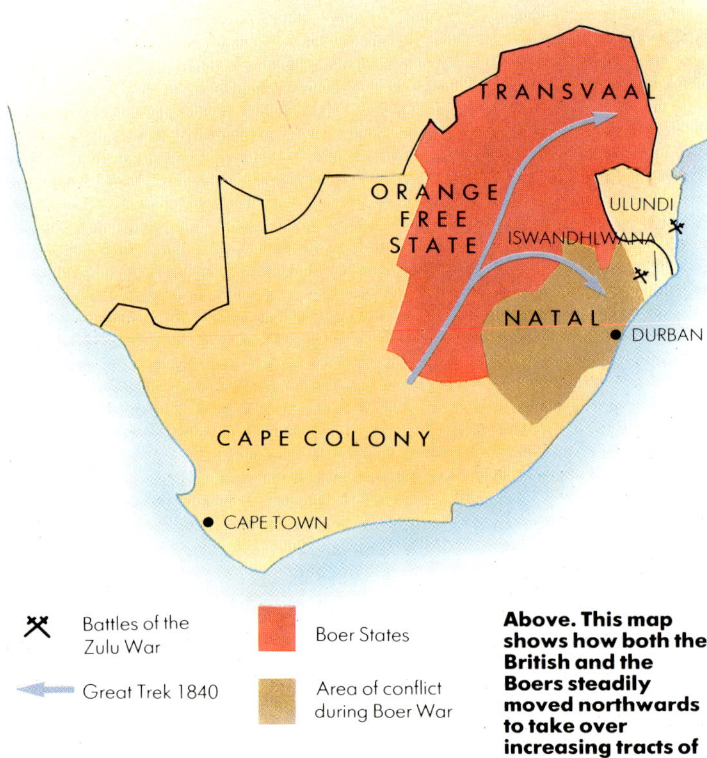

Above. This map shows how both the British and the Boers steadily moved northwards to take over increasing tracts of the tribal lands of South Africa.

The battle of Spion Kop in Natal in January 1900. It was a Boer victory which humiliated the British forces.

The Zulu

The Zulu were the most powerful of the original tribes of southern Africa. In 1810 they chose a new chief, Shaka, who organized the tribe as a conquering army. He introduced the *assegai*, a spear designed for stabbing rather than throwing, and larger shields for extra protection. The Zulu drove back rival tribes and gained control of a large area of eastern South Africa. Shaka was murdered in 1828, but the Zulu conquests continued until they were checked by the Boers 10 years later.

The Zulu had lost land to the Boers and to the British, and there was a new border dispute in 1877. In 1879 the British ordered Chief Cetawayo to disband his troops. When he refused, the British invaded Zululand.

The first British attack was beaten off, but six months later a stronger force invaded and defeated the Zulu. In 1887 the British took direct control of Zululand and 10 years later it became the British colony of Natal. However, Zulu defiance of British rule continued into the twentieth century.

European weapons, drove the tribes back and cleared the country for themselves. By 1856 they had set up two independent Boer republics, Orange Free State and Transvaal.

DIAMONDS AND GOLD The Boers and the British lived alongside each other uneasily until, in 1867, diamonds were discovered on the western border of Orange Free State. This changed the whole future of South Africa, as a poor farming country became a rich supplier of precious stones and metals. The British claimed the territory where the discoveries were made and this was resented by the Boers.

Meanwhile the British were finding it more and more difficult to govern South Africa. Things became worse in 1884 when gold was discovered at what is now Johannesburg in the Transvaal. This turned out to be the biggest gold field in the world and soon there was a 'gold rush' like the one in 1849 in California (see page 419). Prospectors rushed to the Transvaal from all over the world, and once again the Boers felt that they had been cheated of what should have been theirs.

THE BOER WAR By the 1890s the tensions between the Boers and the British had reached boiling point. The British had only a small army in South Africa, but they declared war in October 1899, expecting an easy victory. They were wrong. The Boers fought hard and it took a large army sent from Britain to defeat them. The result was that the Boer republics became part of the Union of South Africa, and remained within the British Empire for the next 60 years.

A Boer farmstead. When they settled in the Orange Free State and Transvaal, the Boers showed much of the same spirit as the American pioneers.

THE SCRAMBLE FOR AFRICA

The African Explorers

David Livingstone (1813–1873)—right, with Stanley—a Scottish doctor and missionary, first went to Africa in 1840 to set up a mission in what is now Botswana. In 1849 he and William Oswell crossed the Kalahari Desert, and over the next few years he explored the Zambezi River, including the great waterfalls which he named after Queen Victoria. His last exploration in 1866 was to search for the sources of the Congo and Nile rivers. He died of fever on 1 May 1873.

Sir Henry Morton Stanley (1841–1904) was a Welsh-born journalist who went to Africa in 1869 to find Livingstone, missing for three years. They met on the shores of Lake Tanganyika in 1871. After Livingstone's death, Stanley led two explorations of the area round the River Congo.

Left. Sir Richard Burton (1821–1890) began to explore Somalia in East Africa in 1854. Later, with a fellow army officer called John Hanning Speke, he led an expedition through Tanzania to find the source of the Nile.

Above. Heinrich Barth (1821–1865), born in Hamburg in Germany, first journeyed in 1845 across North Africa and into Syria. He spent nearly six years in Africa, exploring the northern part of what is now Nigeria.

In 1800, Europe knew very little about Africa apart from the Cape area in the south. Sailors knew the Mediterranean shore and a few trading posts round the east and west coasts. The rest of Africa was a mystery. On the map, it was shown as a great white space.

Yet by 1914 Africa had become a patchwork of colonies. The British, French, Germans, Spanish, Portuguese, Italians and Belgians had carved it up between them.

THE GREAT EXPLORERS It was explorers, not invading European troops, who 'opened up' Africa to European influence. Heinrich Barth of Germany crossed the Sahara Desert from north to south in about 1850. At about the same time David Livingstone, a Scottish missionary, explored the Zambezi River in East Africa. Other explorers traced the course of the River Nile northwards and the Congo River westwards.

Although Europeans were excited to read about

The Suez Canal

The idea of a canal linking the Mediterranean and the Red Sea is as old as the ancient Egyptians. The canal, 160 kilometres long, took 10 years to build and was opened in 1869. It was designed by French engineers and built with French and Egyptian money. In 1875 Britain bought the Egyptian share, forging a link with Egypt which lasted until 1955.

Colonial Africa 1870

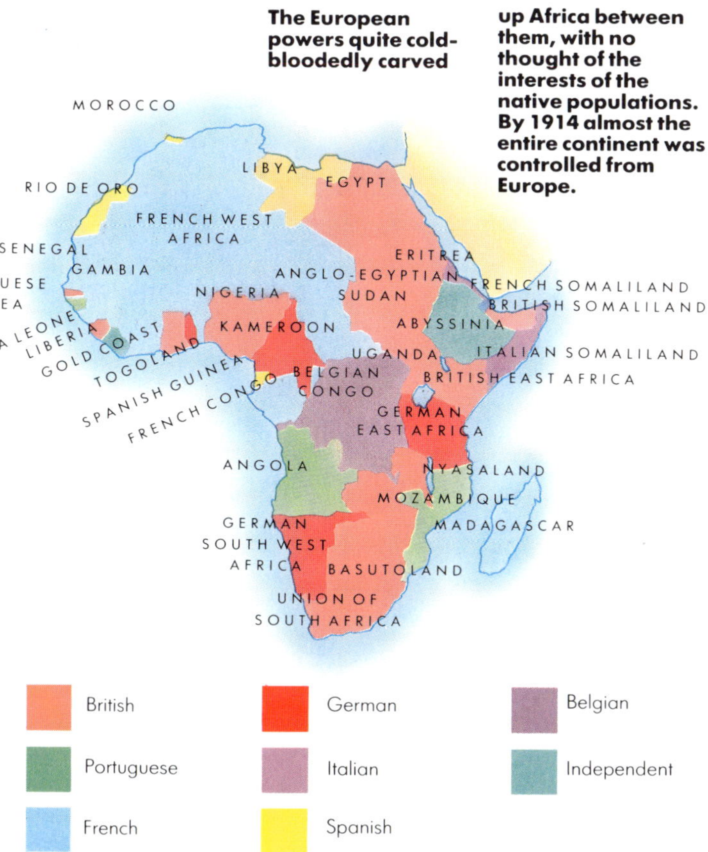

The European powers quite cold-bloodedly carved up Africa between them, with no thought of the interests of the native populations. By 1914 almost the entire continent was controlled from Europe.

these adventures, at first they did not think of taking over the newly mapped areas. The scramble for Africa did not begin until about 1870. There were two reasons for this.

THE SUEZ CANAL One was the opening of the Suez Canal in 1869. As it linked the Mediterranean with the Red Sea, it shortened shipping routes to India and the Far East by several thousand kilometres. It became vital to the European trading nations, especially Britain. To safeguard ships passing through the Canal, Britain took over the 'protection' of Egypt and later gained control of the Sudan. Britain, France and Italy all had colonies at the southern end of the Red Sea. Trade with East Africa could now go through ports in these colonies instead of taking the long way round by the Cape.

SPHERES OF INFLUENCE The second reason for the scramble for Africa was the result of the Franco-Prussian War of 1870–1871 (see page 429). France, which was defeated, looked for an empire to restore its position as a world power. Germany, which was victorious, needed new markets for its industries and colonies for its growing population. In a series of treaties beginning in 1885, European countries agreed among themselves on their 'spheres of influence', the parts of Africa they would take control of, regardless of the feelings of the Africans. The boundaries between European colonies often split up tribal lands or brought together tribes which had been enemies for hundreds of years.

Some Europeans treated the Africans better than others did. In the Belgian Congo (present-day Zaïre), local workers were little more than slaves. In the British and German colonies, either the government or the missionaries did set up schools and provide medical care for the local people. But Europeans were interested in Africa mainly for their own benefit. Many goods that were valuable in Europe—such as precious metals and stones, minerals like copper and nickel, tropical hardwoods and farm produce—were shipped there from Africa, and in return the African colonies provided markets for European manufactured goods. By 1914 only two small areas of Africa, the state of Liberia (set up in 1847 by freed American slaves) and the kingdom of Abyssinia (present-day Ethiopia), were not part of a European empire or under European 'protection'.

The Suez Canal 1869

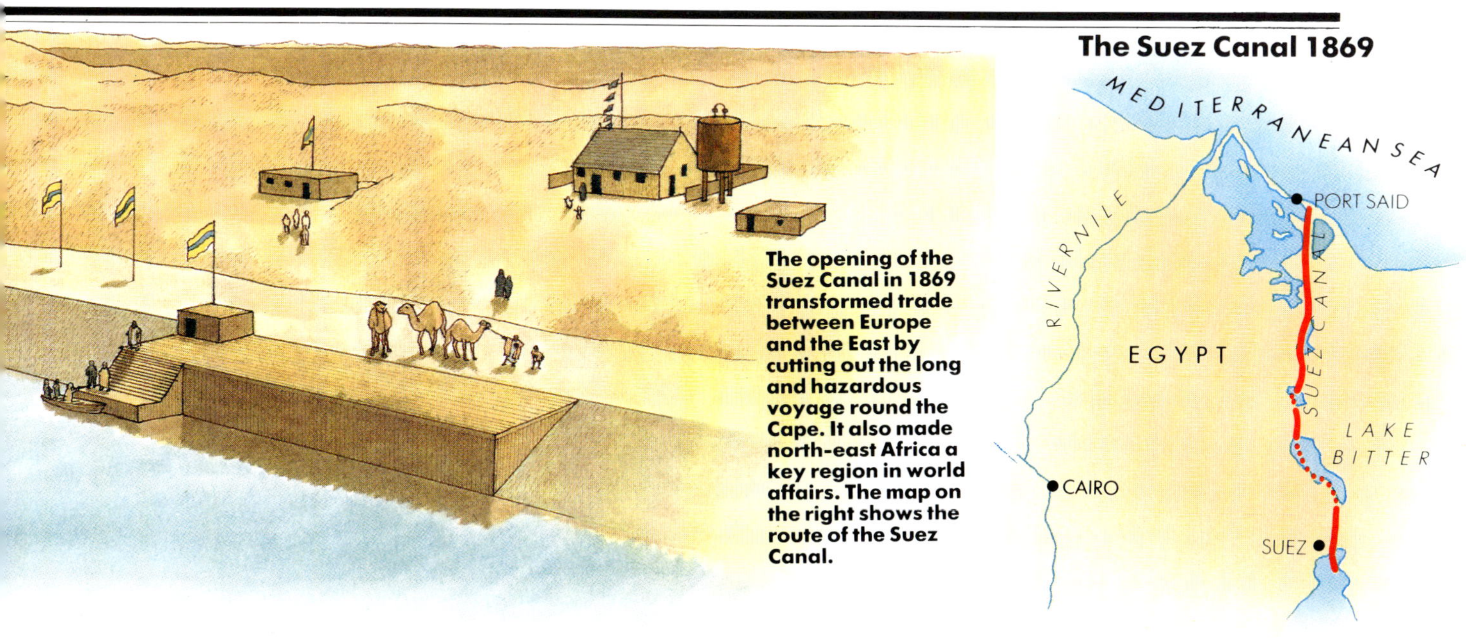

The opening of the Suez Canal in 1869 transformed trade between Europe and the East by cutting out the long and hazardous voyage round the Cape. It also made north-east Africa a key region in world affairs. The map on the right shows the route of the Suez Canal.

AUSTRALIA AND NEW ZEALAND

Australia and New Zealand were the last areas of the world to be added to the British Empire by white settlers, but once settlement began it grew very rapidly.

The new Australians settled round the coast. The outback—the inland desert—was populated by a small number of Aboriginals, the native people of Australia. No European had crossed the outback until 1861, when the explorers Burke and Wills died on their return journey.

Settlers who went to New Zealand found a climate that was similar to that of Britain and they were able to adapt to their new country more easily.

SHEEP AND GOLD Australian settlers in New South Wales found land that was perfect for grazing sheep, and wool became the foundation of Australia's prosperity. By 1850 the country was the largest producer of wool in the world.

Then, in 1851, large deposits of gold were found in New South Wales and Victoria. Later, more was found in Queensland, together with coal, zinc and other minerals. Australia was now able to add industry to its activities and more settlers from Britain arrived to share in its wealth. By the 1890s Australia's two main cities, Sydney and Melbourne, each had populations of nearly half a million.

Above. The route of the ill-fated expedition across the interior of Australia by Burke and Wills who died on their return journey.

Above. The Burke and Wills expedition setting out on their ill-fated journey across Australia from Cooper Creek in 1861.

Left. In 1851, gold was found at Ballarat and Bendigo in Victoria, creating a furious gold rush of men sure they would find a fortune.

Below. Aboriginal spears and boomerangs were no defence against the settlers' guns.

Above. An attempt to suggest settlers and Aboriginals should be friends and would be treated equally.

THE FATE OF THE ABORIGINALS The bad side of the story of white settlement in Australia concerns the treatment of the Aboriginals. There were about 300,000 Aboriginals in Australia when the Europeans arrived. They lived by *hunting and gathering*, in the same way as their ancestors had done for many thousands of years. When the white settlers arrived with their guns, the Aboriginals could do little to resist them. Thousands were killed, many of them simply hunted down for sport. Although Australians prided themselves on their democracy, it was halfway through the twentieth century before the Aboriginals were given any civil rights at all.

MAORI WARS The native people of New Zealand, the Maori, were at first treated no better by the white settlers. Britain claimed New Zealand as part of its empire in 1840, when there were about 2000 whites living there. During the next 20 years this number grew to 100,000 and by the 1880s it had reached half a million. Britain bought South Island from the Maori, but promised that whites would not settle on their land in North Island. This promise was broken and the result was 10 years of fighting between 1861 and 1871, during which 2000 Maori were killed.

Colonisation of New Zealand

MANGONUI
AUCKLAND
NAPIER
NEW ZEALAND
WELLINGTON
CHRISTCHURCH
PACIFIC OCEAN
DUNEDIN
INVERCARGILL

Above. Maori weapons of war reflect their preference for hand-to-hand fighting. They used short hand-spears, top, and clubs, above.

Above. White settlements in New Zealand began in the North Island in 1830. They expanded southwards as coal and gold were found and more farming land was opened up.

Left. Maori chief Hone Heke Pokai. The Maori lived mainly in the North Island of New Zealand. They were tough, intelligent and industrious and they were trained warriors. They lived in villages and farmed the surrounding areas.

NEW ZEALAND'S WEALTH New Zealand was a poor, struggling country, despite the discovery of gold in the 1850s, until the invention of the refrigerated ship. This made all the difference to New Zealand farmers. There was more profit in mutton and lamb than in wool, and New Zealand became a major supplier of cheap meat to Britain. Soon, a large dairy industry was built up after it was found that New Zealand butter could be sold in Britain more cheaply than British butter, despite the cost of shipping it there.

THE AMERICAN BOOM

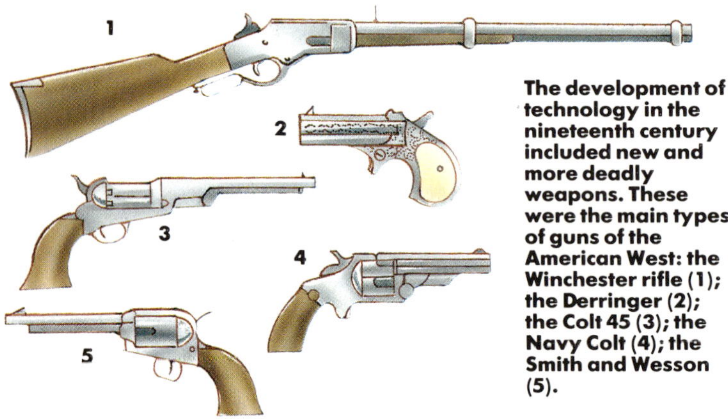

The development of technology in the nineteenth century included new and more deadly weapons. These were the main types of guns of the American West: the Winchester rifle (1); the Derringer (2); the Colt 45 (3); the Navy Colt (4); the Smith and Wesson (5).

The end of the American Civil War in 1865 (see pp. 422–3) was a landmark in the history of the United States. It marked a new start in the development of the farming land of the mid-West and in the build-up of American industry.

GUNS AND BARBED WIRE The great cattle-ranching states lay in a belt stretching from Montana and North Dakota in the north to Texas in the south. In the early days, cattle had been allowed to roam freely and were rounded up twice a year. In 1874 came the invention of barbed wire, which provided a cheap means for ranchers to fence in their cattle. The inventor's factory was soon making 1000 kilometres of the wire a day. But its use also meant the end of the pioneer days when a settler could claim a plot of land and farm it for himself. Now, the big farmers—the 'cattle kings'—saw off new settlers with guns.

GROWING INDUSTRY The amount of steel made in the United States in 1895 was 300 times greater than it had been in 1867. This gives an idea of the rapid growth of industry during those years. America had its own rich resources of coal and metal ores. It had its own vast market for manufactured goods. Many of the new inventions that were to shape modern life, such as the sewing machine, the typewriter, the telephone and the electric light bulb, were American.

United States' industry was the first to develop 'big

MONTANA TERRITORY
DAKOTA TERRITORY
WYOMING TERRITORY
NEBRASKA
COLORADO
KANSAS
MISSOURI
NEW MEXICO TERRITORY
INDIANA TERRITORY
TEXAS

Major Cattle Trails 1870–1890

Goodnight Loving Trail
Western Trail
(Used after 1885)
Chisolm Trail
Shawnee Trail

Above. Hundreds of thousands of cattle were driven the hazardous journey along trails to yards at the newly-opened railheads.

Above. From 1867, the United States built up its influence in the Pacific. The linking of the Pacific and Atlantic Oceans by the Panama Canal in 1914 opened up the eastern US ports to Pacific trade. Until 1979, the United States controlled the canal and surrounding land.

business' methods. Business people built up large groups of companies in order to control wages and selling prices in whole industries. A Scotsman called Andrew Carnegie who had come to America as a poor boy became a multi-millionaire who dominated the US steel industry. Philip Armour, who started his working life on his father's farm, became head of a company which controlled the meat-packing industry. Other millionaires made their money from railways, oil and the telegraph service. These industrial leaders were often called the 'robber barons' because of the methods they used to increase their profits.

LOOKING WESTWARD The opening of the Union Pacific Railroad across the United States in 1869 (see pp. 400–1) led Americans to think of the markets waiting for their goods across the Pacific Ocean in Asia. They had already forced China and Japan to open their ports to American ships (see pp. 430–1 and 432–3). The United States now set about establishing shipping routes across the Pacific, together with a chain of naval bases to protect them. The first of these bases, set up in 1867, was on Midway Island. Over the next 30 years, the map of the Pacific became dotted with US bases.

While European countries split up Africa into 'spheres of influence' (see pp. 436–7), the USA built up its own. It bought Alaska from Russia in 1867. War with Spain in 1898 brought it three former Spanish possessions: Puerto Rico in the Caribbean, and the Philippines and Guam in the Pacific. Hawaii became a United States possession in the same year. Almost unnoticed by the rest of the world, the USA had become a world power.

Left. Pittsburgh, the heart of the US steel industry and nicknamed 'Smoky City'. Its population grew from 21,000 in 1840 to over 321,000 in 1900.

Above. A Cheyenne painting on skin depicting Custer's Last Stand in 1876. Colonel George Armstrong Custer was campaigning against the Sioux Indians led by Sitting Bull. He discovered an Indian encampment near the Little Big Horn river and attacked it against orders. His 264-strong cavalry was outnumbered ten to one and Custer and every one of his men were killed.

GIVE ME YOUR POOR . . .

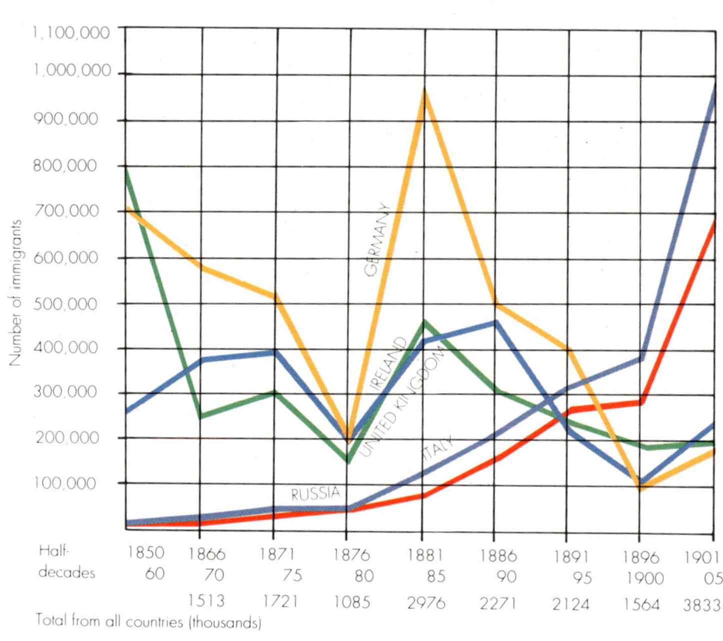

Above. Earlier migrants to the US had come mainly from northern and western Europe. Later, more arrived from southern and eastern Europe.

Above left. Immigrants to the USA leave Ellis Island after medical checks to begin their new lives.

Left. For many, the journey had begun in eastern Europe, from where they had been forced to flee for their lives

The growth of the United States of America would not have been possible without the millions of immigrants who poured into the country. In the 1870s there were nearly three million of them; in the 1880s more than five million entered the country. Immigration reached a peak in the first 10 years after 1900, when almost nine million people arrived.

THE 'NEW' IMMIGRANTS Before 1865, most immigrants to the USA had come from Britain, Ireland and Germany. Slowly, towards the end of the century, the numbers arriving from these countries fell and were replaced by increasing numbers from Italy and Russia. The Italians were fleeing from the poverty of the south of Italy after unification (see p. 428). The Russians were also escaping from poverty. Many Jews from Russia and eastern Europe had a more urgent reason for leaving for America—they were being persecuted and even

The New Americans

Changes in Europe were reflected in the pattern of migration to the USA after the end of the American Civil War. German, British and Irish migrants were in the majority until the 1890s. But as German and British industry grew and developed, more jobs became available to the work force in those countries, and fewer people needed to emigrate to find jobs in order to feed their families. Russians and Italians then began to migrate in huge numbers. Many of the Russian emigrants were Jews, driven into exile by persecution in their own country. Italians were reacting against the dashing of their hopes of a more prosperous future at home after the unification of Italy.

Immigrants had to take whatever work they could get, for the lowest pay. Many worked in the clothing trade, in cramped conditions known as 'sweat shops'.

US Population Density 1890

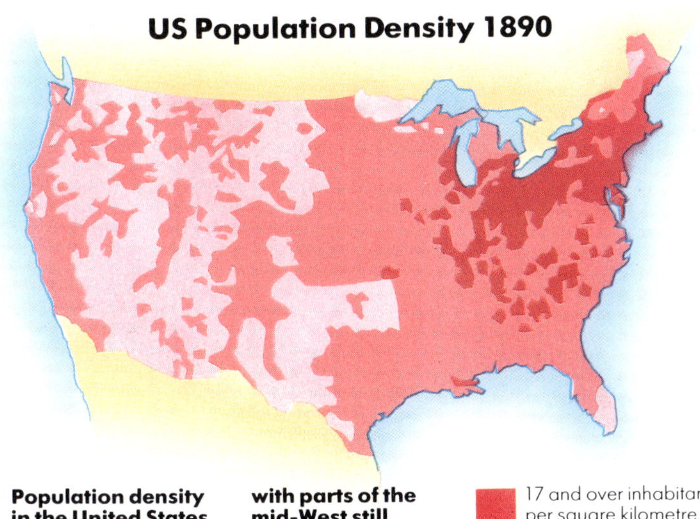

Population density in the United States in 1890. The majority of the population was concentrated in the cities of the east, with parts of the mid-West still almost empty of people.

The Statue of Liberty

After 1886, the first sight that immigrants sailing into New York Harbor had of the United States of America was the Statue of Liberty. Rising more than 90 metres above the water, the statue carries a torch representing liberty in her right hand and a book of laws in her left. On the base a poem specially written for the Statue of Liberty begins:

Give me your tired, your poor, Your huddled masses yearning to breathe free . . .

It was created by the French sculptor F. Bartholdi and was a gift from the French to the American people, commemorating the alliance of France and the USA during the American War of Independence and marking its centenary.

murdered at home. Poles, Czechs, Hungarians, Romanians, Bulgarians, Greeks and Scandinavians all swelled the numbers of immigrants. The millions arriving across the Atlantic Ocean were joined by Chinese who came across the Pacific to California until 1882, when further Chinese immigration was banned.

THE 'NEW' COUNTRY Not everyone was allowed to stay. Immigrants from Europe were first taken to Ellis Island in New York Harbor and given medical checks. If they were unfit, they were sent back home. If they passed the tests, they were allowed in and could go where they wanted.

The United States needed the immigrants, but it wanted them to be proud of their new country. The mixture of races and cultures presented a problem. To become full US citizens the immigrants had to learn English. They were expected to honour the United States flag, the Stars and Stripes, and every school day began with a salute to the flag.

Few of the new immigrants had any money, so they headed for the industrial cities. There, they found work in Chicago's meat factories, the steel mills of Pittsburgh and the textile mills of Philadelphia. Many Italians, Irish and Jews stayed in New York, where they worked long hours for poor pay in industries like clothing manufacture.

Ethnic groups tended to stay together, enjoying the language, culture, religion and cooking they were used to. To save money, they packed their houses with people, causing the problem of overcrowding. The immigrant areas of many American cities quickly became slums. Life for poor immigrants was tough—but not as tough as it would have been if they had stayed at home.

LAND OF OPPORTUNITY America was more a land of hard work than of opportunity for the new immigrants, but their children found the opportunities. They had been born American citizens, and they had no memories of 'the old country' to regret. They had been educated in American schools and had come to accept the American way of life. These second-generation immigrants became absorbed into American culture and proved that, as one writer has said, America was *'the great melting pot where all races of Europe are melting and re-forming'*.

THE OTHER AMERICA

The pampas, or grasslands, of South America were ideal grazing grounds for cattle, and Argentina, in particular, became a leading supplier of meat to Europe.

The United States of America became a world power by using the strength of a large country whose people, after the American Civil War (see pp. 422–3), mostly forgot their arguments and worked together. It might seem strange that the 10 countries of South America did not do the same, once they had become independent in the 1820s. But there were a number of reasons why.

GENERALS AND STRONG MEN One reason was that each country was ruled by a government, usually headed by a general, which enjoyed power and did not want to give it up to a United States of South America. Another was that Spain and Portugal, which had controlled South America for three centuries before independence, had not invested any money there. They had simply taken what they wanted and put nothing back.

A third reason was South America's geography. The Andes Mountains runs down its western side, leaving a thin Pacific coastal strip which was almost entirely cut off from the rest of the continent. On the east, in Brazil, the great tropical rain forest of the Amazon stretches for thousands of kilometres. North of this is a high plateau where South American Indians—whose ancestors had been conquered by the Europeans in the sixteenth century—made a poor living from peasant farming.

The tropical forests, too, were rich in resources. Here, a rubber tree is tapped in a Brazilian forest.

In the interior, away from the cities, there was little real government. A local strong man, called a *caudillo*, would collect a gang round him and take over an area, controlling the small farmers through fear. Some *caudillos* built up armies large enough to start wars and rebellions, and for most of the nineteenth century fighting was going on in one part of South America or another.

Two Strong Men

Francisco Lopez (1827–1870) succeeded his father as president of Paraguay in 1862. At 18 he had been made commander-in-chief of the Paraguayan army and he had come to believe that any problem could be solved by military force. As soon as Lopez became president he built up a huge Paraguayan army — the largest in South America — and set out to pursue his dream of conquering the continent. He declared war on Argentina, Brazil and Uruguay, but his plans ended in disaster. The Paraguayans suffered defeat after defeat, and Lopez himself was killed in battle in 1870. He left his country impoverished and half its population dead.

Dom Pedro II of Brazil (1825–1891), by contrast, was a ruler who devoted his attention to modernizing his country. He became emperor of Brazil in 1831, when he was five, but he was 14 before he obtained real power.

Above. Dom Pedro II.
Left. Francisco Lopez.

Dom Pedro was determined to develop Brazil's trade and industry and so improve the lives of his people. He introduced a European-style banking system and encouraged the development of the coffee and rubber industries. He took an interest in new inventions, such as photography and the telephone, and supported the building of Brazil's first railway and the first submarine telegraph link between South America and Europe. But Brazil's rich farmers still relied on slave labour and when slavery was abolished in 1888 they forced Dom Pedro to abdicate as emperor.

1 One of the results of the new interest in science was the start of the chemical industry. The first synthetic dye was made in 1856 by William Perkin when he was only 18 years old. By the 1870s Germany was in the lead in this field. Other new products included linoleum (1860), the first cheap mass-produced floor-covering.

2 Joseph Lister, a British surgeon introduced antiseptics to the medical world. They reduced the risk of infection and many people survived operations which before would have killed them. They were in widespread use by the 1880s.

3 Experiments with flight were in progress at this time. Otto Lilienthal was building and flying gliders in Germany in the 1890s.

South American States 1888

Above. South America in 1888, showing the major political divisions across the continent.

Right. South American culture extended back thousands of years before the Europeans.

THE LAST SLAVES IN AMERICA Some landowners built up large estates where they grew sugar or coffee. In Brazil, many of these estates were worked by slave labour until 1888, when slavery was at last banned. Brazilian landowners faced ruin, but they were saved by the new demand for rubber, which grew easily in the tropical climate and did not need a large force of workers.

Elsewhere in South America, other new demands created new wealth. Improved methods of canning led to the development of the corned beef industry, using cattle reared on the *pampas*, or grasslands, which were similar to the North American prairies. Tropical hardwood trees were in demand for furniture and a timber industry grew up on the edges of the rain forests. Phosphates and nitrates were mined and exported as fertilizers.

DIVIDED CONTINENT There was no Industrial Revolution in South America. This was partly because of the lack of coal and iron ore, but mainly because no-one wanted to invest money to start industries. Although the 10 South American nations were independent, they still behaved like colonies. They survived by exporting raw materials to North America and Europe in exchange for manufactured goods. The USA was also happy that South America remained divided and did not become a rival power.

THE INDUSTRIAL RACE

On 1 May 1851, more than 30,000 people gathered in a huge new iron and glass building in Hyde Park, London. They had come to see Queen Victoria open the Great Exhibition.

'BRITISH IS BEST' The Great Exhibition included products from all over the world, but pride of place was given to the products of British industry and the British Empire. The exhibition attracted over six million visitors from all over Britain and across the world. The organizers wanted all of them to take home the message that 'British is best'.

In 1851, this was true. Britain's Industrial Revolution had been the first in the world and Britain was still the most important manufacturing country. Its empire was the world's largest and was still growing. Most British people expected things to go on getting better and better.

THE USA CATCHES UP Although Britain did not realize it at first, the industrial world was changing. One of the first signs was another exhibition which was held in Philadelphia, Pennsylvania, in 1876 to celebrate 100 years of American independence. This showed how quickly the United States of America had developed since the end of the Civil War in 1865 (see pp. 422–3). All the products of America's new industries were on display, together with new American inventions.

One of these new inventions was the telephone, which had been invented that year by Alexander Graham Bell, a Scotsman who had emigrated to the United States to make his fortune. This, combined with later American inventions such as the *phonograph*, photographic film and machines for setting printers' type automatically, made the USA the world leader in communications. Americans were the first to make manufactured goods from *mass-produced* parts which were fitted together on a *production line*. By the 1870s many products were made in this way, which took less time and so cost less. America later dominated world industry with such mass-produced products as sewing machines, typewriters, cameras and, in the twentieth century, cars.

In the nineteenth century, steel was an essential part of the machines that manufactured goods and of many goods themselves. By 1890 the USA had overtaken Britain as the world's largest producer of steel. Ten years later it was producing more steel than the other leading countries, Britain and Germany, put together.

The Eiffel Tower, built as the centrepiece of the Paris Exhibition in 1889.

GERMANY JOINS THE RACE Germany, the third runner in the industrial race, had won second place in steel production by 1890. German scientists and engineers had also been busy. Their achievements included important improvements in chemical dyes and the invention of two kinds of *internal combustion engine*—petrol-driven and diesel. The British were still inventive too, but they were more concerned with improving existing machines and methods than with developing new ones. For a while, their huge empire protected their industry from trading rivals, but after about 1880 it was no longer true that Britain was 'the workshop of the world'.

Right. Alexander Graham Bell's first telephone receiver, produced in 1875 under stiff competition from other inventors.

Left. Isaac Singer's 1851 sewing machine. This was to transform the clothing industry which could make garments cheaper and quicker.

Thomas Alva Edison with the first sound recording machine, the phonograph – one of his many inventions. Largely self-taught, Edison set up his first laboratory at the age of 10. He took out more than 1,000 patents during his career.

Right. The Gatling Gun, 1863, which was first used with devastating effect in the American Civil War.

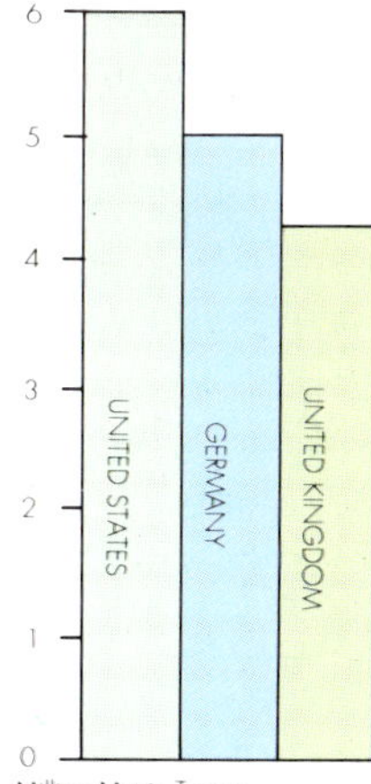

Left. George Eastman's plastic roll film, 1884, marked the beginning of photography as a popular pastime.

Some American Inventions

1851 Singer sewing machine. Isaac Singer's was not the first sewing machine, but it was a great improvement on earlier models and was the first to be mass-produced for the home.

1869 Celluloid. This was the first plastic material, useful but dangerous as it was highly inflammable.

1876 Telephone. Invented by Alexander Graham Bell, a Scotsman who had settled in the USA.

1882 Electric light bulb. Invented by Thomas Alva Edison as a cheaper and better alternative to gas lighting.

1884 Camera film. Invented by George Eastman. Previously, photographers had used cumbersome glass plates.

1886 Linotype. This automatic typesetting machine, which set a line of type at a time, was invented by Ottmar Mergenthaler, a German who had emigrated to the USA.

1886 Phonograph (early record player). Another of Thomas Alva Edison's inventions, this was the first sound system, recording sound on a tinfoil cylinder.

1889 Movie camera. Eastman's invention of camera film led Edison to develop a camera to take moving pictures, which could be watched through a hand-held viewer.

Steel Production 1895

6
5
4
3
2
1
0
UNITED STATES
GERMANY
UNITED KINGDOM
Million Metric Tonnes

Left. A significant year for British industry was 1895, when Germany's steel production overtook Britain's for the first time. Before that, Britain had maintained her lead in the production race, which had been gained by being the first nation to embark on the Industrial Revolution and introduce new machinery and practices.

Exhibition 1851

Full title: The Great Exhibition of the Works and Industry of All Nations
Planning began: 1849
Building began: 30 July 1850
Exhibition open: 1 May–15 October 1851
Exhibitors: 13,937
Visitors: 6,039,205

The Great Exhibition was held in the Crystal Palace on the south side of Hyde Park in London. After the Exhibition, the Crystal Palace was rebuilt at Sydenham in south London. It was destroyed by fire in November 1936.

THE STEAMSHIP AGE

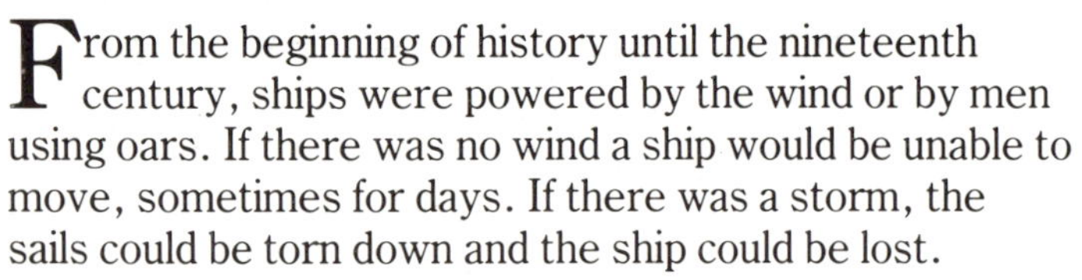

From the beginning of history until the nineteenth century, ships were powered by the wind or by men using oars. If there was no wind a ship would be unable to move, sometimes for days. If there was a storm, the sails could be torn down and the ship could be lost.

THE FIRST STEAMSHIPS Soon after the steam engine was invented in the late eighteenth century, there were several attempts to build steam-powered ships. At first, these were paddle-steamers which were used on canals and rivers and for short voyages between coastal ports. The first steamship to cross the Atlantic Ocean was the *Savannah* in 1819. It had both engines and sails and it travelled most of the way using wind power.

The engines in the early steamships were inefficient and used huge amounts of fuel. But this improved when ship-builders began to use propellers instead of paddles, and to fit more efficient engines, until by the 1860s the steamships could compete with sailing ships. They could also be larger than sailing ships, as their hulls, or basic frames, were made of iron or steel instead of wood.

Mark Twain, author of *Tom Sawyer* and *Huckleberry Finn*, spent about 15 years as a pilot of paddle steamers on the Mississippi river. His real name was Samuel Langhorne Clemens. His pseudonym is a boatman's phrase meaning a depth of water of two fathoms.

Right. The *Savannah* was the first steamship to cross the Atlantic in 1819. The journey took 28 days, 11 hours but was under steam for less than five days.

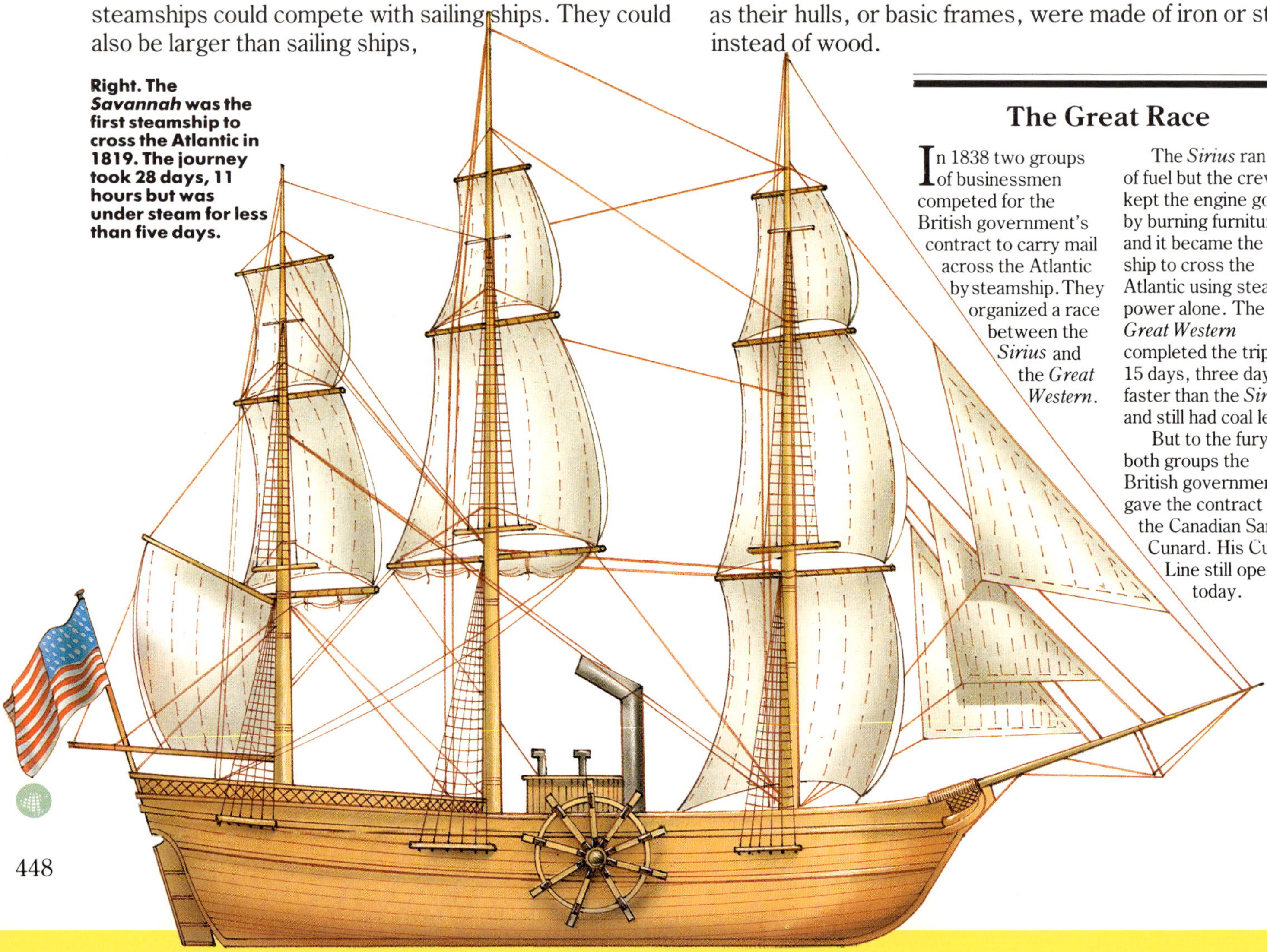

The Great Race

In 1838 two groups of businessmen competed for the British government's contract to carry mail across the Atlantic by steamship. They organized a race between the *Sirius* and the *Great Western*.

The *Sirius* ran out of fuel but the crew kept the engine going by burning furniture and it became the first ship to cross the Atlantic using steam power alone. The *Great Western* completed the trip in 15 days, three days faster than the *Sirius*, and still had coal left.

But to the fury of both groups the British government gave the contract to the Canadian Samuel Cunard. His Cunard Line still operates today.

THE GREAT DAYS OF STEAM Exporting grain and meat from North America, or wool from Australia and New Zealand, together with emigrants travelling from Europe, all created fresh demands for shipping. Ship-owners became prosperous.

In 1882 the *Dunedin*—the first refrigerated ship, carrying a cargo of meat and butter from New Zealand—arrived in London. Increasing supplies of food from abroad lowered prices in Europe, and British farming in particular suffered badly. At the same time, the European market for food encouraged farmers in North and South America, Australia and New Zealand to grow more.

Meanwhile, passenger travel by sea also increased. For the well-off, it became common to travel between America and Europe on business or holiday.

British dock workers were among the first to organize themselves to negotiate better pay and conditions. Here, London dockers vote for a strike in 1889.

SHIPS OF WAR Navies were at first less keen than merchant ship-owners to use steamships. As the early steamships burnt so much fuel, it would have been difficult in wartime to keep them at sea without having to return to port frequently for refuelling. Admirals also thought that iron hulls would be more easily damaged than wooden ones. But these were partly excuses for the fact that senior naval officers had been trained to use sailing ships and did not want to change their methods.

The French navy was the first to adopt steam power for its warships and gradually the advantages of steam and iron hulls came to be accepted by other countries. After about 1860 there was a great increase in building warships. These new ships had iron hulls and thick armour plate made of iron, and they were fitted with sails as well as steam engines. Revolving gun turrets were fitted to some battleships in the American Civil War (see pp. 422–3) and these were so successful that other navies copied them. Later, steel armour plate up to 30 centimetres thick replaced the iron plate. Soon all the major world powers were rebuilding their navies.

Above. The Federal steamer *Monitor* (right) rams the Confederate *Merrimac* in one of the first engagements between steam-powered warships.

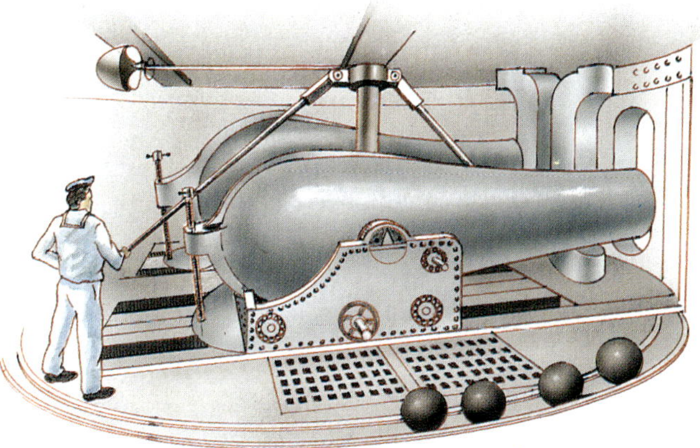

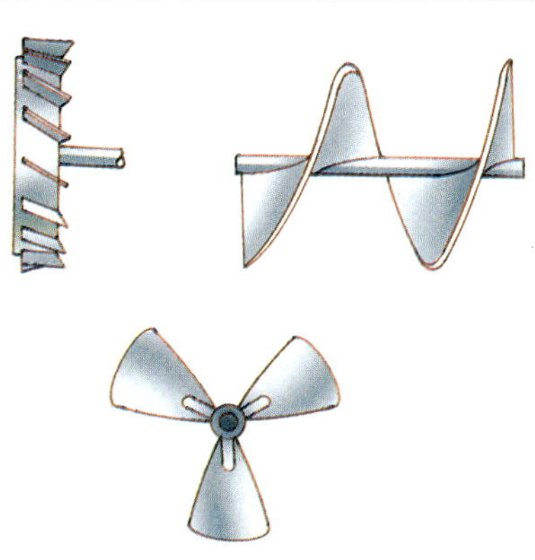

Right. A cannon and far right, types of early propeller.

ADVANCES IN SCIENCE

Above. The ability to generate electricity on a large scale was developed in the 1880s. This tram was operating in Paris by 1898.

Europeans and Americans in the nineteenth century were fascinated by science. They wanted to know more about the world than religious teaching told them. As the century went on, discovery after discovery seemed to provide new answers and opportunities. It seemed as if there was nothing that science could not do.

THE PATTERN OF DISCOVERY Nineteenth-century science followed a regular pattern. First, a scientist would work out a theory or idea about an aspect of science. Then others would try out the theory in experiments to see if it was correct.

In 1831 Michael Faraday (1791–1867) conducted experiments in Britain which demonstrated the laws of electricity. His ideas were taken further by a Cambridge physicist, James Clerk Maxwell, who in 1873 proved the connection between electricity and magnetism. By 1880, the German firm of Siemens had demonstrated the first electric train, making use of Maxwell's theories, and in 1881 the world's first two electric power stations opened in New York and London.

Michael Faraday provided the starting point for another important development. He found that the chemical *ether* numbed pain. At that time there was no way of putting someone to sleep before an operation; patients were fully conscious and had to be held down by strong men. In 1846 an American surgeon first used ether during an operation, but the next year a Scot called James Simpson (1811–1870) tried *chloroform*, which was easier to use. *Anaesthetics* allowed surgeons to carry out operations which had been impossible before.

SCIENCE IN THE UNIVERSITIES Science made great advances during the century in almost every area of human activity. There was a boom in scientific studies. Harvard University in the United States of America, and London, Cambridge, Glasgow, Paris and Berlin Universities in Europe, became centres of scientific research. There was a growth in scientific societies, too. Some, like the Royal Society in Britain, funded expeditions and experiments. Others were more concerned to spread the new scientific knowledge more widely.

POPULAR SCIENCE Everyone could join in this new excitement. Science was not only for the scientists. In many cities, there were lectures and demonstrations which ordinary people could attend. For those who could not reach them, there were popular science magazines like *Chambers' Journal*, founded in Scotland in 1854, and *The Scientific American*.

Left. The first university to be founded in America was Harvard, at Cambridge, Massachusetts, which dates back to 1693. By 1840 it had become one of the great centres of learning in the US and was at the forefront of the scientific revolution.

People of Science

James Clerk Maxwell (1831–1879) was a Scottish physicist whose most important work was done at Cambridge University. His discovery of the link between electricity and magnetism was probably the most far-reaching of the nineteenth century. It led to the use of electric motors, and all the electrical appliances we use today.

Louis Pasteur (1822–1895), a French chemist, devoted his life to investigating the causes and prevention of disease. One of his discoveries was that bacteria in food could be killed by heating the food to 55°C. This process is still called 'pasteurization'.

Pasteur developed *vaccines* for use in the prevention of many diseases, including anthrax and rabies.

Above. Louis Pasteur. Left. James Clark Maxwell.

Below. An Italian scientist lectures on astronomy in London. Events like this were hugely popular and many people came to hear about the discoveries being made.

Above. A fanciful picture of students of the Scottish surgeon James Simpson, who first used chloroform as an anaesthetic. The rapid advance of science made many sceptical of its claims.

Newspapers gave an increasing amount of space to science, and more serious students could buy science encyclopaedias in weekly parts and collect them to make a reference library.

GOING IT ALONE Not all the advances in science were made by trained scientists. Many people worked on their own on their ideas or inventions. One of these was the inventor of the telephone, Alexander Graham Bell (see p. 455), who experimented in his spare time after his day's work as a professor of speech training. Another was Thomas Edison, who went to school for only a few months and taught himself all the science he knew. Some of his inventions are listed on page 447. Scientific knowledge was growing so fast that there were opportunities for everyone to take part.

1 Science led to advances in the treatment of illness – and also in its prevention. Ideas about the causes of disease which were little more than superstition gave way to soundly-based scientific theories. In Britain, for example, Dr John Snow showed that an outbreak of cholera in London in 1854, which caused thousands of deaths, could be traced to the use of one infected street water pump. This led to a Public Health Act forcing all towns to provide clean water.

2 The invention of the telegraph – and later the telephone – had a dramatic impact on newspapers. In 1805 it took two weeks for news of the battle of Trafalgar to appear in *The Times*, in London. By 1851, the paper was able to print European news within hours. By 1866, news from North America could also be sent instantly by cable.

THE DAWN OF THE OIL AGE

The American artist George Luks saw the oil companies as monsters aiming to devour the earth. He called this picture, dated 1899, 'The Menace of the Hour'.

The first oil well in the world was drilled at Oil Creek, Pennsylvania, in the United States of America in 1859. It was only 21 metres deep and produced just 25 barrels of oil a day.

UNWANTED RICHES Oil is a mixture of substances. At that time, people only used some of these. Most of the oil, including the petrol, was burned off or thrown away. What was left was *paraffin*, which was used mainly for oil lamps but also for cooking and heating. People had previously used vegetable or animal oil, particularly whale oil, for these purposes. Coal was the fuel in demand for industry and for use at home.

The oil industry grew very slowly in its early years, but there was a sudden change in the 1880s and 1890s, when petrol and diesel engines were invented. By 1901 there were about 15,000 cars in use in the USA and almost as many in Europe. At about the same time the world's merchant and naval ships began to burn oil instead of coal in their engines. Between 1870 and 1900 the world's oil production multiplied 25 times.

Discoveries of oil brought prosperity to places which had never known it before, for example in parts of the Rocky Mountains in America. In 1901 oil was found in southern Texas and Louisiana, which until then had been among the poorest parts of the United States. Then other countries began to join in the oil boom: Mexico, Peru and, in the twentieth century, other South American countries and the Middle East.

THE OIL COMPANIES Prospecting for oil, and then sinking wells to bring it to the surface, is a long and costly business. In 1884, for example, foreign companies were allowed to prospect for oil in Mexico, but it was 16 years before any was found. Even after oil has been discovered, most of the cost of labour and materials must be spent before a single drop of oil is produced. Only large companies can afford these costs. The result was that from the start the oil industry was dominated by large companies such as Standard Oil in the USA, founded in 1870, and the Royal Dutch Company in Europe, formed in 1890. They were able to control production and prices, making huge profits. For a time in the 1880s Standard Oil controlled almost all the oil produced in the United States, about four-fifths of the world's production.

SHAPING NATIONS The full effect of oil on the world did not appear until the twentieth century, but the first signs of change began to be seen at the end of the 1800s. The USA produced by far the most of the world's oil and

A production field in the early days of the oil industry. In those days, the oil was stored in barrels, and it is still measured in barrels although they are no longer used.

The First Oil Billionaire

Right. A cartoonist's view of the 'oil king' John D. Rockefeller (above).

John Davison Rockefeller (1839–1937) left school at 14 to work as a clerk. Nine years later he became a partner in a small refinery. He found that the industry was badly organized. In 1870 he founded the Standard Oil Company, which soon took over almost all its rivals.

When Rockefeller retired in 1911 he was the richest man in the US. He gave over US $500,000,000 to educational projects, health care and medical research.

The power of oil: this graph shows the growth of US oil production from 1860 to 1900. As new uses were found for oil and people realized the potential profits which could be made, the development of oil production proceeded at an astonishing rate, setting the stage for the power oil would wield in the twentieth century.

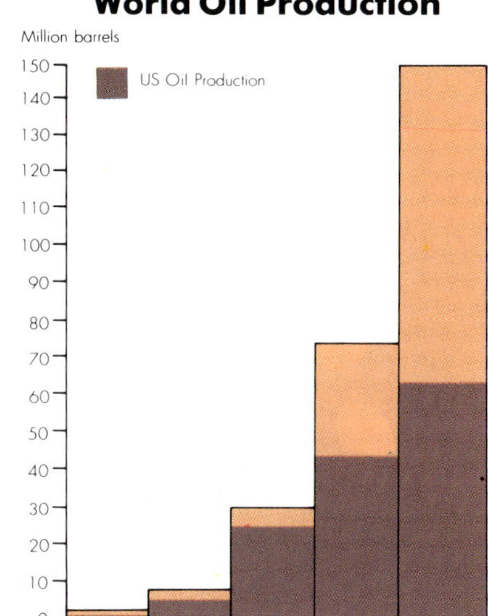

Left. Oil lamps were decorative as well as practical. Until the petrol engine was invented, lighting was the main use of oil.

this gave the country more industrial power. Western Europe did not produce any oil; it all had to be imported, which made it more expensive than it was in America. Many other parts of the world also depended on American oil supplies. Meanwhile, as people changed to oil, lower demand for coal led to the closure of many small mines.

THE COMMUNICATIONS REVOLUTION

The last half of the nineteenth century saw the start of the next revolution in world history—the communications revolution.

In 1800 the only way for most people to communicate over a distance was by letter, which was carried by horse and took several days to arrive. Ships signalled to each other with flags. Armies used *semaphore*, a message system involving either flags or signal arms in different positions.

MESSAGES BY WIRE These primitive methods of communication had been sufficient for a long time, but with the growth of industry and trade something better was needed now. In 1836 an American called Samuel Morse (1791–1872) came up with the first answer—the telegraph. At about the same time, two British scientists called Charles Wheatstone and William Cooke had a similar idea.

Morse's telegraph used electricity and magnetism to send messages in a code of dots and dashes along a wire. The first line to carry telegraph messages was opened between Baltimore and Washington DC in 1845.

A New York street festooned with wires in the early days of the telephone. Later, cables were laid underground in cities.

Telegraphy made communication almost instantaneous, and it was very successful. Telegraph lines quickly spread between the main cities of North America and Europe, and by 1900 across other continents too. Britain and the rest of Europe were linked by underwater telegraph cable in 1851 and by 1865 there was a cable beneath the Atlantic Ocean.

THE TELEPHONE From the telegraph, it was only a step to sending voice messages, rather than coded ones, along a wire. There were many rivals to be the first to do this, but Alexander Graham Bell won the race in 1876. His first telephone was crude and difficult to hear, but improvements soon followed.

By 1878 the town of New Haven, Connecticut, had the world's first telephone exchange (with 21 customers) and by 1879 there were

Before dialling was introduced, every telephone call had to be connected by hand by the operators. Consumers often had to wait for a line to be free, and calls took longer to connect.

Left. The early days of radio. Reactions to Marconi's radio transmissions were cool until he used radio to report on the America's Cup yacht race in 1899. Below. Alexander Graham Bell, inventor of the telephone, opens up a new line from New York to Chicago, 1892.

The Great Telephone Race

Three men were involved in the race to invent the telephone, which promised a great deal of money to the successful inventor. Alexander Graham Bell (1847–1922) was a teacher of the deaf who was interested in the telephone as an aid for the deaf. Elisha Gray (1835–1901), a telegraph engineer, wanted to use telegraph wires to carry voice messages. Thomas Alva Edison (1847–1931) was working on the same idea in secret, financed by the Western Union Telegraph Company.

The three men's applications for a *patent* — the right to profit from an invention — arrived at almost the same time in February 1876. The patent was awarded to Bell, though the decision was disputed. He heard the news on his 29th birthday.

After a slow start, the telephone rapidly became accepted after improved and long-distance lines were developed.

TELEPHONES IN THE USA 1880–1900

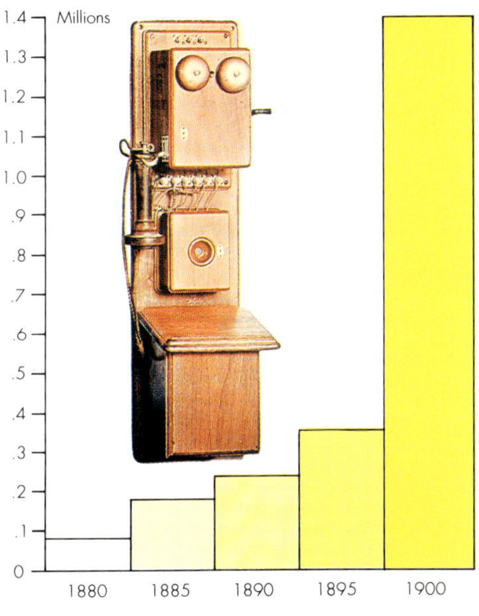

1 Postal communication also made great strides in the 19th century, helped by railways and steam shipping. Britain introduced cheap postage in 1840 and the example was rapidly copied. In 1863 an international agreement was made to co-ordinate the post between different countries.

2 The cinema was developing during the last part of the 19th century. The first clear pictures were shown in the USA by Woodville Latham and in England by Robert Paul, both in 1855. Thomas Edison built the first studio in 1893.

Above. The British 'Penny Black', 1840, was the world's first postage stamp.

Above. The ten cent stamp was one of the first in the USA.

telephone networks in Britain, France and Norway. The telephone had soon become an essential part of doing business, but people were slower to accept it in their homes, partly for fear that their conversations would be overheard! The invention of automatic dialling in 1889 by an American called Almon B. Strowger helped to overcome this worry.

NO WIRES The third important communications invention came at the end of the nineteenth century. Guglielmo Marconi (1874–1937) was an Italian scientist who was interested in wireless telegraphy—sending telegraphic messages through the air by radio waves. He moved to London because the Italian government would not back him. In 1896 he began experiments in Britain and a year later he succeeded in sending a radio message over a distance of 15 kilometres. In 1898 he set up a system so that *lightships* could communicate with the shorc by radio.

The rest of the story of radio belongs to the twentieth century, but its development arose out of the way that nineteenth-century inventors were interested in the possibilities opened up by a greater understanding of electricity and magnetism. Marconi was a pioneer of the technology that has given most of the world its main source of information and entertainment today.

MAKING SALES

Liptons made their reputation by promising good quality food at low prices. This was good news for people who had had to put up with inferior provisions.

The Industrial Revolution spread during the nineteenth century to factory production of almost everything anyone might need, from food to clothes and from toothbrushes to shoelaces. Manufacturers invested heavily in factory buildings and equipment. The way to get back the money they had spent was to make sure that customers bought *their* products and not those of a rival. At the same time, improved transport made it possible to distribute factory-made goods nationally and internationally.

BRAND NAMES Increasingly, manufacturers began to use brand names to identify their products, often with an easy-to-remember symbol or *trade mark*. One of the first people to see the value of giving products brand names and advertising them widely was William Lever (1851–1925), who started a soap business in Lancashire, England, in 1884. Newspapers and magazines were not printed in colour then, so Lever advertised mainly on brightly coloured posters. The idea spread, and soon advertisements were urging people to buy

The new department stores offered shoppers everything they needed under one roof.

particular brands of canned meat, ink, pen-nibs and other everyday products. The advertising industry had been born.

CHAIN AND DEPARTMENT STORES An important change also happened in the shops. Shop-keepers realized that they could negotiate a better price from manufacturers—and so earn a greater profit for themselves—if they agreed to buy goods in large quantities. They then set up, or took over, several shops (a chain) to sell the goods.

One of the British pioneers of this style of shop-keeping was Thomas Lipton (1850–1931). By the 1880s he had a chain of grocery shops all over Britain and attracted customers to them by the clever use of advertising. Then he saw that he could make more money by owning his own tea and coffee plantations and running his own bacon and fruit-canning factories. His ideas were copied by many other grocers trying to attract customers. As wages began to rise towards the end of the century, people could afford to look for better quality goods as well as more varied and tastier food.

An early advertisement for Coca-Cola, originally promoted as a health drink.

ALL UNDER ONE ROOF
Another new type of shop was the department store. This was a large shop which supplied all kinds of goods, divided into separate departments, so that customers could do all their shopping under one roof. The first department store in Britain was Whiteley's in west London, which William Whiteley built up in the 1870s from a small drapery shop. Department stores aimed to make shopping entertaining by providing demonstrations of products, fashion shows and restaurants where musicians played while the customers had their meals. The idea was to make customers loyal to a particular store.

These developments were both good and bad for the customers. They led to better quality goods, because shop-keepers were afraid that disappointed customers might go to a rival. But they also made it harder for the customer to feel that he or she was getting the personal service that could be found in a smaller shop run by one individual. Many shops today are still trying to get this balance right.

The revolution in shopping.
Right. This New York drug store has its merchandise set out invitingly on display. Shops began to look more as we know them today.
Below. Macy's department store in New York. Again, goods are arranged to catch the shopper's eye.

Shopping by Post

Mail order was an important development in retailing towards the end of the nineteenth century. It reached its peak in the USA, where families in the newly settled west were out of reach of the city stores.

One of the most famous American mail order stores is Sears Roebuck, founded in Chicago in 1886 to sell watches by post. It soon extended its merchandise and by 1893 was publishing a 300-page catalogue. This allowed families in remote areas to buy the latest goods and inventions.

Towards Today
TIME CHART

AD	EUROPE	NORTH AND SOUTH AMERICA	REST OF WORLD
1834			The Great Trek from Cape Colony begins
1839>1842			Britain launches First Opium War against China
1850>1864			Taiping Rebellion in China
1851	The Great Exhibition is held in London		Gold found in New South Wales and Victoria in Australia
1852	Cavour becomes prime minister of Piedmont		
1853			US warships sail into Tokyo Bay
1856			South African Boers establish the independent republics of Orange Free State and Transvaal
1856>1860			Britain and France attack China: the Second Opium War
1859	War between Piedmont and Austria		
1860	Rebellion in southern Italy		
1861>1871			The Maori Wars against the British
1865>1868			Civil war in Japan
1866	Prussia defeats Austria in the Seven Weeks' War		
1867		USA establishes a naval base at Midway Island in the Pacific USA buys Alaska from Russia	Diamonds discovered on the border of Orange Free State
1869		North America's first transcontinental railway opens	The Suez Canal opens
1870	Unification of Italy complete except for Vatican City Outbreak of the Franco-Prussian War	Standard Oil Company founded in the USA	
1871	France surrenders to Prussia. Wilhelm I proclaimed Kaiser of the German Empire		Delegation leaves Japan for America and Europe to study Western technology
1873	James Clerk Maxwell publishes his paper on electricity and magnetism		
1874		Barbed wire invented in the USA	
1876		The Centennial Exhibition is held in Philadelphia	
1879			Britain fights the Zulu War
1880	In Germany, Siemens demonstrates the first electric train		
1882	First refrigerated cargo ship arrives in Britain from New Zealand		
1884			Gold discovered in the Transvaal
1884>1885			War between China and France, ending in Chinese defeat
1885	European powers agree on 'spheres of influence' in Africa		
1886		The Statue of Liberty completed in New York Harbor	
1888		Slavery abolished in Brazil	
1894>1895			War between China and Japan, ending in Chinese defeat
1896	Marconi begins experiments with radio		
1898			The Spanish-American War
1899			Britain declares war on the Boers
1899>1900			The Boxer Rising in China

Colonies in 1900

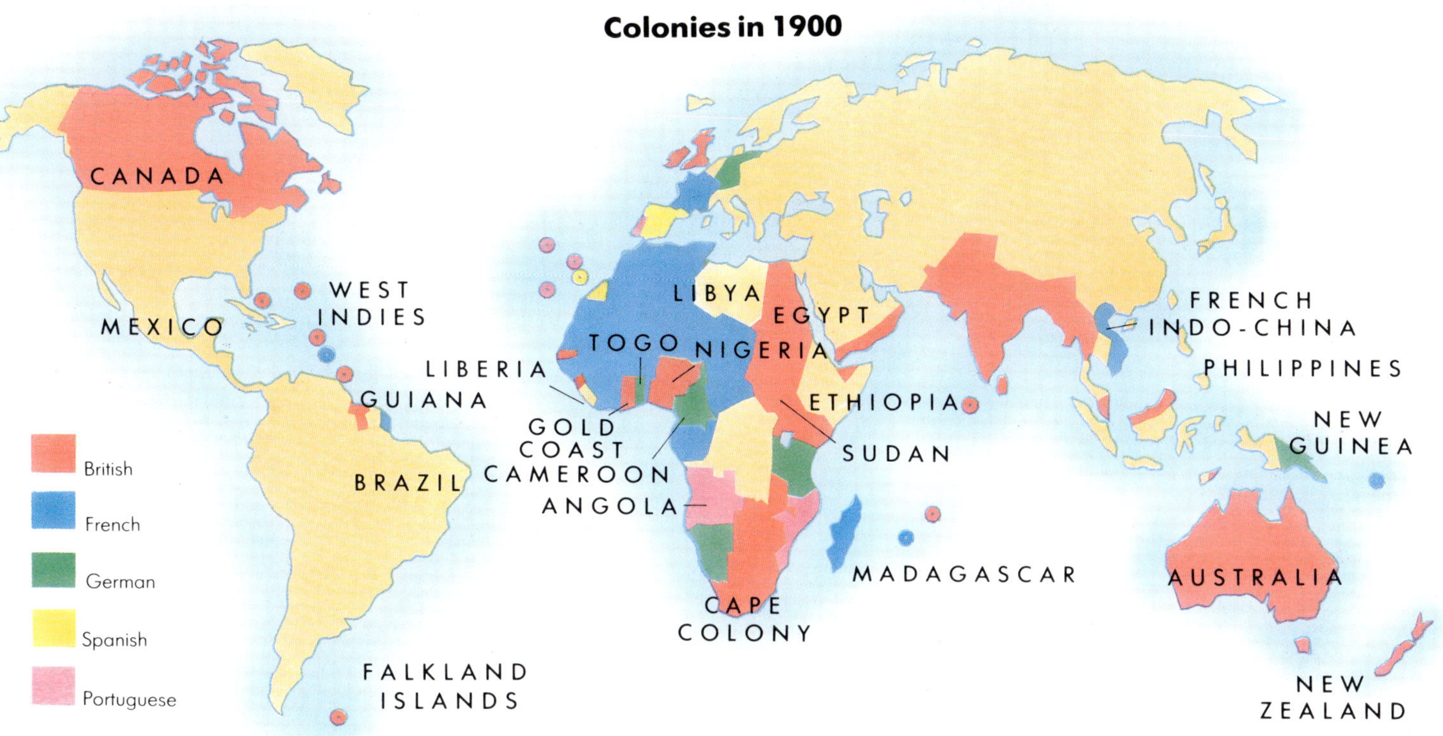

The End of the Old Order

At the beginning of the twentieth century, many areas of the world were ruled by the old colonial powers of Europe, such as Britain, France, Belgium and the Netherlands, which had built up empires during the previous century. However, Germany and Italy, each of which had only become a united country in the second half of the nineteenth century, had very few colonies and little world influence.

RIVALRY BETWEEN BRITAIN AND GERMANY The wealthiest and most successful colonial nation was Britain. It had a tiny army but a large navy, and was powerful enough to govern an empire which included Canada and Australia, the Indian sub-continent and several African states. After 1900, Germany's growing industrial strength led to rivalry with Britain. This found expression in the race to build bigger and better fleets of battleships.

RUSSIA In eastern Europe, the tsars of Russia governed a huge but backward empire which had scarcely been touched by modern agricultural techniques or industrialization. The extreme poverty of many of the Russian people helped the *Marxist* revolution of 1917 to succeed.

TWO WORLD WARS Within western Europe, Germany's alliance with the old Austro-Hungarian Empire posed a threat to neighbouring countries such as France and Belgium in the west and Russia in the east. It was clearly only a matter of time before Europe's old order was destroyed. The war that broke out in 1914 quickly spread to the Middle East and involved Turkey's Ottoman Empire as well.

People called the First World War the 'war to end all wars', but within 20 years war had broken out again. The years between the two wars had seen the growth of *dictatorships* in Germany, Italy and Spain. They were helped by the great poverty and discontent in these countries. During this time, Japan also increased its military power and threatened the colonial interests of Britain and the USA.

OLD EMPIRES AND NEW POWERS

Major changes were on the way at the beginning of the twentieth century. Empires which had lasted for centuries were about to break up, and other nations were becoming more powerful.

THE BRITISH EMPIRE In 1900 the most powerful country was Britain, which ruled an empire that covered a quarter of the world. This empire included India, much of central and southern Africa, the West Indies, Hong Kong and Malaysia. Britain's biggest *colonies*, Canada and Australia, had their own governments but the British monarch still had the final say in what happened there.

Britain had not had to fight a major war since the end of the Napoleonic Wars in 1815. However, between 1899 and 1902 British troops fought and won a war against Dutch *Boer* settlers for control of South Africa.

EMPIRES IN DECLINE The two old empires of eastern Europe, Austria-Hungary and Russia, were now becoming weaker. Austria-Hungary was made up of different peoples, such as the Slovaks, Slavs and Czechs, who all wanted to be independent. Other states such as Serbia also wanted to break away from Austria's influence.

Russia was by far the largest empire of the old world, but now it was facing problems too. Russia's leader, the

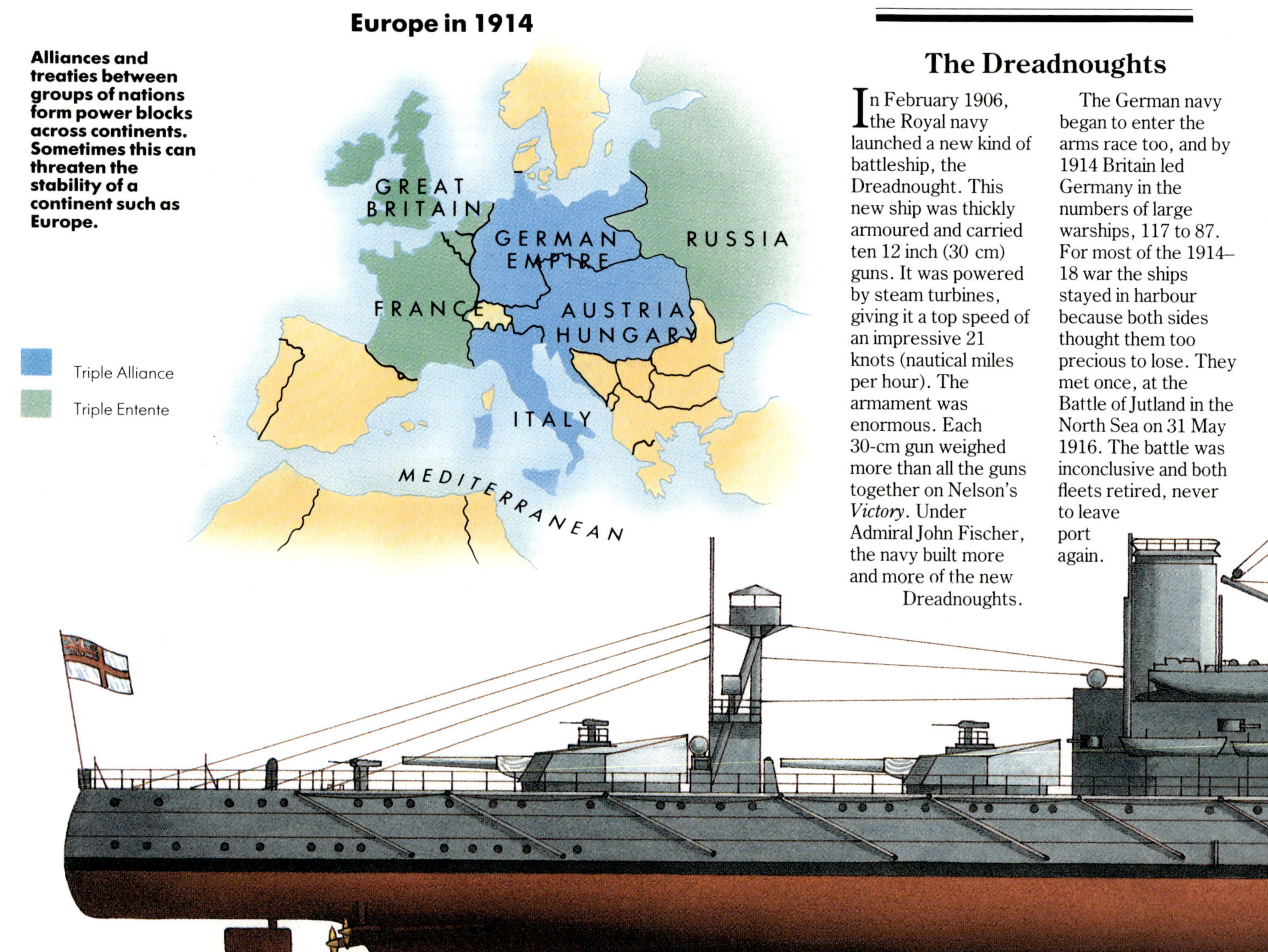

Alliances and treaties between groups of nations form power blocks across continents. Sometimes this can threaten the stability of a continent such as Europe.

The Dreadnoughts

In February 1906, the Royal navy launched a new kind of battleship, the Dreadnought. This new ship was thickly armoured and carried ten 12 inch (30 cm) guns. It was powered by steam turbines, giving it a top speed of an impressive 21 knots (nautical miles per hour). The armament was enormous. Each 30-cm gun weighed more than all the guns together on Nelson's *Victory*. Under Admiral John Fischer, the navy built more and more of the new Dreadnoughts.

The German navy began to enter the arms race too, and by 1914 Britain led Germany in the numbers of large warships, 117 to 87. For most of the 1914–18 war the ships stayed in harbour because both sides thought them too precious to lose. They met once, at the Battle of Jutland in the North Sea on 31 May 1916. The battle was inconclusive and both fleets retired, never to leave port again.

tsar, was an emperor who ruled over a country that covered one-sixth of the Earth's land surface. But, although it was so big, the industrial revolution which had transformed most of western Europe had made little difference to Russia. It was a backward *feudal society* which depended on farming and which was run in an old-fashioned, inefficient way.

Groups of Marxists, who wanted to bring changes to Russia, organized the opposition to Tsar Nicholas II (1894–1917). In 1905 they tried to launch a revolution against him. Nicholas then set up an assembly of representatives who were elected by the middle classes to help govern the country. This move towards *democracy* was not enough to prevent a revolution in 1917 (see pages 474–5).

Turkey's great Ottoman empire was also in decline, but it still ruled over Greece, Palestine and Mesopotamia (present-day Iraq). In 1908 junior officers in the Turkish army, known as the 'young turks', overthrew the unpopular Sultan Abdul Hamid II and set up a western European-style government.

Right. Japan flexes its industrial muscles in a territorial war against the declining Russian empire.

RISING POWERS The United States of America and Japan were two new powers that were about to challenge the domination of the old empires. In 1894 Japan had defeated China and had seized land around Port Arthur, in northern China near to its border with Russia. In a war against Russia in 1904, the Japanese navy sank the entire Russian Baltic fleet at the Battle of Tsushima.

The United States had recently seized the Philippines and Cuba from Spain. In 1903 it used a revolution in Panama as an excuse to take control of that country from Colombia, so clearing the way for the building of the Panama canal.

In 1870 the Prussian leader, Bismarck, had united all the different German states into one empire. By 1900, this was the strongest industrial power in Europe. Its growing influence caused the great empires and nations of Europe to group together in different alliances.

NEW ALLIANCES Germany, Austria-Hungary and Italy formed the Triple Alliance to protect themselves from possible attack by France or Russia. France and Russia joined to form the Dual Entente. In 1904 Britain and France signed the Entente Cordiale, agreeing to help each other in time of war. Europe was ready for a major war.

Above. In 1904, Britain's alliance with France, the Entente Cordiale, settled the two countries' colonial disputes in North Africa and they agreed to help each other in time of war. But the entente provoked Germany into challenging their influence in Morocco. This postcard is a memento of the alliance, and shows President Fallières of France and King Edward VII.

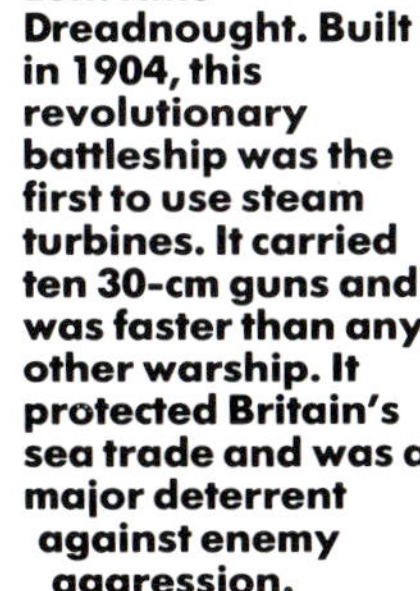

Left. HMS Dreadnought. Built in 1904, this revolutionary battleship was the first to use steam turbines. It carried ten 30-cm guns and was faster than any other warship. It protected Britain's sea trade and was a major deterrent against enemy aggression.

TECHNOLOGICAL DEVELOPMENTS

Great technological changes took place at the beginning of the twentieth century. These developments, particularly in the areas of transport and communications, began to touch on and improve the lives of ordinary people more than ever before.

Technological progress was regarded as a good and necessary thing. There were no worries about the pollution caused by factories and no-one thought that supplies of fuels like coal or gas would ever run out.

The calm water of harbours promised smooth landings for the large passenger-carrying flying boats of the 1930s, although their popularity soon began to wane.

TRANSPORT The motor car was developed towards the end of the nineteenth century. At first it was an expensive luxury that only the rich could afford. But new methods of making large numbers of items, known as *mass-production* techniques, were developed by Henry Ford in the USA, and this made cars more affordable.

Cars had been developed after the *internal combustion engine* was invented in 1876. This engine also made powered flight possible. In 1900, a German called Count Zeppelin built a huge gas-filled airship that was powered by two petrol engines. On 17 December 1903, Orville Wright took to the air in an aeroplane made of wood and canvas at Kitty Hawk, South Carolina, USA.

The airship *Hindenburg* explodes while docking at Lakehurst, New Jersey, USA. There were no survivors.

The First World War (see pp. 466–73) encouraged the development of fighter aeroplanes and bombers. In 1919, two British pilots, Alcock and Brown, made the first flight across the Atlantic Ocean in a Vickers Vimy bomber that had been adapted to fly the long distance.

By the early 1920s, private airlines were advertising regular passenger flights from London to the main European cities. However, for most people, going by sea was still the only way of travelling to another continent.

In the 1930s, airships began regular flights across the Atlantic. But when the German airship *Hindenburg* burst into flames at Lakehurst, New Jersey, in the USA in 1936, people lost confidence in this form of transport.

NEW COMMUNICATIONS The telephone and the phonograph (record player) had been invented in the late nineteenth century.

The Italian electrical engineer, Guglielmo Marconi, invented wireless telegraphy in 1895. This allowed Morse signals – dots and dashes – to be sent over long distances and was mainly used to send messages between ships. But in 1906 an American, Reginald Fessenden, sent continuous waves of sound by wireless. Words and music could be broadcast for the first time.

RADIO, CINEMA AND TELEVISION In Britain, the British Broadcasting Company (BBC) was set up in 1922. Radio was no longer just for the rich, because a radio receiver, a 'crystal set', could be made simply and cheaply at home.

The cinema was also developing rapidly. *The Jazz Singer* (1927) was the first talking picture ever made. Audiences were amazed to hear the film's star, Al Jolson, speak the first famous words: *'You ain't seen nothing yet!'*

The first television system was demonstrated by a Scottish scientist, John Logie Baird, as early as 1926. Ten years later the BBC began regular television broadcasts from Alexandra Palace in London.

Landmarks of Speed and Distance

Top. The *Queen Mary*.
Above. The Wright brothers' biplane *Flyer 3*.
Far left. Model T Ford.
Left. The *Mallard*.

Below. One of the first telephones.

December 17 1903, Orville Wright makes the world's first powered flight in an aircraft, flying 36.5 metres in 12 seconds.
25 July 1909, Louis Blériot makes the first flight across the English Channel.
14–15 July 1919, Capt John Alcock and Lt Arthur Whitten Brown make the first Atlantic flight.
1919 The world's first daily international airline service started by Aircraft Transport and Travel Ltd, from Hounslow, England, to Le Bourget, France.
21 July 1925 Malcolm Campbell, in 350 horse power Sunbeam *Bluebird*, is the first to reach 241 km per hour on land.
21 May 1927 Charles Lindbergh makes the first solo Atlantic flight.
1929 German airship *Graf Zeppelin* completes a round-the-world trip.
5–24 May 1930 Amy Johnson flies solo from Britain to Australia.
1935 Sir Malcolm Campbell, in *Bluebird* 3, breaks the land speed record, reaching a speed of 484 km per hour.
1937 The *Queen Mary* breaks the Atlantic crossing record in 3 days, 20 hours and 42 minutes.
1938 *Mallard* reaches a speed of 202 km per hour pulling seven coaches.

Key Dates in Transport

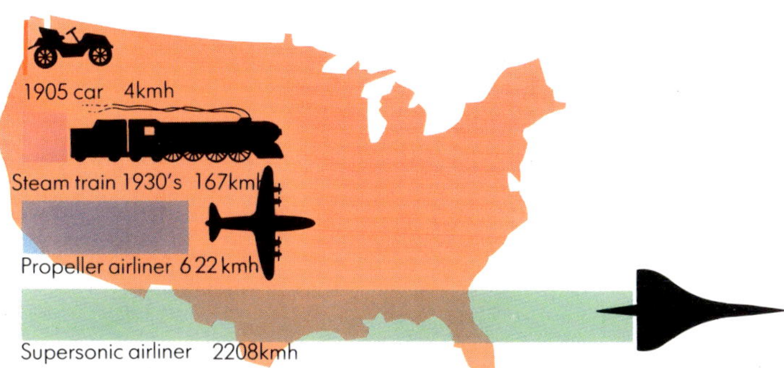

The development of transport this century has been astonishing. *Concorde* can now travel across the USA in under two hours.

5000 BC	Pack animals first used
1500 BC	First wheeled vehicle, in Mesopotamia
900 AD	Chinese invent canals and canal locks
100	Compass reaches Europe
1522	First circumnavigation of the globe. Expedition led by Magellan
1783	Montgolfier brothers make first flight in hot-air balloon
1816	Tarmacadam roads
1829	Stephenson's Rocket
1885	Daimler develops practical internal combustion engine
1903	Wright brothers make first controlled aeroplane flight
1937	Jet engine invented
1947	First plane to break the sound barrier
1959	The first hovercraft built
1961	Yuri Gagarin, first man in space
1969	Neil Armstrong, first man on the Moon

SCIENTIFIC IDEAS AND THE ARTS

Salvador Dali's dream-like painting, *The Persistence of Memory* (1931), is a surrealist painting. Its dream-like imagery is represented in sharp focus and as realistically as possible, almost resembling colour photography.

At the beginning of the twentieth century, new scientific ideas and new movements in art, literature and music reflected the excitement and optimism which people felt as they entered a new century.

SCIENCE Scientists began to question the nature of the world around them and some very important theories were developed at this time. Albert Einstein's Theory of Relativity, published in 1905, explained one of the key secrets of the universe, which was that the smallest particle—the atom—contained an enormous amount of 'locked up' energy. At first it was thought that this energy could never be released, but in 1919 British scientist, Ernest Rutherford, used radioactivity to split a nitrogen atom. This led to the development of nuclear energy and, eventually, to the making of an atomic bomb.

THE INNER MIND Equally important developments occurred in psychology—the study of how the human mind works. Sigmund Freud, an Austrian doctor, used hypnosis to find out his patients' deepest thoughts. He developed a system called *psycho-analysis* to help cure some forms of mental illness.

The increasing knowledge of psychology had an effect on literature and art. Writers like Marcel Proust, James Joyce and Virginia Woolf explored the innermost thoughts of the characters they wrote about, while playwrights like Henrik Ibsen used the theatre to show the problems that can arise between people.

The artists Pablo Picasso and Georges Braque led a movement called *Cubism*, in which an object was seen from many different angles at the same time. Instead of painting something exactly as it was, they wanted to show the ideas and feelings that could be expressed about it. Other artists included *Surrealists* like Salvador Dali and Rene Magritte, whose paintings show a disturbing dream world where anything could happen.

ENTERTAINMENT, DESIGN AND ARCHITECTURE Throughout the 1920s and 1930s, the gramophone (record-player), wireless (radio) and cinema became available to more people. New forms of entertainment were dominated by the USA. Hollywood became the world capital of film-making. Jazz, a type of music developed by blacks in the American southern states, was popular all over the world and it also influenced classical composers like George Gershwin.

Modern designs included *Art Deco*, which got its name from the Paris Exposition des Arts Décoratifs of 1925. It took the idea of streamlining used on planes,

Austrian scientist Albert Einstein's theories about the atom heralded the dawning of the nuclear age and completely changed the way we think about the universe and how it works.

Left. Completed in 1930, New York's Chrysler Building shows the influence of Art Deco in architecture. The decorations represent the rising Sun, a popular basis for designs. Stylized flowers and zig-zag motifs were also common.

Sigmund Freud

Sigmund Freud (1856–1939) developed the theory of psycho-analysis, a way of treating people's mental disorders by encouraging them to talk openly about their hidden thoughts. He was an Austrian doctor who worked mainly in Vienna. He drew up his theory after hearing of a Dr Breur who had cured hysteria by hypnotizing his patients so that they remembered an important event in their life that was buried. They could then begin to understand it and the illness could be cured.

Freud found that not all illnesses could be treated using hypnosis, so he got his patients to talk about their lives in general, and particularly their childhoods.

He also believed that sexual impulses hold the key to human behaviour, even from our earliest years. He was criticized by some doctors because they did not understand his approach and because many of his patients were rich, neurotic, Viennese women who did not represent a cross-section of society. Freud has done much to help us understand how our minds operate.

He wrote many papers and books, one of the most famous being *The Interpretation of Dreams*, which suggests that the subconscious mind is expressed in dreams.

1 Venustiana Carranzo became president of Mexico in 1914 but soon fell out with his lieutenant and civil war and chaos followed. In 1915 Carranzo was recognized as the president by the United States. Local difficulties led in 1916 to the US army mounting raids in Mexico, which were not greatly successful.

2 In 1908 a constitutional convention was held to discuss the future of South Africa. The convention decided that the states, including Natal, Cape Colony, Orange River Colony and Transvaal should form a union. English and Dutch became the official languages and the head of the Union was the King of the United Kingdom.

Right. The architect Le Corbusier loved geometric forms and applied new technical ideas. He believed that buildings should be designed according to their function. This shows the characteristic *pilotis* used to raise buildings off the ground.

Below. Colourful Art Deco ceramic designs by Clarice Cliff are now highly prized by collectors. Art Deco relied on strong colours that were influenced by nature. They had shapes that reflected the new streamlined trains and aeroplanes.

trains and cars, and applied it to everyday objects such as radios, telephones and furniture. These designers used modern materials, such as tubular chrome and an early type of plastic called *bakelite*, in their work.

In the world of architecture, the techniques of building with steel frames and reinforced concrete made it possible to build tall structures, such as the skyscrapers of New York. When the Empire State Building was completed in 1931 it became, at 449 metres high, the tallest skyscraper in the world. It kept this record until 1973.

The French architect, Le Corbusier, put forward the idea of people living in high-rise blocks that contained flats, shops and recreation areas. His Unit d' Habitation was built in Marseilles in France in 1946 and became the model for housing developments in the second half of the century.

OUTBREAK OF WAR

Austrian Archduke Ferdinand is shot in Sarajevo, Serbia. His assassin Princep is led away.

In the early years of the twentieth century, many people believed that the peace in Europe was only temporary. Germany was rapidly becoming a major economic and military power, and some of the older empires saw it as a threat.

France was particularly worried. It had suffered a humiliating defeat in the Franco-Prussian War of 1870–1. Prussia, one of the largest independent states that had later combined to form Germany, had taken the important industrial region of Alsace-Lorraine from the French.

ALLIANCES AND ARMAMENTS France and Russia had agreed in August 1891 that if either country was attacked, the other would give it full military support. In 1904 Britain had made separate agreements with Russia and France, also promising its support if there was a war. In eastern Europe, Russia wanted to prevent the expansion of Germany's ally, the Austro-Hungarian Empire.

Every major European country began to spend more and more money building bigger and better equipped armies and navies. It needed only one small incident to upset the balance of power and spark off a war.

On 28 June 1914, Archduke Ferdinand of Austria was murdered in Sarajevo in Serbia, as a protest against Austrian control of that country. The Austro-Hungarian Empire immediately declared war on Serbia. Russia came to Serbia's aid and ordered its army to prepare for war. Now the leaders of Germany became anxious. If Russia invaded Austria-Hungary, then it might also attack Germany. France, Russia's ally, might seize the opportunity to attack Germany from the west.

THE VON SCHLIEFFEN PLAN In 1905, the chief of staff of the German army, Count Alfred von Schlieffen, had drawn up a plan to deal with this situation. As Russia was so vast, it would take about two weeks after it had declared war before it was ready to fight, because Russian troops would have to travel long distances to reach the *front line*, where the fighting was. The plan was to use this time to send most of the German army through Belgium to attack France from the north.

The German army would surround Paris and force the French army to fight a defensive battle that it would be certain to lose. By the time Russia could equip its army and send it into battle, France would have surrendered and Germany's entire army would be free to concentrate on a war in the east.

WAR IS DECLARED On 1 August 1914, Germany declared war on Russia. Two days later it declared war on France and sent its army through Belgium to attack. Because it had agreed in 1830 to defend Belgium if it was invaded, Britain declared war on Germany on 4 August.

Throughout the 1914–1918 war, most of the fighting was in France and Belgium and on the borders of Russia. Nevertheless, the war was called a world war because fighting spread to eastern Europe, Turkey and the Middle East. In 1917, the United States of America entered the conflict (see pp. 472–3). Indian, Canadian and Australian regiments also fought with the British.

The most successful advertising campaign of all time: Lord Kitchener's appeals recruit a huge army of volunteers.

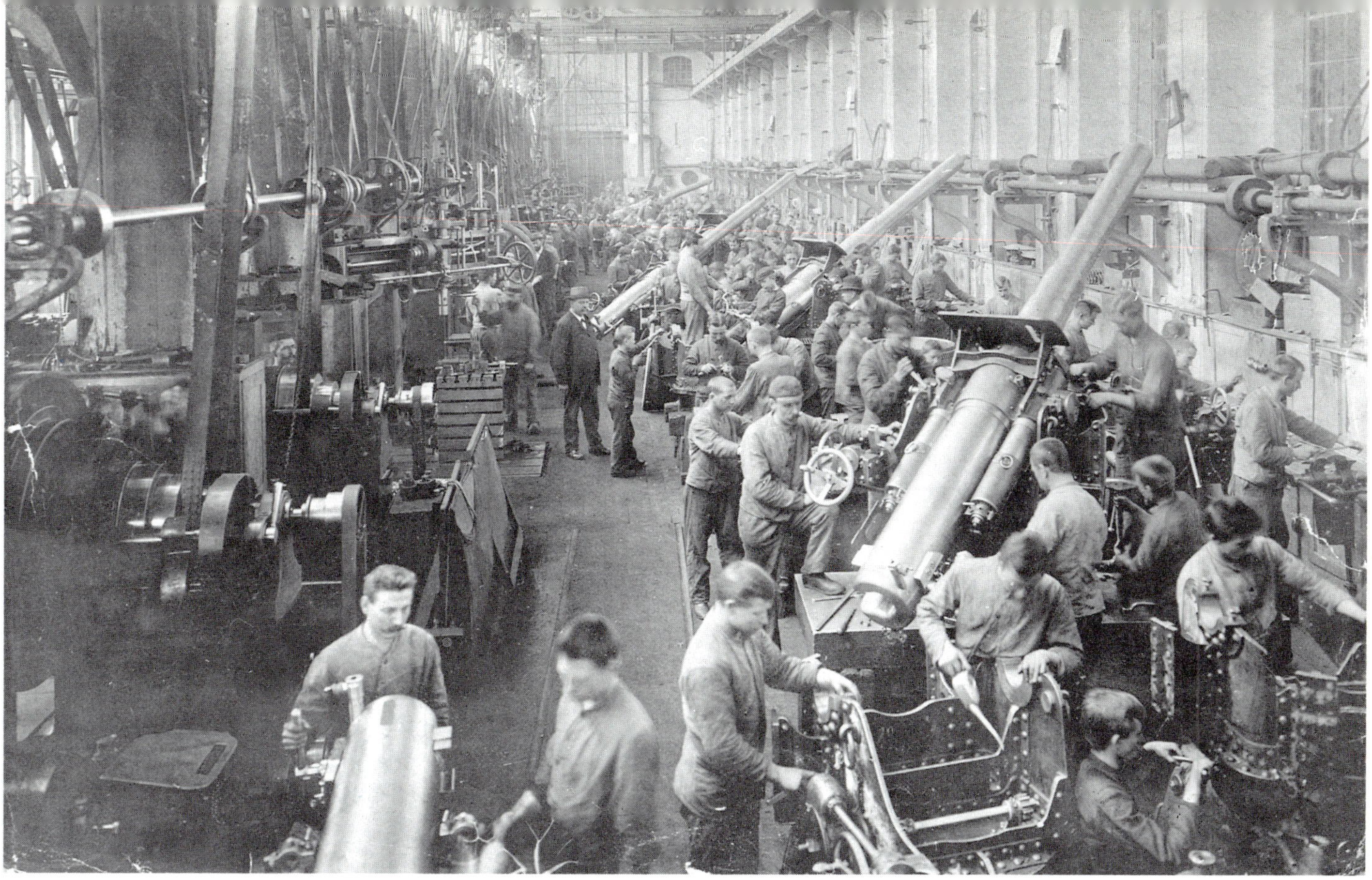

Industrial power. This photograph shows a German armaments factory in full production at the beginning of the First World War. The Germans increased their stores of weapons as all countries prepared for war.

The Size of Regular Armies in 1914

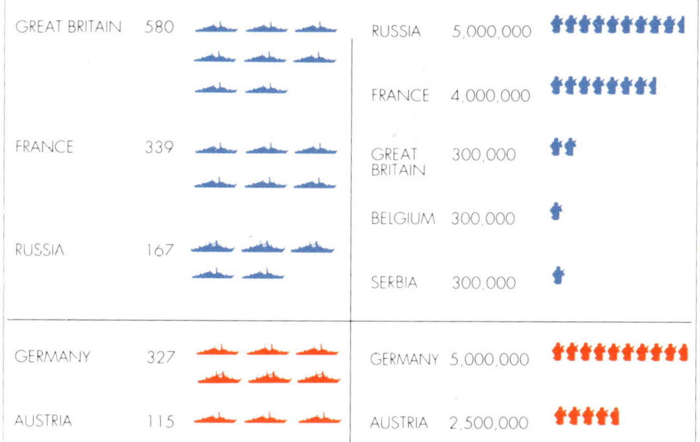

The sizes of the armies ranged against each other at the start of the First World War differed in the relative importance attached to the army as compared to the navy. No air forces were in operation at this time but the types that would form the early warplanes were being developed. France, Russia and Germany all had large standing armies. The French lost many of their men in the early days of the war at Verdun, where they held up the German advance at a cost of 300,000 casualties. The British had only a small standing army, which was swelled in the days to come by volunteers, encouraged by Lord Kitchener. The largest navy was the British Navy, which had entered a ship-building war with the Germans. These great navies met only once, at the battle of Jutland. The stalemate trench-warfare meant that many men were needed to replace those lost at the front.

Germany Invades, August 1914

Right. Von Schlieffen's famous plan was drawn up to combat the possibility of attack on two fronts. Once the French had surrendered, Germany would then move its troops to the east ready to defend its border with Russia.

Austro-Hungarian Empire 1914

A map of Austria-Hungary at the start of the First World War. The empire did not survive the war.

THE WAR IN EUROPE

At first, the war was fought by armies on the move. *Allied forces* had to move quickly to stop the German army's rapid advance. Some early battles were fought by cavalry: soldiers on horseback.

On 12 August, a force of 81,472 British soldiers and 30,000 horses set out for France under the command of General Sir John French. In Britain, people believed that the war would be over by Christmas. After several minor battles with German forces, the British stopped the German advance at Ypres in Belgium in mid-October. Meanwhile, the French army halted the German forces in the valleys of the Somme and the Marne rivers.

TRENCH WARFARE All across western Europe, from the Belgian coast to Switzerland, the opposing armies dug lines of trenches to mark out the territory they had gained. These lines of trenches became known as the Western Front. The ground in between them was called 'no man's land'.

Gradually, the trench systems were enlarged and fortified to make them harder to attack. Thousands of soldiers were needed to defend them. From the shelter of a trench, one soldier with a machine-gun could mow down hundreds of advancing troops. To attack a well-defended enemy trench meant almost certain death.

The Western Front 1914–1918

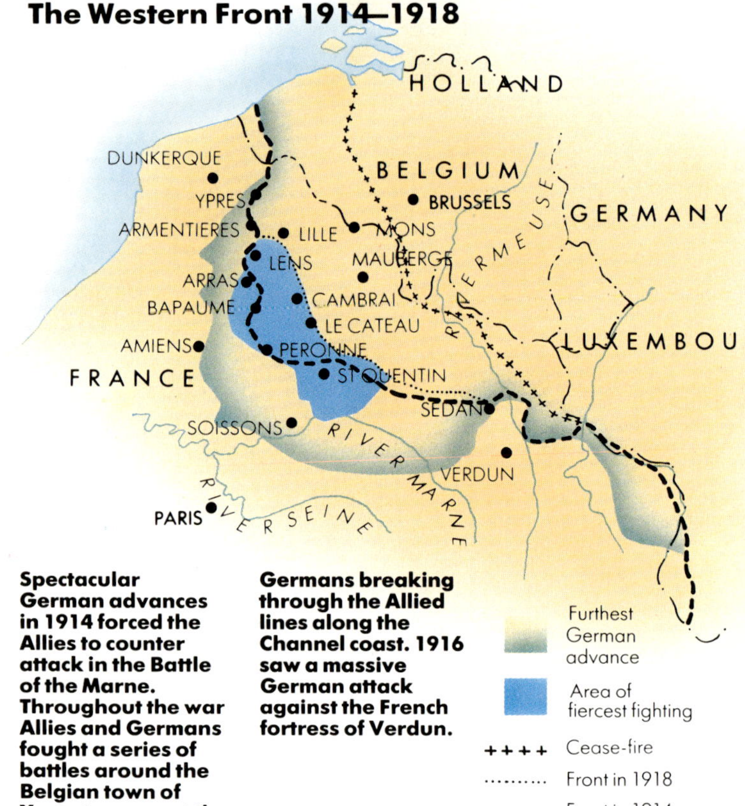

Spectacular German advances in 1914 forced the Allies to counter attack in the Battle of the Marne. Throughout the war Allies and Germans fought a series of battles around the Belgian town of Ypres to prevent the Germans breaking through the Allied lines along the Channel coast. 1916 saw a massive German attack against the French fortress of Verdun.

THE GENERALS' WAR Nevertheless, generals on both sides thought that they could only make progress if they launched massive attacks on the enemy's trenches. In almost every case these attacks failed. Two of the biggest and most disastrous battles came in 1916. On 21 February the German army attacked the French fortress of Verdun. Although the French were heavily outnumbered, General Pétain ordered his troops to fight to the last man. As the number of French casualties rose, so Pétain sent in more and more troops.

For four months the French army held on to the fortress, although the German attacks had reduced it to ruins. In the end the Germans gave up. They had lost about 218,000 men. But the French had lost 315,000. The French army had not given way but its spirit was broken. On 1 July, the British and French launched a combined attack in the valley of the Somme which was to last until November. Troops carrying heavy equipment and moving across open ground were easy targets for the German machine-gunners. On the first day of the battle, 20,000 British soldiers were killed and another 40,000 were wounded, the highest casualties suffered in a single day of the war.

WEARING DOWN THE ENEMY As the war went on, countries *conscripted* (ordered to join the army) huge numbers of men. Allied generals liked large battles because they thought that eventually the Germans would run out of soldiers. In fact, the populations of Germany and its allies were growing, and they had more than enough men to replace those who died. The military power of the Allies was not enough to end the war quickly.

Down the line from death. Wounded British soldiers make their way to a field hospital.

In Flanders Fields

In Flanders fields the poppies blow
Between the crosses, row on row
That mark our place; and in the sky
The larks, still bravely singing, fly
Scarce heard amid the guns below.

We are the Dead. Short days ago
We lived, felt dawn, saw sunset glow,
Loved and were loved, and now we lie
In Flanders fields.

Take up our quarrel with the foe:
To you from failing hands we throw
The torch; be yours to hold it high.
If ye break faith with us who die
We shall not sleep, though poppies grow
In Flanders fields.

John McCrae. Died in Base Hospital, 1918

The last great disaster for the Allies was the Battle of Passchendaele, near Ypres, which started on 31 July 1917. Rain and the heavy bombardment of shells had turned the battlefield to mud. During two and a half months of fighting, British troops suffered 300,000 casualties and the German casualties were 275,000 men.

Left. Soldiers lived their daily lives in the comparative safety of a trench while waiting for orders to go into battle. If the enemy started shelling the trench, soldiers would have to shelter underground in dug-outs.

The Introduction of Tanks

In October 1917, British troops won a minor but significant victory against the Germans at Cambrai, northern France, when they launched a surprise attack using tanks.

The tank was a new weapon which changed twentieth-century warfare completely. It was an armour-plated vehicle with caterpillar tracks which enabled it to move slowly but steadily across rough terrain. The tank had cannons which could fire to the front and to the side.

The sheer size and weight of the tank meant that it could break through the tangled barbed-wire fortifications protecting the German trenches. Foot soldiers following behind the tanks were protected from enemy fire and could move through the gaps created in the barbed wire.

WAR ON ALL FRONTS

Above. The mainstay of the Royal Flying Corps was the Sopwith Camel.

A German Fokker D7 biplane.

Another German fighter, this time a Fokker E1 monoplane, an advance on the earlier models.

The First World War was fought in eastern Europe and the Middle East as well as in Belgium and France.

THE EASTERN FRONT Russia was not well-prepared for war. Now that France and Britain were fighting Germany on the Western Front, Russia moved quickly to support its allies and sent troops into eastern Germany. But the Germans won a decisive victory at the Battle of Tannenburg on 29 August 1914. The remaining Russian forces retreated.

Meanwhile, a third Russian army had suffered heavy losses when it had attacked and defeated the Austrians. Germany sent reinforcements to Austria and succeeded in turning back the Russian advance. The eastern borders of Germany and Austria were now safe from further attack, and so Germany was able to strengthen its attack in the west.

The Germans, who had planned to defeat France quickly so that their armies could fight off a massive Russian attack, found that they could easily fight a war on two borders after all. On 2 May 1915 they attacked Russia along a wide stretch of the Eastern Front and in the middle of the year Germany captured most of Poland, which had previously been controlled by Russia.

Italy joined the Allies on 23 May 1915 by declaring war on Austria-Hungary. This meant that Austrian troops had to leave the Russian front to defend Austria's mountainous southern border with Italy.

TURKEY In October 1914 Turkey entered the war as an ally of Germany and immediately sent an army to attack Russia. Thousands of Turks died in this campaign as a result of the bitterly cold Russian winter.

Turkey's empire included a large part of the Middle East and so it was in a good position to cut off supplies of oil to the Allies. Turkey also threatened to attack the Suez Canal, which would prevent supplies reaching Britain from Australia and India.

One way of hitting at Turkey was to prevent German supplies reaching Turkey through the Balkan states of south-eastern Europe. A British and French force landed at Salonika in Greece, which was neutral (not part of the war). They hoped to join up with the Serbian army and prevent any reinforcements from Germany or Austria-Hungary reaching Turkey.

This Allied army was unable to prevent the defeat of Serbia by the Austro-Hungarian army, which went on to conquer the Balkan states of Montenegro and Albania. In the end it seemed that the Allied army had served no

Gallipoli

Australian and New Zealand (ANZAC) troops land at Gallipoli in 1915.

Turkey controlled the narrow straits of the Bosphorus, and so cut off Russia's most direct sea route to the west. With this route closed, the Allies found it impossible to send supplies to Russia.

In order to distract Turkish troops from attacking Russia, Britain sent a naval force to land troops at Gallipoli on Turkey's Aegean coast. The first landings took place on 25 April 1915. Australian and New Zealand troops (ANZACs) were used as part of the first attack. They suffered heavy losses when they tried to climb the steep cliffs.

The Gallipoli campaign was badly managed from the start. Allied troops suffered appalling casualties and gained little or nothing. They never succeeded in taking the well-defended Turkish positions on the cliff tops, and on 8 January 1916 British commanders organized a safe withdrawal to ships waiting offshore.

The Eastern Front 1914–1918

Below. The war on the eastern front. The Germans won decisive battles at Tannenburg (Aug 1914), and at the Masurian Lakes (Sept 1914), completely destroying two Russian armies. Winter prevented a further German advance. In a second great offensive in 1915 the German army captured the whole of Poland and Lithuania leaving one million Russian soldiers dead. After the Bolshevik Revolution of 1917, Russia was forced to pull out of the war, leaving the Germans in possession of a huge part of western Russia.

Turkey Defeated 1917–1918

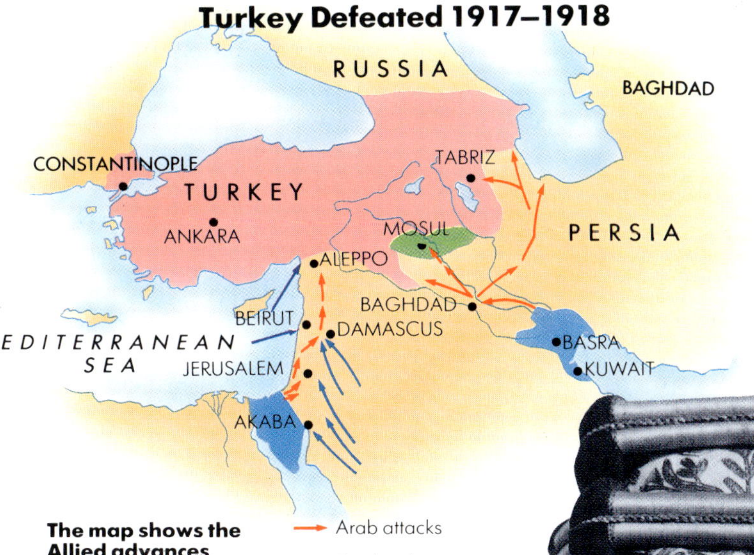

The map shows the Allied advances towards Turkey during the First World War from Palestine in the west and from Mesopotamia (present-day Iraq) in the east.

useful function in this area and had simply drawn troops away from the Western Front, where they were badly needed.

THE MIDDLE EAST The British landed a small army in Palestine to protect the Suez Canal from a Turkish attack. This campaign is best remembered for the heroic actions of Colonel T.E. Lawrence—Lawrence of Arabia—who organized a secret *resistance movement* among the Palestinians, encouraging them to fight the Turks who governed their country.

British forces led by General Allenby advanced against the Turks and on 9 December 1917 drove them out of Jerusalem. Foreign Secretary Balfour announced that Britain intended to create a Jewish homeland in Palestine when the war ended.

Colonel T.E. Lawrence adopted the headgear of the Arab resistance fighters with whom he joined forces.

AMERICA ENTERS THE WAR

An American recruitment poster showing Uncle Sam preparing for a bare knuckle fight with the enemy.

At first, the United States was neutral in the First World War. But the Allies were able to buy essential supplies and weapons there. These supplies had to be sent across the Atlantic by ship.

GERMANY'S U-BOAT BLOCKADE In early 1915, Germany declared a *blockade* of Britain. This meant that it tried to prevent ships going in and out of British ports. It also announced that its submarines (U-boats) would sink any British *merchant ship* they saw.

Germany's war on merchant shipping hit the USA's export trade hard. US ships were sunk and the lives of its citizens were also placed in danger. About 100 Americans died when the British liner *Lusitania* was sunk by a U-boat off the coast of Ireland in May 1915. Germany's U-boat campaign helped prepare public opinion in the USA for war.

On 31 January 1917 Germany announced that it would step up its U-boat war to include any ships from neutral countries that it found in the eastern Atlantic. On 6 April, after protests about US ships being sunk, the USA declared war on Germany.

It would take time for America to raise an army of volunteers, equip them and send them to France. In the meantime, the USA lent money and supplies freely to the Allies. With the industrial might of the USA on the side of the Allies, Germany could not hope to win.

"All the News That's Fit to Print."

The New York Times.

EXTRA 5:30 A.M.

LUSITANIA SUNK BY A SUBMARINE, PROBABLY 1,260 DEAD; TWICE TORPEDOED OFF IRISH COAST; SINKS IN 15 MINUTES; CAPT. TURNER SAVED, FROHMAN AND VANDERBILT MISSING; WASHINGTON BELIEVES THAT A GRAVE CRISIS IS AT HAN

SHOCKS THE PRESIDENT

Washington Deeply Stirred by the Loss of American Lives.

BULLETINS AT WHITE HOUSE

Wilson Reads Them Closely, but Is Silent on the Nation's Course.

HINTS OF CONGRESS CALL

Loss of Lusitania Recalls Firm Tone of Our First Warning to Germany.

CAPITAL FULL OF RUMORS

The Lost Cunard Steamship Lusitania

Cunard Office Here Besieged for News; Fate of 1,918 on Lusitani

Left. The sinking of the *Lusitania* and deaths of 100 Americans helped persuade America to join the war.

HUNGER AND REVOLUTION Throughout the summer of 1917 there were food riots in Petrograd (St Petersburg) in Russia. The advancing German armies had captured the rich farming land of Ukraine. Soon Russia would be overtaken by revolution and would leave the war (see pages 474–5).

But there were also food shortages in Germany. Britain's poweful navy had kept up a blockade to prevent imports reaching German ports. Germany's farms were

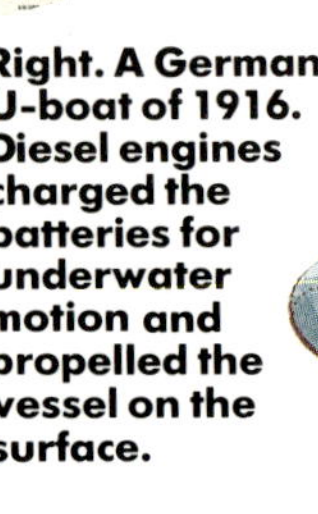

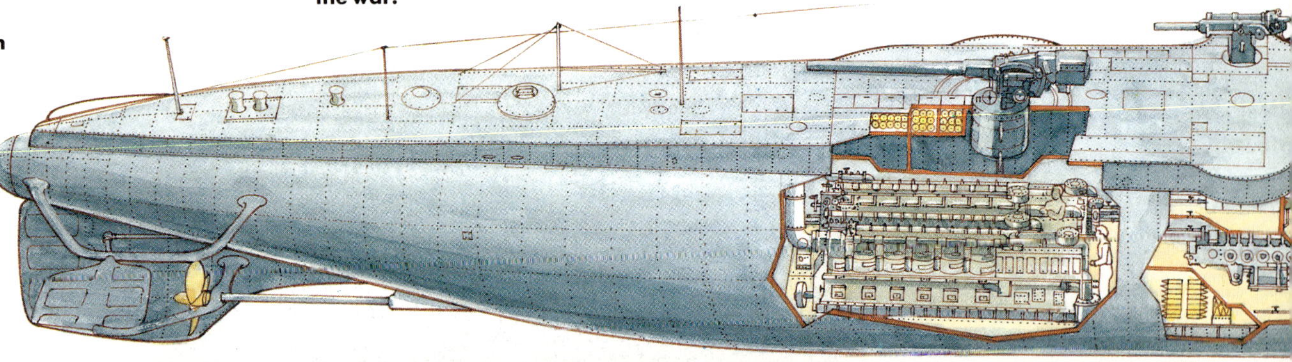

Right. A German U-boat of 1916. Diesel engines charged the batteries for underwater motion and propelled the vessel on the surface.

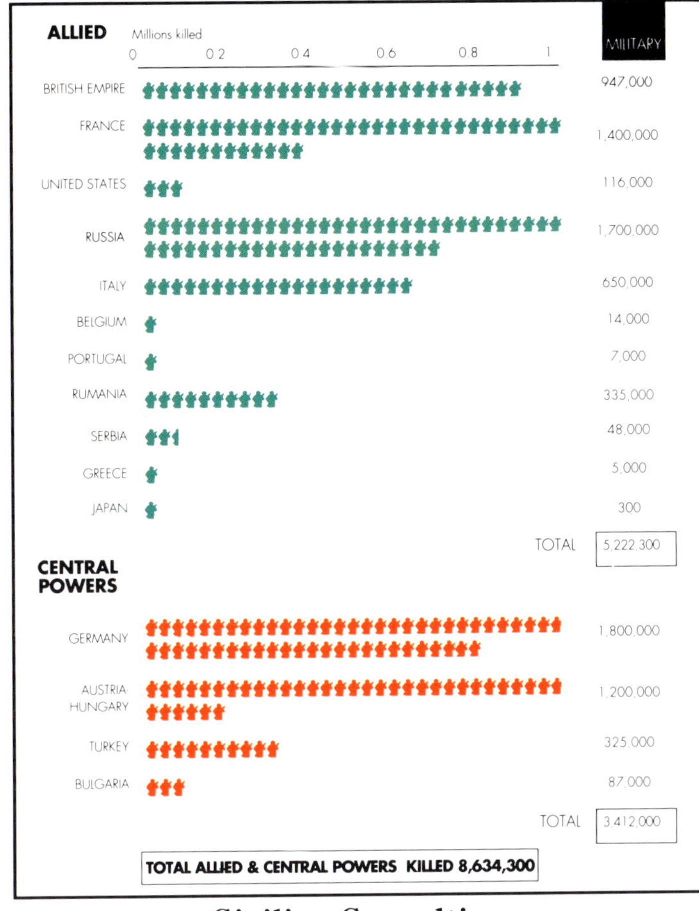

Civilian Casualties

The First World War was the first war to involve large numbers of civilian casualties. The Germans brought war to the British people through naval bombardments of the coastal towns of Scunthorpe and Scarborough. At first, air raids were carried out by giant airships, Zeppelins, but after several of these were shot down, the Germans used aeroplanes. Altogether, just over 1100 civilians were killed in Britain because of the war.

In France and Belgium the civilians were much worse off. As the Germans invaded France in 1914 much of the two countries was overrun and many civilians lost their homes and some their lives as the two armies battled for advances. Some small towns were completely destroyed by shelling from either side.

also failing to produce food, because so many men had gone to fight that there were not enough left to work on the farms. When Germany began to lose more and more battles, its leaders were afraid that shortages at home would lead to a revolution.

The Easter Rising

One unexpected result of the war was an attempt by sections of the Irish volunteer army and nationalist sympathizers to set up an Irish Republic.

On Easter Monday in 1916, seven men set up a headquarters at the central post office in Dublin and proclaimed a republic. After five days of fighting, British troops regained control of the city. The men who had signed the proclamation were shot. Others were charged with treason and sentenced to be hanged. One of the army leaders who escaped the death penalty was Eamon de Valera, later to become the Republic's first president.

Above. World leaders – American president Woodrow Wilson, centre, signed the Treaty of Versailles in 1919 with French prime minister Clemenceau, left, and British prime minister Lloyd George, right.

GERMANY IS DEFEATED Russia left the war after signing the Treaty of Brest-Litovsk on 3 March 1918. Germany was now free to concentrate on the Western Front and made one last effort to defeat the Allies.

In March, a massive German attack broke through the French and British lines on the Somme. Led by Field Marshal Foch, the Allied armies, including a US army under General Pershing, fought back. The Germans soon ran out of supplies and by the end of April their advance halted. Now Allied forces attacked at the Battle of the Marne and Allied tanks advanced towards Germany.

During the final days of the war the old Austro-Hungarian Empire collapsed, as its individual states declared independence and made peace with the Allies.

On 9 November the German Kaiser was forced to resign and a new republican government took over. Germany signed an *armistice*, a cease-fire, with the Allies on 11 November. War was at an end.

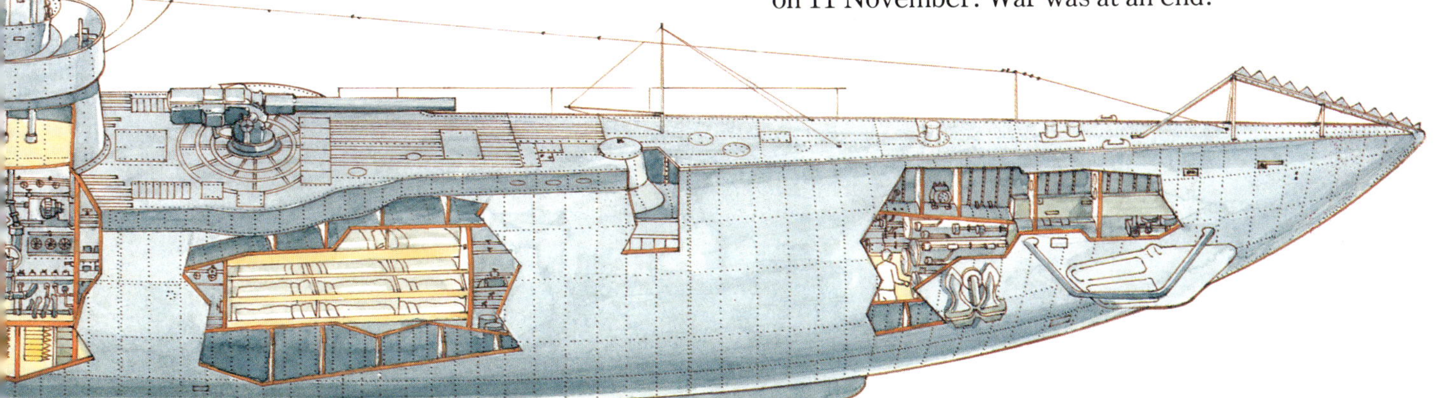

THE RUSSIAN REVOLUTION

St Petersburg in 1917. Violence breaks out as revolutionaries take to the streets to fight for a Communist government.

Russia suffered huge losses during the First World War (see chart p. 473) and its civilian population was starving. Tsar Nicholas II was forced to abdicate in March 1917 and was succeeded by a republican government, led by Prince Lvov, which did not last long. In July, a lawyer called Alexander Kerensky became prime minister, but his government was divided and deeply unpopular.

FALL OF THE GOVERNMENT A number of small but influential Marxist groups led the opposition to Kerensky's government. The most important of these was the *Bolsheviks*, led by Vladimir Ilyich Ulyanov, who was better known as Lenin.

The war was going badly and many Russian soldiers had begun to mutiny. Kerensky had given guns to the committees of workers, called *soviets*, whom he hoped would remain loyal to him. In fact, many members of the soviets were Bolsheviks, loyal to Lenin.

Lenin and Trotsky

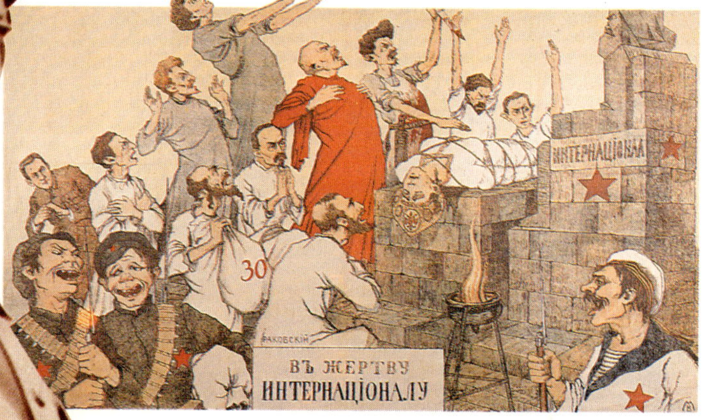

Vladimir Illych Lenin (1870–1924) was leader of the Bolsheviks who seized power in Russia and ruled there for over 70 years. He was born in Simbirsk and attended Kazan University, where he first read Karl Marx. He moved to St Petersburg where he organized a 'Union for the Liberation of the Working Class', for which he was sent to prison. After this, he left Russia but returned to lead an unsuccessful revolution in 1905. He was exiled for this act. At this time most Russians were very poor and were ruled by the autocratic tsar. In 1917, Tsar Nicholas abdicated.

Above. A Russian cartoon depicts Lenin, Trotsky and other revolutionaries sacrificing the spirit of Mother Russia.

Left. Leon Trotsky, Lenin's right-hand man, was later forced from power when he threatened Stalin's position as absolute leader.

Lenin returned to lead the October revolution in 1917 against the interim government. His Bolsheviks gained control of Russia, but civil war followed. Lenin died in 1924.

Leon Trotsky (1879–1940) As a young man, Trotsky was imprisoned for agitating, but he escaped and fled to London where he met Lenin. He was involved in the unsuccessful 1905 *coup* and was again imprisoned. He escaped, then returned to Russia in 1917 to help lead the revolution. After this he built up and led the Red Army to victory in the civil war against the White Russians. He was opposed to Lenin's successor, Stalin, was expelled from the Communist party and was killed in Mexico by one of Stalin's assassins.

Supported by factions from different revolutionary groups, including the *Menshevik* or 'minority' Marxist groups, Lenin called upon Kerensky's government to surrender. Early in the morning of 7 November 1917, groups of revolutionaries, armed with guns and supported by units of the Russian army, advanced upon the Winter Palace in Petrograd (St Petersburg) where the government was based. The ship *Aurora*, which was anchored in the River Neva, fired a few shots at the palace. There was no opposition and in a short while the government had fallen.

Joseph Stalin ruled the USSR with a rod of iron from 1924–1953.

LENIN'S COMMUNIST GOVERNMENT Lenin's Bolsheviks quickly established themselves as the main group in the revolutionary government, keeping the more moderate Mensheviks out of positions of power. The Bolsheviks renamed themselves 'Communists', a name taken from Marx and Engels's *Communist Manifesto* of 1848.

The new government passed laws giving peasants the right to seize land held by the aristocracy. The Communists took control of industry, banks and transport, and confiscated the land and property of the Russian Orthodox Church.

In March 1918, Lenin's government signed the Treaty of Brest-Litovsk with Germany, withdrawing from the war and allowing Germany to keep the parts of Ukraine that it had taken over.

CIVIL WAR IN RUSSIA Any hopes that the tsar would return faded in July 1918, when the Communists ordered the execution of Nicholas II and all his family. Even so, there was civil war in Russia from 1918 to 1920, as supporters of the monarchy (helped by Britain and France) attempted to overthrow the Communist government. It was a time of great bloodshed and hardship.

THE RISE OF STALIN By the time Lenin died in January 1924, he was firmly in control of the new Communist state. After his death, power passed into the hands of one of his party officials, Joseph Stalin. The new leader was not interested in Communism's original ideas about justice and fairness and he became a ruthless tyrant.

War in Russia 1918–1920

Left. A Russian poster calls for opposition to world fascism. It is easy to forget that Russia, more than any other nation, helped to defeat Hitler's Germany.

Above. Nations such as Britain, America, France and Germany aided and encouraged counter-revolutionary forces to fight a civil war against Russia's Bolsheviks.

SOCIAL REFORM

The Russian revolution (see pp. 474–5) provided the world with an example of a state looking after the needs and well-being of all its citizens. Western governments took many years to grant their citizens similar rights. They finally did so because of pressure for reform from workers' organizations and other groups.

In the early years of the century, few countries had pensions for old people, or paid *benefits* to those who were unemployed or too sick to work. New Zealand was the only country where women could vote. In some countries, people were not allowed to form *trade unions*.

SOCIALISM Communism (Revolutionary Socialism) was unpopular in Europe. But Democratic Socialism aimed to bring about social changes through laws passed in Parliament. In Britain, these Socialists were represented by the Labour Party. The first Labour government was elected in 1924 and was led by Ramsay MacDonald. This government lasted less than a year, but the Socialist movement remained important.

The success of this movement was at first due to its close links with trades unions, who used their money to support the election of members of parliament who agreed with their ideas. Before the First World War, trade unions became very powerful in Britain, France, Germany and the USA. They went on strike to force governments to agree to social reforms, and to gain political power for working people.

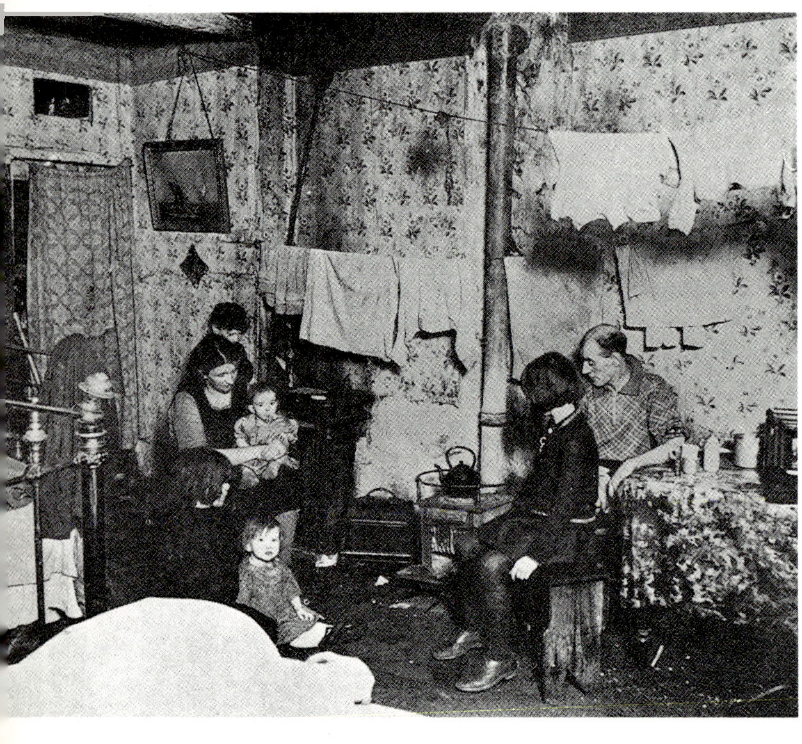

During the depression of the 1930s, many British working class families lived in cramped slum conditions. Many suffered ill-health as a result and the infant mortality rate was high.

ELECTORAL REFORM The slogan, 'votes for women', was heard more and more in the early 1900s. Women who campaigned for the vote were called 'suffragettes', because they wanted 'suffrage' (the right to vote). In Britain, their leaders were Emmeline Pankhurst and her daughter Christabel. The suffragettes drew attention to their cause through actions such as hunger strikes and chaining themselves to the railings of government offices. Many were imprisoned.

At the end of the First World War, the vote was given to women in Britian who were over 30 years of age and were married to householders. But in 1928, with the support of the Labour Party, women were given the vote on the same terms as men. Many other countries were slower to change.

THE WELFARE STATE A *welfare state* is a country which provides money and support to the old, sick, unemployed and so on.

In Britain, the Liberal government of 1906 made the first moves towards this. It introduced small pensions for people over 70 years of age, and a national insurance scheme, covering sickness and unemployment, to which employers, employees and the state all contributed.

In 1942 the British economist, Sir William Beveridge, first used the term 'welfare state' and said that the state should look after its citizens '*from the cradle to the grave*'. The Labour government that came to power after the Second World War put his ideas into practice, and by 1948 Britain had a National Health Service which gave free treatment to everyone. The government also paid cash allowances to mothers to help them bring up their children; improved pensions; unemployment benefits, and sick pay.

Social change was slower to begin in the USA. State pensions were not introduced until the early 1920s. Improvements to conditions of employment came with the Social Security Act of 1935, which increased old age pensions and introduced unemployment benefit and help for poor children.

Child mineworkers in the USA. In the early years of the century most American states had no laws to prevent child labour.

1 In the USA the president, Franklin D. Roosevelt introduced his New Deal. This was legislation set up to help the American economy to recover from the depression of the Thirties. Laws were passed to make farmers produce the right crops, and to give the president powers to oversee many banking and financial deals. Money was also made available to invest in the economy where needed and new taxes were raised.

2 The British power in India began to decline from about 1920 onwards. In 1919, 379 Indians were shot dead and over 1000 injured when British troops fired on a crowd in Amritsar. Mohandas Gandhi called for a non-violent protest against British rule and a boycott of all foreign goods. His following grew and many workers went on strike in protest against British rule. Gandhi's peaceful protest led in 1947 to Indian Independence.

Political Change

In Britain, poor working conditions brought about a general strike in which over three million workers from all industries brought the nation to a standstill for nine days in 1926. Miners whose claim for a living wage had sparked off the strike were defeated and they had no choice but to return to work after six months of near starvation.

But the inter-war years were also years of important political change. War had made people challenge the established political parties and look for new solutions. Britain's first Labour government was elected in 1924 and the general election of 1929 was the first in which all women were allowed to vote.

When Women Got the Vote

One of the most striking features of the 20th century has been the increased part that women play in society. In Britain, until the middle of the last century, they had no right to vote, to enter universities or the professions, or to own property. They could not keep their earnings, or even their children if their husband chose to leave or divorce them. By 1914, some of these wrongs had been corrected but people's attitudes were hard to change.

Two world wars, education and full employment have brought enormous changes in attitudes towards women's rights and such questions as divorce, equal pay and careers for married women. Even so, some people feel that women are still badly off, and that much remains to be done before people recognize that men and women are truly equal.

New Zealand	1893
Australia	1902
Finland	1906
Norway	1913
USSR	1917
Austria	1918
Germany	1918
Britain (partial)	1919
Belgium	1919
Ireland	1919
USA	1920
India	1926
Pakistan	1926
France	1944
Italy	1945
Japan	1945
Israel	1948
Indonesia	1955
Switzerland	1971
Jordan	1973

Women still do not have the vote in many, mainly Muslim countries including Iran, Iraq, United Arab Emirates, Saudi Arabia and Kuwait.

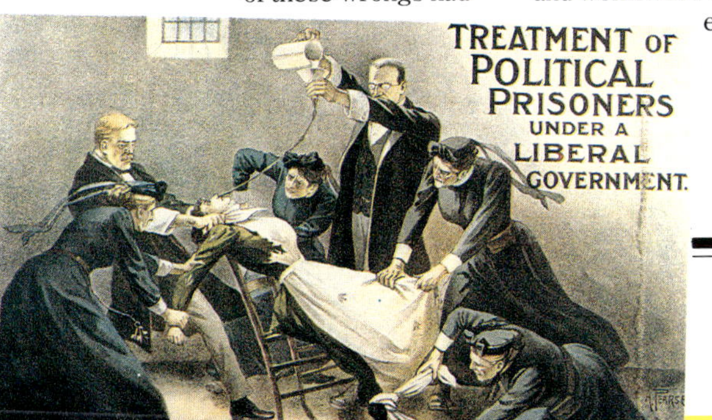

Suffragettes who were imprisoned often went on hunger strike and were brutally force-fed by prison doctors.

DEPRESSION AND DICTATORSHIPS

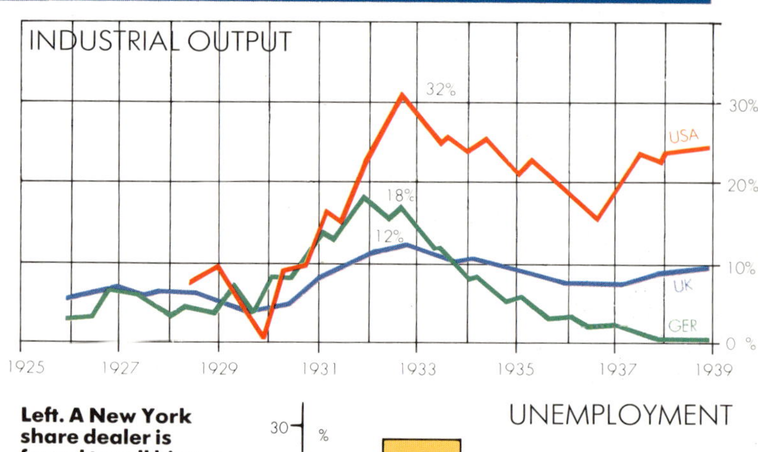

Left. A New York share dealer is forced to sell his car as billions of dollars are wiped off the value of shares in one day.

Above. Industrial output fell to a record low in 1930. Right. World unemployment reached a peak of almost 30 per cent in the early 1930s.

The countries that had fought in the First World War were slow to recover. The high number of casualties in the armed forces meant that nations such as France, Germany, Russia and Britain had lost a generation of young men. Industries which had been producing weapons found it difficult to adapt to the needs of peacetime. There was no money to invest in new machinery, so factories used old working methods which were expensive and inefficient. Soldiers everywhere returned home to unemployment, poor housing, low wages and little hope for the future.

DEPRESSION In October 1929, a world wide *recession* (very bad economic conditions) set in. In the United States of America, eight or nine million workers lost their jobs. There was little or no government help for them. The number of people out of work in Germany rose to six million. This period is known as the Great Depression.

THE NEW DICTATORSHIPS In many countries, people looked for extreme solutions to their economic and political problems. Dictators, rulers with absolute power, took control in some countries. The first was Benito Mussolini, who came to power in Italy in October 1922.

People said of Mussolini that *'he made the trains run on time'*. Il Duce, as he was called, gained popular support because of his major building projects. These provided jobs at a time of unemployment, created a modern transport system, and helped Italian industry to recover. Adolf Hitler (see pp. 480–1), who came to power in Germany in 1933, adopted many of Mussolini's strategies to end unemployment and help industry.

The First World War had been called 'a war to end wars', and after it was over the Allies had set up the League of Nations, where politicians could discuss their problems instead of going to war. However, during the 1930s acts of war increased.

Italy invaded Abyssinia (Ethiopia) in 1935, using planes and modern weapons against the poorly equipped Abyssinian troops. The countries of the League of Nations reduced trade with Italy as a punishment, but this did not stop Italy from adding the independent African state to its small overseas empire.

In 1936 civil war broke out in Spain between the republican government and right wing forces led by General Franco. Britain gave financial aid to Franco and

Right. In Spain, the artist Pablo Picasso captures the world's horror at the killing of innocent civilians in an air raid on the town of Guernica during the Spanish civil war.

Below. General Franco led a fascist revolt against the legitimate left wing republican Spanish government. Franco took over as a dictator in 1939 and ruled until his death in 1975.

Prohibition

On 28 October 1920, the National Prohibition Act became law in the USA. Its aim was to prohibit the making, distribution and sale of alcohol, and it was passed because drunkenness was a widespread social problem among the working classes. A strong religious lobby thought alcohol was evil and should be banned.

Instead of making America a safer place to live, the Prohibition laws actually led to violent gang warfare as rival interests, including the Mafia, sought to gain control of the lucrative but illegal business of distilling and selling alcohol.

The law enforcement agencies and the Government finally realized that the Prohibition laws could not be enforced and they were repealed in 1933.

Italian East Africa 1935

The invasion and dividing-up of the Horn of Africa proved more difficult than the European invaders expected. The Italians colonized Eritrea to the north and Italian Somaliland to the east.

ERITREA
RED SEA
FRENCH SOMALILAND
BRITISH SOMALILAND
ADDIS ABABA
ETHIOPA
ITALIAN SOMALILAND
UGANDA
KENYA

Italian conquests 1935–1936

Germany lent him tanks, planes and pilots, which helped to give him victory three years later.

THE OLD WORLD POWERS During the 1920s and 1930s, Britain and the USA paid no attention to the increasing signs of aggression from the new rising powers within Europe and the Far East.

Meanwhile, the Soviet Union under Stalin (see p. 475) was trying to become an industrial power to compete with the countries of western Europe and North America. Stalin forced small landowners to give up their farms so that they could be joined together to make large *collectivized* farms. New farming methods could then be used to make these farms more productive. Reforms were forced upon the Soviet people and anyone who resisted Stalin was executed or sent into exile in Siberia. During the same period, China suffered a long civil war, in which Jiang Jeshi's government troops fought with Communist forces.

In Italy, Benito Mussolini, Il Duce, rekindled his country's pride through a military-style dictatorship. He provided jobs in a time of high unemployment by starting major building projects. Mussolini came to power in October 1922 following his 'march on Rome' – an armed demonstration that forced Italy's King Victor Emmanuel III to grant him absolute power.

THE RISE OF ADOLF HITLER

The Great Depression which hit all of the Western world in the 1920s and early 1930s was even worse in Germany, because it was paying off heavy debts after the First World War. Prices rose so fast that banknotes became almost worthless. The German people were desperate for a solution to their problems.

THE NAZI PARTY The National Socialist, or Nazi, Party led by Adolf Hitler was rapidly gaining popularity. Hitler blamed low wages and high unemployment on the Jewish businesses in Germany. He organized a small private army called the SA, or Sturm Abteilungen. Dressed in their brown shirts and jack boots, the SA acted as guards at Nazi rallies and beat up Communists and Jews.

In 1925, Hitler used the SA to try to overthrow the state government of Bavaria and seize power. The attempt failed and he was jailed for three years, during which time he wrote a book about his political ideas. It was called *Mein Kampf*, 'My Struggle', and it became a bestseller. Because Hitler was violently opposed to Communism, he was able to make an alliance with the weak Catholic Centre Party. After the 1932 elections, the Nazis and the Centre Party formed a government. Hitler was made chancellor, or prime minister.

THE NAZIS SEIZE POWER In 1933 the German parliament building, the Reichstag, was burnt to the ground, probably by the SA. Hitler said that it was a Communist plot, using this as an excuse to extend his powers and end democracy in Germany.

Above. Adolf Hitler addresses his massed armies at Nuremburg in 1938. In less than a year he was to take his country to war.

Germany in 1919

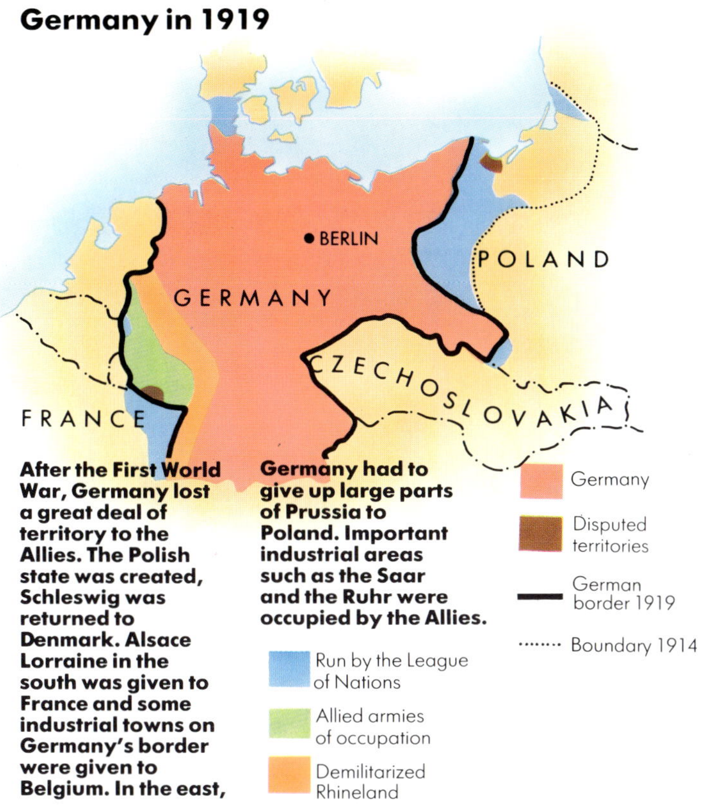

After the First World War, Germany lost a great deal of territory to the Allies. The Polish state was created, Schleswig was returned to Denmark. Alsace Lorraine in the south was given to France and some industrial towns on Germany's border were given to Belgium. In the east, Germany had to give up large parts of Prussia to Poland. Important industrial areas such as the Saar and the Ruhr were occupied by the Allies.

Germany in 1933–39

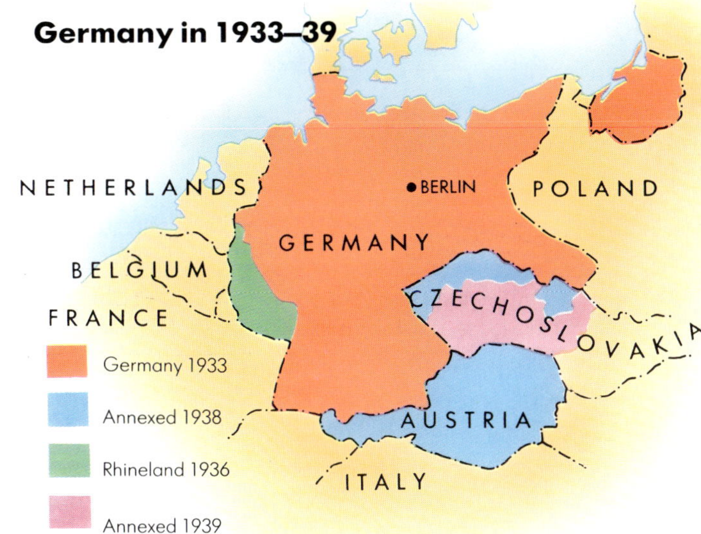

Hitler aimed to recapture German land lost to the Allies after the First World War. He claimed that any countries which had German-speaking communities should become part of the Reich to extend the sway of the Aryan race which he believed was superior. The return of the Saar to German rule in January 1935 marked the beginning of Hitler's ambitions to conquer territory in Europe. In 1938, he annexed Austria. Czechoslovakia was invaded in March 1939 and in May the Germans took over the free port of Danzig. Finally Hitler invaded Poland on 1 September, triggering the Second World War.

But Hitler could not be sure of total power while the SA was strong enough to stage a *coup* and overthrow him. On 30 June 1934, 'Night of the Long Knives', Hitler ordered loyal Nazis to assassinate key members of the SA. Hundreds of SA troopers were killed.

GERMANY PREPARES FOR WAR Hitler then set about building up his armed forces, buying weapons and introducing conscription so that all young men spent a certain amount of time in the armed forces. He wanted to recover the lands that Germany had been forced to give up after the 1914–1918 war. In 1935, Germany regained the Saar area from the French. A year later, German forces re-occupied the Rhineland.

In 1938, Hitler sent tanks into Vienna and forced Austria to agree to be united with Germany. In that same year he said he would take over the Sudetenland, the part of Czechoslovakia that bordered Germany, where about three million German-speaking people lived. The leaders of France, Britain and Italy agreed not to prevent a Germany invasion of Czechoslovakia.

Hitler believed he could not be stopped in his ambition to expand Germany. He now turned his attention to Poland, which in 1919 had been granted a strip of land that gave it access to the port of Danzig. Called the Polish corridor, this strip of land divided the German state of Prussia into two. Hitler demanded that Danzig be handed over to Germany, together with the right to travel through the Polish corridor. Poland refused, and Britain and France guaranteed their support if Germany attacked.

On 1 September 1939 German troops poured into Poland, and as a result Britain and France declared war on Germany.

STADT KÖLN SERIE A
GUTSCHEIN ÜBER
EINE
BILLION
MARK

Left. Runaway inflation meant German notes lost their value almost as soon as they were printed.

Above. Hitler's brownshirts forced Jews to perform menial tasks, such as cleaning the streets by hand.

THE DOMINATION OF EUROPE

The Second World War was sparked off by Germany's invasion of Poland. But, although they declared war on Germany, there was nothing Britain and France could do to help the Poles.

Germany's armies used new tactics called blitzkrieg: lightning war. First, they sent in dive-bombers to do as much damage as possible. Then they attacked by land, using tanks followed by infantry. An hour after the German invasion of Poland, the city of Warsaw had been bombed and half the Polish airforce had been destroyed before it had even taken off. Within a month, Germany had taken over Poland.

THE 'PHONEY WAR' British troops were sent to France to help fight against the expected German attack. But nothing happened immediately. This period is often called the 'phoney war'. People wondered what was going to happen. In Britain, civilians were given gas masks and children were sent from the towns to the countryside in case of a surprise bomb attack.

Then, in April 1940, Germany invaded neutral Norway and Denmark. This was to stop Britain's navy from attacking the supplies of iron ore that Germany obtained from Sweden.

GERMANY ON THE ATTACK After the First World War, France had built a heavily fortified wall along its border with Germany, in case of attack. This wall was known as the Maginot Line. However, in May 1940 German panzer, or tank, divisions rolled through Belgium and the Netherlands, so bypassing the Maginot Line. British and French troops moved north into Belgium to fight, but were surrounded by German panzer forces which had moved through the Ardennes forest. The British and French retreated towards the coast and escaped from Dunkirk to Britain.

After this, Field Marshal Pétain, the leader of France, signed a cease-fire agreement with Germany. France was divided in two. The northern zone was under German military rule and the southern zone was governed by a French government set up at Vichy but controlled by Germany.

BRITAIN STANDS ALONE Britain became the centre of resistance to Hitler's Germany. Members of European

The Spitfire

The Supermarine Spitfire (below left), designed by Reginald Joseph Mitchell, and the Hawker Hurricane enabled a small number of British pilots to gain control of the skies from the many German bombers and fighters, including the Messerschmidt 109 (above left), sent to destroy them.

Europe under Hitler

The map shows the extent of German occupied territory in Europe 1939–1945. Hitler had expanded his empire to its greatest extent right across Europe in November 1942.

Axis and satellite territories

Axis occupied territories

Opponents of the Axis Powers

Neutral countries

The Ghetto

Warsaw, the capital of Poland, was almost completely destroyed by the German army in the Second World War. The Germans surrounded the city in 1939 and the city was badly damaged in the siege. The German troops terrorized the people of Warsaw. They arrested thousands and killed many without trial. They put about 500,000 Jews in a small area called the ghetto. Many died from disease or were killed by the Germans.

governments who had fled from their own countries to Britain encouraged their citizens to help defeat Nazism. People who had managed to escape from occupied France and Poland fought alongside the British forces.

Britain itself was attacked, too. Between 15 August and 15 September 1940, German bombers raided British cities and airfields as the first stage in a planned invasion. These air attacks were known as the Battle of Britain and they ended in victory for the Royal Air Force (RAF). Although the German planes outnumbered the British by two to one, they lost almost twice as many aircraft as the British. Finally their losses forced them to abandon these major bombing raids.

The RAF owed its success partly to the fast and manoeuvrable Spitfire aeroplane. The pilots who fought in the Battle of Britain were known as the 'Few'. Many of them were killed.

At sea, British and neutral merchant ships came under increasing attack from the German submarines, the U-boats. For a long time it looked as if Germany would succeed in cutting the vital supplies of food and raw materials imported into Britain from overseas.

Survivor of the Blitz! German bombs destroyed most of London's centre and East End but St Paul's Cathedral escaped destruction.

The Germans overran Europe with blitzkrieg, lightning war, tactics. Rapidly advancing tanks broke down enemy resistance while infantry followed quickly behind. In this way the German army quickly overran Poland. Following the invasion of Denmark and Norway, German armies overran the Netherlands, Belgium and Luxembourg in May 1940. In the following month the defeat of the French army gave Hitler control of most of Western Europe.

THE WORLD AT WAR

Above. US Marines come ashore during the Pacific war.

Right. This Russian cartoon shows how the Allies would defeat Hitler by fighting Germany on all fronts.

By the end of 1940, Hitler thought that Britain was no longer a threat to his ambitions. He turned his attention to the Soviet Union.

Besides hating Communism, Hitler believed that the Slavs and Russians were inferior to German people. He wanted to take their territory and turn them into slaves to work for the expansion of Germany.

OPERATION BARBAROSSA In 1939, Germany and the Soviet Union had made an agreement not to fight each other, but in June 1941 Hitler turned his back on this agreement and launched Operation Barbarossa: the invasion of the Soviet Union.

Hitler started his campaign hoping for a quick victory. But even though the German army was much better organized and better equipped than the Soviets, the invasion used up valuable German resources and caused heavy casualties. It was on the battlefields of Russia that Germany began to lose the war.

Right. The Allies' main tank in the last part of the war was the American-built Sherman.

THE NORTH AFRICA CAMPAIGN
Italy joined the war as Germany's ally on 10 July 1940. The alliance was called the *Axis*. Italy's dictator, Mussolini, was keen to share in Germany's victories.

In September 1940, Italian forces entered Egypt, where the British had a small army protecting the Suez Canal, which was a vital link between Britain and its empire. The British army soon pushed the poorly-trained and badly-equipped Italians back into Libya, taking thousands of prisoners.

Hitler sent troops and tanks, commanded by General Rommel, to fight in North Africa. For the next two years British and Axis forces fought for control of the area. General Montgomery's Eighth Army finally defeated Rommel's Afrika Corps at El Alamein in Egypt in October 1942.

By the end of that year, the British had defeated the Italian navy, which allowed them to cut off German supplies to North Africa. Allied forces landed in Algeria and Morocco and linked up with Montgomery's forces. The Axis forces in North Africa surrendered in the following May.

AMERICA ENTERS THE WAR After the Japanese attack on the US Pacific fleet at Pearl Harbor (see page 489), Germany, which was Japan's ally, declared war on the USA on 11 December 1941. Three world powers – Britain, the Soviet Union and the USA – were now ranged against Germany. But it was not easy to defeat Germany. The USA had to fight in the East as well as in Europe. Britain and the USA also had to send supplies to the Soviets to help them fight Germany.

By the end of 1941 the Germans had got within sight of Moscow.

The War in Europe 1942–1945

Left. Operation Overlord was launched against beaches in Normandy in 1944.

Left. The Allied offensive in Europe began with the invasion of Italy and the landings in Northern France. To the east the Russians broke through the German lines in Poland in January 1945. On March 7 the Allied armies crossed the river Rhine into Germany, and on May 1 as Soviet forces entered the city of Berlin, Hitler and his wife Eva Braun committed suicide in his bunker.

Right. Infantry uniforms of the Second World War. From left to right, the United States of America, Germany, Britain, Italy and USSR. Many soldiers who had escaped from their own countries, such as Poles, fought in special units with the Allied forces.

THE TIDE TURNS

One of the most savage air raids of the war. In a single night, Dresden was flattened by Allied bombing.

After the Axis forces in North Africa surrendered in May 1943, the way was clear for the Allies to push into Italy and begin to fight the Germans and Italians in a different area. This was the second front that Stalin had been asking for.

THE ALLIES LAND IN ITALY The invasion of the island of Sicily began in July and the Axis forces did not do much to resist it. Mussolini's close advisers told him to resign. A new Italian government approached the Allies to ask for peace.

Allied forces moved to the mainland of Italy and began a rapid advance. By the beginning of 1944, they had reached Rome. But their advance was slowed down by a German army which was determined to hold on to northern Italy. Mussolini was still the ruler there, although he was now controlled by the Germans.

DEFEAT IN RUSSIA After the German forces were pushed back from Moscow at the end of 1941 (see p. 484), Hitler moved his armies south to capture the oil fields of the Caucasus. By the autumn of 1942, he had decided to take the city of Stalingrad (Volgograd).

The Germans besieged the city and bombarded it with *artillery*, heavy field guns. Although they were outnumbered by three to one, the Soviet forces held on to the city, fighting ferociously. In late November, more Soviet troops arrived to relieve the city. It was the Germans' turn to be surrounded. In an attack that lasted from 10 January to 2 February 1943 Soviet troops killed 100,000 German soldiers and took a further 110,000 prisoner. Of those taken prisoner, most died because of the harsh conditions in which they were kept.

The following year the Soviets defeated a major German attack. For the first time in the war they also

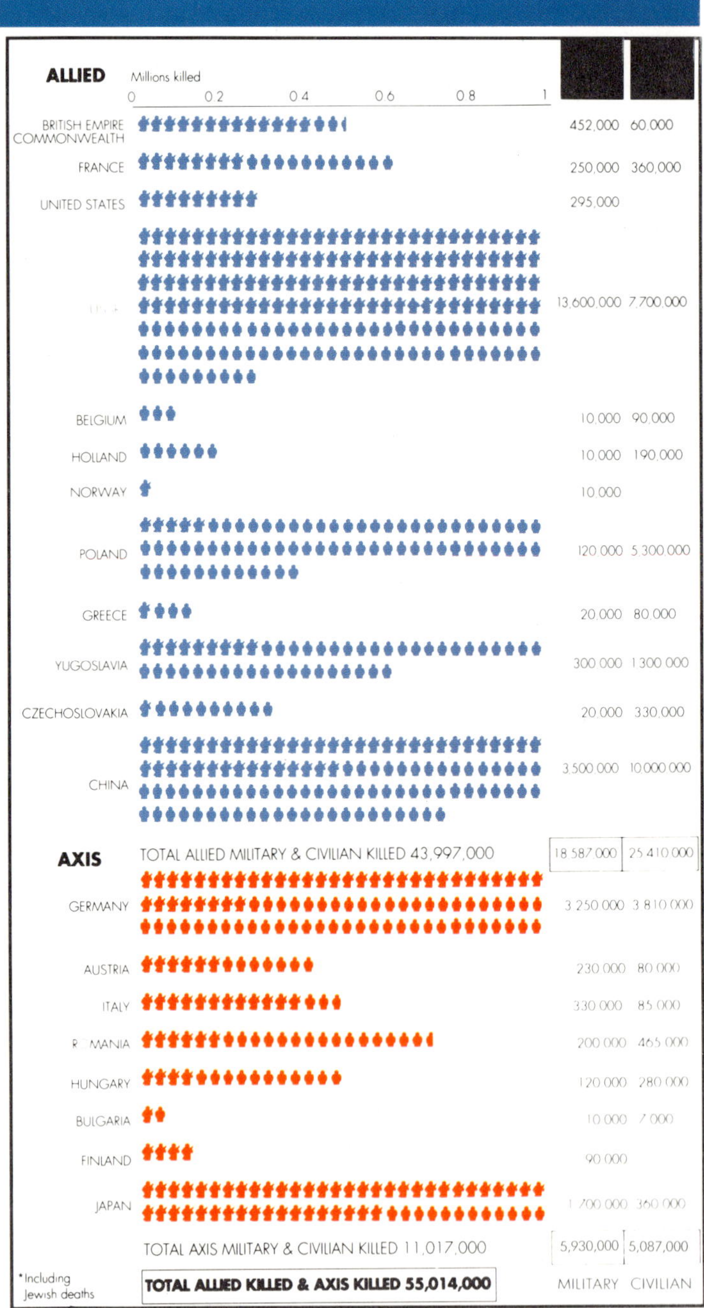

The USSR suffered by far the highest casualty rate of any country fighting in the Second World War, both in military and civilian terms. Poland lost a great number of civilians.

The Holocaust

Hitler wanted to create a strong German master-race of fair-haired blue-eyed 'Aryans', so he set about eliminating people he thought were racially inferior, like the Jews and the gypsies, and also the disabled and mentally handicapped.

But it was the Jews who attracted his particular hatred. Like many other Germans, he resented Jewish businessmen whom he thought were conspiring to rob German people of money and jobs. Hitler planned to kill all the Jews in Europe, in what he called the 'final solution to the Jewish question'.

Prisoners in a concentration camp cheer the soldiers freeing them.

The Germans hated the Jews so much that when Hitler started persecuting them, hardly anyone protested at the terrible cruelty and injustice. First, he took away their rights as citizens. Then he made them live in separate areas called ghettoes. Finally, he began a deliberate programme to exterminate the Jews by taking them away to special *concentration camps* in Eastern Europe, where they were kept in the most dreadful conditions before being gassed, shot, tortured or dying from disease and starvation.

By the end of the war in 1945, Hitler's SS has murdered around six million innocent Jews.

The Attempt to Kill Hitler

On the morning of 20 July 1944, a German officer planted a bomb hidden in a briefcase under the table where Hitler and his generals were planning their military campaign. Minutes later there was an enormous explosion.

Thinking Hitler had been killed, Colonel Claus von Stauffenburg telephoned his fellow conspirators in Berlin.

But the table had turned away the full force of the blast and Hitler was only slightly injured. The conspirators were quickly arrested and some of them, including von Stauffenburg, were shot.

During the Allied campaign to liberate Italy from fascist rule, Italian troops changed sides while German forces counter-attacked and hindered the Allied advance. Allied troops invaded Sicily in July 1943 then southern Italy in September. Despite more Allied landings, Rome was not taken until 4 June.

launched an attack first, forcing the Germans to withdraw.

Supplies were now getting through to the Soviet army, partly because of Allied aid and partly because of great increases in industrial production. The Red Army began a march westwards that only ended when it reached Berlin, the German capital.

OPERATION OVERLORD Just before dawn on 6 June 1944, the Allies landed on five beaches in Normandy, northern France. They had previously spread false information about what they were going to do, so the Germans were expecting them to land further to the east. The first troops ashore soon won through. By the end of the day, 156,000 men had landed in Normandy. More and more Allied troops poured into Europe, forcing the German army to withdraw.

Although the Germans were now certain to be defeated, Hitler launched a campaign of bomb and rocket attacks on Britain. In reply, the Allies stepped up their bombing raids on German cities like Hamburg and Dresden, hoping to end the war more quickly.

On 23 April 1945, Mussolini was captured and shot by Italians who were opposed to his rule. Shortly afterwards the German forces in Italy surrendered. On 30 April 1945, with Soviet troops already entering Berlin, Adolf Hitler shot himself. Eight days later, his successor, Admiral Doenitz, surrendered to the Allies. The war in Europe was over.

THE RISING SUN

The War in the East

Above. The extent of Japan's conquests. Most of the territory was taken in just six months of fighting. From 1943 their overstretched forces were forced to retreat.

Above. US warships are sunk at Pearl Harbor in a surprise attack that signalled the outbreak of war with Japan.
Right. Japanese suicide pilots sacrificed their lives to defend their country.

In the years between the two world wars, Japan rose from a backward feudal nation to become an industrialized world power with a fast-growing population. Yet Japan's system of government was old-fashioned and undemocratic, headed by an emperor who was regarded as a god.

THE ARMY TAKES CONTROL In 1936, army officers took control of the government, with the approval of the emperor. During the late 1930s, Japan took advantage of the civil war in China (see page 506), conquering large sections of that country. Japanese troops treated the Chinese brutally, killing 250,000 civilians in the city of Nanjing alone.

When war broke out in Europe, Japan realized that a weakened British Empire would be unable to prevent it from extending its influence in the Far East and the Pacific.

The United States of America responded to Japanese attempts at expansion by announcing that it would not export any more oil to Japan until the Japanese withdrew all their troops from China. Discussions between the two countries failed to reach an agreement on this issue, and Japan began to consider a military solution to its problems.

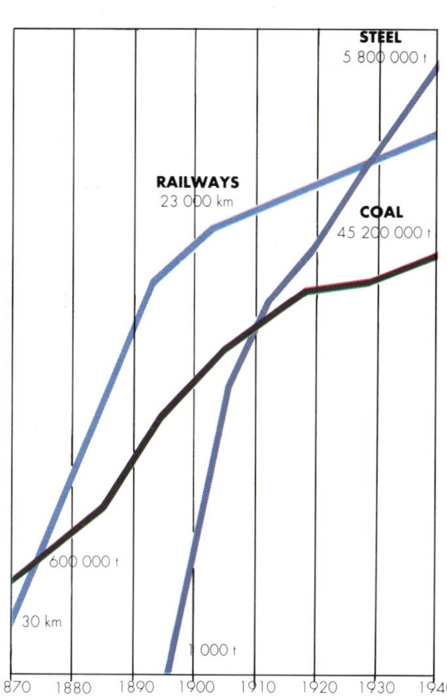

Japanese Industry

Today, manufacturing industry is the most important area of work in Japan. At the turn of the century, the Japanese were not able to produce large amounts of steel, a vital part of building up their country. Between 1900 and 1940 the output of steel rose 1000%, helping to build railways which covered more of the country every year.

Right. The American B29 Superfortress with the atomic bombs used against Japan. In the last stages of the war, waves of bombers rained destruction on Japan's industrial cities.

Below. The first atomic bomb destroyed the city of Hiroshima on 6 August 1945.

Rebuilding Japan

The post-war recovery of Japan was extremely slow but it was helped by an American aid programme. Japan was eventually allowed to rebuild her large industrial companies which had been disbanded after the war. From about 1947 onwards Japan was allowed a limited amount of international trade. Under the terms of her surrender Japan was not allowed to keep an army – and this condition remains unaltered today. But not keeping an army, means Japan has not had to spend money on defence. This has left the country free to invest more money in rebuilding its industry and infrastructure. Japan's disadvantages eventually became its advantages.

PEARL HARBOR On 7 December 1941, Japan launched a surprise bombing raid on Pearl Harbor in Hawaii, sinking almost the entire US Pacific fleet. The following day, the United States and Britain declared war on Japan. Shortly afterwards, Germany and Italy, which were Japan's allies, declared war on the USA.

Japanese forces surprised the Allies by moving swiftly to capture Hong Kong. The following February, the British troops in Singapore surrendered to a Japanese army which had attacked after travelling through jungle that the British had thought no-one could get through.

Within six months the Japanese had conquered the Dutch East Indies, Burma, the Philippines and the islands of the South Pacific. But in June 1942 the American fleet won a decisive victory at the Battle of Midway, sinking Japan's four largest aircraft carriers.

From mid-1943 onwards, Japan's army, which was stretched over too wide an area, began to suffer defeat in the US attacks upon the Pacific islands and the British campaign in the jungle of Burma. To the Japanese, defeat meant dishonour. They would rather die than surrender. This opinion meant that they thought anyone else who surrendered had acted dishonourably. Japanese soldiers treated captured Allied soldiers like slaves and forced them to work on projects such as the Burma railway, where many died of heat, disease and hunger.

DEFEAT OF JAPAN By 1944, the Allies were able to blockade Japan, preventing ships from going in or out of Japanese ports. This meant that Japan could not obtain iron or steel, rubber or oil. As they captured more Pacific islands from the Japanese, the US airforce used them to launch bombing raids on Japanese cities.

The US navy and army advanced towards Japan and fighting became more intense. With just enough fuel left to fly their planes, the Japanese *Kamikaze* pilots flew suicide missions against US warships.

Japan still refused to surrender. On 6 August 1945, a US plane dropped the world's first atom bomb on the city of Hiroshima. Three days later, another bomb was dropped on Nagasaki. Around 160,000 Japanese civilians died in the two raids. The Soviet Union joined the Allies in the war against Japan, and the Japanese finally surrendered on 15 August 1945.

The End of the Old Order

TIME CHART

	EUROPE/USA	RUSSIA/CHINA/FAR EAST	MIDDLE EAST	REST OF THE WORLD
AD				
1901	Death of Queen Victoria			
1902				End of the Boer War in South Africa
1904>1905		Russo-Japanese war		
1905		General strike in Russia, riots in St Petersburg		
1908			Young Turks revolt overthrows Turkey's traditional leadership	
1914>1918	First World War begins with the shooting of little known Austrian Archduke Ferdinand in Serbia			
1915			Turkey enters the First World War on Germany's side	
1916	Easter Rising in Dublin – Irish challenge Britain's rule			Belgian forces occupy parts of German East Africa
1917		Russian Revolution – Bolsheviks overthrow provisional government	Balfour Declaration – Britain favours the setting up of a Jewish state in Palestine	
1918>1920		Civil war in Russia		
1919	Treaty of Versailles – USA, France and Britain demand reparation terms from a defeated Germany. League of Nations established		France is given a mandate by the League of Nations to govern Syria and Lebanon	Britain is given German East Africa which is then renamed Tanganyka (now Tanzania) In India, demonstrators are massacred at Amritsar
1922	Mussolini becomes dictator of Italy			Indian civil rights leader Gandhi is imprisoned
1928				Indian National Congress demands independence from Britain
1929	Wall Street Crash precipitates world recession	China – Mao Zedong sets up Red Army	Arab-Jewish rioting in Palestine	
1933	Hitler becomes chancellor of Germany			
1934	Roosevelt's 'New Deal' legislation introduces social and economic reforms in the USA			
1935				Italy invades Ethiopia
1936>1939	Spanish Civil War			
1937>1945		Japan invades and occupies parts of China		
1939>1945	Second World War – Germany invades Poland. Britain and France declare war on Germany			
1941		Hitler launches Operation Barbarossa, the invasion of Russia Japan declares war		
1943	Allied invasion of Italy		Italy invades Egypt from its colony in Libya	
1944	Allied invasion of Normandy			
1945	Germany surrenders on 8 May, VE Day	USA drops two atom bombs on Hiroshima and Nagasaki. Japan surrenders		

Nuclear Powers 1992

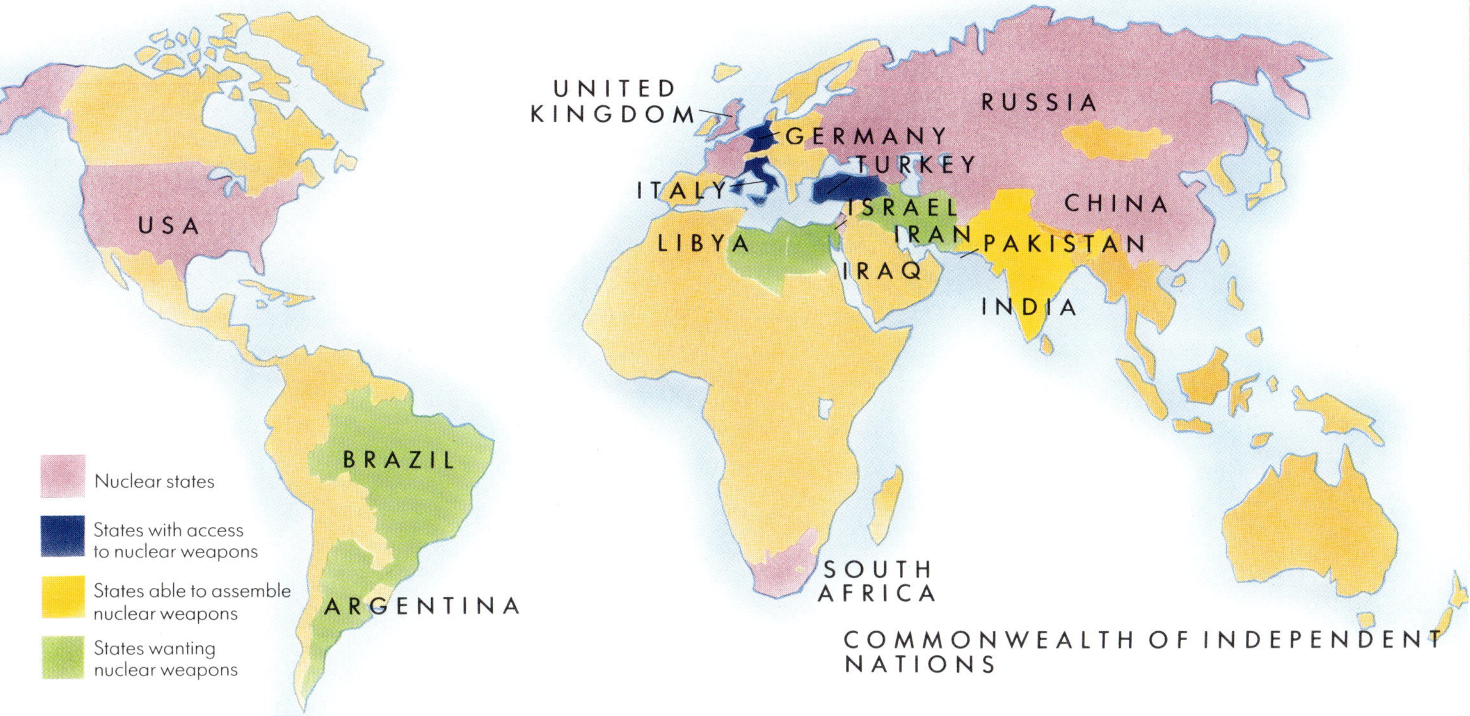

Creating a New World

The balance of world power changed dramatically after the Second World War. The United States of America and the Soviet Union emerged as super-powers and their influence was felt in every country of the world. The rivalry between the two super-powers was illustrated by the space race, in which the USA and USSR developed spacecraft and rockets that were capable of launching satellites.

Through its Marshall aid programme, which it developed in order to stop Communism from spreading, the USA helped European countries to rebuild their bombed-out factories and re-establish their industries. The countries of western Europe joined in a military alliance with the USA against the Soviet Union. This was known as the North Atlantic Treaty Organization, NATO.

In eastern Europe, behind an 'iron curtain', the Soviet Union forced its political ideas of Communism on nations such as the Baltic States, Poland, Hungary, Czechoslovakia (then one country) and Romania which had previously been independent. However, in the late 1980s Soviet power began to fade and many states were able to break away and form their own independent, democratic governments.

Outside Europe, the Middle East has been in an almost constant state of conflict. The Palestinians have been trying to recover their homeland, which became a part of the new Israeli state in 1947. The increasing strength of the Islamic religion has also brought many oil-producing Arab states into conflict with the countries of the West.

The decline of colonial powers led to former colonies, mainly in Africa and Asia, gaining their independence. In spite of being free from colonial control, most are still economically dependent on countries of the developed world and are facing huge problems in feeding and educating their people.

The challenge now facing all the peoples of the world is to find a way in which the human race can live in balance with the Earth's resources.

THE DIVISION OF EUROPE

Left. Millions of refugees trudged across Europe, trailing their few possessions in broken carts, in search of permanent homes.

Below. The three most powerful Allied leaders, Churchill, Roosevelt and Stalin, met at Yalta after the war to divide Europe into zones of influence which would stop German aggression. They decided to give part of Poland to Russia and part of East Germany became part of Poland.

At the end of the Second World War, people all over the world had to rebuild their lives.

THE RESISTERS During the war, groups of people – known as resistance movements – in countries that had been taken over by the Germans, worked against the soldiers occupying their countries. For example, they bombed trains carrying supplies to the German army. Towards the end of the war, these groups helped the Allies to free their countries from Nazi rule. Communist groups formed the core of many resistance movements. When the war ended, resistance groups temporarily governed their newly liberated countries and helped to restore civilian governments.

Resistance movements gave rough justice to people who had supported the Nazis. In France, for example, it is thought that around 5000 of these people were executed without trial.

Meanwhile, those leaders of Nazi Germany who had been captured were put on trial at Nuremburg in Germany. Altogether, 12 Nazis were sentenced to death and seven were given long prison sentences.

REFUGEES At the end of the war, there were millions of *refugees* in Europe trying to find their way home. Some of them were people who had been taken from their homes by the Germans and sent to other countries to act as slave labour, for example in factories in Germany itself. Others were Jews and political prisoners who had spent the war in *concentration camps* and were lucky to have survived. Some people had lost their homes in the fighting, or were now moving westwards because they were afraid of coming under the control of the Red Army in eastern Europe.

The Allies had to identify and care for these people, and somehow return them to their homes. This was a difficult task, as many had no papers to show where they came from.

Among all these innocent refugees there were also

Above. The fall of Berlin, 30 April 1945, liberated by the Soviets. A Russian soldier plants the red flag on top of the chancellory building, the Reichstag, in the centre of the city. Berlin suffered horribly in the final days of the war and much of it was completely destroyed.

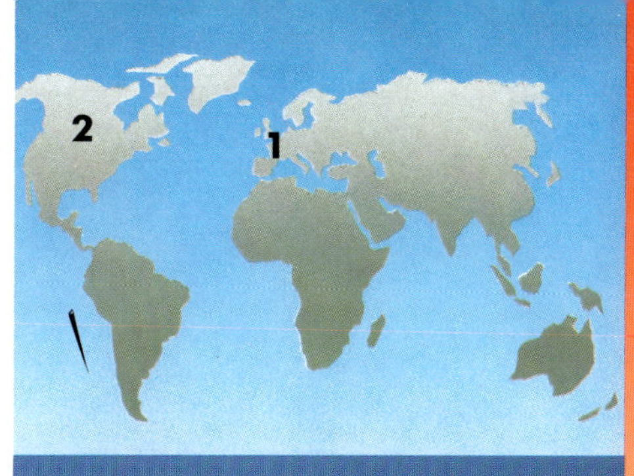

Above. Christian Dior's 'New Look': post-war women's fashions went for soft, sweeping lines when clothing eventually came off ration.

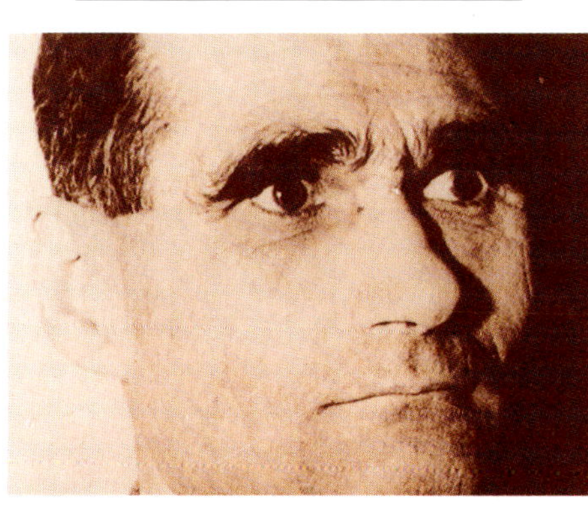

Rudolf Hess (1894–1987)

Rudolf Hess was one of the most important members of the German Nazi Party at the beginning of the war. In 1941, on the eve of the German invasion of Russia, Hess flew to Scotland to try and persuade the British to make peace with Germany. He was immediately arrested and imprisoned in the Tower of London. At the end of the war a series of trials were held to punish those who had been involved in war crimes. Hess was tried for his part in running the Nazi regime. He was found guilty and imprisoned for life.

some Nazis trying to escape from justice. Because of the confused situation, it was easy for some of these men to 'disappear', and to reappear months or years later in a different town or country, using different names. Many escaped to places such as South America, where they made new lives for themselves.

EAST AND WEST At the end of the war, Soviet troops occupied half of Germany and almost all of eastern Europe. At a conference between the Allies in 1945, President Roosevelt of the USA had promised Stalin a '*sphere of influence*' in the countries that the USSR had occupied.

The Soviets took over Latvia, Lithuania and Estonia in north-west Europe. They also encouraged the setting up of Communist governments in countries on the USSR's eastern border – Poland, Hungary, Romania and Czechoslovakia (then one country). They drew new boundaries for Poland, absorbing the eastern parts of that country into the Soviet Union and adding a large part of what was once Germany to the west.

The eastern part of Germany, which had been occupied by Soviet troops, became the Communist state of East Germany. Within East Germany, however, the city of Berlin remained under the joint control of the Allies: Britain, France, the USA and the USSR.

1 In 1949 the communists won control of the Hungarian Parliament. The new Soviet style constitution was unpopular and in 1956 riots broke out in the capital, Budapest. Some concessions were made but then Soviet troops moved in to crush the uprising and many more communist reforms followed. In 1989 Hungary returned to democratic rule.

2 In Canada in 1968 the French-speaking population of Quebec moved to become a separate state. President de Gaulle of France encouraged the split but the Canadian government remained firm in wishing to keep Quebec as part of Canada, and Prime Minister Trudeau used the police and troops to keep order.

THE COLD WAR

The 'Cold War' is the name given to the period following the Second World War when relations between the Soviet Union and the United States of America became very bad and even hostile. After the war, the countries of east and west formed themselves into two opposing groups. On the west was the North Atlantic Treaty Organization (NATO), made up of the United States of America and its European allies, including Britain and France. On the east, the USSR and the Communist states around it formed an alliance called the Warsaw Pact.

THE SPREAD OF COMMUNISM Communist groups in Europe which had helped organize resistance to the Nazis during the war (see p. 492) attracted popular support. In countries such as France and Italy, many Communists were elected as politicians and trade union organizers. The United States of America tried to prevent the spread of Communism in Europe by giving financial aid to countries which had been ruined by the war. This programme, called the Marshall Plan, was launched in June 1947.

Above. In 1955 the 8 eastern European communist governments came together to sign the Warsaw Pact. Under the agreement the armies of these states were placed under one command. A large part of the Warsaw Pact army was stationed in East Germany to act as a threat to Western Europe. These countries lay behind what Churchill called the 'iron curtain'.

The Berlin Wall

In June 1948, trouble broke out when the USSR tried to blockade the Allied-controlled sectors of Berlin to force the British and American occupying forces to leave. Berlin was cut off from West Germany but Allied aircraft flew in food and essential supplies.

The Berlin airlift lasted until May 1949 when the Soviets re-opened the borders. However, in 1961 the Soviets built a high fortified wall around their sector of the city. Many east Berliners were shot trying to escape over the wall to the freedom of the West. The notorious Berlin Wall was finally removed in 1989.

Above. Soviet tanks set up a road block in the city of Prague. When Czechoslovakia threatened to leave the Soviet Union in 1968, the Red Army was sent to restore Soviet rule and to depose the Czech president, Alexander Dubcek, who had tried to break away from Soviet control.

THE IRON CURTAIN In 1948 the USSR encouraged a revolution in Czechoslovakia which brought in a Communist government. Every country in eastern Europe now had a Communist government, all controlled from Moscow. The Soviets tried to stop people in these countries from going to western Europe. The British prime minister, Winston Churchill, compared this to *'an iron curtain'* coming down across Europe.

The USA and its European allies were determined to halt the spread of Communism in Europe and around the world. The Cold War started in 1948, when the Soviets besieged the western part of Berlin which was controlled by Britain, France and the USA. The West responded by flying in supplies.

The first open conflict between Communist and Western forces was the Korean War, which began in 1950. The Communist army of North Korea, supported by the USSR and China, invaded South Korea. The USA sent troops to support the South Koreans. The North Koreans were defeated in 1953.

THE ARMS RACE In 1949 the Soviets successfully tested a nuclear bomb. This was the start of a race between the USSR and USA to see who could build the most nuclear weapons.

Technology developed for space travel became part of the arms race. In 1957, the USSR launched the satellite *Sputnik I* into orbit around the Earth. It was now possible to build a rocket with a nuclear warhead that could hit a target accurately from a long distance. The Americans and the Soviets stationed missiles in Europe that were aimed at each other. The ever-increasing number of missiles made the risk of a third world war seem more likely.

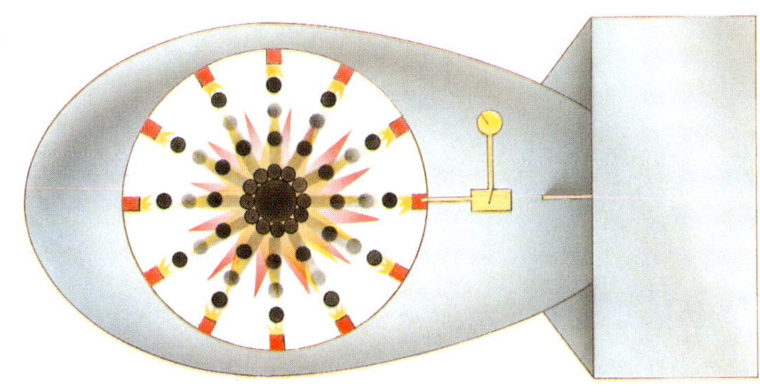

An atomic bomb, like the ones dropped on Hiroshima and Nagasaki in 1945. Both the USA and the USSR made enough weapons to destroy the Earth many times over.

TREATIES The Nuclear Test Ban Treaty of 1963 was the first step in a gradual process of talks between the USSR and the USA about the development of nuclear weapons. Both sides began to reduce their numbers of these weapons after the first Strategic Arms Limitation Talks, SALT 1 in 1972.

In spite of regular talks, the Cold War continued to exist between the two world powers for many years. However, after Mikhail Gorbachev became leader of the USSR in 1985, these attitudes began to change. Partly because they believed Gorbachev was making efforts to improve life in the Soviet Union for his people, the USA trusted him more. The Cold War came to an end.

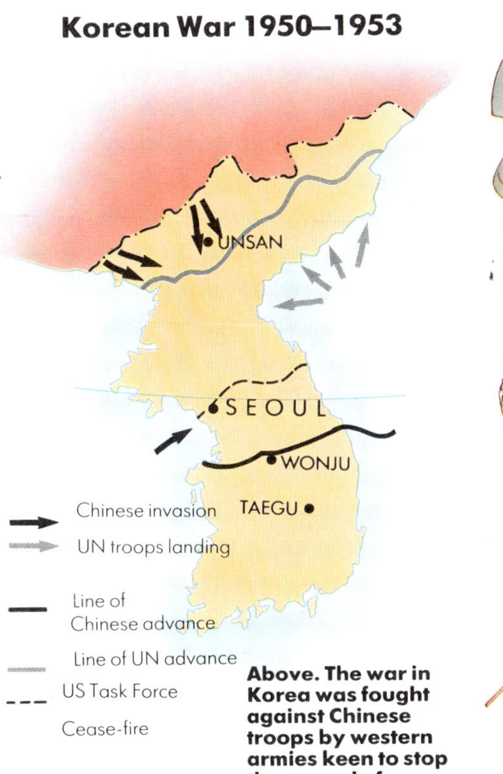

Above. The war in Korea was fought against Chinese troops by western armies keen to stop the spread of communism.

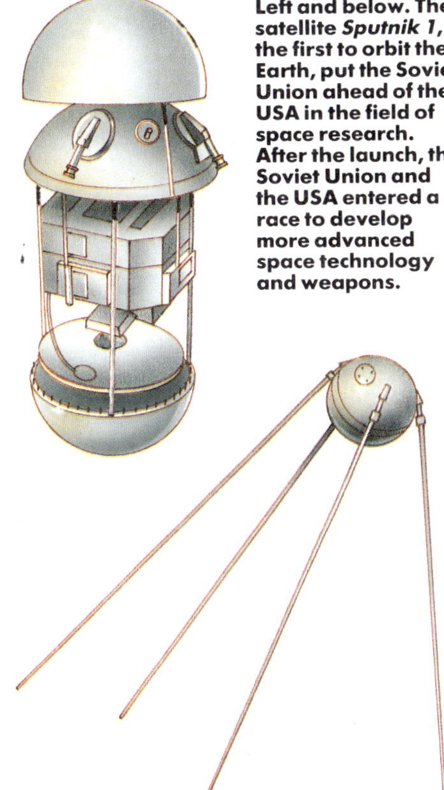

Left and below. The satellite *Sputnik 1*, the first to orbit the Earth, put the Soviet Union ahead of the USA in the field of space research. After the launch, the Soviet Union and the USA entered a race to develop more advanced space technology and weapons.

Gorbachev

In 1985, Mikhail Gorbachev was elected leader of the Soviet Union. He wanted to change the Soviet political system through *perestroika*, restructuring, and *glasnost*, openness. Following electoral reforms, East European peoples held democratic elections in 1989 and got rid of their communist leaders, and East and West Germany were reunited.

Gorbachev achieved reductions in nuclear and conventional weapons through talks with US President Reagan. He pledged a return to a capitalist system, but lost power in 1992.

THE DECLINE OF EMPIRES

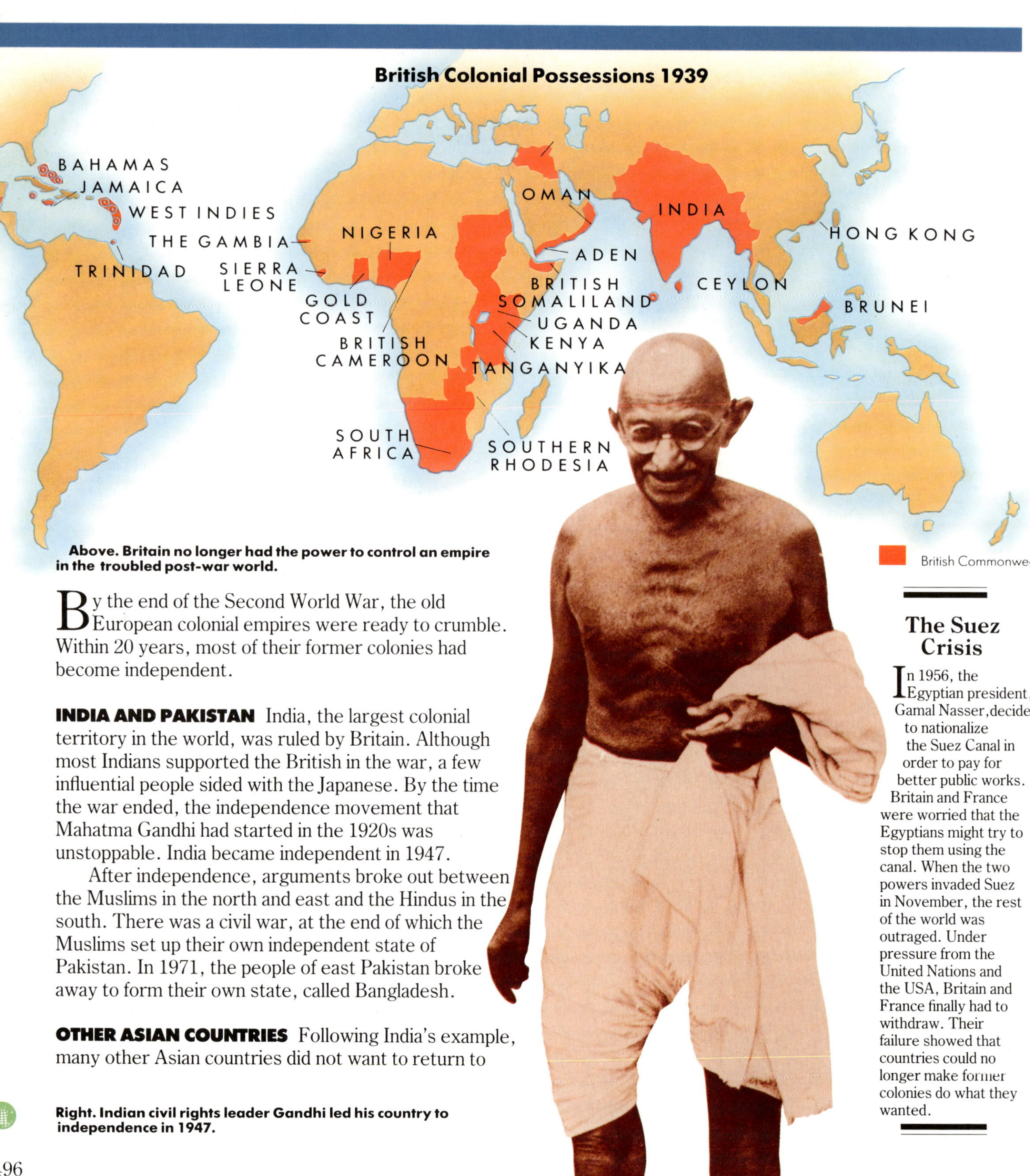

Above. Britain no longer had the power to control an empire in the troubled post-war world.

By the end of the Second World War, the old European colonial empires were ready to crumble. Within 20 years, most of their former colonies had become independent.

INDIA AND PAKISTAN India, the largest colonial territory in the world, was ruled by Britain. Although most Indians supported the British in the war, a few influential people sided with the Japanese. By the time the war ended, the independence movement that Mahatma Gandhi had started in the 1920s was unstoppable. India became independent in 1947.

After independence, arguments broke out between the Muslims in the north and east and the Hindus in the south. There was a civil war, at the end of which the Muslims set up their own independent state of Pakistan. In 1971, the people of east Pakistan broke away to form their own state, called Bangladesh.

OTHER ASIAN COUNTRIES Following India's example, many other Asian countries did not want to return to

Right. Indian civil rights leader Gandhi led his country to independence in 1947.

The Suez Crisis

In 1956, the Egyptian president, Gamal Nasser, decided to nationalize the Suez Canal in order to pay for better public works. Britain and France were worried that the Egyptians might try to stop them using the canal. When the two powers invaded Suez in November, the rest of the world was outraged. Under pressure from the United Nations and the USA, Britain and France finally had to withdraw. Their failure showed that countries could no longer make former colonies do what they wanted.

The Mau Mau

From 1952 until 1956, the Mau Mau, an African group dedicated to removing the British, directed terrorist attacks against white settlers in the British colony of Kenya. Many settlers and their families were killed and their farms were set ablaze. Britain sent troops to track down the killers and the Mau Mau leader, Jomo Kenyatta was imprisoned. In 1961, Kenyatta was released from prison. Three years later, he became Kenya's first president after winning democratic elections. Meanwhile the British colonies in Africa were gaining their independence. Ghana was first to go in 1957, followed by Nigeria (1960), Tanganyika and Sierra Leone (1961), Uganda (1962) and The Gambia (1963).

Left. The French president General de Gaulle granted independence to the former French colonies Morocco and Tunisia in 1956. Britain set the pace for decolonization before the Second World War by granting independence to Canada, Australia, New Zealand and South Africa, then to India and Pakistan in 1947. Gradually the empires began to change to allow peoples the freedom to govern themselves.

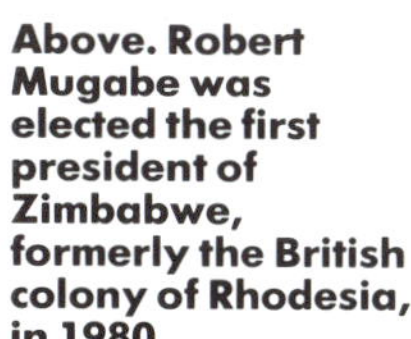

Above. Robert Mugabe was elected the first president of Zimbabwe, formerly the British colony of Rhodesia, in 1980.

Western rule in 1945. A rebellion in Indonesia led to independence from the Netherlands in 1949. In Indo-China, the Communists rebelled against their French rulers. The French, supported by the USA, fought back but were defeated at the Battle of Dien Bien Phu in 1953 and were forced to leave. Indo-China was broken up to form Cambodia (Kampuchea), Laos and Vietnam.

Malaysia became independent from Britain in 1957. Now the only British colony in Asia is Hong Kong, which is due to be returned to Chinese rule in 1997.

AFRICA After the Second World War, the Allies freed Italy's former African colonies, Ethiopia and Libya. France granted independence to Morocco and Tunisia after rebellions there. But the French settlers in Algeria, who made up 10 per cent of the population there, were fiercely opposed to any move towards Arab independence. The result was a war between the settlers and the Algerians that lasted four years and cost many lives. The defeated white settlers finally had to leave the country.

In many African countries, white settlers not only governed the country but also controlled its economy, legal system and armed forces. When these countries became independent, they had to begin to rebuild all these systems and that sometimes led to problems. For example, after independence, there were civil wars in the former Belgian Congo, now Zaïre, and Nigeria.

RHODESIA AND SOUTH AFRICA Algeria was not the only country where the white settlers wanted to remain in control. In 1965, for example, Rhodesia rejected Britain's plans for its independence and the white government remained in place. The Africans in Rhodesia were kept out of power. Finally, after talks with the British government and African politicians, Rhodesia was renamed Zimbabwe and a democracy was set up in 1980.

South Africa was once part of the British Empire. Its white government voted to leave the Commonwealth and become a republic in 1961, because it did not want to share its power with the black South Africans.

Other countries tried to persuade the country's white politicians to introduce changes to the country. Many countries refused to sell certain items, such as weapons, to the South African government until it agreed to allow black people to vote. In the early 1990s the government finally relaxed its *apartheid* policy. The first black president, Nelson Mandela, was elected in 1994.

INTERNATIONAL UNITY

Above. A United Nations peacekeeping force keeps warring Greek and Turkish factions apart in Cyprus.

At the end of the First World War, the League of Nations (see p. 478) was set up to help solve problems between countries, but it was not successful. Since the Second World War, other international organizations have replaced it.

THE UNITED NATIONS The United Nations (UN) was founded in 1944. Representatives of countries meet to discuss international problems. Its aim is to reduce tension in the world and thus make war less likely.

The UN is headed by a secretary-general who is elected to lead the UN for five years. The General Assembly is made up of representatives from every country. If a majority of nations criticize the behaviour of one member state, this can put pressure on that state to behave differently. In 1956, for example, the UN condemned France and Britain for invading Egypt over the Suez Canal (see p. 496). This succeeded in preventing a war.

The UN Security Council has 11 members. Five of these – the USA, Russia, Great Britain, France and China – are permanent members. They can vote to take action against a member nation, or to send an armed force to keep the peace in an area where war is likely to break out. For example, UN troops were sent to Cyprus in 19XX to prevent a civil war between the Greek and Turkish communities.

But the UN has not always been successful. For instance, it could not prevent conflicts which involved the interests of the USA or the USSR. This is because any decision by the Security Council has to be unanimous: every member must agree with it. Each member has the right to veto, or say no to, any of the council's proposals. The USA and the USSR often used their vetoes in the past to protect their own interests.

The former Allies failed to agree on common aims once Germany had been defeated.

SETTING UP THE EEC After the damage done by the Second World War, the European countries needed to rebuild their bombed factories and start manufacturing goods for export. Some politicians called for western European countries to work together to re-establish trade links. This led to the Treaty of Rome in 1957,

The European Union

The United Nations

The United Nations has a number of specialized agencies which were set up to deal with major world problems.

The World Health Organization (WHO) aims to eradicate killer diseases such as malaria and AIDS and improve the health of people all over the world through immunization and education programmes.

The United Nations Educational, Scientific and Cultural Organization (UNESCO) is working to put an end to illiteracy and to ensure that people all over the world are given a basic education free.

The Food and Agriculture Organization (FAO) seeks to raise standards of nutrition by improving the quantity and quality of foods available around the world.

The Red Cross

The International Red Cross is an organisation dedicated to the relief of human suffering. Each country has an individual branch, but all work together to help others. The Red Cross was founded by a Swiss man called Jean Hentri Dunant. He had witnessed the suffering of the wounded in the Austro-Sardinian war, and he wanted to find a way to help others in this situation. In 1863 a group of delegates met in Geneva to discuss the idea of an organisation, and by 1864 the First Geneva (Red Cross) Convention had been signed by 12 European nations. The convention laid down the way that prisoners-of-war should be treated and how the wounded should be helped. The symbol of the Red Cross, the red cross on a white background is the reverse of the Swiss flag in honour of the founder.

which set up the European Economic Community (EEC). The Treaty was signed by six countries – Belgium, the Netherlands, Luxembourg, France, West Germany and Italy. Its main aim was to make it easier for these states to trade with each other. For instance, most countries put a tax on goods that are imported from other countries. The EEC wanted to abolish these taxes.

The six countries set up a European Parliament in Brussels, Belgium, to discuss matters that concerned all of them. They also set up a European Court in Strasbourg in France, to which people living in EEC countries could complain if they thought their country was treating them unfairly.

FROM THE SIX TO THE 12 In 1973 Britain, Ireland and Denmark joined the EEC. Since then, Spain, Portugal and Greece have also joined, bringing the number of members up to 12.

The EEC is now usually called the EU – the European Union – because it is no longer only interested in trade. It has become more involved in political issues relating to member states.

1 In 1979 the Soviet Union sent its troops into the Asian republic of Afghanistan. They set up a leader sympathetic to the communists and claimed that they were invited guests of the new government. The Afghans waged a guerrilla war against the occupying forces and in 1989 the Soviet troops withdrew. They were beaten by American funded groups of Islamic fighters called Mujahadeen, who then became locked in a civil war to find out who would run the country after the Russians had gone.

2 In 1982 the Argentine army invaded the Falkland Islands, which are British territory. The invasion was a result of a long dispute over who owned what the Argentinians called the Malvinas. The British government sent a task force to recapture the Islands. They landed on the Islands and after fierce fighting they defeated the poorly-equipped Argentinian army, and re-took Port Stanley, the capital. This defeat led to the downfall of the military regime in Argentina and saw a return to democratic government.

ISRAEL AND THE ARAB WORLD

American president Jimmy Carter, centre, brings together Egyptian leader Anwar Sadat, left, and Israeli president Menachem Begin, right, for peace talks at Camp David.

The Jewish State of Israel has only been in existence since 1948, but for most of its short life it has been in conflict with its Arab neighbours. The reasons for the dispute can be traced back to the defeat of Turkey's Ottoman Empire in the First World War, when the League of Nations put Britain temporarily in charge of Palestine.

THE BALFOUR DECLARATION In November 1917 the British government issued the Balfour Declaration: a promise to make Palestine a national home for the Jewish people who were scattered around the world.

Under British rule, Jewish *emigrants* began to settle in Palestine. These settlers often set up communities called kibbutzim, the Hebrew word for 'groups', where everyone worked together.

By 1936 the stream of emigrants from Europe turned into a flood as Jews fled to escape *persecution* in Hitler's Germany (see p. 487). This led to an uprising in Palestine. In order to keep the peace, Britain put a strict limit on the number of Jews coming to Palestine. As a result, several ships carrying Jewish emigrants were turned away. One ship sank, killing all the people on board.

SETTING UP OF THE JEWISH STATE After the war, it was discovered that millions of Jews had been slaughtered in Nazi death camps. Britain and the rest of the Western world felt the time had come to give the Jews a permanent home.

Britain handed Palestine over to the Jews, who proclaimed the new State of Israel in May 1948. Jews from all over the world came to settle in Israel and began to build the country, which developed rapidly.

WAR WITH THE ARABS Shortly after proclaiming its independence, Israel was attacked on all sides by five neighbouring Arab states. By July, a well-organized Israeli army had defeated the Arabs. But Jordan captured Israeli land on the West Bank of the River Jordan, including the city of Jerusalem.

In June 1967, Israeli planes attacked the Arab forces that had been gathering on its borders. This was the start of the Six Day War. Within hours, Israel had destroyed the airforces and the airfields of Egypt, Syria and Jordan. Israeli land forces captured the whole of Jerusalem and the West Bank of the Jordan, and also took the Sinai Peninsula to the south. The UN arranged a cease-fire.

INVOLVEMENT OF THE SUPER POWERS On 5 October 1973, the Jewish holy day of Yom Kippur, Arab armies – equipped and trained by the Soviet Union – launched a surprise attack on Israel. At first it seemed that they would overcome the unprepared Israeli army.

On the fifth day of the war, the USA, which was Israel's ally, sent urgently needed equipment and modern fighter aircraft to help Israel's airforce. The tide of war began to turn in Israel's favour.

Symbol of a divided city: the Golden Mosque in Jerusalem which covers the rock from which Muhammad ascended into heaven.

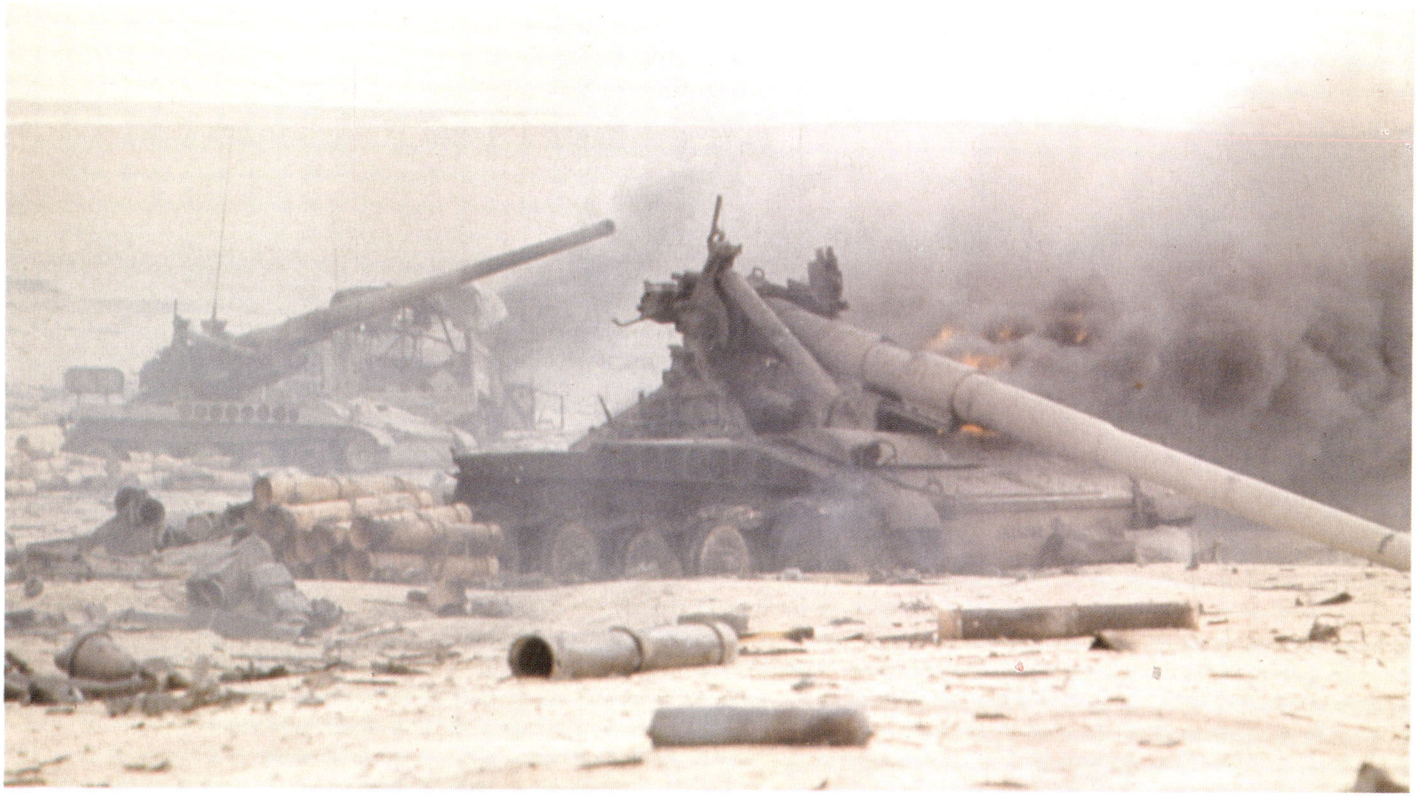

Above. During the Six Day war in 1967, the Israelis scored major victories against the Arabs.

The Expansion of Israel 1947–1990

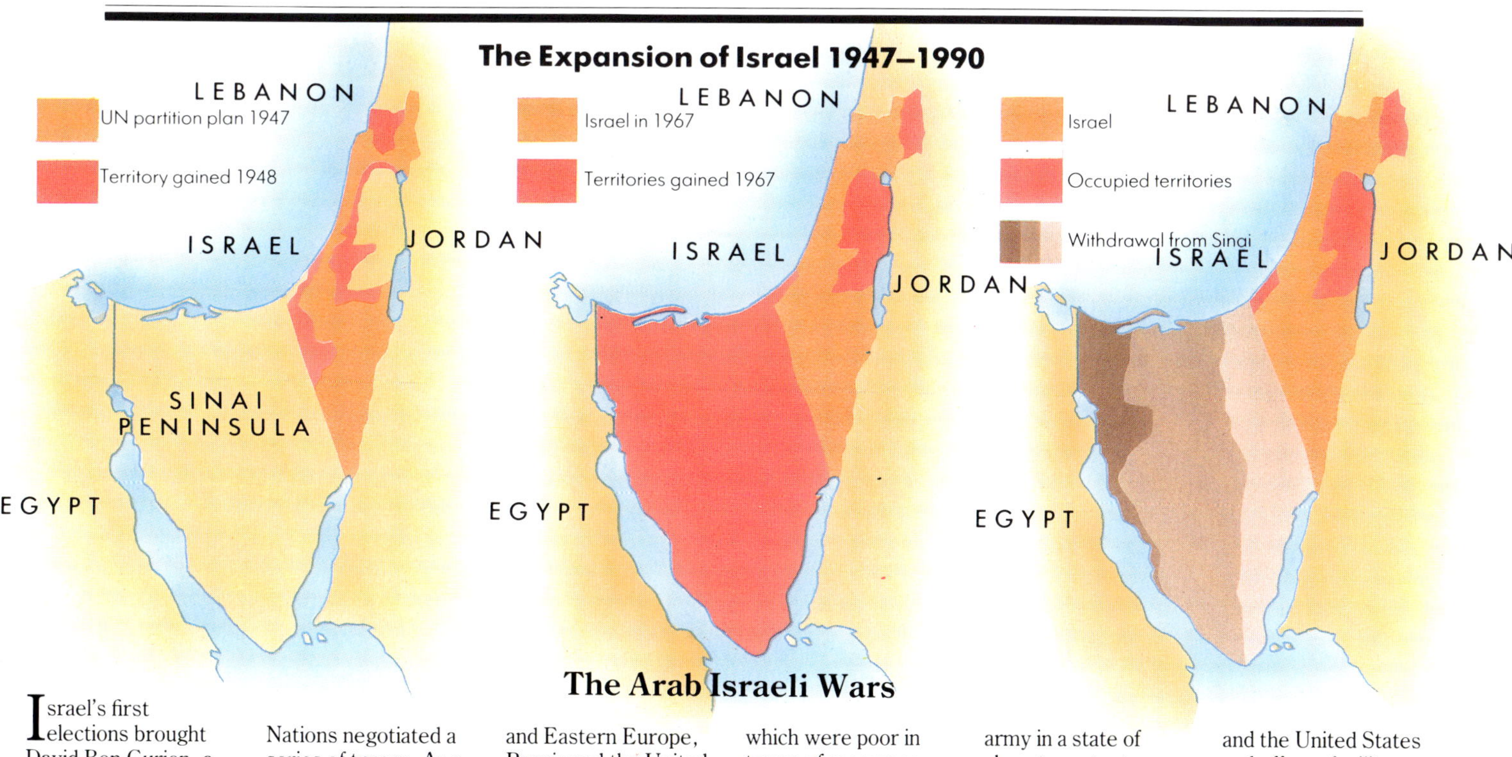

The Arab Israeli Wars

Israel's first elections brought David Ben Gurion, a former guerrilla leader, to power. Following the defeat of the Arab League nations in the war of 1948, the United Nations negotiated a series of truces. As a result of the threat to the fledgling state, Israel encouraged the immigration of massive numbers of Jews from Western and Eastern Europe, Russia and the United States. The influx of Jews tended to mean that Israel's native Palestinian people were pushed out into separate communities which were poor in terms of resources and land.

The rapidly growing population and the need to spend large amounts of money on keeping an army in a state of almost constant readiness caused Israel serious economic difficulties. But the country has had influential friends particularly in Britain and the United States and offers of military assistance were particularly helpful in the Yom Kippur war of 1973.

OIL AND ISLAM

OPEC

The Organization of Petroleum Exporting Countries was launched in 1960 to improve trading conditions for Third World petroleum-exporting states. It has 13 member states including Iran, Iraq, Kuwait, Libya, Qatar, Saudi Arabia and the United Arab Emirates. At the time, most oil wells in the Middle East were owned and operated by Western companies. By the early 1970s most wells had been nationalized by their respective Arab governments.

During the 1973 war against Israel, the Arab states realized they could exert pressure by cutting off oil supplies to Israel's allies. Iran took the lead in raising prices, and between 1973 and 1974 the price of oil increased by 500 per cent, leading to a deep recession in the West.

Since the late 1970s, Saudi Arabia, an ally of the USA, has kept its oil production high and this has tended to stabilize the price of oil.

Iranians celebrate the return of Ayatollah Khomeini, their religious leader.

The area we know as the Middle East stretches from Libya in the west to Iran in the east. This area produces over half the oil and natural gas used in the Western world. Oil has made some countries, like Saudi Arabia, Qatar and the United Arab Emirates, very rich indeed. However, other countries in the area are among the poorest in the world.

SUEZ Although the Arab countries had been dominated by colonial powers for many centuries, after the Second World War they began to show their independence. One of the first examples of this was the decision of Egypt's President Gamal Nasser to seize control of the Suez Canal in 1956. At that time the Canal was owned and operated jointly by Britain and France. Nasser's action led to a force of British and French troops invading Suez. Pressure from the United States and the United Nations soon forced them to withdraw (see p. 496).

IRAN The most important religion of the Middle East is *Islam*. When the people of Iran rose up against their Shah, the monarch, in 1979, Islamic holy men helped to organize the revolution. An Islamic republic was set up under Ayatollah Khomeini, a religious leader who had been outlawed by the Shah and who had been forced to live in exile in France.

The new Islamic state introduced strict religious laws and cut off relations with the West. A group of students took over the US embassy in Tehran, the capital of Iran, and held its staff hostage to bargain for the release of Iranian property in the USA, which had previously belonged to the Shah's government.

War also broke out with Iraq over territory around the oil port of Basra, which both countries claimed. Religious differences in the war soon developed, as Iraq's government did not follow the *fundamentalist* form of religion that was practised by Iran.

Western countries such as Britain, France and West Germany sold arms openly to Iraq, while the USA made secret arms deals with Iran in order to speed the return of the US embassy hostages. The hostages were finally released in 1981.

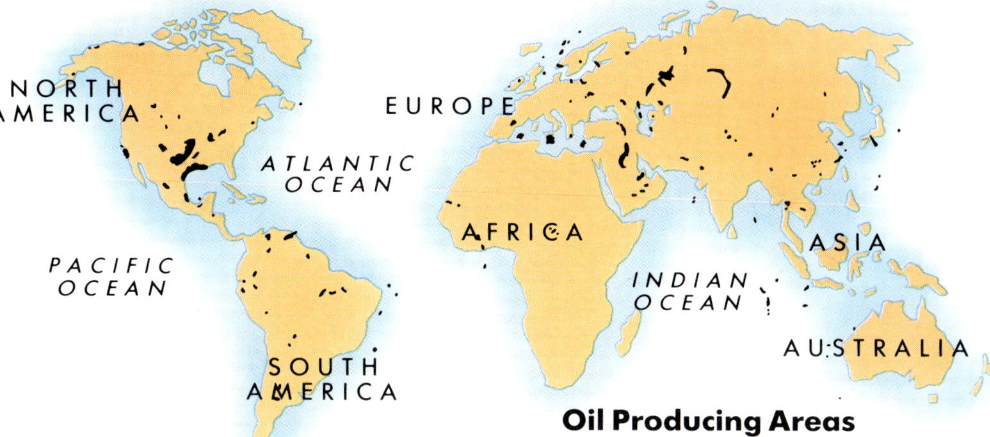

Above. This map shows the positions of important oil fields around the world.

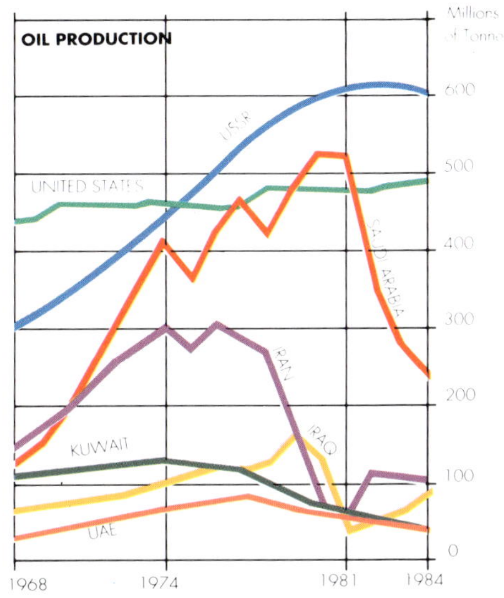

Left. A graph to show the output of some of the world's major oil-producing countries. The Soviet Union was the world's largest producer.

Above. Some Middle-Eastern oil producers have deliberately lowered their output to force other states to pay more for their oil.

The Gulf

The Gulf States include Saudi Arabia, Bahrain, Oman, Qatar, Kuwait and the United Arab Emirates (UAE).

In spite of being the richest Arab nations, they are also among the most backward-looking. The tiny states are governed by old-fashioned monarchies, there is little democracy, and members of the Arab royal families fulfil the functions of ministers of state.

Most Gulf States observe a very strict Islamic law with prohibition of alcohol and traditional penalties such as the use of corporal punishment to deal with some crimes.

The reason for the political stability is that a high standard of living is enjoyed by all Arab families; income per head is among the highest in the world. Their very high standard of living has enabled many wealthy families to enjoy luxury goods bought from the West and also to invest overseas.

However, the fact that the Arab populations of these states are so small means that they have to employ large numbers of overseas workers, particularly in their armed forces, domestic service and construction industries.

Saudi Arabia is by far the richest oil state with the biggest oil reserves and the highest oil production of any Arab nation. Saudi produces roughly three times as much oil as the other Gulf States put together and almost as much oil as the rest of the Arab oil-producing nations. Saudi exports most of its oil to the West and, more than any other nation, is responsible for setting a world price for oil by either increasing or decreasing its production.

Beirut, capital of Lebanon, is the focus for the civil war that has raged in the country since 1975.

THE GULF WAR The Iran-Iraq war ended in 1988, but in August 1990 the Iraqi leader, Saddam Hussein, invaded Kuwait. He claimed that Kuwait had originally belonged to Iraq before the Western powers had established a monarchy there after the fall of the Ottoman Empire in 1918. The United Nations condemned this invasion and some Western countries, led by the USA and Britain, sent troops to the area. Some Arab countries, including Saudi Arabia and Syria, supported this action. When the Iraqis had not withdrawn from Kuwait by January 1991, the Allies attacked the Iraqi troops in Kuwait. Within a few weeks, the Allied forces had pushed Saddam Hussein's army back to the borders of Iraq.

LEBANON The conflict between Israel and its Arab neighbours (see pp. 500–1) spilled over into Lebanon in 1975 after Israel attacked Palestinian bases in Lebanon. Civil war broke out. Even after the Palestinians withdrew from the capital city of Beirut, fighting continued between Christian *Druze* forces and Shi-ite Muslims who were supplied with arms by Iran and Syria.

VIETNAM

In February 1965, at the height of the Cold War (see pp. 494–5), American troops arrived in South Vietnam to fight the spread of Communism in Asia. The South Vietnamese government was under attack from North Vietnam and from rebels – the Viet Cong – within its own country.

AN UNWINNABLE WAR The Americans tried without success to fight a traditional war against the Viet Cong. But the Viet Cong moved about constantly and avoided open battles. By day, they hid their weapons and looked like ordinary peasants; by night they launched small-scale raids. On many occasions, American forces killed innocent Vietnamese peasants, mistaking them for their enemy.

But killing innocent civilians only made the Americans more unpopular in Vietnam and helped the Viet Cong to win more support. When the US forces stepped up the action against North Vietnam by bombing stores of weapons and supplies, the Viet Cong became more determined to fight back. In any case, no amount of American bombing could ever cut off the supply of arms to the rebels, as the Soviet Union and China were supplying weapons and aid to North Vietnam.

All around the world, people became more and more opposed to the American involvement in Vietnam as the war dragged on. This opposition increased when the Americans bombed Vietnamese villages with a substance called *napalm*, which set fire to the villages.

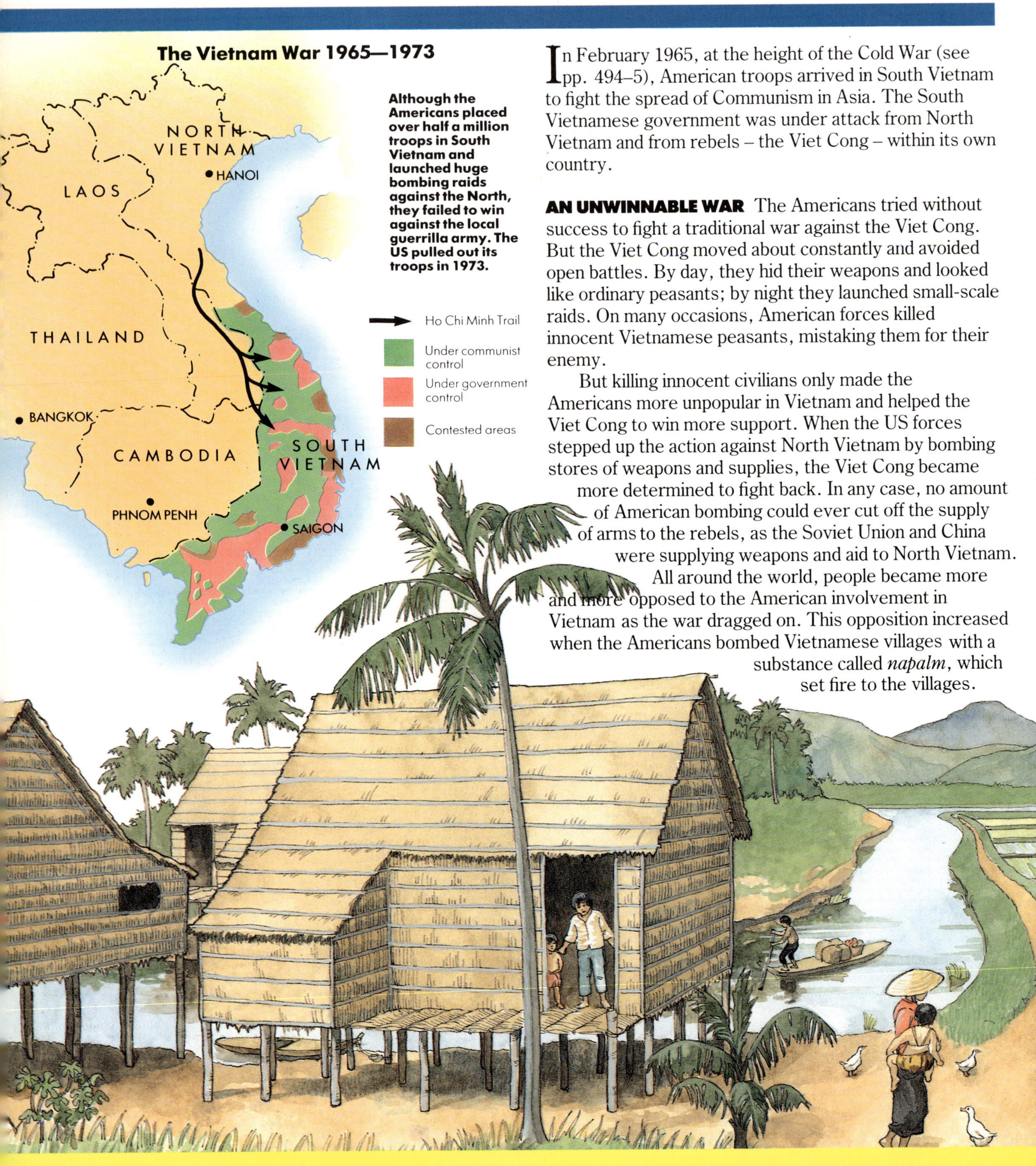

Although the Americans placed over half a million troops in South Vietnam and launched huge bombing raids against the North, they failed to win against the local guerrilla army. The US pulled out its troops in 1973.

Bring Our Boys Home

American public opinion could no longer tolerate the high casualty rate among the troops and the seemingly senseless destruction of North Vietnam and Cambodia by mass bombing raids. A very strong anti-war movement gathered force within the USA. President Johnson did not stand for re-election. His successor, Richard Nixon, reduced the number of American troops and increased aid to help the South Vietnamese strengthen their own army.

Left. South Vietnamese children run in terror from their burning village, destroyed by fighting between the US troops and the Viet Cong guerrillas.

Above. North Vietnamese leader Ho Chi Minh founded the Vietnamese Communist Party in 1930. He led North Vietnam until his death in 1969.

THE TET OFFENSIVE On 31 January 1968, the Viet Cong and the North Vietnamese launched a major attack, called the Tet Offensive, against the US and South Vietnamese forces. Although the Viet Cong attack was defeated, the fact that they could launch an attack at all after all the bombing raids that had been carried out against them, made politicians in America realize that they could not win the war.

During the early 1970s, the USA increased its bombing raids on North Vietnam and on neighbouring Cambodia, which it thought was supplying arms to the Viet Cong. The United States hoped to force the North Vietnamese to begin peace talks.

THE US WITHDRAWAL In 1973, the United States of America and the North Vietnamese finally signed a cease-fire. The USA began to withdraw most of its forces, leaving South Vietnam to defend itself. But peace between the North and the South was only temporary. By the beginning of 1974, North Vietnamese forces had begun to advance on the South. In April, President Thieu of South Vietnam escaped to Taiwan. Within days, the last American soldiers left Vietnam and the longest war in the USA's history came to an end. A few hours later, North Vietnamese troops captured the South Vietnamese capital city of Saigon and took over the country.

A Vietnamese village. The Americans found fighting against the North Vietnamese difficult as conventional methods of fighting failed. The Viet Cong soldiers lived as normal peasants in the villages and came out at night in small groups to attack the enemy.

RED CHINA

The 'Great Leap Forward' organized people into self-sufficient groups, producing everything they needed to eat and all their clothes and household and farming equipment.

The history of China after the Second World War is the history of the Chinese Communist Party. It is a history shaped by just one man – Mao Zedong.

After the Japanese had been driven from China at the end of the Second World War, Mao's Red Army fought to take control of the vast country from Jiang Jeshi's Chinese Nationalist Party. The Communists finally captured the capital, Beijing, in January 1949. Mao proclaimed the People's Republic of China in October.

REFORMS Like Russia in the nineteenth century, China was a vast country containing many different ethnic groups. Most of the population were peasants, who lived in villages in conditions of great poverty. One of Mao Zedong's first acts on becoming chairman (leader) of the new People's Republic was to take large farms away from wealthy private landlords and divide the land up among the poor. The landlords were treated harshly. Most were executed; it is believed that during the early years of the new republic between one and two million landlords were killed.

However, the change in land ownership was not enough to feed China's rapidly growing population, which

The Long March 1934–5

Above. Mao Zedong led his communists on the 'Long March' to escape enemies and set up a new power-base.

In 1934, Mao Zedong tried to lead a communist uprising with a large force of peasant volunteers – the Red Army. When Chinese government troops surrounded his base, Mao decided the only way to keep Chinese communism alive was to retreat towards the northern mountains.

Thus began the famous Long March. Mao led an army of 90,000 people for 10,000 kilometres over 368 days. At the end of the Long March, Mao was elected Chairman of the Chinese Communist Party.

Left. A Communist poster shows members of the armed forces and workers cheering their leader, Mao Zedong.

Right. Deng Xiaoping was leader of the Chinese Communist party during the pro-democracy student uprisings in 1989.

Above. Hong Kong, on the coast of southern China, is one of the world's most important financial and trading centres. After a war with China, Britain was granted the right to govern Hong Kong for 99 years. This lease expires in 1997 when Britain will have to return the colony to China.

was then 650 million. So, from 1954 onwards, Mao encouraged the peasants to increase their production from farming by pooling their land in collective farms.

The government also invested in building roads and railways and in power generation projects. Because of high taxes, industrialists often preferred to hand over their businesses to the government, which then employed them as managers.

CHINESE ISOLATION During the 1950s, the Soviet Union helped China to develop its economy by giving it large amounts of financial aid and by sending scientists and technicians to help the Chinese set up modern factories. From 1960, relations between the two Communist countries became strained as China turned inwards and became concerned only with rebuilding its society.

The Chinese government introduced two important changes to the country. The 'Great Leap Forward' in 1958 reorganized people into living in groups that were self-sufficient, producing all their own food and goods. Both agricultural and industrial output fell dramatically and so too did China's exports to the rest of the world.

The 'Cultural Revolution' of 1966 forced all artists and intellectuals to work on the land. This resulted in an enormous waste of talent and a decline in standards of education. During this period, many books were burned and people were encouraged to read *The Little Red Book of Collected Thoughts of Chairman Mao*.

PRESENT-DAY CHINA When Chairman Mao died in 1976, two rival groups fought for control of the country. On one side, Deng Xiaoping wanted limited reforms and some development of Western ideas. On the other side was the 'Gang of Four', including Mao's widow, who wanted to continue the strict policies of the Cultural Revolution.

Deng Xiaoping became head of state in 1977 and began to open up trade with the West. He also introduced a strict policy of one child per family in an attempt to stop the country's huge population from growing any further. However, the Chinese government has dealt harshly with many of its people who have called for the country to become a democracy. China has also dealt harshly with the independence movement in Tibet.

RELIGION

Religion gives people moral rules by which to live their lives, but when it is taken to extremes it can make some people very intolerant of other people's beliefs.

EASTERN EUROPE When the Communists took power in Russia in 1917 (see pp. 474–5), they wanted to put an end to religious beliefs, which they thought were nothing more than superstitions that would divide people's loyalty to the state.

Governments in eastern Europe after the Second World War disapproved of all religions. In some countries, such as the Soviet Union, it was against the law to practise religion. Believers could be sent to prison or to a psychiatric hospital if they were caught worshipping together. Jews were treated especially badly. They were not allowed to worship, and for many years they were also refused permission to emigrate to Israel.

When Communist control of eastern Europe crumbled at the end of the 1980s, so too did the ban on religious activities. Romanian revolutionaries celebrated the fall of their Communist dictator, Nikolai Ceaucescu, with church services held in the open air. In 1989, *Russian Orthodox* Christians celebrated Christmas openly in Moscow for the first time since the Revolution.

THE MIDDLE EAST The foundation of the Jewish state in Israel and the involvement of the United States of America in the politics of the Middle East has sparked off a revival of the traditional Arab religion of Islam.

Most Arab states are hostile towards Israel, mainly because of their support for the Palestinian Arab population which lived in the area before Israel was founded. Civil war broke out in Lebanon when Palestinian refugees from Israel settled there and upset the delicate balance between the country's Christian and Muslim

Above. After years of suppression under communist rule, a Russian orthodox priest holds an Easter service in St Valentine's Cathedral, Kiev, Ukraine.

Right. Religion can lead to conflict. This graffiti in Belfast, Northern Ireland, is a symbol of revolt by the IRA against British rule in the province.

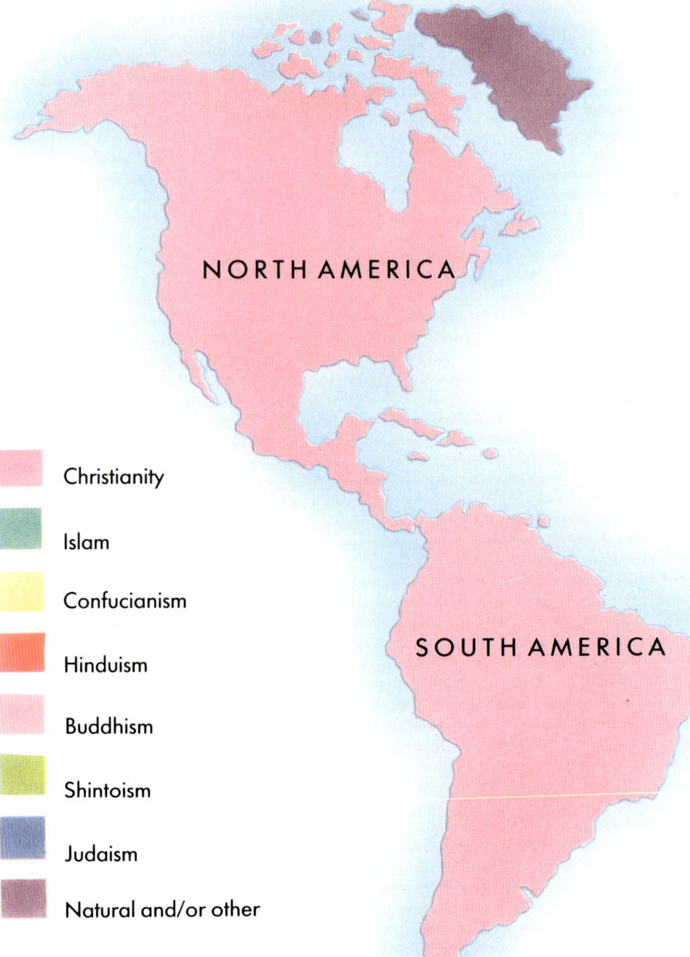

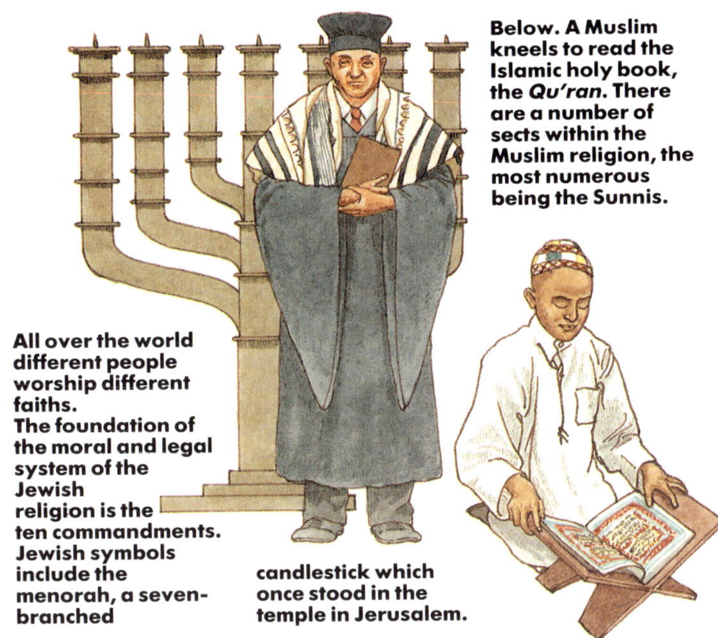

Below. A Muslim kneels to read the Islamic holy book, the *Qu'ran*. There are a number of sects within the Muslim religion, the most numerous being the Sunnis.

All over the world different people worship different faiths. The foundation of the moral and legal system of the Jewish religion is the ten commandments. Jewish symbols include the menorah, a seven-branched candlestick which once stood in the temple in Jerusalem.

communities.

There have also been wars between Islamic groups and nations. Iran and Iraq were at war for most of the 1980s, even though they were both Muslim countries. In the Gulf War of 1991 (see p. 503), President Saddam Hussein of Iraq attacked both the Islamic kingdom of Kuwait and the Jewish state of Israel.

NORTHERN IRELAND When southern Ireland became independent in 1921, the northern province of Ulster stayed within the United Kingdom. Unlike the rest of Ireland, Ulster had a large Protestant community, whose ancestors were British. Its Catholic population was in a minority. Catholics who tried to get good jobs or houses were treated less favourably than Protestants and the community was sharply divided into two distinct religious groups. The Catholics began to protest about this.

Rioting broke out between the Protestant and Catholic communities in 1969 and the British army was sent to restore order. The army has been in Northern Ireland ever since.

By January 1970 the Provisional IRA (Irish Republican Army) had been formed to fight against the British army. It also attacked members of the Protestant community. Protestants formed a similar organization, called the Ulster Defence Association or UDA. The IRA wants Northern Ireland to be united to the Irish republic in the south, while the UDA wants it to remain part of the United Kingdom.

Since the unrest started, hundreds of soldiers, police and civilians have been killed, as well as many terrorists. Mistrust and hatred between the two religious communities continues, and a solution is as distant as ever.

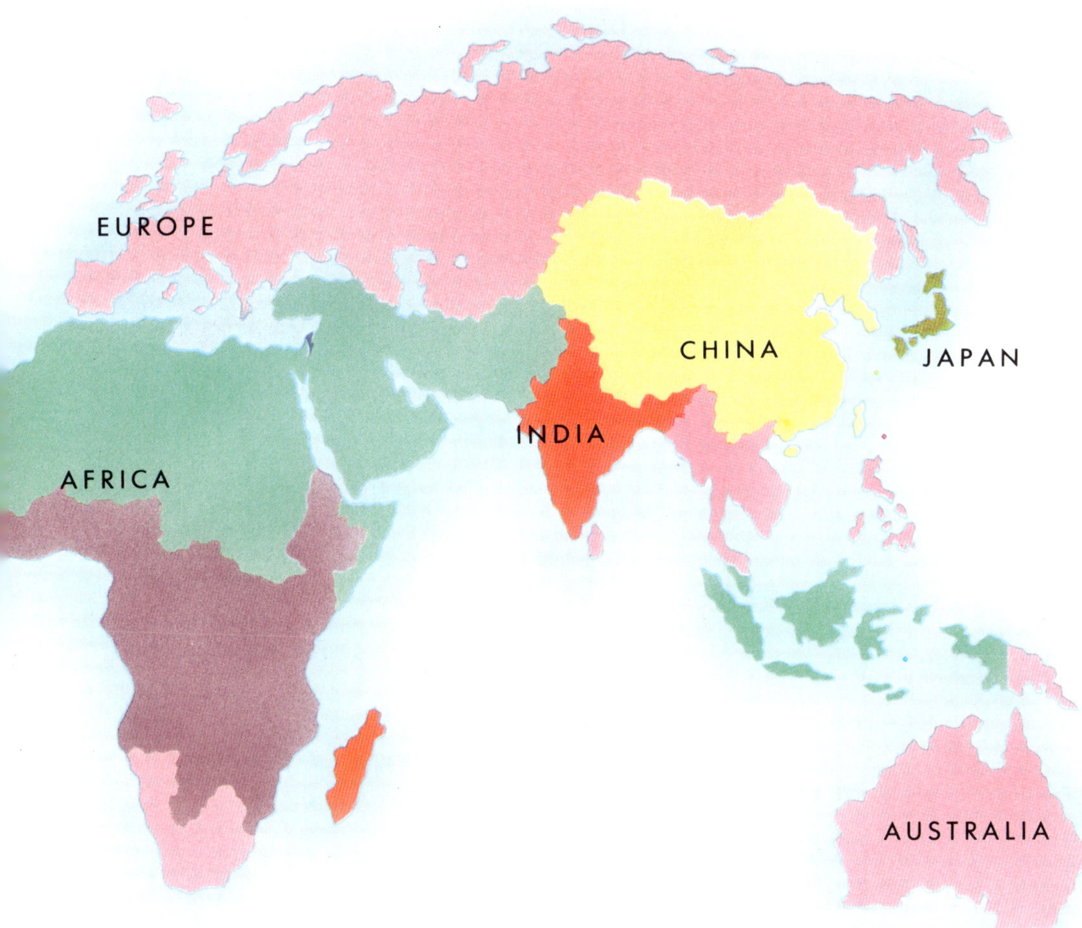

World Religions

The different belief-systems of the world. The religion with the most followers is Christianity. The followers of Christianity are spread all over the world, but concentrated in the Western hemisphere. Followers of Islam are found mainly in the Middle East and North Africa. The areas covered by particular religions generally follow the routes of trade or conquest of that people of that particular faith. Islam has moved from the Middle East towards Western Europe, as did Christianity, which has spread from what is now Israel to the rest of the world.

THE STRUGGLE FOR HUMAN RIGHTS

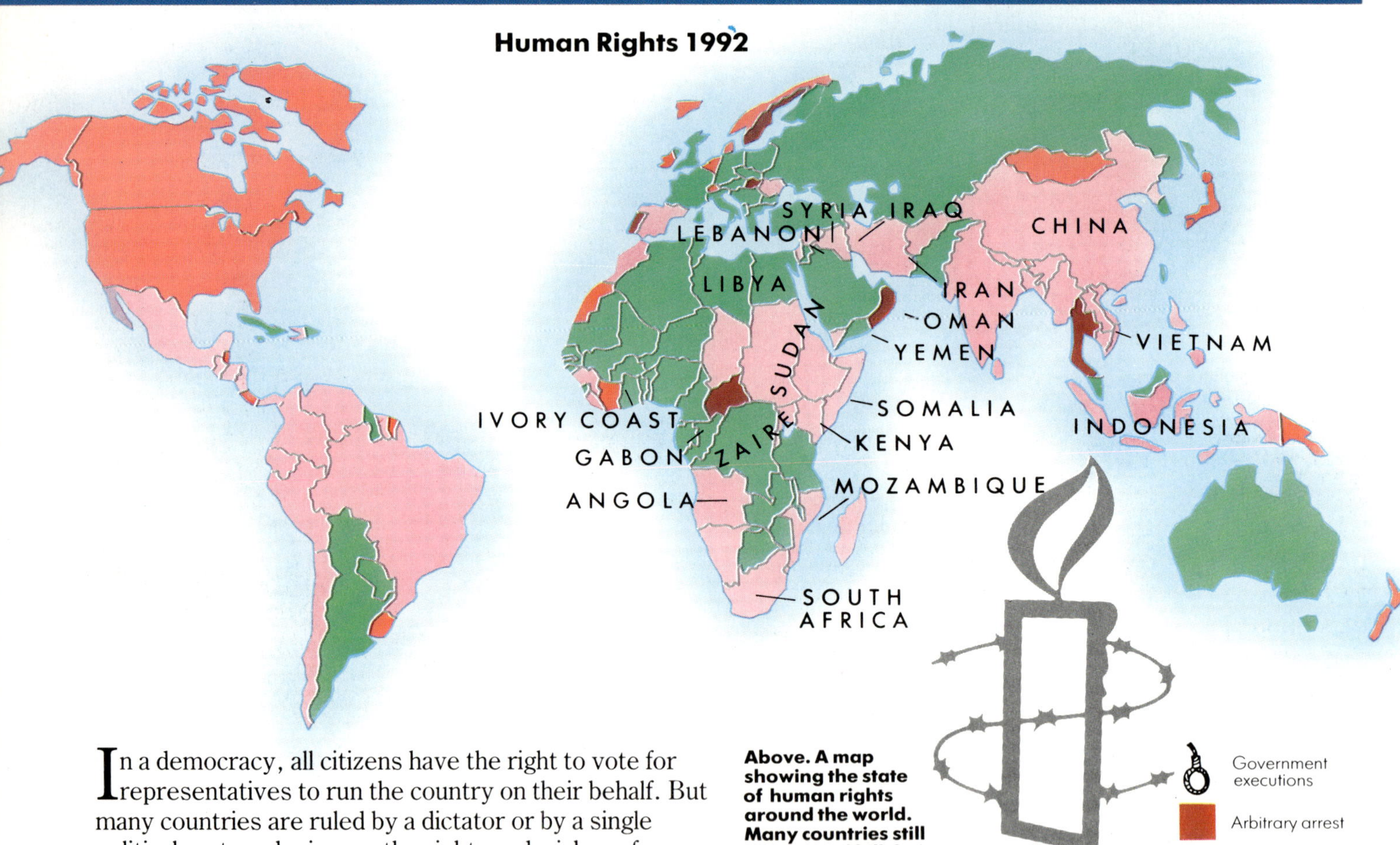

Above. A map showing the state of human rights around the world. Many countries still torture and kill their citizens. More common still is imprisonment without trial and punishment for speaking out against the government.

Above. The symbol of Amnesty International. This group works for the release of political prisoners in any country.

In a democracy, all citizens have the right to vote for representatives to run the country on their behalf. But many countries are ruled by a dictator or by a single political party, who ignore the rights and wishes of large sections of the population. Even democratic governments can sometimes fail to protect the rights of their citizens.

Nowadays, journalists and television cameras have made people more aware of the struggle for human rights all over the world. When unarmed students were killed by troops in Tianenmen Square in Beijing, China, in June 1989, the world's attention was focused on the Chinese people's demand for a more democratic form of government.

HUMAN RIGHTS The Universal Declaration of Human Rights, issued by the United Nations in 1948, says that everyone should be treated 'without distinction of any kind such as race, colour, sex, language, religion, political or other opinion.' But these human rights are not always upheld. According to the campaigning organization, Amnesty International, torture is still practised in one third of the countries in the world.

RACE Racial discrimination is the term for one *ethnic* group treating another group unfavourably simply because that group is different. Sadly, this behaviour can be found in almost any part of the world.

During the 1960s, black people in the southern states of the USA campaigned for the right to have the same education and job opportunities as white people. One of the leaders of this campaign was Dr Martin Luther King. He was assassinated in 1968, but his 'Freedom Riders' campaign was successful.

In South Africa, government has remained in the hands of a white minority. After 1961, when white South Africans voted to leave the British Commonwealth and

Andrei Sakharov

Andrei Sakharov (1921–92) won the Nobel Peace Prize in 1975 for his efforts in promoting human rights in what was the Soviet Union. He first became well-known as a physicist. His work on controlled thermonuclear reactions helped the Soviet Union to develop the hydrogen bomb in the 1950s. He was exiled from Moscow in 1980 for speaking out against the government. Later he became an elected member of the Congress of People's Deputies.

Above. In 1989, Chinese students filled Tianenmen Square in Beijing. They protested against the government and demanded democracy. Many were killed as the protest was brutally broken up.

Right. For many years, blacks in South Africa were banned from white areas.

Right. Martin Luther King fought for equal rights for black people. He was shot dead in Memphis, USA, in 1968.

become a republic (see p. 497), the black population was treated completely differently from the white population. This policy, called *apartheid* or 'apartness' in Afrikaans, meant, for example, that black and white people could not live in the same areas. The white government passed very tough laws to control its black population. They banned public meetings. Anyone who was suspected of being involved in anti-government activities was arrested and held without trial for 90 days.

Some of these rules were changed in the late 1980s, and the first free elections were held in 1994.

Nelson Mandela

Opposition to apartheid centred on an organization called the African National Congress (ANC). Nelson Mandela, one of the ANC leaders, was imprisoned from 1962 to 1989. He was elected president of South Africa in the first free elections, held in 1994.

POLITICAL OPPOSITION Originally, the Russian Revolution had aimed to make people more free by ending the power of the tsars. But Joseph Stalin, the leader from 1924 to 1953, returned the country to a state of terror. His secret police arrested huge numbers of innocent Russian citizens who were suspected of plotting against him, and either executed them without trial or sent them to labour camps in Siberia, where many died. Several million people disappeared in this way.

Later Soviet leaders did not follow Stalin's extreme example, but they did use harsh treatment against anyone who criticized the Soviet system. People could not discuss ideas freely. Many books were banned and many writers were *exiled* to remote parts of the Soviet Union.

Mikhail Gorbachev (see p. 495) began a policy of openness or *glasnost* when he became the Soviet leader in 1982. For the first time Russian newspapers were allowed to criticize the Communist system and writers were allowed to return from exile.

NEW IDEAS IN THE ARTS

Elvis Presley in 'Jailhouse Rock'. He brought a new excitement to rock and roll.

Since the Second World War, the culture and lifestyle of the United States of America has had an enormous influence on the rest of the developed world. The USA was by far the wealthiest country after the war. It was also the first to develop a *consumer society*, where more people had more money and looked for more things on which to spend that money.

By the early 1960s, most European countries had overcome the economic problems of the post-war years. Many people, particularly the young, found that they had greater incomes and increased leisure time.

THE ROCK AND ROLL YEARS After the war, classical music built upon the changes that had occurred during the early years of the century. But more people were listening to a new type of music called rock and roll. American musicians such as Bill Haley, Chuck Berry, Fats Domino, Little Richard, Buddy Holly and Elvis Presley sang about rebelling against authority and became very popular with young people.

Films such as *Rebel Without a Cause*, starring James Dean, and *The Wild One*, starring Marlon Brando, were also about the problems and concerns of young people. The word 'teenager' was used for the first time, and teenagers began to develop their own culture.

THE SWINGING SIXTIES In the 1960s, London became a centre for pop culture and fashion. Groups like the Rolling Stones and the Beatles created their own unmistakable sound, while designers like Mary Quant and Barbara Hulaniki of Biba made Carnaby Street the fashion capital of the world. Clothes changed dramatically. Young women threw away girdles and stockings in favour of mini-skirts, tights and T-shirts.

Fashion was not the only thing that changed. People were more tolerant and broad-minded about what they saw and read. In many countries, *censorship* was relaxed. It was only after a court case in 1960 that people in Britain were allowed to read D.H. Lawrence's novel, *Lady Chatterley's Lover*. In 1968 two British theatre productions, *Oh Calcutta!* and *Hair*, shocked the world when nude people appeared on stage. The second half of the century also produced some new novels which explored difficult themes such as the nature of violence and sexuality. Some of the most influential of these were William Golding's *Lord of the Flies*, J.D. Salinger's *Catcher in the Rye* and Hubert Selby's *Last Exit to Brooklyn*.

POP ART Youth culture created its own art, known as pop art. Its most famous artist was Andy Warhol. Pop art was almost anti-art; in fact, some people said it wasn't art at all.

Marlon Brando in the 'Wild One'. This leather-clad look inspired generations of teenaged rebels.

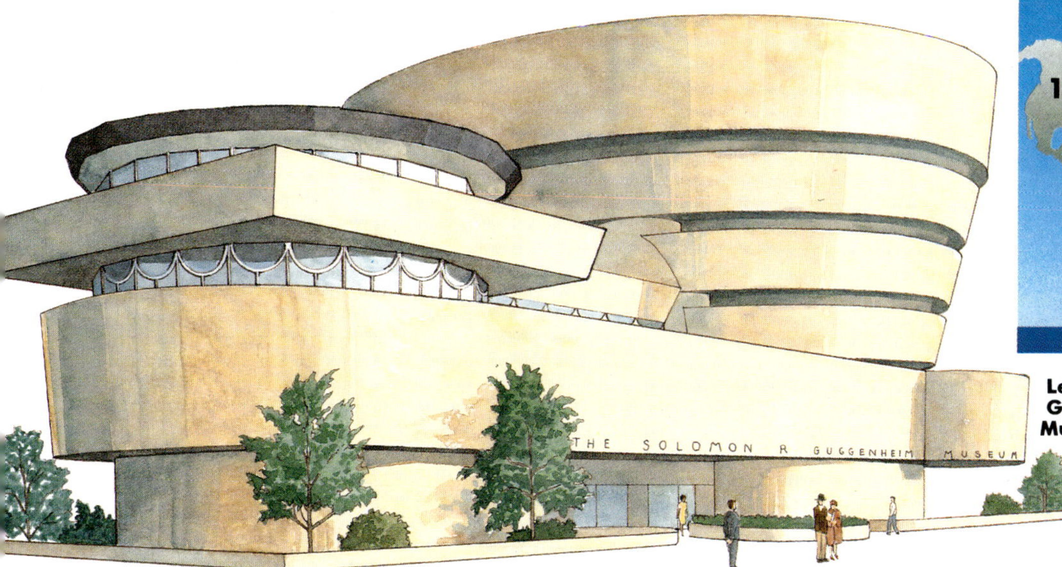

Left. The Guggenheim Museum in New York. It exhibits modern art.

Frank Lloyd Wright

One of the most influential of all twentieth-century architects was the American, Frank Lloyd Wright. Wright's career began in 1890 and spanned six decades.

Wright's imaginative designs were applied not just to large public buildings but to houses which he believed should fit in with the surrounding landscape. He made bold use of both traditional and new building materials like ferro-concrete and always claimed that his inspiration lay 'in the nature of materials'.

Wright's last major work and his most famous was the Guggenheim Museum in New York City.

1 Sport during the 1960s saw the development of the competitor as star. Cassius Clay, later Mohammed Ali, became heavyweight boxing champion of the world. At the Olympics in Mexico in 1968 black American athletes gave the 'black power' salute when they collected their medals, to protest for equal rights.

2 Increasing affluence began to give people more time for leisure activity. The blockbuster film was very popular, with films like *Ben Hur* costing millions but taking more. More people than ever before (in the West) owned televisions and cars.

Left. 'Whaam!' by Roy Litchenstein. Pop art explored the images of a consumer society and modern mass-production. Other examples include Andy Warhol's pictures of a soup tin and of screen idol Marilyn Monroe.

Above. Jean Paul Satre, the French existentialist thinker and writer. His theory that we only become something through thought and deed was very influential.

Right. London became the fashion capital of the swinging sixties. Mary Quant and other designers worked from Carnaby Street, which was filled with shops selling the new look.

Left. The student riots in Paris in 1968. There was rioting in many countries against the ruling parties.

THE DEVELOPING WORLD

Left. Women wash their cooking pots in an open drain in the street in a village in Bangladesh.

Below. A flooded village in Africa. Such disasters in developing countries require immediate aid from richer nations both to solve the immediate problems of providing food, shelter and medical aid as well as trying to re-establish the stricken communities.

The developing world, also known as the Third World, consists of poor countries which have little manufacturing industry of their own, where the majority of the population are peasants who live in extreme poverty in the countryside.

GEOGRAPHY AND CLIMATE Most of these countries are situated in Africa, the Indian sub-continent, South America, the Middle East and the Far East. The hot climate in these areas, combined with too much or too little rainfall and poor soils, makes farming difficult.

Unfortunately, these areas also tend to suffer from natural disasters, such as earthquakes, high winds and flooding, which destroy life, property, farming land and livestock. In Bangladesh, for example, a tidal wave in 1991 flooded a vast area of low-lying agricultural land, killing at least 100,000 people. Most of the cattle were also drowned, and the survivors were left with no food and no way to rebuild their ruined farms.

Mother Theresa won the Nobel Peace Prize in 1979 for her work in looking after orphans in Calcutta.

SERVICES AND JOBS The governments of developing countries are not usually able to provide the services that people in the developed world take for granted, like well-made roads, transport, education, health care and sick pay. Employment is scarce and low-paid. Often, an employed person has to support a large number of dependants, such as children or elderly relatives.

Aid Programmes

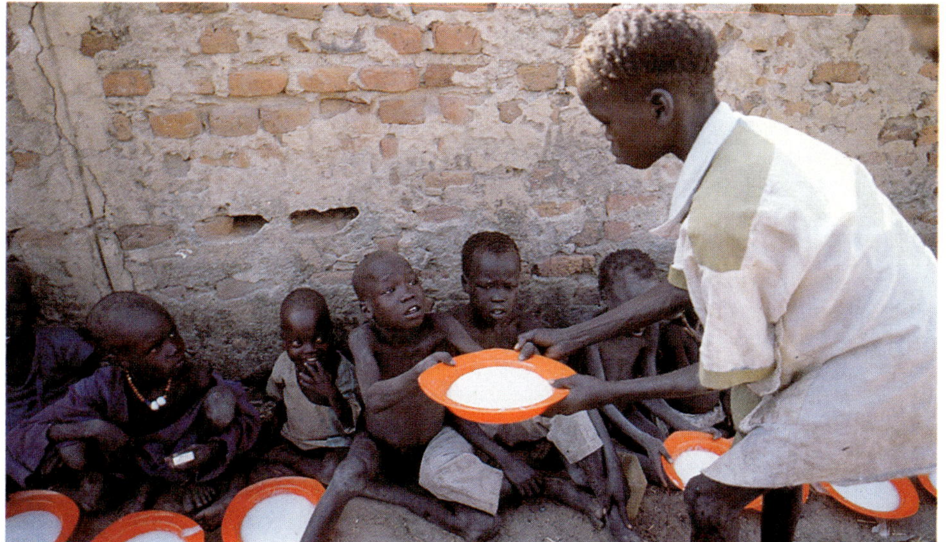

It is in the interests of the developed world to help Third World countries improve their own industries and reduce their dependence on single commodities. Many aid packages provide money for major civil engineering projects, such as building dams or power stations, that will improve a nation's economy. Over a number of years, aid will improve trade links and be of mutual benefit.

As well as receiving direct aid, many developing countries have borrowed from richer countries. High interest on loans has made many of them even poorer. If they could borrow money more cheaply, they would be better able to carry out aid programmes.

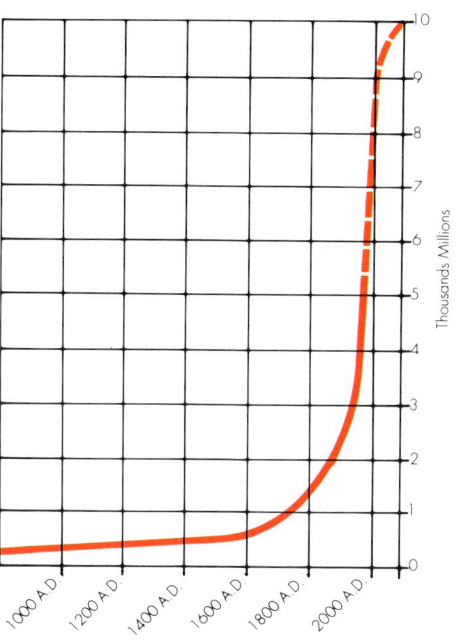

Above. This graph shows how the human population has increased since 800AD. Until 1600 the number of people grew steadily. After this the numbers began to grow very rapidly. Today the world population is close to six billion. If the rate stays the same there will be ten billion people on the planet by the end of the 21st century, on a planet which cannot adequately feed half that number.

The world is sharply divided into wealthy and poor nations.

CASH CROPS Many developing countries were once colonies whose economies were organized to suit the needs of their colonial rulers. As a result, they were never allowed to grow all their own food, or to develop manufacturing industries. Instead, the land was used to produce a limited number of food crops to send to the country that governed them.

This history can be seen today in countries that still concentrate on growing one type of crop, which is exported for cash to pay for imports such as industrial machinery. Examples of such *cash crops* are coffee from Kenya, tea from Tanzania, cotton from Sudan and cocoa from Ghana. Zaïre's economy depends largely on mining copper.

Under the cash crop system, less land is available for growing crops and raising livestock to feed the country's population. It is very risky for a country to depend too much on one crop. If a disease affects the crop, or there is a drought, the country has nothing to export. If too much of the crop is produced, this may lead to a sudden fall in the price on the world market.

POPULATION GROWTH AND POVERTY The chief problem faced by most developing countries is that their population is expanding faster than their income. Traditionally, many people have large families because many of their children die when they are babies, and they want to ensure that at least one child will survive to look after them in their old age. But improvements in medical care mean that more of these children are growing up to be adults, so the populations are soaring. Meanwhile, the money that is received from trade is not enough for the growing populations. These countries are still dependent on the West for aid, or cash help.

Poverty is made worse by the increasing problem of famine. If the government is weak, this can lead to a revolution. It seems unlikely that these countries will become settled and peaceful until their citizens have won a greater share of the world's prosperity and food.

SCIENTIFIC DISCOVERIES

Above. The ENIAC, Electronic Numerical Integrator and Calculator, was the first modern computer, invented in 1946. It took up a whole room.

Right. Robots can now perform the work previously done by men, including building and painting cars.

The twentieth century has seen huge changes in science and technology, which have affected everyone's lives.

COMPUTERS The first American computer, ENIAC (Electronic Numerical Integrator and Calculator) was so big that it occupied a huge room. Despite its size, it was no more powerful than a small modern home computer.

Today's computers contain *microchips* that allow them to store vast amounts of information. This information can be called up instantly and used to carry out difficult tasks such as making financial calculations, monitoring factory production, drawing up timetables, and designing complex machines. Some computers can even be programmed to control robots which are used in factories to carry out special tasks.

THE COMMUNICATIONS REVOLUTION It is possible for computers to communicate with each other, not simply within one country but even across continents, by using satellites. When two or more computers are linked together this is called a *network*.

More and more office work is being carried out by people who communicate with each other by means of computer terminals and fax machines. In the future, it will be possible for people to see and talk to each via their computer screens.

MEDICINE The Scottish scientist, Sir Alexander Fleming, discovered penicillin in 1928. It was first available as a medical drug towards the end of the Second World War. Penicillin is an *antibiotic*. It works by destroying the cell walls of bacteria that cause infection within the human body. Doctors use antibiotics to treat many diseases, like tuberculosis and pneumonia, which were previously responsible for many deaths.

THE BUILDING BLOCKS OF LIFE In 1953, two scientists, James Watson and Francis Crick, identified a mechanism by which all living things pass on genetic characteristics to their offspring. In humans, this substance controls the features, such as hair colour or height, that a person inherits from his or her parents. Earlier in the century it had been discovered that the central nucleus of the cells of all living things contain chromosomes that govern the cell's growth and formation.

Watson and Crick discovered that the chemical within the chromosomes, called deoxyribonucleic acid or DNA, was formed of two separate threads coiled around each other in a double helix. In DNA the order of the molecules within the helix forms a chemical code which governs the cell's growth. It is the complex pattern of DNA in cells that indicates differences between the species of plant and animal life, as well as between individuals.

The study of DNA has helped scientists discover more about inherited diseases in humans. By isolating the parts of the DNA that cause such diseases as cystic fibrosis, muscular dystrophy and Down's syndrome, scientists can work towards finding a cure for these and

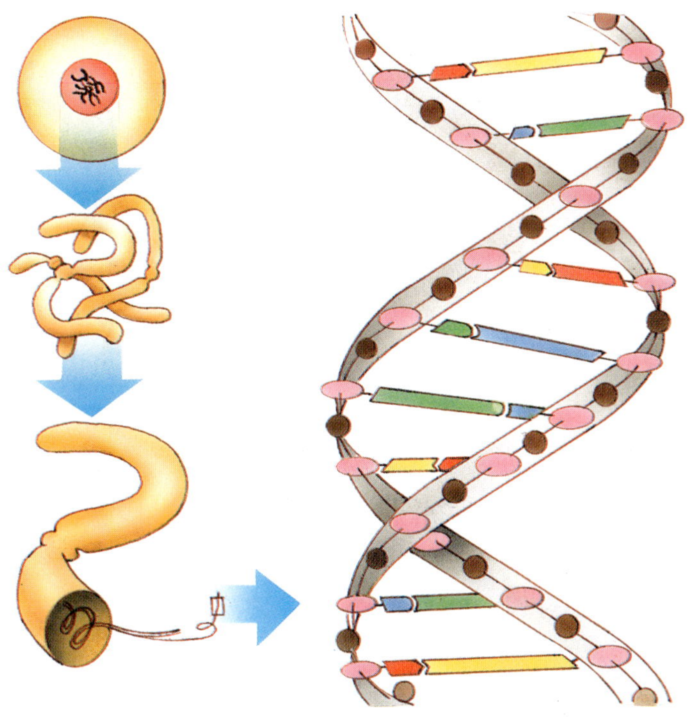

Left. In 1953, James Watson and Francis Crick discovered the structure of the molecule of life – DNA – which is a major part of the chromosomes within our body cells. DNA molecules carry the genetic information which make our body's cells work. It also carries the genes which give us our particular characteristics, such as whether we have blue or brown eyes, whether we are tall or short, and so on. The structure of DNA is like a spiral ladder. The strands can separate to form new DNA and pass on characteristics. Sometimes this can go wrong, leading to diseases which are inherited by children from their parents.

Above. Information is stored on a compact disc as pits on a plastic dish. A laser reads this and reproduces the sound.

Above. The cassette tape holds information as patterns on a magnetic tape, in this case in a compact cassette.

Invented in 1876 by Alexander Bell, the telephone works on the same principle, although calls are now transmitted as light pulses along optic fibres.

Synthetic rubber is made from chemicals. It can be used to make anything from elastic bands to car tyres.

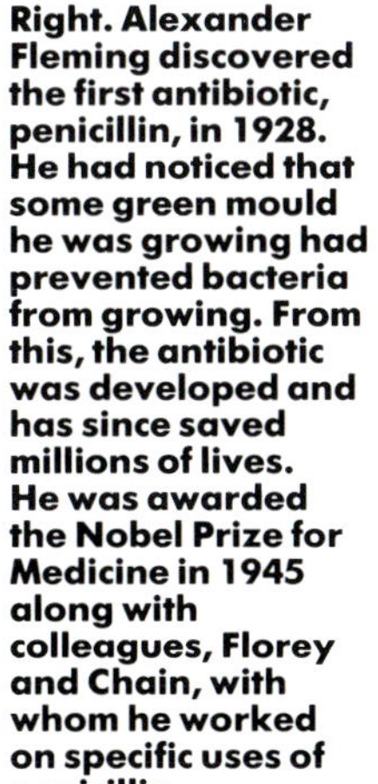

Right. Alexander Fleming discovered the first antibiotic, penicillin, in 1928. He had noticed that some green mould he was growing had prevented bacteria from growing. From this, the antibiotic was developed and has since saved millions of lives. He was awarded the Nobel Prize for Medicine in 1945 along with colleagues, Florey and Chain, with whom he worked on specific uses of penicillin.

Organ Transplants

South African surgeon Christiaan Barnard performed the first successful heart transplant operation in 1967. For many years the operation remained risky and many patients died when their bodies rejected the tissue of another human. However, the success rate for heart transplant operations has risen dramatically, with a high percentage of patients surviving and going on to live for 10 or more years after the transplant.

Livers, kidneys, hearts and lungs and bone marrow have now all been transplanted and have helped save many lives.

other diseases. A study of DNA is helping scientists produce crops that are resistant to disease and which have characteristics that enable them to be grown in specific climatic and soil conditions.

One major achievement that has come from research into the structure of cells is the 'test tube baby' technique developed by Patrick Steptoe in 1978. An egg was taken from the mother's body and fertilized in a test tube. The growing embryo was later put back inside its mother's womb, where it developed normally. Since it was developed, this technique has helped many childless couples to have children.

Scientists and doctors have made enormous advances in controlling the spread of infectious diseases by a process known as vaccination. In this, an individual's own immune system is primed to counteract a disease by being injected with a tiny quantity of the disease.

In 1955 Dr Jonas Salk produced a vaccine to prevent polio which has been so successful that the disease, which once crippled many children, is now almost unknown. Other potentially fatal diseases such as typhoid and cholera have disappeared from many areas of the world.

But there are always fresh challenges for the medical profession and one of the greatest of these will be how to halt the spread of the AIDS virus – which causes acquired immune deficiency syndrome – and to treat patients who develop the disease.

Much scientific research is concerned with putting people into space, and exploring the outer reaches of the universe. The results can help in everyday life. Teflon for example, was invented for the Apollo space programme, and new fabrics came about from space-suit design.

THE RACE TO SPACE

'That's one small step for a man; one giant leap for mankind.' These words were spoken by American astronaut Neil Armstrong on 20 July 1969 and told the world that people had landed on the Moon for the first time. Over 500 million viewers around the world watched this event on television.

The successful Apollo 11 mission to the Moon was the result of a race between the Americans and the Russians to see who could become the most technologically advanced nation.

Yuri Gagarin was the first man to travel in space in April 1961.

THE START OF THE RACE A German scientist, Werner von Braun, developed the first high altitude rocket, called the V2, which was used against Britain towards the end of the Second World War. After the war, von Braun was invited to the United States of America to continue his research. However, it was the Russians who made the first breakthrough in space travel on 4 October 1957, when they launched a satellite, Sputnik 1, into orbit around the Earth. Sputnik circled the Earth for 96 days before breaking up.

Above. The stages in the launch of an Apollo moon rocket. The boosters fall away from the craft as it leaves the Earth's atmosphere. The lunar module fires its rockets, propelling it towards the Moon where it makes a soft landing. Meanwhile, the command module orbits above the Moon's surface.

Left. A Second World War German V2 rocket. The Germans devoted considerable effort towards rocket development and the head of their research team, von Braun, went to the USA to help develop NASA's space rockets.

Above. Vostok 1 was the Soviet spacecraft which carried Yuri Gagarin into orbit in 1961.

On 12 April 1961, the Russian cosmonaut Yuri Gagarin became the first person in space. His spacecraft, Vostok 1, completed one orbit of the Earth. Alan Sheppard became the first American to make a space flight three weeks later.

In that same year, President John F. Kennedy of the USA set his scientists the challenge of landing people on the Moon by the end of the decade. America put an increasing amount of money into its space programme and unmanned space craft were sent to photograph and to land on the Moon.

NEW DIRECTIONS After the Moon landings in 1969, the Americans sent another five missions there. On these occasions, the astronauts gathered rock samples and even drove a 'moon buggy'. The last Moon landing was the Apollo 17 mission in December 1972.

After then, the US and Soviet space programmes concentrated on building space stations that can stay in orbit around the Earth, and on developing space craft that can be used over and over again. Soviet cosmonauts stayed in space for longer and longer periods, in order to test the effect of weightlessness. In 1988, a Soviet stayed in space for 366 days.

During the 1980s, the United States launched its space shuttle programme. This developed a re-usable craft, rather like an aeroplane, to carry passengers and cargo on short flights into space. The shuttle has been used to launch satellites.

THE FUTURE One day, people may colonize the planets in order to mine rare minerals or to create new towns and cities if the Earth becomes too crowded. The technology already exists to build colonies on the Moon or Mars. Food crops could be grown inside clear plastic domes there.

At present, travelling even to the nearest star would take many years.

The Solar System

Both the former USSR and the USA have launched unmanned craft to explore the planets of our solar system. The *Viking 1* and *2* expeditions have landed on Mars, photographed it and collected soil samples. It is possible that people will land on Mars in the not too distant future.

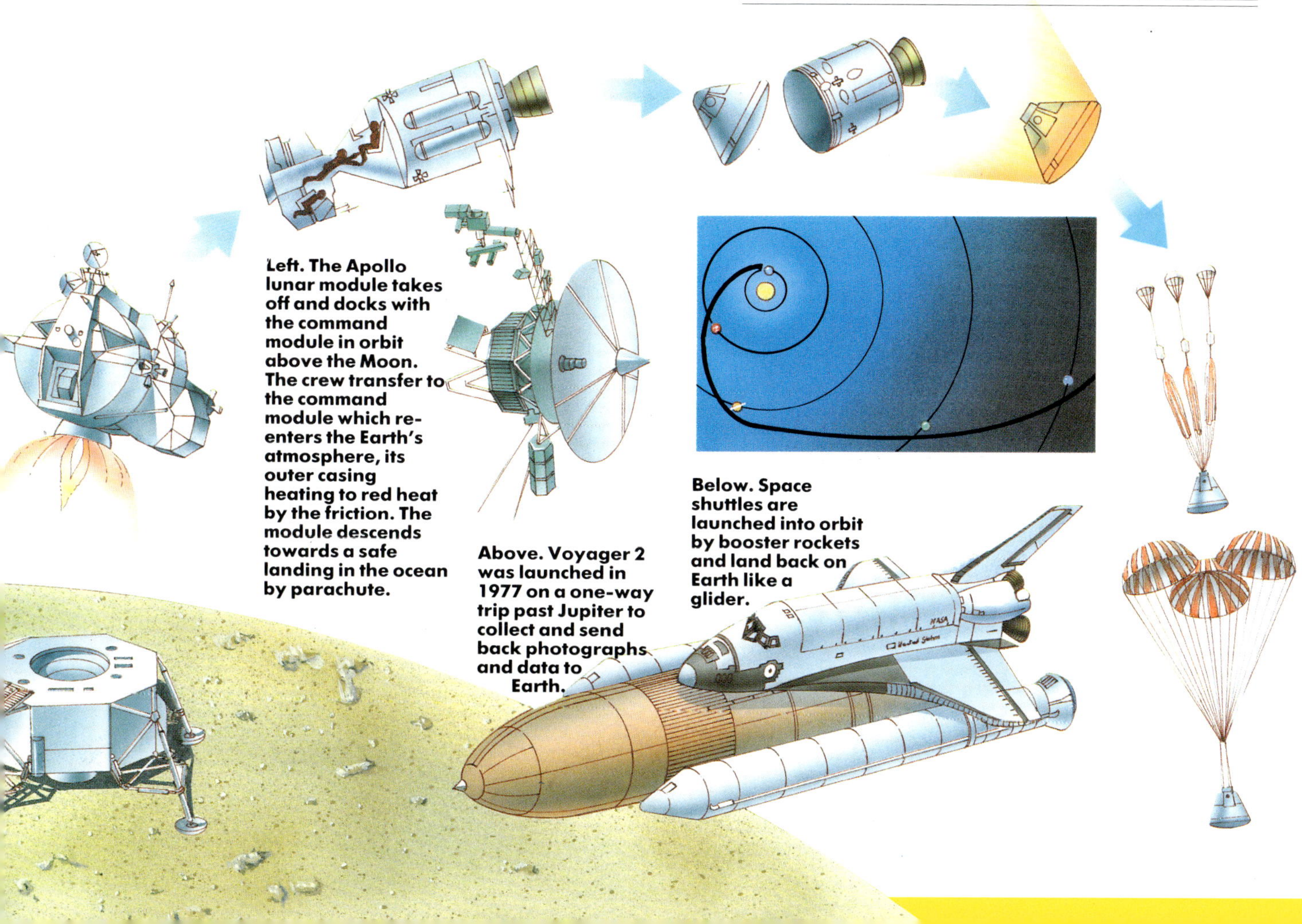

Left. The Apollo lunar module takes off and docks with the command module in orbit above the Moon. The crew transfer to the command module which re-enters the Earth's atmosphere, its outer casing heating to red heat by the friction. The module descends towards a safe landing in the ocean by parachute.

Above. Voyager 2 was launched in 1977 on a one-way trip past Jupiter to collect and send back photographs and data to Earth.

Below. Space shuttles are launched into orbit by booster rockets and land back on Earth like a glider.

THE WORLD TODAY

Cutting down the rainforests, such as this one in Guatemala, for farming or development, means fewer trees to absorb the increasing amounts of carbon dioxide being produced.

The greatest problem facing the world today is not war, famine or natural disasters. It is over-population.

POPULATION AND THE ENVIRONMENT In 1991, the world's population was around 5300 million. It is expected to rise to around 6500 million by the year 2000. In 100 years time, the world's population will be more than double its present size. This growth means that people will need to use more natural resources, such as *fossil fuels*, minerals, farming land and timber.

The rate of population increase is highest in developing countries (see p. 515). In some of these countries, more than 40 per cent of the population is under the age of 16. When they grow up and have children of their own, the results will be far worse poverty, famine and disease than has been seen so far.

THE DEVELOPED WORLD The expanding world population is also threatening developed countries, where more people are living longer and want a better lifestyle. If this continues, there will be more and more cars on the roads, while factories will be producing more and more goods which use more of the Earth's scarce resources.

Improvements in farming, fishing and industry have helped the developed countries to become wealthy. But people are now realizing that these improvements have disadvantages as well. Farmers use chemical fertilizers which sink into the soil and pollute our water supplies. Modern fishing methods are so effective that not enough fish are surviving to breed, so the numbers of fish are falling. Fish are also being killed by the chemical pollution which factories release into our rivers and seas.

THE GREENHOUSE EFFECT Every year, more and more of the rain forests of South America, Africa and the Far East are being cleared for timber and farming. Some scientists believe that cutting down forests is adding to the amount of carbon dioxide in the Earth's atmosphere, creating a 'greenhouse effect' which is raising temperatures worldwide.

These changes in the Earth's climate are causing more land to turn to desert, which means that there are more frequent droughts in countries like Ethiopia and

Oil Pollution

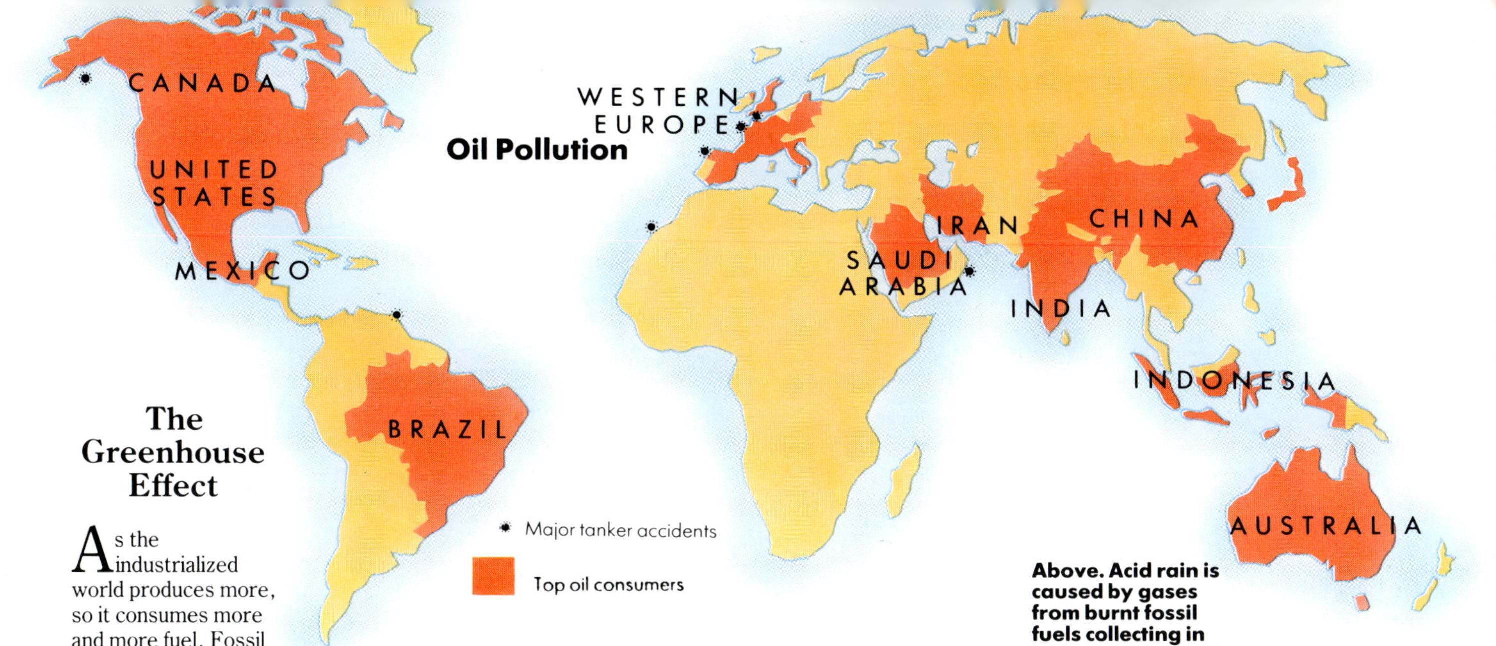

CANADA
UNITED STATES
MEXICO
BRAZIL
WESTERN EUROPE
IRAN
SAUDI ARABIA
CHINA
INDIA
INDONESIA
AUSTRALIA

* Major tanker accidents

Top oil consumers

The Greenhouse Effect

As the industrialized world produces more, so it consumes more and more fuel. Fossil fuels such as coal, gas and oil were formed from decaying trees and vegetation many millions of years ago. When they are burned, they release carbon dioxide.

Carbon dioxide has always been present in the atmosphere, and trees absorb the gas through their leaves. But the vast forests of the world are rapidly being cut down. As more and more fossil fuel is burned so more gas is released, and the remaining trees cannot absorb it all.

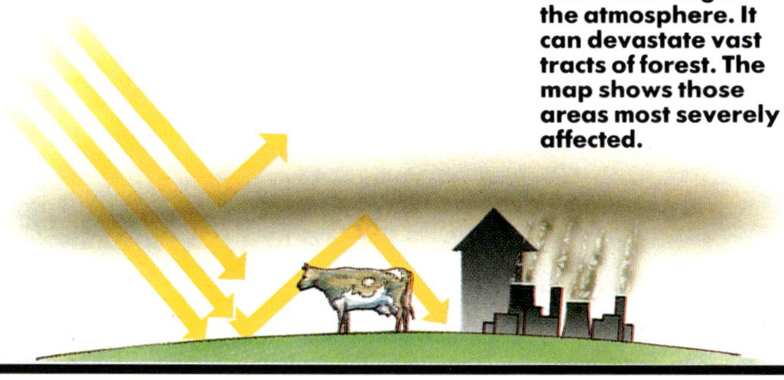

Above. Acid rain is caused by gases from burnt fossil fuels collecting in the atmosphere. It can devastate vast tracts of forest. The map shows those areas most severely affected.

Left. Carbon gases in the atmosphere can trap sunlight and heat, known as the greenhouse effect. This may cause a rise in temperature, or global warming.

Sudan. Increased temperatures also cause parts of the ice caps at the North and South Poles to melt, which raises the sea level and causes flooding in coastal areas all over the world.

FINDING A SOLUTION The survival of our world will depend not just on stopping the population from growing too fast, but also on greater co-operation between developed and developing countries. At the moment, the Earth's resources are unfairly divided between rich and poor countries, and the demand for consumer goods in Western societies threatens to use up all these resources within a few decades. If we can all agree to divide up what we have more equally, and find ways of living which are less wasteful, there is some chance that our planet can recover.

People everywhere will have to use less energy, for example by finding more efficient manufacturing methods, giving up private cars, using public transport and recycling household waste. We will have to make greater use of alternative sources of energy from the Sun, the winds and tides. And of course we will all have to agree to have fewer children, so that we have sufficient resources to care for the children that we do have, in both the rich first-world countries and those where food is short.

Humans have been responsible for many species of plants and animals becoming extinct, either through hunting or through the destruction of their natural habitats for farming or development. However, international conservation agencies are doing what they can to save those which are now under severe threat, such as, from left, the Japanese crane, tiger, oryx, bison, white rhino and leather back turtle.

Creating a New World

TIME CHART

AD	EUROPE/USA	RUSSIA/CHINA/FAR EAST	MIDDLE EAST	REST OF THE WORLD
1945	The United Nations is formed with its headquarters in New York			
1946			Formation of the state of Israel	
1948>1949	Berlin is blockaded by the Soviet Union. The Allies have to mount an airlift to supply food to the city			
1949	The formation of the North Atlantic Treat Organization (NATO)	People's Republic of China is proclaimed. Mao Zedong is elected chairman of the people's council (head of state)		
1950>1953		Korean War. USA intervenes to halt the advance of North Korea's communist forces into South Korea		
1957	The Treaty of Rome: six European nations form the Common Market			
1959				Revolution in Cuba – Marxist leader Castro comes to power
1961	The Berlin Wall is built			South Africa becomes a republic
1962				Cuban Missile Crisis
1964			Civil war breaks out in Cyprus	Kenya achieves independence
1967			The Six Day War – Israel is attacked by neighbouring Arab states but defeats them	
1965>1973		Vietnam war		
1973			The Yom Kippur War – Arabs launch a surprise attack on Israel which is celebrating the religious feast of Yom Kippur	An extreme right wing coup led by Col Pinochet sweeps Allende from power in Chile
1979			The Shah of Iran is deposed and Iran becomes an Islamic state	
1979>1989				Soviet invasion and occupation of Afghanistan
1980				The all-white government of Rhodesia concedes power to a black majority government and a new constitution. Zimbabwe is born
1982				Falklands conflict
1985		Mikhail Gorbachev becomes leader of the Soviet Union		
1989		China – massacre of anti-communist demonstrators in Tianenmen Square, Bejing		
1989>1990		East Germany's communist government topples and with it the Berlin Wall. Anti-communist revolutions depose regimes in Czechoslovakia and Romania		
1990>1991			The Gulf War. Iraq invades Kuwait but is forced out by UN troops	

GLOSSARY

absolute ruler A leader who has complete power. He or she makes.all the laws and every decision about governing the country.

acropolis The highest part of an ancient Greek city, where the temples and other sacred structures were situated.

aediles Four elected officials of ancient Rome, in charge of public works and state records.

Alans One of the *barbarian* tribes from the east that attacked the Roman Empire, closely related to the Persians.

alchemy An early form of chemistry, concerned with finding a way to change ordinary metals into gold.

alliance An agreement between different countries or governments to co-operate with each other.

Allies Term used for the UK, USA and others who fought with them in the twentieth century.

alloy A mixture of metals, for example bronze, which is a mixture of tin and copper.

alluvium Fertile soil carried down-river and deposited on surrounding land by flooding.

alphabetic A writing system in which each symbol represents a sound. First used by the Phoenicians and adopted by the Greeks.

Amerindians The original inhabitants of the American continents.

amphitheatre Translates as 'theatre in the round' because of its oval shape. Used for *gladiatorial* and animal fights in the Roman Empire.

amphorae Huge pottery jars used to transport and store wine, olive oil etc.

amulets Magic charms.

anaesthetic A drug that stops patients feeling pain or renders them unconscious before an operation.

anthropologist One who studies how people in different societies live and behave.

antibiotics Drugs that fight *bacterial* infection.

apartheid South African policy of separating black people from white people. Until recently, laws prevented black people from entering 'whites only' areas and made mixed marriages illegal.

aqueduct An overground water channel, often raised on arches over rivers, ravines or buildings.

archaeologist One who studies the remains of antiquity and excavates to find evidence.

armistice A permanent cease-fire.

Art Deco Decorative arts of the 1920s and 1930s, characterized by bold colours and streamlined shapes.

artillery Heavy long-range guns.

Aryans A large group of people using *Indo-European* languages. Originally used to describe the *Sanskrit*-speaking invaders of India in ancient times. The Nazis used the term to mean white people, especially northern Europeans.

assegai A light spear tipped with iron, used for hand-to-hand fighting by the Zulu.

astrolabe An ancient instrument used for calculating the position of the sun and the stars.

astronomer Someone who makes a scientific study of the stars and planets.

australopithecenes The earliest known hominids to walk on two feet.

Axis powers Germany and its allies in the Second World War.

back-to-back A house which shares its back wall with another, so that there is no back door.

bacteria Minute living organisms. Some cause dangerous diseases.

bakelite An early twentieth-century type of plastic.

Bandkeramik Pottery decorated with incised linear designs and used by the earliest farming people of central Europe, who are named for this.

bankrupt Someone whose business fails, usually leaving large debts.

Bantu An African tribe. The word is also used to mean all the original peoples of southern Africa.

barbarians The name used by the ancient Romans for anyone who was not Roman or did not speak Latin.

bard A poet or singer.

basilicas Large aisled buildings in Roman town centres, used as law courts and for public ceremonies.

Bastille The fortress and prison in Paris at the time of the French Revolution. For ordinary people, it symbolized the harsh way they were treated.

benefits (state) State payments for people who are ill, out of work or retired. The money to pay benefits is raised by taxing people who are in work.

Berbers A nomadic tribe that inhabited northwestern Africa.

Black Death An old name for bubonic plague.

blockade Blocking a country's borders with the army or navy of another country, to stop it trading.

bloomery A simple furnace where iron ore is smelted into metal.

Boer South African of Dutch descent.

Bolshevik Member of a Russian group which favoured revolutionary tactics and led the October 1917 revolution.

Book of Common Prayer Prayer book used by the Church of England.

Bronze Age The period when bronze was used for tools and weapons. The actual time period varies from region to region; in northeast Europe it embraces the second millennium BC.

Buddhism A religion founded by Siddhartha Gautama, who died in c. 483

BC. Buddhists believe that the universe works according to principles that cannot be altered by people or gods.

bureaucracy A system in which government officials control the way a country is run.

Burgundians One of the *barbarian* tribes that attacked the Roman Empire. They moved into eastern France and established a kingdom there around AD 480.

caliphs The rulers and religious leaders of the medieval Islamic world.

calligraphy The art of beautiful writing.

Calvinism The beliefs of a group of *Protestants* who follow the strict ideas of John Calvin.

canabae Civilian settlement which grew up outside a Roman fort.

canopic jars Egyptian funerary jars into which the organs of a dead person were placed.

cantons The different areas which make up the country of Switzerland.

caravan Originally, a group of people, usually traders, travelling together for security, especially in the deserts.

caravanserai A staging-post on a camel *caravan* route where rest and refreshment were available.

Cardinal One of the most important figures in the Catholic Church. The College of Cardinals elects the Pope and helps to decide on Church policy.

cash crop A single crop grown only for the export market and sold to earn money to pay for imported goods. Examples are tea, coffee and sugar.

caste system Strict social order of classes or castes in India originating from the four main groups of *Aryan* society.

caudillo A gang leader who controlled an area of South America.

cavalry The part of an army that is made up of soldiers on horseback.

cells Originally, small rooms in a monastery inhabited by priests or monks.

censor Originally, an elected official who kept a register of all citizens in ancient Rome. Today, **censorship** means limits put on the freedom of people to write (and read) whatever they like in book and newspapers.

Chalcolithic Stone Age period when copper and stone were in use.

Ch'in The *dynasty* from which China takes its name.

chivalry The code of behaviour that *knights* were meant to follow, including being brave, bold, loyal, honourable, faithful, devout, charitable and loving.

chloroform A general *anaesthetic* first used in 1847.

circus Originally, a stadium used for chariot racing in ancient Rome.

citadel Raised fortress protecting a city or village.

city-states Cities which were large and important enough to have their own systems of government.

collectivism A political system based upon people working together in groups.

colony Originally, a town set up for retired Roman soldiers and their families in the *provinces*. In modern use, an area ruled by another country.

Communism A system of government where all power rests in the hands of a single party which controls all economic activity and provides all social services.

concentration camp Prison used in wartime to hold people thought to be a danger to the state. During the Second World War, the Nazis also put people such as Jews and gypsies in these camps, where millions were killed.

Confucianism Chinese religion based on the teachings of Confucius (c. 551–478 BC). It had a great influence on the development of Chinese civilization.

congregations (Puritan) Groups of people who gather together to worship according to *Puritan* ways.

conscription Compulsory recruitment to the armed forces.

consul Originally, the highest political office in Roman government. Some other countries later adopted the term, too.

consumer society A society where the freedom of individuals is expressed in their power to spend money in whichever way they choose.

Coptic A sect of Christianity which broke away from the mainstream Church in AD 451.

corpus vigilum Roman army unit which provided police protection and a fire service for towns.

coup The overthrow of a government.

courtiers Companions or advisors to monarchs or other rulers.

crop rotation A system of farming where a different crop is grown in the same field each year. This is because each crop takes different minerals out of the soil, so changing them round allows the soil to recover these minerals.

Cubism Twentieth-century school of painting where a subject is seen as a series of interconnected geometric shapes.

cuneiform Wedge-shaped writing system, using a reed stylus on clay tablets. It was invented by the Sumerians.

curator aquarum Super-intendent of the aqueducts and water supply in an ancient Roman town.

cursus publicus Official courier service set up by the Roman Emperor Augustus.

Cyclopaean Used to describe massive walls, as at Tyrins in ancient Greece. It comes from the word

'Cyclops', the one-eyed giants of Greek legend.

Cyrillic alphabet The Slavonic alphabet formed in the ninth century AD, believed to have been developed by St Cyril.

daimyo A *feudal* lord in Japan.

Danelaw The parts of England that the Vikings ruled.

democracy Originating in ancient Greece, a system of government in which authority rests ultimately with the people. In modern use, simply a system where all adults can vote.

dhow A light sailing ship, designed to carry goods across the Indian Ocean and the Arabian Sea.

dictator Originally a man appointed by the Roman *consuls* to rule for six months, with absolute power, in times of emergency. Now used of any ruler who has complete power.

diocese Originally, one of twelve districts set up by the Roman Emperor Diocletian to govern the empire. Now a group of *parishes* controlled by a bishop.

discrimination Treatment of a group of people in a way that gives them inferior rights.

dissection Cutting up dead bodies (people or animals), to find how they work and to improve the treatment of disease.

dissent To disagree with views that are generally accepted.

Divine Right The idea that a monarch rules a country as God's representative on Earth.

Druze Religious and political *Islamic* sect involved in Lebanon's civil war after 1976.

dynasty Family which rules a country or empire, passing power on from generation to generation.

dykes Ditches or channels which are dug in order to drain water from low-lying land.

earthworks Solid mounds or walls made of earth, often used as military defences.

embalming Method of drying and preserving a dead body.

emigrant A person who travels from one country to settle in another.

Enlightenment Eighteenth-century movement among *philosophers* in western Europe, who questioned tradition and authority.

epic poems Long narrative poems relating heroic events.

eques singularis Member of the Roman emperor's mounted bodyguard.

equites Roman citizens who owned property. Originally called equites (*knights*) because they were rich enough to provide a horse and armour in war.

ether A general *anaesthetic* made by mixing acids with alcohol.

ethnic group People who belong to a recognizable cultural or racial group who have arrived in another country to improve their economic prospects.

excommunication Cutting off a person from the Church and forbidding him or her to take part in any of its services.

exile Prohibition from living in one's own country.

fallow A field left free of crops (usually for a year), to let the soil rest.

feudalism A way of organizing early or medieval society, stretching from one powerful, wealthy person down to those with no power at all, in which land is granted in return for military or labour services.

fire ships Old ships which are filled with gunpowder, moved close to enemy ships and then set on fire.

First Estate The nobility, particularly the French nobility before the Revolution.

forum Originally the open market area of an ancient Roman town. Most public buildings were grouped around the forum.

fossil fuels Organic materials that were trapped at a time when prehistoric muds and sands were being compressed to form layers of rock, and which then formed coal, oil or natural gas.

Franks One of the '*barbarian*' tribes that attacked the Roman Empire. They settled in Gaul (France) and are the ancestors of the French.

front line The outer limit of territory held by an army in battle.

fulling-mill In medieval times, the place where woollen cloth was taken to be washed after it had been taken off the *loom*.

fundamentalist A fanatical person who holds extreme religious beliefs.

garrison Building where whole regiments of soldiers are lodged.

gladiators Fighters in the Roman *amphitheatre* who usually fought to the death against each other or animals.

glasnost A Russian word for openness. President Gorbachev used the word to characterize a new spirit of freedom in the Soviet Union in the mid-1980s.

Gothic architecture A graceful, elegant style of building and design which developed in medieval northern Europe.

Goths One of the '*barbarian*' tribes that attacked the Roman Empire. They set up kingdoms in Italy, southern France and Spain.

gorytas A quiver or bow-case of a particular style, used by the Scythians.

grammar schools Schools originally founded in the sixteenth century to teach boys Latin.

grammaticus Teacher of Roman children from about 12 years of age.

greaves Armour covering the legs from knee to ankle.

guild halls The places where groups of medieval craftsmen, called guilds, held their meetings.

guillotine An instrument that was used in France to behead people found guilty of certain crimes. During the French Revolution it was used to behead the king and queen, and many others.

heathen A word used by followers of the Christian or Islamic religions to describe someone who does not share their beliefs.

Hegira The word used to describe the flight of Muhammad from Mecca in AD 622. It marks the beginning of the Muslim era.

Hellenistic Age The period from the death of Alexander the Great to the rise of the Roman Empire.

helot A slave in the town of Sparta in ancient Greece.

herders People who live off the animals that they herd.

heretic A member of a religious group who believes something that is opposed to the authorized teaching of that religion.

hierarchy An ordered structure of control or command.

hieroglyphic Form of writing using drawings to indicate words, syllables or letters. Used by the ancient Egyptians.

Hinduism An eastern religion with no known founder or date of founding. Hindus worship vast numbers of deities and many animals and plants are sacred to them.

hippodrome A stadium for chariot racing in ancient Rome.

Holy Roman Empire An area of Europe which included much of Germany, Austria and Hungary and was usually ruled by the Habsburg family in medieval times.

holy sacraments The ceremonies of the Church, including baptism, communion and burial.

hoplite Foot soldier in ancient Greece.

Huguenots French *Protestants*.

humanist A Renaissance *philosopher*.

Huns A nomadic Asian race that overran Europe under their leader, Attila (ruled AD 433–53).

hunting and gathering The lifestyle of mankind in the earliest times, when people survived by hunting birds and animals and gathering wild fruits, nuts and berries.

Ice Ages Ancient periods when part of the Earth was covered with ice.

Iliad Homeric epic relating the destruction of Troy by the Greeks.

immigrant A person who arrives in another country to settle there.

indigenous The original inhabitants, animals and plants of a country.

Indo-European A group of languages that includes *Sanskrit*, Greek, Latin, Persian and most modern European languages, whose speakers must therefore have common ancestors—historians do not know who.

indulgences Documents offering people pardon for all their sins, sold by the medieval Church in return for a money payment, usually to a charitable cause.

inflation Increasing prices.

Inquisition Medieval Roman Catholic court which tried people who had been accused of *heresy*.

internal combustion engine An engine fuelled by petrol or diesel oil.

irrigation The provision of water for farming by using canals or small channels of water.

Islam The Muslim religion founded by Muhammad in the seventh century AD.

Jacobins A powerful political party in France at the time of the revolution.

Janissaries Well-trained soldiers, originally from Christian families, who fought in the army of medieval Ottoman sultans.

junk A Chinese sailing ship, designed to carry heavy loads of cargo across the South China Sea.

Kamikaze Japanese suicide pilot.

knights Soldiers on horseback, protected by chain-mail or plate armour and well equipped with weapons. Only rich men could afford this, so 'knight' came to mean someone from a high-status family and was used as an honourable rather than a military title.

koine The common Greek language spoken in the *Hellenistic* world.

Kremlin A fortified building in the centre of any Russian town, especially the one in Moscow.

lacquerwork Form of art used by the ancient Chinese. Objects of wood were coated with a shiny lacquer which gave them a sheen.

larnax Rectangular-shaped box or chest.

latitude The distance of a place north or south of the Equator.

legio Roman legion, the main unit of the army, usually made up of about 5,500 men.

lightship A ship fitted with a powerful light which takes up a stationary position to warn other shipping of hazards.

limes Permanent defended barrier built by the Romans at an edge of their empire.

limited liability A type of company where the shareholders'

financial responsibility towards investors is limited by law.

Lindisfarne Gospels Richly illuminated Bibles produced in the late seventh century AD on the island of Lindisfarne, off the northeast coast of England.

longitude The distance of a place east or west of Greenwich in London.

Lombards One of the '*barbarian*' tribes that attacked the Roman Empire. They eventually settled in northern Italy.

loom A machine for weaving cloth.

Lutherans Protestants who follow the teachings of Martin Luther.

magazine A store-house or place for military stores.

magister equitum Second-in-command to a Roman *dictator*. He was in charge of the *cavalry*.

magister ludi Teacher of reading, writing and arithmetic to Roman children aged seven to 12.

Magna Graecia Literally 'Great Greece', was land in southern Italy and Sicily settled by the ancient Greeks.

Magyars Nomadic people who lived on the plains of eastern Europe in medieval times.

Mahabharata An *Aryan*/*Hindu* epic cycle which tells of a colossal war fought between two royal families.

maize A tall cereal crop also known as 'corn' or 'sweetcorn'.

malnutrition Illness caused by not eating enough healthy food.

mandarin An official in the *Chinese Empire*.

manes Originally the word for the souls of the dead in ancient Rome. Came to mean their gods of the dead.

manioc A tropical root crop, originating in the Americas.

Marathas The *Hindu* rulers of western India in the *Middle Ages*.

Marxist Someone who believes in Karl Marx's *Communist* theories.

mass-produced Identical goods made in large numbers.

megaliths Monumental ancient stone structures, for example Stonehenge in England.

megaron Large hall with a central hearth. This word was used in Mycenaean Greece.

Menshevik A member of a minority group of the Russian Socialists who opposed the *Bolsheviks*' violent tactics in the early 1900s.

mercenaries Soldiers hired for money to fight in the service of countries of which they are not citizens.

merchant ship A ship that carries cargo.

mesa A flat-topped hill.

microchip A small miniaturized component that is part of a computer.

militia Men who are signed up as soldiers to defend their local area.

mimus Short sketch about city life performed in a Roman theatre.

minaret The tower of a mosque from which the call to prayer is given in the religion of *Islam*.

Minoan The *Bronze Age* culture of Crete, named after King Minos.

missionaries People, usually Christians, who attempt to spread their own religion and beliefs, usually overseas.

moa Giant flightless bird of New Zealand, now extinct.

Mongols Nomadic peoples on the plains of central and northeastern Asia. They set up an empire in China in the thirteenth century.

monopoly A right to deal in a certain product which is granted to just one person, or claimed by one country.

monotheism Term used to describe a religion which worships only one god.

Moor A person of mixed Arab/*Berber* descent. The Moors conquered and occupied Spain from AD 711 to 1492.

mosaic Floor or wall decoration made up of many very small fragments (called lesserae) of stone, tile or glass.

'mule' A machine for spinning cotton, invented by Samuel Crompton in 1779.

mummy The dead body of an ancient Egyptian, bandaged and treated to endure for eternity.

musketeer Soldier who used a gun known as a musket.

mutiny An uprising of soldiers or sailors against their officers.

mystic Someone who seeks to communicate with God through prayer and meditation, and who perhaps also receives visions or other experiences of God.

nabobs British merchants who made their fortunes in India after the seventeenth century.

napalm A highly inflammable petroleum jelly made into bombs. It was used by the US air force to bomb villages in North Vietnam.

nation-states Countries that rule themselves.

natron A sulphur-like chemical used in ancient Egypt to dry out bodies before mummification.

Neolithic New *Stone Age*.

Nestorian A form of Christianity founded by Nestorius, the patriarch chief bishop of Constantinople from AD 428 to 431.

network (computer) A series of work stations linked together.

New World The Americas.

noble savage A term used during the *Enlightenment* to describe native peoples, who were thought to be honest and unspoilt by 'civilization'.

nomad Someone who does not live in a fixed, settled home, but who moves from place to place, in order to find food or water.

nosegay Bunch of sweet-smelling flowers, carried to disguise unpleasant smells. In the past, people believed that nosegays would also help to ward off disease.

Odyssey Homer's epic poem of the 10-year journey undertaken by the hero, Odysseus, after the fall of Troy.

oligarchy Government by the few over the many.

open fields Medieval system of farming in which each villager worked a number of strips of land in the same field. They were called open fields because they had no hedges or walls.

opus sectile Type of Roman marble flooring. Small pieces of marble made up patterns or pictures. The pieces of marble were larger than in *mosaic* floors.

Orthodox Christian One who follows the beliefs of the part of the Christian Church which broke away from Rome in 1054.

Ostrogoths One of the '*barbarian*' tribes that attacked Rome. They settled in parts of Italy.

pa A Maori fortress.

packhorses Horses that were used to carry packs of goods for sale, at a time when the roads were too rough for wheeled vehicles.

pagan A word used by followers of a religion to describe someone who does not share their beliefs.

pagoda A *Buddhist* temple tower of several storeys.

Paleolithic Old *Stone Age*.

pampas Grasslands of South America.

pantomimus Ballet with music usually about legends of the Roman past.

papyrus Writing material made by the ancient Egyptians from the stem of the papyrus plant.

paraffin A fuel derived from oil and used for cooking, heating, diesel and aviation fuel. Also known as kerosene.

parfleche A receptacle made from dried buffalo skin.

parish An area with its own church and priest or vicar.

parliament An assembly of people who have been elected to govern a country.

patent The exclusive right to make, use or sell an invention.

patricians Wealthy land-owning people in the Roman Empire.

penance A punishment for a religious sin.

penitents People who are sorry for their past sins and who say special prayers, or perform special rituals, to ask God for forgiveness.

perestroika A Russian word for restructuring, specifically of the Soviet economy in the mid-1980s.

persecution Treating people badly because of their religious or political beliefs.

petition A request for change made to those in authority and signed by a number of people.

phalanx A solid formation of infantry in battle.

philosophy Seeking for wisdom and knowledge, especially about people, their ideas and beliefs.

phonograph An early record-player which used tinfoil cylinders instead of discs.

pictograms Earliest form of writing, invented in Mesopotamia, which used pictures to indicate objects, animals, people and nature.

pictographs Early form of Chinese writing using simplified pictures of objects.

pike-man Soldier who fought with a weapon called a pike, rather than with a gun.

Pilgrim Fathers The settlers who sailed from England to America in 1620.

pilgrimage A journey undertaken by religious people to a holy shrine or other holy place.

pioneer Name given to members of the families who moved westwards and began to develop the farmland of the American west.

pithoi Large Greek ceramic storage jars.

plague An epidemic disease that can be caught by people from fleas that live on rats.

plantation A large farmstead, especially in the southern United States.

plebeians Ordinary working people in the Roman Empire.

pollution Damage to the environment caused by human activity.

pontifex Ancient Roman priest who carried out ceremonies and sacrifices for the gods.

praetors Officials elected as judges of the ancient Roman state.

prism A triangular shape of glass used to split white light up into seven separate colours.

production line A factory system in which the manufacturing processes are arranged in sequence to maximize production and minimize time.

prophet Someone believed to be a messenger from God.

Protestants Christians who broke away from the Roman Catholic Church during the *Reformation*.

provinces Originally, lands conquered or taken over by the Romans outside Italy, which became part of the Roman Empire.

psycho-analysis Method of determining a person's mental state from patterns of behaviour.

Puritans Groups of Protestants after about 1560 who had very strict beliefs and simple ('pure') church services.

qipu A knotted string, used by the Inca people of Central America to keep accounts and other records of business and military affairs.

quadrant An instrument shaped like a quarter of a circle and used for measuring angles.

quadrivium Part of the curriculum in medieval European schools and universities. It covered mathematics, music and astronomy.

quaestors Officials elected to look after the finances of the Roman state.

Quakers A religious group founded by George Fox (1624–1691).

Qur'an The collection of holy scriptures of the religion of *Islam*.

Ramayana An *Aryan epic poem* which tells the story of Rama a dispossessed prince, and the abduction of his wife, Sita.

rampart Bank, usually of earth strengthened with wood or stone, around a fort or town.

raw materials The basic items from which a manufactured product is made.

rawhide Untanned leather.

recession Extreme decline in economic conditions.

reclaiming land Draining low-lying marshy land on the coast and using it for farming, etc.

refugee Person who is forced to flee from *persecution*.

relics When associated with the Christian religion, relics are objects (sometimes parts of the body) thought to have belonged to saints or other people of religious significance.

relief Form of carving or moulding where the forms stand out from the background.

Renaissance A word meaning 're-birth', used to describe a movement in the arts, literature, music and philosophy, which flourished in late-medieval Europe.

republican Believer in a system of government which has no monarch.

resistance movement An underground network of freedom fighters operating in a country that is occupied by an enemy power.

rhyton A drinking cup or pottery horn with a hole in the point to drink through.

Rig Veda An *Aryan* epic poem.

Romance languages General name for the modern languages that developed out of the Latin spoken throughout Europe during the era of the Roman Empire. They include French, Spanish, Italian, Portuguese and Romanian.

runes A system of writing consisting of simple strokes, devised by Germanic people in the third century AD.

Rus Vikings who settled on the trade route between Novgorod and Kiev in the ninth century AD. The name Russia comes from the Rus.

salons Entertainments or parties given by rich people, especially in Paris.

Salvation The religious belief that one can please God through prayer and good deeds.

samurai A Japanese warrior. Like *knights*, samurai came from the upper ranks of society and were meant to follow a strict code of brave, honourable behaviour.

Sanskrit Language of the *Aryans*.

satrapy An ancient Persian province.

scribe A professional writer, employed to write letters, keep accounts and make copies of books.

Second Estate The clergy, especially in France before the revolution.

secret ballot A system of voting using anonymous slips of paper.

semaphore A visual communications system using the position of flags to represent the letters of the alphabet.

Senate Originally a group of ex-officials of the Roman state who gathered to discuss and debate government business. The term is now used for one branch of *parliament* in some countries (eg the USA).

sepoy An Indian soldier in the British army.

serfdom A system in which peasants had to work in one particular place for one particular landowner and had no right to move or to own property.

Shinto The name given to a wide variety of religious practices which developed in prehistoric Japan. It basically states that there is a supernatural living form in all natural objects, such as mountains, trees and animals.

shoguns Powerful army leaders in Japan, who controlled the emperor and the country from the twelfth century until 1868.

spectrum The range of colours produced by splitting white light with a *prism*.

Spinning Jenny A machine for spinning cotton, invented by James Hargreaves in 1764.

squash Plants related to melons, gourds and cucumbers, sometimes known as pumpkins.

stelae Standing pillars of stone with inscriptions carved on them.

steppe A dry, grassy, generally treeless plain, as in the southeast of Europe and in Asia.

stock market A place where company shares are bought and sold.

Stone Age Early period when stone was used for tools and weapons.

stucco Form of plasterwork used to produce mouldings or picture decorations on walls and ceilings.

stupa Round building (originally a mound of earth) in the centre of *Buddhist* monasteries used for rituals.

superpower A large nation with considerable world influence, such as the USA today.

Surrealism Twentieth-century artistic movement which portrays images from the unconscious mind in realistic detail.

sutra hall The building in a Japanese *Buddhist* temple complex where the scriptures are kept.

tapu A Maori word meaning 'forbidden', from which we get 'taboo'.

Tartars Another name for the *Mongols* who invaded Russia in medieval times.

tenement A building containing a number of homes on separate floors.

tenter-frame In medieval times, a large, wooden frame on which wet cloth was stretched into shape after it had been to the *fulling-mill*.

terracotta Kiln-fired pottery moulding used mostly for decoration on buildings and statues.

Third Estate The ordinary people, especially of France before the revolution.

trade mark A name or design adopted by a company to distinguish the goods it makes or sells.

trade union An organization of workers aimed at improving pay and conditions of work.

transhumance The rearing of stock in two places: in the uplands in summer and in the lowlands in winter.

tribune One elected by the Roman *plebeian* class to look after their interests in government.

tribuni militum Officers in the Roman legion who recruited the soldiers and served the legionary commander.

tribute An amount paid in goods or money by a conquered people to their conqueror.

trivium Part of the curriculum in medieval schools and universities. It covered grammar, linguistics and philosophy.

tundra An Arctic plain. The vegetation is mainly mosses, lichens and stunted shrubs.

unification The bringing together of a number of small states into one country.

vaccine A substance injected into the body to prevent disease.

Vandals One of the '*barbarian*' Germanic tribes which attacked the Roman Empire in the fifth century AD.

Varangians Vikings who pushed south to Constantinople. Many of them became merchants for Byzantinium.

verjus The juice of unripe grapes, used as a seasoning and preservative.

vestments Special robes worn by priests during a church service.

vicarius Governor of a *diocese*, or district, appointed by the Roman Emperor Diocletian.

viceroy Someone who rules in a *colony* on behalf of a monarch of another country.

villa Roman term for a house or estate in the country or by the sea.

Visigoths One of the '*barbarian*' tribes that attacked the Roman Empire. They went on to settle areas of France and all of Spain.

water-frame A machine for spinning cotton, run by water power, invented by Richard Arkwright in 1769.

welfare state A country which looks after its people by providing state benefits for those who are ill, retired, sick and so on.

wood-block printing An early form of printing.

Zen Japanese Buddhist movement which developed in the thirteenth century. Zen aims at harmony in living and uses everyday arts, such as tea-making and calligraphy, to develop skills.

ziggurat Temple tower built in Mesopotamia. The god's sanctuary was built at the very top.

Zoroastrianism Persian religion founded by the *prophet* Zoroaster.

INDEX

Further Reading

The World at War by Mark Arnold-Foster (William Collins, 1973)
A History of the Pacific by Glen Barclay (Sidgwick & Jackson, 1978)
The Times Concise Atlas of World History edited by Geoffrey Barraclough (3rd edition, Times Books, 1989)
Everyday Life in Colonial America (Batsford)
The Land of Ur by Hans Baumann (Oxford University Press, 1969)
Mummies, Masks and Mourners by Margaret Berrill (Hamish Hamilton, 1989)
James I of England by Caroline Bingham (Weidenfeld & Nicolson, 1981)
James VI of Scotland by Caroline Bingham (Weidenfeld & Nicolson, 1979)
Cultural Atlas of China by Caroline Blunden and Mark Elvin (Phaidon, 1983)
Bismarck by Martin Booth (Harrap, 1975)
The Atlas of Archaeology by Keith Branigan (Ed.) (Macdonald, 1982)
The Twentieth Century the Pictorial History foreword by Lord Briggs (Hamlyn, 1989)
Historical Atlas of the Ancient World by J. Briquebec (Kingfisher, 1990)
Arms and Armour: Eyewitness Guide by Michèle Byam (Dorling Kindersley, 1989)
Europe Round the World by Trevor Cairns (Cambridge University Press, 1981)
The First Civilizations by G. Caselli (Macdonald, 1983)
Life through the Ages: Window on the World by Giovanni Caselli (Dorling Kindersley, 1989)
The Middle Ages: History of Everyday Things by Giovanni Caselli (Macdonald, 1985)
Renaissance and New World: History of Everyday Things by Giovanni Caselli (Macdonald, 1985)
The Roman Empire and the Dark Ages by Giovanni Caselli (Macdonald, 1981)
In Search of Tutankhamun by G. Cesarini and P. Ventura (Macdonald, 1985)
The First Americans by R. Claiborne (Time Life)
The Eighteenth Century Europe in the Age of Enlightenment by A. Cobban (Thames and Hudson)
Atlas of Ancient America by Michael Coe, Dean Snow and Elizabeth Benson (Facts On File, 1986)
The Roman Army by Peter Connolly (Macdonald, 1975)
Ancient Rome: Cultural Atlas for Young People by Mike Corbishley (Facts On File, 1989)
The Middle Ages: Cultural Atlas for Young People by Mike Corbishley (Facts on File, 1990)
Secret Cities by Mike Corbishley (Hamish Hamilton, 1989)
What Do We Know About the Romans? by Mike Corbishley (Simon & Schuster Young Books, 1991)
China by A. Cotterell (John Murray, 1988)
Penguin Encyclopedia of Ancient Civilizations by Arthur Cotterell (Ed.) (Penguin, 1980)
Money: Eyewitness Guide by Joe Cribb (Dorling Kindersley, 1990)
The Greeks by Judith Crosher (Macdonald, 1975)
A History of Southern Africa by Christopher Danziger (Oxford University Press, 1983)
The Story of Africa by Basil Davidson (Mitchell Beazley, 1984)
The Ancient Kingdoms of Mexico by Nigel Davies (Penguin, 1982)
What Do We Know About the Egyptians? by Joanna Defrates (Simon & Schuster Young Books, 1991)
The Ancient Persians by B. Dicks (David and Charles, 1979)
Atlas of Twentieth Century World History by Michael Dockrill (Harper Collins, 1991)
Warfare in History by G. A. Embleton (Wayland, 1984)
The Flowering of the Middle Ages edited by Joan Evans (Thames and Hudson, 1985)
The Romans by Joan Forman (Macdonald, 1975)
Encyclopaedia of Twentieth Century Warfare ed. Dr Noble Frankland (Mitchell Beazley, 1989)
Cromwell: our chief of men by Antonia Fraser (Mandarin, 1989)
Mary Queen of Scots by Antonia Fraser (Weidenfeld & Nicolson, 1969)
The Great Moghuls by Bamber Gascoigne (Jonathan Cape, 1987)
The North American Indian by Michael Gibson (Theorem, 1978)
Photohistory of the Twentieth Century by Jonathan Grimwood (Blandford Press, 1986)
The Hamlyn Historical Atlas (Hamlyn)
The Arab-Israeli Issue: Flashpoints Series by Paul Harper (Wayland 1986)
Europe in the Nineteenth Century by H. Hearder (Longman, 1966)
The Story of America by Louis Heren (Times Books, 1976)
Oxford Illustrated History of Medieval Europe edited by George Holmes (Oxford University Press, 1988)
The Voyage of the Armada by David Howarth (Collins, 1981)
Medieval People by Sarah Howarth (Simon & Schuster Young Books, 1991)
Medieval Places by Sarah Howarth (Simon & Schuster Young Books, 1991)
The Conquistadors by Hammond Innes (Collins, 1986)
Ancient Rome by Simon James (Dorling Kindersley, 1990)
Ancient Japan by Edward Kidder (Phaidon, 1977)
Trade and Religion: A Kingfisher Historical Atlas (Kingfisher, 1989)
Early Modern Europe, 1500–1789 by H. Koenigsberger (Longman, 1987)
Daily Life at Versailles in the 17th and 18th Centuries by J. Levron (Allen and Unwin)
City: A Story of Roman Planning and Construction by David Macauley (Collins, 1975)
The World of Islam to the 1500s: Living History by Fiona Macdonald (Collins Educational, 1991)
A Medieval Castle: Inside Story by Fiona Macdonald (Simon & Schuster Young Books, 1990)
A Medieval Cathedral: Inside Story by Fiona Macdonald (Simon & Schuster Young Books, 1991)
The Penguin Atlas of Medieval History by Colin McEvedy (Penguin Books, 1961)
World History Factfinder by Colin McEvedy (Cresset Press, 1984)
China: Great Civilizations by Beth McKillop (Franklin Watts, 1987)
Technology in War by K. Macksey (Arms and Armour Press)
The Collins Illustrated Encyclopaedia of Famous People by K. and V. McLeish (Collins, 1990)
The Spanish Armada by Colin Martin & Geoffrey Parker (Penguin, 1989)
Chronicle of the Twentieth Century ed. Derrik Mercer (Longman, 1988)
How People Lived: Window on the World by Anne Millard (Dorling Kindersley, 1989)
Bourbon and Stuart by John Miller (George Philip, 1987)
The Rise of Modern China by Dorothy Morrison (Oliver and Boyd, 1988)

Cultural Atlas of Africa edited by Jocelyn Murray (Phaidon, 1981)
Atlas of Twentieth Century History by Richard Natkiel (Hamlyn Bison, 1982)
Japan's Modernization by Edmund O'Connor (Harrap, 1975)
The Angles, Saxons and Jutes by Pamela Odijk (Macmillan, 1989)
The Egyptian World by Margaret Oliphant (Kingfisher, 1989)
The Thirty Years' War by Geoffrey Parker (Routledge & Keagan Paul, 1984)
The World, An Illustrated History edited by Geoffrey Parker (Times Books/Channel 4, 1986)
Farm Tools Through the Ages by M. Partridge (Osprey, 1973)
Japan: Great Civilizations by Mavis Pilbeam (Franklin Watts, 1987)
The Vikings: Great Civilizations by Robin Place (Longman, 1980)
Empires and Ideas by Michael Pollard (Blackie, 1981)
The Victorians by Michael Pollard (Heinemann, 1979)
The First Industrial Society: England in the Mid-19th Century by Ronald Posner (Collier Macmillan, 1975)
The Greek World by Anton Powell (Kingfisher, 1989)
Elizabeth I by Jasper Ridley (Constable, 1983)
Henry VIII by Jasper Ridley (Constable, 1984)
Mary Tudor by Jasper Ridley (Weidenfeld & Nicolson, 1973)
The Earliest Men and Women by J.M. Roberts (Penguin, 1980)
The First Civilizations by J.M. Roberts (Penguin, 1980)
The Illustrated Atlas of Archaeology by Sue Rollin (Longman, 1982)
Before 1066: History of Britain by Philip Sauvain (Macmillan)
History of Africa by K. Shillington (Macmillan, 1989)
The World the Romans Knew by Nigel Sitwell (Hamish Hamilton, 1984)
The Making of the Modern Age by Peter and Mary Speed (Oxford University Press, 1983)
Seventeenth Century Interior Decoration In England, France and Holland by P. Thornton (Yale University Press, 1978)
The Times Atlas of Past Worlds
Past Worlds: The Times Atlas of Archaeology (Times Books Ltd, 1988)
Everyday Life of the Barbarians by Malcolm Todd (Batsford, 1972)
Saxon Britain: History in Evidence by Tony Triggs (Wayland, 1989)
Viking Britain: History in Evidence by Tony Triggs (Wayland, 1989)
Ivan the Terrible by Henri Troyat (New English Library, 1984)
The Time of the Indian by Kenneth Ulyatt (Penguin, 1975)
Age of Machines R.J. Unstead (Macdonald, 1974)
Emerging Empire by R.J. Unstead (Macdonald, 1972)
Looking at History: The Twentieth Century by R.J. Unstead (A & C Black, 1974)
See Inside an Ancient Greek Town by R.J. Unstead (Kingfisher, 1986)
See Inside an Egyptian Town by R.J. Unstead (ed.) (Kingfisher, 1986)
The Assyrians by R.J. Unstead and W. Forman (Ward Lock, 1980)
A Concise History of India by Francis Watson (Thames and Hudson, 1979)
Europe Since 1945 by J. Robert Wegs (Macmillan, 1977)
The Sea Dogs by Neville Williams (Weidenfeld & Nicolson, 1975)
Victorian New Zealanders by June A. Wood (A.H. and A.W. Reed, 1974)
In Search of the Dark Ages by Michael Wood (BBC Books, 1981)
The Medieval and Renaissance World by Esmond Wright (ed.) (Hamlyn, 1979)
The Expanding World by Esmond Wright (ed.) (Hamlyn, 1979)
Daily Life in Rembrandt's Holland by Paul Zumthor (Weidenfeld & Nicolson, 1962)
Daily Life in Rembrandt's Holland by P. Zuruther (Weidenfeld & Nicolson, 1962)

Picture Acknowledgements

The author and publishers would like to acknowledge, with thanks, the following photographic sources:

p. 15 AKG; p. 20 (upper) Trustees of the British Museum; p. 21 Trustees of the British Museum; p. 23 Michael Holford; p. 25 (upper) C.M. Dixon, (centre and lower) Trustees of the British Museum; p. 26 (upper) Robert Harding Picture Library, (lower) Trustees of the British Museum; p. 27 C.M. Dixon; p. 28 AKG; p. 29 (left) C.M. Dixon; p. 31 (upper) Michael Holford, (lower left) Michael Holford, (lower centre) Douglas Dickins, (lower right) Michael Holford; p. 32 (left) AKG, (centre) Robert Harding, (right) AKG; p. 34 C.M. Dixon; p. 35 (left) C.M. Dixon, (right) Sonia Halliday Photographs; p. 36 AKG; p. 37 (left) Sonia Halliday Photographs, (right) Robert Harding Picture Library; p. 38 (left and right) MacQuitty Collection; p. 41 (upper) C.M. Dixon, (centre left) C.M. Dixon, (centre right) Ancient Art & Architecture Collection, (lower) Robert Harding Picture Library; p. 45 (left and right) Ancient Art & Architecture Collection; p. 47 (upper left) Ancient Art & Architecture Collection; (centre) Michael Holford, (upper right) Michael Holford, (lower right) Michael Holford; p. 49 (left and right) Werner Forman Archive; p. 51 (upper left and right) Michael Holford, (centre) Sonia Halliday Photographs, (lower) Werner Forman Archive; p. 52 Werner Forman Archive; p. 53 AKG; p. 54 (upper) M. Oliphant, (lower left and right) Trustees of the British Museum; p. 55 (left) Mansell Collection, (right) Robert Harding Picture Library; p. 56 MacQuitty Collection; p. 57 (upper and lower) Douglas Dickins; p. 58 C.M. Dixon; p. 59 (upper, centre, left and lower) Trustees of the British Museum, (centre right) Werner Forman Archive; p. 61 (upper and lower left) Michael Holford, (lower right) Olympia Museum; p. 63 (upper) Sonia Halliday Photographs, (lower) C.M. Dixon; p. 64 Michael Holford; p. 65 (all photographs) Ministry of Culture, Archaeological Receipts Fund, Thessalonika Museum; p. 66 (upper and lower) Mansell Collection; p. 69 (upper) M. Oliphant, (lower) Sonia Halliday Photographs; p. 70 Macquitty Collection; p. 72 (upper and lower) Ancient Art & Architecture Collection; p. 73 (left) The Bridgeman Art Library, (right) Werner Forman Archive; p. 76 (upper) Archiv für Kunst und Geschichte (AKG), (lower) AKG; p. 77 (left) AKG, (right) Michael Holford; p. 78 C.M. Dixon; p. 80 Ancient Art & Architecture Collection; p. 83 (left) M. Corbishley, (right) Michael Holford; p. 85 Mansell Collection; p. 87 (all photographs) Ancient Art & Architecture Collection; p. 88 Michael Holford; p. 89 (left and right) AKG; p. 90 C.M. Dixon; p. 92 C.M. Dixon; p. 93 (left) Trustees of the British Museum, (upper centre) Judges Postcards Ltd, Hastings, (right) Tyne & Wear Museums, (centre) Werner Forman Archive; p. 94 (upper and lower) C.M. Dixon; p. 96 C.M. Dixon; p. 97 Michael Holford; p. 99 (upper and lower) C.M. Dixon; p. 100 (left) Michael Holford, (centre and right) Sonia Halliday Photographs; p. 101 Trustees of the British Museum; p. 102 C.M. Dixon; p. 105 (left and upper) C.M. Dixon, (centre) Ancient Art & Architecture Collection, (right) Werner Forman Archive; p. 108 Robert Harding Picture Library; p. 109 MacQuitty Collection; p. 110 (upper) Robert Harding Picture Library; p. 112 (left) Werner Forman Archive, (right) Michael Holford; p. 113 (upper and centre) MacQuitty Collection, (lower right) Werner Forman Archive; p. 116 (left) C.M. Dixon, (right) Douglas Dickins; p. 118 Douglas Dickins; p. 119 (left) MacQuitty Collection, (upper and lower right) Robert Harding Picture Library; p. 120 Michael Holford; p. 121 (upper) Ann & Bury Peerless, (lower) Michael Holford; p. 122 Ancient Art & Architecture Collection; p. 123 (upper) C.M. Dixon, (lower) Ancient Art & Architecture Collection; p. 124 Douglas Dickins; p. 125 (left) Michael Holford, (upper, centre and lower right) C.M. Dixon; p. 126 MacQuitty Collection; p. 127 MacQuitty Collection; p. 128 Sonia Halliday Photographs; p. 129 (left) Douglas Dickins, (right) C.M. Dixon; p. 130 (left and lower right) Ancient Art & Architecture Collection, (upper right) MacQuitty Collection; p. 131 (upper) Ancient Art & Architecture Collection, (lower left and right) MacQuitty Collection; p. 132 Werner Forman Archive; p. 133 (left) Ancient Art & Architecture Collection, (right) Alan Hutchison Library; p. 134 Werner Forman Archive; p. 135 Sonia Halliday Photographs; p. 136 Sonia Halliday Photographs; p. 137 (upper and lower) Sonia Halliday Photographs; p. 140 C.M. Dixon; p. 141 Ancient Art & Architecture Collection; p. 142 Barbara Heller Photo Library; p. 143 (left) Ancient Art & Architecture Collection, (right) C.M. Dixon; p. 145 Ancient Art & Architecture Collection; p. 147 (upper left) Sonia Halliday Photographs, (upper right) Werner Forman Archive, (lower) C.M. Dixon; p. 149 (left) SCALA, (right) C.M. Dixon; p. 150 (left) AKG, (right) Ancient Art & Architecture Collection; p. 151 (all photos) Stanley E. West; p. 152 AKG; p. 155 (upper and lower) Ancient Art & Architecture Collection; p. 156 (upper) Werner Forman Archive, (centre) C.M. Dixon; p. 157 AKG; p. 158 SCALA; p. 159 Sonia Halliday Photographs; p. 161 Sonia Halliday Photographs; p. 162 SCALA; p. 164 (upper and lower left) Ancient Art & Architecture Collection, (centre) Werner Forman Archive; p. 166 Werner Forman Archive; p. 167 Werner Forman Archive; p. 168 (upper) Michael Holford, (lower) Ancient Art & Architecture Collection; p. 169 (upper left) The British Library, (upper right) Ashmolean Museum, Oxford, (lower) Michael Holford; p. 172 (upper) Robert Harding Picture Library, (lower) Sonia Halliday Photographs; p. 174 Sonia Halliday Photographs; p. 175 Sonia Halliday Photographs; p. 176 (upper) Robert Harding Picture Library, (lower) C.M. Dixon; p. 177 (upper left and right) C.M. Dixon, (lower) Michael Holford; p. 178 (upper) C.M. Dixon, (lower) Ancient Art & Architecture Collection; p. 180 Ancient Art & Architecture Collection; p. 181 The Chester Beatty Library; p. 182 (upper) Ancient Art & Architecture Collection, (lower) Réunion des Musées National; p. 183 Sonia Halliday Photographs; p. 184 C.M. Dixon; p. 185 (upper) Robert Harding Picture Library, (middle) Osterreichische Nationalbibliothek, Vienna, (lower) William MacQuitty; p. 186 Michael Holford; p. 187 Robert Harding Picture Library; p. 188 William MacQuitty; p. 189 (upper and lower) Ancient Art & Architecture Collection; p. 191 (upper) Ancient Art & Architecture Collection, (lower) Robert Harding Picture Library; p. 193 Werner Forman Archive; p. 194 Ancient Art & Architecture Collection; pp. 196 and 197 Trustees of the British Musuem; p. 199 Werner Forman Archive; p. 200 Michael Holford; p. 201 Werner Forman Archive; p. 204 AKG; p. 205 (left and right) C.M. Dixon; p. 206 The British Library; p. 208 (left) Sonia Halliday Photographs, (right) The British Library; p. 210 By Gracious Permission of Her Majesty the Queen, The Royal Collection; p. 212 AKG; p. 213 The British Library; p. 214 AKG; p. 216 AKG; p. 217 (left) AKG, (right) Michael Holford; p. 218 Robert Harding Picture Library; p. 219 (left and upper right) AKG, (lower) C.M. Dixon; p. 220 C.M. Dixon; p. 221 (upper) AKG, (lower) Michael Holford; p. 223 Werner Forman Archive; p. 224 Werner Forman Archive; p. 225 Robert Harding Picture Library; p. 227 C.M. Dixon; p. 230 The British Library; p. 232 The British Library; p. 233 (left and right) Sonia Halliday Photographs; p. 236 Mary Evans Picture Library; p. 237 The Bodleian Library, Oxford; p. 238 Ancient Art & Architecture Collection; p. 240 Sonia Halliday Photographs; p. 241 Sonia Halliday Photographs; p. 242 Michael Holford; p. 243 (upper) The British Library, (lower) William MacQuitty; p. 244 (upper) Robert Harding Picture Library, (lower) AKG; p. 247 (upper, centre, centre right and lower left) AKG, (lower centre) Mary Evans Picture Library; p. 248 Robert Harding Picture Library; p. 249 (left and right) Sonia Halliday Photographs; p. 251 (upper) Werner Forman Archive, (lower) Michael Holford; p. 253 (left) Robert Harding Picture Library, (right) Douglas Dickins; p. 254 Robert Harding Picture Library; p. 255 C.M. Dixon; p. 256 Douglas Dickins; p. 257 Werner Forman Archive; p. 258 Robert Harding Picture Library; p. 260 The British Library; p. 261 (upper) Philadelphia Museum of Art; Gift of John T. Dorrance Jr., (lower) The British Library; p. 262 (upper) Michael Holford, (lower) Michael Holford; p. 264 C.M. Dixon; p. 265 (upper and lower) AKG; p. 268 Bridgeman Art Library; p. 269 (upper) Giraudon; p. 269 (centre and lower) AKG; p. 270 Robert Harding Picture Library; p. 271 Bulloz; p. 272 Mansell Collection; p. 273 AKG; p. 275 Mary Evans Picture Library; p. 276 (left) Bridgeman Art Library; p. 276 (centre) AKG; (right) Michael Holford; p. 278 Tiroler Landesmuseum Ferdinandeum; p. 279 (upper) AKG, (lower) Mansell Collection; p. 280 (upper) Mary Evans Picture Library, (lower) Mansell Collection; p. 281 Ancient Art & Architecture Collection; p. 282 Crown Copyright; The Royal Armouries; p. 283 Robert Harding Picture Library; p. 284 Ancient Art & Architecture Collection; p. 285 Giraudon; p. 286 Robert Harding Picture Library; p. 287 Bridgeman Art Library; p. 289 Robert Harding Picture Library; p. 290 Giraudon; p. 291 Mary Evans Picture Library; p. 292 Musees Royaux de Beaux-Arts de Belgique; p. 293 (left) Giraudon, (right) AKG; p. 294 (upper) Robert Harding Picture Library, (lower left) Mansell Collection, (lower centre) Bulloz, (lower right) AKG; p. 295 Mansell Collection; p. 296 Guttenberg Museum; p. 301 (left) Mansell Collection, (right) AKG; p. 303 Michael Holford; p. 304 Werner Forman Archive, p. 305 (left) National Portrait Gallery, (right) Sheepvaartmuseum; p. 307 (upper and lower) Mansell Collection; p. 308 Hulton-Deutsch Collection; p. 309 Mansell Collection; p. 310 Sonia Halliday Photographs; p. 311 Michael Holford; p. 313 (left) Osterreichische Nationalbibliotek, (right) National Museum, Copenhagen; p. 314 Roger Hammond, p. 315 (upper) Robert Harding Picture Library, (lower left and right) Michael Holford; p. 316 Bridgeman Art Library; p. 320 Werner Forman Archive; p. 321 (upper left) Hulton-Deutsch Collection, (upper right) Robert Harding Picture Library, (lower left, centre and right) Trustees of the British Museum; p. 322 (upper) Trustees of the British Museum, (centre) Hulton-Deutsch Collection, (lower left) Werner Forman Archive, (lower right) Trustees of the British Library; p. 324 AKG; p. 325 (upper and lower left) South American Pictures, (upper right) Michael Holford, (lower right) Courtesy of the Hispanic Society of America; p. 327 Mansell Collection; p. 328 Trustees of the British Museum; p. 329 Hulton-Deutsch Collection; p. 332 Mansell Collection; p. 333. Ancient Art & Architecture Collection; p. 334 Mansell Collection; p. 335 Bridgeman Art Library; p. 337 (left) Institute of Agricultural History & Museum of English Rural Life; p. 337 (right) Mansell Collection; p. 339 Walker Art Gallery; p. 340 Bridgeman Art Library; p. 341 Ancient Art & Architecture Collection; p. 343 Michael Holford; p. 345 (upper and lower) AKG, (right) Reunion des Musees Nationaux; p. 346 Michael Holford; p. 347 By Gracious Permission of Her Majesty the Queen; p. 348 Sonia Halliday Photographs; p. 349 AKG; p. 350 AKG; p. 351 (left) Ancient Art & Architecture Collection, p. 351 (right) AKG; p. 352 Giraudon; p. 353 (upper, centre, upper right and lower left) AKG, (lower centre and right) Mary Evans Picture Library; p. 355 (left) Mary Evans Picture Library, (right) National Maritime Museum; p. 356 Bridgeman Art Library; p. 359 (left) Michael Holford, (right) Robert Harding Picture Library; p. 361 (left) Michael Holford, (right) Bridgeman Art Library; p. 365 Robert Harding Picture Library; p. 366 Mansell Collection, (below) AKG; p. 367 Peter Newark's Western Americana; p. 368 AKG; p. 369 (upper) Peter Newark's American Pictures, (lower) Mansell Collection; p. 370 AKG; p. 371 (upper left) Ancient Art & Architecture Collection, (upper and lower right) Bridgeman Art Library, (lower left) Mansell Collection; p. 372 AKG; p. 373 AKG; p. 374 AKG; p. 375 (upper) Bulloz, (lower) Giraudon; p. 379 Scala; p. 380 Michael Holford; p. 381 (upper) British Library, (lower) Rijksmuseum Foundation; p. 382 (upper) National Portrait Gallery, (lower) British Library; p. 383 British Library; p. 385 Werner Forman Archive; p. 386 Mansell Collection; p. 388 AKG; p. 389 (upper and centre) Toula Antonakos; p. 389 (right) Robert Harding Picture Library; p. 390 Aukland City Art Gallery; p. 391 (left) Michael Holford, p. 391 (right) Aukland City Art Gallery; p. 392 Hulton-Deutsch Collection; p. 393 Werner Forman Archive; p. 396 Photographie Bulloz; p. 397 Communist Party Archive; p. 399 (left) Berlin National Gallery, (right) Hulton-Deutsch Collection; p. 400 Mansell Collection; p. 402 Western Americana Picture Library; p. 403 (upper) Bridgeman Art Library, (lower) Hulton-Deutsch Collection; p. 405 (upper left) Mansell Collection, (upper right) RIBA, (lower left) Bridgeman Art Library, (lower right) Mansell Collection; p. 406 Fotomas Index; p. 407 (upper) AKG, (centre left and right) Hulton-Deutsch Collection, (lower) AKG; p. 408 Mansell Collection; p. 409 Museum of English Rural Life; p. 410 AKG; p. 411 (upper) Hulton-Deutsch Collection, (centre) John Massey-Stewart, (lower) Wellcome Institute Library; p. 412 Visual Arts Library; p. 413 (centre) Ancient Art & Architecture Collection, (right) Michael Holford; p. 414 (upper left) The 1st Queen's Dragoon Guards, (upper right) Punch, (lower) Bridgeman Art Library; p. 417 (upper) Mansell Collection, (lower) New York Historical Society; p. 420 Wedgwood Museum; p. 421 (upper and lower left) Hulton-Deutsch Collection, (upper and lower right) Mary Evans Picture Library; p. 422 (centre) Western Americana Picture Library, (right) Hulton-Deutsch Collection; p. 423 (upper and lower) Western Americana Picture Library; p. 425 (left) National Portrait Gallery, (right) AKG; p. 425 (lower left) Bridgeman Art Library, (centre) Robert Harding Picture Library; p. 428 AKG; p. 429 (left) Hulton-Deutsch Collection, (right) AKG; p. 430 Wayland Picture Library; p. 433 (left) Fotomas Index, (right) Bridgeman Art Library; p. 435 Mary Evans Picture Library; p. 436 (left and centre) Hulton-Deutsch Collection, (right) Mary Evans Picture Library; p. 438 Ancient Art & Architecture Collection; p. 439 (left) State Library of Victoria, (right) Hocken Library, University of Otago; p. 441 National Museum of the American Indian; p. 442 (upper) Bettmann Archive, (centre) Hulton-Deutsch Collection; p. 443 Bettmann Archive; p. 444 Ann Ronan; p. 445 (upper) Mary Evans Picture Library, (lower) Mansell Collection; p. 447 (upper) Mary Evans Picture Library, (lower) ET Archive; p. 448 Western Americana Picture Library; p. 449 (upper) Mary Evans Picture Library, (centre) Hulton-Deutsch Collection, p. 451 (upper and centre left, right) Mary Evans Picture Library, London Planetarium, (lower left) Wellcome Institute Library; p. 452 Western Americana Picture Library; p. 453 (left) Hulton-Deutsch Collection, (centre) Western Americana Picture Library Rockefeller; p. 455 (upper) Mary Evans Picture Library, (centre) AT&T; p. 456 Hulton Picture Library; p. 457 (upper) Advertising Archive, (lower) Bettmann Archive; p. 461 (left) Edimedia, (right) Popperfoto; p. 462 Hulton-Deutsch Collection; p. 464 (upper) Bridgeman Art Library, (lower) Mansell Collection; p. 465 Mary Evans Picture Library; p. 466 Bettmann Archive; p. 467 Ullstein Bilderdienst; p. 469 Camera Press; p. 471 (upper) Hulton-Deutsch Collection, (lower) Camera Press; p. 472 (upper) ET Archive, (lower) Bettmann Archive; p. 473 Hulton-Deutsch Collection; p. 474 (upper) Mansell Collection, (lower left) Hulton-Deutsch Collection, (lower right) SCR Photo Library; p. 475

(upper and lower) SCR Photo Library; p. 476 Mansell Collection, p. 477 (upper) Bettmann Archive, (lower) Mary Evans Picture Library; p. 478 Topham Picture Source; p. 479 (upper) Bridgeman Art Library, (centre) Hulton-Deutsch Collection, (lower) AKG; p. 480 Hulton-Deutsch Collection, (lower right) AKG; p. 481 (right) Imperial War Museum, (lower) Illustrated London News Picture Library; p. 483 (upper) Hulton-Deutsch Collection, (lower) Popperfoto; p. 484 (upper) Imperial War Museum, (centre) ET Archive; p. 486 Hulton-Deutsch Collection; p. 487 Hulton-Deutsch Collection; p. 488 (upper and lower) Hulton-Deutsch Collection; p. 489 Camera Press; p. 492 (upper) AKG, (lower) Popperfoto; p. 493 (upper) SCR Photo Library, (lower) Popperfoto; p. 494 (left and centre) Rex Features, (right) Popperfoto; p. 495 Popperfoto; p. 496 Camera Press; p. 497 (left) Robert Harding Picture Library, (upper right) Frank Spooner Pictures, (lower right) Rex Features; p. 498 Camera Press; p. 500 Camera Press; p. 501 Topham Picture Source; p. 503 (left, centre and right) Popperfoto; p. 507 (left) ET Archive, (upper and lower right) Rex Features; p. 508 (upper) SCR Photo Library, (lower) John Arthur/Impact Photos; p. 511 (upper) Topham Picture Source, (lower left) Orde Eliason/Link, (right and lower centre) Popperfoto; p. 512 (upper and lower) Kobal Collection; p. 513 (upper) Bridgeman Art Library, (lower left and right) Camera Press, (lower centre) Hulton-Deutsch Collection; p. 514 (upper) Mark Edwards/Still Pictures, (centre) Frank Spooner Pictures, (lower) Hulton-Deutsch Collection; p. 515 Frank Spooner Pictures; p. 516 (upper) IBM, (centre) Ford Photo Library; p. 517 Hulton-Deutsch Collection; p. 518 Popperfoto; p. 520 Still Pictures.

Wherever possible the copyright holder has been notified but we apologise if any material appears in error.